TECHNICAL METALS

*Dedicated
to the memory
of my wife,
Gertrude*

TECHNICAL METALS

By
Harold V. Johnson
Spoon River College
Canton, Illinois

CHAS. A. BENNETT CO., INC.
Peoria, Illinois 61614

VH   10   9   8   7   6   5   4   3   2   1

Library of Congress Catalog Number: 67-12639
PRINTED IN THE UNITED STATES OF AMERICA

ISBN 87002-139-7

ACKNOWLEDGMENTS

Every effort has been made to bring this book completely abreast of the many technological developments that have occurred in recent years.

The author wishes to express his thanks and appreciation to the many industrial firms who have so generously contributed information and illustrations. Without such cooperation a book of this type would not be possible.

The author also wishes to express his thanks to the editors and others of Chas. A. Bennett Co., Inc., who, through their advice and patience, have made their contribution to this book.

He is indebted to his family members for their interest and encouragement, and is especially grateful to Carol Harkless for assistance in reading the proof.

The following firms contributed illustrations used in this text:

Acro Welder Mfg. Co.
Air Reduction Co.
Aluminum Co. of America
All Metal Screw Products Co.
Allegheny Ludlum Steel Corp.
Allis-Chalmers Mfg. Co.
American Art Clay Co.
American Foundrymen's Society
American Gas Furnace Co.
American Iron and Steel Institute
American Machinist—
 Metalworking
 Manufacturing
American Tech. Society
American Tool Works Co.
Armstrong Brothers Tool Co.
Atlas Press Co.
Automation Industries Inc.
Banner Welder Inc.
Beard Mfg. Co.
Beloit Tool Co.
Beverly Shear Mfg. Co., Inc.
Black and Decker Mfg. Co.
Boice Crane Div. of Wilton Corp.
Boral Industrial Corp.
Brown & Sharpe Mfg. Co.
Butler Mfg. Co.
Cadillac Gage Co.
Carpenter Steel Co.

Caterpillar Tractor Co.
Cerro Sales Corp.
Chambersburg Eng'g Co.
Cincinnati Milling Machine Co.
Cincinnati Shaper Co.
Clausing Div. Atlas Press Co.
Cleveland Automatic Machine Co.
Cleveland Twist Drill Co.
Columbian Vise & Mfg. Co.
Covel Mfg. Co.
Crescent Tool Co.
Cushman Chuck Div. Cushman
 Industries Inc.
Di-Acro Corp.
Delta Power Tool Div.,
 Rockwell Mfg. Co.
DeVlieg Machine Co.
Diamond Clamp & Flask Co.
W. C. Dillon Co., Inc.
Harry W. Dietert Co.
Divine Bros. Co.
DoAll Co.
Dumore Co.
Duro-Metal Products Co.
Elox Corp.
Enterprise Mach. Tools, Inc.
Erie Foundry Co.
Ex-Cello Corp.
Federal Products Corp.

Friden, Inc.
Gallemeyer & Livingston Co.
Gemaco
General Motors Corp.
Giddings & Lewis Machine Tool Co.
Gleason Works
George Gorton Machine Co.
Great Western Mfg. Co.
Greenfield Tap and Die Corp.
Haag Machine Co., Inc.
Hamilton Watch Co.
Hardinge Brothers, Inc.
Hossfeld Mfg. Co.
Heald Machine Co.
Heller Tool Co.
Hilland Griffith Co.
Hines Flask Co.
Hobart Brothers Co.
The A. F. Holden Co.
Index Machine & Tool Co.
International Harvester Co.
International Silver Co.
Johnson Gas Appliance Co.
Jones and Lamson Machine Co.
Jones & Laughlin Steel Corp.
Kent Owens Machine Co.
Landis Tool Co.
Lea Mfg. Co.
R. K. LeBlond Machine Tool Co.
Lincoln Electric Co.
Lindberg Engineering Co.
Linde Co.
Lodge & Shipley Co.
Lufkin Rule Co.
Macklandburg Duncan Co.
Magnaflux Corp.
Mahr Gage Co., Inc.
Marquette Corp.
Meta-Dynamic Div. the Cincinnati
    Milling Machine Co.
Metallizing Co. of America, Inc.

Metco, Inc.
Metric Association, Inc.
Millers Falls
Minnesota Mining & Mfg. Co.
Montgomery & Co., Inc.
H. E. Morse Co.
McEnglevan Heat Treating
    & Mfg. Co.
National Crucible Co.
National Cylinder Gas
National Machinery Co.
National Twist Drill & Tool Co.
Niagara Machine Works
Nicholson File Co.
North American Aviation, Inc.
Northern Business News Service
Norton Co.
Oliver Machinery Co.
O'Neil-Irwin Mfg. Co.
Osborn Mfg. Co.
Peck, Stow & Wilcox
Phoenix Products Co., Inc.
Pratt & Whitney Machine Tool
    Div. Colt Industries
Price and Rutzebeck
Propellex Div. of Chromalloy
    American Corp.
Pyrometer Instrument Co., Inc.
Racine Hydraulics & Machinery,
    Inc.
Reid Bros. Co., Inc.
Republic Steel Corp.
Rockford Engineered Products Co.
Rockwell Mfg. Co. Delta Power
    Tool Div.
Scherr-Tumico Inc.
Scientific Cast Products
Screw & Bolt Corp. of America
Sebree's Photography
Sellstran Mfg. Co.
Sheffield Corp.

Shell Process Inc.
Shore Instrument & Mfg. Co., Inc.
Simonds Saw and Steel Co.
J. T. Slocomb Co.
South Bend Lathe Co.
Spincraft Inc.
Standard Tool Co.
Stanley Tools
L. S. Starrett Co.
Superior Electric Co.
Supreme Products Corp.
Sutter Products Co.
Swartz Standard Fixture Co. Div.
    Universal Vise & Tool Co.
Swayne, Robinson and Co.
Taft-Pierce Mfg. Co.
Technical Education & Mfg., Inc.
Henry G. Thompson & Son
Thomas C. Thompson Co.
Threadwell Tap & Die Co.
Timken Roller Bearing Co.
Tinius Olson Testing Machine Co.
Turner Corp.
Tweco Products Co.
U. S. Dept. of Labor
U. S. Steel Corp.
Union Twist Drill Co.
United Engineering and Foundry Co.
Vesuvious Crucible Co.
O. S. Walker Co., Inc.
Warner & Swasey
Wassco Glo Melt Div.
    American Electric Heater Co.
Waterbury Farrell Co.
Weller Electric Corp.
Whiting Corp.
Whitman & Barnes
Whitney Metal Tool Co.
J. H. Williams & Co.
Williams-White & Co.
Wilson Mechanical Instrument Div.
Zenith Foundry Co.

LIST OF COLOR ILLUSTRATIONS

PREFACE...

Almost every product of American industry *contains metal parts* or is manufactured by machines made of metal parts. Metal products in our homes have done much to make them convenient places to live.

This text is planned for use in most school metalworking courses. Even potential engineering students can acquire information and develop skills that are considered basic in many technical and engineering programs.

A course in general metals should be a part of the general educational program, contributing not only to the student's skills, but also to his ideals, appreciations, and attitudes.

This text has been planned for the general metal shop, or it can be used in the general metal area of the general shop.

The book is divided into *several main sections,* including the uses of bench tools, bench and wrought metal, metal spinning, art metal, sheet metal, forging, foundry, welding, machine shop, and heat treating. Also included is a section on the introduction to metalworking and one on present-day trends in machining metals. There are numerous *projects* in the book, and each section is divided into units which cover the *basic tools, related information, materials,* and *processes.*

In addition to covering the various manipulative processes, this text places emphasis on the principles of *good design,* and on *consumer knowledge* which involves the ability to select products properly.

Moreover, the book stresses safety, which is all important to both the instructor and the student. The ability to plan a job in advance and then do the operations without injury to the student or another worker is perhaps the most important thing for the student to learn through experiences in metalworking. Good safety practices are stressed in a separate unit in the book and also integrated where appropriate throughout the book.

Opportunities are given for developing independent planning, and following through a specific job to a successful completion. All illustrations have been carefully selected and represent the best illustrative approach to instruction. Emphasis is placed on encouraging the student to appreciate good design and careful workmanship in the projects shown in this book.

The author's experience leads him to believe that the aims stated in this preface reflect a need that definitely exists in American education today. It is his confident hope that TECHNICAL METALS will meet this need in a way that will mutually benefit students, instructors, and —ultimately—an important segment of our nation's industry, the metalworking trades.

HAROLD V. JOHNSON

Contents...

Contents

Contents

Section One

Introduction to Metalworking

Before you do anything that is *systematic,* what is the first requirement?

You have to make plans. Therefore this book begins with a section on the very important part of Technical Metals that is related to planning.

It takes up *occupations* that you might enter—such as in the vast aircraft and space exploration industries and the automobile industry. It covers *safety, drawing and sketching, project development,* a *consumer's* look at metals, *design, measurement,* and *layout.*

Section One is an introduction to the planning and procedures that lead to the study of basic metalworking. In this connection to help avoid injuries on the job, you will take up safe practices early. Refer to this Unit constantly as you work.

Next, no product can be designed or made under industrial conditions unless technical workers such as yourself can read plans and make sketches. Uses of metals by the consumer, product design, measuring and layout—all make up the "know-how kit" of the metals technician.

vices by an intelligent, skilled, and flexible work force.

Employment in the individual machining occupations is expected to increase. In the years ahead, the broad field of semi-skilled work will provide jobs for many production machine operators. Applicants for skilled jobs, however, will have to meet increasingly high standards. Industry will need craftsmen who can do difficult machining and fabricating operations.

The automated or numerical control of machine tools is a technological advance which may affect machining workers. Fig. 1-1. Numerical control may greatly simplify their jobs and increase their production efficiency. The need for maintenance technicians will increase.

The earnings of skilled machining workers compare favorably with those of other skilled industrial workers. Tool and die makers and instrument makers are the highest paid workers in the machining group, and among the highest paid skilled workers.

Occupations in the Metalworking Trades

Almost every product of American industry contains metal parts or is manufactured by machines made of metal parts, which are shaped or formed by machining workers, who make up the largest occupational group in metalworking trades. In the 1960's, more than a million workers were employed as all-around machinists, machine tool operators, tool and die makers, instrument makers, set-up men, and layout men. Others were employed in trades that involved the working of metal such as foundry occupations, forging, welding, and sheet metalwork.

In the metalworking trades, young people with manual or mechanical abilities do not need college training to find opportunities which range from those of machine tending to the highly skilled tool and die maker.

The economic and military strength of our country depends to a great extent on the initiative and competence of our craftsmen. The contributions of engineers, chemists, and other scientists are transformed into goods and ser-

1-1. Numerically controlled grinder.

Most machine shops are fairly clean, well lighted, and free from dust. Safety instructions are an important part of job training. Because they work with high speed machine tools and sharp cutting instruments, workers in these occupations need good safety habits.

Machining work is not physically strenuous. The machine tools do the actual cutting while the worker sets the machine, watches the controls, and checks the accuracy of the workpiece.

Some of the most important metalworking jobs available today are described in this unit.

Opportunities in Technical "Space" Programs

It is astonishing how great the opportunities are for a metals technician in the vast space transportation program. As pointed out in the report sponsored by the National Aeronautics and Space Administration, much of the production comes under the heading of craftsmanship. The things that you learn in a study of technical metals often have direct application.

From the report of the committee which studied the relationships between school industrial-technical training and space, conducted under the general direction of Dr. John L. Feirer at Cape Kennedy—and from subsequent developments—an extensive unit came out on the subject of metals alone.

Flights in space cannot be "rubber stamped." Each component of a spacecraft, or of experimental devices connected with the space program, must be given individual attention. In other words, the work is *not put on a production line.*

Included in the occupational skills of over a million manufacturing employees are such basic considerations as—layout, measurement, tolerance allowance, metal properties, heat-treat, hand forming and machining operations, casting, spinning, drilling, joining, and finishing.

"Space" includes the entire aircraft production industry, as well as the immense government program. Hundreds of thousands of persons are employed in an aircraft industry that includes the development of prototypes, which cannot be automated. You can see how closely related such work must be with the basic metalworking factors covered here, in a textbook that goes beyond all previous publications of its kind.

Forge Shop Workers

Forging is the process in which workers use drophammers and presses to shape glowing hot metal. This is similar to the work of the oldtime blacksmith, except that large mechanical equipment is substituted for the blacksmith's hand tools. Fig. 1-2.

1-2. One of the many jobs that are performed in a forge shop—forming the bowl on a spoon.

1-3. All-around machinist.

Because forged metal is strong, such items as automobile crankshafts, gears, pliers, wrenches, and aircraft and missile parts are produced by forging.

Most forge shop workers learn their skills through on-the-job training and work experience.

A few companies offer apprentice programs for the more skilled forge shop jobs, such as die sinker, heat treater, hammersmith, hammerman, and press-smith. The programs generally last four years, provide 8,000 hours of classroom training and practical experience in using the tools of his trade.

All-around Machinists

The all-around machinist, Fig. 1-3, is a skilled worker who makes metal parts with machine and hand tools. He can set up and operate most types of machine tools, select the tools and materials required for each job, and plan all the operations necessary to complete the job according to specifications and blueprints. He has to be able to use a variety of precision measuring instruments and to make standard shop computations relating to dimensions,

15

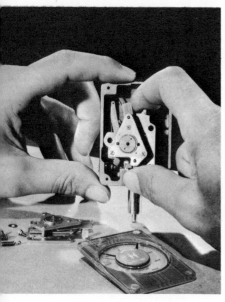

1-4. Instrument maker.

1-5. A model of the design is fashioned in wax about twice the size of a table-spoon to permit every detail of the design to be brought out and perfected. A plaster of paris mold of this model is used to make a bronze casting in reverse. It requires many hours of painstaking tooling to prepare the pattern for the steel die.

feeds, and speeds of machining. He also has to have a knowledge of heat-treating operations on cutting tools.

Coremakers

In foundry work, cores—hollow-mold forms—are placed on molds to form cavities or pockets in castings. When the metal is poured it solidifies, and when the core is removed, the desired cavity or pocket remains. Coremakers make the cores either by hand or by machine.

When done by hand, small cores are made on the workbench by *bench coremakers;* larger ones on the foundry floor by *floor coremakers.*

A wide range of skills is required in this occupation. Completion of a four-year apprenticeship is needed to become a skilled hand coremaker. Only a brief period of on-the-job training is needed for less skilled handwork and for most machine core-making.

Instrument Makers

Instrument makers (also called *experimental machinists* and *model makers*) work closely with scientists and engineers in translating ideas and designs into experimental models, special laboratory equipment, and non-standard instruments. The instrument parts and models range from simple gears to such intricate parts as those used in guided-missile navigation systems. Fig. 1-4.

Most instrument makers advance from the ranks of machinists or skilled machine tool operators. Others learn their trade through apprenticeships which last 4 or 5 years.

Jewelers and Jewelry Repairmen

Jewelers make rings, pins, necklaces, bracelets, and other ornaments by hand. They frequently use precious, semiprecious, or synthetic stones and set them in gold, silver, or platinum. They also repair jewelry, make rings larger or smaller, reset stones, and refashion old jewelry.

Jewelers may follow their own design or one by another person who specializes in design work. Fig. 1-5. The jeweler has to have the ability not only to design, coupled with an artistic sense, but he has to have the skill to use small hand and machine tools, such as drills, files, saws, soldering irons, and jewelers' lathes.

Young persons learn this particular trade by on-the-job training while working for an experienced jeweler, by serving a formal apprenticeship, or in a trade school.

Layout Men

In his highly specialized work, the layout man marks metal stock, castings, and forgings to indicate where and how much machining is necessary. Fig. 1-6. This requires the ability to use many types of measuring instruments and to read and interpret blueprints and working drawings.

It takes 6 to 10 years training and experience to develop the skills needed in this occupation. The trade is usually learned through a machinist apprentice program.

Machine Tool Operators

Many tool operators, Fig. 1-7, are essentially machine tenders who perform simple, repetitive

1-6.   Layout men.

1-7.   Machine tool operator.

1-8.   Metal spinner.

operations. However, some machining operations are complex and require highly skilled operators.

The work of the machine tool operator is similar to that of the all-around machinist except that it is often limited to a single type of machine. The skilled operator has to be able to adjust the speed, feed, and other controls, and select the proper cutting tools for each operation.

The great majority of these workers learn their skills on the job. Skilled operators can work in production, maintenance shops, and toolrooms.

Metal Spinners

Few people realize the increasing importance of metal spin-

ning. This process now meets such varied metal-forming needs as in the manufacture of dairy equipment, lighting fixtures, and guided missiles.

The demand for accomplished metal spinners is great and will increase. Many of the men who do this work in the United States today learned their trade in Europe. Young persons in this country can now learn metal spinning by working with craftsmen who have this skill. Fig. 1-8.

Millwrights

Millwrights are skilled workers who move and install heavy industrial equipment and machinery. They must have a knowledge of the equipment on which they work because frequently it is

1-9. Molder.

necessary to take apart, repair, and assemble it. Also, these men are trained to use a wide variety of hand tools, to fit bearings, to align gears and pulleys, and to install electrical and hydraulic equipment. They often use measuring devices such as calipers, squares, plumb bobs, levels, and micrometers. A further necessity is the ability to read blueprints.

Workers learn this trade as helpers to skilled millwrights over a period of years or through an

1-10. An apprentice at work on a lathe.

apprenticeship program. High school courses in mechanical drawing, mathematics, and machine shop practice are useful to young men interested in this career.

Molders

The molder, Fig. 1-9, is a foundry worker who uses a special type of sand to prepare a mold which contains a cavity in the shape of the product to be made. Molten metal is poured into the cavity where it solidifies and forms the required casting. A molder is highly skilled in the use of slicks, trowels, and many other hand tools. Molds for small castings are usually made on the workbench by *bench molders*. *Machine molders* operate various types of equipment which rapidly make large quantities of identical castings.

A molder today receives his training through a 4-year apprenticeship program, or equivalent

experience under a qualified molder.

Ornamental Ironworkers

The work of these craftsmen is very similar to that of the blacksmith, but more artistic. By heating metal in a forge or furnace, hammering it on an anvil, or shaping it with bending tools and machines, the ornamental ironworker makes such products as lamps, door knockers, fireplace implements, porch railings, gates, and doors.

Most workers enter the occupation by getting jobs as helpers in blacksmith shops where they gradually learn the trade.

Patternmakers

Patternmakers are highly skilled craftsmen who manually build patterns for molds from which foundry castings are formed.

The patternmaker must be able to work from blueprints prepared by an engineering department. He makes a precise pattern for the product, after allowing for shrinkage of the molten metal when it cools in the casting process, different alloys, and for other factors.

The wood patternmaker prepares the master patterns. He has to have the ability to select the proper wood stock, lay out the pattern, and shape the wood to the final form using hand tools and machines such as lathes, planers, bandsaws, and sanders.

The metal patternmaker prepares patterns from metal stock. He must be able to use a wide variety of metalworking machines to shape and finish patterns.

There are also patternmakers

1-11. Set-up man.

1-13. Punches and dies made by a tool and die maker.

that work with other materials such as plaster and plastic.

Because such great skill is required, patternmaking is very difficult to learn informally. Apprenticeship, Fig. 1-10, or similar on-the-job training programs are the principal means of qualifying as a journeyman. Some trade schools offer preparatory courses.

Set-up Men (Machine Tools)

The set-up man is a skilled specialist employed in plants and machine shops which do machin-

1-12. Tool and die maker.

ing on a production basis. His job is to get machine tools ready for operation by semi-skilled operators. He also instructs the operator how to run the job. Working from drawings, specifications, blueprints, and job layouts he has to be able to determine the proper speeds, feeds, tooling, and operation sequence. He may make trial runs and adjust the machine until the parts conform to specifications.

Most set-up men work in plants that produce aircraft, automobiles, and machinery.

A set-up man, Fig. 1-11, must be thoroughly trained in the use of all types of machine tools such as turret lathes, screw machines, grinders, shapers, milling machines, and all types of production machines. Most set-up men come from the ranks of highly skilled machinists.

Tool and Die Makers

Tool and die makers, Fig. 1-12,

are highly skilled, creative workers whose products are tools, dies, and special guiding and holding devices such as drill jigs and fixtures (which hold metal while it is being drilled, stamped, shaped, etc.). They also make gages and other measuring devices which are used in manufacturing precision metal parts. Die makers construct punches, Fig. 1-13, which are used in stamping and forging operations.

In comparison with most other machinists, tool and die makers have a broader knowledge of machining operations, shop practices, mathematics, and blueprint reading, and usually can work to closer tolerances and do more precise handwork.

Persons entering the trade should have good mathematical and mechanical abilities, and some understanding of physics. Several years of formal apprenticeship or on-the-job training are needed to learn this trade.

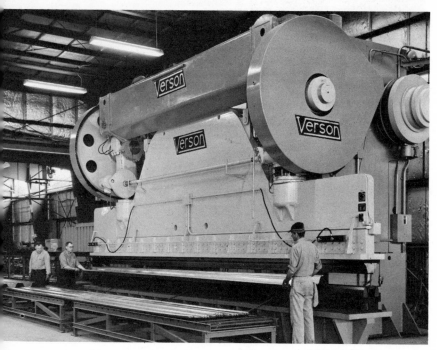

1-14. Sheet metalworkers dwarfed by the size of the machine.

Welders and Oxygen and Arc Cutters

Welders, Fig. 1-15, join metal by applying intense heat and sometimes pressure to melt edges and surfaces to form a permanent bond with or without the use of filler metal. Closely related to welding is *thermal cutting* (also called oxygen and arc cutting). Oxygen and electric arc cutters also use torchlike devices to cut or trim metal objects to shapes, and remove excess metal so a workpiece is of manageable size for machining. The method is automatic in production work.

Of the more than thirty-five different ways of welding metals, most fall under three basic categories: arc, gas, and resistance welding. Arc welders perform their work either with hand or machine methods. Gas welders join metals by hand or with automatic and semi-automatic equipment. Semiskilled oxygen cutters work either with oxygen-fuel or oxyacetylene cutting machines. Resistance welding is mainly a machine process performed by semiskilled operators. Heat builds up by direct contact of surfaces, using electric current.

Sheet Metalworkers

Sheet metalworkers fabricate and install ducts used in heating, air-conditioning, and ventilating systems. They also fabricate and install a wide variety of other products made from thin metal sheets, such as roofing, siding, and commercial steel kitchen equipment. Skilled sheet metalworkers should not be confused with assembly-line operatives who also make sheet-metal products, but are trained in only a few specific operations. Fig. 1-14.

The worker must be able to read blueprints, lay out the job, and form metal with bending machines, hammers, and anvils. Other required skills are soldering seams and joints, welding, and riveting.

The best way to learn this trade is through a 4- or 5-year apprenticeship program. However, some have acquired the necessary skills by working for many years as helpers of experienced craftsmen. Also, some knowledge of this work can be gained in trade schools.

1-15. Welder.

Check Your Knowledge

1. Do the metalworking trades provide jobs for individuals with no skills?

2. Approximately how many people in the United States are directly or indirectly employed in some phase of metalworking?

3. Is there a demand for semi-skilled workers in industry today?

4. What are some of the skills necessary to become an all-around machinist?

5. What does a blacksmith do?

6. What are cores, and for what are they used?

7. How does a jeweler learn his trade?

8. What is another name for an instrument maker?

9. What is meant by the term apprentice?

10. What type of training is necessary to become a good layout man?

11. Give some of the requirements for becoming a machine tool operator.

12. Name some products made by a metal spinner.

13. What is the job of a millwright?

14. Explain the work of a molder. How does he get his training?

15. What does an ornamental iron worker do?

16. Name four materials from which patterns are made.

17. What is the job of a set-up man?

18. Explain the work of the tool and die maker.

19. Name some products that are fabricated by the sheet metal worker.

20. Name two sources of heat used when welding manually.

Terms to Know and Spell

mechanical	forging	millwright
skilled	die-sinker	hydraulic
fabricating	coremaker	ornamental
technological	solidifies	journeyman

---

2 ▷ Safe Practices in the Metal Shop

It is important to be not only an able worker but also a safe one. Anyone without proper safety attitudes has no place in the school shop. He is both a menace to himself and to fellow students or workers.

Your instructor is interested in your welfare and safety. When he insists on safe practices, pay close attention and follow his instructions. This not only shows that you appreciate his interest but also protects you from the possibility of serious injury.

General Safety Measures

• **Dress correctly.** To protect your clothes, wear either an apron or a short-sleeved, beltless shop coat. An apron fits snugly, offering little chance of being caught by moving parts of a machine tool. Fig. 2-1. Avoid carrying waste or cloths in the pockets. Remove outer garments or any loose clothing, such as a sweater or necktie, that may be caught in the moving parts of a machine.

• **Remove rings and wrist watch.** Jewelry worn on the

2-1. Even though this operator is using measuring instruments, his eyes are protected with safety glasses and he is observing all the safety rules.

hands or wrists may get caught in the moving parts of machines and cause serious injury.

• **Always walk in the shop.** Running is not safe. There is always danger of colliding with another student operating a machine, which might cause injury. A fall, especially while carrying a sharp-edged tool, can be serious, or you might contact a high-temperature job unit or hard-edged object that would do injury.

• **Protect your eyes.** Eyes should be protected at all times with safety glasses or an eye shield. Even though working with measuring instruments in a safe part of the shop, you may be called to a machining area. Fig. 2-2. There is always danger from flying chips or particles from grinding wheels. They can cause eye damage or a total loss of eyesight.

2-2. What violations of safety practices can you find in this picture?

21

2-3. This operator knows his machine. He is dressed properly and has his eyes protected from flying particles.

- **No horseplay.** Never be tempted to liven things up with a little horseplay such as tossing tools or small parts to other students. Always attend strictly to the job at hand and focus your attention on what you are doing. Horseplay can cause serious accidents.
- **Scrap materials on floor.** Do your part in keeping the shop clean. Scraps or shavings on the floor may cause falls, sprains, cuts, and broken bones to you and other students who might trip over them. Place all scrap material in containers provided for that purpose.
- **Know your machine.** Check the machine to see that all guards are in place. Stop the machine before taking measurements on the work. Check to see that all clamps or other work holders are tight before turning on a machine. Be sure keys and wrenches are cleared from the work area before starting the machine. Fig. 2-3.
- **Never try to remove chips with the fingers.** Chips have sharp edges. Always use a brush or stick to remove them.
- **Keep hands away from moving parts.** Shut off the machine when adjusting the work. The temptation to feel the work sur-

face while the machine is running can result in disaster.
- **Take care of injuries.** No matter how small, report all accidents to the instructor. He will administer first aid or get you to a doctor in case of a serious injury.

Safety Precautions— Hand Tools

1. Be certain all files are fitted with handles to prevent the tang from piercing the hand.
2. When using the cold chisel, direct chips away from others working near you. Use only sharp edged tools. Blunt tools are dangerous. Why?
3. When using a wrench, be sure it fits the bolt or nut head properly. A loose-fitting wrench will round the corners and slip, resulting in possible hand injuries. A small wrench has a limited capacity. When it is used beyond that capacity, it may fail and cause injury. To work safely, select a tool the right size.
4. Make sure that hammer heads and screw driver blades are in their handles securely.
5. Grind "mushroomed" head edges and burrs off cold chisels.
6. Do not carry tools with sharp points or edges in your pocket.
7. Do not use a wrench in place of a hammer. It is also dangerous practice to pound the handle of a wrench with a hammer.

Safety Precautions—Bench and Wrought Metal

1. The general safety measures also apply in this area.
2. Wear special protective clothing during operations involving the use of hot metal.

3. Use a hammer only in good condition—with a smooth, rounded face and firm head.
4. Wear goggles when chipping, filing, or otherwise working on metal.
5. Hold the cold chisel so that your hand will not be injured if the hammer misses the head of the tool.
6. Make a file cut to start a hacksaw. This is to prevent the saw from slipping and cutting the hand.
7. In using a portable drill, support the drill with one hand and apply the correct pressure with the other. Too much pressure may break the drill and cause injury.
8. Never wear gloves when using the portable drill. They can be caught in the revolving chuck.

Safety Precautions— Metal Spinning

1. Stand out of line with the revolving metal disc when the lathe is started. The disc may fly out.
2. Never permit other students to stand on the side of the lathe opposite you while doing the spinning. Why?
3. Wear a leather glove on left hand during the spinning and trimming processes. A severe cut can result if a bare hand slips and contacts the flying disc.
4. Do not adjust the spinning rest while the lathe is in motion.
5. Do not touch the revolving disc while the lathe is running.
6. *Always wear safety glasses.*

Safety Precautions— Art Metal and Jewelry

1. Follow all general safety precautions.

2-4. Pouring green sand molds on a conveyor line. The molder is properly dressed for this work.

2. Wear rubber gloves when using corrosive chemicals.

3. Mix acid into the water in a glass or earthenware jar when doing etching.

4. When buffing art metal projects, hold the work below center as the wheel revolves toward you. Should the work be pulled from your hands by the buffing wheel, it will be thrown away from you rather than toward you.

5. Hold the work being buffed with two hands. Cloth buffers have a tendency to grab and pull the work from the hands of the operator.

Safety Precautions— Sheet Metal

1. Review the safe practices for the use of hand tools. Many also apply when working with sheet metal.

2. When using squaring shears, keep fingers away from the cutting blade at all times.

3. Remove sharp burrs and edges on sheet metal being formed.

4. When using the bar folder, keep your fingers in the clear.

5. Avoid breathing fumes from sal-ammoniac.

6. Use care in handling a soldering copper. You cannot tell if it is hot or cold by looking at it.

7. Never use a soldering copper with a loose tip or handle.

Safety Precautions— the Foundry

1. Be certain molding sand is properly tempered. Too much moisture in the sand will cause the mold to "blow" when the metal is poured. Fig. 2-4.

2. Molds rammed too hard will cause a "blow" when they are poured.

3. Use the vent wire with care. Avoid sticking the fingers with the sharp point.

4. Do not throw damp or wet metal into furnace, crucible, or ladle of molten metal. It causes an explosion that will make the metal spatter around.

5. Before using crucibles, check for cracks or flaws.

6. Ladles should be thoroughly dry before metal is poured into them.

7. Leggings should be worn to protect against splashes of molten metal.

8. Blow air through a crucible furnace before you light it.

9. Use properly fitted tongs and shanks when handling crucibles of molten metal.

10. Do not wedge pieces of metal into a crucible when charging it. The metal will expand when heated and crack the crucible.

11. Do not place your face directly over sprues and risers.

2-5. This lathe operator is following good safety practices with his eyes protected and sleeves rolled up.

Safety Precautions— Machine Shop

1. Follow the general safety measures. Fig. 2-5.

2. Become familiar with the operation of any machine you use. Fig. 2-6.

3. Never use a drill without clamping the work securely, in a vise or otherwise.

4. On off-hand grinders,

2-6. This operator has only one pair of eyes. He could lose his eyesight by not taking the necessary time to put on a pair of safety glasses or face shield.

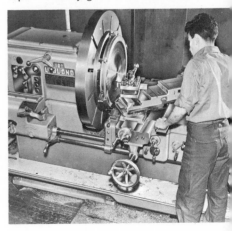

2-7. Proper dress for working on the grinder. Note the rolled up sleeves, the apron, and the safety glasses.

make sure that the protective shields are in place.

5. Stand to one side of a grinding wheel when first starting the machine. Check the wheel speed and machine speed. If the wheel is defective or if it is attached to the shaft with flanges of different sizes or types, it is likely to break up violently, almost like an explosion. Fig. 2-7.

6. Wheels out of round must be trued. Worn wheels that will not respond to truing or dressing should be replaced.

7. Wheels for wet grinding should not be permitted to stand partly immersed in water, because absorption will destroy their balance. Fig. 2-8.

8. Set the work rest 1/16″ from the wheel. If too much space is left the tool may become wedged in this space and cause the wheel to break.

9. Use the left-handed method when filing on the lathe.

10. Do not attempt to oil the

drill press while the machine is running.

11. Run the drill on a drill press at the proper speed; forcing or feeding too fast may result in broken drills and possible injury.

12. The two most common injuries around a shaper are from flying chips and getting fingers caught between the workpiece and the tool. Take utmost care with this tool.

13. Never take measurements while the ram is in motion.

14. To avoid striking the hands on a milling machine cutter while setting up, the set-up should be done as far away from the cutter as possible.

15. Do not use compressed air to blow chips from a milling machine table. Use a brush.

Safety Precautions— Heat Treating

1. Make sure furnaces and other heat treating equipment have protective devices.

2. All piping and valves should be identified by standard code color.

3. Valves should be readily accessible with their open and shut positions clearly visible.

4. Gas ovens should be adequately purged before lighting.

5. The furnace should be checked to be sure that, in event of any instrument failure, the safety device will work.

Check Your Knowledge

1. How should a student be dressed to work safely around machinery?

2. Why should sleeves be rolled up above the elbows?

3. How may a wrist watch or ring cause an accident?

4. What should be worn on the hands when using corrosive chemicals?

5. How can a loosely hanging necktie cause an accident?

6. Why should files be fitted with a suitable handle?

7. Blunt edges of tools are dangerous. Why?

8. Why is it important that a wrench fit a nut properly?

9. Safety glasses are necessary when working around machinery. Why?

10. Name some dangers in operating a spinning lathe.

11. What is especially dangerous about working with sheet metal?

12. What happens when hot metal is poured into a mold if the sand is improperly tempered?

13. What is the danger of throwing damp or wet metal into a crucible of molten metal?

14. Name the type of accident that can happen when an object being drilled is not securely held.

15. How should chips be removed from a machine table?

16. Name two causes for a

2-8. Goggles protect the eyes from flying particles when using a lathe grinder.

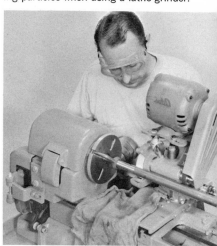

grinding wheel to break up violently.

17. Should grinding wheels be permitted to stand partly immersed in water? Explain your reason.

18. Are safety devices necessary on gas heat-treating furnaces? Why?

1. A great deal of emphasis is placed on safety in industry. Discuss fully.

Terms to Know and Spell

eye shield	*capacity*	*earthenware*
accident	*dangerous*	*squaring shears*
adjusting	*protective*	*precaution*
administer	*injured*	*explosion*
safety	*corrosive*	*purged*

3 ▷ Reading Drawings and Sketching

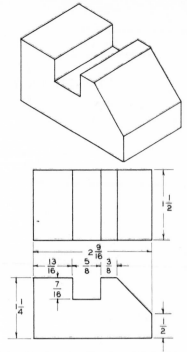

3-1. The two-view drawing of the guide block, showing dimensions, is a working drawing. The one without dimensions is an isometric drawing.

3-2. Two views of a cylindrical shape.

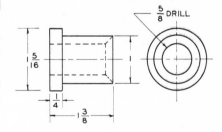

In the metalworking shop you need a working drawing or sketch for any project you make. You also have to develop the ability to interpret a working drawing or blueprint, and transfer the dimensions to your project. Blueprints and other graphic guides are the universal language of the industrial world.

Drawings can include information on what material to use, the size and shape of each part, and what the finished object will look like.

Types of Drawings

The type of drawing most commonly used in the metal shop is the working drawing (orthographic projection). Fig. 3-1. It may have one or several views. Two views are usually required for a simple cylindrical shape. Fig. 3-2. For most objects, however, a three-view drawing is necessary. Fig. 3-3. Usually required are the front, top, and side or end views.

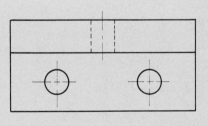

3-3. An example of a three-view drawing of an angle block.

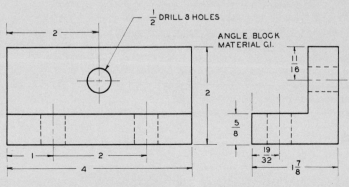

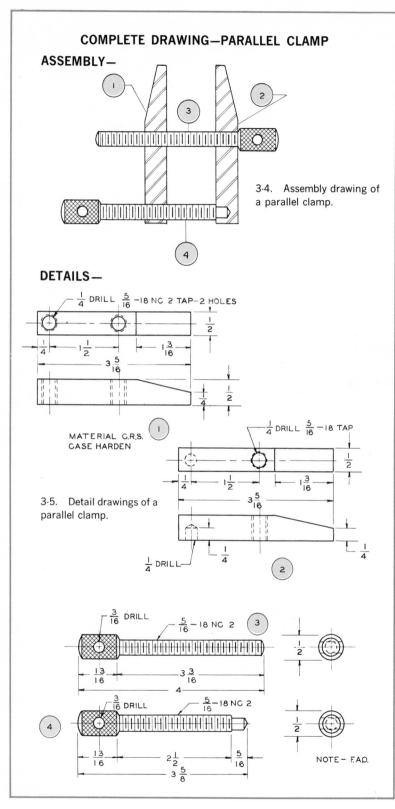

COMPLETE DRAWING—PARALLEL CLAMP

ASSEMBLY—

3-4. Assembly drawing of a parallel clamp.

DETAILS—

¼ DRILL 5/16 —18 NC 2 TAP—2 HOLES

MATERIAL C.R.S.
CASE HARDEN

3-5. Detail drawings of a parallel clamp.

¼ DRILL 5/16 —18 TAP

¼ DRILL

3/16 DRILL 5/16 —18 NC 2

3/16 DRILL 5/16 —18 NC 2

NOTE— F.A.O.

Most sets of drawings also include an assembly and a detail drawing of each part. The assembly drawing shows how the parts fit together, Fig. 3-4, and the detail drawing, Fig. 3-5, gives complete dimensions and notes for making the parts.

Meaning of Lines

Reading a drawing consists of studying all the views of an object to see what the lines, dimensions, and instructions mean, and then deciding how the surfaces are to be shaped. It may not be necessary for the metalworker to make a working drawing, but it is important that he know the types and meanings of lines, symbols, and other information.

In order to give meanings to drawings, different types and "weights" of lines are used. Lines common to working drawings are shown in Fig. 3-6.

• **Object lines,** or outline of parts, are used to show the shape or outline of the part to be made. The object line is heavier than a dimension or center line.

• **Section lines.** On some drawings we have to visualize how the inside would appear if the part were cut in half or a solid piece cut along a certain line. Section lines are thin and equally spaced. Various symbols for these lines are also used to indicate different kinds of materials and to save work. These symbols can be found in a drafting handbook. See description of "section" later in this unit.

• **Hidden lines** are used when parts of an object are concealed by front surfaces. They are sometimes called invisible lines because they represent an invisible surface of the object.

• **A center line** represents the axis of a symmetrical part, such as circles and arcs. They are light broken lines consisting of alternately long and short dashes, closely and evenly spaced.

• **Dimension lines** are unbroken except at the dimension and have an arrowhead at each end to indicate the limit of the object.

• **An extension line,** or witness line as it is sometimes called, extends the edge of the object that is to be dimensioned. The extension line should start about 1/32″ from the object and extend about 1/8″ beyond the point of the arrowhead. It is easier to read many times than are dimensions within a view.

• **Cutting plane** lines are heavy, long and short dashes (one long, two short, one long, two short, etc.) alternately and evenly spaced. They are used to show a section that is to be removed.

• **Break lines** indicate the continuation of the object, which cannot be included in the drawing because of space limitations. Two styles are shown in Fig. 3-6.

Dimensions

In the early days of machine manufacturing in this country, drawings often lacked many necessary dimensions. Not only was this a severe handicap to the worker, but often only the original design plans were available.

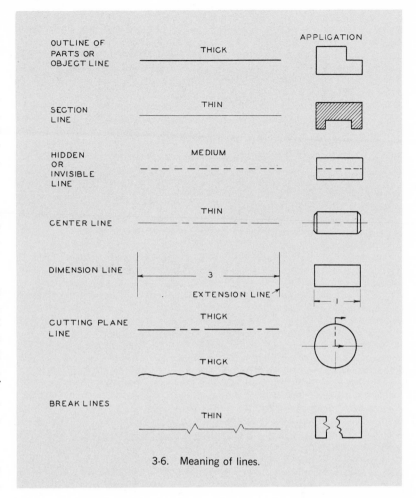

3-6. Meaning of lines.

Later full dimensioning became the practice and, when blueprinting came into use, workmen in widely separated localities could use the same drawings. This development was necessary for successful mass production.

At one time, dimensions on the prints were all in inches and fractions of an inch, the smallest being 1/64″. Then when improvements were made in the control of manufacturing processes, demand arose for specifications that were easier to use and provided a more accurate fit. You can see the difficulty of working with smaller fractions such as 1/128,

and that decimal fractions, such as 3.125 or 4.875, are much better for dimensions requiring accuracy. As a result, decimal dimensions became common in close-tolerance manufacturing.

However, many small articles manufactured today require only inch units and common fractions for dimensioning. The machinists' rule is satisfactory for general shopwork.

A drawing today may be dimensioned entirely with whole numbers, or entirely with decimals, or with a combination of the two, the last being most common. Fig. 3-7. A decimal

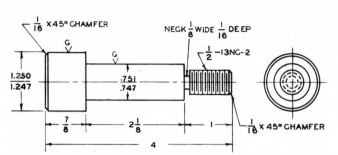

3-7. Dimensions shown in both fractions and decimals. Tolerance is also given in two dimensions written as decimals.

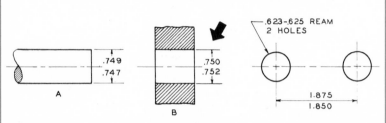

3-8. Method of giving limits. (A) For a shaft the high limit is placed above the low limit, since the shaft is machined from "large to small." (B) For hole dimensions (see arrow) the low limit is placed above, since the hole is machined from "small to large."

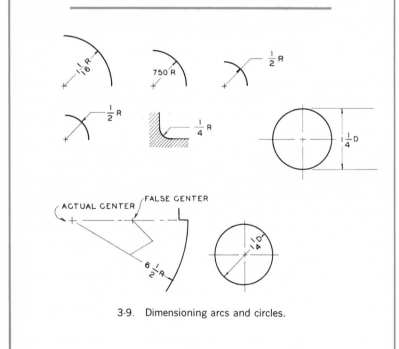

3-9. Dimensioning arcs and circles.

dimension indicates that a greater accuracy in making the part is required. As said, the decimal system also helps eliminate mathematical errors and makes it easier to show allowances and tolerances for each part. Fig. 3-8. Tolerance is the amount of variation permitted in the size of a part or in the location of points or surfaces. For example, a dimension given as 1.375 ±.002″ means it may measure 1.377″ or 1.373″, or anywhere between these dimensions. The tolerance, or total amount of variation "tolerated," is .004″.

Decimal measuring must be done with precision measuring tools such as a micrometer or vernier caliper.

When working from a drawing or blueprint, the dimensions must be followed carefully; the drawing is never measured to determine the size of the parts. Decimal dimensions are read from left to right and from bottom to top.

A circular arc is dimensioned in the view in which its true shape is shown, by giving the numeral denoting its radius, followed by the abbreviation R as shown in Fig. 3-9. Centers are indicated by small crosses except for small or unimportant radii. Fig. 3-10 shows how the various types of lines are used in a drawing.

Sections or Sectional Views

By means of a limited number of carefully selected views, the exterior of most complicated objects can be shown.

However, it is sometimes necessary to show more or less complicated interiors of parts that cannot be shown by means of hidden lines. This is accomplished by slicing through the object as one would cut through an apple. A cutaway view is then drawn of the object and, as said, is called a sectional view or simply a section.

There are many kinds of sectional views. For example, if the cutting plane line passes halfway through the object, the result is a half-section. Fig. 3-11 (B). When the cutting plane passes "fully" through the object it is called a full section. Fig. 3-11 (A).

Scale Drawings

A part may be too large to be drawn full size. Or it may be so small that the actual-size drawing would be hard to read. Draftsmen solve these problems by making scale drawings. The part is drawn in a convenient size, exactly in proportion to the object.

Of course, to interpret scale drawings, you have to know exactly how much larger or smaller the drawing is, compared with the part. This information is usually shown on the drawing, expressed as a *ratio*. For example, if the drawing is half size, the scale would read 1:2 (the ratio of 1 to 2). If the drawing is twice actual size, the scale is expressed as 2:1. If the drawing is full size, the scale would be given as 1:1.

Symbols

Besides the views and dimensions, more information is usually needed to produce a part. The kind of material, its treatment, the number of parts required, tools and dies needed—all of this and more have to be conveyed to the worker.

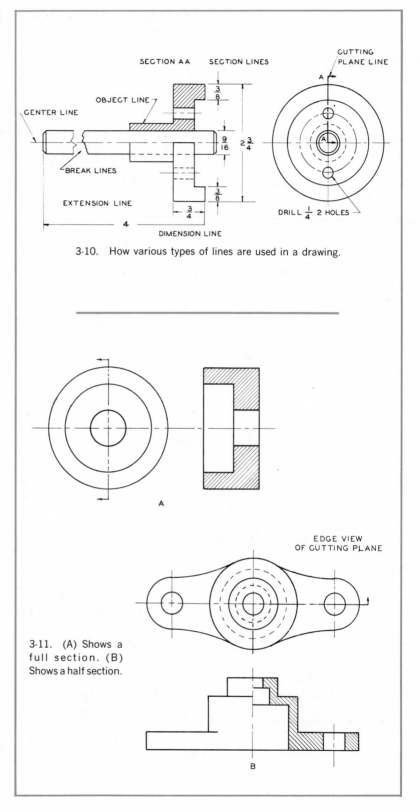

3-10. How various types of lines are used in a drawing.

3-11. (A) Shows a full section. (B) Shows a half section.

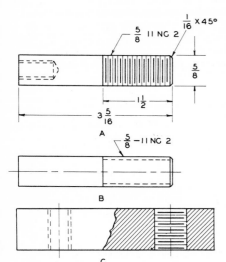

3-12. Symbols for threads: (A) external, (B) simplified external, (C) internal.

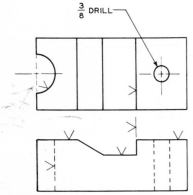

3-13. A simple casting having several finished surfaces. The two views show how finish marks are indicated on the drawing.

The use of symbols saves a great deal of time yet conveys to the worker necessary information. The two most common symbols used on machine drawings are those that show screw threads and finish marks. The screw thread symbols may be either regular, Fig. 3-12 (A), or simplified, Fig. 3-12 (B). Finished or machined surfaces are indicated by a V-like mark. Two styles of finish marks are approved by the ASA, the newer V symbol and the older *f* symbol. Fig. 3-13 represents a simple casting showing several finished surfaces and how they are indicated on a drawing. The point of the V should rest on the line of the metal in a manner similar to that of a tool bit.

When it is necessary to control surface roughness of finished surfaces, the V is used as a base for more elaborate surface quality symbols.

Notes

Holes that are to be drilled, bored, reamed, punched, cored,

3-14. Holes that are to be drilled, reamed, etc., and parts that are to be threaded or knurled are usually specified by standard notes.

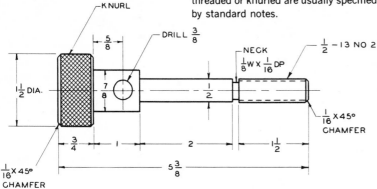

etc., are usually specified by standard notes, as shown in Fig. 3-14. The order of items in a note corresponds to the order of procedure in the shop producing the hole. Specifications include information such as special instructions for machining, kind of material, heat treatment, and finish.

Notes are classified as *general notes* when they apply to an entire drawing, or *local notes* when they apply to specific items.

Abbreviations

There are many abbreviations placed on drawings. A few of the most common ones are listed in Table 3-A.

Sketching

Sometimes it is necessary to convey an idea to a metalworker by means of a simple drawing in freehand. Most designs made by an engineer are first prepared in

COMMON ABBREVIATIONS	
Abbreviations	**Meaning**
THD.	Thread
NC	National Coarse
NF	National Fine
UNC	Unified N.C.
UNF	Unified N.F.
DIA.	Diameter
R	Radius
RH	Right Hand
LH	Left Hand
FAO	Finish All Over
CSK.	Countersink
CBORE	Counterbore
CI	Cast Iron
CRS	Cold-rolled Steel
HDN.	Harden
RPM	Revolutions per Minute
ASSY.	Assembly
CP	Circular Pitch
DR.	Drill
GA.	Gage or Gauge

Table 3-A.

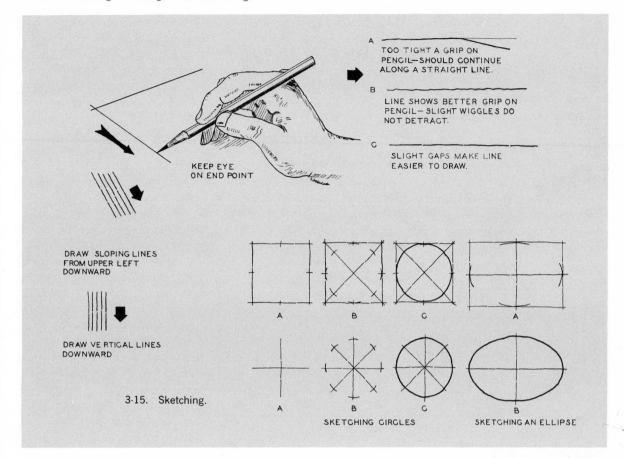

A — TOO TIGHT A GRIP ON PENCIL—SHOULD CONTINUE ALONG A STRAIGHT LINE.

B — LINE SHOWS BETTER GRIP ON PENCIL— SLIGHT WIGGLES DO NOT DETRACT.

C — SLIGHT GAPS MAKE LINE EASIER TO DRAW.

KEEP EYE ON END POINT

DRAW SLOPING LINES FROM UPPER LEFT DOWNWARD

DRAW VERTICAL LINES DOWNWARD

3-15. Sketching.

SKETCHING CIRCLES

SKETCHING AN ELLIPSE

the form of freehand sketches and then turned over to the draftsman who draws them with instruments to scale.

Freehand sketches are of great assistance to the designer in organizing his thoughts and recording his ideas. The degree of perfection required in a sketch depends upon its use.

Soft pencils such as HB or F should be used for freehand sketching. Drafting offices usually have a supply of sketch pads with sheets ruled horizontally and vertically eight squares to the inch.

The chief difference between a mechanical drawing and a freehand sketch lies in the character or technique of the lines. A good freehand line need not be rigidly straight or exactly uniform. The quality of a freehand line lies in its heavy and light variations.

Since most of the lines in sketching are straight, it is important to learn how to make them well. Hold the pencil about 1½″ from the point, approximately at a right angle to the line to be drawn. Draw horizontal lines from left to right with a free, easy wrist-and-arm movement. Draw vertical lines downward with finger-and-wrist movement. Fig. 3-15. Inclined lines may be drawn the same.

Small circles and arcs can easily be sketched in one or two strokes. For a larger circle, Fig. 3-15, sketch the enclosing square lightly, mark the mid-points of the sides, draw light arcs tangent to the sides of the square, then use a heavier line to make the final circle.

Check Your Knowledge

1. What is a working drawing?

2. What is meant by the term "orthographic projection"?

3. Name the three most common views used in a drawing.

4. Distinguish between an assembly and a detail drawing.

5. Why is it important for a metalworker to know the meanings of lines?

6. What is the purpose of a cutting plane line?

7. *What created the need for more accurate dimensions on drawings?*

8. *What is a decimal dimension?*

9. *Why shouldn't a drawing be measured to obtain the required dimensions?*

10. *What is meant by a half-section? A whole section?*

11. *Why is it necessary to make a drawing to scale under some circumstances?*

12. *What is a symbol? How are they used?*

13. *What is a finish mark? Explain how it is used.*

14. *Explain the importance of notes on a drawing.*

15. *Why is it necessary to use abbreviations on a drawing?*

16. *Why is it important to be able to make a freehand sketch?*

For Class Discussion

Explain why the working drawing is the language of the industrial world.

Of what importance is the draftsman to industry?

Terms to Know and Spell

working drawing	*symmetrical*	*proportion*
sketch	*dimension*	*view*
assembly drawing	*fraction*	*finish mark*
cutting plane	*sectional*	*horizontal*
symbols		

---

4 ▷ Planning Your Project

In the industrial world today the importance of planning is clearly realized.

A well-planned product pleases the consumer and is successful. One that is poorly planned may never reach the market, or it may do so only after much waste of costly materials and workers' time.

Consequently, before a new model of a car or airplane, for instance, is placed in production, many skilled and well-paid people contribute to its planning.

Some of the most important work is done by designers and engineers who make the necessary plans and drawings.

Accuracy and efficiency are required in this work and in other phases of planning, such as writing specifications and making shop orders. By following the same procedures and striving for the highest standards in the school shop, you will gain valuable knowledge of how our great industries work.

You should develop the skills to make your own plans, including these important items:

A bill of materials showing: (1) number of pieces for each part, (2) sizes of stock, (3) name of each part, (4) kinds of material and a (5) list of standard parts such as bolts and nuts.

Before starting your project you will also need:

A working drawing, blueprint or shop sketch of the project, and a planning sheet. The planning sheet, or plan of procedure as it is sometimes called, is a list of the steps needed to complete the project. These steps, called operations, should be listed in careful order. Certain operations have to be done before others can be performed. If the operations are carefully planned much time can be saved in the construction of the project. All tools and equipment needed should be listed on the planning sheet. This will save many trips to the tool crib and results in a more efficient work schedule.

4-1. An assembly drawing of a depth gage.

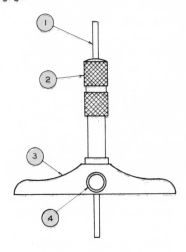

ASSEMBLY-DEPTH GAGE

Planning Procedure

In making a plan of procedure, Table 4-A, break down the project into the smallest parts and list all steps necessary to make each part. Analyze the drawing carefully to see that you understand all the construction details. If in doubt, consult with your instructor.

After all the parts have been made, carefully check the assembly drawing that goes with the detail drawing. This will show you how the parts are assembled. Fig. 4-1 shows a typical assembly drawing and Fig. 4-2 a detail drawing of the parts.

Table 4-A lists materials used in the construction of the depth gage. A stock list, catalog or handbook of materials can be obtained from manufacturers and metal supply companies.

Tools and Equipment

Engine lathe, metal-cutting band saw or milling machine, drill press, drill chuck, center punch, knurling tool, ⅛″ drill, ⁵⁄₁₆″ drill, files, dividers, scriber, 10-32 tap and die, layout dye and abrasive paper.

Procedure

1. Secure blueprint or make sketch of project.

2. Cut all pieces to size as shown on Bill of Materials.

3. Base
   (a) Coat stock with layout dye.
   (b) Layout shape on stock.
   (c) Cut to shape on band saw or milling machine.
   (d) File all sides smooth.
   (e) Drill ⅛″ hole through base.

PLANNING SHEET

Name _____ Grade _____

Date project started _____

Date project finished _____

DEPTH GAGE (See Figs. 4-1 and 4-2)

(See Tools and Equipment and Procedures in adjoining column.)

BILL OF MATERIALS

No. of Pieces	Size	Part Name	Kind of Material	Cost
1	½″ x ⅝″ x 3½″	Base	Cold-finished steel	
1	⅝″ x 4″ Round	Barrel	Cold-finished steel	
1	½″ x 2″ Round	Thumb screw	Cold-finished steel	
1	⅛″ x 4½″	Rod	Drill rod	

(See Pages 453 and 454 for materials used in metalworking.)

Table 4-A

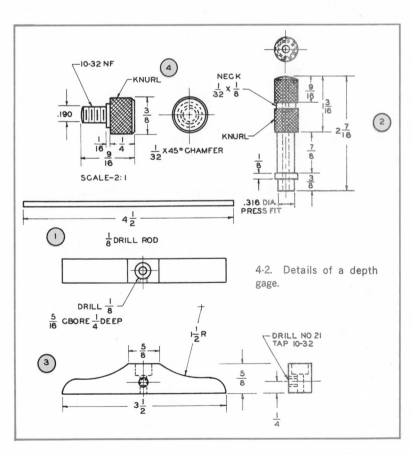

4-2. Details of a depth gage.

(f) Counterbore ⁵⁄₁₆″ deep with ⁵⁄₁₆″ drill.

(g) Polish with abrasive paper.

4. Barrel

(a) Center drill both ends.

(b) Mount between centers on lathe.

(c) Turn to dimensions.

(d) Knurl.

(e) Place in chuck and drill ⅛″ hole.

(f) Round knurled end.

(g) Polish with abrasive paper.

5. Thumbscrew

(a) True the stock in the chuck.

(b) Turn to dimensions.

(c) Knurl.

(d) Face radius on threaded end.

(e) Cut threads with 10-32 die.

6. Rod

(a) Cut a piece of ⅛″ drill rod to length.

(b) File ends smooth.

7. Assemble. Barrel should press into base.

Check Your Knowledge

1. Why is it important to plan a project before you build it?

2. Prepare a bill of materials for a project of your choice.

3. Make a list of the tools, materials, and equipment needed to construct this project.

4. Work out the correct plan of procedure.

5. What does a planning sheet contain?

6. What does the bill of materials contain?

5 ▷ Metals in Our Everyday Lives

Have you ever thought how important metals are? Consider the transportation and communication fields, for example. Without steel and aluminum we would have no automobiles, no aircraft, no railroads. For electronic communications, copper is a vital element.

So it is throughout industry. Even those manufacturers who do not use metal as a raw material rely on it for their production machinery and in countless other ways. The high living standard of which we Americans are justly proud would be unachievable without rich metal resources.

This unit will help you understand the uses of metal in industry and your work will become more meaningful. Also you will be better able to decide whether a job in the important metals industry has a place in your future.

Raw Materials Used in Making Steel

Iron

The term iron refers loosely to the many alloys of which iron is a base. Iron has been known from prehistoric times. No one has found out how man discovered the utility of iron, or how he learned the art of extracting the metal from ores.

The early history of iron is confused with mythology, religion, and folklore. Man's first iron probably came from meteors which contained nickel-iron alloys and could be used without refinement for weapons and tools.

The first production of iron from oxides (rust) probably occurred about 1500 B.C., in the area between the Black and Caspian seas. By 1350 B.C. the art of iron smelting had spread to Mesapotamia, Palestine, and Egypt, and then through the entire Mediterranean.

Iron Ore

Two-thirds of the ore used in American steel mills comes from domestic mines. In 1962, this amounted to some 74 million tons.

To produce a ton of steel, a typical steel mill requires almost two and three-fourths tons of raw materials.

Although deposits of iron ore are found in a number of states, the Lake Superior area has long been the major supplier in the United States. The greatest deposits are in Minnesota, where the famous Mesabi Range is located. In 1962 this area supplied over 57 million tons of iron ore.

The ore is carried from the mines in freight cars and is dumped into bins holding several carloads each. The ore is then transferred to large boats and carried to Chicago, Gary, Cleveland, Detroit, and other cities along the Great Lakes. These boats are capable of carrying about 12,000 tons of ore each. Fig. 5-1.

American ores consist chiefly of natural iron oxides containing minor percentages of non-metallic impurities known as gangue. The ore from the vicinity of Lake Superior is a heavy, reddish, stone-like mineral called hematite. It contains two parts of iron and three parts of oxygen. Another ore, magnetite, is a black magnetic oxide which contains 72.5 per cent iron. The high quality magnetite ores of Sweden are a source of that country's steel, famous for its freedom from sulphur and phosphorus. Incidentally, as said, purest iron in its natural state comes not from the earth at all, but from the sky in the form of meteors.

Iron is combined with carbon and other alloys to make steel. Coal, which is used for heat in the production of steel, is mined in twenty-four states. West Virginia, Kentucky, Pennsylvania, and Illinois are the largest suppliers, providing nearly three-fourths of the coking coal mined in the United States.

Another requirement in steel production is limestone. Its use will be explained in the following pages. Nearly every state has deposits of limestone; those near Cacite, Michigan, are particularly important to the steel industry.

Smelting Iron Ores

PIG IRON

Although iron is relatively abundant in the chemical compounds making up the earth's crust, as it comes from the mines, Fig. 5-2, iron ore must go through processing which is expensive and complicated.

Making pig iron is the first step in purifying the iron. The iron ore becomes pig iron when the impurities are burned out in a

5-1.   A boat used to transport iron ore on the Great Lakes.

5-2.   Mining iron ore.

5-3. Blast furnace, showing down-comers from furnace to dust catcher and electronic precipitator for further removing of dust.

the hot blast. Some of the gas from the top of the furnace is used to preheat this air.

It takes about 2 tons of iron ore, 1 ton of coke, and ½ ton of limestone, to make 1 ton of pig iron. The ore, coke, and limestone are dumped into the top of the blast furnace. In operation the furnace may be considered as a tall column of iron oxide and gangue, coke, and limestone, all mixed together but remaining in lumps large enough to allow free passage of air up through the mixture.

The burning coke and the blast of very hot air melt the iron ore. The carbon of the coke unites with the oxygen of the air to form carbon monoxide, which passes up through the column along with nitrogen from the air. The carbon monoxide becomes cooler, though

still very hot, and unites with more oxygen to form carbon dioxide. As the material in the bottom of the column is consumed, the iron settles and reaches the hottest part of the furnace; it then becomes molten and runs down to collect in the bottom of the furnace.

The limestone is used as a flux to carry off the gangue. These two substances combine to form a slag which, because it is lighter than the molten metal, floats to the top. The slag and the iron are drawn off from time to time, the slag through a cinder notch and the iron through a lower iron notch or tapping hole. Fig. 5-4.

As it comes from the furnace, the iron is known simply as hot metal. Not until it is cast in molds is it called pig iron. A large blast furnace can yield from 500 to

blast furnace. Though still containing some impurities, pig iron has a high metal content.

The blast furnace is a steel shell about 90 to 100 feet high, lined with fire brick. Fig. 5-3. The internal diameter varies, being about 25 feet at the widest part. Fig. 5-4 shows a cross-section of a blast furnace with the important parts labeled. The furnace top consists of a hopper and double-bell arrangement for control of the entering charge (the load of ore, coke, and limestone), and for inhibiting the loss of gases. The gases are carried off through a pipe near the top of the furnace and used as a fuel. Air is blown into the furnace through nozzles called tuyeres which are located at intervals around the bottom. Usually three or more stoves heat the air for

5-4. Cross-section of a blast furnace. Alternate layers of coke, ore, and limestone are charged through the top and pass downward through the furnace where the iron is separated and melted.

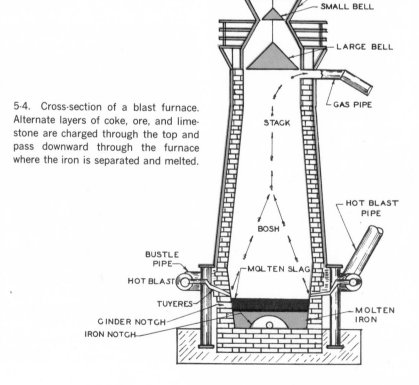

1,000 tons of hot metal in 24 hours.

CAST IRON

Cast iron is formed by remelting pig iron and other materials—including limestone and prepared fluxes—in a cupola furnace. Fig. 5-5. The limestone and fluxes aid in separating the impurities from the pig iron. The limestone also acts as a flushing agent to carry off the oxides and ash from the fuel. The cupola is fired with coke to produce the high temperature required for melting iron. The fuel is lighted at the bottom, and the blast from the blower enters through the tuyeres. The air blast furnishes the oxygen. With the carbon in the coke it brings on the combustion necessary to create the heat to melt the metal.

The amount of air supplied to the furnace is carefully calculated to produce efficient operation. As the charge of metal descends in the furnace, it is preheated until it reaches the area where the melting takes place. This area is called the melting zone. The metal melts in small drops, and these drops pass down through the bed charge of coke to the well of the furnace, where they collect to form a bath of liquid metal.

The furnace is tapped by the furnace tender, who uses a sharpened metal tapping bar to remove the clay plug from a tap hole, as shown. The metal flows through the hole down the spout into the receiving ladle.

Cast iron is brittle and gray in color. It is the most common material for making castings such as for automobile engine blocks and can be machined on the lathe,

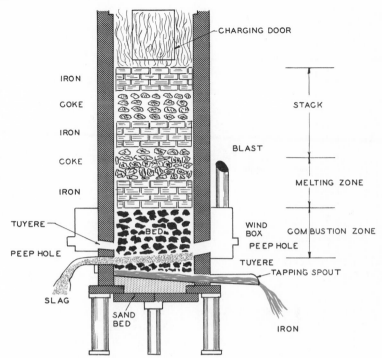

5-5.   Cross-section of a cupola furnace.

GAGE NUMBERS		
Gage No.	Brown & Sharpe or American Standard for nonferrous wire and sheet metals	United States Standard for iron and steel plate
16	0.0508	0.0625
18	0.0403	0.0500
20	0.0320	0.0375
22	0.0253	0.0313
24	0.0201	0.0250
26	0.0159	0.0188
28	0.0126	0.0156
30	0.0100	0.0125

Table 5-A

shaper, milling machine, and other machine tools. It contains from 1.50 to 6.00 per cent carbon. It melts at about 2,200 degrees Fahrenheit.

Ferrous metals in plate and sheet are measured by the United States Standard (USS) gage. See Table 5-A.

MALLEABLE CAST IRON

Malleable iron is cast iron which has been made softer, stronger, and tougher by baking in an oven for a prolonged period. This tends to burn out some of the carbon. The annealing process necessary to convert white cast

37

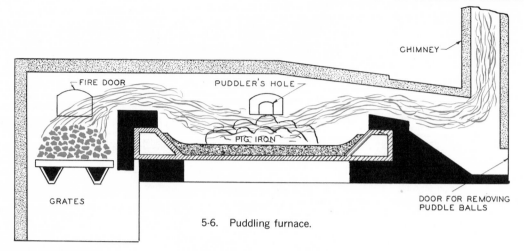

5-6. Puddling furnace.

iron into malleable cast iron is as follows:

1. The castings are packed in cast iron pots with a pack-material supporting them to prevent warpage.

2. The pots are then placed in an oven. Their joints are sealed with clay to prevent oxidation.

3. The temperature is raised to 1,550 to 1,650 degrees F., as measured by temperature controls and held at that point for 40 to 60 hours.

4. The temperature is slowly lowered to 1,275 degrees F. The oven doors are opened, and the pots are removed.

WROUGHT IRON

Wrought iron is a product of the puddling furnace. Fig. 5-6. Pig iron is charged on a heated hearth which has been covered with iron oxide. As the pig iron melts, silicon, phosphorus, manganese, and carbon are oxidized. The oxides of these elements form a slag which, because of the iron oxide lining of the furnace, is high in iron oxide content. After the charge has become liquid, the heat is reduced and the iron oxide of the slag reacts with the remaining silicon, manganese, phosphorus, sulphur, and carbon in the charge.

The liquid charge is stirred or puddled. This is done so that every part of the melted iron is touched by the flame. Most of the carbon and other impurities are burned out and the iron forms a pasty, metallic mass. This paste is worked into lumps or balls, called puddle balls, which are removed from the furnace and squeezed, hammered, and rolled into bars while hot.

Wrought iron is very tough, but it can be hammered, bent, twisted, and stretched with relative ease. Because of these characteristics many beautiful projects can be made with it in the school.

The purest wrought iron is made in Norway and Sweden. Therefore it is known as Norwegian iron and Swedish iron.

STEEL

In the early Colonial days, steel was rare. It was imported for swords, bayonets, and cutting tools. Several attempts had been made to produce steel, but it remained for Samuel Higley of Simsbury, Connecticut, to be credited with the first steel produced in America, around 1725.

What is believed to be the first steelworks in America was established in Trenton, New Jersey, in 1734. Apparently the steel was made by packing charcoal around wrought iron bars and heating the whole mass for a week in a closed furnace. The bars absorbed enough carbon from the charcoal to become steel.

Between 1850 and 1860, the Age of Steel was really born. This was due to the invention of the Bessemer process for steel making. Until then, steel had been available only by the pound. The Bessemer process (which will be described later), followed by the invention not many years later of the open hearth furnace, made

Composition of Wrought Iron by Weight	
Iron	96.76 per cent
Carbon	0.10 per cent
Manganese	0.01 per cent
Silicon	0.20 per cent
Sulphur	0.03 per cent
Phosphorus	0.20 per cent
Slag	2.70 per cent

Table 5-B

steel available by thousands of tons.

What Is Steel?

After learning how pig iron is made in the blast furnace and is ready to be converted into steel, this is a good time to ask, "What is steel exactly and how does it differ specifically from iron?"

Pig iron contains a number of elements such as manganese, silicon, phosphorus, and particularly carbon, in high enough proportions to make it brittle. The amount of carbon varies from 3.5 to 4.4 per cent. To make steel, these elements are largely burned out or oxidized from the iron, and the carbon usually reduced to less than 1 per cent and sometimes as little as 0.02 per cent.

Ordinary steel is an alloy of iron with carbon, which is malleable, in the form of a cast block or ingot. Such steel is called plain carbon steel.

Plain carbon steels constitute about 92 per cent of all steel pro-

5-8. Structural mill.

duced. The remaining 8 per cent of steel production consists of alloy steels. A more detailed explanation of these will be made later in this unit.

Making Steel

Steel is produced by one of the following methods:
- Bessemer converter.
- Open hearth furnace.
- Crucible furnace.
- Electric furnace.
- Basic oxygen process.

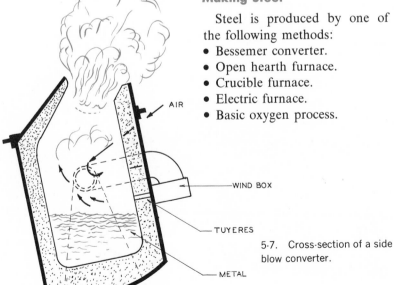

5-7. Cross-section of a side blow converter.

THE BESSEMER CONVERTER

An English engineer, Sir Henry Bessemer, developed a process of blowing a stream of air through a molten mass of pig iron in a pear-shaped furnace. Fig. 5-7 shows a cross-section of such a furnace, called a Bessemer converter.

The first steel made by the Bessemer process in the United States was produced in 1864 at Wyandotte, Michigan. The peak of Bessemer steel production was reached in 1906 when nearly 13,800,000 tons were produced here. Three years later, open hearth steel surpassed it for the first time. Bessemer steel production since 1939 has averaged a little under 6 per cent of total American steel production, although improvements are now being developed in the process.

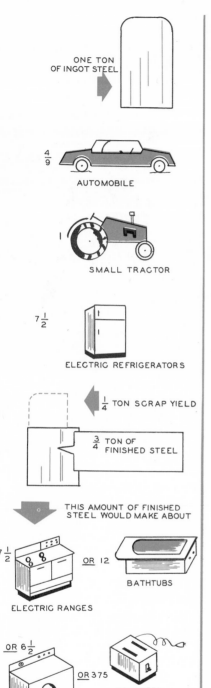

ONE TON OF INGOT STEEL

$\frac{4}{9}$ AUTOMOBILE

1 SMALL TRACTOR

$7\frac{1}{2}$ ELECTRIC REFRIGERATORS

$\frac{1}{4}$ TON SCRAP YIELD

$\frac{3}{4}$ TON OF FINISHED STEEL

THIS AMOUNT OF FINISHED STEEL WOULD MAKE ABOUT

$7\frac{1}{2}$ ELECTRIC RANGES   OR 12 BATHTUBS

OR $6\frac{1}{2}$ AUTOMATIC WASHERS   OR 375 TOASTERS   OR 1,000 ELECTRIC IRONS

5-9. How big is a ton of ingot steel? Note what it will make.

The Bessemer converter is a large, pear-shaped steel shell lined with a material that resists acid or basic melting. It is supported by two trunnions or pins. One is hollow to carry the air blast to the wind chamber; the other is geared to a motor so that the furnace can be tilted. The removable bottom contains the wind chamber and tuyeres. The converter is 15 to 22 feet high and holds 30 tons of metal.

A charge of molten cast iron is poured into the converter, which is tilted to a horizontal position. The air blast is turned on to prevent the metal from flowing into the tuyeres. The furnace is then raised to a vertical position. The air blowing through the metal oxidizes the silicon, manganese, and carbon out of the charge. Sparks and flame belch from the open mouth of the converter. At first brilliant sparks burst forth, followed by brown fumes and tongues of flame, which means that the oxygen is burning out the impurities. Next the flame be-comes longer and intensely bright as the carbon burns out.

After 12 to 15 minutes the flame suddenly dies out. The oxidizing process has been completed. The furnace is then turned to a horizontal position, and the blast is shut off. The heat created by this process is so great that the mass of metal is white hot. It is then poured into a ladle, where additions are made to recarburize it to the point required for that particular melt. The hot metal finally is cast in ingot molds.

Some of the largest uses of Bessemer steel are for nails, screws, wire, rails, and building materials such as beams. Fig. 5-8, page 39.

Fig. 5-9 shows the many products that can be made from a ton of ingot steel.

THE OPEN HEARTH FURNACE

The open hearth furnace, Fig. 5-10, is a regenerative type consisting of a hearth lined with highly refractory material, dish-shaped, about 2 feet deep. Above

5-10. The open hearth furnace is charged through seven large doors and steel is tapped from the opposite side.

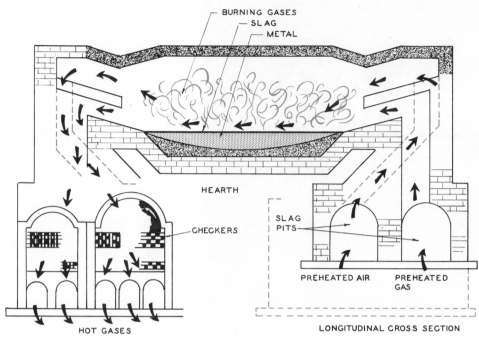

BURNING GASES
SLAG
METAL

HEARTH

CHECKERS

SLAG
PITS

PREHEATED AIR   PREHEATED
GAS

HOT GASES

LONGITUDINAL CROSS SECTION

5-11. Schematic cross-section of an open hearth furnace.

each end of the hearth is a burner. Gas and air unite at the burners and burst forth in a long flame which plays over the surface of the metal in the hearth, supplying terrific heat. The gas and air are preheated in chambers filled with firebrick laid in checkerboard fashion and called checkers. Fig. 5-11.

In operation, the flame coming from the right end of the furnace passes over the hearth. The burnt gases from the flame are drawn down through the checkers at the left end, heating these compartments. At the end of 10 or 15 minutes the direction of the fuel, air, and flame is reversed from left to right, improving combustion. This change of direction takes place every 10 or 15 minutes until the steel is ready to be drawn from the furnace.

The furnace is charged with limestone and iron ore, followed by iron or steel scrap. Iron ore

constitutes 2 to 20 per cent, scrap 30 to 40 per cent, and the rest is molten pig iron. About half of the scrap comes from waste steel that collects in the mills. The rest comes from junked automobiles, machinery, railroad cars, and other discards. The charge is heated for about 2 hours and then molten pig iron is added.

After 8 to 12 hours, the furnace is tapped into a large ladle and the final alloying elements are combined to give the steel the composition called for by the purchaser.

CRUCIBLE FURNACE

The crucible furnace, Fig. 5-12, is the oldest device used for the

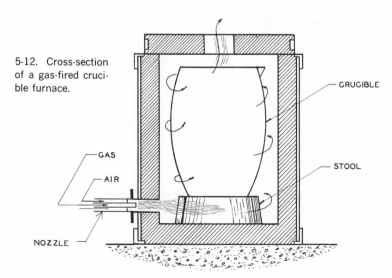

5-12. Cross-section of a gas-fired crucible furnace.

CRUCIBLE

STOOL

GAS

AIR

NOZZLE

5-13.   A 140-ton top-charge electric-arc melting furnace.

Excellent-quality tool steel was made in crucible furnaces, but since each crucible can hold only a small amount of metal, the process is slow, expensive, and has been largely replaced by the electric furnace.

ELECTRIC FURNACE

The electric furnace, Fig. 5-13, is used to make stainless steel, heat-resistant, and tool steels. The feature of this process is the heat generated by an electric arc.

The electric furnace makes superior alloy steels because it can be more rigidly regulated than the Bessemer converter or the open hearth furnace.

The main charge introduced into the furnace consists of steel scrap. In operation, the current is turned on and the electrodes, Figs. 5-14 and 5-15, are lowered until an arc strikes from them to the scrap. The intense heat generated by the arcs melts the entire charge. This is called a cold melt process. There are two principal stages in this process:

1. The scrap is completely melted and silicon, phosphorus, manganese and carbon are removed. The oxidization of these elements form a slag which floats

manufacture of high-carbon and alloy steels. It is now virtually obsolete. However, by studying it briefly you can learn some important principles of making steel.

High-carbon steel is made by melting wrought iron, scrap steel, and carbon in a barrel-shaped, graphite crucible 20 inches high and 12 inches in diameter. The desired hardness of the steel determines the amount of carbon to be placed in the crucible. For alloy steel, materials such as tungsten and chromium are also placed in the crucible.

5-15.   Tapping a 70-ton electric furnace.

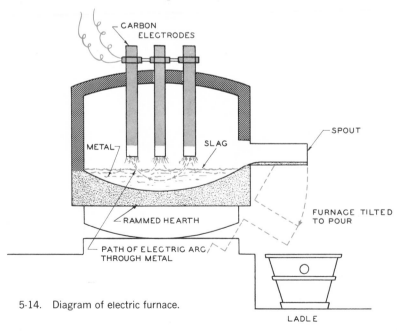

5-14.   Diagram of electric furnace.

5-16. Coreless induction furnace.

on top of the molten steel and is skimmed off.

2. Some of the sulphur and other undesirable elements are eliminated in a new slag. It is during this period that the exact chemical composition of the steel is made as ordered. This is done by adding the right amounts of alloying elements such as chromium, nickel, or tungsten. After 4 to 12 hours the furnace is tapped.

The coreless electric induction furnace, Fig. 5-16, is a newer type used for making fine steel. It operates on the principle of an electric transformer.

Basic Oxygen Process

The making of steel by the basic oxygen process has grown rapidly in the past few years and shows promise of greater growth in the years ahead. In this process a water-cooled lance is lowered into the top of the container or vessel and oxygen of 99.5 purity is forced into the furnace at supersonic speed. The oxygen quickly burns off the unwanted elements contained in the charge of molten iron and scrap.

Only a few years ago basic oxygen vessels produced steel at a rate of about 50 tons an hour. Today a vessel has a potential almost ten times that amount. To reach this high level of output requires vast quantities of oxygen —about 2,000 cubic feet per ton of steel. See chart below.

Types of Steel

Carbon Steels

Carbon steels are classified by the amount of carbon that they contain. This is expressed in points or by percentage (100 points is equivalent to 1 per cent).

• *Low carbon steel,* often called mild steel, contains 0.10 to 0.30 per cent carbon (10 to 30 points). The low carbon content makes it impossible to harden this type of steel. However, it is easily machined and is suitable for many school projects.

• *Medium carbon steel* contains 0.30 to 0.60 per cent carbon. Such machine steel can be used for bolts, shafts, and school projects such as hammer heads and parts that require hardness.

• *High carbon steel,* known as tool steel or high carbon tool steel, contains from 0.60 to 1.50 per cent carbon. The best grades are made in the electric and the crucible furnace. It is called tool steel because such tools as taps, dies, drills, and reamers are made from this type of steel. Alloying elements are added to tool steel during the process of melting so that it will do things that plain carbon steel cannot do.

Hot-rolled Steel

Some steel is formed into ingots. Ingots may be rolled while hot between a series of rollers which are moved closer together as the steel goes back and forth between them. Hot water is sprayed on the steel as it passes the last set of rollers, leaving a black scale surface, to be cleaned off later. This is a low carbon, general purpose steel. It is made in the open hearth furnace.

Cold-finished Steel

This steel is made either by drawing the metal through a die or rolling the metal through rollers to form the bars to shape. Round

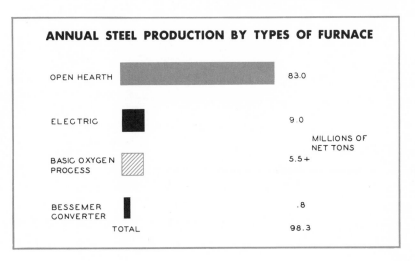

ANNUAL STEEL PRODUCTION BY TYPES OF FURNACE	
OPEN HEARTH	83.0
ELECTRIC	9.0
	MILLIONS OF NET TONS
BASIC OXYGEN PROCESS	5.5+
BESSEMER CONVERTER	.8
TOTAL	98.3

steel bars are formed by drawing the steel through dies. The squares and flats are put through rollers to obtain their shape. These bars have a smooth finish and a shiny surface. Round bars or wires may also be called *cold-drawn* steel because they are drawn through dies, while flats and squares may be called cold-rolled steel because they are passed through rollers.

ALLOY STEELS

Alloy steel is a carefully made steel with sufficient alloying metals added to modify the properties of plain carbon steel. An alloying compound or element is one that is more or less soluble in the major metal and one that participates in physical or chemical reactions at various temperatures, thus modifying the properties. Alloying metals vary, from very low (0.0005%) boron or 0.1% vanadium to very high (20% chromium or more).

Alloys are needed for parts that are subject to severe stresses, strains, corrosion, and wear. Each grade has specific properties. Silicon steel, for instance, has a high electrical resistance and is therefore excellent for transformer cores.

Properties are also determined by the amount of an alloy. Alloying elements are added to the steel during the process of melting. Properties include:

- Hardness, for cutting or resistance to wear.
- Strength and toughness.
- Ability to hold its size and shape during hardening.
- Ability to withstand heat so great that it would soften plain carbon steel.

Some of the most common of the alloying elements used in alloy steels are described below:

- *Manganese* when added to steel in the amounts from 1% to 15%, produces an alloy with hardness and resistance-to-wear properties. Manganese makes steel easier to hot roll or forge. In simple terms, the effect of adding more manganese to a plain carbon steel is to increase the degree of hardness.
- *Chromium,* when alloyed with steel, causes the hardness to penetrate deeper and when present in sufficient quantity will give oil-hardening properties. Chromium contributes high-polish quality, wear resistance, and toughness but raises the temperature necessary for hardening.

Plain carbon-chromium steels may contain from .25 to 1.50% chromium and find their largest use in household appliances and such tools as twist drills, reamers, machine knives, mandrels, and car bumpers.

- *Nickel* is used as an alloying element in steel to increase its strength and toughness and to resist certain heat-treatment strains. Nickel lowers the hardening temperature somewhat and tends to make the steel oil-hardening rather than water-hardening. For general use, the amount of nickel varies from 1% to 4%. Nickel plating is used under chromium plating, on trim for automobiles and appliances.
- *Vanadium* is sometimes added in small quantities (about .15%) to an otherwise straight carbon steel. It acts as a deoxidizer and cleanser and helps make a fine-grained steel. In tool steel it resists shock and jarring better than straight carbon steel.

- *Silicon.* Practically all tool steel contains a small percentage of silicon (usually from .10% to .30% —note the *decimal points*) which is added for much the same purpose as small quantities of manganese to facilitate casting and hot working. In tool steel, silicon imparts hardening and toughening qualities.
- *Tungsten.* Tungsten is added to straight carbon steel to produce a fine, dense grain structure. It must be added in fairly large quantities to be effective. Using 12% to 20% in conjunction with chromium, it gives the steel a new property—namely red-hardness. A cutting tool steel containing 18% tungsten and 4% chromium can continue to cut, even after the cutting edge has been heated to a dull red color (about 1,000 degrees F.). This high-speed alloy is undoubtedly the most important tool steel in existence.
- *Molybdenum* somewhat shares the properties of both chromium and tungsten. When used between a ratio of only .25% and 1.50%, in conjunction with silicon, manganese, chromium, or other elements, molybdenum increases the toughness and strength of tool steel.

TOOL AND DIE STEELS

Any steel that is used for the working parts of tools may be called "tool and die" steel.

Tool steel must contain, alloyed with iron, some elements that give it the ability to harden. The most important of these is carbon. In general, tool steels do not contain less than .60% or more than 1.30% carbon. Other alloying elements are frequently used to supplement the carbon. There are so many different types of tool and die steels that often steel manufacturers give them trade names.

Properties of Metals

Modern industry uses many different types of steel and other metals. Each type is selected for its special properties. Some of these properties are described below.

• *Ductility* is the property or characteristic of a softer metal such as wrought iron that permits it to be hammered, drawn out, molded, or shaped without fracturing or shattering. It is the opposite of "brittle."

• *Brittleness* means that a metal breaks or cracks easily. Some cast iron and hardened steels are brittle. A spring is hard but not brittle.

• *Elasticity* is the property which permits metal to return to its original shape after being bent or twisted. A spring is elastic.

• *Malleability* means metal can be rolled, hammered, or bent without cracking or breaking.

• *Hardness* is the resistance to being penetrated or dented. Hardness of certain types of steel can be increased by heat-treating.

• *Toughness* is the ability of the metal to resist bending, breaking, cracking, or stretching. It also resists impact; is not easily penetrated—hard but not brittle.

Identifying Steels

There are three basic methods used in identifying steels:

• The number system.
• The color code.
• The spark test method.

The first two are reference systems. They are very valuable, but can be used only after the steel has been labeled or when

CLASSIFICATION OF CARBON AND ALLOY STEELS

Type of Steel	AISI No. 1942	SAE No. 1942	Common Uses
Plain carbon	C 1020	1020	Tacks, nails.
Free cutting	C 1115	1115	Studs, screws, bolts.
Manganese	A 1330	1330	Burglarproof safes.
Nickel	A 2317		Armor plate, steel rails, wire cables.
Nickel-chromium	A 3130	3130	Gears.
Molybdenum	A 4140	4140	Ball and roller bearings, machine parts.
Chromium-vanadium	E 6150		Springs, frames, and axles.
Stainless-chromium	414	51310	Stainless cooking utensils, sinks.

Table 5-C

certain information is known about it. The third method can be used when no information is provided.

THE NUMBER SYSTEM

The Society of Automotive Engineers (SAE) and the American Iron and Steel Institute (AISI) have developed a system or series of numbers for identifying carbon and alloy steels. Actually the AISI method is somewhat more comprehensive than the SAE, but there is no conflict. Any steel catalog or the New American Machinists' Handbook, Section 25, gives complete information about these numbering systems. However, by referring to Table 5-C, which gives some examples, and by reading the following paragraphs you can see basically how they work.

A = Basic open hearth alloy steel
B = Acid Bessemer carbon steel
C = Basic open hearth carbon steel
D = Acid open hearth carbon steel
E = Electric-furnace steel

The letters preceding American Iron and Steel Institute numbers tell the kind of furnace in which the steel was made. Thus the letter A in the number A 2317 means that the steel was made in the basic open hearth furnace.

Both systems are based on the use of four or five digits.
• The first digit tells the kind of steel; 1 is carbon steel, 2 is nickel steel, 3 is nickel-chromium, etc.
• The second digit of the number tells the percentage of the alloy represented by the first digit. The last two digits (sometimes three) show the carbon content in points (100 points equal 1% by weight). For example, SAE 3130 or AISI A 3130 has the following analysis: The first digit (3) indicates nickel-chromium steel. The second digit (1) indicates the per cent of this alloy and the last two digits (30) a carbon content of 0.30 points.

COLOR CODE

Most manufacturers of steel identify their products with colors.

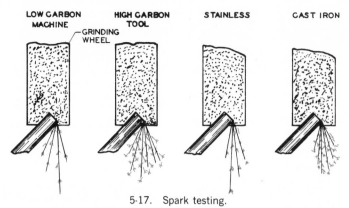

LOW CARBON MACHINE   HIGH CARBON TOOL   STAINLESS   CAST IRON

GRINDING WHEEL

5-17. Spark testing.

Each type of steel has a corresponding color painted on the ends of the bars. The codes vary from one company to another, so to interpret them you must know the manufacturer's marking system.

THE SPARK TEST

It is often possible to learn the general identity of a piece of iron or steel by the spark test. Fig. 5-17. When the metal piece is held against a grinding wheel, sparks result. Metals produce their own characteristic kinds of sparks, of which some common types are described in Table 5-D. Comparison of the sparks with those from a known piece of metal can also aid in identification.

It is important that the wheel be clean. Dress with an emery wheel dresser.

Standard Shapes and Sizes of Common Bar Stock

Bar stock can be purchased in common lengths of 10, 12, 14, and 16 feet. The following table gives the diameters, widths, and thicknesses that can usually be purchased from steel suppliers, and Fig. 5-18 shows standard shapes. See next page.

Nonferrous Metals

Many nonferrous metals are in use, but only a few find their way into the school shop. Some are too difficult to work and therefore do not lend themselves to school objectives. Others are too expensive.

Nonferrous metals may be grouped as follows:
- Base metals: copper, aluminum, tin, nickel, zinc, and lead.
- Alloys: brass, bronze, britannia metal (pewter), gar-alloy, and nickel silver.
- Precious metals: gold, silver, and platinum.

PROPERTIES OF NONFERROUS METALS
- *Base metals*

COPPER is one of the most useful metals. It is extremely malleable and ductile, so can be rolled into very thin sheets. Its electrical conductivity is greater than any except the most precious metals, and it also conducts heat excellently. Copper does not corrode in dry air, although in a moist atmosphere it becomes coated with a film of green carbonate which seals out deep oxidation. Copper is the basis of all important alloys known as the brasses and bronzes.

ALUMINUM is a comparatively soft metal of dull silvery appearance. Geologists tell us that approximately 8 per cent of the surface layer of the earth consists of aluminum, about 5 per cent iron, and less than 0.02 per cent of zinc, lead, and copper. It is never found in the native state; its compounds are principally the silicates and oxides. A great deal of

DESCRIPTIONS OF IRON AND STEEL SPARKS

Metal	Color	Spark description
Wrought iron	Straw	Long shafts ending in forks.
Low carbon or machine steel	White	Short shafts that end in forks and appendages.
Medium carbon steel	White	Bright starlight explosions— brighter as carbon increases.
High carbon steel	White	Short bushy sparks of large volume. Many sparks follow around wheel.
Alloy or high speed steel	Dull red	Forked spurts that resemble streaks, with explosions.

Table 5-D

electrical power is required to separate the chemical combinations. The metal is at present produced from ore—mineral bauxite.

Mining Bauxite. Bauxite, as a rule, is found near the surface of the earth and is mined by open-pit operation. However, it may be located at a considerable depth, overlaid with sand, clay, limestone, and similar materials which require underground methods of mining.

Purification of the Ore. The bauxite is taken from the mines, crushed into small pieces, washed, screened, and dried.

After being dried it is shipped to a refining mill where the impurities are removed. The Bayer process is used in most refining operations. The aluminum hydrate of the ore is dissolved out by means of caustic soda, reprecipitated, and calcined to form pure aluminum oxide.

Pure aluminum oxide is desired for the production of pure aluminum. Two pounds of aluminum oxide will make about 1 lb. of aluminum. Separating the aluminum from oxygen is accomplished by dissolving the aluminum oxide (alumina) in molten cryolite, a compound of sodium, aluminum, and fluorine. An electric current is passed through large carbon lined smelting pots filled with molten cryolite. When the alumina is placed in the bath the electric current frees the oxygen and the molten aluminum settles to the bottom of the tank. The molten aluminum is drawn out, Fig. 5-19, and poured into molds to form "pigs." The metal is then sent to the rolling mills for final processing.

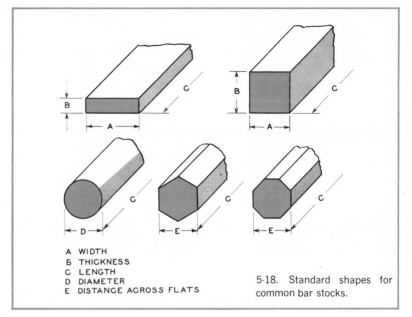

A WIDTH
B THICKNESS
C LENGTH
D DIAMETER
E DISTANCE ACROSS FLATS

5-18. Standard shapes for common bar stocks.

COMMON BAR STOCK

Kind	Sizes (in inches)
Rounds (shafting)	$3/16$ to 9
Squares	$1/4$ x $1/4$ to $4\frac{1}{2}$ x $4\frac{1}{2}$
Flats	$1/8$ x $5/8$ to 3 x 4
Hexagons	$1/4$ to 4
Octagons	$1/2$ to $1\frac{3}{4}$

Table 5-E

5-19. A craneman is manipulating a giant crucible into position to tap one of the electrolytic cells containing molten aluminum. Assisting him is a pot serviceman. One spout of the crucible is lowered into the pot, then, through vacuum, molten metal is drawn into the crucible from the pot bottom.

5-20. Light gage aluminum sheet for rigid containers and other applications begins with massive rolling ingots such as this one.

Properties. An outstanding characteristic of aluminum is its light weight. It is unusually malleable and ductile and may be worked and shaped with comparative ease. Its melting point is 660° C. (1220° F.). It possesses high thermal and electrical conductivities. Commercially pure aluminum (99%) has a tensile strength of about 13,000 lbs. per square inch but this can be doubled by cold-rolling processes. Fig. 5-20. It can be alloyed with other metals, and together with the use of heat-treating processes, the tensile strength may be increased to as high as 70,000 lbs. per square inch. This would place it in the range of structural steel. The most common alloying elements are chromium, iron, nickel, zinc, manganese, copper, silicon, and magnesium.

It is readily adaptable to making sand castings, permanent mold castings, and die castings. Fig. 5-21. The many aluminum alloys make them particularly adaptable to such metalworking processes as machining, rolling, Fig. 5-22, forging, Fig. 5-23, drawing, extruding, and spinning.

Identification of Aluminum. A uniform system has been adopted by the aluminum industries to identify the various types.

In the Aluminum Association (A.A.) number, the first digit identifies the major alloying element as shown in Table 5-F.

Designations for Aluminum	
1	pure aluminum or better
2	copper
3	manganese
4	silicon
5	magnesium
6	magnesium and silicon
7	zinc
8	other elements
9	special

Table 5-F

Group 1 has no alloying material in the metal.

The last two digits of Group 1 indicate the degree of aluminum purity, which is expressed in hundredths of 1 per cent.

5-21. This is one of the world's largest die castings—hot from a mammoth "griddle."

The last two numbers identify specific alloys in the group. These digits are the same as used to identify similar alloys before adoption of the new marking system. For example, 2024 was formerly known as 24S, and 6061 was referred to as 61S.

Applications. One of the first major applications for aluminum produced by the electrolytic pro-

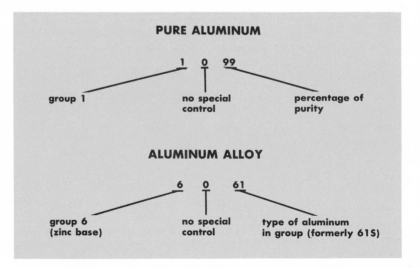

PURE ALUMINUM

1   0   99

group 1   no special   percentage of
               control   purity

ALUMINUM ALLOY

6   0   61

group 6   no special   type of aluminum
(zinc base)   control   in group (formerly 61S)

48

cess was the production of cooking utensils.

Since the early nineties, the metal's usefulness has extended widely. Vacuum cleaners and washing machines are built of aluminum alloys because of its lightness and resistance to corrosion. Being a good conductor of heat and electricity, electric irons, mangles, and waffle molds have been made from this metal.

Architects use it in building construction for windows, storm doors, screen cloth, store fronts, etc. Aluminum siding for homes is rapidly replacing older type siding due to its lasting qualities and easy care.

The transportation industry consumes the largest percentage of this metal for trains, trucks, buses, and other vehicles.

The aircraft industry today is a large user of aluminum alloys in the construction of civilian and military aircraft. The space program also uses its share.

It is not in the scope of this text to name all of the applications of aluminum. What the future holds for this metal no one knows, but it has already demonstrated its usefulness to mankind.

Tin is a lustrous, silvery white metal. Moisture has very little effect on it, so tin provides good protection against rust. This largely accounts for its use in the canning industry. Actually, tin cans are often made of a thin layer of iron, coated with tin. One of the softest metals, tin also has excellent malleable qualities.

Nickel is a white metal, almost as bright as silver. It is malleable, ductile, and can be welded. Because it adds strength, nickel is

often used as an alloy. Its most important such use is in certain steels in which it is the only alloying metal.

Zinc is a bluish gray metal with a distinct crystalline fracture when broken. Because it is brittle, this metal must be heated between 200 and 300 degrees when it is rolled into sheets or drawn into wire. Zinc is often used as an alloying element with copper and aluminum.

Lead is bright, almost white, when freshly cut, but quickly oxidizes to gray on the surface when exposed to air. One of the heaviest metals, lead is very malleable and ductile and can be hammered or rolled into thin sheets.

Lead will alloy with many other metals. When combined

5-22. Tapered sheet emerges from a rolling mill. The worker in the foreground uses a micrometer to gage the metal after rolling, then signals the operator with results of the tapered reduction.

5-23. A 50,000-ton hydraulic press die-forges an aircraft wing spar.

with tin, antimony, and sometimes copper, it is the basis of bearing metals, solders, and type metal, among its numerous uses.

• Alloys

BRASS varies in color from a reddish shade, which indicates a high percentage of copper, to a higher golden brass which has a zinc content of about 35 per cent. Brass may be obtained in rods, bars, flat sheets, tubes, and wire.

BRONZE is a copper-tin alloy. It has other names such as gun metal and bell metal. Certain alloys of bronze are made by adding aluminum, manganese, nickel, and other metals, each contributing its own qualities.

PEWTER or the more modern version of it, BRITANNIA METAL, is an alloy having a distinctive appearance and many desirable properties. Old-time pewter contained a considerable amount of lead. However, present-day pewter has been converted to an alloy composed of approximately 91 per cent tin, 7.5 per cent antimony, and 1.5 per cent copper. The best grades contain no lead. The antimony serves to whiten the metal and to impart a hardness unknown to old pewter. Pewter is softer than brass, bronze, and similar alloys. It exceeds most other metals in ease of working and ductile properties. This metal presents a beautiful silvery white sheen when polished. It does not work-harden under tools as copper and brass do.

GAR-ALLOY has a zinc base, with silver and copper added for strength. It is often used in metal spinning because it is relatively inexpensive. It can also be drawn and hammered, and buffs to a high polish.

NICKEL SILVER, sometimes called "German silver," is a copper-zinc-nickel alloy. It usually contains 64 per cent copper and 18 per cent nickel. Nickel silver has much the same physical properties as brass. It can be soldered, formed, and annealed, and is used for rings, bracelets, and other jewelry.

• Precious Metals

SILVER is a lustrous, soft, very ductile and malleable metal. When pure, it is nearly white. This metal is an excellent conductor of heat and electricity, and its low degree of chemical activity keeps surface corrosion at a minimum. Common uses are for jewelry, coins, and plating tableware. Coins often consist of 90 per cent silver with 10 per cent copper added for hardness.

STERLING SILVER contains at least 0.925 parts of silver. Alloys of copper and other elements provide hardness. Sterling silver is widely used in tableware and jewelry. It may be spun, etched, or chased.

GOLD, besides its beautiful and distinctive appearance, has other valuable properties. It is highly malleable and ductile, and an excellent conductor of electricity. Moisture does not corrode it, nor is it affected by oxygen or ordinary acids. A relatively soft metal, gold is usually hardened by alloying with copper, silver, and other metals. Alloying with copper is particularly important in the manufacture of jewelry.

PLATINUM is grayish white, malleable, ductile, and resistant to corrosion. One of its chief uses is in alloys for jewelry. It is also used in making laboratory utensils, electric wires, and certain dental supplies. Its most important alloy is with iridium.

Check Your Knowledge

1. Name three important metals and give a key industrial use of each.

2. Why is it important that you have an understanding of the materials of industry?

3. What is iron ore? Where are the greatest deposits found?

4. What is magnetite?

5. What is pig iron?

6. Explain the difference between iron ore and pig iron.

7. Describe the operation principles of a blast furnace.

8. What types and amounts of materials are needed in making a ton of pig iron?

9. Where does the blast furnace get its name?

10. How is cast iron formed?

11. Explain the operation of a cupola furnace.

12. What is malleable iron? Nodular iron?

13. The uses of pig iron are?

14. What is wrought iron?

15. Name four methods of producing steel.

16. Explain the open hearth process.

17. From what materials is steel made?

18. What is the difference between cast iron, wrought iron, and steel?

19. Name four kinds of furnaces for making steel.

20. Describe the difference between pig iron and steel.

21. Describe the Bessemer process.

22. Describe the open hearth process.

23. Is the open hearth furnace entirely charged with pig iron?

24. What type of furnace makes the greatest portion of steel? Why?

25. Describe the crucible way of making steel.

26. For what is crucible steel used?

27. What is low carbon steel?

28. Name three grades of carbon steel.

29. What is the basic oxygen process of making steel?

30. What is high carbon steel?

31. What is an alloy?

32. Name four reasons alloys are added to steel.

33. Name at least three common alloying elements.

34. Name three methods of steel identification.

35. Briefly explain the SAE and AISI numbering systems.

36. What is the purpose of the spark test?

37. Explain the difference between the properties of ferrous and nonferrous metals.

38. What are the main properties and uses of copper?

39. What is brass?

40. What are other names given to bronze?

41. Name four nonferrous metals and describe each.

42. Describe some industrial uses for aluminum.

43. What is pewter or britannia metal and describe some of its uses.

For Class Discussion

What would our civilization be like without iron? Without copper?

Would lack of gold or silver affect us as much as a lack of aluminum? Discuss consumer uses.

Terms to Know and Spell

iron oxide	puddling furnace	silicon
gangue	converter	molybdenum
hematite	crucible furnace	ductility
magnetic oxide	graphite crucible	malleability
limestone	alloying elements	conductivity
carbon dioxide	manganese	bauxite
cupola	chromium	aluminum hydrate
combustion	vanadium	cryolite

6 ▷ Project Design

Countless familiar objects, from knives and forks to cars and houses, have originated with an idea in a designer's mind.

Design has far-reaching effects in our daily lives. It plays a major role in our nation's economy. Industrial progress could not take place without the excellent designs that are continually being developed for products and processes.

To do this interesting, well-paid work, you must not only develop knowledge and skill but also a mind that is both imaginative and practical. You must have experience. Your metalworking course provides excellent opportunities for experience through project design.

The Elements of Design

All visible objects have certain characteristics which are so obvious that we sometimes take them too much for granted. These are basic "tools" of design; we can learn about them by observing them in the objects about us.

• **Line.** Although things differ as much as trees and cars, buildings and clouds, they have shapes and internal details that may be represented by three basic types of lines: straight, circular, and curved. Fig. 6-1.

• **Shape.** Many irregular shapes are found in nature, but four basic roots—round, square, triangular, and rectangular—are observable and very useful in design. Fig. 6-2. They serve effectively

6-1. A variety of straight and curved lines. Notice that a straight line can be diagonal as well as vertical or horizontal, and that curves can be combined in various ways.

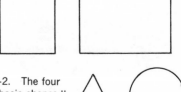

6-2. The four "basic shapes."

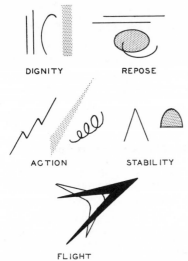

DIGNITY   REPOSE

ACTION   STABILITY

FLIGHT

6-3. Lines may induce a feeling of motion. They add interest and control attention, as well as forming shapes.

(Gen. Motors Corp.)

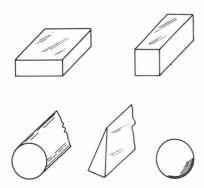

6-4. Metal products have solid shapes or masses.

6-5. A bowl finished in its natural color. The contrast between the wood and metal enhances the beauty of both.

in planning an article that is both functional and pleasing to the eye. Lines may induce a feeling of motion. See Fig. 6-3 in the adjacent column.

● **Mass.** When applied to design, mass means the three-dimensional aspect of an object. A plane rectangle has only length and width, but a bar of metal has depth or thickness as well. Thus it has mass, while the rectangle does not. Mass can have an infinite variety of forms involving cubes, cylinders, and other three-dimensional shapes. Fig. 6-4.

● **Texture** is the surface character of a material. Largely this means the feel of the surface, but some surfaces look smoother or rougher than they are. Such visual effects also are included under texture. By hammering, rolling, perforating, pressing, or expanding, the texture of metal can be altered.

● **Color.** All metals have a natural color which is typical. Fig. 6-5. Copper, for instance, is a pleasing bright reddish brown when polished.

Aluminum can be given a variety of pleasing colors by anodizing. Anodizing is accomplished by immersing the metal in an electrolytic bath. An electric current, when passed between the aluminum and a bath containing a solution of sulphuric acid, chromic acid, boric acid, causes an oxide to form on the metal. The coating produced can be dyed in a wide range of colors and become part of the surface of the metal. Also, metals can be finished in many colors by the use of lacquer, enamel, heat, or other treatments. A piece of fine workmanship can be enhanced by the

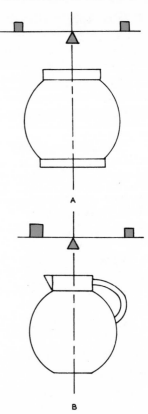

A

B

6-6. (A) Formal balance. (B) Informal balance.

application of a well chosen color, or it can be made unsightly if an inappropriate color is used.

Principles of Design

There are certain fundamental principles in the over-all design of a project:

● **Balance.** An object is said to have balance when its corresponding parts seem equal in weight or appearance. There are two types of balance: formal (or symmetrical) and informal (asymmetrical). When the parts on both sides of the object are alike, this is formal balance. When they are different but give the appearance of equality, because of position or relative size, this is informal balance. Fig. 6-6.

6-7. Unity, harmony, and good balance are easy to observe in this formal design.

6-8. A project that has utility as well as beauty and is a good example of formal balance.

• **Unity** is achieved when the parts combine to make one—when the object does not look disjointed or "stuck together." Fig. 6-7.

Attention to these principles will go a long way toward helping you design a project that has utility as well as beauty. Figs. 6-8 and 6-9.

• **Proportion** is the relationship between the dimensions of an object. Fig. 6-10. Some objects look better than others because of this relationship. For example,

a rectangular serving tray is more pleasing to the eye than a square one. In ancient times designers learned that 5:8 was an excellent proportion for rectangles. Can you find illustrations in this chapter in which this "golden rectangle" proportion has been followed?

• **Harmony** is achieved when the shapes, colors, and textures of an object look well together. When colors clash, or too many textures are used, appearance suffers.

• **Rhythm** is best obtained by the repetition of shapes, colors, or lines at regular intervals. This gives the object a pleasing appearance and may impart an interesting feeling of movement. Fig. 6-11.

• **Emphasis** is the process of focusing attention on a certain part of an object by its position, color, shape, or other decorative effect.

Modern Trends in Design

Over the years trends in design have changed, partly because of general financial conditions and partly because people's tastes are affected by changes such as wars, better communications, and education. Labor and other production costs are high. This has

6-10. A good example of proportion is shown in this laundry hamper made of perforated metal.

6-11. Well-balanced curves show good proportion and rhythm.

6-9. A group of projects that have utility as well as beauty, designed and produced by students.

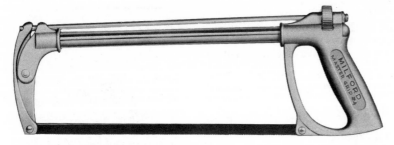

6-12.   A well designed hacksaw. Features have been added that make this saw a more useful and practical product.

6-13.   A useful silent butler that can be made with a minimum amount of material at a reasonable cost.

led designers to avoid many frills, which would cause added expense. The public often wants products which are inexpensive, not only to purchase, but also to maintain. Fig. 6-12.

Again, the result is that the designer strives for simplicity and streamlined effects. At the same time, extras are added to satisfy our craving for distinctive features, such as chrome strips on cars.

Design Selection

There are many points to remember in selecting a design. Fig. 6-12.
• Is the design practical? Will it really contribute to the usefulness of the project? Fancy brasswork on a wood lamp might be pretty, but if it made the switch hard to reach it would be impractical.
• Is the design appropriate for the project? The shape of a fish is well suited for an ash tray, but

not many people would want a name plate of the same shape. List some other common design shapes, and projects for which they would not be appropriate.
• Is the project designed to fit in well with its surroundings? A

6-14.   A disc sander is a utility project that can be made in school.

lamp should not be designed in contemporary style if it is meant for use in a room with traditional furnishings, nor is a small, carved coffee table the best design choice for a large room with "big" needs.
• Can the design be carried out safely and easily with the tools and equipment on hand? Are your tools in good condition?
• What about materials called for in the design? Are they available or can they be obtained easily at reasonable cost? Fig. 6-13. Have they been well chosen, both for function and appearance?

How To Design a Project

In design the basic point to be decided is how to make the fullest use of tools, materials, and processes, in your specific situation. This leads to other questions.
• Where can I get ideas?
• If I am following someone else's design, how can I improve upon it for my own needs and taste?
• What choice of materials do I

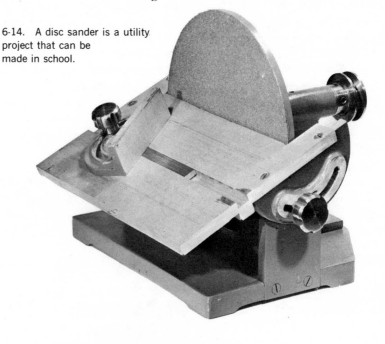

have? Should I combine materials for better appearance?

● How strong does the object need to be? How can I make it strong enough?

● What is the best way for me, with my abilities, equipment and materials, to make the project attractive and functional?

By answering these questions *for yourself* you will find that the project becomes more interesting and meaningful, and learning is easier. Of course, important sources of help are available to you.

Your greatest help will come from your instructor. For example, your project may be a fireplace set. Your teacher may demonstrate or assist in your learning the fundamental processes involved. Then he will guide and encourage you to experiment with the materials you will be using. This lets you discover for yourself the many things you can do with your materials, such as heating, bending, forming, and twisting metal.

You can get design ideas from the great variety of fireplace sets shown in catalogs and displayed in hardware stores and fixture shops.

When your instruction, experimentation, and outside research have enabled you to answer the important questions about your project, proceed with the following steps:

1. Make several freehand sketches of your idea, revising until you are satisfied.

2. Discuss the design with your teacher, and improve it in any way you can. Make working drawings as a guide in constructing the project. NOTE: Full scale drawings should be made of any irregular parts.

3. Make a Bill of Materials and a Plan of Procedure.

A project such as a fireplace set has a great many applications in metalworking. It will deepen your first-hand experience of materials and processes. It will give you practice in planning, making sketches and working drawings, and following directions. If you cooperate on the project with several classmates, you can learn something about the team approach, which is so important in modern industry. Finally, and this is important, you will have a fine opportunity to exercise your creative talent.

Types of Designs

In selecting a design make sure that the product will not be a waste of time and material. Many school projects can be utility items such as the disc sander illustrated in Fig. 6-14. Although utilitarian, it still requires style and skill.

Some projects have a decorative value in the home. Fig. 6-15. Perforated and lattice metal is available for such popular uses.

Check Your Knowledge

1. Name two ways in which design affects our everyday lives.

2. How will the study of design aid you as a consumer?

3. A bar of metal has mass,

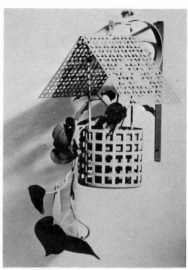

6-15. This project made of perforated metal is an example of good design.

but a rectangle does not. Explain.

4. What are the four basic shapes used in design?

5. What is balance in design?

6. Explain the difference between formal and informal balance.

7. What is proportion? Give an example of good proportion.

8. What is emphasis in project designing?

9. How do high labor costs affect the designer of consumer products?

10. Name four important points in selecting a design.

11. Who is your most important source of help in designing a shop project? Where else can you find ideas?

12. How important is the proper selection of materials?

Terms to Know and Spell

three-dimensional	*anodizing*	*rhythm*
mass	*symmetrical*	*design*
texture	*proportional*	*functional*
perforating	*harmony*	*utilitarian*
expanding		

7 ▷ How To Use Measuring and Layout Tools

The rule is the basic measuring tool. Many other tools have been developed from it.

Because rules are essential to the machinist's trade, they are available in a wide selection, to meet the needs of the precision worker. Some are only ¼″ in length, for measuring in grooves, recesses, and keyways, while some others are 12 feet long. Many machinists prefer the 6″ rule because it is convenient to carry and use.

The #8 stamped on the rule in Fig. 7-1 indicates that each graduation on the bottom edge is equal to ⅛″. You will notice that the lines are not all the same length. For instance, look at the first inch of the rule shown in Fig. 7-1. The shortest lines are used for those measurements which would usually be referred to in eighths—⅛″, ⅜″, ⅝″, and

⅞″. Where the measurement would be in fourths a somewhat longer line is used, and a still longer one at the ½″ mark. The longest line is used at the end of the inch, and the number 1 is stamped there to make the rule as easy as possible to read.

The most commonly used rule has four sets of graduations, with 16ths and 8ths of an inch on one side, 64ths and 32nds on the other. Fig. 7-2 shows the edge of this rule which has ¹⁄₁₆″ graduations. Fig. 7-3 shows the back-side of the rule graduated in 64ths and 32nds of an inch. Besides the large numerals at the end of each inch, this side of the rule also has smaller numbers which make it still easier to read. For instance, on the edge graduated in 32nds, a number appears every ⅛″ which gives the measurement in 32nds. Thus when measuring ²¹⁄₃₂ it is not necessary to count all 21 graduations; merely by referring to the mark at ²⁰⁄₃₂ and adding ¹⁄₃₂, the result is obtained much more simply.

Hook rules, Figs. 7-4 and 7-5, can be used for taking measurements through holes in gears or pulleys. The hook makes it possible to locate the end of the rule to take accurate measurements. Hook rules are made in both wide and narrow styles. The narrow style is used to measure through small diameter holes.

Table 7-A shows Brown and Sharpe graduations for rules.

A **circumference rule** is a decided convenience for sheet metal layout, Fig. 7-6. On one edge is a regular rule for measuring diameters, while on the opposite edge a scale shows the corresponding circumferences. For example, if you want to lay out a piece of sheet metal that is to be rolled into a 5″ cylinder, find the length by locating the 5-inch mark on the rule; then look across to the mark on the scale, which will be 15²³⁄₃₂″. Such rules are available in lengths up to 48″ and are very accurate.

The outside caliper, Fig. 7-7, is used to make external measurements when a ¹⁄₆₄″ tolerance is permitted.

Round stock is measured by setting the caliper to the approximate diameter of the stock. Hold the caliper square with the workpiece and move the caliper legs down on the stock. The distance between the legs can be measured with a steel rule.

To develop habits of consistent accuracy, it is well to remember that we are primarily dependent upon two senses in making nearly all measurements—the sense of sight and the sense of touch. These are most important when using contact measuring tools.

Inside calipers are used for taking internal measurements of cylindrical workpieces. To set the caliper, hold a rule square on a flat surface, then set one leg of the caliper on this surface and adjust the other leg until it points to the center of the proper mark on the rule. A hole diameter can be measured, Fig. 7-8, by setting the caliper to the approximate size of the hole and inserting the legs into the opening.

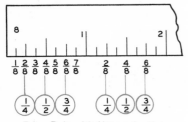

7-1. Rule with ⅛″ graduations.

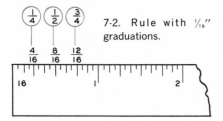

7-2. Rule with ¹⁄₁₆″ graduations.

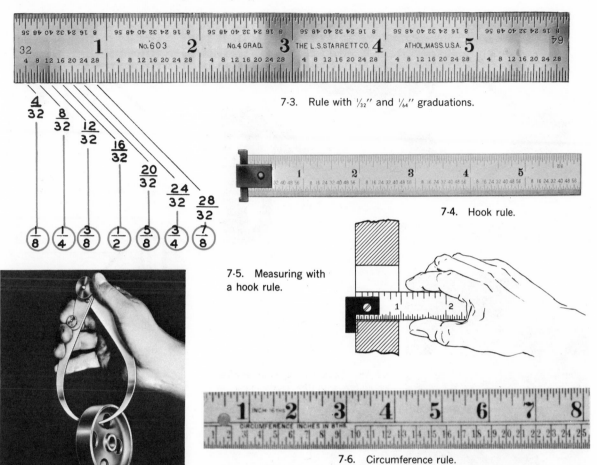

7-3.   Rule with ¹⁄₃₂″ and ¹⁄₆₄″ graduations.

$\frac{4}{32}$ $\frac{8}{32}$ $\frac{12}{32}$ $\frac{16}{32}$ $\frac{20}{32}$ $\frac{24}{32}$ $\frac{28}{32}$

$\frac{1}{8}$ $\frac{1}{4}$ $\frac{3}{8}$ $\frac{1}{2}$ $\frac{5}{8}$ $\frac{3}{4}$ $\frac{7}{8}$

7-4.   Hook rule.

7-5.   Measuring with a hook rule.

7-6.   Circumference rule.

7-7.   Outside caliper.

7-8.   Inside caliper.

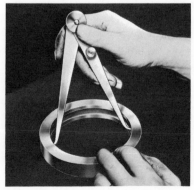

BROWN AND SHARPE GRADUATIONS FOR STEEL RULES

Graduations	No. 4	No. 6
1st edge	8ths	10ths
2nd edge	16ths	50ths
3rd edge	32nds	
4th edge	64ths	
	No. 8	**No. 9**
1st edge	32nds	16ths
2nd edge	64ths	32nds
3rd edge	10ths	64ths
4th edge	100ths	
	No. 10	**No. 11**
1st edge	32nds	64ths
2nd edge	64ths	100ths
3rd edge		
4th edge		

Table 7-A.

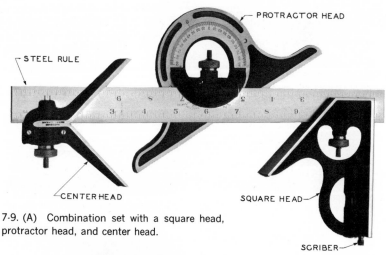

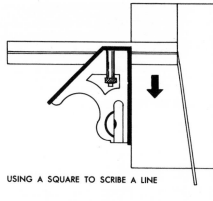

7-9. (A) Combination set with a square head, protractor head, and center head.

USING A SQUARE TO SCRIBE A LINE

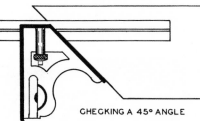

CHECKING A 45° ANGLE

7-10. (B) Uses of the combination set.

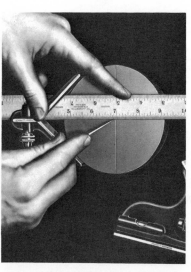

7-9. (B) Locating the center of a round workpiece with the center head of a combination square.

7-10. (A) Using the combination square to measure part on a die. The part at left is the protractor head, and at right is the center head.

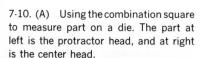

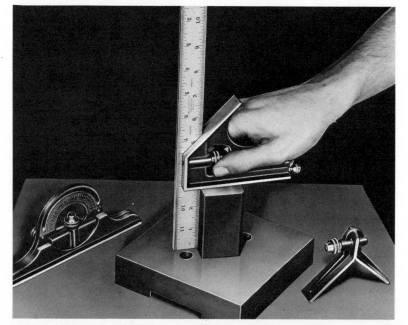

Squares

A square has one right angle and two straight edges for measuring and marking. Several types of squares are used in the metalworking trades. They have a variety of uses: layout work, testing the accuracy of two surfaces that must be square or at right angles to each other, laying out lines that must be parallel to each other, setting up workpieces in the shaper or milling machine.

The combination set, Fig. 7-9 (A), consists of three separate tools and a steel rule that may be used with each. It consists of a graduated, hardened steel blade with a sliding try square head that also combines a mitre and level. Thus it can be used as a rule, square, mitre (for various angles), depth gage, height gage, and level. The protractor head has direct-reading double graduations with a full 0 to 180 de-

58

7-11. Hard steel try square.

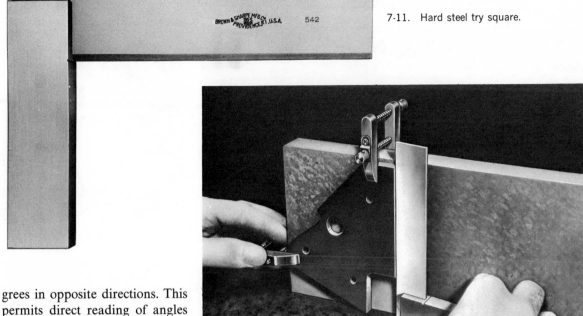

7-12. To assure true vertical mounting, a machinist checks the workpiece against a hard steel square before final clamping.

7-13. (A) A prick punch.

grees in opposite directions. This permits direct reading of angles either above or below the blade and eliminates troublesome figuring of graduations. In addition, an auxiliary centering head for finding the centers of cylindrical pieces can be substituted for the square head. Fig. 7-9 (B). Along the center of the rule is a groove that serves as a guide for clamping the head in a fixed position. Each head may be fastened at any point along the length of the rule by means of a thumb screw. One use of the tool is shown in Fig. 7-10 (A). Another use is shown in Fig. 7-10 (B).

Hardened steel squares, Figs. 7-11 and 7-12, are used for setting up and checking precision work on surface plates and machine tools. The beam and the blade are lapped. At the inner corner the beam is grooved to provide clearance for burrs and dirt.

Squares are fine precision instruments and therefore should be handled with care.

Prick Punch

A prick punch is a layout tool used to mark the location of holes after the lines have been scribed on the workpiece. Prick punch marks are generally placed along a layout line so that the machinist can tell if the workpiece is being machined correctly. Layout lines are sometimes difficult to see, and the line of prick punch marks serves as a guide. A prick punch has a sharp point ground to an angle of from 30 to 60 degrees. Fig. 7-13 (A).

Center Punch

The center punch resembles a

prick punch in appearance. The difference is that the point of the center punch is ground to an angle of about 90 degrees. It is used to enlarge prick punch marks so that a drill can be started accurately and easily. Fig. 7-13 (B) shows a set of center punches. See next page.

Dividers

Dividers have straight legs that terminate in points. They are made with spring joints and firm joints and are used like a compass to lay out regular curves—primarily to indicate the location and size of holes to be drilled.

7-13. (B)   Set of center punches.

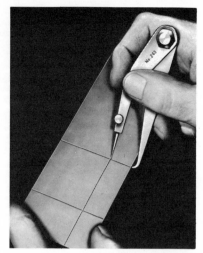

7-17.   Using a hermaphrodite caliper to lay out a line parallel to an edge.

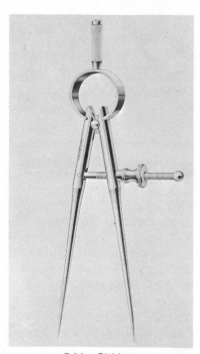

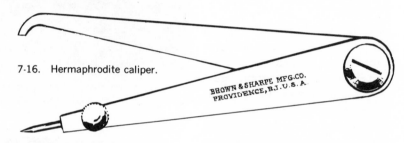

7-16.   Hermaphrodite caliper.

7-14.   Dividers.

Care should be taken to keep the points sharp and of the same length. Fig. 7-14.

To set the dividers, place one leg or point on a mark on the steel rule and open the other leg until the desired dimension is obtained. Fig. 7-15 (A). To scribe a circle, Fig. 7-15 (B), place one point on the prick punch mark, tip the divider slightly, and scribe the circle. Do not make over one turn of the dividers, as turning the dividers several times can

result in making more than one line on the workpiece.

Hermaphrodite Caliper

The hermaphrodite caliper, Fig. 7-16, has one pointed leg, as on dividers, and one hooked leg, similar to that of an outside caliper. Among its uses are locating centers of cylindrical workpieces, and scribing lines on a workpiece parallel to its side. Fig. 7-17.

The tool is set by placing the hooked leg on the end of the rule and adjusting the scriber point to the desired setting.

The Trammel

The trammel, Fig. 7-18, is a layout tool used to measure between two points, or to scribe

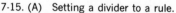

7-15. (A)   Setting a divider to a rule.

7-15. (B)   Scribing circles with dividers.

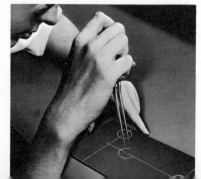

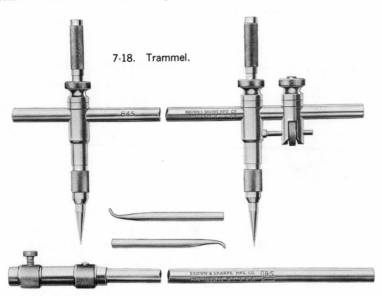

7-18. Trammel.

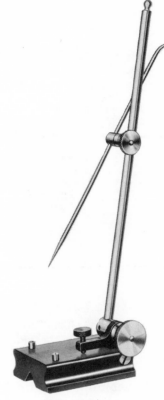

7-20. Surface gage.

large circles or arcs too large for ordinary dividers. It consists of a long rod, called a beam, on which are mounted two sliding heads used to hold scribing points. The points are adjustable in spring chucks. They can be replaced by pencils, caliper legs, or ball points. Fig. 7-19 shows a trammel being used to scribe an arc on a workpiece.

7-19. A trammel in use. Scribing an arc with a trammel. The bent scriber is held against the flat of the casting.

Surface Gage

The surface gage, Fig. 7-20, locates distances from a base and locates points at a given height on the opposite ends of an object lying on a flat surface. It can be used to draw a line at a given height on an irregularly shaped object, or to level workpieces on a machine table. The gage can also be used with an indicator attached for inspecting various parts and checking the work-piece. Fig. 7-21.

7-21. Indicator attached to surface gage for inspection.

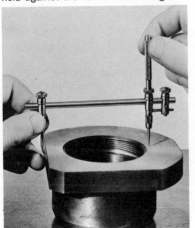

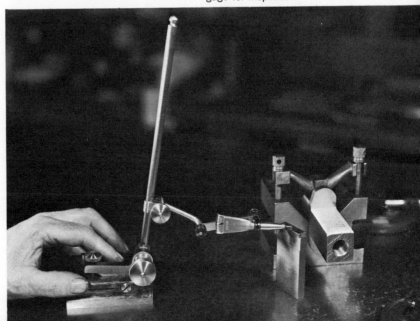

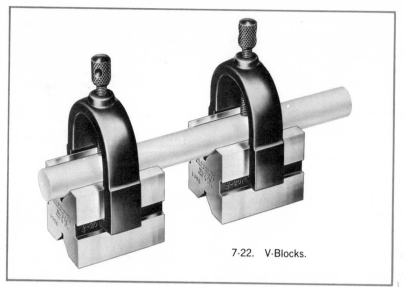

7-22. V-Blocks.

V-blocks

V-blocks, Fig. 7-22, have many uses around the metalworking shop. An important use is holding round stock for layout work in drilling, milling, grinding, and other machining operations. V-blocks are commonly made in pairs, and are usually manufactured from hardened and ground tool steel. The V's are carefully centered and ground to exact dimensions. The workpiece is usually clamped in the block.

7-23. Toolmaker's clamps.

Toolmaker's Parallel Clamps

Toolmaker's parallel clamps, Fig. 7-23, are used for holding small work together during machining operations or layout. The jaws are rounded and tapered at the ends to permit clamping under shoulders or in recesses.

What Is Layout?

As used in the metal shop, the term *layout* means transferring lines, centers, and other informative markings from the blueprint directly onto the workpiece. This information serves as a guide for shaping the finished piece.

Layout is similar to mechanical drawing, but it differs in one important way. The lines on a mechanical drawing are used only for reference and are not actually measured or transferred.

In laying out, even a slight error in the placement of a line or a center will result in a similar error, often costly, in the finished workpiece. Therefore all the transferred information must be clear and correct, and all lines made with scribers, dividers, or

center points must be exact and sharp.

Preparing the Surface

As an aid in making scribed lines stand out clearly, the workpiece is coated with a colored solution which varies depending upon the kind of metal to be worked.

A blue layout dye which dries instantly when brushed onto a clean metal surface is commonly used. It provides an opaque blue background that eliminates glare and eyestrain, besides strengthening the lines.

Layout dye can be made in the school shop by adding gentian violet dye to white shellac, then diluting with denatured alcohol so that the dye has the proper consistency to flow evenly upon the work. A small brush is used to apply the dye.

For rough-surfaced work such as castings or for simple work where no great accuracy is required, chalk or a mixture of white lead and turpentine will serve adequately as a coating. For fine, exact layouts on smooth or finished surfaces, there is a special marking solution which gives a dull-copper appearance. It is one ounce of copper sulphate to four ounces of water to which a little nitric acid has been added.

Equipment for Layout

All marking tools such as scribers, surface gages, and trammels should have sharp, well-tempered points. Straight edges, as on rules and squares, should be frequently inspected for dents and nicks, and checked against a master square.

Care in using a center punch

is extremely important, because it can easily drift off its true mark. A great asset for fine work is an automatic center punch in which a built-in, adjustable spring provides the striking force. It enables the operator to have both hands available to steady the tool, and lets him keep his eyes focused on the exact point of contact. Figs. 7-24 and 7-25.

A plane surface of reliable levelness is required as a base for the workpiece and for measurement tools. Special plates such as surface or laying-out plates are available for this purpose. Fig. 7-26.

Laying Out a Workpiece

The following information is basic. Of course, layout jobs vary greatly, so not all of these steps may have to be done on any given job. However, if you are familiar with this information you can adapt it easily to meet specific needs.

1. Any burrs on the material should be removed with a file. If possible, square the ends of the workpiece. This is not always possible with a rough casting.

2. Coat the surface with layout dye. Fig. 7-27.

3. Place the workpiece on a surface plate so that all dimensions can be made from the surface plate. If the lines fall below the workpiece, the work can be raised by placing it on parallels.

4. When several parallel lines are to be scribed, a temporary line can be made near the bottom of the workpiece to act as a check point, in case the work should move during layout.

5. If the dimensions for lines do not have to be exact, the

7-24. Automatic center punch.

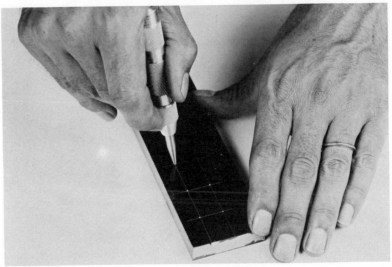

7-25. Automatic center punch in use.

7-26. Surface plate.

7-27. Coating a workpiece with dye preparatory to layout work.

63

7-28. Using a surface gage, rule, and rule holder to transfer measurements.

7-29. Steps in making a simple layout showing the order in which lines, arcs, and holes are laid out.

A– REFERENCE LINES

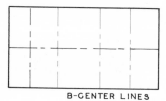

B–CENTER LINES

C– $\frac{9}{32}$ AND $\frac{3}{16}$ RADIUS ARCS

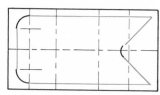

D–OUTLINE OF PATTERN

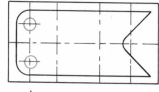

E– $\frac{1}{4}$ DIAMETER CIRCLES

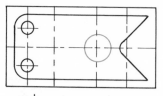

F– $\frac{1}{2}$ DIAMETER CIRCLE
COMPLETED LAYOUT

scriber point on a surface gage can be set to the graduations on the blade of a combination square, or a rule held in a rule holder as shown in Fig. 7-28.

6. In laying out the locations of holes, and all necessary lines, first scribe the center line along which they are to be drilled. Fig. 7-29. A line then can be scribed with a square held at right angles to the workpiece, as shown in Fig. 7-30. Prick punch at the intersection of these two lines. Fig. 7-31. If more than one hole is to be drilled, use a pair of dividers to space the holes. Prick punch each intersection before stepping off the next one so that the distances will be accurate. A spacing punch can be used to locate centers for a series of accurately spaced holes as shown in Figs. 7-32 and 7-33.

7. Scribe a circle with a pair of dividers. Then enlarge the prick punch mark with a center punch.

8. Lines parallel and close to an edge or end may be made with a hermaphrodite caliper.

9. Angular lines may be laid out with a simple bevel protractor or a universal bevel protractor.

10. In using a steel rule, make sure the rule is kept parallel to the workpiece in order to obtain the correct length.

11. In squaring a line across the workpiece, hold the square firmly against the side of the work and mark the line across the work with a scriber, as shown in Fig. 7-34.

12. A pencil can sometimes be used for making bend lines on sheet metal. A soapstone crayon can be used for marking lines on metal plate.

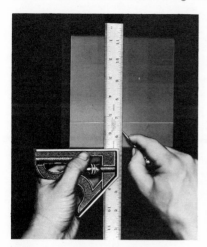

7-30. Laying out with a combination square held at right angle to the workpiece.

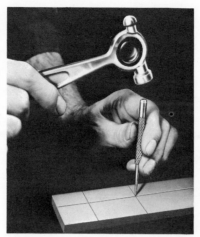

7-31. Prick punching at the intersection of two lines. Note that the hammer has a magnifying glass to check fine work.

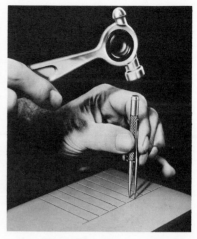

7-32. The combination center punch and spacing tool is handy for quick, accurate layout of work for drilling.

Check Your Knowledge

1. Describe a steel rule.

2. Why do machinists prefer the 6″ rule?

3. What does the No. 8 refer to when it appears on the left end of a steel rule?

4. How many 16ths are there in one inch? How many 64ths are there in ⅜″?

5. What are the four most common graduations on a steel rule?

6. Name some uses of the hook rule.

7. What is a circumference rule?

8. Name the parts of a combination set.

9. Name four uses of a combination set.

10. What two angles can be made with a combination square?

11. Why do you think a solid square is more exact than a combination square?

12. Set the bevel protractor at 35 degrees. What other angle can be measured with this setting?

13. Explain the difference between a prick punch and a center punch.

14. Explain some uses of the dividers.

15. What is a hermaphrodite caliper and explain its uses?

16. What type of work can be done with the trammel?

17. Describe the surface gage. What is its use?

18. Give some of the uses of V-blocks.

19. For what is a parallel clamp used?

20. What is a layout?

21. Name some of the coatings that can be applied to metal to make layout lines easier to see.

22. When is chalk used on a surface?

23. Name some of tools used in layout work.

24. What advantages does an automatic center punch have over the conventional type?

25. Describe the method used in setting a pair of dividers.

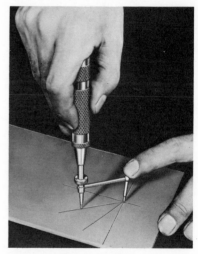

7-33. Spacing attachment for automatic center punches, used for accurately spacing center distances. It can be instantly screwed into the punch shank in place of the regular point.

7-34. Using a hard steel try square and scriber to square a line across the workpiece.

26. What is a surface plate? For what is it used?

27. List the steps in making a layout.

28. What is a spacing punch?

29. What instrument do you use to lay out lines close to and parallel to an edge?

30. What type of instrument is used to lay out angular lines?

31. Why is it necessary to lay out workpieces in the shop?

Why is careful, accurate layout work important in the metal trades?

Discuss the advantages of modern measuring tools.

Is a knowledge of mathematics important in layout work?

Discuss the advantages of using accurate measuring tools.

Compare the accuracy of tools used by machinists and those used by carpenters.

Terms to Know and Spell

measuring	parallel
caliper	transferred
circumference	denatured
combination set	intersection

graduations
layout
hermaphrodite
trammel

Section Two

Using Bench Tools

IN STUDYING bench tools, you learn to use hand tools for filing, sawing, thread cutting, reaming, and assembling, as well as related information.

It may seem surprising, but the use of hand tools is often

more difficult to learn than the operation of some machine tools. For instance, a tool and die maker or a bench worker must have great skill with hand tools, and so must machine repairmen, automobile mechanics, and metal patternmakers.

Thus you see how important these tools are for industry. Their uses extend to the home, also, of course. Even on big construction, when machine tools are not available, their work must be done with bench tools.

Study this section well, and master these tools. They will benefit you in many ways all through your life.

8 ▶ Non-edge Tools

Vises

The bench or machinist's vise, Fig. 8-1, is used to hold workpieces for hand-tool operations such as filing, tapping, threading, and reaming. Vises come in a variety of sizes, so you can choose one suitable for the size and shape of the workpiece to be held.

Vises consist essentially of a fixed jaw, a movable jaw, a screw, and a handle. Some have a swivel feature, Fig. 8-2, that lets the vise rotate on its base. The faces of the jaws have either smooth or serrated plates. To hold and protect workpieces made of soft metal, caps also made of soft metal, Fig. 8-3, are mounted on the jaws.

Hammers

The machinist's hammer, or ball-peen hammer, has a flat face for general work and a round end for riveting and peening. Fig. 8-4. The size is determined by the weight of the head, which varies from 4 ounces to 3 pounds. When doing layout work, a 9-ounce hammer is ordinarily used.

Soft hammers, Fig. 8-5, are made of brass, lead, rawhide, plastic, rubber, and wood. They are used for driving machine parts, seating workpieces in a machine vise, or striking a finished surface.

Screwdrivers

BLADE TYPE

A screwdriver consists of a handle, commonly of plastic, and a blade with the tip properly shaped to fit a screw slot.

For general purposes, screwdrivers are classified by size, according to the combined length of the shank and blade. Sizes run from 2½ to 12 inches. The diameter of the shank and the width and thickness of the blade are proportionate to the length. However, there are many specials with long thin shanks, short thick shanks, and wide or narrow blades. Sometimes a joint in

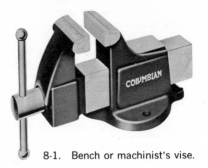
8-1. Bench or machinist's vise.

8-2. Machinist's vise with swivel base.

8-3. Jaw caps for a machinist's vise.

8-4. Ball-peen hammer.

8-5. Soft hammer made of plastic and metal.

8-6.   Screwdriver with plastic handle.

8-7.   Screwdriver with square shank.

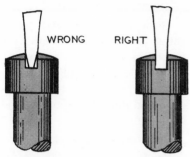

WRONG   RIGHT

8-8.   This close-up view of a blade in a screw slot shows right and wrong blade shapes. Note that the correctly shaped blade fills the slot exactly.

8-9.   Phillips screwdriver for Phillips-head screws.

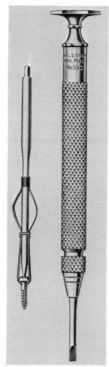

8-10.   Jeweler's screwdriver.

8-11.   Offset screwdriver for getting into hard-to-reach places.

8-12.   Offset screwdriver of Phillips type.

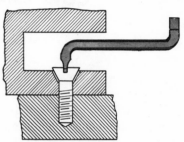

8-13.   How to use an offset screwdriver.

metal is difficult to reach, and blades must be specially sized to fit a large or small slot.

Fig. 8-6 represents the type of screwdriver most commonly used. Handles may be made of wood or plastic. Plastic handles are usually molded around the end of the shank.

The blades of smaller screwdrivers are often round; the larger ones have a square shank to which a wrench can be fitted to aid in turning. Fig. 8-7.

It is important to select the size of a screwdriver so that the thickness of the blade is a good fit in the screw slot. Fig. 8-8. This prevents burring the slot and reduces the force required to hold the blade in place. Always keep the blade squarely in line with the axis of the screw.

• *Regrinding.* When grinding the tip of a screwdriver, care should be taken that the temper is not drawn out. Do not allow to heat. Stop and go frequently. To regrind the blade, grind the sides so that they are either parallel for a short distance or slightly concave. This will help keep the bit in the slot even when a severe twisting force is applied. Excessive flare at the sides of the blade often prevents it from getting down into counterbores. When grinding, make sure the end is ground straight across, and never grind the faces so that they form a sharp edge at the tip.

OTHER TYPES

Recessed-head screws, commonly called Phillips head, have a cavity style, X-shaped, requiring a specially shaped screwdriver tip as shown in Fig. 8-9.

Watch and clock makers, jewelers, opticians, and toolmakers use the screwdriver shown in Fig. 8-10, which is specially adapted to fine delicate work. When not in use the blade can be reversed in the body for convenience in carrying the screwdriver in the pocket.

In close quarters, the offset screwdriver is invaluable. It is usually made of round, square, or hexangular stock, with blades at opposite ends turned in opposite directions so that it can operate in quarter turns. They are in a regular form and in shapes to fit Phillips screws, Figs. 8-11 and 8-12. The use of this screwdriver is illustrated in Fig. 8-13.

Check Your Knowledge

1. Name some non-edge tools which are commonly used in the metal shop.

2. Name the parts of a vise.

3. What are vise caps? What are they used for?

4. What determines the size of a machinist's hammer or ball-peen hammer?

5. Name the uses of a soft hammer.

6. Why are some screwdrivers equipped with a square shank?

7. Name some of the types of screwdrivers.

8. Where can an offset screwdriver be used to advantage? (Think this question out by examining machines.)

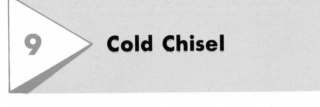

9 ▷ Cold Chisel

The metalworking cold chisel is a forged tool used to shear, cut, and chip cold metal. One end is hardened and ground to make a good cutting edge. For certain types of work, metal can actually be cut faster and better with a cold chisel and hammer than by machine, but considerable skill is needed.

When chipping, *always wear safety glasses,* and be sure the work is held firmly in a vise.

Hold the chisel at an angle that will cut a chip that is not too thick to move. Keep your eyes focused on the *edge* of the chisel constantly during this operation. (1) Strike the head of the chisel a firm blow. (2) Reset the chisel after each blow. (3) Cut a small amount at a time. NOTE: If this exact procedure is followed you will work more efficiently and the cutting edge of the chisel will last longer.

After the workpiece has been chipped, use a file for finishing.

Four types of cold chisels are commonly used in the metal shop.

Fig. 9-1. They come in a variety of sizes and usually are made of octagonally shaped tool steel which is often called *chisel steel.*

• The **flat** cold chisel is used for general chipping and cutting purposes, including the removal of rusted rivet and nut heads.

• The **diamond point** chisel is used for chipping V-shaped oil grooves and sharp corners. It has a tapered square shape at the cutting end. The chisel gets its shape by having the cutting edge ground diagonally from one corner to the opposite one, creating a diamond shaped cutting surface. It is like a facet corner on a diamond.

• The **cape** chisel is forged to produce a cape or flare, forming a cutting edge that is narrow in comparison with the thickness of the body, to keep the chisel from sticking in the groove or slot. This chisel is used for cutting narrow slots or keyways and rectangular grooves.

• The **round nose** chisel is used for producing oil grooves and

other concave or in-curved surfaces. The chisel is ground so that the face of the cutting edge is an ellipse. This chisel can be used for chipping a groove to draw a drill back to the true location of the hole to be drilled.

Grinding a Cold Chisel

Through use the head of a cold chisel becomes mushroomed, as shown in Fig. 9-2. The cutting edge also becomes dull or nicked. The chisel should then be sharpened and the head again ground to shape.

CAUTION: *A mushroomed head is dangerous because one of the ragged edges may fly off when struck with a hammer and cause injury to you or others working near you.*

1. When sharpening a flat chisel, hold the cutting edge at the correct angle against the face of the grinding wheel and move the chisel back and forth. Grind the cutting edge at an angle of

9-1. Four types of cold chisels.

FLAT COLD CHISEL

CAPE CHISEL

DIAMOND POINT CHISEL

ROUND NOSE CHISEL

60 to 70 degrees. This angle can be checked with a center gage. Fig. 9-3. The edge should be very slightly curved in instead of straight across.

2. Do not press the chisel hard or hold it too long against the grinding wheel, for too much pressure will cause the metal to heat, thereby removing the temper.

3. While grinding, dip the chisel in water frequently to keep it cool.

4. Grind first one side, then the other, to form the proper edge. Check frequently with a center gage.

CAUTION: *When grinding be sure to wear safety glasses or a face shield.*

Cutting Out a Shape with a Flat Chisel

Also always wear a protective device for your eyes during this operation.

1. Scribe an outline of the pattern on the metal.

2. Place the metal on a soft steel plate. Do not use a surface plate, anvil, or vise.

3. Grasp the chisel with tips of fingers and thumb of one hand. Hold the chisel in a perpendicular position with the cutting edge on the layout line. Fig. 9-4.

4. Strike the head of the chisel with the hammer, keeping your eyes focused on the line to be cut. *Do not cut clear through.*

5. Move the chisel along the layout line, overlapping slightly the cut just made, and strike again.

6. Continue cutting around the layout line until the chisel is almost through the metal.

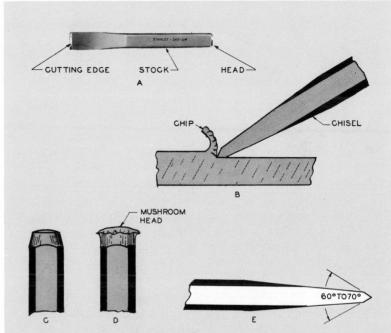

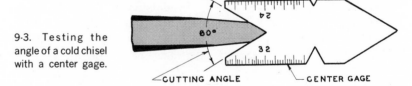

9-2. (A) Parts of a cold chisel. (B) Wedge action of cold chisel. (C) Correctly ground head. (D) Mushroom head is dangerous. (E) Correct cutting angle.

9-3. Testing the angle of a cold chisel with a center gage.

7. Start back at the beginning of the cut and finish cutting through the metal.

Shearing in a Vise

1. Clamp the workpiece in a vise with the line to be cut just above the top of the jaws, unless the metal is to be filed afterward; then the line should be placed even with the vise jaws or very slightly below, to allow for filing later.

2. The bevel of the chisel's cutting edge should be placed flat on the vise jaw. The top side of the edge will then be parallel to the layout line. Be careful not to

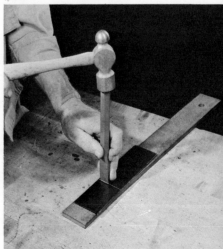

9-4. Using a cold chisel with the work-piece held on a metal plate.

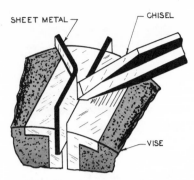

SHEET METAL — CHISEL
VISE

9-5.   Shearing with a cold chisel.

hold the chisel higher, or it will dig into the vise jaw.

3. Strike the chisel with the hammer.

4. After each cut, advance the chisel along the metal until shearing is completed. Fig. 9-5.

Bench Shears

THROATLESS

Hand operated shears are made in many styles, each designed for a particular type of cut.

One of the most important and versatile styles is the throat-less shears. Figs. 9-6 and 9-7. Designed to make straight, curved, or irregular cuts, the form of the shears makes it possible to turn metal to any position while the cut is being made. This type of shears cuts soft sheet metal as easily as a pair of scissors cuts paper. Throatless shears are made in various sizes for thicknesses up to $3/16''$ in mild steel.

All cuts should be started at the vertex of the blades because this is the point of greatest power. The sheet should always be kept flat on the bed of the shears.

SLITTING SHEARS

Another style is the slitting shears used primarily for such purposes as making straight cuts in heavy sheets, trimming, and cutting iron bar stock and strapping. Fig. 9-8.

Inside slotters, Fig. 9-9, which permit cutting inside edges of a sheet, are extremely valuable to the sheet metal worker.

9-7.   Zig-zag cuts are easily made on a throatless shears.

9-8.   Slitting shears being used to cut bar stock. Notice the adjustable hold-down which keeps material flat during the cut.

9-6.   Hand operated, throatless bench shears.

9-9. The inside slotter will cut inside a sheet, slit through, and do many types of design work inside or outside.

CAUTION: *Always keep your fingers away from the sharp cutting edges!*

Check Your Knowledge

1. Explain the uses of a cold chisel.

2. Name the different types of cold chisels.

3. Explain the danger of using a chisel with a mushroomed head.

4. Name some important points in grinding a cold chisel.

5. What are bench shears?

6. Name some uses of bench shears.

7. Try out use of slitting shears and the inside slotter.

Terms to Know and Spell

cold chisel	*ellipse*	*shearing*
chipping	*mushroomed*	*vertex*
octagonally	*dangerous*	

---

10 ▷ Files

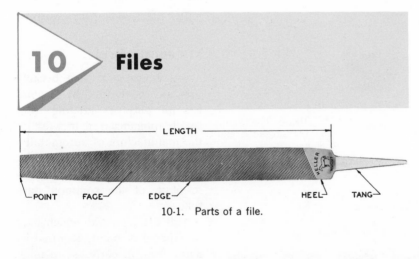

10-1. Parts of a file.

POINT · FACE · EDGE · HEEL · TANG · LENGTH

10-2. The length of a file. For example, this measures 10″.

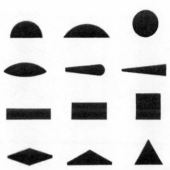

10-3. Cross-section of file shapes.

A file is an instrument having cutting ridges or teeth on a surface or surfaces, used for smoothing or abrading metal and other materials. Fig. 10-1. Most files are made of hardened, high-grade tool steel. A similar tool is the rasp, which has coarser, pointed teeth.

General Characteristics

Files and rasps are distinguished in three ways: by their *length,* their *kind* (or name), and their *cut.*

• **Length.** The length of a file, Fig. 10-2, is the distance between its heel and its point. The tang (pointed end for holding the handle) is never included. File lengths vary from 4 to 18 inches; the lengths most commonly used are 6, 8, 10, and 12 inches. In general, the longer a file is the greater is its cross-section.

• **Kind.** Files are often identified by certain familiar terms, such as flat, mill, or half round, describing either the general appearance or the common use of the tool. Files are sometimes described by a geometrical term, such as triangular, circular, or quadrangular. This refers to the cross-sectional shape of the file. Fig. 10-3. Special shapes are required in die making and jewelry work.

73

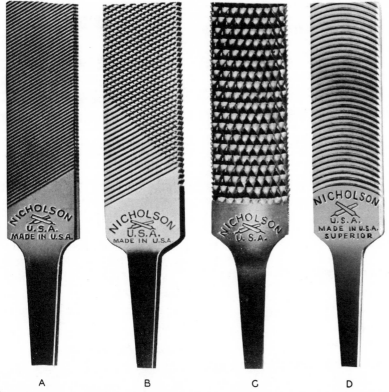

10-4. The cut of files. (A) single cut, (B) double cut, (C) rasp cut, (D) curved tooth.

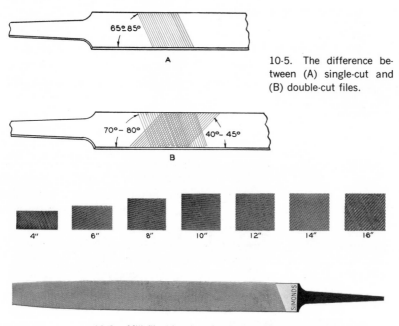

10-5. The difference between (A) single-cut and (B) double-cut files.

10-6. Mill file, showing the coarseness range.

• **Cut.** The cut of a file may be described in two ways: by the coarseness of the cutting surface, and by the number and arrangement of teeth or cutting edges. Coarseness is indicated by such terms as *rough* (the coarsest), *coarse, bastard, second cut,* and *smooth cut.* Three common arrangements of cutting edges, *single cut, double cut,* and *curved tooth,* are shown in Fig. 10-4 and compared with a rasp.

A single-cut file has just one series of cuts, at an angle of 65 to 85 degrees across the face. A double-cut file has two rows of cuts that cross each other diagonally to form individual diamond-shaped cutting points. Fig. 10-5.

File Classification

Files can be classed in three groups: machinist's files, Swiss pattern files, and special purpose files.

MACHINIST'S FILES

These are so named because they are widely used by machinists for purposes ranging from small appliance repair work to the manufacture of automobiles, ships, and aircraft. Most machinist's files are double cut. A description of the common ones follows:

• **Mill file.** This file, which may be tapered or blunt, acquired its name from its early use in filing mill or circular saws. Now it is commonly used for drawfiling, to produce a fine smooth surface on a workpiece. Being single cut, it is an exception to the rule that most machinist's files are double cut. Fig. 10-6.

• **Flat file.** This double-cut file comes in a bastard cut for rough

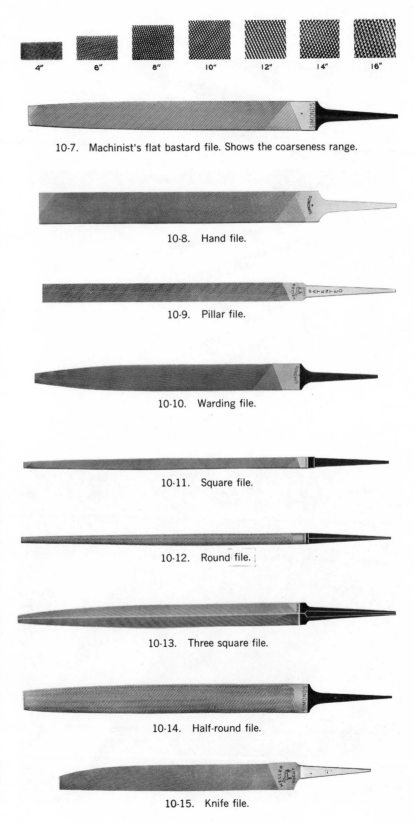

filing and in a second cut for finish filing. It is cut on both edges and sides, and can remove a large amount of stock. Fig. 10-7.

● **Hand file.** This thick, rectangular file has parallel edges. One edge, called the *safe* edge, does not contain teeth. The file is tapered in thickness. Fig. 10-8.

● **Pillar file.** This parallel file has a rectangular cross-section of narrow width and extra thickness. It is used for making slots and keyways. Fig. 10-9.

● **Warding file.** A thin rectangular file of sharply tapered width and uniform thickness, this tool is named for its most common traditional use—filing ward ridges on locks and notches on keys. It is good for any notching job. Fig. 10-10. (Ward means "prevent" in this sense. It stops other keys from fitting.)

● **Square file.** This instrument may either be tapered or blunt. It is used for enlarging square holes and for filing slots and keyways. Fig. 10-11.

● **Round file.** Tapered in shape, this file is used on curved surfaces. Fig. 10-12.

● **Three square file.** This file has a triangular cross-section and is usually double cut. It is for internal filing and cleaning up square corners. Fig. 10-13.

● **Half-round file.** One side is flat; the other is curved. The flat side is double cut, and the rounded side either single or double cut, depending upon the length and coarseness required. A half-round file is used on concave (in-curving) surfaces. Fig. 10-14.

● **Knife file.** This file resembles a knife blade—thick at one edge and thin or sharp at the other.

10-7. Machinist's flat bastard file. Shows the coarseness range.

10-8. Hand file.

10-9. Pillar file.

10-10. Warding file.

10-11. Square file.

10-12. Round file.

10-13. Three square file.

10-14. Half-round file.

10-15. Knife file.

It is used for the clean filing of sharp cut-in angles or inside corners. The sharp edge does not damage a surface while filing the other at the point where they meet. Fig. 10-15. See page 75.

Swiss Pattern Files

These are fine finishing tools, used for truing up grooves, keyways, and notches. Fig. 10-16. Tool and die makers, jewelers, model makers, and delicate part finishers are among those who use them.

Swiss pattern files are made to more exacting measurements than conventional American pattern files. Their points are smaller and their tapers longer. They have very fine cuts, ranging from No. 00 to No. 6—the finest.

Curved Tooth Files

Curved tooth files cover a distinct need and have a considerable range of shape and structural characteristics. They are widely used in automobile manufacturing and repairing industries for fine work on curved aluminum and sheet steel or for smoothing flat surfaces. They are also used on softer metals such as brass and babbitt. Because of their curved teeth they readily clear themselves of chips and allow quick adjustments and correct rake for speed and economy. Fig. 10-17.

Safety and File Care

It is dangerous to use a file *without a handle,* as the sharp tang can puncture the flesh and cause painful injury. There are two types of handles. One is driven on the tang and the other has screw threads. Do not strike the file with a hammer to drive

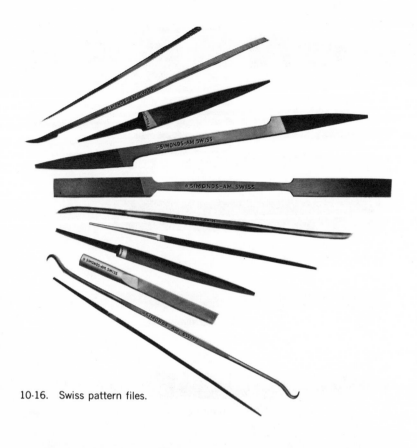

10-16. Swiss pattern files.

10-17. Curved tooth files.

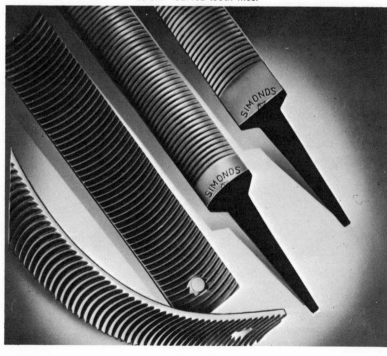

on a handle. Instead, tap the handle on the bench until it is tight.

A **file card** or **brush,** Figs. 10-18 and 10-19, should be used to help keep the file clean. Brush in the direction of the teeth.

Files not in use should be hung on a *rack* to prevent them from rubbing together and blunting the teeth.

When filing, keep the teeth well *chalked* with ordinary blackboard chalk. Chalking helps to prevent the teeth from becoming clogged with chips. Small chips that remain in the teeth are called *pinnings.* They can be removed with a piece of wire flattened on one end. A special "scorer" of this kind comes with each file card. NOTE: A clogged file will scratch the workpiece. Non-ferrous metals have a tendency to clog the teeth more rapidly than ferrous metals. It is therefore especially important to keep a file clean and well chalked when filing aluminum, brass, or copper.

Never rap a file against a metal vise as this ruins the teeth and may break the file.

How to Use a File

There are three basic methods of using a file:

• **Straight filing,** which means pushing a file lengthwise—parallel with or slightly diagonally to the workpiece.

• **Drawfiling** is done to obtain a very smooth and level surface.

• **Lathe filing,** which means stroking the file against a workpiece which is revolving on a lathe.

How To Do Straight Filing

1. Workpieces to be filed are

10-18.   File card and combination card and file brush.

usually held in a vise. For most filing, the vise should be about elbow high.

2. Cover the jaws of the vise with jaw caps. (See page 89.)

3. Select the right file for the job. It must be fitted with a handle.

4. Stand in a comfortable working position. An awkward position can be tiring, especially if the job requires considerable time. Fig. 10-20.

5. With the right hand (if your are right-handed—otherwise, with the left), grasp the end of the handle so that it fits snugly against the fleshy part of the palm. The thumb should lie along the top of the handle and parallel to it; the fingers should point up toward your face.

6. With the thumb and first two fingers of the other hand, grip the tip of the file. Hold the hand in such a way that the ball of the thumb will be pressing down on the file, in line with the

10-19.   Cleaning teeth with a file card.

10-20.   Stand in a comfortable position when filing. Notice correct method of holding the file. Left thumb is crosswise to the file, for a light stroke. NOTE: Files not in use are hung on a rack.

10-21. Proper way to hold a file. Thumb is in line with the handle, or lengthwise to the file, for a heavy stroke.

scratch rather than "shave" or shear the metal.

1. Use a mill file of bastard cut or a long-angle lathe file for routine drawfiling. When a considerable amount of metal is to be removed, a flat hand file (double-cut) may be used.

2. Grasp the file at both ends. Move it in short strokes back and forth, cutting only on the forward stroke. If the file is held at a slight angle, it will produce a better finish. Turn the file as you begin work, until you obtain the best cutting position.

3. Apply moderate pressure. Shift the file along after a few strokes so that the same teeth are not in constant use. NOTE: For the last few strokes the file should be held square with the workpiece.

4. Clean the file after its entire face has been used.

5. When finished remove the burr as in straight filing.

LATHE FILING

In filing a workpiece as it revolves on a lathe, the file should not be held rigid or stationary, but should be stroked constantly. A slight gliding or lateral motion assists the file to clear itself of chips, and also helps prevent scoring the workpiece. Fig. 10-25.

A long-angle lathe file is best for this work, although a standard mill file can also be used. The long-angle file provides much cleaner shearing, eliminates drag or tear, and overcomes "chatter." Sections without teeth protect any shoulders on the object which are not to be filed.

For work requiring a smoother finish, the file can first be rubbed against flat cast iron, to reduce

handle, when heavy strokes are required. Fig. 10-21.

7. When a light stroke is desired, and the pressure demanded becomes less, the thumb and the fingers of the hand holding the tip may change position so the thumb lies at right angles to the length of the file.

8. *Do not attempt to cut on the return stroke;* your file cuts only in one direction. Fig. 10-22.

9. Attempt to keep pressure on the file equalized. For flat filing, proceed in an almost straight line, changing its course just enough to prevent "grooving." In Fig. 10-23 the operator is putting too much pressure on the file. The grip should be more relaxed. Also, the file isn't held level, which will cause it to "rock"

and leave the work surface rounded instead of squared.

10. Apply just enough pressure to keep the file cutting during the entire cutting stroke.

11. Keep the file free of chips by using chalk, scorer, and the file card or brush.

12. After the surface has been filed smooth, remove the burr from the edge of the workpiece by holding the file at an angle and moving it lightly across the ridge.

DRAWFILING

Drawfiling is done to obtain a smooth finish by removing rough file marks from the workpiece. Fig. 10-24. NOTE: A file with a short-angle cut should never be used, because it may score or

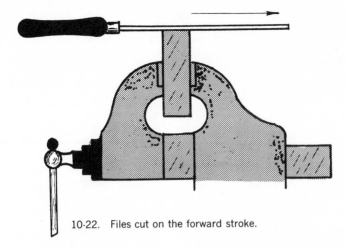

10-22. Files cut on the forward stroke.

10-23. File not held properly. Note the "desperate" grip.

the extreme sharpness of the teeth. Be careful not to dull them too much. The best practice is to use a separate file, of course.

Swiss pattern files are more satisfactory for lathe-filing workpieces which have surfaces that curve along an axis, such as elliptical or oval shapes.

PRECISION FILING

Many production devices today require precision filing. In making dies, patterns, models, and measuring instruments, and in the electronic field, precision files are needed. These small files have innumerable shapes, sizes, cuts, and purposes.

General instructions for straight filing also apply to precision work. Remember especially to use a smooth, slow, and slightly diagonal forward stroke with a

flat, precision file. Do not attempt to file on the backward stroke. Turn a round or half-round file clockwise as the stroke is made, to assure a deeper cut and a smoother finish.

Check Your Knowledge

1. What is a file?

2. What are the three general characteristics of files and rasps?

3. What is meant by the "kind" of file?

4. What is a single-cut file?

5. How are files classified?

6. Name six different types of machinist's files.

7. What is a double-cut file?

8. Why is it important to keep a file clean?

9. Distinguish between straight filing and drawfiling.

10. Discuss use of precision filing in local industries and trades.

10-24. Drawfiling.

10-25. Filing on the lathe.

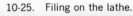

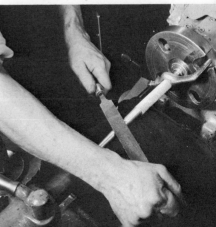

Terms to Know and Spell

tang	*concave*	*lateral motion*
cross-sectional	*nonferrous*	*shearing*
bastard	*drawfiling*	*elliptical*
smooth cut	*burr*	*diagonal*
single cut		

11 ▷ Assembly Tools

Pliers

There are many types of pliers, some of which are described in this unit. They are used to cut or twist wires and to grip small parts. Pliers should not be used on nuts or bolts because the teeth of the jaws round off the corners of the bolt head or nut, causing a wrench to slip.

Common Types of Pliers

Combination or slip-joint pliers are the most common. The slip joint permits the jaws to be opened wider at the hinge pin for gripping larger diameters. They are used for holding round bar or pipe. Fig. 11-1. They should never be used for holding hardened material, as this dulls their gripping power. The flat jaws may be used for holding or pulling sheet metal or wire. Some combination pliers are made with side cutting arrangement for cutting wire. Fig. 11-2.

Side cutting pliers are convenient for cutting and bending wire, and frequently have insulated handles for protection in electrical work. They are used a great deal by linemen. Fig. 11-3.

Diagonal pliers have a nose and full cutting bite that make them handy for cutting wire at a diagonal slant in a tight place. They are also useful for installing and removing cotter pins, cutting them to length, and spreading the ends. Fig. 11-4.

Long-nose pliers are used by radio and telephone workers, for making loops and bends of all sizes. The nose allows them to reach into tight places. These pliers are very popular for ignition and other close electrical work. Fig. 11-5.

Other types of pliers include the **round nose** and **needle nose** for forming springs and bending wire; **parallel-jaw pliers** for greater holding power. Fig. 11-6.

Wrenches

Wrenches are commonly classified according to the following terms, which are fairly self-explanatory: open-end and socket types, adjustable and nonadjustable.

In selecting a wrench be sure it fits the nut or bolt head on which it is to be used. A poorly fitted wrench can ruin the head and cause injury to the user. Fig. 11-7.

Nonadjustable open-end wrenches fit standard-sized bolt heads and nuts. Fig. 11-8 shows a **double open-end** wrench, with different sized fixed jaws at each end.

The **adjustable open-end** wrench, Fig. 11-9, has one fixed jaw part and another which can

11-1. Combination or slip-joint pliers.

11-2. Side cutting slip-joint pliers.

11.3. Side cutting pliers.

11-4. Diagonal pliers. The nose slants down.

11-5. Long-nose pliers.

11-6. Parallel-jaw pliers.

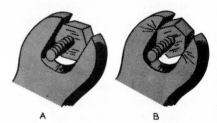

A RIGHT

B WRONG

11-7. Use a wrench that fits the nut properly. Do you see how misfit wrenches can cause injury to the user as well as damage to materials?

11-8. Double open-end wrench.

11-9. Adjustable wrench.

11-10. Combination box and open-end wrench.

11-11. Box wrench with both ends offset.

11-12. Offset L-socket wrench.

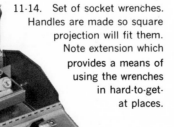

11-13. T-handle socket wrench.

be adjusted. Two sizes, small and medium, can take care of a wide range of bolt head and nut sizes.

The **box wrench** uses a socket to fit down over the bolt head or nut. It is circular, with twelve notches inside. The closed shape helps prevent slipping. These wrenches are available combined with open-end wrenches. Fig. 11-10. Also they are made with one or both ends offset, for reaching into difficult places. Fig. 11-11. Sizes range from ⅜″ to 1¼″.

Among the common types of **socket wrenches** are the **L-socket,** Fig. 11-12, which is one of the simplest, and the **T-socket.** Fig. 11-13. Most socket wrenches are sold in sets. Fig. 11-14.

The **spanner wrench** is another useful type. **Hook spanners** are used on ring nuts with square slots cut on the outside diameter. Figs. 11-15 and 11-16. **Pin spanners** are used on nuts that have matching holes in their faces. Fig. 11-17.

The **pipe wrench** is used to turn pipe, fittings, and other round members. The jaws' sharp teeth bite into the metal when pressure is applied to the handle. This wrench should never be used on an unprotected, finished surface. Fig. 11-18.

11-14. Set of socket wrenches. Handles are made so square projection will fit them. Note extension which provides a means of using the wrenches in hard-to-get-at places.

11-15. Fixed hook spanner.

11-16. Adjustable hook spanner.

11-17. Pin spanner wrench.

11-18. Pipe wrench.

Check Your Knowledge

1. Why should pliers not be used to tighten bolts or nuts?

2. What are combination pliers? For what are they used?

3. Name four common types of pliers.

4. What are the two main classifications of wrenches?

5. What is a box wrench?

6. Discuss the purposes and uses of socket and spanner wrenches.

7. Why should a pipe wrench not be used directly on a finished surface?

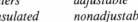

Terms to Know and Spell

pliers	*adjustable*
insulated	*nonadjustable*
diagonal	*wrench*
socket	*spanner*

12 ▷ Cutting Screw Threads with Taps and Dies

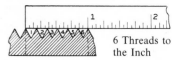

6 Threads to the Inch

12-2. Counting the number of threads per inch with a rule.

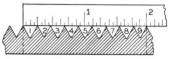

9 Threads to Two Inches Equals 4½ Threads to the Inch

12-3. By counting all the threads in two inches and dividing by two, an odd number of threads can be determined.

Perhaps the easiest way to describe a screw thread is to compare it with a flexible form, such as a piece of string, that is wound around the outside or down inside a cylinder. The *rate of advance* (or rate of winding) is uniform, and so is the *ridge section* of the thread (which would be like the width of the string). The finished thread has a spiral form, called a *helix*. Fig. 12-1.

Screw threads transmit motion or power, make delicate final adjustments on certain types of equipment, and fasten parts together, among other uses.

Threads may be cut on a lathe, a screw machine, or a thread grinding machine. Those that are cut on the outside of a cylinder are called *external* threads, and those on the inside are called *internal* threads.

Screw threads are identified by the number of threads per inch. Often this number can be learned by measuring with a rule.

Fig. 12-2 shows the measurement of a screw which has an even number of threads per inch. At first glance you may think there are seven threads because there are seven high points or *crests*. A closer look will show that there are five threads in the middle and only one-half at each end, for a total of six.

When there is an odd number of threads per inch you will find it easier to count the threads in two inches and divide by two. Fig. 12-3.

Parts of a Screw Thread

Fig. 12-4 shows the parts of a screw thread. Definitions follow:
• **Major diameter** is the larger or outside diameter of the thread.
• **Minor diameter** is the smaller diameter of a thread, measured at its root or bottom.
• **Pitch diameter** is the diameter of an imaginary cylinder drawn, the surface of which would pass through the threads at such points

as to make equal the width of the threads and the width of the spaces between the threads.
• **Pitch (P)** is the distance from any given point on the crest of a thread to a corresponding point on the crest of the next thread. A thread pitch gage is used to measure this. Figs. 12-5 and 12-6.
• **Lead (L)** is the distance a given screw thread advances axially in one complete turn.
• **Crest** is the top surface where the two sides of a thread join.
• **Root** is the bottom surface where the sides of two adjacent threads join.
• **Axis** of screw is the center line through the screw lengthwise.
• **Depth of thread** is the distance between the crest and the root of the thread, measured perpendicularly to the axis.
• **Thread angle** is the angle included between the sides of the thread measured in a plane through the axis.
• **Form of thread** is the cross-section of thread cut by a plane containing the axis.
• **Series of thread** is the standard number of threads per inch for various diameters.

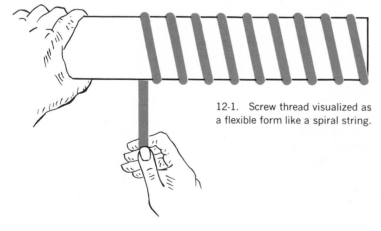

12-1. Screw thread visualized as a flexible form like a spiral string.

A *single thread* is composed of one ridge; the lead is equal to the pitch. *Multiple threads* are composed of two or more ridges running side by side. You must study this to understand it. As shown in Fig. 12-7, the *slope line* is the hypotenuse of a right triangle whose short side equals ½ P for single threads, P for double threads, 1½ P for triple threads, etc. This applies to all thread forms. In *double threads,* the lead is twice the pitch; in *triple threads* the lead is three times the pitch, etc. In odd-numbered measurements, the root is opposite the crest: in a double or quadruple thread, the root is opposite a root. A double thread advances twice as far as a single thread and a triple thread advances three times as far.

Multiple threads are used where quick motion but not great strength is important, as on valve stems, fountain pens, and toothpaste caps.

A *right-hand* thread requires a bolt or nut to be turned clockwise or to the right to tighten it.

A *left-hand* thread requires a bolt or nut to be turned counterclockwise or to the left to tighten it.

Standard Screw Threads

The angles, depths, and pitches just described could be cut in countless different ways. Yet internal and external screw threads must match exactly. Obviously, this requires precision and also *standardization.* You can imagine the confusion and maintenance problems that would arise if manufacturers did not try to agree on certain standard shapes and dimensions.

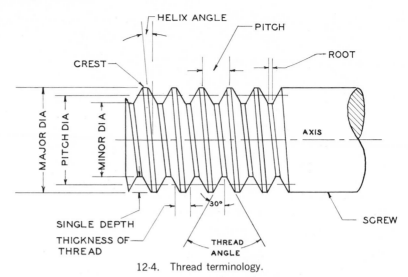

12-4. Thread terminology.

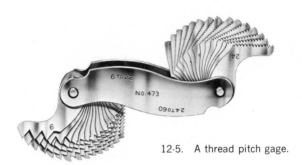

12-5. A thread pitch gage.

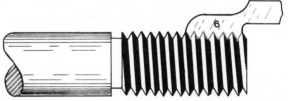

12-6. Checking the number of threads with a pitch gage.

12-7. Multiple threads with leads indicated.

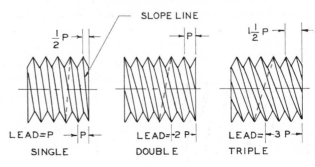

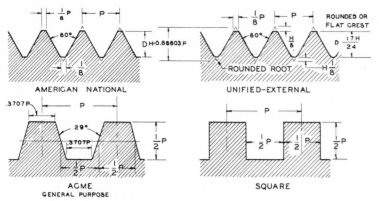

12-8. Four standard screw-thread forms.

There has been agreement in this matter, not only among manufacturers but even among nations. Still, we do not have just one kind of screw thread. Some variation is necessary, partly because it takes time to replace equipment after new standards are approved, and partly because one form will not meet all needs. Fig. 12-8 shows four common thread forms.

• **American (National) Standard.** This system was established in 1935 as a standard for the U.S.A. The National Screw Thread Commission was authorized by Congress for the task.

This thread has an included angle of 60 degrees; the crest and root are flat. Within this system there are six different *series* which vary as to diameter and threads per inch: (1) National Coarse—N.C., (2) National Fine—N.F., (3) National Extra Fine—N.E.F.,

12-9. Single right hand external square thread.

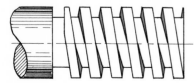

(4) National 8-pitch series, (5) National 12-pitch series, (6) National 16-pitch series. The first two are the most widely used.

Sizes of screw threads in these series are indicated by a two-part number. The first part gives the major diameter, and the second tells the number of threads per inch. A 10-24 (N.C.) screw has a number 10 diameter and 24 threads per inch. The number 10 is a code number that enables you to find the exact diameter in decimal fractions of an inch. To do this, multiply the code number by 0.013 and add 0.060.

Example

Find the major (outside thread) diameter of a 6-32 screw.

$$6 \times 0.013 + 0.060 = 0.138$$

The number of threads per inch varies on each screw of a given size. A number 10 screw in the N.C. series is made with 24 threads to the inch; number 10 in the N.F. series is made with 32 threads to the inch.

• **Unified.** In 1948 a slight revision of the old standard was approved, not only by the United States, but also by Great Britain and Canada. In this system the

crest of the external thread may be flat or rounded, and the root is rounded. Otherwise, this thread form is basically the same as the American National. A gradual change to this type of thread is taking place in industry. In this system the two series in most common use are the Unified Coarse (U.N.C.) and the Unified Fine (U.N.F.).

• **Acme.** This form is classified as a power-transmitting thread. It is strong and capable of carrying a heavy load. The 29 degree included angle reduces friction.

• **Square.** In this form the opposite sides of the ridge are square with each other and perpendicular to the center axis of the threaded part. Used in power transmission. Fig. 12-9.

• **American Pipe Threads.** These come in three series. The Taper Pipe Thread (T.P.T.) has a taper of ¾″ per foot. In lamp projects in this book, ⅛″ pipe is frequently used. Fig. 12-10.

Thread Fit

Thread fit describes how tightly a bolt and nut fit together. In the American National thread system there are the following four general classes:

• *Class 1* fit is recommended only for screw thread work in which shake or play is not objectionable. This fit is used in parts that are essential for rapid assembly.

• *Class 2* is for threaded parts that can be put together entirely with the fingers. There may be a little shake or looseness between the parts. Recommended for the great bulk of interchangeable screw thread work.

• *Class 3* is for a higher grade of threaded parts, requiring greater

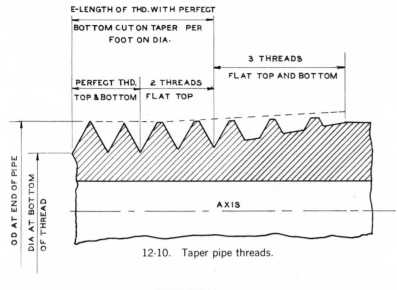

12-10. Taper pipe threads.

12-11. Adjustable tap wrench.

12-12. T-handle tap wrench.

different starting end taper but the same diameter. The threaded portion of the tap has flutes running lengthwise to provide cutting edges for the threads. The end of the tap is squared off for the tap wrench, which can either be adjustable, Fig. 12-11, or a T-tap wrench, Fig. 12-12.

A tap set is comprised of one each of a *taper tap,* a *plug tap,* and a *bottoming tap.* Fig. 12-13. See page 86.

Hand Tapping

Before a tap can be used, a hole must be drilled in the workpiece with a tap drill. The correct drill may be found in Table 12-A.

Theoretically, a hole drilled to the size of the minor diameter should be correct for tapping the thread. But for practical purposes the hole would be too small, or too "tight," as it does not allow sufficient working clearance.

accuracy and is recommended only in cases where the high cost of precision tools and continual checking are warranted.

• *Class 4* is for the finest threaded work. A screwdriver or wrench may be necessary to assemble the parts. Not adaptable to quantity production.

Taps

Taps are used to cut internal threads. They are made in all standard diameters and pitches.

Standard hand sets consist of three taps, each of which has a

TAP DRILL SIZES
National Screw Threads Commission—Standard*

AMERICAN NATIONAL FINE (NF)			AMERICAN NATIONAL COARSE (NC)		
Size of Tap	Threads per Inch	Tap Drill	Size of Tap	Threads per Inch	Tap Drill
#4	48	43	#4	40	43
#6	44	37	#5	40	38
#8	40	33	#6	32	36
#10	36	29	#8	32	29
#10	32	21	#10	24	25
#12	28	14	#12	24	16
1/4	28	3	1/4	20	7
5/16	24	I	5/16	18	F
3/8	24	Q	3/8	16	5/16
7/16	20	25/64	7/16	14	U
1/2	20	29/64	1/2	13	27/64
9/16	18	33/64	9/16	12	31/64
5/8	18	37/64	5/8	11	17/32
3/4	16	11/16	3/4	10	21/32
7/8	14	13/16	7/8	9	49/64
1	14	15/16	1	8	7/8

*Based on 75% full thread.   Table 12-A.

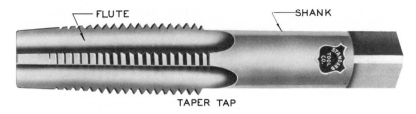

FLUTE — SHANK

TAPER TAP

PLUG TAP

BOTTOMING TAP

12-13. A set of hand taps. The taper tap cuts either all the way through or far enough to set up a plug tap, which does not finish the bottom of a blind (closed) hole. The bottoming tap is used for cutting threads to the bottom of the hole.

Therefore, the diameter of the drilled hole must necessarily be slightly larger than the minor diameter of the thread.

One generally accepted rule for this is that the diameter of the tapped hole should be approximately equal to the major diameter, D, of the screw, less 75% of the double depth of the thread. **When a hole has been drilled,**

it is referred to as "allowing 75% of full thread."

If no table is available the correct tap drill size may be calculated as follows:

If a hole is to be tapped ⅜-16 NC, the tap drill size may be found by subtracting the pitch from the diameter.

$$\frac{3}{8}'' - \frac{1}{16}'' = \frac{5}{16}''$$

1. Lay out the location of the hole.

2. Select a tap drill of the correct size.

3. Place the workpiece in a vise or other holding device and drill the hole.

4. Select a tap wrench and insert the tap. If a "blind hole," Fig. 12-14, is to be tapped, start with a taper tap and follow with

plug and bottoming taps. (A blind hole is one that does not extend completely through the workpiece.)

5. Apply pressure downward, Fig. 12-15, turning the tap clockwise and applying cutting oil regularly. Use lard oil in tapping steel. NOTE: Cast iron and brass do not need a lubricant. When it is started, the tap must be held vertically, at right angles to the workpiece. Check this angle with a hardened steel square.

6. Once the tap is started it is not necessary to apply pressure, because the tap will feed itself into the hole.

7. Back the tap about a quarter turn for each half or complete turn. This serves to break the chip and permits oil to reach the cutting edge.

8. If the tap sticks, work it carefully back and forth. Never force a tap, as this can cause it to break.

9. It may be necessary to back the tap out of a blind hole several times to clean chips from the cutter and the hole.

Cutting Threads With a Die

A die is used to cut external

12-14. Illustration is an example of a blind hole.

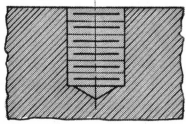

12-15. Cutting an internal thread.

12-16. Round adjustable split die.

12-17. Two-piece threading die.

12-18. Solid square die.

12-19. (A) Die stock.

12-19. (B) Die stock used to hold the die. Note the guide ring which serves to keep the die square.

threads on a rod or bolt. There are three kinds of threading dies:
- **Round adjustable split die,** Fig. 12-16. This type is most commonly used because it can be adjusted to cut a thread of the required fit.
- **Two-piece threading die.** Fig. 12-17.
- **Solid square die,** Fig. 12-18.

Threads are cut as follows:

1. Grind a chamfer on the end of the workpiece so the die will start more easily.

2. Fasten the die in a *die stock*, Fig. 12-19, so that the chamfered portion is on the bottom side. NOTE: Some die stocks have a guide or ring that fits on the workpiece and keeps the die square with the work.

3. Adjust the guide on the die stock for a free fit, just so it will turn. If the guide does not fit freely, it will bind.

4. Clamp the workpiece in the vise and place the die on the end of the piece.

5. Hold one hand over the center of the workpiece and apply pressure to get the first threads started.

6. Apply cutting oil and turn the die stock clockwise. Check to see if the stock is square with the workpiece. Fig. 12-20.

7. Turn the die stock back frequently to break the chips.

8. Back off the die when the desired length of threads is cut and check the threads with a thread gage, nut, or the part it is

12-20. Cutting external threads with a die stock and die.

to fit. If the thread is too tight, adjust the die and run over again. NOTE: If the die has not been started square, the result will be a "drunken" or crooked thread.

Check Your Knowledge

1. What is a screw thread?

2. What is an external thread?

3. To what is the pitch diameter equal?

4. Describe two ways to measure the number of threads per inch.

5. What is meant by the minor diameter?

6. What is meant by the term "thread fit"?

7. Name and describe the four classes of thread fits.

8. What is a Unified thread?

9. Describe an Acme thread.

10. What is a tap and for what is it used?

11. Name the three common types of taps.

12. What does ⁵⁄₁₆ -18 stamped on a tap refer to?

13. What is a tap drill?

14. Why is it necessary to back up the tap?

15. What is a two-piece die?

16. What is a threading die?

17. Do you think the end of the workpiece should be chamfered before threading? Why?

Terms to Know and Spell

ridge section	*thread angle*	*included angle*
helix	*hypotenuse*	*unified*
external	*form of thread*	*tap*
crest	*thread fit*	*minor diameter*
axis of screw	*die*	*clockwise*
root	*pitch*	*die stock*

13 ▷ Hand Reaming

Reaming is an operation for finishing a hole very smoothly to the exact size. In precision work it is often impossible to drill a hole of the exact size or degree of smoothness required. In such cases the hole is drilled slightly undersize, then finished (or perfected) with a reamer.

Hand reamers can produce very accurate holes when properly used. They are made with a square end for attaching a tap wrench.

Machine reamers have the shank tapered to fit the machine spindles in which they are going to be used.

Types of Hand Reamers

Hand reamers are solid, straight devices with either straight or spiral flutes, designed for sizing holes. Figs. 13-1 and 13-2. They are made either of carbon or high speed steel. They are turned in the hole by placing a tap wrench on the squared end. Hand reamers come in sizes from ⅛″ to 1½″. A spiral fluted reamer has greater shearing action than one with straight flutes.

Expansion hand reamers, Fig. 13-3, are used for the purpose of enlarging a hole a few thousandths of an inch. The reamer is constructed with a hollow center and has a tapered piece with threads that fits into the end of the reamer. When the screw is tightened, the cutting edges expand in diameter. When resharpened, a solid reamer has to be ground to a smaller size, but the expansion hand reamer can be adjusted back to standard size after sharpening. However, the limits of expansion are small, as shown in Table 13-A. The reamer is not meant to be used for perfecting odd size holes.

Taper reamers are used for finishing taper holes smoothly and accurately. Fig. 13-4. They have either straight or spiral flutes. The spiral fluted reamer has a shearing action that eliminates chatter and is generally preferred. Larger size taper reamers are made in both roughing and finishing types. When a large

LIMITS OF EXPANSION FOR STRAIGHT EXPANSION REAMERS	
Reamer Size	**Limits of Expansion**
¼″ to ¹⁵⁄₃₂″	.005 of an inch
½″ to ³¹⁄₃₂″	.008 of an inch
1″ to 1- ²³⁄₃₂″	.010 of an inch
1¾″ to 2½″	.012 of an inch

Table 13-A.

amount of stock is to be removed, a **roughing reamer,** Fig. 13-4 (B), is used. It has spaces ground into the cutting edges or teeth to prevent overloading the entire length of each tooth. These nicks or spaces are staggered on the various teeth to help in stock removal.

The **finishing reamer,** Fig. 13-4 (A), is used to size and smooth the hole.

Taper reamers are made in a range of sizes for tapers such as Brown & Sharpe and Morse and for various taper pins. Fig. 13-5.

Reaming Holes

1. Drill the correct size hole. The amount of stock left for reaming depends upon the diameter of the hole and the quality of the work desired, but it should not exceed .010″ to .012″. In schools the general practice is to use a drill 1/64″ smaller than the reamer size—often referred to as the *reamer-drill* size.

2. Fasten the workpiece securely in the vise so that the hole can be reamed in a vertical position.

3. Attach an adjustable tap wrench to the square end of the reamer.

4. Put cutting oil in the drilled hole or on the teeth of the reamer.

5. Turn the reamer clockwise, applying light pressure. Fig. 13-6. If the hole is the correct size the tool will align itself correctly. Keep it cutting or "chatter" will develop. Chatter is a series of rough lines or marks in the surface. If not corrected, the chatter marks get worse. Chatter can be eliminated by keeping the reamer cutting and increasing the down-

13-1.   Hand reamer with straight flute.

13-2.   Hand reamer with spiral flutes.

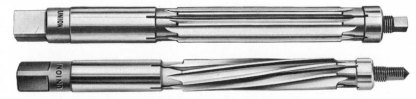

13-3.   Expansion hand reamers. Straight and spiral flutes.

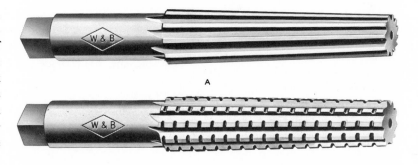

A

B

13-4.   Large-diameter hand taper reamers: (A) finishing reamer, (B) roughing reamer.

13-5.   Typical long taper reamers.

ward pressure. Continue until the entire length of the hole is reamed. Do not force reamer or it will become jammed in the hole. When using a straight reamer with a tapered tip, run the reamer deep enough so the bottom of the hole is reamed to full diameter.

13-6.   Hand reaming.

6. Do not reverse the direction of the reamer. This will ruin the delicate cutting edges.

7. Remove the reamer by withdrawing it carefully from the hole, while continuing to turn it clockwise.

Check Your Knowledge

1. What is reaming?

2. In drilling the hole for reaming, why must it be drilled undersize?

3. Name the typical hand reamers.

4. What makes an expansion reamer different from a solid hand reamer?

5. What are taper reamers used for?

6. What is a roughing reamer? A finishing reamer?

---

14 ▷ Hand and Power Sawing

Metal stock that is too small to be cut on a machine can be placed in a vise and cut to size with a *hand hacksaw*. This saw has two essential parts, the *frame* and the *blade*. Fig. 14-1. Other work also is done, as in cutting off a bolt head when a bolt is jammed. Pipe, tubing, and rod, for special or custom fitting on the job, may be hand cut. An example would be concrete reinforcement or plumbing.

Frames

There are two types of frames, the *solid,* which will take only one size of blade, and the *adjustable,* which will hold blades ranging from 8″ to 12″ in length. A wing nut generally is used to place proper tension on the blade.

Saw Blades

Choosing the right blade for the job is important. There are three things to consider:
- Type of steel (regular or high speed).
- Type of blade (rigid or flexible back).
- Pitch (number of teeth per inch).

Both standard (regular) and high speed steel blades are recommended for precision cutting when the workpiece can be held in a vise. The flexible type is best for maintenance men, plumbers, electricians, and others whose work makes rigid support of the workpiece impossible.

Pitch Selection

Selecting the correct pitch (number of teeth per inch) for the material to be cut is important. Table 14-A gives the general rules governing hand hacksaw blade selection, and may be applied to power units. The following suggestions will also help:

At all times at least two teeth should be engaged in the material to be cut.

- Use a fine tooth for small or thin stock and a coarse tooth for larger sections.
- Soft, easily machined metals require a coarse tooth because larger spaces between teeth are needed to carry away the larger chips and prevent clogging. For

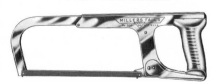

14-1. Hand hacksaw.

SELECTION CHART FOR HAND HACKSAW BLADES

Number of teeth per inch	Diameter of material to be cut	Type of material to be cut
14	1″ or more	Aluminum, babbitt, bronze, brass, cast iron, cold-rolled steel, iron
18	¼″ to 1″	Angle (light and heavy), cast iron, drill rod, tool steel; also for general cutting
24	1/16″ to ¼″	Brass pipe, BX heavy, heavy sheet metal, iron pipe
32	less than 1/16″	Sheet metal over 18 gage, tubing over 18 gage, flush pipe, BX light

Table 14-A.

very hard metals, use a finer tooth than you would choose for a very soft metal of the same size section.

Set of the Blade

The set of the blade means the manner in which the teeth are bent. Set is necessary so that the *kerf* (the slot cut by the saw) will be wider than the blade. This keeps the blade from sticking in the kerf.

There are two types of set for hand hacksaw blades (Fig. 14-2):

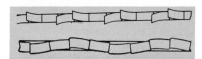

14-2. Two types of set for hand hacksaw blades.

Raker set, in which one tooth is set (or bent) left, the next one set right, the next not set at all, and so on.

Wavy set, in which several adjacent teeth are bent in one direction; then a similar number are bent in the opposite direction, giving a sort of rolling or wavy effect.

Using the Hand Hacksaw

1. Whenever possible clamp

14-3. Clamp thin sections of metal between wood, sandwich fashion. The cut edges are left smooth. Prevents bending of the workpiece.

14-4. All hand hacksaws are designed to cut on the forward stroke. Make sure the teeth point forward and the blade is properly tensioned.

the workpiece firmly in a vise, remembering to put soft "jaw caps" on the vise if necessary. When cutting thin sheet material, clamp between two pieces of wood and cut through wood and metal, as shown in Fig. 14-3.

2. The broadest side of the workpiece should be up, so you can use coarse teeth for rapid cutting. The layout line should be as close to the ends of the jaws as possible.

3. Fasten the blade in the frame so that the teeth are pointing away from the handle. Fig. 14-4.

4. In starting a cut, hold the front of the frame as well as the handle to guide the saw and help produce an even, steady downward pressure. Fig. 14-5. Push the saw straight across the surface of the workpiece in a full-length stroke. Press down with both hands.

5. Then release the pressure and return the saw evenly to the starting position. Do not twist the blade or raise it up out of the cut, as this may cause jamming. Strive for an even, powerful stroke.

Common Mistakes to Avoid

1. Don't start sawing on a

14-5. Correct method of holding the hacksaw for starting the cut.

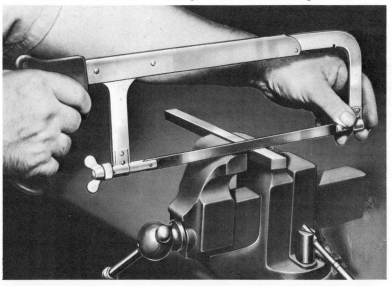

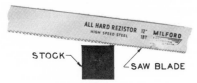

CORRECT SLANT APPROACH

14-6. Do not start sawing at a corner or at sharp angles. Start the saw at a low angle.

corner or at a sharp angle to the work surface. Fig. 14-6.

2. If you get off the guide line, don't try to straighten the cut. Turn the workpiece over and start a new cut from the opposite side at a point that will remove the first groove when completed. Fig. 14-7.

3. Don't force a new blade into a cut started with an old blade; the set of the new blade will be wider, and the blade may break if you try to force it.

4. Don't force the saw with too much pressure or too rapid strokes. "Steadier and easier" will do it faster.

Power Sawing

There are three general types of power saws for cutting metals: (1) the power hacksaw, (2) the horizontal band saw, (3) the vertical band or contour saw.

14-7. If you get off the guide line, don't try to twist the blade to straighten the cut. Turn the work over and start a new cut from the opposite side. Take care in starting, as here shown.

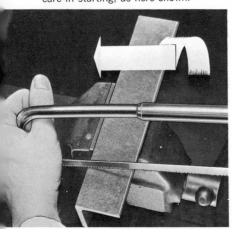

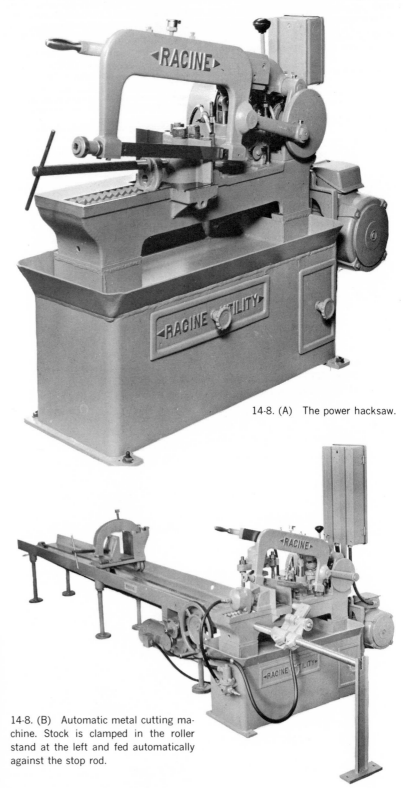

14-8. (A) The power hacksaw.

14-8. (B) Automatic metal cutting machine. Stock is clamped in the roller stand at the left and fed automatically against the stop rod.

The Power Hacksaw

The power hacksaw is capable of turning out accurate, reasonably close-tolerance work, provided it is used carefully.

Figs. 14-8 (A) and 14-8 (B) show typical power hacksaws. The hacksaw can be used for cutting stock square, or the vise can be swiveled to cut stock at an angle. A saw frame holds the blade. Sawing takes place on the forward stroke; on the return stroke the frame lifts slightly to reduce wear on the blade. Most saws are equipped with oil hydraulic feed to provide accurate control throughout the cut.

WORK SET-UP

The following rules will help you in clamping most types of work in the conventional hacksaw machine vise:

1. Thin strips should be laid flat.

2. Short ends of stock should be cut singly to assure firm clamping and accurate dimensions.

3. Round stock or tubing, when gang cut, should be held tight by clamps or chain vise. See Fig. 14-9, showing "multiple rounds."

4. Round stock or tubing can be cut two bars at a time by attaching a tapered wedge—thick end up—to both jaws, or by placing a double V-block or wedge of leather or wood between two bars. Fig. 14-9.

POWER BLADES

Power hacksaw blades are quite different from hand blades in size, shape, type, and number of teeth. Power blades are heavier, and have a coarser tooth pitch.

SELECTION CHART FOR BLADE AND FEED OF POWER HACKSAW

Type of cutting	Feed Pressure	Width of blade	Thickness of blade
Light angle iron, pipe, rods	Light to moderate	1″	.050″
General purpose cutting	Moderate	1¼″ to 1½″	.062 to .075″
Large sections	Heavy	1¾″ to 2″	.088 to .100″

Table 14-B.

Power blades are available in ten different lengths, from 12″ to 36″. Widths include ⅝″ through 4½″. Thickness ranges from 0.032″ to 0.125″; however, the extremes of width and thickness are not common.

The pitch of teeth may be 2½, 3, 4, 6, 10, 14, or 18 per inch of cutting length. The most common pitches are 4, 6, 10, and 14.

CUTTING OFF STOCK

1. If a square cut is to be made, be sure the vise jaws are square with the blade. If stock is to be cut at an angle, the vise has to be set accordingly.

2. Place bar stock in the vise and support one end on a roller stand.

3. Push down on the handle of the frame until the blade just

14-9. Various methods of work set-up for power hacksawing.

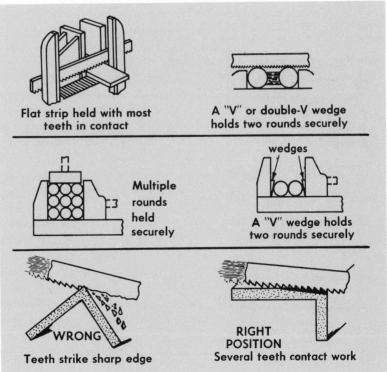

Flat strip held with most teeth in contact

A "V" or double-V wedge holds two rounds securely

Multiple rounds held securely

wedges

A "V" wedge holds two rounds securely

WRONG
Teeth strike sharp edge

RIGHT POSITION
Several teeth contact work

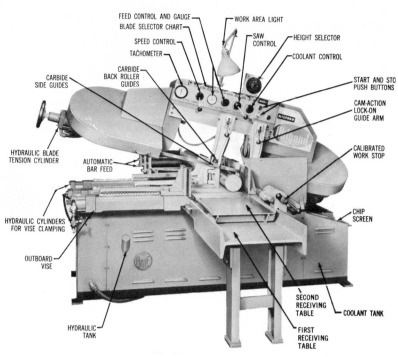

FEED CONTROL AND GAUGE
BLADE SELECTOR CHART
SPEED CONTROL
TACHOMETER
CARBIDE
BACK ROLLER
GUIDES
CARBIDE
SIDE GUIDES
WORK AREA LIGHT
SAW
CONTROL
HEIGHT SELECTOR
COOLANT CONTROL
START AND STO
PUSH BUTTONS
CAM-ACTION
LOCK-ON
GUIDE ARM
HYDRAULIC BLADE
TENSION CYLINDER
AUTOMATIC
BAR FEED
CALIBRATED
WORK STOP
HYDRAULIC CYLINDERS
FOR VISE CLAMPING
OUTBOARD
VISE
CHIP
SCREEN
HYDRAULIC
TANK
SECOND
RECEIVING
TABLE
FIRST
RECEIVING
TABLE
COOLANT TANK

14-10.   Horizontal metal-cutting band saw.

Horizontal Metal-cutting Band Saw

This saw has a continuous blade which travels in a horizontal plane or slightly inclined from the horizontal.

Blades used are made of high carbon steel with a flexible back and hardened teeth. They may have from 6 to 24 teeth per inch, with raker set, and may vary in width from $1/16''$ to $1''$.

The saw shown in Fig. 14-10 has a hydraulically operated feed, an adjustable vise, an adjustable stock stop, and a means of varying the cutting speed. It can cut stock square or at an angle.

CUTTING OFF STOCK

1. Adjust the vise at right angles to the blade if a square cut is desired.

2. Adjust the blade guides so that they are only slightly wider than the stock to be cut.

3. Vary the cutting pressure on the stock by moving the weight on the frame.

4. Turn on the power and grasp the handle of the saw frame, while releasing the ratchet lever with the other hand.

5. When the cut is completed, the machine will turn off automatically.

The function of this saw is the same as the power hacksaw's, described previously, except that its continuous cutting action is similar to that of the vertical band saw. This permits more pieces to be cut than by the power hacksaw in the same length of time.

The Vertical Band Saw

This saw, Fig. 14-11, is made in different sizes to handle stock from 18" to 24" in thickness and

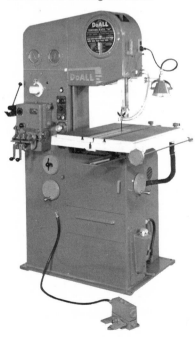

14-11. Band or contour sawing machine. Note device mounted on the machine for welding the blade.

clears the top of the stock. With a steel rule held against the right side of the saw blade as a guide, move the bar of stock until its cutoff line meets the edge of the rule.

4. Tighten the vise securely. If loose, the stock will roll and break the blade. If several pieces are to be cut the same length, set the stop rod or cutoff gage, which is used to control the length of cut.

5. Turn on the power and push in the clutch handle to start the saw frame moving. It will feed itself into the stock automatically.

6. When the cut is completed, the frame raises itself from the work automatically and stops cutting.

7. Loosen the vise and move the stock forward against the stop rod to cut the next piece if several pieces of the same length are required.

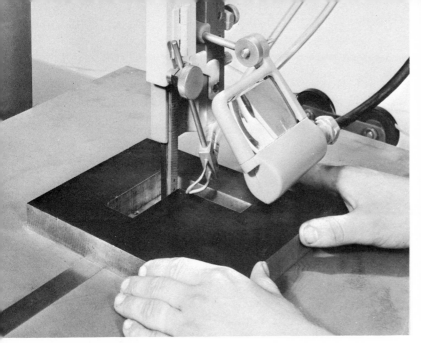

14-12. Filing on the metal-cutting band saw.

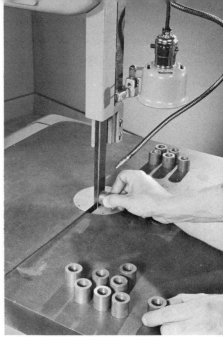

14-13. Polishing on the metal-cutting band saw.

with throat capacities that vary from 16″ to 60″. The best saws are equipped with variable speed control which permits easy adaption to the characteristics of different metals.

Blades for the saw also vary as to width and pitch. Blades are usually purchased in 100′ lengths, then cut as required and the ends for the loop welded on the butt welder. Pitches available are 6, 8, 14, and 18. Common widths are ¼″, ⅜″, ½″, ⅝″, ¾″ and 1″.

Filing and polishing can also be done on this saw. Figs. 14-12 and 14-13.

Profile or contour sawing is a fast, accurate, and efficient method of producing intricate curved or irregular cuts in almost any machinable metal. Radii as small as 1/16″ can be cut, and either internal or external contours can be sawed. Where internal contours are involved, it is first necessary to drill a hole within the contour to admit the saw blade. The blade is cut at a convenient point, threaded through the pilot hole, and rewelded on the butt welder. Fig. 14-14. Blades are always raker set to provide the necessary clearance.

Sawing with the Contour Saw

1. Guide lines should be drawn on the workpiece unless a machine guide is used.

2. Select the proper blade for the job.

3. Consult the job selector chart to determine the correct cutting speed.

4. Lower the saw guide until it is about ½″ above the thickest part of the workpiece, and clamp the saw guide in position.

5. Start the saw and bring the workpiece up to the blade. Advance the workpiece against the blade with steady pressure.

14-14. Preparing to make an internal cut on a vertical band saw. Starting holes are drilled in the workpiece and the saw blade threaded through one of them. The blade is then welded into an endless band to make the cut, on the butt welder at the left side of the machine.

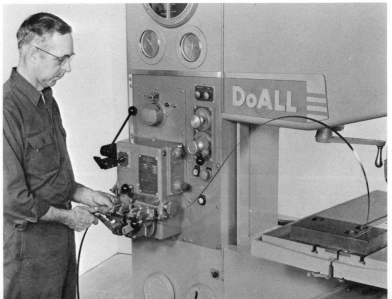

14-15. Cutting an internal contour. Drill hole within the contour area to admit the saw blade.

6. If round stock or irregular workpieces are to be cut, they must be held securely in a clamp.

7. If internal cutting is to be done, starting holes are drilled in the workpiece and the saw blade threaded through one of them. The blade is then welded on the butt welder into an endless band. The cut can then be made. Figs. 14-14 and 14-15.

The vertical band saw or con- tour machine is used in produc- tion work in many manufacturing plants. A jig is mounted on the saw table to hold the workpiece and any number of pieces can be cut. Fig. 14-16.

The vertical band saw has taken over much of the work formerly done on the milling ma- chine and shaper, at a great sav- ing in time.

Friction Sawing

Friction sawing differs from other metal sawing methods be- cause it is not actually a cutting operation; instead it is a burning process, similar to torch cutting. It is not only much faster than conventional sawing methods but is effective for very hard materials which could not normally be sawed.

Friction cutting involves the use of a blade running at very great speeds, between 6,000 and 18,000 feet per minute. Friction heat is built up where the work- piece contacts the blade, and burning occurs. Held to the fast moving blade with constant pres- sure, the workpiece is rapidly heated to about 1,700 degrees F. At this point, oxygen forced into the cut by the tooth gullets causes the metal to burn. Since any given part of the blade is out of con- tact with the metal 99% of the time, the blade itself remains at a temperature that does it no harm.

While friction sawing has solved many difficult metal cut- ting problems, it has a distinct limitation imposed by size and thickness of the work, so is not suitable for all types.

Check Your Knowledge

1. Name three types of power saws.

2. Why is the proper selection of blades for the power saw important?

3. Name two types of metal cutting band saws.

4. What is meant by profile or contour sawing?

5. Besides sawing, what other operations may be done on the vertical band saw?

6. Why are various speeds nec- essary on the band saw?

7. What is friction sawing?

14-16. Slotting of swivel ratchet wrench handles on a vertical band saw. The handles are made of A-8260 steel. Production rate: 120 an hour.

Terms to Know and Spell

tension
flexible
pitch selection
clutch handle
butt welder
raker set
contour saw
hydraulic
profile
friction sawing
wavy set
close-tolerance
tapered wedge
pilot hole

15 ▷ Metal Fasteners

15-1.   Machine bolt with nut.

Fasteners are used to join and hold two or more pieces of metal either temporarily or permanently. Some of the most common are bolts, screws, nuts, rivets, and pins.

Machine Bolts

The term machine bolt is generally used to denote a "through bolt" which has a head on one end, is threaded on the other and passed through clearance holes in two or more aligned parts to receive a nut for tightening and holding parts together.

Unless otherwise specified, machine bolts are made with National Coarse (N.C.) or National Fine (N.F.) threads, in diameters from ¼″ to 4″ and in lengths from ½″ to 30″. These bolts are either made with a black, rough finish or are machined all over, with the underside of the nut finished to resemble a washer. Fig. 15-1.

Machine bolts are available with either square or hexagonal heads.

Cap Screws

Cap screws differ from machine bolts in that they are used for fastening two pieces together by passing through a tolerance hole in one piece and screwing into a tapped hole in the other.

There are five types of American Standard cap screws: *hexagonal head, flat head, round head, fillister head,* and *hexagonal socket.* These are shown in Fig. 15-2.

The heads may be slotted for a screwdriver or may have a socket. To turn the socket-head type, special hexagonal keys are required. Cap screws are regularly produced in finished forms for use on machines and machine tools requiring precision fit and good appearance.

Machine Screws

Machine screws are similar to cap screws but are generally smaller (0.060″ to 0.750″) in diameter. Machine screws are made with oval, round, flat, fillister, truss, binding, and pan heads. Fig. 15-3. They come with either National Fine or National Coarse threads. American Standard machine screws are regularly produced with a naturally bright finish, not heat-treated, and supplied with plain-sheared ends, not chamfered. Below ¼″ in diameter the sizes of machine screws are stated by numbers, such as 8-32. The 8 refers to the diameter, and 32 to the threads per inch.

Machine screws are adapted to fastening thin material. Hence all the smaller numbered screws are threaded nearly to the head. They are also used in dies, jigs, fixtures, and the construction of firearms. Fig. 15-4 shows a screw style guide, page 98.

Set Screws

Set screws are used for arresting the movement of assembled parts, such as a door knob or the

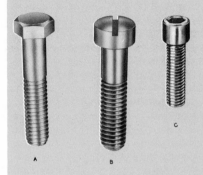

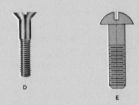

15-2.   Cap screws. (A) Hexagon, (B) fillister head, (C) socket head, (D) flat head, (E) round head.

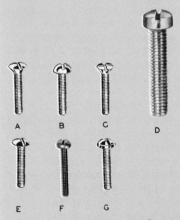

15-3.   Machine screws. (A) Oval head, (B) round head, (C) flat head, (D) fillister head, (E) truss head, (F) binding head, (G) pan head. Machine screws are used for assembling small mechanical and electrical products.

97

SCREW STYLE GUIDE

SLOTTED HEAD	PHILLIPS RECESSED	HI-TORQUE RECESS	TORQ-SET RECESS	HEXAGON SOCKET	SPLINE SOCKET
DRILLED SPANNER	SLOTTED SPANNER	KNURLED HEAD	ROUND ONE WAY		SAFETY MODIFIED PHILLIPS
WELD UNDER	WELD OVER	HEXAGON TRIMMED	HEXAGON UPSET		SLOTTED HEXAGON
ROUND	FILLISTER	TRUSS	100° FLAT		82° FLAT
OVAL	FLAT FILLISTER	PAN	BINDING		UNDER CUT
SQUARE HEAD SET	SOCKET SET HEX SPLINE	FILLISTER DRILLED	WASHER HEAD		DRILLED HEXAGON
CUP POINT	CONE POINT	FLAT POINT	OVAL POINT	HALF DOG POINT	FULL DOG POINT

15-4.

Thread-forming Screws

These screws cut or form threads when they are driven or turned into the proper size hole. Thus they eliminate tapping, riveting, and soldering. Sometimes called "self-tapping," they are available with all common types of heads. Fig. 15-8.

Stove Bolts

Stove bolts are commonly used to secure stove parts and similar work. Fig. 15-9. Flat, round, or oval heads are standard. Standard body diameters range from ⅛″ to ½″ and lengths from ½″ to 6″.

Carriage Bolts

Carriage bolts have a round head, Fig. 15-10. The part of the body under the head is square. They come in a black, rough finish and have a National Coarse thread.

A carriage bolt is usually used to fasten a wooden piece to metal. The square part under the head is sunk into the wood to prevent the bolt from turning while the nut is being screwed on. Standard body diameters range from ³⁄₁₆″ to ½″ and lengths from ½″ to 6″.

Stud Bolts

A stud bolt has no head and is threaded on both ends, one more than the other. Stud bolts seldom exceed 12 inches in length. One end of the bolt is screwed into a tapped hole. The part to be held is slipped over the stud or studs and a nut is used at the top of the stud to hold the parts together. Fastening the cylinder head to the block of an automobile engine is a good example of its use. Fig. 15-11. By removing the nuts the head can be lifted

hub of a pulley on a shaft, Fig. 15-5. They come either with square heads or headless, Fig. 15-6, and with variously shaped points, Fig. 15-7. The headless type is either slotted or has a socket for a hexagonal wrench known as the Allen hex. key or an Allen wrench. It sinks completely so as not to interfere with use of the part.

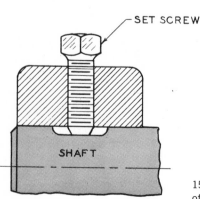

15-5. Set screw used to prevent slipping of a pulley on a shaft.

while the stud bolts remain in the block.

Nuts

There are many different shapes and sizes of nuts. Fig. 15-12. Most common are hexagonal and square. These are graded in a general way as *regular* and *heavy*. The heavy line is thicker and slightly larger across the flats. Regular square nuts do not have a finished surface. A washerlike face is machined on the bearing surface of finished and semifinished nuts.

CASTLE NUTS

Castle nuts and slotted nuts have grooves in their upper face to receive a cotter pin. The bolt also has a hole in it to receive the pin. This holds the bolt firmly in place. Fig. 15-13.

JAM NUTS

These hexagonal shaped nuts are much thinner than a regular hexagon nut. Jam nuts are used in narrow spaces to lock regular nuts into position. They are fully machined and have a washerlike face. One end of the nut is chamfered, or it can be obtained with both ends chamfered.

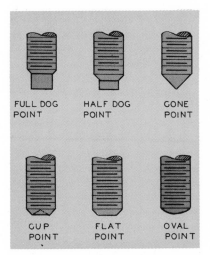

15-7. American Standard set screw points.

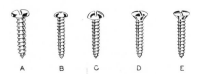

15-8. Thread-forming screws. (A) Binding, (B) truss, (C) round, (D) countersunk oval, (E) countersunk flat.

15-9. Stove bolts. Flat countersunk head and round (button) head. Rolled threads.

15-6. American Standard set screws. (A) Square head cup point set screw, (B) slotted set screw, (C) hex. socket set screw, (D) hex. socket, cup point, (E) Allen hex. key.

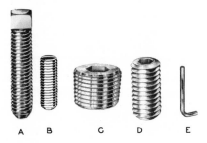

15-10. Carriage bolt.

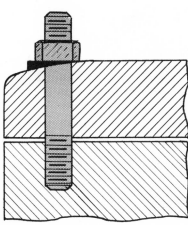

15-11. Showing use of a stud bolt in automobile engine work. As the nut turns, the force drives the bolt in at the same time.

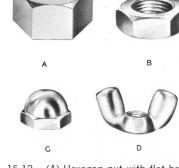

15-12. (A) Hexagon nut with flat bearing surface, (B) jam nut, beveled both sides, (C) acorn nut, (D) wing nut.

15-13. Castle or castellated nut.

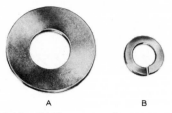

15-14. (A) Flat washer, (B) lock washer.

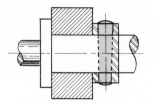

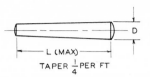

15-16. Taper pin application.

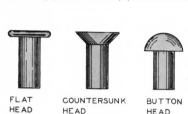

FLAT HEAD   COUNTERSUNK HEAD   BUTTON HEAD

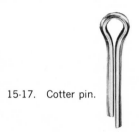

15-17. Cotter pin.

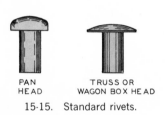

PAN HEAD   TRUSS OR WAGON BOX HEAD

15-15. Standard rivets.

CAP OR ACORN NUTS

Cap or acorn nuts are usually made of plated brass, for work that requires a decorative appearance.

WING NUT

A wing nut is suited for frequent adjustment or quick removal. It is made with both National Fine and National Coarse threads. The wings provide a method of tightening the nut by hand.

Washers

Washers are placed under bolt heads and also between a nut and a workpiece. There are two general types, *flat* and *lock*. Fig. 15-14 (A). A lock washer, Fig. 15-14 (B), is used to prevent a nut from working loose, especially on a machine where there is excessive vibration. A flat washer protects the finished surface of the work, which may be marred when the bolt or nut is tightened. It also provides a bearing surface for the bolt or nut.

Rivets

Rivets are regarded as *permanent* fastenings. This is their main difference, compared with removable fastenings, such as machine bolts and cap screws. Rivets are made from wrought iron, mild steel, copper, or aluminum, among other metals. They are available with round, oval, flat, countersunk, button, pan, or truss heads. Fig. 15-15 shows a few common types used in the school shop.

The most common sizes are 1/8″ and 3/16″ in diameter. A rivet should be .003″ to 1/64″ smaller in diameter than the holes in the pieces to be riveted. It should be long enough to extend out. Allow enough length to form a head about double the diameter of the rivet. Proper methods of riveting will be shown in Unit 22.

Machine Pins

American Standard machine pins include taper pins, straight pins, dowel pins, clevis pins, and cotter pins. For light work, the taper pin is used for fastening hubs or collars to shafts, as shown in Fig. 15-16.

Taper pins are cylindrical and tapered in shape and are used to keep two parts in a fixed position and preserve alignment of parts.

The cotter pin, Fig. 15-17, is fitted into a hole drilled crosswise in a shaft and prevents parts from slipping or turning off.

Check Your Knowledge

1. What are some of the most common types of metal fasteners?

2. Explain the difference between a machine bolt and a cap screw.

3. Name five types of American Standard cap screws.

4. How does a cap screw differ from a machine screw?

5. Where are carriage bolts used?

6. Describe a stud bolt. For what is it used?

7. How are nuts graded?

8. Name two general types of washers.

9. Name several types of materials used in the construction of rivets.

10. What are some of the shapes of rivet heads?

11. What is a taper pin? For what is it used? For what is a cotter pin used?

Terms to Know and Spell

fastener	fillister	hexagonal
clearance	sheared	carriage
machined	assembled	stud
slotted	headless	cylinder

---

16 ▷ Hand Polishing with Coated Abrasives

A coated abrasive consists of a flexible backing, to which a rough, grainy surface is applied and held by a film of adhesive. The backing may be cloth, paper, vulcanized fibers, or a combination of materials. Aluminum oxide and silicon carbide are widely used for the abrasive surface. Natural abrasives—flint, emery, and garnet—are also used but are not as satisfactory.

The development of modern coated abrasives began toward the end of the nineteenth century when it became possible to produce granules of silicon carbide and aluminum oxide of uniform standard in an electric furnace. Since then there has been a steady improvement in quality and economical manufacture.

Many crystalline forms of silicon carbide are available. Most are hexagonal particles, made up of masses of interlocking crystals. Aluminum oxide abrasives are produced by purifying bauxite to a crystalline form and adding various amounts of titania to impart extra toughness.

Aluminum oxide has a tougher grain than silicon carbide, so is particularly well adapted to the polishing of high carbon steel, alloy steels, and tough bronze.

Processing Abrasive Grains

As the abrasive is produced, either in a lump mass or as looser crystallites, it is first fed through powerful jaw crushers, and then through roll crushers to reduce to grain sizes. Since it is not possible to crush the grains to any one size, a series of vibrating silk screens is used to separate the grains in commercial grit sizes. Batteries of screens, ranging from fine to coarse, sift the grains. These screens are carefully made from threads of exact size and number per square inch to insure extreme accuracy in the size of the apertures through which the abrasive particles are sifted. Sub-sieve grades, called "flours," are graded by hydraulic separators and air classifiers.

Silk screens for this process are made in Switzerland, where this art has been passed from father to son for generations.

Accurate grading is all important to eliminate damage that could be caused by oversizes. Abrasive grades are numbered from 12, the coarsest, to 600.

COMPARATIVE GRADING CHART*
Aluminum Oxide, Silicon Carbide, Garnet and Flint

Mesh	Symbol	Mesh	Symbol
600	—	80	0
500	—	60	½
400	10/0	40	1½
360	—	36	2
320	9/0	30	2½
280	8/0	24	3
240	7/0	20	3½
180	5/0	16	4
150	4/0	12	4½
120	3/0		
100	2/0		

*The way the symbol is written is very important. For instance, 3 is much coarser than 3/0. Also, 3 is finer than 4, but 3/0 is coarser than 4/0. This may seem confusing at first, but it will become clear as you use the symbols.

Table 16-A

As said, there are four general groups of backings used in the coated abrasive industry: paper, cloth, vulcanized fiber, and combinations of these laminated together. Cloth backing is durable, and well suited for general school metalworking. Abrasive cloth can be purchased in 9″ x 11″ sheets or in rolls ½″ to 3″ wide.

Polishing with Abrasive Cloth

Abrasive cloth is quite expensive; care should be taken in its use.

1. Tear a strip of abrasive cloth, the size needed, from a sheet or roll.

2. For polishing pieces by hand, wrap the abrasive material around a flat piece of wood, sized to fit your grip. Apply oil to the surface of the cloth or place a few drops on the workpiece.

3. Use coarse abrasive to start with; if the condition demands finer polishing, follow with a medium grade and finish with a fine grade.

4. When polishing on the lathe, place a few drops of oil on the abrasive cloth before using.

CAUTION: *Do not bring your hands near the lathe dog.*

Check Your Knowledge

1. What is a coated abrasive?

2. Name some of the backings used in a coated abrasive.

3. Name three natural abrasives.

4. How are aluminum oxide abrasives produced?

5. Explain how the abrasive particles are sized.

6. Why is it important to have accurate grading of abrasives?

7. Describe the methods used in hand polishing.

Terms to Know and Spell

coated abrasive	*crystalline forms*	*air classifiers*
adhesive	*interlocking crystals*	*vulcanized fiber*
aluminum oxide	*grit sizes*	*laminated*
silicon carbide	*subsieve grades*	

Section Three

Wrought Metal

Only a few years ago wrought metal was thought to be suitable only for exterior open work or filigree and for kitchen and outdoor furniture. Today it is used throughout the home.

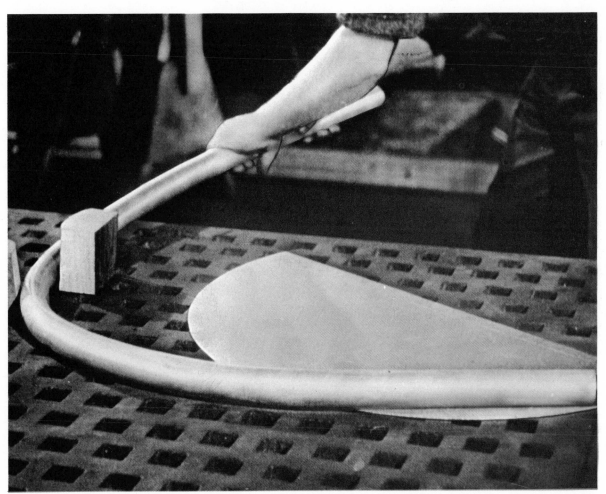

Because metal has a range of working characteristics, contemporary designers have adapted it to diverse modern home requirements. Metal can be bent in a wide variety of designs and yet stronger types are relatively easy to use in long, slender functional supports and braces which are essential to graceful appearance. Metal can be combined with materials such as plastic, plywood, fiber glass, formica, leather, fabric, plate glass, and other materials.

The popularity of metal in home furnishings is shown by the fact that its use has grown until it now represents about one-fourth of the total sales in the field.

Metal furnishings are suited to today's informal type of living. Smaller homes and apartments require furniture that is strong, versatile, non-bulky, and easy to maintain. Metal furniture is easy to clean and is not susceptible to warping. It is not basically affected by temperature changes or moisture.

Early wrought iron designers and craftsmen forged their pieces hot because heavy metal was used in this particular era. Today most pieces are cold-formed.

17-1. Shows the method of enlarging a pattern. The form at the left represents the original drawing. By enlarging to 1″, a full-size pattern can be made. (Note that neither drawing is actual dimension size here.)

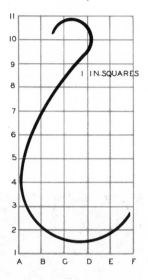

17 ▷ Designing the Scroll

A scroll is a strip of metal which has been bent to a circular shape similar to an open clock spring. Scrolls tend to break up the monotony of straight lines and add to the interest of the project. Devices such as forks and jigs are used to form these scrolls.

Before a scroll can be made, a layout or pattern has to be drawn. Sometimes the pattern has to be enlarged to full size so that the length of stock can be determined and to check with the workpiece as the bending proceeds.

1. Lay out the design or pattern on squared paper.

If it is not laid out on squared paper, proceed as follows:

2. Rule over the original drawing with squares of a fractional-inch size, depending upon the scale to which the design has been made.

3. *For example:* If the original drawing has been made one-fourth full size, lay out ¼-inch squares.

4. Then by laying out 1 inch squares for the full size pattern, the enlargement will be the correct size.

5. The full size pattern should be laid out on heavy wrapping paper or cardboard.

6. Down the left hand side of the original drawing place numbers for each horizontal ruled line. Along the bottom, letter each vertical line. Number and letter the enlarged graph in the same manner.

7. On the original drawing locate a point and lightly dot the same point on the enlarged pattern. Continue this process until you have marked enough points to draw the pattern layout full size. Fig. 17-1.

8. Using a straightedge for straight lines and a French curve or bent wire for curved lines, connect the points with a pencil line. If both sides of the design are alike, only half of the outline needs to be drawn.

18 ▷ Forming the Scroll

1. Measure the length of stock needed by laying a soft wire along the pattern. Then straighten the wire and measure.

2. Cut the stock to the required length.

3. The end of the stock is flared by holding it on the anvil and striking with glancing blows. Fig. 18-1.

4. Start bending the scroll by placing the stock flat on the anvil, with one end extending slightly beyond the edge. Start the curve by striking the metal with the flat of the ball-peen hammer, using glancing blows. Fig. 18-2. Move the workpiece forward a little at a time, as the beginning of the scroll is formed.

5. After the curve has been started, turn the workpiece over and complete the first part of the scroll, Fig. 18-3, by striking it with the flat of the hammer. Fig. 18-4 shows these first steps.

Check the curve by placing it upon the pattern to see if it conforms to the outline.

6. The remainder of the scroll can be completed on a bending jig or fork. There are various types, as shown in Figs. 18-5 (A), 18-5 (B), and 18-5 (C).

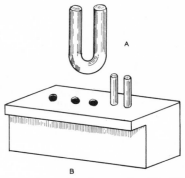

18-5. Jig for bending scrolls. (A) "U" shaped bending fork made from round rod. (B) Metal block with removable pins that can be adjusted for different workpiece thicknesses.

18-5. (C) Adjustable bending jig. The large bar, attached off center, may be adjusted to different workpiece thicknesses.

18-1. Flaring the end of the stock preparatory to forming the scroll.

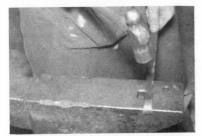

18-2. Starting the scroll. One end extends slightly beyond edge of the anvil.

18-3. Completing the first bend.

18-4. Steps in starting and forming a scroll.

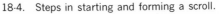

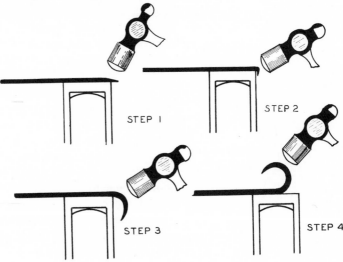

STEP 1

STEP 2

STEP 3

STEP 4

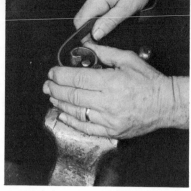

18-6. Completing the scroll on a bending jig.

18-7. Workpiece laid on pattern to see if the scroll is being formed correctly.

18-8. Feed the workpiece a little at a time to complete the scroll.

18-9. The pipe and metal are both clamped in a vise. The curve is formed by pulling the metal down over the pipe.

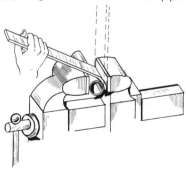

7. After the bending device is locked firmly in a vise, adjust the pins to the proper opening. Slip the workpiece between the pins at a point where the metal has just been bent. Hold the scroll between the pins firmly with one hand and grasp the straight end with the other. Pressure may now be applied with the thumb and fingers of one hand to continue forming the curve.

8. Feeding the workpiece a little at a time into the jig, continue bending. Fig. 18-6.

9. Check the work frequently by holding it over the pattern to see if the scroll is being formed correctly, as shown in Fig. 18-7. If too great a bend is formed it will be necessary to open the scroll to fit the pattern.

10. Sometimes the pattern calls for two scrolls to be formed on the same piece in opposite directions, as shown in Fig. 18-8. In this case the curve should be continuous and smooth from one scroll to the other to obtain a pleasing design.

11. After the scroll has been completely formed, check to see if it lies flat on edge. If the scroll needs to be straightened, place it in a vise edgewise and lift it to the correct level by hand.

Bending Curves

Curves can be formed by bending the metal around a bar of round stock or a pipe. Fig. 18-9. There are two methods of bending metal in this manner:

1. Select a short piece of pipe or rod equal to the inside diameter of the curve to be formed. Clamp one end of the workpiece and the rod in a vise. Grasp one end of the workpiece and pull it

18-10. Bending metal over a pipe or rod. Alternately move and strike the work a little at a time.

18-11. Steps in forming an eye. In Step 3, the strip is bent as indicated by the arrow. Step 4 shows the finished eye.

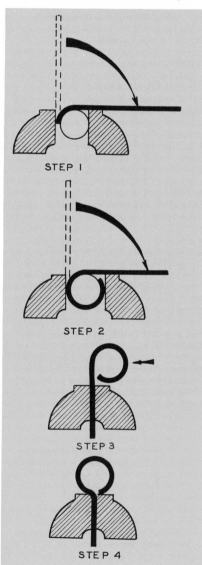

STEP I

STEP 2

STEP 3

STEP 4

toward you. Loosen the vise jaws, feed the workpiece in around the rod, and again clamp both the rod and workpiece in the vise. Continue bending.

2. Another method is to clamp the rod in a vise. Place the metal over the pipe. Strike the workpiece glancing blows with the flat of a ball-peen ham-mer, Fig. 18-10. Move the metal forward, continuing to strike the workpiece until the curve is formed.

A small eye can be formed by clamping the stock in with a piece of round rod or pipe equal to the inside diameter of the eye. Fig. 18-11 shows the four steps used in this method.

19 ▶ Bending and Twisting

Many projects will require the bending of metal at right, acute, and obtuse angles. For the most part, strips or bars ¼ in. or less in thickness can be bent cold. When making angular bends in the metal, the following proce-dure is suggested:

1. Make a full size layout of the part to be bent, so that you can determine the amount of straight metal to allow for the bends. Add an amount equal to one-half the thickness of the met-al for each right angle bend. For instance, if you are using stock ¼″ thick, and are going to make two right angle bends, add ¼″ to the length of the stock. Fig. 19-1.

In bending round stock, first estimate the point where the bend should begin. A full-size drawing of the finished form should be made on paper. A tan-gent point for each arc to be formed can then be located on a piece of scrap stock, as shown in Fig. 19-2. The points of bend can be marked with chalk or soapstone.

2. The order in which the metal is to be bent is important. Decide which bend is to be made first. Fig. 19-3.

3. Clamp the stock vertically with the bend line at the top of the vise jaws. Use a square to check the workpiece being sure that the extra material which has been allowed for the bend is above the jaws.

4. Bend the stock by striking near the vise jaws with the flat of the ball-peen hammer. If the piece is long, apply pressure with one hand while striking the metal at the same time. Fig. 19-4.

5. To obtain a square bend, place the workpiece in a vise, as

19-1. Allow one-half the thickness of the stock for each bend.

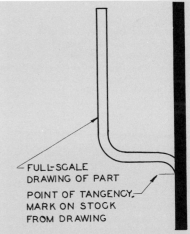

19-2. Estimating the point of bend on round stock. The metal is laid over straight parts of the drawing to cover them in finding tangent points.

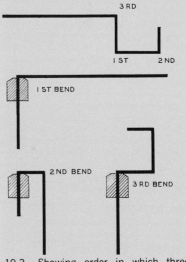

19-3. Showing order in which three bends are made. Allow extra material for each bend.

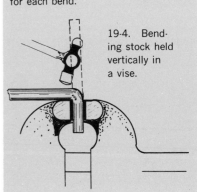

19-4. Bend-ing stock held vertically in a vise.

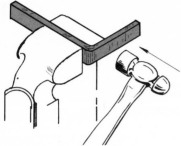

19-5. Squaring a bend in a vise.

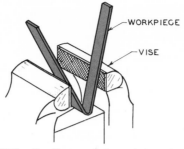

WORKPIECE

VISE

19-7. Bending an acute angle in a vise.

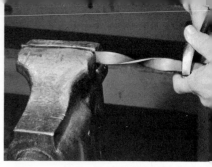

19-10. Twisting long, light stock with a crescent wrench.

shown in Fig. 19-5, and strike directly on the bend.

6. To make an obtuse angle bend (greater than 90 degrees), use an adjustable wrench as a bending tool. Fig. 19-6.

7. To make an acute angle bend (a bend that is less than 90 degrees), place the right angle bend between the jaws of a vise and squeeze the two sides together until the desired angle is obtained. Fig. 19-7.

Sheet metal can be bent by placing the metal between steel bars or angle iron and striking with a wooden or rawhide mallet along the sheet. Fig. 19-8.

Twisting Metal

Interest can be added to a project by twisting some of the pieces. Fig. 19-9. Twisting also strengthens supporting parts. Square rods of mild steel up to ½″ in width can be turned cold, as can band iron ¼″ in thickness to 1″ in width. Large diameters must be worked hot.

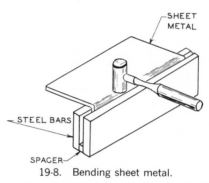

SHEET METAL

STEEL BARS

SPACER

19-8. Bending sheet metal.

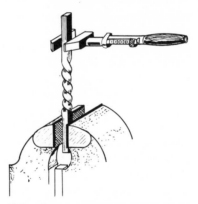

19-9. Begin work just above point where twist is to start. Experience is needed in learning how to space between turns. Use a sharp action, making a 180° twist each time.

1. Since metal decreases in length when twisted, cut stock longer than the finished piece. Allow ¼″ for each twist.

2. Mark off section to be twisted.

3. If twisting a short length, place it vertically in the vise. Fig. 19-9.

Long pieces of light material should be held in a horizontal position. The first limit mark should be even with the working edge of the vise jaw. Place an adjustable wrench at the other limit of the section to be twisted. Fig. 19-10. Rotate the wrench at the same point until the desired number of twists are made. NOTE: A piece of pipe—the right diameter, not too large—slipped over the section to be twisted will help prevent the workpiece from bending out of line.

Bending Small Pipe or Tubing

1. To bend small pipe or tubing construct a jig as shown in Fig. 19-11. If the bend is to be sharp, fill the pipe or tubing with wet sand or molten lead. This tends to prevent the tubing from collapsing.

CAUTION: *Molten lead is never recommended in small work for beginners.*

2. Place the tubing or pipe in the jig; then slowly and carefully draw around the form. The sand can be removed after the proper shape has been obtained.

19-11. Pipe or tubing can be bent by using wood form blocks. Tube is bent around the hollowed out curved piece.

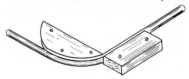

19-6. Starting an obtuse angle bend using a monkey wrench.

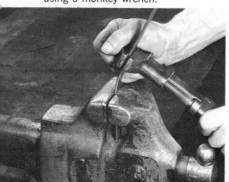

20-3. Making a sharp angle bend, with flat rollers and the wedge unit. Use the power of the vise to bend the proper angle.

20

Bending and Forming Metal on a Machine

There are several types of machines that are available for bending and forming metal smoothly and accurately. Described in this unit are the "Metl-Former," the Universal bender, and the "Di-Acro" bender.

How To Use the "Metl-Former"

This handy combination tool forms, shapes, rolls, and bends aluminum, wrought iron, soft steel, brass, and copper (flat, sheet, or round stock) into intricate shapes. Fig. 20-1.

The tool is capable of easily rolling and shaping wrought iron stock up to ⅛″ x 1¼″. It can also handle copper and aluminum tubing up to ½ in.

1. On heavy paper, make a full size drawing of the project form. Determine the length of material needed. A soft piece of wire can be used for this.

2. Open the jaws of the machine enough to admit a strip of stock between the drive (power) roller and the driven rollers.

3. Close the jaws so that the first two rollers contact the metal.

4. Tighten the vise jaws approximately one-fourth turn, and turn the crank until the right length of turn is formed.

5. Tighten the vise a small amount at a time and crank the metal back and forth until the proper radius is formed. Fig. 20-1. The metal is reversed in the rolls if the curve extends too far.

6. To form tubing, insert concave-grooved tubing rollers in the machine and proceed as above. Fig. 20-2.

7. Fig. 20-3 shows the method of making an angle bend. Fig. 20-4 shows the method used in bending sheet metal, which is limited to a 2½″ edging with this type of device.

20-1. Basic metal forming kit used to form flat stock.

20-2. Using tubing or rod rollers. Note three groove sizes for standard tube dimensions. Stock must fit the groove used.

20-4. To make an edge bend in sheet metal, insert the stock between the jaws and move it along gradually. The triangular unit is attached to one vise jaw, as shown.

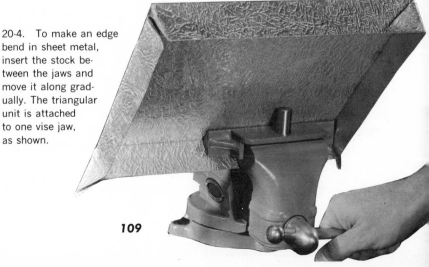

How To Use the Universal Bender

The Universal iron bender is a practical tool for bending pipes, rounds, flats, squares, tubing, conduit, and angle iron. Thoroughly adjustable, it can be easily, quickly, and accurately set up for bending problems encountered in the school shop.

Descriptions for bending ¾" and 1" pipe sizes are given below (Fig. 20-5):

1. Connect frames with No. 20 center pin.

2. Place the No. 14 grooved forming die between frames on No. 20 center pin. When bending ¾" pipe, mount the No. 14 grooved pipe die so that the ¾" groove is on top, and when bending 1 in. pipe so that the 1 in. groove is on top.

3. Place the No. 11 bending block square on the No. 19 "U" shaped pin in the third ⅝" hole, in the main frame, on the No. 22 support plug.

4. Place the No. 10 "V" grooved roller on the No. 18 eye pin in the third ⅝" hole in the swinging frame.

5. Place pipe between block

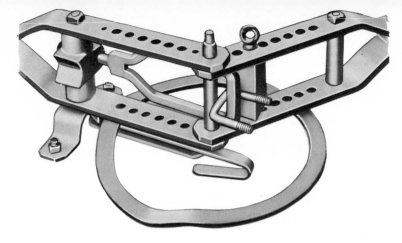

20-6. Bending "U" bolts.

and roller and the No. 14 grooved forming die.

6. Pull on the swinging frame handle and bend the pipe about 20 degrees. Feed the pipe along 1 to 2 inches for each pull on the swinging frame. NOTE: Keep the pivot pins well lubricated.

This device is capable of bending "U" shapes of ½" round or square stock or 3/16" x ½" flat stock cold. For hot bending, the capacity is about double.

Self locking cam shaped dies for bending "U's" of 1¾", 2", and 2¼" inside spread are furnished with regular equipment. The dies can be built up to any larger size desired by simply bending a piece of flat stock around them. With these cam

shaped dies, clevises can be bent so that both ends will come out exactly even. Fig. 20-6 shows a "U" bolt being bent to shape. Scrolls can easily be formed on this machine. See Fig. 20-7.

How To Use the "Di-Acro" Bender

Another type of bending machine used in school shops is the "Di-Acro" bender. Fig. 20-8. This machine consists of (1) a form that has the same shape as the bend to be made and (2) a forming roll that moves around the form to shape the metal.

The following procedure is suggested in operating this machine:

1. On heavy paper, make a full-size drawing of the part to be bent.

2. Use a soft wire to determine the length of stock needed.

3. A tangent to the arc of the bend to be formed can be located on scrap stock. This point is marked on the material with chalk or soapstone.

4. Place the stock in the bender with the mark against the radius collar.

5. Make a trial bend. If the bend does not conform to the pattern, move the mark on the drawing the amount the bend should be changed.

20-5. Bending pipe and tubing ¾" to 1" in diameter in the Universal machine.

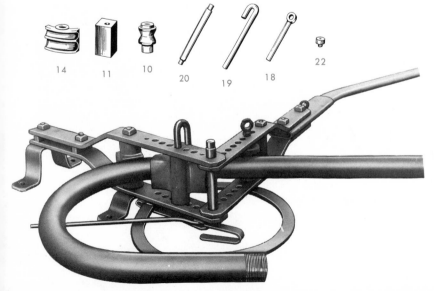

14   11   10   20   19   18   22

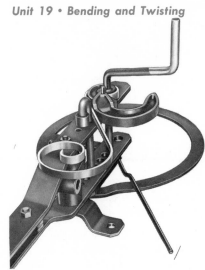

20-7. Forming a scroll on a Universal bender.

6. Set the stop for the desired bend angle. (This is generally done by trying it out till you have the correct angle.)

7. Move the operating arm until the metal starts to bend. After a short bend has been made, check against the drawing.

Scrolls and other shapes of irregular radii can be readily formed with the Di-Acro bender in rigid materials even though the forming nose revolves in a perfect circle. This is accomplished by using a collar having the same contour as the shape

to be formed, as illustrated in Fig. 20-9, and adjusting the forming nose to come only the thickness of the workpiece away from the "high point" of the contour collar.

As the material will bend only where this contour collar offers resistance, the forming nose can lead the material around until it contacts the "high point" and exerts sufficient pressure to force it into shape of the collar.

Fig. 20-9 illustrates the main steps in producing a scroll with this bender.

Various contour collars can be made from steel plate or even from a cast aluminum blank, either of which can be cut on a metal-cutting band saw.

Since all metals are somewhat elastic, they will spring back more or less after they are formed, and for that reason the bending form must usually have a smaller radius than the required bend. The amount of springback is dependent upon the type of material, its size and hardness, as well as upon the radius of the bend. It is usually necessary to experiment to determine the exact size of the bending form.

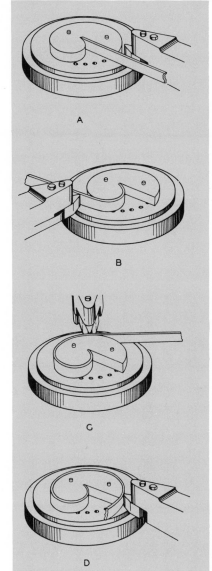

A

B

C

D

20-9. Forming a scroll. (A) Adjust the forming nose so the material will fit snugly between the nose and the "high point" of the contour collar and insert material. (B) Advance the operating arm with steady, even pressure. Note how the material bends only where resistance is offered by the contour collar. (C) Material continues to bend and take the shape of the contour collar as the arm is advanced. (D) As the forming nose reaches the "high point" of the contour collar, material is "set" in new shape.

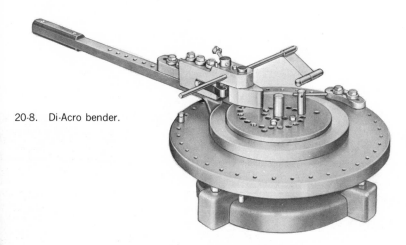

20-8. Di-Acro bender.

21 ▷ Drilling

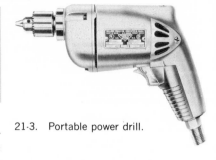

21-3.   Portable power drill.

The parts of wrought iron projects can be joined with rivets, machine screws, bolts, or by welding.

When rivets, machine screws, bolts, or other fastening devices are used, it will be necessary to drill holes to accommodate them, When a drilling machine is not available, a hand drill or a portable electric hand drill can be used. (See the Unit on Drilling Machines and Drills.)

Drilling by Hand

A hand drill, Fig. 21-1, can be used for holes ¼″ D. or smaller. The following procedure is suggested:

1. Hold the shell of the chuck in one hand. Open the jaws and insert the drill with the other. Tighten the jaws so that the drill is held firmly.

2. Locate and mark points to be drilled. Clamp the workpiece in the vise so that the drilling can be done horizontally. Fig. 21-2.

3. Place the point of the drill on the center punch mark and crank at a moderate speed. Apply enough pressure to keep the drill cutting.

4. Ease up on the pressure when the drill point is about to break through the workpiece. After the drill bit has broken through, continue to crank clockwise but pull back on the handle.

Drilling with a Portable Power Drill

The portable electric drill, Fig. 21-3, does a faster job than the hand drill. Electric drills vary in size. The two most common sizes have a capacity for holding drills up to ¼″ D. and ½″ D.

Proceed as follows:

1. Fasten the workpiece securely in a vise or clamp. NOTE: The drilling can be done either vertically or horizontally.

2. Insert the proper size drill bit for the job.

3. Tighten the jaws with a chuck key.

4. Place the drill point on the workpiece as marked.

5. Turn on the power and proceed, applying steady pressure. Fig. 21-4.

6. Ease up on the pressure when the drill point is about to break through; otherwise the drill might be broken.

See the Unit on Running Drilling Machines and Drills.

21-1.   Hand drill. For vertical drilling, note the hold handle on this side. If left-handed, you may hold with the right hand and turn with the left. The gear mesh is precise but can be loosened by abuse. CAUTION: Use only a sharp drill bit.

21-2.   Horizontal drilling with a hand drill. Note position of hands and support against body.

21-4.   Drilling with a power drill.

22 ▷ **Riveting and Decorating**

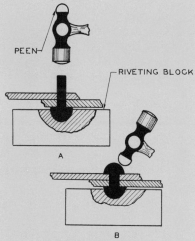

22-2. (A) Flange the rivet with the flat end of a ball-peen hammer. (B) Round off the rivet by striking with glancing blows.

The most common method of fastening band iron or wrought iron parts together is by riveting. Rivets are made of soft iron, brass, copper, or aluminum. (See Unit 15.) Soft iron rivets are used for wrought iron projects. They are available with round, oval, flat, and countersunk heads. The most common sizes are 1/8" and 3/16" D. The length is determined by the thickness of the part to be joined. Suggested procedure is as follows:

1. Measure the thickness of the pieces to be joined and select the correct rivet diameter and length. Fig. 22-1. NOTE: Round-head rivets should be used if they are to be part of the ornamental effect. The rivets should be long enough to extend through both pieces of metal and beyond by 1½ times the diameter of the rivet if it is to be rounded at both ends. If the design calls for a rivet to be *flush,* countersink both sides of the material and allow just enough head to fill the countersunk holes.

2. Mark and drill the holes. If the rivet is to be flush with the surfaces, countersink each side.

If several rivets are to be used, drill one hole and rivet at this point. Then drill the other holes. This makes it easier to line up each joint accurately.

3. Insert the rivet in the hole and place the head against the metal riveting block, which is made with a concave pocket on the surface. A round-head rivet should rest in the pocket of the riveting block and riveting set (Fig. 22-3) to prevent damage to the rivet head and to shape the other end.

4. Upset or flange the rivet by striking the end with the flat of a ball-peen hammer. Fig. 22-2 (A). This tends to fill up the hole. Then round it off with glancing blows. Fig. 22-2 (B). If the surface is to be flat, strike the rivet with the peen of the hammer to fill the countersunk hole. Finish by striking with the flat of the hammer. Fig. 22-3 shows the use of a rivet set.

5. In riveting scrolls or curved parts together: (A) Cut a piece of round stock that will fit the curve under the rivet. (B) Drill a conical countersink in the round stock to fit the rivet head. (C) Place the rivet in the hole and complete the joint. Fig. 22-4.

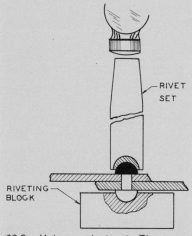

22-3. Using a rivet set. The cone-shaped hole is used to form the shank or head the rivet.

22-4. A rod in a vise can be used to rivet scroll work. A conical hole has been drilled in the rod to keep the head from being damaged.

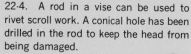
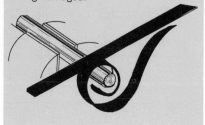

22-1. Amount of rivet necessary to form head.

Decorating Metal

The appearance of most wrought-metal projects can be greatly improved if the surface is hammered or peened. A variety of designs can be used.

Hammering or Peening

The ball-peen hammer is used most often for decorating the ends. However, for some designs a cross-peen or straight-peen hammer is preferred.

1. Decide whether one side or both sides are to be peened.

2. Choose the proper weight hammer for the job to be done. A 14-ounce hammer is generally used.

3. Lay out the area to be peened.

4. Place the metal either on an anvil or other heavy, flat metal surface.

5. Flare the end of the metal by placing it near the edge of the anvil and striking with a ball-peen hammer. Work from edge to edge with closely spaced blows until the end is properly flared. Grind ends to the desired shape. They can be trued with a file if uneven.

Decorating End Surfaces

Fig. 22-5 shows some of the ways that the ends of metal can be decorated. The following procedure is suggested:

1. Lay out the desired end shape upon the metal.

2. File or grind the end to the shape marked.

3. Hold the workpiece in one hand, with the other end held flat upon the anvil. Strike the metal with the peen end of the hammer, using firm, even blows that leave marks touching one another. NOTE: Care should be

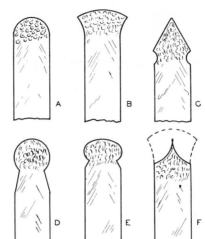

22-5. Traditional designs for wrought metal tipping: (A) rounded, (B) flared, (C) arrowhead, (D) ball, (E) pinched, (F) arrowhead.

taken not to stretch the metal. Work from one edge to the other, filling in the space to be decorated. If the reverse side is to be decorated, lay a piece of soft copper on the anvil to protect the peened surface and use heavier blows to obtain the required effect on the second side.

Check Your Knowledge

1. Why is wrought iron furniture popular in modern homes?

2. What is a scroll?

3. Explain how a pattern may be enlarged.

4. What kind and thickness of metal can be bent cold?

5. Explain how bending a scroll is started.

6. Describe some of the devices used in bending metal.

7. How do you find the length of metal necessary to form a scroll?

8. Describe the hand method for forming a scroll.

9. What allowance in length must be made for each bend?

10. Describe briefly the method of forming an eye.

11. In making a square bend in metal, how is it determined?

12. How do you strike the metal to make the proper square bend?

13. Explain how the metal should be placed in a vise for a square bend.

14. How is metal twisted?

15. What tool is used for twisting metal?

16. Why is it difficult to bend tubing or pipe smoothly?

17. How can a good bend be obtained to avoid kinks in the material?

18. Name typical bending machines.

19. What are some of the advantages of a bending machine?

20. What are some of the fasteners used to join parts of wrought iron projects?

21. What is meant by heading?

22. Why are metal pieces riveted?

23. Describe four shapes of rivet heads that are used the most.

24. How long should a rivet be?

25. What is a rivet set?

26. How are rivet holes formed?

27. What is a riveting block?

28. What does the term peening mean?

Terms to Know and Spell

formica	*tangent*	*concave-grooved*
designers	*conical*	*conduit*
scroll	*adjustable*	*clevises*
fractional-inch	*collapsing*	*radii*
acute angle	*intricate*	*peened*

Section 3, Project 1
MAGAZINE RACK

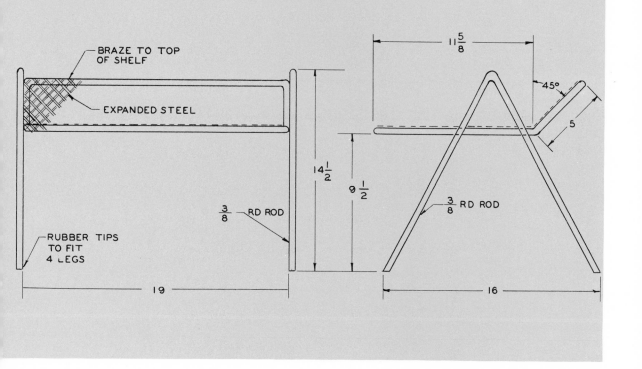

BRAZE TO TOP
OF SHELF

EXPANDED STEEL

$14\frac{1}{2}$

$\frac{3}{8}$ RD ROD

RUBBER TIPS
TO FIT
4 LEGS

19

$11\frac{5}{8}$

45°

5

$9\frac{1}{2}$

$\frac{3}{8}$ RD ROD

16

Section 3, Project 2
FIREPLACE SET

Brush

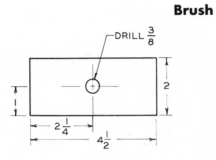

DRILL $\frac{3}{8}$

2

$2\frac{1}{4}$

$4\frac{1}{2}$

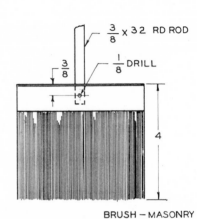

$\frac{3}{8}$ X 32 RD ROD

$\frac{1}{8}$ DRILL

$\frac{3}{8}$

4

BRUSH — MASONRY

Shovel

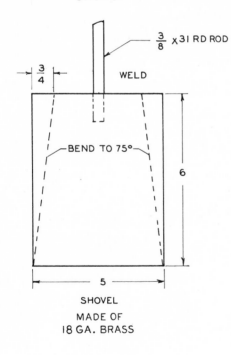

$\frac{3}{8}$ X 31 RD ROD

WELD

$\frac{3}{4}$

BEND TO 75°

6

5

SHOVEL
MADE OF
18 GA. BRASS

Poker

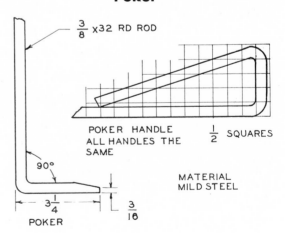

$\frac{3}{8}$ X32 RD ROD

POKER HANDLE
ALL HANDLES THE
SAME

$\frac{1}{2}$ SQUARES

90°

$3\frac{1}{4}$

$\frac{3}{16}$

POKER

MATERIAL
MILD STEEL

Section 3, Project 3
FLOWER POT HOLDER

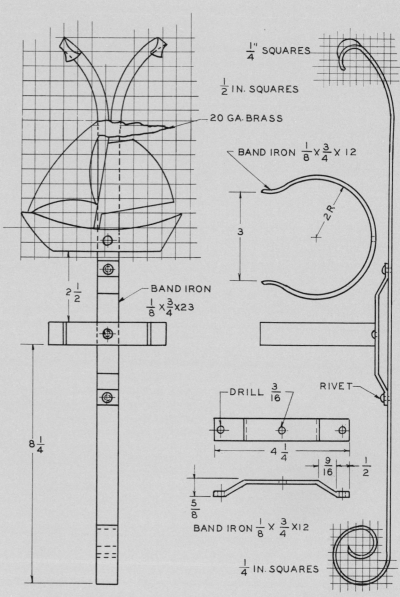

$\frac{1}{4}$" SQUARES

$\frac{1}{2}$ IN. SQUARES

20 GA. BRASS

BAND IRON $\frac{1}{8}$ X $\frac{3}{4}$ X 12

2 R

3

2 $\frac{1}{2}$

BAND IRON
$\frac{1}{8}$ X $\frac{3}{4}$ X 23

8 $\frac{1}{4}$

RIVET

DRILL $\frac{3}{16}$

4 $\frac{1}{4}$

$\frac{9}{16}$ $\frac{1}{2}$

$\frac{5}{8}$

BAND IRON $\frac{1}{8}$ X $\frac{3}{4}$ X 12

$\frac{1}{4}$ IN. SQUARES

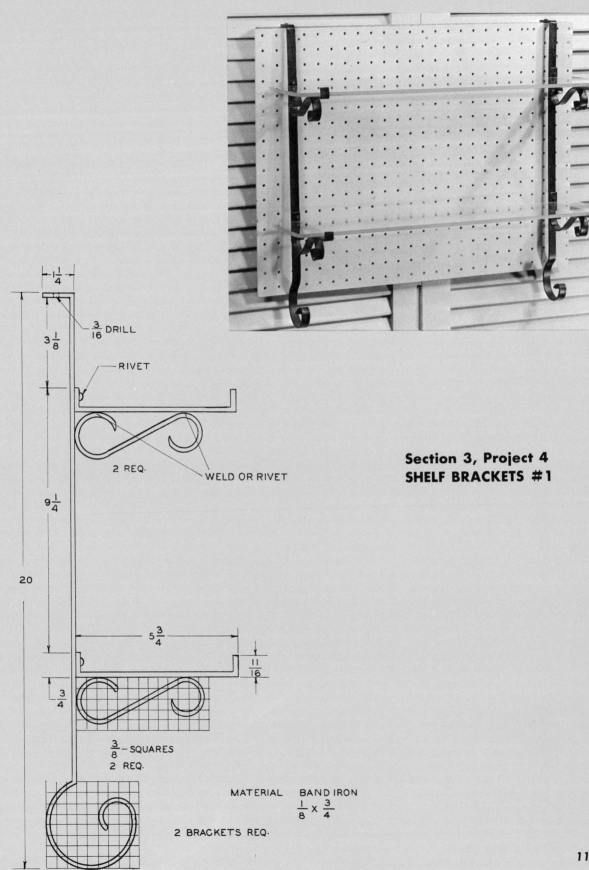

$1\frac{1}{4}$

$\frac{3}{16}$ DRILL

$3\frac{1}{8}$

RIVET

2 REQ.

WELD OR RIVET

Section 3, Project 4
SHELF BRACKETS #1

$9\frac{1}{4}$

20

$5\frac{3}{4}$

$\frac{11}{16}$

$\frac{3}{4}$

$\frac{3}{8}$ – SQUARES
2 REQ.

MATERIAL   BAND IRON
$\frac{1}{8}$ × $\frac{3}{4}$

2 BRACKETS REQ.

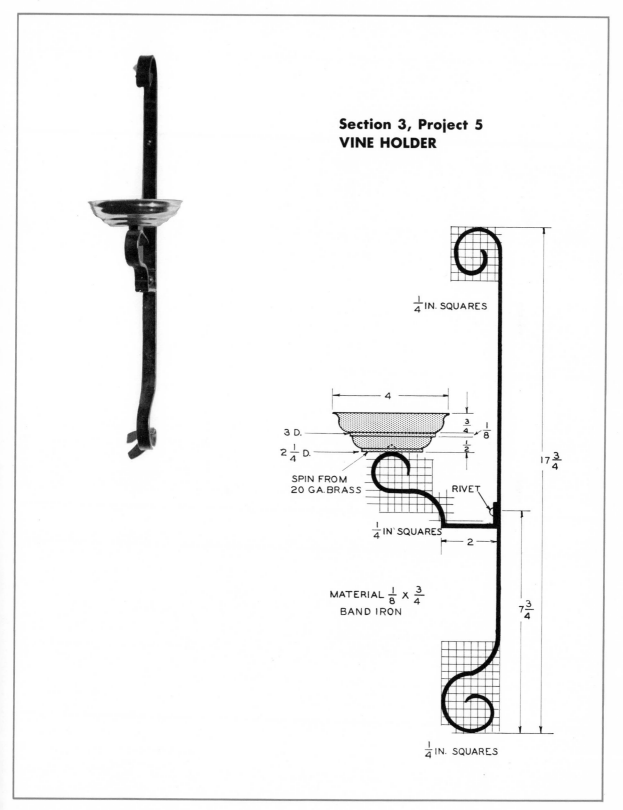

Section 3, Project 5
VINE HOLDER

$\frac{1}{4}$ IN. SQUARES

4

$\frac{3}{4}$ $\frac{1}{8}$

$\frac{1}{2}$

3 D.

$2\frac{1}{4}$ D.

SPIN FROM
20 GA. BRASS

RIVET

$17\frac{3}{4}$

$\frac{1}{4}$ IN. SQUARES

2

MATERIAL $\frac{1}{8}$ X $\frac{3}{4}$
BAND IRON

$7\frac{3}{4}$

$\frac{1}{4}$ IN. SQUARES

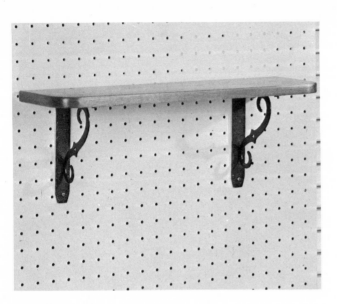

**Section 3,
Project 6
SHELF
BRACKETS #2**

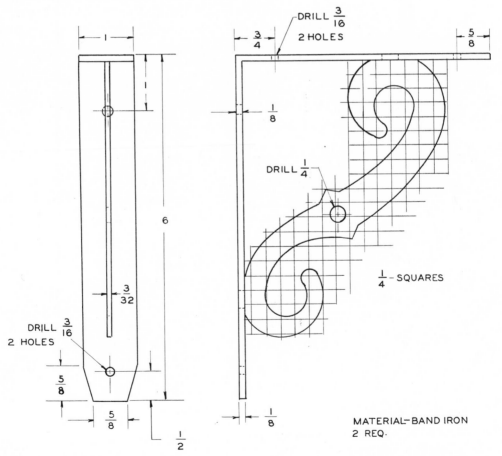

DRILL $\frac{3}{16}$
2 HOLES

$\frac{3}{4}$

$\frac{5}{8}$

$\frac{1}{8}$

DRILL $\frac{1}{4}$

$\frac{1}{4}$ – SQUARES

1

6

$\frac{3}{32}$

DRILL $\frac{3}{16}$
2 HOLES

$\frac{5}{8}$

$\frac{5}{8}$

$\frac{1}{2}$

$\frac{1}{8}$

MATERIAL–BAND IRON
2 REQ.

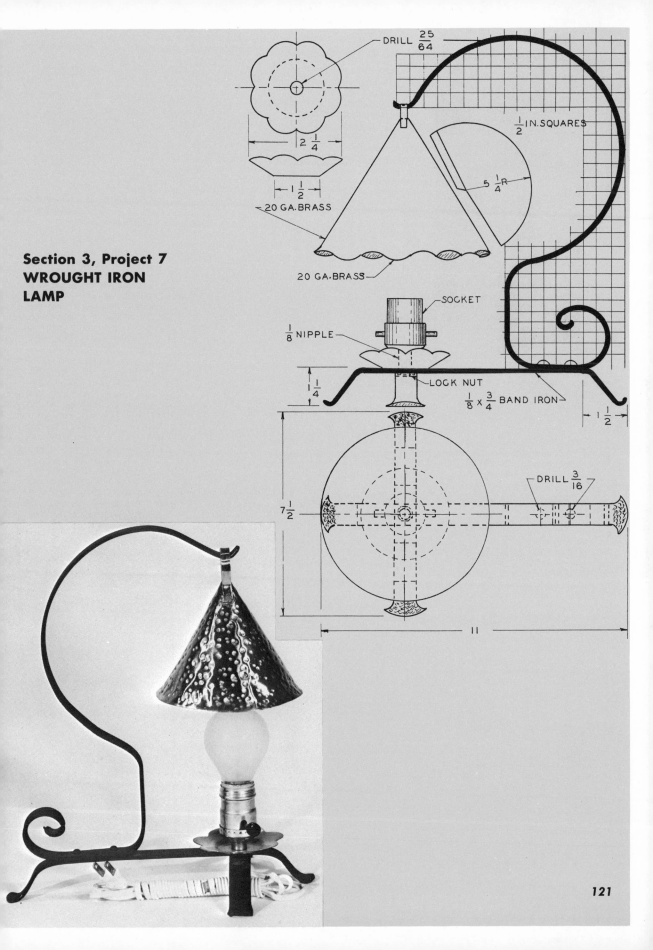

Section 3, Project 7
WROUGHT IRON
LAMP

DRILL $\frac{25}{64}$

$\frac{1}{2}$ IN. SQUARES

$2\frac{1}{4}$

$5\frac{1}{4}$R

$1\frac{1}{2}$

20 GA. BRASS

20 GA. BRASS

SOCKET

$\frac{1}{8}$ NIPPLE

$1\frac{1}{4}$

LOCK NUT

$\frac{1}{8} \times \frac{3}{4}$ BAND IRON

$1\frac{1}{2}$

DRILL $\frac{3}{16}$

$7\frac{1}{2}$

11

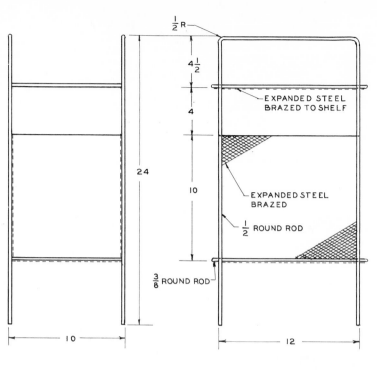

Section 3, Project 8—TELEPHONE STAND #1

$\frac{1}{2}$ R

$4\frac{1}{2}$

EXPANDED STEEL
BRAZED TO SHELF

4

EXPANDED STEEL
BRAZED

10

$\frac{1}{2}$ ROUND ROD

24

$\frac{3}{8}$ ROUND ROD

10

12

Section 3, Project 9—TELEPHONE STAND #2

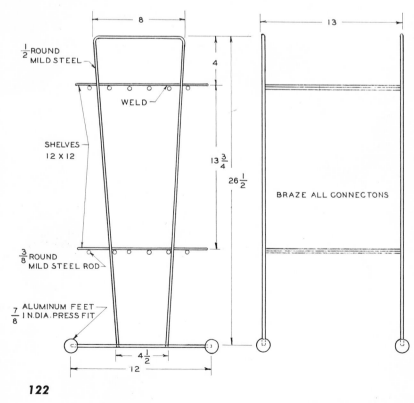

8

$\frac{1}{2}$ ROUND
MILD STEEL

WELD

SHELVES
12 X 12

$\frac{3}{8}$ ROUND
MILD STEEL ROD

$\frac{7}{8}$ ALUMINUM FEET
I N.DIA. PRESS FIT

4

13

$13\frac{3}{4}$

$26\frac{1}{2}$

BRAZE ALL CONNECTONS

$4\frac{1}{2}$

12

Metal Spinning

M ETAL SPINNING is the art of raising sheet metal discs into contoured forms on the lathe. The end of a tool forced into a metal disc revolving in a lathe makes a dent. If the tool is held in this dent and if the metal is rotated about a center,

the dent will turn into a groove extending entirely around the disc. It may then be said to have been "spun" into a changed form.

To secure this result, however, it is necessary that the metal, in bending, meet a resistance in the form of a "chuck" around which the metal can take shape. The chuck is usually made of wood. However, it can be of metal or metal covered wood.

The Eygyptians originated metal spinning. Our present-day knowledge of this craft, however, has come from the Greeks and Romans, who spun many of their articles from pewter.

During the reign of Edward III (1327-1377), metal spinning was introduced into England as a trade. Metal spinners formed their own guild systems to maintain uniform standards in the craft. About 1840, metal spinning was introduced into the United States.

The growth of metal spinning has been due to demands in the field of fine household wares, lighting fixtures, aircraft parts, and, more recently, missile components.

23 ▷ The Spinning Lathe

Of course, the most important piece of equipment for metal spinning is the lathe. Special lathes are manufactured for the work. Fig. 23-1 shows a 15″ spinning lathe suitable for use in schools. It turns the chucks as well. Other lathes give excellent service. Fig. 23-2 shows one that was built for the purpose of spinning various metals. It is capable of handling work up to 15″ in diameter. Smaller spinning lathes are suitable for use in the school, as the one shown in Fig. 23-3. The lathe shown in Fig. 23-4 is an industrial type that is built to do heavy work.

Many schools have wood turn-ing lathes that can easily be used for metal spinning. Metal cutting lathes can be converted for spinning by making a few necessary changes.

The lathe spindle must be able to withstand high pressures required in spinning. Thrust bearings strong enough to take this pressure are a necessity.

Spinning lathes should operate at speeds ranging from 480 to 2750 rpm. As a rule, the speed should be inversely proportional to the diameter of the work. It is best for beginners to operate the lathe at a slow speed and use higher speeds only as experience is gained.

The hand-wheel tailstock used on wood-turning lathes is satisfactory for spinning. But many commercial lathes are equipped with a cam lever and sliding spindle for rapid adjustment of the tailstock, as shown in Fig. 23-5 on page 126.

The lathe must be equipped with a spinning T-rest.

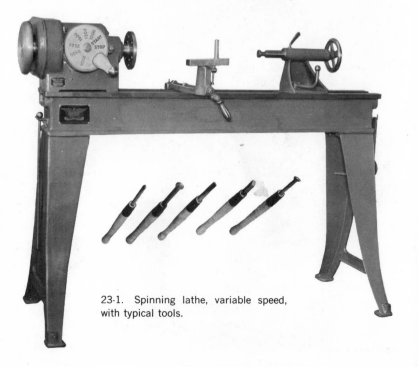

23-1. Spinning lathe, variable speed, with typical tools.

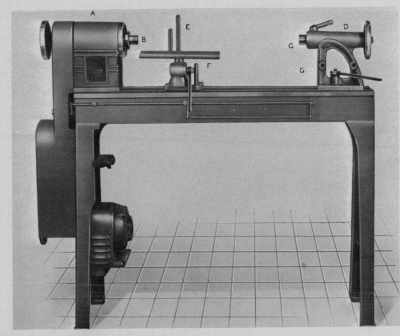

23-2. A type of spinning lathe capable of spinning discs up to 15″. (A) Headstock; (B) spindle; (C) poppet; (D) tailstock; (E) spinning pin; (F) T-rest; (G) rest bank.

23-3. Small spinning lathe with all the necessary accessories.

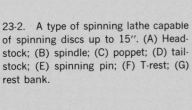

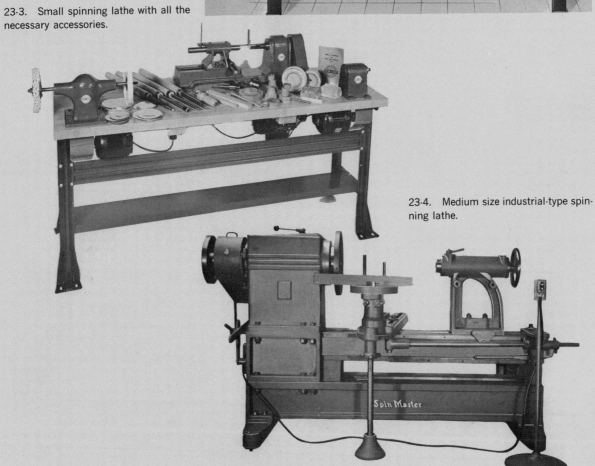

23-4. Medium size industrial-type spinning lathe.

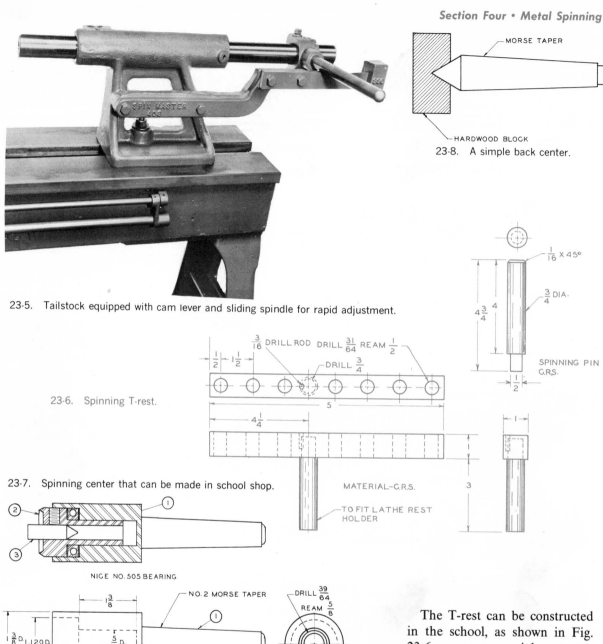

23-8. A simple back center.

23-5. Tailstock equipped with cam lever and sliding spindle for rapid adjustment.

23-6. Spinning T-rest.

23-7. Spinning center that can be made in school shop.

MATERIAL—C.R.S.

TO FIT LATHE REST HOLDER

NICE NO. 505 BEARING

ALL PARTS TOOL STEEL HDN AND TEMPER

The T-rest can be constructed in the school, as shown in Fig. 23-6, or a commercial type may be purchased.

The spinning center can be purchased from a manufacturer of spinning lathes and accessories, but Fig. 23-7 shows one that can be made in the school machine shop. If no spinning center is available, a wood block can be used on a lathe as shown in Fig. 23-8.

24-2. Industrial-type spinning tools.

The number of tools used depends upon the skill and experience of the spinner.

There are many types of spinning tools. Fig. 24-1 illustrates a set of tools suitable for use in the school. Fig. 24-2 illustrates the tools used by skilled industrial spinners.

Hand spinning tools may be divided into three general classes: rounded or blunt tools, tools with sharp cutting edges for trimming, and beading tools. The tools with rounded forms are supplied in a variety of shapes and diameters.

For general use, the only tools required for the beginner are the flat back tool, the trimming or diamond point, the ball, planishing, and beading tools.

The *flat back tool,* Fig. 24-1 (A), is the most important. The larger portion of spinning is done with it. One side of the tool is flat and the reverse side is rounded and shaped somewhat like a spoon. It is made from tool steel, so it can be hardened and polished.

The *pointed* tool, Fig. 24-1 (B), is convenient for forming sharp corners and small radii.

The *trimming* tool, Fig. 24-1 (C), trues the disc and reduces it to size. It must be kept sharpened to a keen edge.

The *ball* tool, Fig. 24-1 (D), with a round end, is generally used for heavier gages of metal in breaking-down operations.

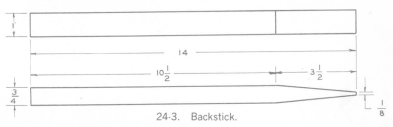

24-3. Backstick.

24-1. Set of small spinning tools. (A) flat back tool; (B) pointed tool; (C) diamond point trimming tool; (D) ball tool; (E) beading tool; (F) back center; (G) beading tool roll.

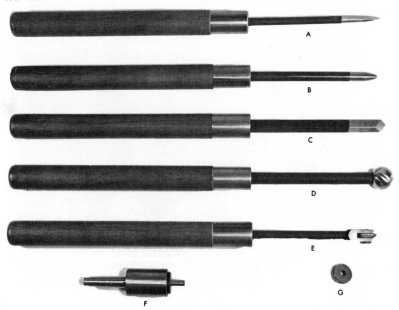

The *beading* tool, Fig. 24-1 (E), forms beads on the edges of spun projects. The wheel may vary in diameter from 1″ to 2″. The concave part of the wheel varies with the diameter.

Other tools used by industrial spinners have such identifications as knob, bead, staff, tucker, riffler, smoothing, and finishing.

Tools used for spinning *steel* are made from brass or bronze.

To spin *aluminum* or *britannia metal,* a tool made from hickory, such as a pick handle, is recommended for beginners. It lessens the risk of marring the metal.

A *backstick* of hardwood, such as shown in Fig. 24-3, is necessary in spinning.

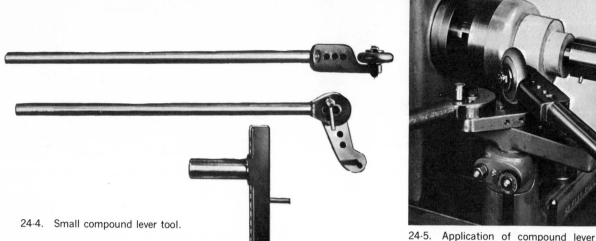

24-4. Small compound lever tool.

24-5. Application of compound lever tool.

A *compound lever* tool, Fig. 24-4, is often used by commercial spinners. Fig. 24-5 demonstrates the application of this tool.

Spinning pliers, Fig. 24-6, are often used for crimping the edge of a blank to stiffen it or to aid in removing wrinkles.

24-6. Spinning pliers.

25 ▷ Chucks for Metal Spinning

25-1. An assortment of hardwood chucks. The faceplate is inserted in the chuck.

The chucks used in metal spinning are of two types, solid and sectional.

Chucks are generally made from solid or laminated hardwood blocks. Fig. 25-1. They can also be turned from cast iron or steel. Industry uses a great number of chucks turned from laminated blocks. Wooden chucks can be covered with sheet metal to prolong their usefulness.

An ordinary faceplate such as used on a wood turning lathe may hold the block while being turned to shape and also in the spinning operation. The most satisfactory method is to construct faceplates as shown in Fig. 25-2 and use them as a permanent part of the chucks. Changing faceplates from one chuck to another is never practical, because the chuck cannot be placed back exactly in the same position, causing it to run out of true.

Follow blocks are made of hardwood, to hold the metal blank against the chuck. The follow block must revolve freely so that it rides between the ball-bearing tailstock center and the disc at the same speed as the chuck.

The follow block should be at least 1″ thick and never larger than the diameter of the base to be spun. If it is too small, there is the possibility that the metal may be spun back over it. If too large, working close to the base is difficult.

A hole is drilled at the center of the follow block to fit the friction unit of the tailstock center. The block is centered directly behind the chuck. Then, after bringing it up to the tailstock friction unit, turn it to match the base.

For turning a chuck, make a template for checking its shape. Allow enough length to the chuck so that when trimming or beading the outer edge of the blank, working space between the headstock and blank is allowed.

The bases of chucks for bowls and trays are turned slightly concave so the finished article stands more solidly. See Fig. 25-3.

Deep spun articles require breakdown chucks. These allow stage-by-stage forming, which prevents the metal from becoming too thin. The workpiece is spun over each of these until the desired shape has been secured for final spinning over the original chuck. Fig. 25-4.

Projects that require spinning the open end down to a smaller diameter are spun with sectional

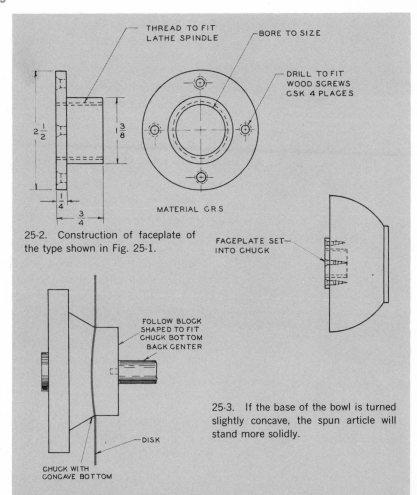

25-2. Construction of faceplate of the type shown in Fig. 25-1.

25-3. If the base of the bowl is turned slightly concave, the spun article will stand more solidly.

25-4. The breakdown process. (A) Disc centered; (B) first drawing to chuck; (C) disc laid down to chuck; (D) shell from breakdown chuck fitted over final chuck; (E) stages in spinning metal to final form.

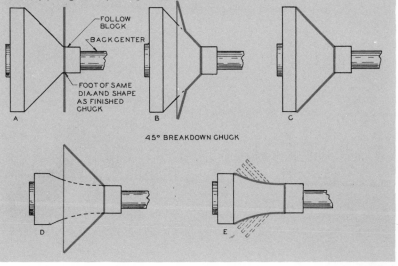

25-5. Sectional chuck. A metal ring holds the sections together.

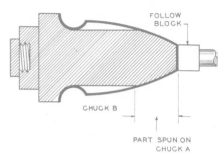

CHUCK A

FOLLOW BLOCK

CHUCK B

PART SPUN ON CHUCK A

25-8. A chuck for "spinning on air."

chucks. Figs. 25-5 and 25-6. When the article is completed, the chuck is collapsed and removed.

The sectional chuck consists of a backing block to which a face-plate is fastened, an arbor, segments, and cover plate or ring.

How to Construct a Sectional Chuck

1. Select a block of hardwood large enough to make the chuck. If necessary glue several pieces together for the block.

2. Drill a hole through the center. Then turn a mandrel with a slight taper to fit the hole.

3. Mount the block between centers in the arbor and turn to shape.

4. Fasten a block of wood of suitable thickness to the face-plate and turn a recess in the block to fit the chuck and arbor.

5. Turn a recess in the end of the chuck for the locking plate or ring made from pipe. If a

25-6. Sectional chuck with breakdown chuck.

locking plate is used, it is turned from wood. Fig. 25-7 (A).

6. The chuck is removed after it has been turned to shape.

7. Lay out the sections. Be sure the key piece has the correct angles so that it can easily be removed.

8. Set the chuck on end and cut the sections on a band saw or back saw. The saw kerf can be filled with cardboard of the same thickness.

9. The locking plate or ring is now put in place. In spinning, the follow block will fit against this plate. Fig. 25-7 (B).

Some spinning projects are spun "on air." Two chucks are used. The shell is spun over the first chuck. Fig. 25-8. It is then placed on a partial, straight-sided chuck and the operator uses a tool to form the desired shape. In this type of spinning, the inside of the shell has to be supported with the backstick. The unsupported remainder of the radius is spun by eye "on air."

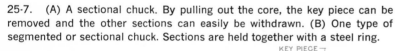

25-7. (A) A sectional chuck. By pulling out the core, the key piece can be removed and the other sections can easily be withdrawn. (B) One type of segmented or sectional chuck. Sections are held together with a steel ring.

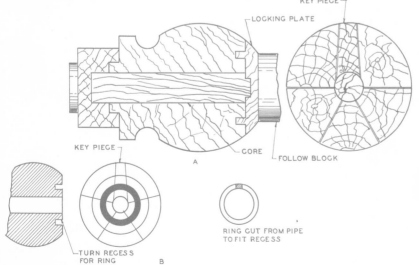

KEY PIECE

LOCKING PLATE

KEY PIECE

CORE

FOLLOW BLOCK

A

TURN RECESS FOR RING

B

RING CUT FROM PIPE TO FIT RECESS

26 Metals Adaptable for Spinning

A great deal of skill is required to spin some metals. For example, copper, brass, stainless steel, and monel metal work-harden during the spinning process and have to be annealed.

Because aluminum is one of the easiest metals for the beginner to master, it should be used until fundamental skills are developed. The softer grades work-harden very little, and many beautiful projects can be spun from this metal. However, much practice is required before any deep spun article can be turned by the novice.

The best grade of aluminum for spinning is 1100.0 (formerly 2S-00). This and 3003 (formerly 3S-0) are the most commonly used.

The thickness of metal used depends on the article to be spun. Recommended thicknesses are from 28 to 12 ga. Twenty and 18 ga. aluminum are ideal for the beginner.

Modern pewter or britannia metal is an alloy with many desirable properties that can be polished to look like silver. This very soft metal does not work-harden under pressure from spinning tools. Modern britannia metal contains no lead, so can be used in utensils.

Copper is suitable for spinning, works up beautifully, and takes a high polish. It is rather difficult for beginners to spin as it work-hardens and has to be *annealed* during the spinning process.

To *anneal copper,* heat it to an iridescent color and then plunge in clear cold water.

Many beautiful projects can be spun from brass. Its spinning properties are about the same as copper. See Table 26-A.

ANNEALING TABLE FOR METALS USED IN SPINNING			
Metals	**Thickness**	**Degrees Heat**	**Lubricant**
Aluminum	18 to 22 ga.	650°—just chars pine	Commercial stick wax.
Copper	20 to 26 ga.	1000°—very dull red	Stick wax, cup grease, tallow candle, laundry soap.
Brass	20 to 26 ga.	1000°—very dull red when oil burns off	Same as above.
Britannia Metal		No annealing required	Commercial stick wax.
Monel	20 to 26 ga.	1700°—bright yellow	Laundry soap.
Steel	24 to 26 ga.	1200°—bright cherry red	Laundry soap.
Zinc	20 to 26 ga.	212-375°, boiling water—spin hot	Tallow or soap.
Gar-alloy	18 to 24 ga.	270°F.	Any lubricant.

Table 26-A.

27 Metal Spinning Lubricants

A lubricant is needed to reduce friction. Many kinds of lubricants can be used, depending upon the type of metal being spun. If considerable heat is generated, lubricant of higher viscosity is required.

A good lubricant can be purchased in stick form that works well on copper, brass, and aluminum. Special lubricants can be purchased from suppliers specializing in this material.

Ordinary naphtha soap or mut-ton tallow makes a good lubricant. Some spinners mix one-half pound of oil to two pounds of tallow. These ingredients are heated together until the mixture is melted.

A good lubricant can be made by shaving a cake of naphtha laundry soap into fine pieces and heating the chips in about two pints of water until melted. After the mixture is dissolved, add a quart of No. 30 engine oil. Mix thoroughly.

28 ▷ The Fundamentals of Metal Spinning

The beginner should start on shallow saucer shapes until he gets the feel of the flow of metal.

In the spinning process, although the metal is cold and hard it appears to flow somewhat like clay on a potter's wheel. When metal is spun it has a tendency to change thickness. Excessive pressure in one spot will thin it rapidly and rupture the metal. Also, as the outer edge of the disc shrinks in circumference, it has a tendency to form wrinkles. By combining the use of the backstick and flatback tool these can be removed.

A detailed explanation of the basic spinning process follows:

1. Prepare a working drawing of the article to be spun.

2. Turn a hardwood chuck of the required shape.

3. Select a metal disc of the proper size. This can be determined as shown in Fig. 28-1.

4. For beginners the center of the disc can be laid out with dividers and a circle scribed on the metal the diameter of the follow block.

For more advanced work, center the disc between the chuck and the follow block. Draw the follow block tight against the blank. Move the T-rest back about 2″ and lock it in place. Start the lathe at slow speed. With a flat piece of hardwood held as in Fig. 28-2 (A and B), press gently on the edge of the blank while releasing the hand-

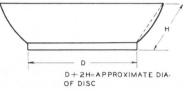

28-1. How to determine the diameter of the disc.

28-2. (A) Centering the disc.

28-2. (B) Centering the disc.

wheel of the tailstock lightly. When the disc is centered, quickly tighten the tailstock.

Caution: *Never stand directly behind the disc as there is danger of its flying out of the lathe.*

5. Determine the correct spindle speed. See Table 28-A.

SPEEDS FOR ALUMINUM

Diameter of Chuck	Speeds in rpm
3″ to 6″	2000 to 3400
7″ to 10″	1500 to 2300
11″ to 14″	1000 to 1200
15″ to 20″	500 to 800

Table 28-A.

Expert spinners prefer to use the highest speed possible, because the metal flows more easily at high speeds. Beginners should use speeds from 900 to 1200 rpm.

6. Select the proper tool for the project. For spinning aluminum this can be hickory. It will not mar the soft aluminum as a metal tool is inclined to do. In industry a tool made of forged tool steel having a highly polished surface is used.

7. Insert the spinning pin in the T-rest and adjust the rest so that when the tool is placed against the pin it will form a slight angle with the face of the disc. In spinning, do not try to reach too far on either side of the pin.

8. Turn on the power and apply suitable lubricant to the outer surface. Fig. 28-3.

9. Hook the disc to the base as rapidly as possible. This eliminates the danger of the blank flying from the lathe. Fig. 28-4.

10. Grasp the tool in the right hand, with the handle under the right arm held close to the body. Place the tool against the right

28-3. Applying lubricant to the disc.

28-4. Hooking the disc to the chuck.

13. Place the tool against the spinning pin. Then, holding it below center, move it upward. Fig. 28-7. Exert pressure against the blank, sweeping from the center to the outside, making sure that the sweep is carried all the way to the edge. NOTE: Spin the metal with the rounded side of the tool, not the point. Then, beginning at the edge, sweep back to the center. If the tool movement is in one direction only, the metal will thin excessively and the tool will puncture it.

Move the spinning pin as often as necessary while laying the metal down to the chuck.

Do not try to spin the complete shape in one stroke, or the outer edge will collapse and wrinkles will develop. At the first sign of a wrinkle, use the backstick, which acts as a movable chuck. Draw both tools toward the outer edge of the disc. The backstick is placed opposite the spinning tool, holding it as shown in Fig. 28-8. (See next page.)

CAUTION: *In reversing the movement of the tool toward the follow block, watch carefully that the metal does not bulge and flow back over it. If the metal becomes hard and springy, remove and anneal it.*

14. Before the final edge is laid down, use the backstick and flat back tool to turn the edge at a right angle to the chuck. Move the T-rest to within ¼″ of the edge of the disc. Trim the edge to size. Smooth with a file. NOTE: The amount of edge left is determined by the size of the roll desired. If a rolled edge is not needed, lay the metal down to the chuck.

side of the spinning pin with the left hand around the pin and the tool. The rounded side of the tool is held against the blank with the end slightly below center.

11. Apply pressure, moving the tool point down and to the left. Then apply pressure near the center and sweep toward the outside. NOTE: All spinning is done with body force, not with the arms. Fig. 28-5.

12. After the metal is hooked on, trim the edge of the blank with the diamond point tool as shown in Fig. 28-6. When metal is rolled, grain is produced. When metal is spun, especially if the article is deep, it has a tendency to flow more easily across the grain and the blank becomes out-of-round and will wrinkle. The edge should be trimmed frequently as the metal has a tendency to crack from the outside toward the center. Trimming will remove these cracks.

CAUTION: *Wear safety glasses and a leather glove on the left hand during spinning operations. There is always danger of the left hand coming in contact with the sharp disc.*

28-5. Apply pressure, moving the tool down and to the left.

28-6. Trimming the edge. Wear glove on the left hand to prevent coming in contact with the sharp edge of the disc.

28-7. Hold the tool against the spinning pin, starting below center. Then move upward.

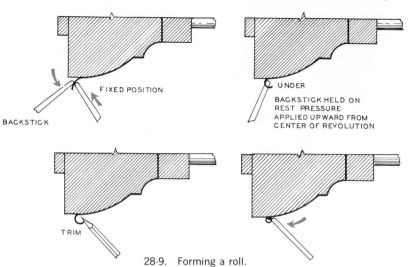

FIXED POSITION

BACKSTICK

UNDER

BACKSTICK HELD ON REST PRESSURE APPLIED UPWARD FROM CENTER OF REVOLUTION

TRIM

28-9. Forming a roll.

15. Hold the backstick against the left edge of the metal while the flat back tool is against the right side. Fig. 28-9. Apply pressure with the backstick until the edge starts to turn over. Check the roll; if necessary trim again. Using the flat back tool, apply final pressure to form the roll.

A beading tool can be used to form an edge bead, which is a small flange left at right angles to the spun piece. Hold the tool at a slight angle at the start; then gradually straighten it until the bead is formed. Fig. 28-10.

Hints for the Spinner

1. Sometimes a project will spin so tightly that it is almost impossible to remove it from the

chuck. In this event, drill a ⅛" or ¼" hole all the way through the chuck. This will permit air to enter the spun part for easy removal. Another method is to go over the spun piece with a planishing tool. This enlarges the spun part slightly so that it can be removed.

2. CAUTION: *Never insert the metal disc while the lathe is in motion. Experienced spinners are capable of doing this, but it is dangerous for beginners.*

3. If the tool sticks while spinning aluminum, it may be due to excessive speed, work-hardening, or lack of lubricant.

The inside of a bowl may be polished with steel wool. Fig. 28-11.

28-10. A bead or flange may also be formed with a beading tool.

28-8. Hold the backstick directly behind the spinning tool.

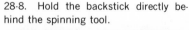

28-11. Polishing inside a bowl with steel wool.

134

Soldering Spun Projects

Many spun projects require the joining of two or more parts with solder. Each type of metal calls for a different technique in soldering.

The first essential is that the metal be clean. The second requirement is that the proper heat source be used. Some of the heating devices are an alcohol blowtorch, propane torch, soldering copper, and electric copper.

Solders

Solder is available in bar, solid wire, acid or resin core wire.

Most soft solders are a mixture of tin and lead. Solder must have a lower melting point than the metal to be joined. The most common solder is an alloy of lead and tin known as half-and-half or 50-50 solder. It melts at about 420°F. A freer-flowing solder with about 60 percent tin, melting at about 360 to 370°F., can be used for britannia metal. Special solders are made for aluminum.

A solder with a very low melting point is the 63-37 type, known as "eutectic" solder because of this trait, although there is a type which melts still lower, an alloy of lead, tin, and bismuth. Known as bismuth solder, it may be used where special precautions are necessary.

Fluxes

A flux is needed in all soldering. Flux prevents the formation of metallic oxide that hinders the flow of solder. It also acts as a cleaning agent.

For soldering britannia metal, the most commonly used flux is composed of glycerine with about 10 drops of hydrochloric acid added to each ounce.

Soldering Britannia Metal

Soldering britannia metal requires special techniques. Because britannia metal melts at a temperature of 425°F., care must be taken in soldering it. Never use a soldering copper. A sharp torch flame is the best heat source. Either an alcohol blowtorch, a blowpipe and Bunsen burner, an alcohol lamp and blowpipe, or a small gas torch may be used. The procedure is as follows:

1. Set the project on a piece of asbestos.

2. It may be necessary to wire the parts together to hold them while being soldered. They can also be held on an asbestos board with nails. Fig. 29-1.

3. Coat the seam or joint with a liberal amount of flux. Place snippets of solder along the joint or hold the solder wire on the joint. Fig. 29-2. Move the torch flame back and forth along the seam or joint. Fig. 29-2. If the flame is concentrated on one spot for even an instant, the metal will melt. Watch closely for the flux to smoke and boil. Very suddenly thereafter the solder will melt and run into the joint. It will run toward the hottest part of the metal, so draw it along with the flame.

29-2. Hold the soldering wire on the joint and move the flame of the torch back and forth to avoid concentration of heat at one point.

29-1. For soldering, parts may be wired together or held on an asbestos board with nails.

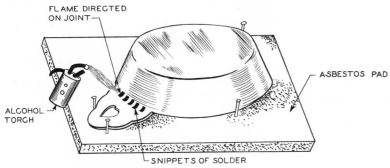

FLAME DIRECTED ON JOINT

ALCOHOL TORCH

ASBESTOS PAD

SNIPPETS OF SOLDER

30 ▷ Polishing Spun Projects

30-2. Buffing the finished project.

A well executed project calls for an equally well-planned and executed finish. The finish brings out the natural beauty of the project itself.

Polishing is generally done in four steps: roughing, oiling, buffing, and coloring. The first two steps are to remove scratches from the surface and prepare it for buffing. Buffing brings out the luster of the metal, while coloring brings out a high degree of gloss.

For the roughing operation felt wheels, sewed muslin wheels or those made of canvas or muslin cemented together are coated with abrasive grit. To prepare a roughing wheel, coat it with hot hide glue. When it is almost dry, rotate, scrape smooth, and shape the wheel with the sharp end of a file. When it is thoroughly dry,

recoat with hot glue or waterglass and, while the wheel is wet, roll a rougher cutting wheel in No. 60 grit and a finer wheel in No. 100 grit emery or fused aluminum oxide. Recoat when the grit works down smooth.

A lubricant may be used in polishing. For the oiling operation, a felt wheel, Fig. 30-1, charged with No. 100 or 220 grit is used. Buffing tallow, oil, or beeswax will serve as a lubricant, depending upon the finish desired.

For buffing, use a wheel made of muslin sewed together, Fig. 30-2. The abrasive is applied to the wheel in a grease binder, in stick form. Tripoli is the material commonly used.

For the final polishing, use a loose wheel of unsewed flannel discs. The abrasive is a soft silica or lime in a grease binder.

CAUTION: *Canvas gloves and face shield should be worn when polishing.*

The project being polished should be held below center and moved upward. Fig. 30-1. The metal should be revolved, alternated in direction, and constantly moved.

30-1. Polishing with a felt wheel.

31 ▷ Modern Trends in Metal Spinning

Spinning metal to shape dates back to hieroglyphic Egypt. Historically, the art has depended upon the skill of the worker as he applied pressure with a hand tool to make the metal flow over a chuck, or pattern. In more recent years, hand power has been complemented with mechanical and hydraulic assists, considerably broadening the application of the process.

Large hydraulically controlled

lathes, weighing in excess of 400,000 lbs., enable the operator to skillfully apply enormous amounts of "controlled" tool pressure to shape discs up to 170″ in diameter and 2″ in thickness. These lathes with hydraulic power have the sensitivity of manual operation. This sensitivity permits the operator to retain the same feel that metal spinners have relied upon for centuries.

The lathes are equipped with

31-1. Industrial spinning of 1⅜″ aluminum plate to a 36¾″ hemisphere on a lathe with pushbutton controls.

pushbutton controls that govern the actions of starting, stopping, and braking the machine. The operator merely manipulates two control levers—one for applying pressure, the other for traversing the roller across the workpiece. Fig. 31-1.

The Aerospace program required higher and higher strength/weight ratios. As a result, techniques have been developed to spin the higher strength aluminum alloys (2219, 6061, 5456 and 7075) to name a few—also magnesium alloys and titanium and ultra-strength steels.

Power spinning is considerably different from conventional hand spinning. In conventional spinning, hand tools must be skillfully used to form the metal over the chuck under moderate pressures. Since any reduction of the metal cannot be accurately estimated, thickness is not always uniform, and close tolerances cannot always be maintained. Power

spinning assures accuracy. Much larger shapes may be formed.

Economy of Metal Spinning

One of the major reasons for the economy in metal spinning as a means of fabricating metal is the low cost of making the form over which the metal is spun. Industry uses mandrels or chucks of low-cost hardwood or soft metal. They have fewer components than draw dies and represent only a fraction of the cost. When several sizes of a similar item are required for prototype samples, chucks may be re-cut at a considerable savings. Small quantities can be produced more economically than by forging, deep drawing, or machining.

The spinning process is so versatile that the same plant may turn out everything from dog dishes, Fig. 31-2, to an elliptical dome for Titan III.

Many conical shapes, such as metal television tubes, centrifuge separator discs, hoppers, and other products are not readily adaptable to drawing but are to

31-2. Stainless steel dog-feeding dish.

spinning. Missile fuel-tank bulkheads and tanks can be spun over inexpensive maple chucks. Figs. 31-3 to 31-6. See following page.

Check Your Knowledge

1. What is meant by metal spinning?

2. Describe a metal spinning lathe.

3. Explain the difference between a lathe used in the school and an industrial spinning lathe.

4. Name some types of spinning tools.

5. What is a compound lever tool? How is it used?

6. Of what material is a tool made for spinning steel?

7. What are spinning pliers?

31-3. Stainless steel hemisphere spun from ¾″ thick material.

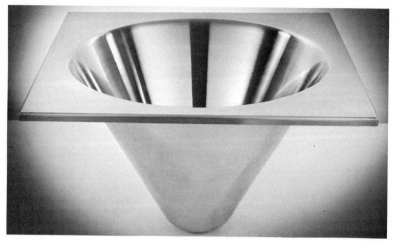

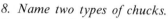

31-4. Stainless steel mixing bowl for food processing machine. One piece construction.

31-5. Unicel pressure filter used in hospitals and laboratories. Parts are spun.

31-6. Aluminum spheres for high-voltage test apparatus. Spun to 1,000 millimeter size, .125 thick wall. Assembled complete to cast and machined shaft.

8. Name two types of chucks.

9. Are wood chucks suitable for spinning metal? Explain.

10. How is a chuck held on the lathe spindle?

11. What is a follow block?

12. Why is the bottom of a tray or bowl made slightly concave?

13. What is meant by the "breakdown process"?

14. Explain the construction of a sectional chuck.

15. On what type of projects would you use a sectional chuck?

16. What is meant by the term "spinning on air"?

17. What is a backstick? Explain how it is used.

18. Why is aluminum the easiest type of metal to spin?

19. What is britannia metal?

20. What is meant by the term "work-harden"?

21. Why is it necessary to anneal copper or brass when spinning articles of some depth?

22. Name some types of lubricants used in spinning.

23. Explain spinning process.

24. Describe the method used in centering a disc.

25. What are some of the dangers involved in spinning metal?

26. How are a bead and a roll formed on a spun article?

27. Name some heating devices used in soldering spun projects?

28. What is "eutectic" solder?

29. Explain some of the difficulties in soldering britannia metal.

30. What is a flux and why is it used in soldering?

31. What are the four steps in polishing?

32. What is meant by "power spinning"?

33. Why is metal spinning more economical than deep drawing?

Terms to Know and Spell

guild systems	template	metallic oxide
spindle	fulcrum	fused
planishing	backstick	prototype

Section 4, Project 1
HURRICANE LAMP

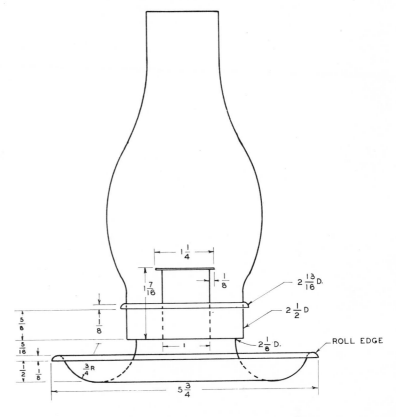

Section 4, Project 2
ASH TRAY #1

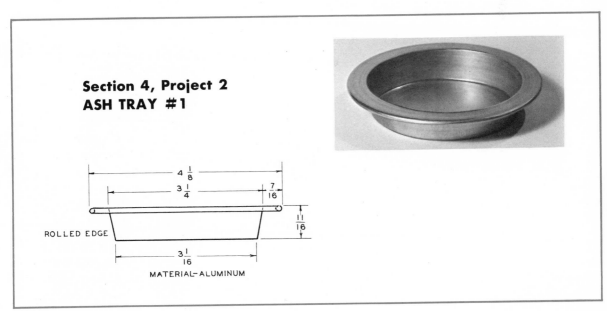

ROLLED EDGE

MATERIAL—ALUMINUM

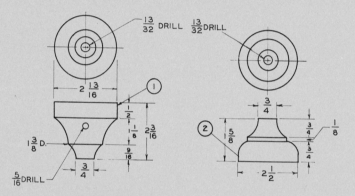

Five different discs are used in making this lamp. The parts are held together with a piece of ⅛-inch pipe to which a socket is attached. Shade holder can be purchased from a lamp store. Made from brass, it makes a beautiful project.

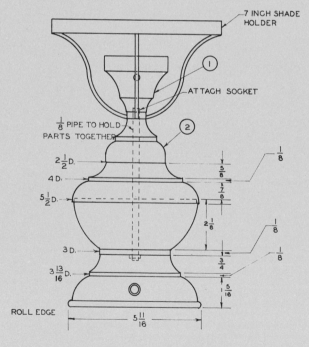

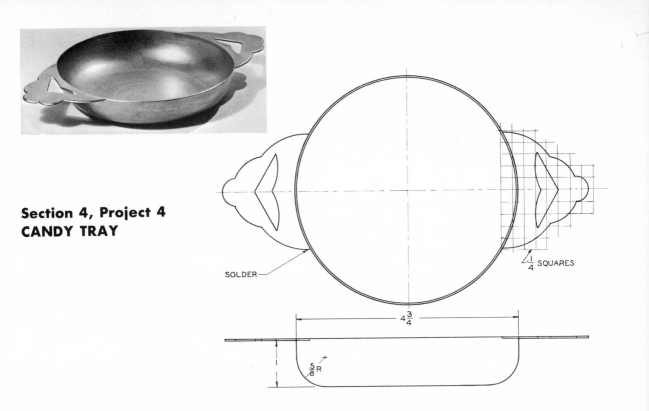

**Section 4, Project 4
CANDY TRAY**

SOLDER

$\frac{1}{4}$ SQUARES

$4\frac{3}{4}$

$\frac{5}{8}R$

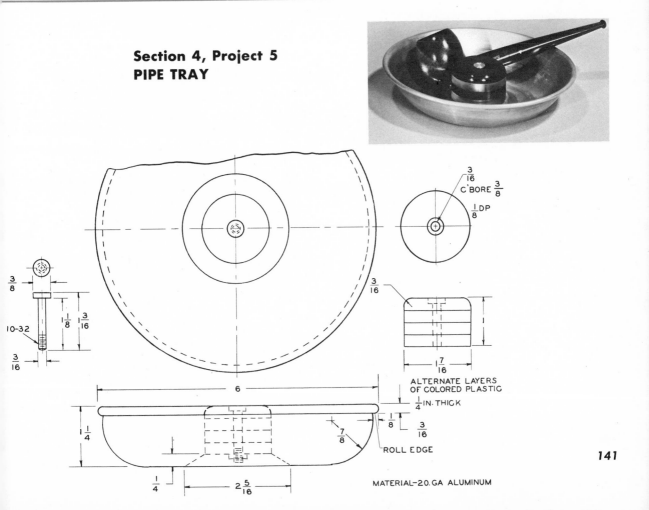

**Section 4, Project 5
PIPE TRAY**

$\frac{3}{16}$

$\frac{3}{16}$

C'BORE $\frac{3}{8}$

$\frac{1}{8}$DP

$\frac{3}{8}$

$\frac{3}{16}$

$1\frac{1}{8}$ $1\frac{3}{16}$

10-32

$\frac{3}{16}$

$\frac{3}{16}$

ALTERNATE LAYERS
OF COLORED PLASTIC
$\frac{1}{4}$ IN. THICK

$1\frac{7}{16}$

6

$1\frac{1}{4}$

$\frac{1}{8}$

$\frac{3}{16}$

$\frac{7}{8}$

ROLL EDGE

$\frac{1}{4}$

$2\frac{5}{16}$

MATERIAL-20. GA ALUMINUM

141

Section 4, Project 6
CANDY BOWL WITH LID

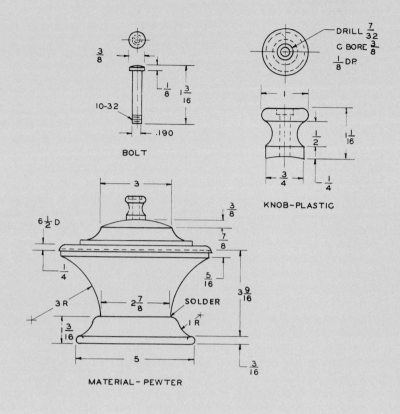

BOLT

10-32

$\frac{3}{8}$

$\frac{1}{8}$

$1\frac{3}{16}$

.190

DRILL $\frac{7}{32}$
C BORE $\frac{3}{8}$
$\frac{1}{8}$ D.P.

1

$\frac{1}{2}$

$1\frac{1}{16}$

$\frac{3}{4}$

$\frac{1}{4}$

KNOB-PLASTIC

3

$6\frac{1}{2}$ D

$\frac{3}{8}$

$\frac{7}{8}$

$\frac{1}{4}$

$\frac{5}{16}$

$3\frac{9}{16}$

3 R

$2\frac{7}{8}$

SOLDER

1 R

$\frac{3}{16}$

5

$\frac{3}{16}$

MATERIAL - PEWTER

Section 4, Project 7—TIER TRAY

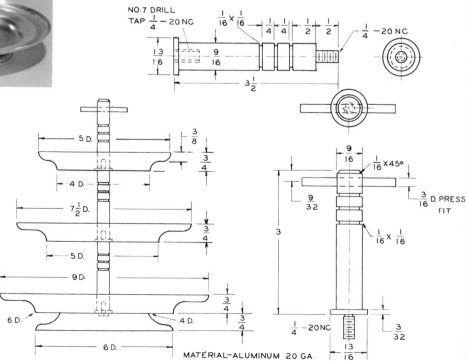

NO.7 DRILL
TAP $\frac{1}{4}$ — 20 NC

$\frac{1}{16}$ X $\frac{1}{16}$

$\frac{1}{4}$ $\frac{1}{4}$ $\frac{1}{2}$ $\frac{1}{2}$

$\frac{1}{4}$ — 20 NC

$\frac{13}{16}$

$\frac{9}{16}$

$3\frac{1}{2}$

5 D.

$\frac{3}{8}$

$\frac{3}{4}$

4 D.

$\frac{3}{4}$

$7\frac{1}{2}$ D.

5 D.

9 D.

$\frac{3}{4}$

6 D.

4 D.

$\frac{3}{4}$

6 D.

$\frac{9}{16}$

$\frac{1}{16}$ X45°

$\frac{3}{16}$ D. PRESS FIT

$\frac{9}{32}$

3

$\frac{1}{16}$ X $\frac{1}{16}$

$\frac{1}{4}$ — 20 NC

$\frac{13}{16}$

$\frac{3}{32}$

MATERIAL—ALUMINUM 20 GA.

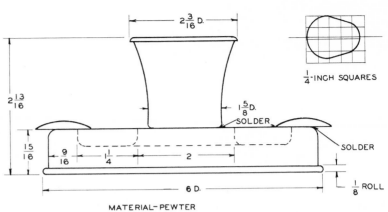

**Section 4, Project 8
ASH TRAY #2
with Cigarette Holder**

$2\frac{3}{16}$ D.

$\frac{1}{4}$-INCH SQUARES

$2\frac{13}{16}$

$1\frac{5}{8}$ D.
SOLDER

SOLDER

$1\frac{5}{16}$

$\frac{9}{16}$

$\frac{1}{4}$

2

6 D.

$\frac{1}{8}$ ROLL

MATERIAL—PEWTER

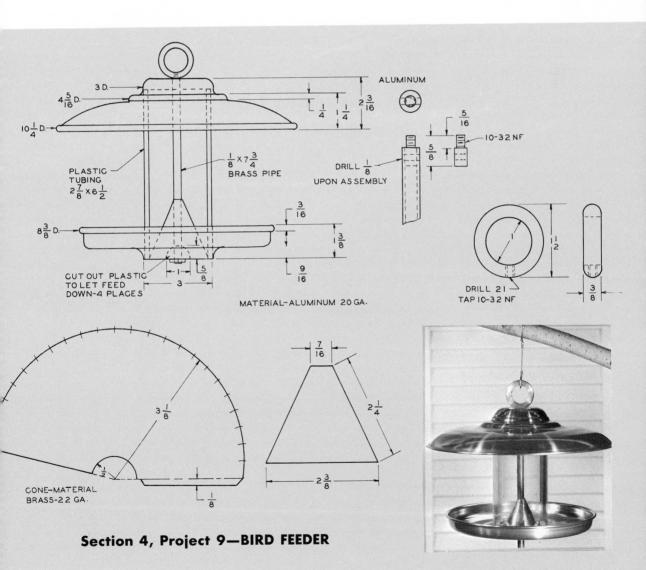

ALUMINUM

3 D.

$4\frac{5}{16}$ D.

$2\frac{3}{16}$

$\frac{1}{4}$ $1\frac{1}{4}$

$10\frac{1}{4}$ D.

$\frac{1}{8} \times 7\frac{3}{4}$
BRASS PIPE

$\frac{5}{16}$

10-32 NF

$\frac{5}{8}$

DRILL $\frac{1}{8}$
UPON ASSEMBLY

PLASTIC
TUBING
$2\frac{7}{8} \times 6\frac{1}{2}$

$8\frac{3}{8}$ D.

$\frac{3}{16}$

$1\frac{3}{8}$

$\frac{9}{16}$

CUT OUT PLASTIC
TO LET FEED
DOWN—4 PLACES

1

$\frac{5}{8}$

3

$1\frac{1}{2}$

$\frac{3}{8}$

DRILL 21
TAP 10-32 NF

MATERIAL—ALUMINUM 20 GA.

$3\frac{1}{8}$

$\frac{1}{2}$

$\frac{1}{8}$

CONE—MATERIAL
BRASS—22 GA.

$\frac{7}{16}$

$2\frac{1}{4}$

$2\frac{3}{8}$

Section 4, Project 9—BIRD FEEDER

143

Section 4, Project 10
FRYING PAN

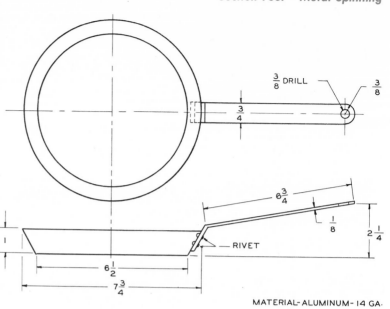

$\frac{3}{8}$ DRILL

$\frac{3}{8}$

$\frac{3}{4}$

$6\frac{3}{4}$

$\frac{1}{8}$

$2\frac{1}{4}$

RIVET

1

$6\frac{1}{2}$

$7\frac{3}{4}$

MATERIAL-ALUMINUM- 14 GA.

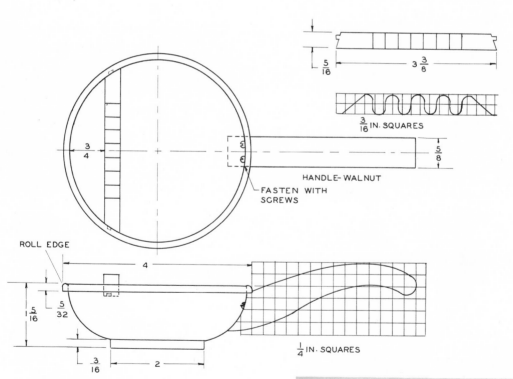

$\frac{5}{16}$

$3\frac{3}{8}$

$\frac{3}{16}$ IN. SQUARES

$\frac{5}{8}$

HANDLE- WALNUT

$\frac{3}{4}$

FASTEN WITH
SCREWS

ROLL EDGE

4

$1\frac{5}{16}$

$\frac{5}{32}$

$\frac{3}{16}$

2

$\frac{1}{4}$ IN. SQUARES

Section 4, Project 11
ASH TRAY #3
with Walnut Handle

Art Metal

ART METALCRAFT is one of the oldest fields of metalworking. Centuries ago man found that some metals were so extremely malleable they could be formed into various shapes by hammering. Because there was a need by man for cooking utensils, art metalcraft was born.

A flatware pattern begins with the artist who sketches the design.

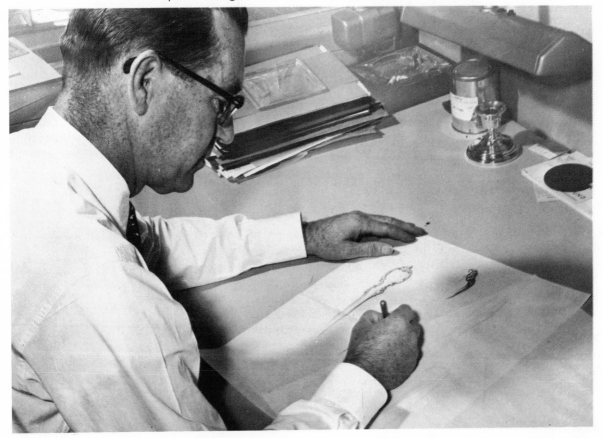

Early records reveal that copper was discovered by ancient man in the Carpathian Mountains about 4500 B.C. and found acceptance by many peoples of the Near East. In Egypt art metal and spinning techniques were developed; pieces made by these ancients have been found dating back to 1900 B.C. Egyptian craftsmen were highly skilled in the forming of copper, bronze, pewter, silver, and gold.

It was natural that other peoples would also make use of this craft. The Greeks and Romans improved upon the Egyptian designs and created products that show a high degree of craftsmanship and skill.

In this section, operations such as shaping and forming—along with skills in surface decorations such as piercing and planishing, fluting, flaring, coloring, and etching—are described.

Many of the technical processes in use today are essentially the same as those employed in ancient times. The early metalworker was familiar with many processes for shaping and ornamenting metal. These included hammering, embossing, chasing and inlaying.

All decorative metalwork was originally executed with the hammer, since hammering naturally preceded casting among early peoples. The parts were hammered out separately and then put together with rivets, soldering having not been invented.

Everything attributable to the Assyrian, the Etrurian, and the Greek goldsmith was wrought by the hammer and punch.

32 ▷ Tools Used in Forming and Raising Metal

A great variety of hand tools have been developed through the years for forming and raising metals. Following are brief descriptions of the ones most commonly used in art metalwork.

Hammers

Forming or **silversmith** hammers, Fig. 32-1, represent essential equipment for art metalwork.

Used for the shaping of bowls and trays, they are of forged steel with highly polished, rounded faces which make a smooth impression on soft metals.

Raising hammers, Fig. 32-1, are generally used on the outside surface in earlier stages of the work to drive or raise the metal, forcing it into the bowl or vase shape, or other desired forms.

Planishing hammers, Fig. 32-1, are used to surface or smooth off irregularities, following the original shaping or raising operation, or embossing, done with other hammers. They also produce the bright, glittering faceted surfaces often seen on bowls or vases. Work to be planished is usually supported on stakes of suitable shapes.

Mallets, Stakes, and Sandbags

Mallets are used principally during the preliminary stages of much of the raised work done on sheet metal over anvils, and sometimes for the entire piece, particularly in pewter work, as they do not leave hammer marks when handled correctly. They are also employed in tray work and for numerous bending and forming operations, a suitable mallet in size and shape being selected for the work at hand. Fig. 32-2 shows several types of mallets.

Stakes, Fig. 32-3, are devices for supporting the metal being shaped. They are made in a wide variety of sizes and shapes. Stakes have square tangs which may be held in a bench vise or in a multistake holder, Fig. 32-4.

32-1. Typical art metal hammers.

FORMING

RAISING

PLANISHING

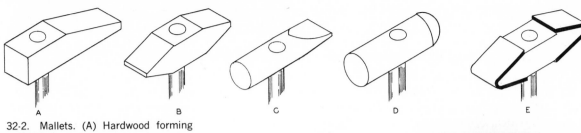

32-2. Mallets. (A) Hardwood forming mallet, (B) double wedge forming mallet, (C) round end forming mallet, (D) round end forming mallet, (E) leather-faced forming mallet used for forming the softer metals. After forming with a mallet, the piece is finished with a hammer.

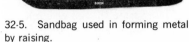

32-5. Sandbag used in forming metal by raising.

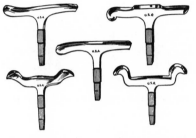

32-3. (A) Stakes of typical varieties. These stakes are used for bending, forming, raising, and planishing.

32-4. Multi-stake holder for all types of stakes.

Use of a multi-stake holder permits the use of every standard anvil stake without the necessity of adapters.

The **sandbag,** Fig. 32-5, is used in raising and forming metal. It is of strong canvas, partially filled with fine sand. Since it is only partially filled, it will fit in the contour or shape of the article worked on.

32-3. (B) Stakes such as these are used to smooth a bowl. The metal is placed over the stake so as to make the shape needed at a certain point.

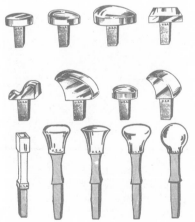

33 ▷ Forming Metal by Beating Down

In beating down, the object is to hammer and stretch a metal disc to the rough shape of a bowl, which is the usual preliminary to any regular forming and shaping. A hammer with a ball-like head is used. Many projects such as shallow trays, plates, and bowls can be entirely formed in this manner.

There are three common methods of forming metal by this process: (1) Sinking or beating down in a wooden or metal form, (2)

beating down over a wooden or metal block, (3) sinking rectangular plates in a vise.

Beating Down a Plate or Tray

Shallow plates or trays can be formed by beating down over a block or down into a form. Both methods will be described in this unit. They require very little equipment. Fig. 33-1 (see following page) shows a round plate 10″ in diameter with a well 6½″ in diameter.

Beating Down Over a Wooden Block

Method 1

1. Select a 10″ disc of 18 gage copper, brass, or aluminum.

2. If the metal has to be cut from sheet stock locate the center and punch with a center punch. Scribe the circle with dividers.

3. Cut to the line with snips and file the edge if necessary.

4. Scribe the inner circle.

5. Select a piece of hardwood and cut to 2 x 3 x 5 inches. Shape to guide the curve of the well. Your teacher will help here, or a ready-cut block may be used.

6. Place the metal disc on the end of the block and draw a pencil line along the circumference so that two nails may be placed as guide pins for sinking the well of the plate.

7. Place the metal disc against the two pins as shown in Fig. 33-2 and begin hammering with a plate or forming hammer. The work should be rotated slowly so that the well is sunk evenly all the way around the disc. Fig. 33-3. *Sink only part way* the first time around.

8. During this process the plate may become slightly out of shape and may have to be straightened as in Fig. 33-4. For this operation use a flat block of hardwood with the corners rounded.

9. Place the work against the end of the block and sink it to the desired depth all around, Fig. 33-5.

10. Straighten the plate again with the block of wood and mallet. Fig. 33-7.

11. When the required shape of the plate is formed, the outside edge may be enriched in many different ways by simple tooling. Design may be drawn on the metal before sinking.

12. If the metal becomes hard during the beating process it can be annealed by heating to a dark red and plunging in cold water.

Beating Down a Tray into a Form

Method 2

One of the simplest methods of beating down metal is with form blocks. Fig. 33-6. There are two types, wooden and metal. Care must be exercised in using the metal block as the sharp edge can cut the disc. Wood blocks are usually made from close-grained maple or birch. When making form blocks that have irregular shapes, cut on a jig saw from ¾″ material and glue this piece to another piece of ¾″ flat stock.

1. Construct a form block that has the recessed portion of the proper size. Round forms can be turned on the lathe.

2. With a pair of snips cut the disc slightly larger than the size of the finished project, as some of the metal will be drawn in during the beating down process. Large trays should be made from 20 to 18 gage metal; 24 to 22 gage can be used for smaller trays.

3. Scribe a line showing the section to be beaten down.

4. Fasten the metal on the form with wood screws or nails at the corners. See Fig. 33-8.

33-2. Starting to sink the well. Note the two nails in the wood block for guidance. They keep the edge distance equal all around. The hidden part of the wood block is shaped to form the curve of the plate.

33-1. Dimensioning and planning a plate made by beating down.

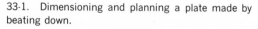

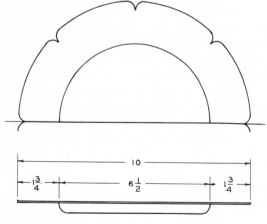

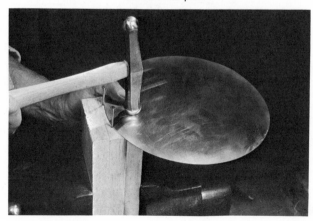

33-3. The first round of hammering completed.

33-4. Straightening the plate with a wood block and a ball-peen hammer.

33-5. Finishing the sinking with the raising hammer.

33-6. Wooden form for beating down Such forms can be made by turning to shape on the wood lathe.

33-7. Rim of the plate straightened with mallet and block of wood.

33-8. Rectangular metal is fastened on the block with nails or screws.

33-9. Circular metal can be held on the form block with the hands.

149

33-10. Strike the metal first in the center and work toward the outside.

33-11. As the metal takes shape, work towards the center until the disc is stretched to the bottom of the form, using a forming hammer or mallet.

If the metal has been cut circular, it can be held down with the hands. Fig. 33-9.

5. Choose a forming hammer or, if the metal is pewter or aluminum, a soft hammer faced with wood, rubber, horn, or leather.

6. Start striking the disc in the center, hammering clockwise toward the outside of the pattern. Fig. 33-10. Hold the hammer so that it strikes the metal squarely.

7. The metal will workharden during the hammering process and must be annealed. Then pickle and wash before refastening it to the form. Annealing creates an oxide scale which will be beaten in unless it is so treated. (See Unit 42, Annealing and Pickling Metal.)

8. Repeat the beating down process. As the work takes shape,

33-12. Flattening the edge with a planishing hammer.

work towards the center in rows until the metal is stretched to the bottom of the form. Fig. 33-11.

9. If the metal is not fastened to the form it will be necessary to keep the edge flat by striking it with the side of a wooden mallet, Fig. 33-12, or with a planishing hammer.

10. Finish the tray by cutting it to shape and filing the edges smooth. A design can be added to the edge, if so desired.

---

34 ▷ Forming Metal by Raising

Raising is a forming process whereby the sides of the metal give shape to the project. The general objective is to hammer and stretch a metal disc to the shape of a bowl, by deep forming.

Two common methods are used: raising over a hardwood form and forming over a sandbag.

1. Make a drawing of the project. The diameter of the material needed can be determined as shown in Fig. 34-1. Another method is bending a

piece of wire to follow the outer shape of the bowl. By straightening the wire, the diameter of the disc can be determined.

2. From stock, cut a circular disc.

3. Locate the center of the disc and with a pencil compass or dividers draw concentric circles about ½ inch apart. Fig. 34-2. These lines are used as a guide in hammering. If using dividers, mark the lines very lightly.

4. Construct a forming block as shown in Fig. 34-3, from hard-

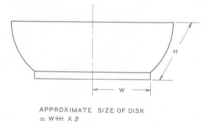

APPROXIMATE SIZE OF DISK
= W+H X 2

34-1. Method of determining the diameter of disc required.

34-2. Measure and draw concentric lines ½″ apart.

wood. Carefully measure and gouge out a shallow cavity in the end grain of the wood, sanding to finish smoothly. Or use a ready-cut block.

5. Lay the metal disc on the cavity in the block so that the edge of the metal lies across the depression.

6. Strike the metal along the outer circle of the disc with a raising hammer, Fig. 34-4, rotating the disc a little after each blow. Avoid striking the edge of the metal. Continue hammering in concentric circles until the center of the disc has been reached. Do not allow the metal to wrinkle so that it folds over, as this will ruin the piece.

7. Since by now the disc has work-hardened, it will be necessary to anneal and pickle the piece. (See Unit 42.) Rinse in running water.

8. When the disc is clean, restore the concentric lines with a pencil compass or dividers.

9. Continue hammering the metal inside the edge as you rotate it over the depression. Anneal and pickle the metal again and continue forming until it is the proper shape. Fig. 34-5.

10. After the final shape has been obtained, Fig. 34-6, anneal and pickle the bowl; scour it with pumice powder and water; rinse and dry.

11. Choose a metal stake and place it in a stake holder. The stake should have about the same curvature as the bowl. Place the bowl upside down over the stake. Fig. 34-7.

12. Select a wooden or rawhide mallet and work out the dents and irregularities. Fig. 34-8.

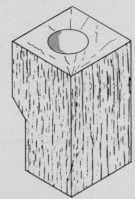
34-3. Hardwood forming block.

34-6. The final shape has now been obtained.

34-4. In raising a bowl place the disc over the form. Hold at slight angle, striking the edge with a raising hammer.

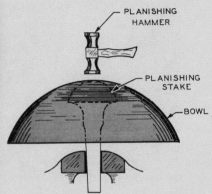
34-7. Set-up: The bowl is placed over a metal stake for the planishing operation.

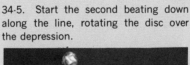
34-5. Start the second beating down along the line, rotating the disc over the depression.

34-8. Working out irregularities with a wooden mallet.

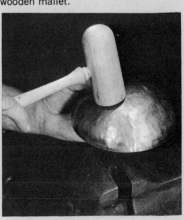

151

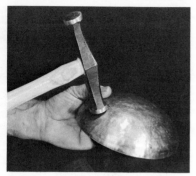
34-9. Planishing with a hammer.

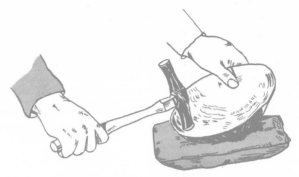
34-11. Forming a bowl on a sandbag.

34-10. Marking an edge line with a surface gage.

13. With a planishing hammer start planishing the exterior covering one area at a time. Fig. 34-9. The hammer blows should fall squarely on the work where it comes in contact with the stake. NOTE: Each blow of the hammer should slightly overlap the preceding one.

14. Place the bowl on a surface plate as shown in Fig. 34-10 and mark an edge line with a surface gage. Trim to the line with snips.

15. The edge may be decorated and a base added; or appendages may be added to the bowl as supports.

16. The bowl is cleaned and a coat of clear lacquer applied to prevent the project from tarnishing.

17. The forming can also be done on a sandbag. Fig. 34-11. Proceed as with the wooden form, but note that the disc must be shaped carefully. Experience is very important.

---

35 ▷ Decorating the Project

For interesting variations, the beauty of a project can be improved by treating the surface or edge of a bowl, tray, or plate. Common methods are: planishing, fluting, scalloping, and overlaying.

Planishing

As shown in Unit 34, planishing is smoothing and stiffening the metal by hammering.

A considerable amount of skill is required to avoid producing heavy hammer marks. When planishing only faint marks should be left, to make the surface of the project more attractive.

1. Select (a) a round-faced stake that is free from blemishes, (b) a smooth-faced planishing hammer.

2. Start at the center and work outward in circles. Strike the metal with light, square, overlapping blows. Cover the entire surface but avoid coming too close to the edges. The flat edges or rims should be planished in the same manner as the flat portion of the bottom. NOTE: Light, well placed blows on the edges will prevent them from becoming uneven.

3. In planishing plates or trays, use a solid hard-metal block or a lead block as a back-up.

4. If the surface is to be high-lighted, polish with fine abrasive paper till the effect pleases you. Spray with clear metal lacquer to preserve finish.

Laying Out for Edge Decoration

In laying out the position for edge decorations such as flutes, domes, scallops, and others that have to be spaced equally, the following procedure is suggested:

1. With a pencil compass, draw a circle on a sheet of heavy paper, the size of the project. Then fold four times carefully, to make "spokes" for your design.

2. With scissors cut out the design at both outside corners.

3. Fasten the paper to the metal with Scotch tape or paper clips.

4. Draw around the design, Fig. 35-1, and cut to shape with snips. If flutes or domes are to be made, draw a line from the edge to the center for each section, as a guide for the hammer.

Fluting

Fluting is a type of surface enrichment that adds to the structural quality as well as making a pleasing appearance. Strength is added.

For fluting a bowl, cut a wooden form that fits the shape of the curve. Fig. 35-2. Use a gouge for this work. Then hold the bowl over the form and hammer in the flute. Fig. 35-3.

To flute the edge of a *plate,* shape a groove in the end of a hardwood block. Shape another piece of hardwood the size of the flute to be made. Divide the plate into the required number of spaces for the flutes. Place the rim of the plate on the hardwood block and hammer in the flutes. Fig. 35-4. The edges of an ash tray may be fluted with a soft piece of wood and a round rod of the same diameter as the flute. Fig. 35-5 (A).

35-1. Outlining the design on a plate. The decoration may then be cut with snips.

35-4. Sinking flutes with a hardwood block.

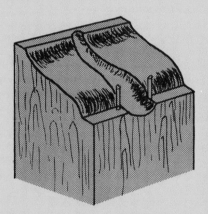

35-2. Wooden form for fluting.

35-3. With the bowl held over the form, the flute is shaped with a forming or ball-peen hammer.

35-5. (A) The edge of this ash tray has flutes formed with a round rod.

35-5. (B) Set of punches and tapping block.

Doming

Domes are formed after the project has been raised to the shape desired. A dome is a raised, conical shape, usually placed at equal intervals or in groups around the rim of a project. Domes may be formed over the end of a piece of pipe with an opening equal to the diameter of the dome. Round the inner edge of the pipe to avoid cutting the metal. Select a ball-peen hammer that will fit partway into the pipe. Place the center of the part to be domed over the center of the pipe and drive the metal into the recess.

Another method of doming is by use of a dapping block and punches. Fig. 35-5 (B). Punches come in a variety of diameters.

Also, one of the simplest methods of doming is to gouge a small conical shape in a block of wood. Lay the part to be domed over the hole and strike the metal with a round-faced punch or ball-peen hammer. Fig. 35-6.

Overlaying

Overlaying consists of applying to the main body of an object a metal decoration of the same or contrasting color. The overlay should be of appropriate design and size.

1. Make a full size drawing of the project and overlay.

2. Cut patterns to shape.

3. Lay the main pattern of the project on the disc and mark the shape.

4. With a jeweler's saw or tin snips, cut the metal to the shape desired.

5. File edges smooth with a fine file.

6. Cut metal for overlay to shape and place the overlay in position on body of the project. Mark with a pencil.

7. Apply flux. Tin both the marked section of the project and overlay.

8. Fasten the overlay in place with clips and heat uniformly with a torch.

9. When the solder begins to flow from the edges, remove the source of heat.

10. Polish with fine steel wool or a fine abrasive cloth and apply a coat of clear metal lacquer.

Scalloping

A wood jig can be made to scallop the edge of a dish. Fig. 35-7. Lay out the desired number of spaces on the dish, place in the opening of the jig, and bend it. NOTE: A commercial type jig, Fig. 35-8, can be purchased or the operation can be performed with a pair of round-nose pliers. The jaws must be heavily taped.

35-6. To form a simple dome, hold the metal over a small conical depression in a wooden block.

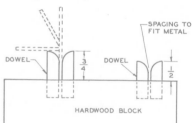

35-7. Construction of jig for scalloping the edge of a tray.

35-8. Using a commercial type of bending jig for scalloping.

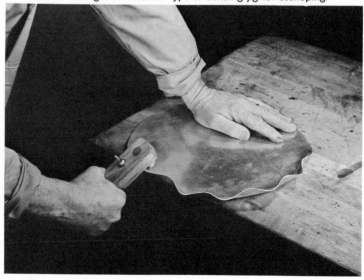

Metal Tooling

Metal tooling is a process that creates a bold-relief design in thin metal.

Foil may be used to face many projects such as wall plaques, lamp bases, picture frames, overlays for book-ends, and others, for surface enrichment.

Metals and Tools

There are three types of metals used in tooling—aluminum, brass, and copper. No. 36 gage metal is best for the beginner. Copper foil is the easiest of the metal foils to tool because it seldom needs annealing.

Fig. 36-1 shows some of the common modeling tools.

Pointed tools, called liners or tracers, are used for tracing the design and for tooling of very fine lines. Fig. 36-1 (A). You can also use a pointed dowel rod, a dry ball-point pen, nut pick, or leather modeling tools. The modeling tool, Fig. 36-1 (B), is used for raising, contour work, and general tooling.

The double ball tool, Fig. 36-1 (C), is used for tooling of detail and fine lines, border work, and fine raising.

Smoothers are wood tools, Fig. 36-1 (D), used for final finishing.

Procedure for Tooling Metal Foil

1. For your first project select a design that is simple without too much depth or detail.

2. Trace the design on tracing paper.

3. Secure a sheet of heavy metal foil and cut to size with snips, being careful not to kink it. An allowance should be made for mounting around the edges. Remove oxides from the foil with No. 3/0 steel wool.

4. Attach the pattern to the foil with masking tape or paper clips, at all four corners.

5. Place the foil on a soft pad made up of several sheets of newspapers, or of felt, rubber, or cork.

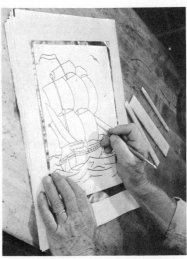

36-2. Tracing the design to metal foil.

36-3. With the spatula end of the modeling tool, work out the design from the back.

36-4. All areas which are to be raised are pressed out with a maple spatula.

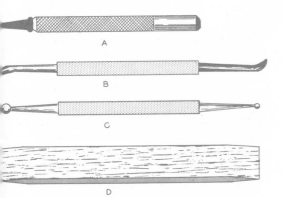

36-1. Modeling tools for tooling foil: (A) Tracing tool, (B) modeling tool, (C) double ball tool, (D) smoother.

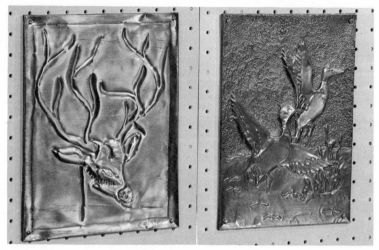

36-5. Samples of metal tooling.

6. With a tracer tool carefully trace the design to the metal, making sure the line can be seen. Fig. 36-2.

Remove the pattern and place foil face down on padding.

8. With the spatula end of the modeling tool, trace the design about 1/32″ inside the line of the original tracing. Fig. 36-3. Work the design from the outline toward the center. Using long sweeping strokes, continue until the design is raised to the proper height.

9. As you work there is a tendency for the background to rise and become distorted. To overcome this, place the metal face side up on a hard surface such as glass, retrace the original design, and flatten the background with the square end of the tool or with a wooden spatula.

10. Place the metal on the pad again face down, and continue with the tooling until the design is raised to the required height. Smooth with wooden spatula, Fig. 36-4.

11. If a background is desired, it may be stippled with a pointed tool, on the top side of the metal. Stamping tools may also be used for this purpose. Fig. 36-5 shows some samples of metal tooling.

37 ▷ Chasing

The process of tooling sheet metal with punches (chasing tools) and a chasing hammer is also referred to as repoussé. Chasing tools look like small punches and cold chisels with blunt, rounded, polished ends and edges. Figs. 37-1 and 37-2. Simple chasing tools may be made from drill rod by rounding off, hardening, and polishing the points. Outlined sections of surfaces may be given emphasis by chasing. This method of decorating the project will improve the final appearance.

Procedure for Chasing on a Wood Block

1. Draw the design and transfer to the sheet metal by using carbon paper.

2. Fasten the metal on a board with escutcheon pins or small screws.

3. In chasing, hold the tool on the metal all the time, even between hammer blows.

4. Move the tool a very small distance toward you on the line, tapping with the hammer.

5. Chase the entire line lightly. Then go over the outline, deepening the grooves a little at a time. Fig. 37-3.

6. Turn the project over and true the design by repeating the operation on the forward side. The background can be worked in with matting tools.

Chasing on Pitch

Chasing large designs is done with the metal mounted on chasing pitch, which can be purchased in bulk, then melted and poured into a pan 1″ or more deep and slightly larger than the metal to be chased.

1. Oil the back side of the sheet and heat both metal and pitch.

2. Press metal slightly into the pitch, oily side down. When both metal and pitch have cooled, the work is ready to be chased.

37-1. Chasing tools.

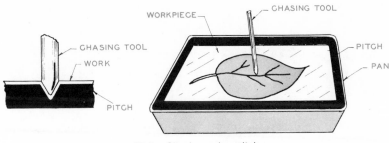

WORKPIECE — CHASING TOOL

CHASING TOOL

WORK

PITCH

PITCH

PAN

37-4. Chasing using pitch.

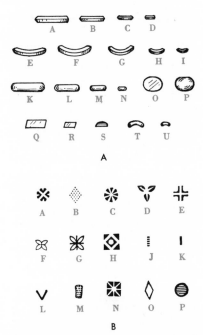

A B C D

E F G H I

K L M N O P

Q R S T U

A

A B C D E

F G H J K

L M N O P

B

37-2. (A) Chasing tool patterns suitable for chasing and repoussé work. (B) Patterns for background work on copper or other soft metals.

3. Place the tool on the outline so that the top is slanting slightly away from you. Fig. 37-4.

4. Tap the tool with the chasing hammer, moving toward you. Movement of the tool should overlap its previous mark.

5. When the design is traced, heat the metal and remove from the pitch. Clean any pitch from the metal with solvent.

6. Oil the raised side of the metal and place this side on the pitch.

7. Work up the design with a round nose and oval chasing tools, within the raised outline on the back side of the design.

8. Work the project on the face side until smooth. Fig. 37-5.

9. Polish with 3/0 steel wool; then color or "antique" the surface by applying black lacquer and sanding as desired. Apply a coat of clear lacquer to prevent tarnishing.

10. The back is filled with plaster of paris, molding clay, cold solder, or paraffin wax.

11. The finished project can be mounted on wood with escutcheon pins. NOTE: A pebble-grain matte board can be used in mounting a foil wall plaque.

37-5. A handmade fork in sterling silver is completely hand chased by a master craftsman to show, in detail, the height and depth of the design.

37-3. Chasing on a wood block.

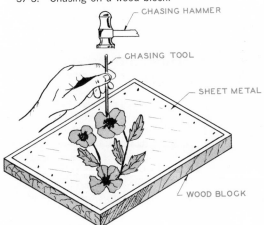

CHASING HAMMER

CHASING TOOL

SHEET METAL

WOOD BLOCK

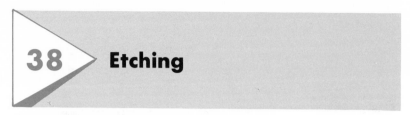

38 ▷ Etching

Etching is a process of applying a reactive solution to the surface of metal to form a design.

Styles of Etching

There are two styles of etching: line and area.

In line etching the complete metal surface is covered with a protective resistant and lines are cut through the resist with a sharp instrument.

Area etching—more often used than line etching—is done by applying a resist to areas that are not to be etched. These areas are in high-relief and the etched background is low-relief.

Materials Used in Etching

Materials often used for chemical resists are asphaltum varnish, acid-resist enamel, stove pipe enamel, lacquer, and—for line etching—beeswax. For straight pattern work, the metal can be covered with masking tape, and the area which is to be etched can be cut away with a sharp knife.

Chemicals used to etch metals are called mordants. Safe commercial non-acid etching mordants can be purchased that do a satisfactory job on aluminum.

For the acid etching of brass, copper, pewter, and other metals Table 38-A can be consulted.

In mixing acid and water—mix the acid into the water in a glass or earthenware jar.

CAUTION: *Always pour acid into the water—never water into the acid!*

Etching Procedure

1. Clean the surface to be etched with fine abrasives or in an acid bath. Do not touch the surface to be etched after it is cleaned. Fingerprints will leave an oily film on the metal and act as a resist.

2. Transfer the design to the metal by tracing on carbon paper. Fig. 38-1. Paint asphaltum varnish on the areas not to be etched by the mordant. NOTE: If the entire project is to be immersed in acid, both surfaces must be covered with resist. Fig. 38-2. Also, cover the edges with two or three coats. If the project is to be a tray or bowl, only the front surface requires painting, as the acid can be poured directly into the tray. Allow to dry for 24 hours.

3. Pour the acid into the project or, if required by the shape, dip the project into the acid with clamps. Inspect the etching frequently. After a few minutes the acid will begin to boil and eat away the unprotected parts of the metal. If the solution boils too fast, dilute it with water. A solution that is too strong raises the edge of the resist.

Break any small bubbles with a pipe cleaner or feather to prevent pitting the metal.

4. When the design has been etched enough, pour off the solution and wash the project in cold, running water until all of the solution has been removed. If the etching is not deep enough, repeat the process. The etching process varies with the strength of the acid. Usually the process requires from 15 to 45 minutes.

38-1. Tracing the design.

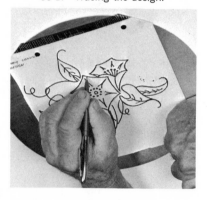

MORDANTS USED FOR ETCHING ART METALS	
Metal	**Mordant**
Aluminum	3 parts water, 1 part hydrochloric acid or commercial mordant
Brass	3 parts water, 1 part nitric acid
Copper	3 parts water, 1 part nitric acid
Monel	1 part nitric, 1 part acetic acid
Nickel silver	3 parts water, 1 part nitric acid
Pewter	3 parts water, 1 part nitric acid
Zinc-base alloy	3 parts water, 1 part nitric acid

Table 38-A.

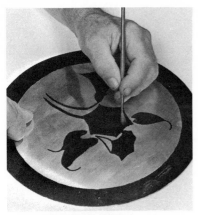

38-2. Cover the background with resist so that the design is etched.

38-3. Cleaning off the resist.

39 ▷ Metal Enameling

Metal enameling is the art of applying a permanent glassy surface. The enamels used are fritted or ground vitreous compounds and colorants which fuse to metals.

Metal enameling is used in industry to add a coating to metal appliances, for appearance and better function. This use ranges from teakettles to refrigerators. Other products such as pins, trays, cuff links, earrings, and bowls are enhanced with enamel. Figs. 39-1 and 39-2.

The permanence and glossy beauty of enameling, plus the speed and ease of applying, make it a favorite with hobbyists and professionals alike. It is an easily acquired skill.

Materials and Tools

Three types of enamels are commonly used: transparent enamels which allow the passage of light, revealing the color or texture of the metal or other enamel underneath; opaque enamels which allow no passage of light; overglazes in liquid form, which are used to paint designs on metal which has been previously enameled.

Although many metals may be enameled, pure copper is the least expensive and most universally used. Copper of 18 gage is recommended. A thinner sheet is more likely to warp; heavier copper is more difficult to form.

Preformed bowls and slightly curved shapes may be purchased, or they may be formed by spinning on a lathe. Fig. 39-3.

An electric enameling kiln or oven that will have a maximum heating temperature of 2,000°F.

5. Remove the asphaltum with turpentine, gasoline, or benzine and wash with soap and hot water. Rinse. Fig. 38-3.

6. Polish the project with 3/0 steel wool. NOTE: A two-tone effect can be obtained by leaving only the etched surface unpolished.

7. If the masking-tape method is used, cover the article with masking tape and transfer the design to the tape. With a sharp knife cut around the area to be exposed, lifting the tape from this section.

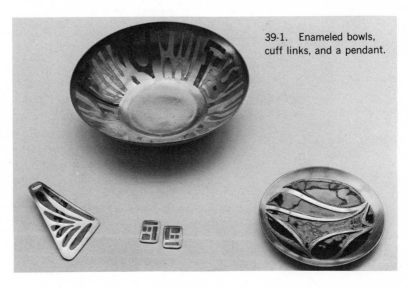

39-1. Enameled bowls, cuff links, and a pendant.

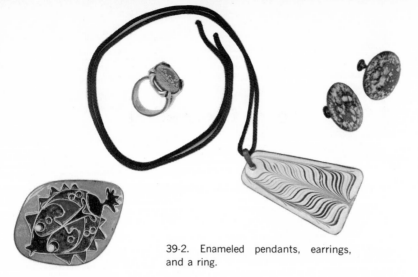

39-2. Enameled pendants, earrings, and a ring.

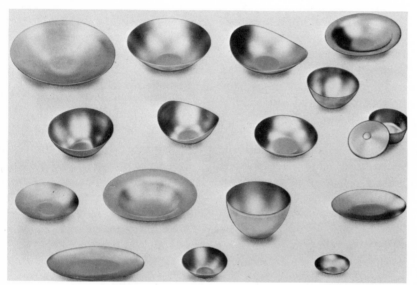

39-3. An assortment of bowls, saucers, and trays made of copper for enameling.

is a requirement for general enameling, Fig. 39-4. A welding torch or gas burner can also be used on small items.

A pickling solution is also a necessity. This can be made by adding one part nitric acid to two parts water.

CAUTION: *Never add water to acid when making this solution.*

An adhesive is necessary to hold the enamel in place before firing in the kiln. It can be made from 1 part of powdered gum tragacanth mixed in 2 parts of alcohol. Or use a commercial gum solution, gum arabic, or lavender oil.

Other materials needed include:
Refractory blocks
Nichrome wire
80 mesh sifters
Enameling forks
Enameling racks
Kiln shelves
No. 3/0 steel wool.
See Fig. 39-5.

Enameling Procedure

1. Check firing equipment. Understand its operation, possibilities, and limitations.

39-4. Metal enameling kiln with pyrometer which indicates temperatures.

39-5. (A) Refractory blocks and wire, (B) atomizer, (C) brushes, (D) carborundum hand stone, (E) water applicator, (F) spatula, (G) sifter, (H, I, J, K) trivets, (L) silver solder, (M) pyrometer, (N) enameling tools.

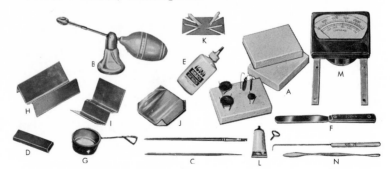

2. Pre-heat the kiln to 1,500° F. Time required depends upon the size and type of kiln. Firing chamber when ready will appear orange yellow. Clean all impurities from the metal. Fig. 39-6. Place in the kiln for a few seconds to burn off the grease coating, Fig. 39-7, and then clean in acid pickling solution. Fig. 39-8. Rinse the cleaned copper thoroughly in running water. Wear rubber gloves to avoid finger marks. Fig. 39-9.

3. Spray or dust a thin coat of adhesive solution over the clean metal surface to be enameled. Fig. 39-10.

4. Place the project on a clean, dry sheet of smooth paper.

5. With an 80-mesh screen basket or shaker-top jar, dust on a fine, uniform coat of dry enamel. Fig. 39-11. (Figs. 39-11, 12, 13 on next page.) Tap the screen gently, beginning at the edge and working around the piece toward the center until the surface is completely covered and no metal shows through. To avoid finger marks, touch only the edges or handle with a paper towel, cloth, or rubber gloves. Pour excess enamel back into the jar.

6. If lavender oil has been used as a base, the piece may be fired immediately. As the oil burns off, the piece will smoke or flame briefly soon after it is placed in the kiln. If gum solution has been used, overspray the piece with the solution to hold the enamel particles in place. Fig. 39-12.

7. Lift the article into the kiln with a wide spatula. Fig. 39-13. Bare metal can be placed directly on the enameling rack. Pieces enameled on both sides

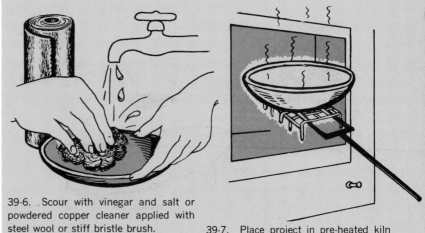

39-6. Scour with vinegar and salt or powdered copper cleaner applied with steel wool or stiff bristle brush.

39-7. Place project in pre-heated kiln to burn off grease or oil.

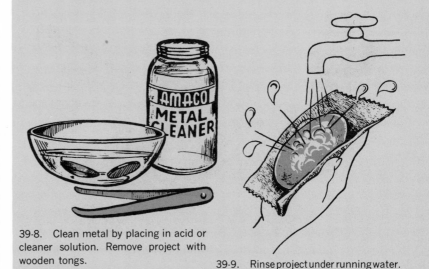

39-8. Clean metal by placing in acid or cleaner solution. Remove project with wooden tongs.

39-9. Rinse project under running water. To avoid finger marks, hold with clean cloth or paper towel.

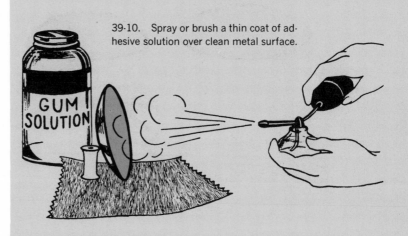

39-10. Spray or brush a thin coat of adhesive solution over clean metal surface.

161

39-11. Dust on a fine, uniform coat of dry enamel. Tap screen gently.

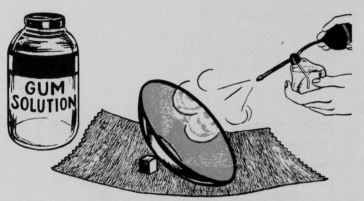

39-12. If gum solution has been used, overspray the piece lightly to hold enamel particles in place. If lavender oil is used as a base, the piece may be fired immediately.

39-13. Sift the dry enameled piece into the kiln with a wide-blade spatula or firing holder.

39-14. Universal trivets can be easily fastened on the surface of the firing rack and are adjustable.

must be supported on metal trivets, Fig. 39-14; on tiny wire prongs; on star stilts, Fig. 39-15; or in special holders, Fig. 39-16. Most holders are placed on racks for easy lifting in and out of the kiln.

CAUTION: *An enameled surface will adhere to anything it touches during firing.*

8. Check after the first minute, then at 15 second intervals. In 2 or 3 minutes both enamel and the copper piece will be a rosy red color; the enamel will melt and become smooth and glistening.

9. Remove the piece at once from the kiln when the enamel looks shiny and glossy. If the surface is still rough return to the kiln and fire a little longer.

10. Place the article and rack on a sheet of asbestos or on a transite board to cool.

11. Remove oxidation with emery, crocus cloth, or steel wool. Dip in pickling solution. You can add more color or interest by applying adhesive again and then applying a different colored enamel or bits of copper, glass, or thread, before applying more enamel. Consult your teacher.

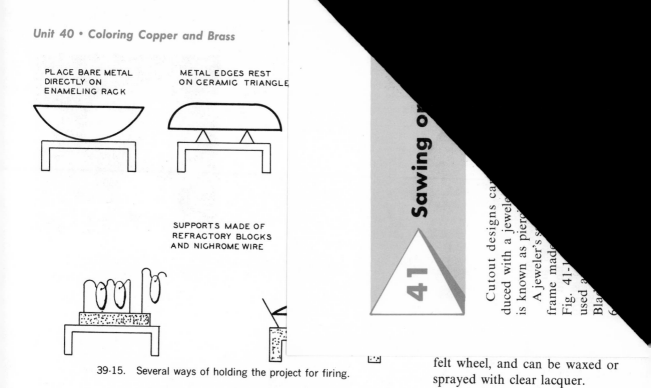

PLACE BARE METAL DIRECTLY ON ENAMELING RACK

METAL EDGES REST ON CERAMIC TRIANGLE

SUPPORTS MADE OF REFRACTORY BLOCKS AND NICHROME WIRE

39-15. Several ways of holding the project for firing.

felt wheel, and can be waxed or sprayed with clear lacquer.

40 ▷ Coloring Copper and Brass

Color adds to the beauty of projects.

Coloring Copper

Before using chemical solutions, clean the base metal thoroughly. The formulas used here were furnished by the Copper and Brass Research Association:

Light to dark brown. Mix:
A solution of
copper sulphate 4 oz.
Potassium chlorate 8 oz.
Water 1 gal.

The depth of color will depend upon how long the project is immersed in this solution. Generally it is immersed from 5 to 10 seconds at 100°F. Then rinse in cold water and dry by air blast, using a hand bellows or air hose.

The surface of copper may also be colored by applying *heat*.

1. Clean the surface of the metal.

2. Apply heat evenly with a blow pipe or alcohol torch.

3. The colors appear in this order: orange-red, red, blue-purple, yellow, dark-red, deep purple, rainbow colors, and chestnut brown.

4. Withdraw heat when the desired color is obtained.

Coloring Brass

To obtain light brown color.

Mix:
Copper sulphate
crystal 4 oz.
Potassium
chlorate 8 oz.
Water 1 gal.

The project is immersed in this solution at room temperature. When the desired color is obtained, it is removed and dried. The formula will produce a variety of brown colors.

Deep blue. Mix:
Sodium
thiosulfate 8 oz.
Lead acetate 4 oz.
Water 1 gal.

At a boiling temperature, immerse until the desired color is produced.

To complete the project, coat with nitrocellulose lacquer by spraying or brushing. Careful spraying will produce a better finish.

163

Piercing

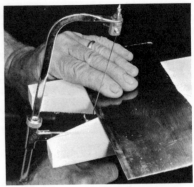

41-2.　Hold the workpiece firmly.

...n be pro-
...er's saw. This
...ng.
...aw has a U-shaped
... in different depths.
... The most commonly
...re the 2½″ and 5″ frames.
...des come in sizes from No.
...0, which is very small, to No. 14,
which is about ¹/₁₆″ wide. Use
the type of blade suitable for the
job to be done. For light work a
No. 2/0 or No. 1/0 can be used.
For cutting heavier metal, a No. 1
or No. 2 will be more satisfactory.

How to Use the Jeweler's Saw

1. Fasten the blade in the
frame with the teeth pointing
toward the handle. NOTE: This is
the reverse of inserting a blade
in a hacksaw.

2. Fasten a V-cutting block
in a vise or onto a bench. The
block should be at the proper
height for cutting while you are
seated.

3. Place the metal so that the
cutting can be done in the V
part of the block. Fig. 41-2.

4. Apply a little soap or wax
to the blade. The saw will cut
easier. Start sawing in the waste
stock, working up to the layout
line. The cutting is done on the
down stroke of the saw.

Do not force the blade around
a sharp corner, as these blades
are easily broken.

5. Follow the outside of the
layout line carefully. If it is necessary to back out of the saw

kerf, continue moving the blade
up and down while removing it.

6. File the edges of the work.

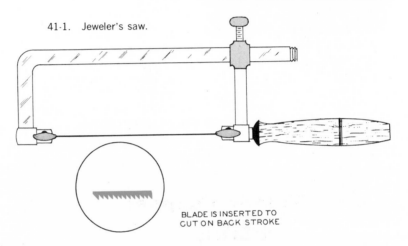

41-1.　Jeweler's saw.

BLADE IS INSERTED TO
CUT ON BACK STROKE

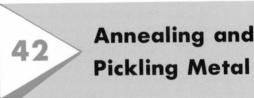

42 ▷ Annealing and Pickling Metal

When metals are being formed
they have a tendency to work-
harden. They must be softened
by annealing. Annealing is done
by heating the metal slightly
above the recrystallization temperature and then cooling.

Metal when being formed also
accumulates dirt and oxide, so
cleaning in an acid bath becomes
necessary. Annealing and pickling
are done at the same time during
forming operations.

Annealing temperatures for art
metals are given in Table 42-A.

METAL	Annealing Temperature
Aluminum 2S	650°F.
3S	750°F.
52S	650°F.
Brass	1100°F.
Copper	1100-1300°F.
Jeweler's bronze	1100-1300°F.
Nickel silver (65-18)	1100°F.
Sterling silver	1100-1500°F.
Zinc-base alloys	250-270°F.

Table 42-A.

Annealing Procedure

Art metals can be heated for annealing in a soldering furnace, or with a gas torch or surface burner such as a gas stove plate. Hold the metal with tongs; heat slowly and evenly.

1. For copper and a simple alloy such as brass, heat the metal to a dark red color.

2. Apply heat slowly and evenly to bring the metal up to annealing temperature. If annealing aluminum, touch it with a piece of white pine. When the pine leaves a brown char mark, remove the metal from the heat and cool at room temperature.

3. After copper and brass have reached the correct annealing temperature, remove the piece with tongs and plunge in clear, cool water.

Pickling

A pickling solution can be made with 1 part sulphuric acid and 9 parts water.

Pickling solutions must always be mixed in acid-proof containers.

Caution: *Always pour the acid into the water slowly!*

To mix the solution, secure a glass or earthenware container large enough to hold the project.

Pour the water into the container and add acid to the water slowly. Mix the solution with a stick as you are adding the acid. This will prevent the mixture from overheating.

Caution: Goggles should be worn to protect the eyes.

Handle the metal with tongs made of copper or plastic. Dip the article into the solution and allow to stay 5 to 10 minutes. Wash in water before drying in clean sawdust or with paper towels. *Do not touch the project with fingers before applying the finish.*

43 ▷ Soldering Art Metal Projects

In some instances special techniques are necessary in soldering such metals as britannia metal, silver, and aluminum.

Britannia metal is difficult to solder for the average beginner due to the low melting point of this metal. An ordinary bunsen burner, alcohol torch, or small gas torch may be used. Britannia metal should never be soldered by using a soldering copper. The concentration of heat caused by touching the point of the copper to the britannia metal will melt a hole through the metal.

A type of solder known as 60-40, which contains 60 parts of tin and 40 parts of lead should be used. This type of solder has a low melting point which is necessary for soldering britannia.

A flux made up of glycerine with about 10 drops of hydrochloric acid added to each ounce is used.

To solder two parts together— coat the seam with a liberal amount of flux and place snippets of solder along the joint with a tweezer or small brush. Fig. 43-1.

Pass the flame back and forth along the joint. Keep the flame moving constantly. If allowed to stay in one spot for even an instant the metal is likely to melt.

It is important that the proper type of flux be selected for all metals used in art metal work. Aluminum requires a special type of flux. The other art metals can be fluxed with muriatic acid, rosin, or a paste type flux.

Art metal projects that have spouts and handles that require soldering can be held together with black iron oxide wire as shown in Fig. 43-2. See illustration which appears on the following page.

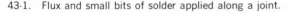
43-1. Flux and small bits of solder applied along a joint.

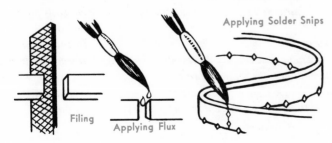
Applying Solder Snips

Filing

Applying Flux

43-2. Parts held together with black iron oxide wire while being soldered.

Check Your Knowledge

1. Where was copper discovered?

2. What tools were used by early craftsmen in shaping metals?

3. What is a forming hammer?

4. What are mallets used for in art metalwork?

5. Name some of the uses of art metal stakes.

6. In what three ways can metal be shaped into trays, plates, and bowls?

7. Describe the simplest method of forming a plate.

8. Why is it necessary to anneal the metal during the forming process?

9. What is a form block?

10. What is the purpose of the two guide pins?

11. What causes a plate to become out of shape during the forming process?

12. Name two types of form blocks.

13. What thickness of metal is commonly used for small projects? For large projects?

14. What does the term "work-harden" mean?

15. What is raising?

16. What kind of stake and hammer are required in raising a bowl?

17. Name two common methods in raising a bowl.

18. How is the size of material determined in raising a bowl?

19. How can irregularities be smoothed out after shaping?

20. What is planishing?

21. What type of stake is used in planishing?

22. Describe the method of laying out a decoration that is to be repeated around the edge.

23. How can flutes be made on an edge?

24. What is doming?

25. What is a dapping block?

26. Describe the process of overlaying.

27. What is metal tooling?

28. Name the types of metal best suited for metal tooling.

29. Name the tools required for this process.

30. What type of padding is needed?

31. How is background raised?

32. What is meant by chasing?

33. Describe the process of etching a design on metal.

34. What is resist and how can it be applied?

35. Explain the difference between line etching and area etching.

36. What is a mordant?

37. What safety precautions should be observed in handling mordants?

38. Why is it necessary to clean the metal thoroughly?

39. Can the same mordants be used for all metals?

40. What is enameling?

41. Why must an adhesive be used in enameling? Describe two types and their characteristics.

42. What is a trivet and how is it used?

43. How is enamel applied to the project?

44. What is meant by the term oxidation?

45. What is the purpose of coloring the project?

46. How can the finish be preserved?

47. Why is it necessary to anneal and pickle nonferrous metal?

48. What is a pickling solution?

49. Why is a flux used?

50. Why is it important to select the right type of flux?

51. How is solder applied?

Terms to Know and Spell

embossing	*kiln*	*metal tooling*
chasing	*gum arabic*	*metal foil*
planishing hammer	*trivet*	*spatula*
work-hardened	*patina colors*	*chasing pitch*
anneal	*saw kerf*	*etching*
pickle	*flux*	*metal enameling*
concentric lines	*flutes*	*refractory block*
appendages	*domes*	*nichrome wire*
pitch block	*scallops*	*oxidation*
mordants	*dapping block*	*snippets*

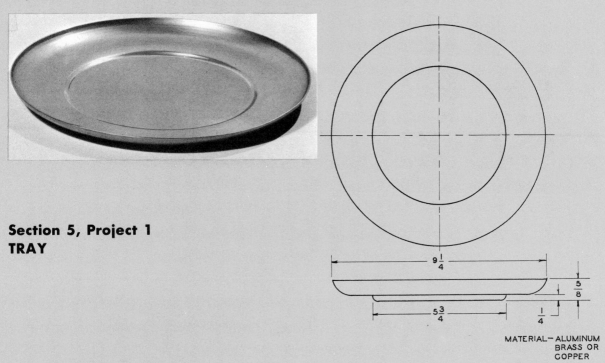

Section 5, Project 1
TRAY

MATERIAL— ALUMINUM
BRASS OR
COPPER

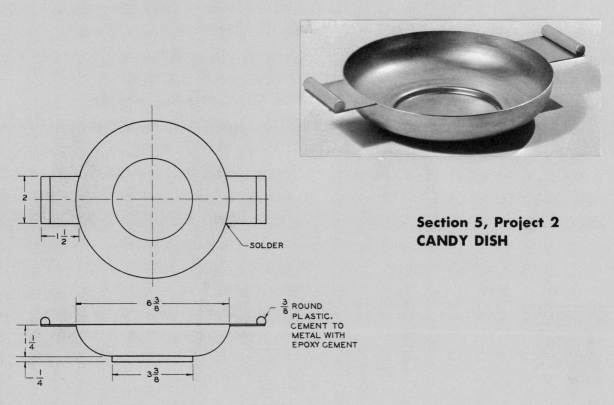

SOLDER

Section 5, Project 2
CANDY DISH

$\frac{3}{8}$ ROUND
PLASTIC.
CEMENT TO
METAL WITH
EPOXY CEMENT

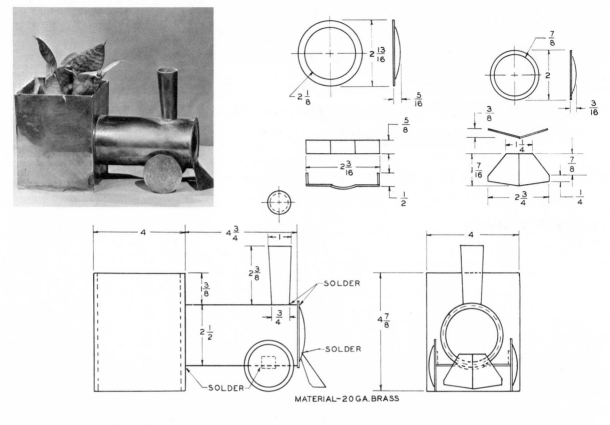

Section 5, Project 3—LOCOMOTIVE PLANTER

SOLDER

SOLDER

SOLDER

MATERIAL—20 GA. BRASS

Section 5, Project 4—SUGGESTIONS FOR METAL ENAMEL PENDANTS

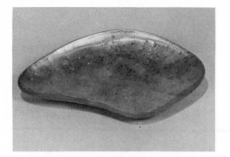

Section 5, Project 5
A FREE FORM
ASH TRAY

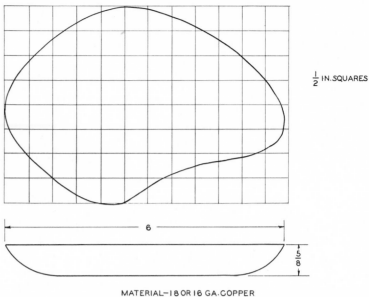

$\frac{1}{2}$ IN. SQUARES

6

$\frac{5}{8}$

MATERIAL—18 OR 16 GA. COPPER

Section 5,
Project 6
LETTER
OPENER

$\frac{5}{8}$

$\frac{1}{2}$

$3\frac{5}{8}$

$8\frac{3}{8}$

$\frac{15}{16}$

A

$\frac{3}{4}$

$\frac{1}{4}$

$\frac{1}{2}$

$\frac{1}{8}$ R

A

$\frac{3}{8}$

SECTION A A

MAKE HANDLE IN TWO PIECES
REGESS FOR THE BLADE
GLUE TOGETHER

Section 5, Project 7
PUNCH LADLE

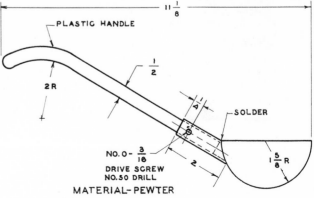

$11\frac{1}{8}$

PLASTIC HANDLE

$\frac{1}{2}$

2 R

$\frac{1}{4}$

SOLDER

NO. 0 - $\frac{3}{16}$
DRIVE SCREW
NO. 50 DRILL

2

$1\frac{5}{8}$ R

MATERIAL—PEWTER

169

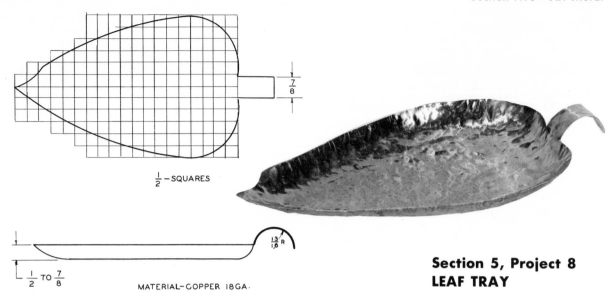

$\frac{1}{2}$ − SQUARES

$\frac{7}{8}$

$\frac{13}{16}$ R

$\frac{1}{2}$ TO $\frac{7}{8}$

MATERIAL—COPPER 18GA.

Section 5, Project 8
LEAF TRAY

Section 5, Project 9
ANGEL FISH PLAQUE

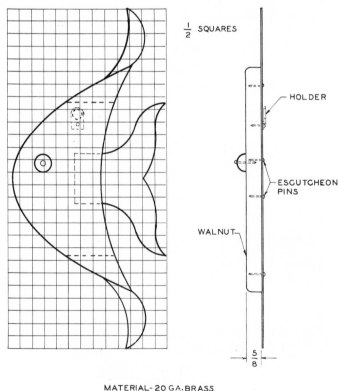

$\frac{1}{2}$ SQUARES

HOLDER

ESCUTCHEON PINS

WALNUT

$\frac{5}{8}$

MATERIAL—20 GA. BRASS
WALNUT

$\frac{1}{2}$ SIZE

Sheet Metal

BENDING is basic to most sheet metalwork. During the bending operation the outside surface is stretched while that on the inside of the bend is compressed. To avoid breakage or severe strain, a larger radius must be used, or the alloy

or temper of the metal must be changed to provide material with better bending characteristics.

In school, you will learn the fundamentals of sheet metalwork, consisting of learning to cut, form, shape, and assemble typical projects.

It is not only important for the sheet metalworker to know the tools and machines of the trade but also to know the materials that are used. Using the wrong type of material for a project can make it practically useless. Another important aspect is work safety.

Materials Used in Sheet Metalwork

44

In industry, operations such as bending, rolling, flanging, and beading are performed on heavy machines, as shown in Figs. 44-1 and 44-2. The most widely used materials in sheet metalwork are metal sheets, wire, band iron, and angle iron. The sheets may be plain, ribbed, or corrugated. They are made of such materials as galvanized iron, black iron, tin plate, copper, aluminum, monel metal, and stainless steel.

Galvanized Iron

This is a traditional name for soft *steel* which is coated with molten zinc to resist corrosion and to improve its appearance. The zinc coating helps to prevent oxidation. It also helps make soldering easier.

Galvanized iron is used for gutter work, furnaces and air conditioners, ventilators, tanks, guards, and similar structures.

The zinc coating is applied in several different ways, the most common being the hot dip process. Annealed sheets are cleaned and pickled in acid. The sheets are then dipped into a bath of molten zinc to reduce flaking when subjected to some types of forming operations.

Galvanized sheet steel ("iron") is sold in a variety of sizes and gages as shown in Table 44-A.

STANDARD GAGE AND WEIGHT OF GALVANIZED SHEET STEEL

U.S. gage	Thickness in inches (approximate)	Weight in lbs. per . sq. ft.
10	.1345	5.781
12	.1046	4.531
14	..0747	3.281
16	.0598	2.656
18	.0478	2.156
20	.0359	1.656
22	.0299	1.406
24	.0239	1.156
26	.0179	0.906
28	.0149	0.781
30	.0120	0.656

Table 44-A.

Tin Plate

Tin plate is made by coating iron sheets with pure tin. The coating has different thicknesses. Sheets with a light coating of tin up to 2 lbs. per base box are called coke tin plate. Plates with a heavier coating, up to 7 lbs. per base box, are called charcoal tin plates. Plates with a coating of 7 to 14 lbs. per base box are called dairy plate.

The weight of coating has reference to the lbs. of coating for one box of 112 14″x20″ sheets.

44-1.   Forming sheets for corrugating in a heavy press.

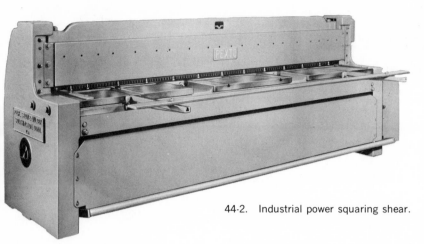

44-2. Industrial power squaring shear.

long-lasting roofing material or for containers and ducts that demand resistance to corrosion. The metal is easily fabricated because of its malleability.

Aluminum

Sheet aluminum has become popular in sheet metalwork. The sheets may be purchased in sizes such as 36″ x 96″ or 48″ x 144″ as well as in bundles containing a variety of sizes. The thickness is usually specified in decimals and gage numbers, based on the Brown & Sharpe table.

Because aluminum is a rust-proof metal, is light, and has long-wearing qualities, it is used for utensils, boats, other industrial products, gutters, flashing, roofing materials, and as house siding.

Tin plate is identified by trade symbols as IC, IX, or by the total weight of the sheets in a base box. Table 44-B gives the data on various grades.

Galvannealed Iron

Galvannealed steel ("iron") has a dull, bonded, zinc surface which takes and holds paints. This metal is easy to form and bend. The coating does not peel or crack and the metal is easily soldered. The gages, weights, and sizes of the sheets are the same as for galvanized steel.

Zinc

Zinc is made in the same gages, weights, and sizes as other metal

sheets. Care has to be taken in bending, as a sharp bend can cause the metal to crack. It is largely used for coating purposes, similar to galvanizing.

Black Iron Sheets

These are uncoated sheets rolled from iron or soft steel of low carbon content.

Black iron sheets are used for pans, cabinets, hoods, safety guards, tanks, and other jobs that are to be given a coat of paint or enameled.

Sheet Copper

Sheet copper is high in cost but is used in certain types of sheet metalwork. It may be selected as

Stainless Steel

Stainless steel has a high percentage of chromium. Stainless sheets are sold in any gage and can be formed, bent, drilled, or sawed in the same manner as other steel. This type of steel has a higher tensile strength and hardness than ordinary steel, therefore is harder to work.

Stainless steel is used for utensils, sinks, and other products that require strength, hardness, beauty, and resistance to corrosion.

TIN PLATE

Base weight in lbs.	Trade symbol	Approximate U.S. gage	Approximate thickness in inches	Weight, lbs. per sq. ft.
100	ICL	30.5	.0113	.459
107	IC	30	.0120	.491
128	IXL	29	.0144	.588
135	IX	28	.0152	.620
155	2X	27	.0175	.712
175	3X	26	.0197	.804
195	4X	25	.0220	.895
215	5X	24	.0246	.987

Table 44-B.

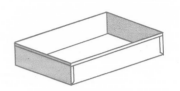

45

Sheet Metal Pattern Development

Sheet metalwork requires a knowledge of pattern development and drawing, which includes applying principles of geometrical construction.

An example of a simple layout for a box is shown in Fig. 45-1. To make this proceed as follows:

1. Draw a square or rectangle equal to the size of the bottom of the box.

2. Draw the two sides and the ends.

3. Draw the hems and seams.

4. Indicate where the metal is to be bent by making small X's on the bend lines.

In developing a pattern, allowances have to be made for hems, edges, and seams.

A *hem* is a folded edge used to increase the strength of the work, eliminate sharpness, and also to improve the appearance of the project. A single hem may be made any width depending upon the gage of the metal and the requirements of the job to be done. A double hem is used when additional strength is required. Fig. 45-2. Sizes of hems may vary from ¼″ for a small shop project to from ⅜″ to ¾″ for an industrial product.

A wired *edge*, Fig. 45-2, is formed on such articles as funnels, pails, cups, and trays. An allowance of 2½ times the diameter has to be made as shown in Fig. 45-3. If a wire of ⅛″ diameter is used, then ⁵⁄₁₆″ must be allowed for it in the metal.

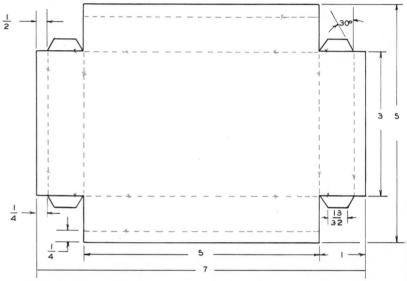

45-1. Planning for a metal utility box is an example of parallel line development

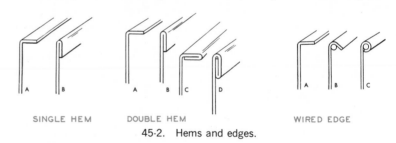

SINGLE HEM   DOUBLE HEM   WIRED EDGE

45-2. Hems and edges.

45-3. Typical allowances for a single hem, double hem, and wired edge.

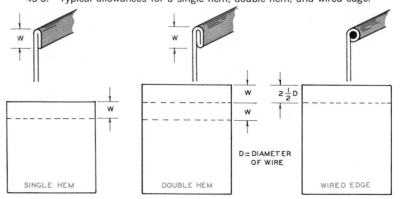

D = DIAMETER OF WIRE

SINGLE HEM   DOUBLE HEM   WIRED EDGE

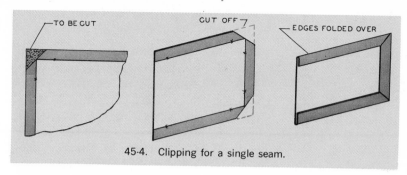

45-4. Clipping for a single seam.

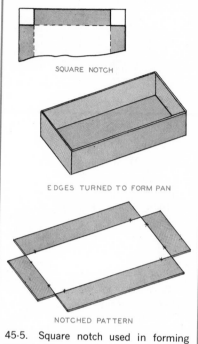

45-5. Square notch used in forming pans and boxes.

Seams are used to join sheet metal. These will be explained in Unit 50.

Laying Out the Pattern

The pattern consists of a layout or "stretchout" of the project, to be used later in cutting pieces. This pattern may be made of paper or metal. If several duplicate pieces are required, as in production work, it is customary to lay out the pattern on metal because metal patterns retain their shape and can be used for an indefinite period. A metal pattern is known as a master pattern or template.

The ability to visualize the finished job from a flat layout is one of the requirements of a good sheet metalworker. NOTE: It is well for an inexperienced person to draw all layouts on paper first so they can be checked for errors before transferring to metal.

Paper patterns can be laid out on heavy drawing paper and the outline cut to shape. Accuracy in laying out the pattern is very important, as you can see.

Under average school conditions, a *prick punch* is used to mark where metal is to be bent and where holes are to be drilled or punched. A *scratch awl* or scriber is used to mark the cutting lines when transferring the pattern to the metal.

Notching and Clipping

Overlapping seams are eliminated by notching and clipping the places where the seams cross. Fig. 45-4. The raw edges are wired.

The square notch, Fig. 45-5, is used on boxes so the corners fit together neatly. Notches eliminate excess material that would make the project bulky. The size of the notch is determined by the bend lines.

The 45° notch is used when double seaming the ends of articles such as pans, or when making a 90° bend on a project with an inside flange, as shown in Fig. 45-6.

45-6. Method of laying out notches. (A) Unshaded area is cut out to make possible the bending of the sheet metal to form an outside corner. (B) A 45° notch is used when making a 90° bend on any job with an inside flange. (C) Straight cut for outside flange. (D) In places where wired edges cross seams, the pattern is notched to prevent material from overlapping.

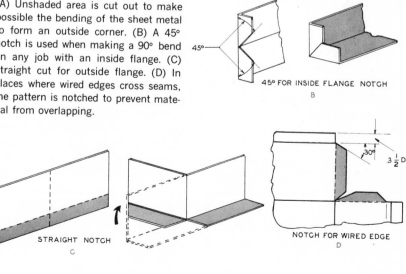

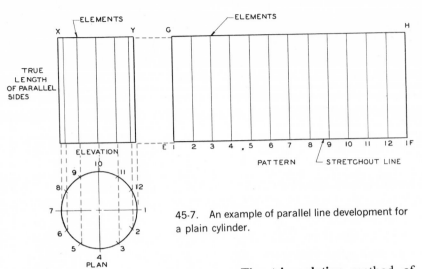

45-7. An example of parallel line development for a plain cylinder.

Developing a Pattern for a Plain Cylinder

The following steps can be used in the development of patterns by the parallel line method.

1. Draw the plan and elevation views as shown in Fig. 45-7. These views are clearly indicated. The elevation is the view that indicates the height of the object. Draw this view first. It should be drawn so that it shows the true length of the parallel sides.

2. Draw the plan view next below the elevation view.

3. Divide the plan view into any number of equal parts. The greater the number the more accurate the pattern will be. In Fig. 45-7, twelve divisions were used for this reason.

4. Draw the stretchout line for the pattern at right angles to the vertical lines in the elevation.

5. Set the dividers at the same distances as used in the plan view and step off the same number of spaces.

6. Draw the elements for the pattern at right angles to the stretchout line.

7. Obtain the true elements or lengths from the elevation view and draw these on the stretchout line at right angles. Connect these points with line GH. The elements for a plain cylinder shown in Fig. 45-7 are all the same length.

Developing a Pattern for a Pipe Cut at an Angle

Fig. 45-8 shows the method most commonly used for developing a pattern for a pipe cut at an angle. The following procedure can be used.

1. Draw the elevation view first. The sides should represent

When a single seam meets at right angles, the pattern is clipped at a 45° angle, as shown in Fig. 45-6. Other angles may be used depending upon the shape of the pattern. A combination of notches on some patterns may have to be used to obtain the necessary fit.

Types of Patterns

There are four types of pattern development used in the sheet metal trade.

● **Straight-line** or **angular** development. Used in making such projects as trays, boxes, and other containers.

● **Parallel-line** development. This method is used for products having parallel sides such as cylinders, squares, elbows, rectangles, offsets, and T-joints.

● **Radial-line** development. Since a great many projects do not have parallel sides, methods other than the parallel method must be used to develop products having tapered sides such as pails, funnels, tapered pipe, or flaring pans. The basic shapes usually take the form of cones, pyramids or frustums.

● The **triangulation** method of development is used for products with non-parallel sides. This consists of dividing the surface of a view into triangles, finding the true lengths of the slant lines that make up cuts for forming, and laying out each part one at a time.

To develop a pattern by this method, three steps have to be followed: (1) Construction of the plan view or elevation, (2) development of true lengths, and (3) layout of the pattern.

Developing Parallel-line Patterns

The parallel-line method of development for sheet metal projects is extensively used because many articles have parallel sides. In parallel-line development, all measuring lines and edges are perpendicular to the stretchout line and parallel to each other. Since the edges are parallel to the front plane, true lengths are always shown in the front view. Planes may be represented as flat sheets of paper, marked off horizontally. Holding a sheet of paper at right angles to this sheet represents the vertical plane.

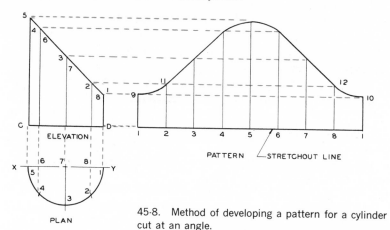

45-8. Method of developing a pattern for a cylinder cut at an angle.

the true lengths of the longest and shortest elements.

2. The pipe is cut at a 45° angle. Draw this line.

3. Draw the line CD in the view equal to the diameter of the pipe.

4. Scribe an arc forming a half circle, as the plan view. Divide this half circle into any number of equal parts and number as shown. Four parts will be sufficient, as shown in the drawing.

5. Project the lines called "elements" to the elevation and number as shown.

6. Draw the stretchout line to the right of the elevation by projecting line CD. Step off eight spaces, each equal to one of the spaces in the half circle, which will give the correct length of the stretchout line. Number each space as shown.

7. Project dotted lines at right angles to the parallel sides of the elevation view from point 1 in the elevation. Project lines 2, 3, 4, and 5 in the same manner.

8. At their corresponding point of intersection with the elements, connect the points of intersection of these lines to complete the pattern.

Intersection of Cylinders

The method of numbering the elements in the plan view is important in the development of patterns for intersecting cylinders.

1. Draw the elevation (A), making both cylinders the same size. Use any convenient length. Do not draw the miter lines at this time. Fig. 45-9.

2. Draw the plan views (B) and (C). Divide into equal spaces and number them as shown. For simplicity, only one-quarter of the eight spaces are numbered in the plan view (B). However, the other views are numbered in the same manner.

3. From the numbered parts in plan (C), project broken lines at right angles to the side of the vertical cylinder.

4. Project dotted lines from the numbered points in plan (B) parallel to the sides of the vertical cylinder to intersect the broken line drawn from (C). Mark the points of intersection and connect these points to form the miter line.

5. Draw stretchout lines at right angles to the sides of cylinder. Mark off eight spaces. Number the same as shown in plan view (C).

45-9. Intersection of cylinders. Development of a pattern for a T joint of 90°.

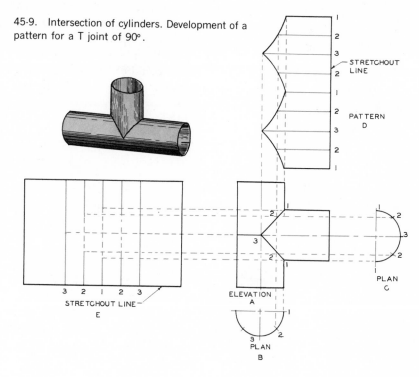

6. The opening for the vertical cylinder is developed by drawing a stretchout line at right angles to the side of the cylinder. Locate the center of this line.

7. Mark off two spaces on each side, equal to one of the spaces in plan (B). This is the length of the opening. Number to correspond with plan (B). Draw elements at right angles to the stretchout line.

8. True lengths can be found by projecting lines from numbered points in the elevation to intersect elements just drawn.

9. Mark the points of intersection. Draw a curved line connecting these points with an irregular curve.

Developing Patterns
FOR SQUARE OR RECTANGULAR PIPE CUT AT VARIOUS ANGLES

1. Draw line XY. Draw lines XC and YD at right angles to line XY. Fig. 45-10.

2. On line XC measure the length of the pipe.

3. From points C and D draw 45° angles.

4. Below the elevation view and parallel to line CD, draw

line EF. Project line from C and D intersecting line EF, forming one side of a rectangle. Complete rectangle to form plan view.

5. Draw the stretchout line. Set dividers equal to line CD and lay out four sides on the stretchout line as shown in the pattern.

6. Draw elements 1, 3, 4, 6, and 1 of the same length as the line YD and at right angles to the stretchout line.

7. Extend broken lines from K to points M and N. From 2 and 5 draw dotted lines 2M and 5N at right angles to the stretchout line. Draw lines 1M, 3M, 4N, and 6N at 45° angles to complete the pattern.

Radial Line Development
DEVELOPING A PATTERN FOR A RIGHT CONE FRUSTUM

1. Draw the elevation ABC with frustum line parallel to BC, Fig. 45-11. Using the base BC of the triangle as a diameter, draw a circle and divide it into any number of equal parts.

2. With A as a center and a radius equal to AC, scribe an arc of indefinite length. Draw arc HI.

3. Set the dividers to equal one of the spaces in the plan view.

4. Starting at any point on the large arc, mark spaces equal to twice the number in the plan view. The stretchout will then be equal to the circumference of the base of the cone. Number as shown and draw lines IG and HF, completing the pattern.

Triangulation Method of Development
TRANSITION OF SQUARE TO ROUND

There are three important steps in the development of patterns by the triangulation method: (1) Construction of the plan or elevation, (2) development of true lengths, (3) layout of the pattern.

45-11. Radial line development. Developing pattern from the frustum of a right cone cut parallel to base.

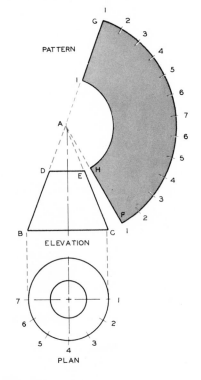

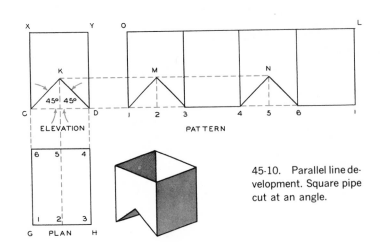

45-10. Parallel line development. Square pipe cut at an angle.

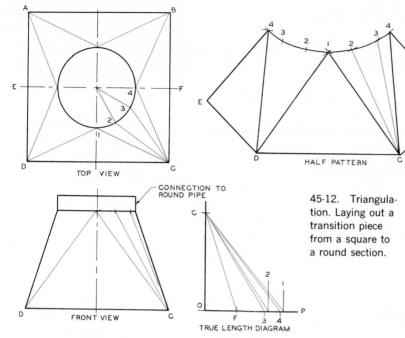

TOP VIEW

HALF PATTERN

CONNECTION TO
ROUND PIPE

FRONT VIEW

TRUE LENGTH DIAGRAM

45-12. Triangulation. Laying out a transition piece from a square to a round section.

1. Draw front and top views as shown in Fig. 45-12. Divide one-fourth of the circle into any number of equal parts.

2. From point C draw a line to each point on the circle as represented by C1, C2, C3, and C4.

3. Draw a true length diagram as shown. Line OP is drawn of indefinite length and the verti-

cal line CO is equal to the height of the transition piece as shown in the front view.

4. Using O as a center and F4, C1, C3, and C4 on the top view as radii, construct arcs intersecting the line OP at F, 1, 2, 3, and 4. These points are connected to C. The lengths correspond to lines in the top view.

5. Draw line DC as a base for the half pattern and using CF, C4, C3, C2, and C1 as radii, draw arcs of indefinite lengths.

6. With points 1, 2, and 3 on the half pattern as centers and distances 1-2, 2-3, and 3-4 of the top view as radii, draw arcs at D2, D3, D4 and C2, C3, C4. Connect the intersecting arcs at 4, 3, 2, 1. 1, 2, 3, and 4 with a line. Draw lines D4, D1, C1, and C4.

7. With D and C as centers of the half pattern and CF of the top view as a radius, draw arcs of indefinite length. With C and 4 on the half pattern as centers and CF from the true length diagram as a radius, draw arcs to intersect lines DE, E4, CF, and F4.

46 ▷ Cutting Sheet Metal

Squaring shears are used to cut large sheets of metal into smaller pieces. After suitable sizes are obtained and the layout made for the project, hand snips can be employed to cut the sheet metal into the sizes called for by the pattern.

Cutting Sheet Metal With Hand Snips

• **Straight snips** are used for cutting straight lines in different sizes from 2″ to 4½″. They will cut sheet metal 22 gage or thinner. Fig. 46-1 (A). (See next page.)

• **Double cutting snips** are for cutting light gage sheet metal pipe. Fig. 46-1 (B).

• **Hawk-bill snips** make curved cuts; therefore they have narrow curved blades. Fig. 46-2.

• **Aviation snips** are used for cutting compound curves and intricate designs. They cut right, left, or universal. Fig. 46-3.

• **Circular cutting snips** are designed especially for cutting out intricate patterns and curves. They cut smoothly and leave the metal unbent. Fig. 46-4.

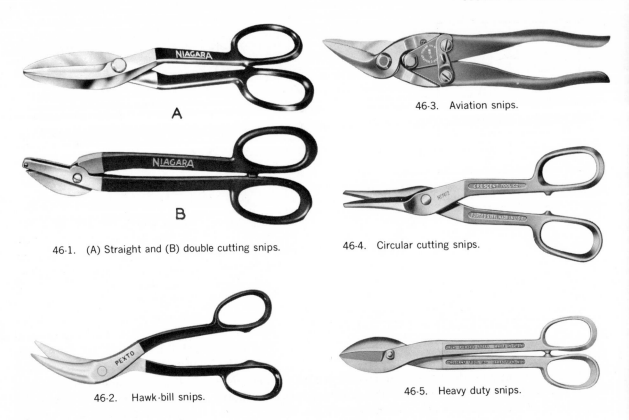

46-3.   Aviation snips.

A

46-1.   (A) Straight and (B) double cutting snips.

B

46-4.   Circular cutting snips.

46-2.   Hawk-bill snips.

46-5.   Heavy duty snips.

● **Heavy duty snips,** Fig. 46-5, are used for extra heavy cutting jobs. Cut curves as well as straight lines.

Cutting Straight and Curved Lines

Sharp snips are necessary in cutting sheet metal. When snips become dull they can be sharpened on a grinding wheel. The blades should be taken apart and ground to an included angle of 85°. In reassembling, adjust the blade tension by turning the nut on the pivot bolt till just tight enough to remain at a set position when opened.

1. Select the proper type snips for the job to be done.

2. Open the snips as far as possible to make long cuts almost the full length of the blades.

3. Cut to the right of the layout line whenever possible, as shown in Fig. 46-6.

4. When cutting outside curves, rough cut within ⅛" of the layout line and then finish the work by cutting around the layout line as shown in Fig. 46-7. (See following page.)

5. When cutting inside curves, drill or punch holes in the waste stock large enough to allow the snips to start. Insert the snips from underneath and cut inside the opening to about ¼" of the layout line. Then, after this cut has been made, cut the hole to size. Fig. 46-8.

6. In cutting notches, Fig. 46-9, open the snips part way and cut with the portion of the blade near the point to avoid cutting past the layout lines.

46-6.   Cutting sheet metal to a right angle. Whenever possible, cut to the right of the layout line.

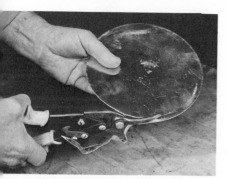

46-7. Cutting an outside curve with aviation snips.

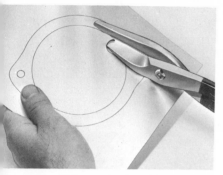

46-8. Using a circular cutting snip to cut an inside hole.

46-9. Cutting notches.

Using the Hollow Punch

Hollow punches punch larger holes than those made with a solid punch. They are used on light sheet metal.

1. Select the proper size punch. Fig. 46-10.

2. Mark the center of the hole with a prick punch.

3. Scribe a circle slightly larger than the punch.

4. Place the metal on a flat lead block or over the end-grain of a hardwood block.

5. Hold the punch in the center of the scribed circle.

6. With a ball-peen hammer, strike the punch a medium blow.

7. Raise the punch to see if it has been evenly centered. Return punch to the impression and punch out the metal. See Fig. 46-11.

8. With the burr side up flatten sheet smooth with a mallet.

Cutting Sheet Metal with Portable Power Shears

Portable power shears, Fig. 46-12, are used for cutting sheet metal which is 18 gage or lighter. Both straight and curved cuts can be made with this machine. It has a minimum cutting radius of about 1".

Cutting Sheet Metal on Rotary and Lever Slitting Shears

The rotary shear, as shown in Fig. 46-13, is designed for cutting sheet stock. The shearing action is done by the edges of two revolving cutting rolls, while the power is provided by a crank handle.

The lever slitting shear, Fig. 46-14, is used to cut bar and sheet stock to rough sizes.

46-10. Hollow punch.

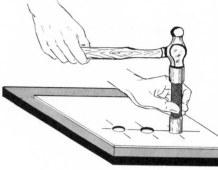

46-11. Using a hollow punch.

46-12. Cutting sheet metal with portable power shears.

46-13. Rotary slitting shear.

46-14. Lever slitting shear for irregular inside and outside cutting. The small illustrations are of work cut from blanks to a scribed line.

46-15. (A) Combination notcher, coper, and shear. (B) Illustrations of operations that can be done on this combination machine.

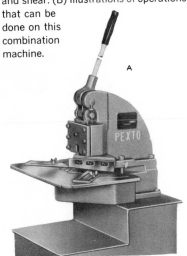

A

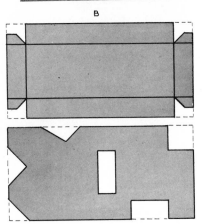

B

Most shears are limited to cutting metal up to ¼″ in thickness. Fig. 46-15 shows a combination notcher, coper, and shear.

Cutting Sheet Metal on the Squaring Shears

Foot-operated squaring shears are used to square and trim sheet metal. The shears shown in Fig. 46-16 are suitable for use in the school. The size of the shears is determined by the width of the sheets that can be cut on the machine. The machine has a bed, two cutting blades, foot treadle, front and back gage, and two side gages. To simplify cutting pieces to specific sizes, the face of the bed has a scale graduated in sixteenths.

1. To cut sheet stock, insert the sheet from the back of the machine. When cutting several pieces to the same size, set the front gage to the required length.

2. Press the left edge of the sheet against the left gage and the end of the sheet against the front gage.

3. Using both hands to hold the sheet firmly on the bed, apply pressure to the foot treadle with your foot.

CAUTION: *Be sure your hands are away from the cutting blade. Fig. 46-16.*

4. To cut several pieces of smaller size, set the back gage and feed the metal in from the front.

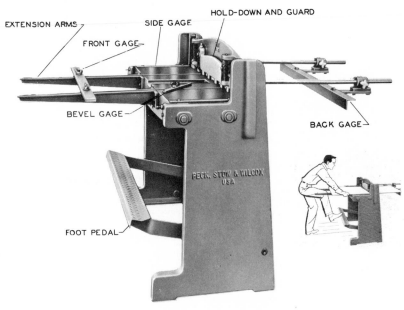

EXTENSION ARMS

FRONT GAGE

SIDE GAGE

HOLD-DOWN AND GUARD

BEVEL GAGE

BACK GAGE

FOOT PEDAL

PECK, STOW & WILCOX USA

46-16. Squaring shears.

47

Bending Sheet Metal by Hand

When machines are not available it becomes necessary to bend sheet metal by hand methods. Usually, developing these hand skills is extremely important in the school situation.

Bending Equipment

DESCRIPTION AND USE OF STAKES

There are many different types of metal stakes used in bending sheet metal. Some of the most common are shown and described in this unit.

- **Bench plate** or **stakeholder,** Fig. 47-1 (A), is a rectangular cast-iron plate that has conveniently arranged tapered holes so that the stakes may be used in different positions.
- **Beakhorn stake,** Fig. 47-1 (B), is used for forming, riveting, and seaming articles not suitable for the blowhorn stake. It has a thick, tapered horn at one end, and a rectangularly shaped horn at the other.
- **Bottom stake,** Fig. 47-1 (C) is used for burring and flanging circular bottoms. It has a fan-shaped, beveled edge, slightly rounded.
- **Coppersmith stake,** Fig. 47-1 (D), is used for general operations. This stake has a rounded edge on one side of the head and a rectangular edge on the other.
- **Common square stake,** Fig. 47-1 (E), has a flat, square shaped head with a long shank. It is a general-purpose stake.

- **Beveled-edge stake,** Fig. 47-1 (F), is made with an offset shank and has a flat, square head with a bevel edge on the outside for double seaming.
- **Double-seaming stake,** Fig. 47-1 (G), is used for laying down bottom seams and has two horns with upset heads on the ends.
- **Round-head stake,** Fig. 47-1 (H), is used for forming operations.
- **Hatchet stake,** Fig. 47-2 (I), is used for making sharp bends, bending edges, and forming boxes and pans by hand. This stake has a sharp straight edge, beveled along one side.
- **Creasing stake,** Fig. 47-2 (J), has a round horn for forming conical shaped pieces. The other end has a tapering square horn with grooved slots for wiring and beading.

- **Needle case stake,** Fig. 47-2 (K), for general bending purposes. It has a round slender horn for forming wire rings and tubes.
- **Candlemold stake,** 47-2 (L), has two horns for different tapers when forming, seaming, and riveting long, flaring articles.
- **Blowhorn stake,** Fig. 47-2 (M), is used in forming, riveting, and seaming tapered articles such as funnels.
- **Conductor stake,** Fig. 47-2 (N), has two cylindrical horns of different diameters, is used when forming, riveting, and seaming small sized pipes and tubes.
- **Hollow mandrel stake,** Fig. 47-2 (O), has a lengthwise slot in which a bolt slides, permitting the stake to be fastened to the bench at any angle or length. The rounded end is used for forming laps, riveting, and double seaming corners of pans and boxes.
- **Double-seaming stake with four heads,** Fig. 47-3, is used for double-seaming large work of all types. (See illustrations, Figs. 47-2 and 3 on following page.)

47-1.   Bench plate and stakes used in sheet metal work.

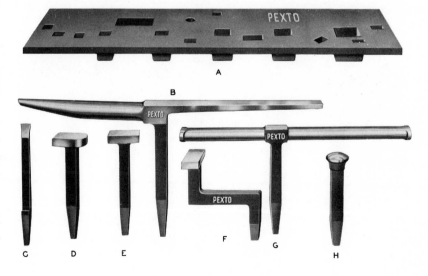

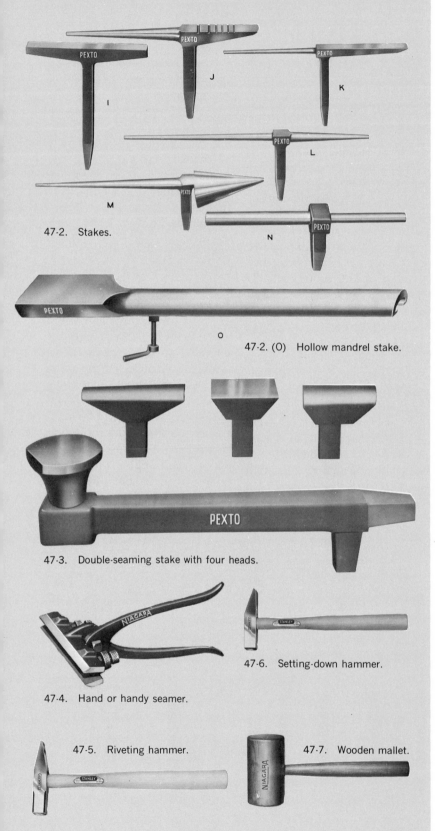

47-2.   Stakes.

47-2. (O)   Hollow mandrel stake.

47-3.   Double-seaming stake with four heads.

47-4.   Hand or handy seamer.

47-6.   Setting-down hammer.

47-5.   Riveting hammer.

47-7.   Wooden mallet.

• The **hand** or **handy seamer,** shown in Fig. 47-4, has 3½″ blades and an adjustable gage. This tool is used in hand seaming operations.

• The **riveting hammer,** Fig. 47-5, has a square, slightly curved face with beveled edges. It is used for riveting.

• The **setting-down hammer** has a square, flat face, used for setting down hems and flanges and for making certain types of seams. Fig. 47-6.

• A wooden or rawhide **mallet** is used for bending operations, as a metal hammer has a tendency to dent the metal. Fig. 47-7.

Making Angular Bends by Hand

1. Between two pieces of hardwood or angle iron, clamp the sheet metal in a vise. Fig. 47-8. If the sheet is too large for a vise, use two C-clamps and the edge of a bench top.

2. The bending line should be even with the upper edge of the jig. Bend the metal down by striking it with a mallet until the required bend is obtained. Fig. 47-8. Continue tapping with the mallet until the required bend is obtained.

3. A hatchet stake can also be used to make a sharp angle bend. Place the bend line of the piece over the sharp edge of the stake. Press the metal down with the hands as in Fig. 47-9 (A) and then square up the bend with a wooden mallet. Fig. 47-9 (B).

4. In making a box by hand, bend the two ends over a suitable stake or vise.

5. Cut a block of wood the exact width of the box. Clamp in position as shown in Fig. 47-10 and bend up the sides of the box.

Bending Cylindrical Shapes by Hand

A cylindrical object can be formed by bending sheet metal around a rod, stake, or pipe, which should be less than or equal to the diameter of the finished cylinder.

1. Place the metal over the rod and, holding one edge securely against the rod, bend the metal to the desired shape. Fig. 47-11.

2. If heavier metal is to be formed, hold the metal on top of the rod or stake with one hand and, with a mallet, strike the metal glancing blows as you feed it across the stake. Fig. 47-12.

Forming Cone-shaped Articles

Cone-shaped articles can be formed over a blowhorn stake. Fig. 47-13. A funnel or similar article can be formed by bending by hand over this stake if the gage of the metal is light enough. Heavier gages can be formed by using a mallet.

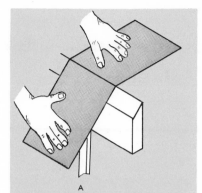

47-9. (A) Making a sharp angle bend over a hatchet stake.

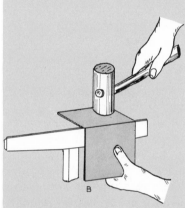

47-9. (B) Squaring off a sharp bend over a hatchet stake with a mallet.

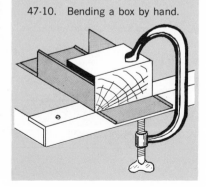

47-10. Bending a box by hand.

47-8. Bending sheet metal by hand between two hardwood blocks clamped in a vise.

47-11. Bending sheet metal over a rod or stake by hand.

47-12. Bending sheet metal into a cylindrical shape by striking as you hold it on a stake.

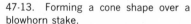

47-13. Forming a cone shape over a blowhorn stake.

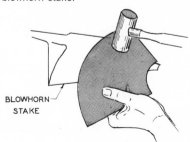

BLOWHORN
STAKE

48

Bending Sheet Metal on a Bar Folder

The *bar folder*, Fig. 48-1, is used to form narrow bends and folds of the type shown in Fig. 48-2. A better job can be done in making bends on the bar folder than can be done by hand.

The most common size bar folder used in school shops is the 30″ size. This machine will form open and closed locks in widths of ⅛″ to 1″ on metal up to 22 gage. A scale on the gage indicates the depth of the fold. After the correct setting is obtained, the gage is locked by turning the lock screw. To regulate the sharpness of the fold, loosen the lever on the wing, which lowers it.

OPERATION OF THE BAR FOLDER

- *Making a Single Hem*

Fig. 48-3 illustrates the method of making a single hem on the bar folder. The procedure is as follows:

1. Set the gage to the width of hem desired by means of the adjusting screw. Fig. 48-3 (A).

2. Tighten the lock screw.

3. Loosen the wedge lock, which is located in the rear of the bar folder.

4. Adjust the wedge screw to get the desired fold. Tighten the wedge lock nut.

5. Set the stop to maximum angle.

6. Adjust the folder for the thickness of the metal.

7. Insert the metal between the blade and the jaw, resting it against the gage fingers. Fig. 48-3 (A).

8. Pull the handle forward as far as it will go. Fig. 48-3 (B).

9. Hold the sheet metal back on the beveled part of the blade, as close to the wing as possible.

10. Hold the metal with the left hand and pull the handle, flattening the seam. Fig. 48-3 (C).

- *Making a Wired Edge by Hand*

1. Determine the size of wire and lay out the edge.

2. Form a rounded hem to receive the wire, over a stake or wooden block. The hem can also be made on a bar folder.

3. Place the wire in the rounded hem, hold in position with a pair of pliers, and fold the metal over the wire by hammering with a mallet. Fig. 48-4 (A).

4. Complete the bend by striking the metal with the peen end of a setting hammer. Fig. 48-4 (B).

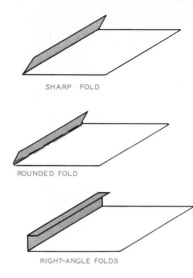

SHARP FOLD

ROUNDED FOLD

RIGHT-ANGLE FOLDS

RIGHT-ANGLE FOLD

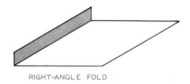

HEM

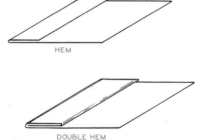

DOUBLE HEM

48-2. Types of bends which can be made on the bar folder.

48-1. Bar folder, used for bending sheet metal.

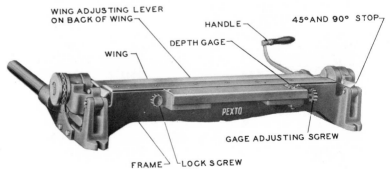

WING ADJUSTING LEVER ON BACK OF WING

HANDLE

45° AND 90° STOP

DEPTH GAGE

WING

PEXTO

GAGE ADJUSTING SCREW

FRAME — LOCK SCREW

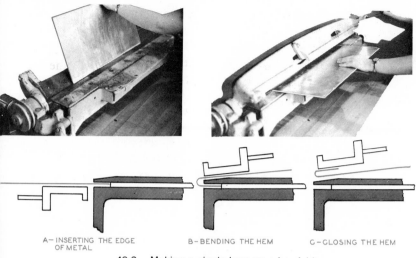

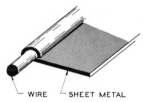

A—INSERTING THE EDGE OF METAL   B—BENDING THE HEM   C—CLOSING THE HEM

48-3. Making a single hem on a bar folder.

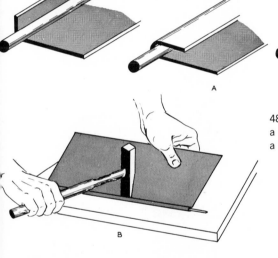

—WIRE   —SHEET METAL

A

B

48-4. (A) Steps in making a wired edge. (B) Completing a wired edge.

48-5. Cornice brake.

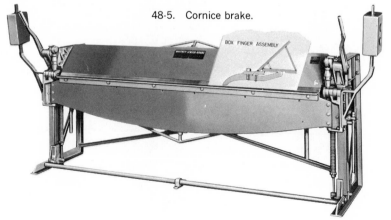

Bending Sheet Metal on a Brake

• The *cornice brake,* Fig. 48-5, and the *box and pan brake,* Fig. 48-6, are used in sheet metalwork for a variety of bending operations. The cornice brake has a solid bending edge bar, while the box and pan brake has fingers that are of different widths. On this brake it is possible to form right angle bends on four sides of a piece such as a box. Proceed as follows:

1. Make a layout on the metal.

2. Bend the four hems, if hems are to be used.

3. Bend one side to 90°.

4. Bend the second side to 90°.

5. Fit just enough fingers together to equal the width of the box and bend one end.

6. Bend the other end. Fig. 48-7.

48-6. Box and pan brake.

48-7. A box being formed on a small box and pan brake.

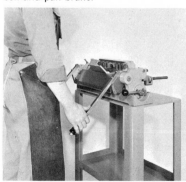

49 ▷ Roll-forming Sheet Metal

A roll-forming—or slip roll-forming—machine, Fig. 49-1, is used to form cylindrical shapes. Typical machines have rolls that are 30″ to 36″ long and 2″ in diameter. The machine is equipped with three rolls. The two front rolls are gear-operated and the back roll is an idler roll. The back roll does the forming and exerts the pressure which causes the metal to be formed to shape. The lower front roll can be moved up and down by adjusting screws to accommodate different thicknesses of metal. One end of the top roll can be raised so that the cylinder can be removed after it has been formed to shape. The right end of one bottom and one back roll has grooves around the circumference for forming cylinders with a wired edge. The steps in forming a cylinder are as follows:

1. Lock the upper roll in position.

2. Turn the adjusting screws, Fig. 49-1, so that the lower roll is parallel with the upper roll. The rolls should be adjusted so that a slight pressure is exerted on the metal as it is fed through.

3. Adjust the back roll so that it will exert enough pressure on the sheet metal to form the desired shape. Make sure the back roll is parallel to both the other rolls.

4. Insert the metal sheet between the front rolls, Fig. 49-2 (A), and turn the crank. As the metal enters the rolls, raise it slightly to start the forming operation, and then lower it as you turn the handle, to catch the back roll. Fig. 49-2 (B).

5. Continue turning the handle to shape the cylinder. To secure the desired radius for the cylinder, readjust the back roll. Raising the rear roll will decrease the diameter of the cylinder while lowering will increase the diameter. Fig. 49-3.

6. Remove the cylinder from the rolls by releasing the slip or upper roll. Fig. 49-4 shows a cylinder being formed on a power roller.

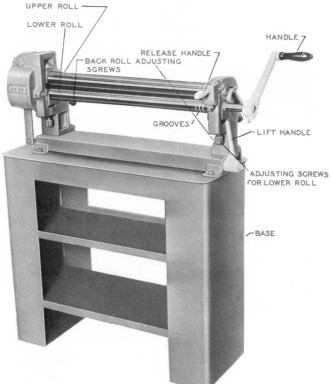

49-1. Roll-forming machine.

UPPER ROLL
LOWER ROLL
BACK ROLL ADJUSTING SCREWS
RELEASE HANDLE
HANDLE
GROOVES
LIFT HANDLE
ADJUSTING SCREWS FOR LOWER ROLL
BASE

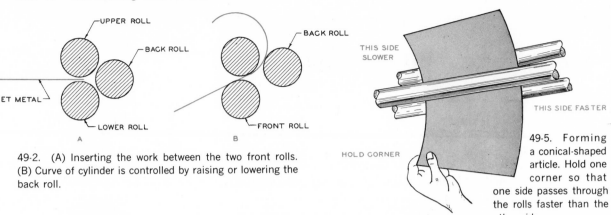

49-2. (A) Inserting the work between the two front rolls. (B) Curve of cylinder is controlled by raising or lowering the back roll.

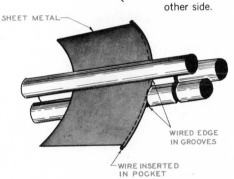

49-5. Forming a conical-shaped article. Hold one corner so that one side passes through the rolls faster than the other side.

49-3. Back roll beginning to form the cylinder.

49-6. Forming a cylinder with a wired edge.

49-4. Power rollers are equipped with a movable foot control that enables operator to use both hands for controlling material and operating the cam actuated idler roll.

To form cone shapes on the slip-roll former, adjust the front rolls as for forming a cylinder. Set the rear roll at an angle that is the same taper as the cone, with the left end nearer the front rolls. Insert the metal with the short side to the left and hold the narrow end back so that the short side passes through the rolls more slowly than the long side. Fig. 49-5.

To form a cylinder with a wired edge, adjust the front rolls with a wider space at the right side than at the left. The grooves of varying sizes in the right end of the lower and rear rolls are for wired edges. Place the sheet metal, with the wired-edge down in the proper size groove, and proceed by turning the crank handle. Fig. 49-6.

50 ▷ Sheet Metal Seams

There is a variety of methods for joining the edges of sheet metal. Some consist simply of lapping the edges and soldering. Special formed seams are used for other articles.

Some of the most common types of seams are lap, single, double, grooved, cap strip, and Pittsburgh.

● The **lap seam** is made by lapping one edge of the metal over the other edge and soldering or riveting the seam. Fig. 50-1.

● A **single seam** is folded to stand at right angles to the surface of the product. Fig. 50-2 (A). This seam can be made by hand or by machine. When a setting down machine is not available, it can be completed by hand.

The single seam is used to fasten bottoms to cylindrical, square, or rectangular containers. The construction procedure is described as follows:

1. For a *cylindrical* container prepare the bottom and body as shown in Fig. 50-2 (B). These edges may be turned on a burring or flanging machine.

2. After the flanges have been made, snap the body into the bottom piece, and with the face of the setting hammer bend the burred edge of the bottom over the burred edge of the cylinder to a 45° angle.

3. Bend the edge of the bottom with the face of the setting hammer until the edge is flat.

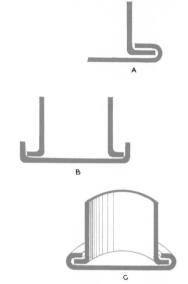

50-2. (A) Single seam, (B) preparation of seam, (C) completed seam on a cylindrical container.

50-3. When making a single seam with straight edges, notch the corners on the bottoms.

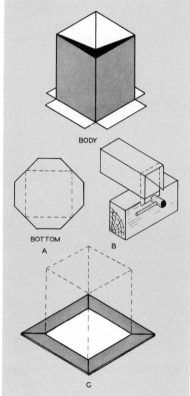

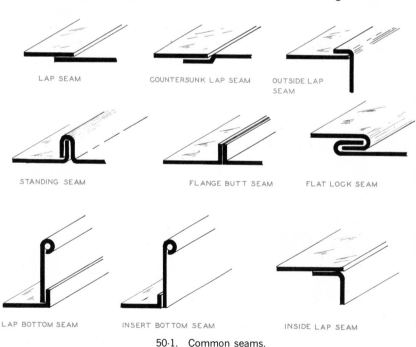

50-1. Common seams.

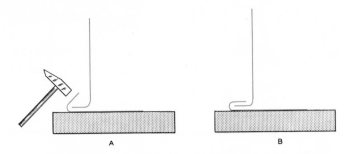

50-4. Making a single seam on a straight-edged container.

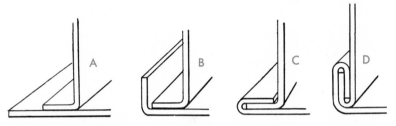

50-5. Double seam. (A) Forming the flange on the body, (B) forming the flange on the bottom, (C) single seam, (D) single seam bent up to the sides of the article to form the double seam.

50-6. Double seam on a cylindrical shaped article. (A) Bending single seam to 45° angle, (B) flattening seam with mallet, (C) two sections, (D) two sections snapped together, (E) forming the single seam, (F) completing the double seam.

4. With the peen of the setting hammer, finish the flattened edge. Fig. 50-2 (C).

5. On *square* or *rectangular* articles, the single seam is either soldered or riveted.

6. Lay out the required flange on the bar folder or brake. Cut the corners off at a 45° angle before bending. Fig. 50-3 (A). Bend the necessary flange on the bottom edge over a block of wood. Fig. 50-3 (B). Insert the body into the bottom piece and, with a setting hammer, bend the flange of the bottom piece over the flange on the body and close the edges with the peen end of the hammer. Figs. 50-3 (C) and 50-4.

• The **double seam** is a single seam bent back against the body of the article, especially used where strength in a joint is required. Correct allowances for the seam should be made to secure good results.

This type of seam can be finished by hand or machine. The machine method is limited, as only a very narrow seam can be made on light metal with a machine.

The double seam does not depend upon solder or rivets to hold it in place. Where strength is required, double seams are used on circular, square, or rectangular jobs such as pails, tanks, boxes, and for square or rectangular duct work.

Double-seaming a Bottom on a Cylinder

1. Form the sides of the container, allowing an extra amount for the flange on the bottom.

2. Turn this edge on a burring machine to a 90° angle. Fig. 50-5.

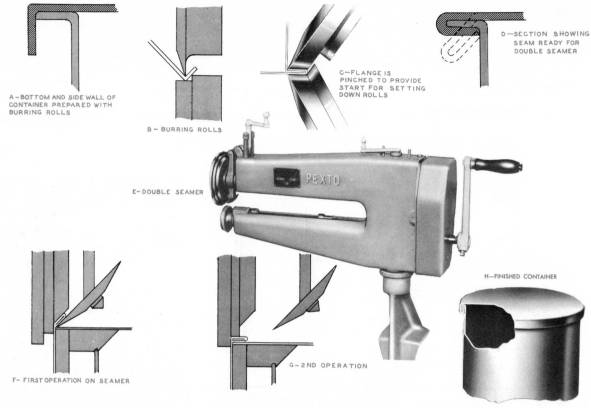

A—BOTTOM AND SIDE WALL OF CONTAINER PREPARED WITH BURRING ROLLS

B – BURRING ROLLS

C—FLANGE IS PINCHED TO PROVIDE START FOR SETTING DOWN ROLLS

D—SECTION SHOWING SEAM READY FOR DOUBLE SEAMER

E—DOUBLE SEAMER

PEXTO

F— FIRST OPERATION ON SEAMER

G—2ND OPERATION

H—FINISHED CONTAINER

50-7. Setting down and double seaming.

3. Cut out the metal for the bottom, allowing for the width of the flange. This can be found by measuring across the turned edges. To this diameter add an amount equal to the thickness of the metal.

4. Turn the edge of the metal, Fig. 50-5 (B), on the burring machine.

5. Snap the metal in place, and close the seam with a setting hammer. Fig. 50-6 (A).

6. Place the container on a double seaming stake. With the hand, hold the container firmly against the end of the stake. Bend the single seam to about a 45° angle by striking inward blows with a mallet, Fig. 50-6 (B), gradually turning the article around with each blow. Keep the con-

tainer and bottom firmly against the stake to avoid crushing the seam.

7. Finish bending the edge with the mallet until the seam is flat. Fig. 50-6 (B).

8. Place the container on a square head stake and tap the bottom with the mallet to square the edge and straighten the seam.

9. Place the container on a double seaming stake and flatten the seam.

Double-seaming a Square or Rectangular Article

1. Bend the edges, sides, and bottom on a bar folder or brake.

2. Bend the ends.

3. Place the end on the article. Hold the end of the box or other container on a square stake.

4. Starting at the top of the container, bend the seam flat with a mallet.

5. Bend the seam to a 45° angle.

6. Turn the container and bend all sides.

7. Strike the seam from the inside with a setting hammer to smooth and tighten the seams. Finish all sides in the same manner.

Double-seaming can be performed on a machine, Fig. 50-7, for the final bending operation after the flanges have been made on the burring rolls. In using the double-seaming machine, place the work over the horn and against the face of the lower roll. Move the upper roll outward with the handwheel. Turn the crank

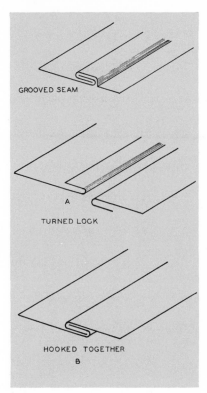

50-8. Grooved seam. (A) Bending the ends, (B) hems hooked together.

screw to bring the angular surface of the upper roll against the side of the edge of the seam. The small wheel then backs up the metal. To deflect the edge of the seam turn the crank handle. Turn the handwheel to shift the upper face so that when the crank handle is turned, the flat portion of the upper roll presses down the deflected edge and forms the seam.

• A **grooved seam,** Fig. 50-8, consists of two folded edges, called locks. The two edges are hooked together and locked with a grooving tool called a hand groover. The hand groover, Fig. 50-9, is used to offset an outside grooved seam. This tool is hardened with one end grooved to offset the grooved lock.

Grooving tools come with grooves of various widths and vary in size. The most common are No. 0, 2 and 4. The groover should have a groove about $1/16''$ wider than the width of the seam to be made.

Proceed as follows:

1. In making a grooved seam, an allowance for the amount of material for the lock should be added. For 24 gage, or lighter, multiply 3 times the width of the lock; for 22 gage or heavier, 3 times the width of the lock plus 5 times the thickness of the metal. Half of the allowances must be added to each side of the pattern.

2. Bend the ends by hand or on a bar folder and hook them together. Fig. 50-8 (B). Flatten the seam slightly with a mallet over a hollow mandrel, or solid mandrel stake if the work is cylindrical.

3. Place the hand groover over one end of the seam and strike with a hammer. Groove the other end in the same manner. Fig. 50-10.

4. Groove the balance of the seam by moving the groover along. Fig. 50-11.

5. Flatten the seam with a mallet to make it smooth.

• The **cap-strip seam** is generally used for assembling cross seams of ducts. As shown in Fig. 50-12, it provides strength and good appearance.

1. Turn locks, as in Fig. 50-12 (A), to the desired size.

2. Turn locks on another strip of metal of the proper width. Fig. 50-12 (B).

3. Piece (B) is then slipped over piece (A). Fig. 50-12 (C). (Fig. 12 appears on next page.)

50-9. Hand groover.

50-10. To lock the seam, start at one end and tip the hand groover at a slight angle. Hook the groover over the edge of the seam and strike a firm blow.

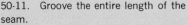

50-11. Groove the entire length of the seam.

• The **Pittsburgh lock** is a corner seam used for pipe and fittings. This seam is sometimes used instead of a double-seam on many jobs, such as boxes and machine guards.

The pocket for a Pittsburgh lock. Fig. 50-13 (A), can be prepared in a bar folder or a Pittsburgh lock former. The allowance for the pocket is $W + W + \frac{3}{16}''$. Make the width of the flanged edge less then the depth of the pocket. After the pieces are fitted together, Fig. 50-13 (B), the projecting edge can be bent over with a mallet. Fig. 50-13 (C).

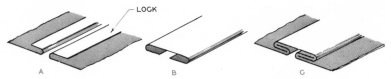

50-12. Cap-strip seam. (A) Turning lock, (B) cap strip with edges turned, (C) completed cap-strip seam.

50-13. Pittsburgh lock. (A) Preparation, (B) edges joined, (C) finished lock.

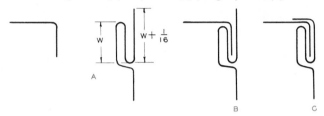

51 ▷ Using a Rotary Machine

A deep-throat combination rotary machine, Fig. 51-1, with selected sets of rolls will perform a variety of operations in sheet metalwork, such as turning, wiring, burring, beading, and crimping. It replaces a separate machine for each operation. Fig. 51-2.

Making a Wired Edge

A rotary machine with two sets of rolls is used for this operation.

1. Place the turning rolls on the machine.

2. Set the gage a distance equal to 2½ times the diameter of the wire, from the center of the groove.

3. Place the metal between the two rolls with the edge firmly against the gage. Fig. 51-3 (A).

4. Tighten the upper roll by turning the crank screw until it

makes a slight depression in the metal. Then turn until the metal has passed through.

5. Lower the upper roll by tightening the crank screw a little more. Tilt the work upward slightly. Fig. 51-3 (B). Turn the crank handle until another revolution has been made. Continue this process until the groove is large enough to receive the wire. Fig. 51-3 (C).

6. Cut a mild steel wire to the correct length. The size is measured by the American Wire gage. The most common sizes are Nos. 10, 12, 14, and 18, depending on how thick the roll must be. Form the wire into a ring in the forming rolls or, if the article is rectangular, over a stake.

7. Slip the wire in the edge and close the metal around it

with a pair of pliers and mallet or a setting-down hammer.

8. Insert the wiring rolls in the machine and adjust the gage a distance from the edge of the upper roll equal to the diameter of the wire, plus 2 times the thickness of the metal.

9. Place the article between the rolls with the wired edge up, against the gage, Fig. 51-4 (A), and lower the upper roll until it grips the work.

10. Turn the handle as you feed in the metal, to set the wired edge. Fig. 51-4 (B). On the last pass, tilt the work upward to force the edge of the metal under the wire.

11. Loosen the upper rolls and remove the work.

Beading

You bead the surfaces of sheet-metal products for a different and neater appearance and to increase the strength of the article. Beading is done with a rotary machine and beading rolls, Fig. 51-5. (See illustrations on following pages.)

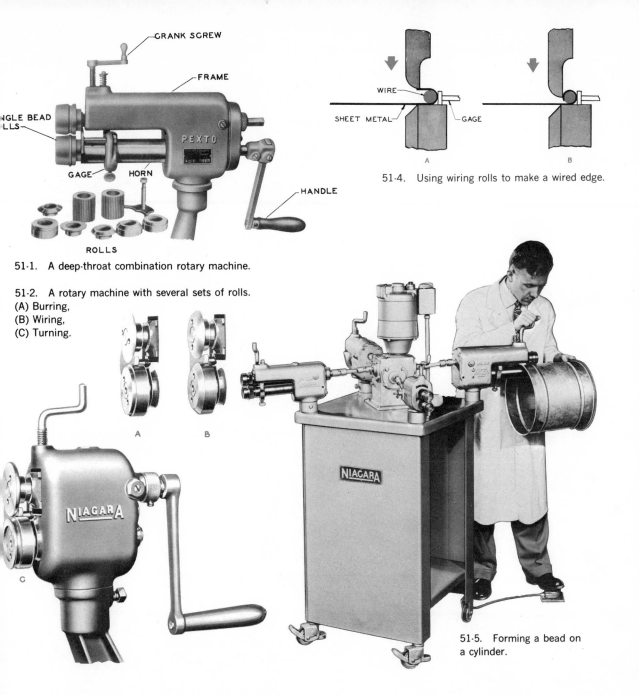

51-1. A deep-throat combination rotary machine.

51-2. A rotary machine with several sets of rolls.
(A) Burring,
(B) Wiring,
(C) Turning.

51-4. Using wiring rolls to make a wired edge.

51-5. Forming a bead on a cylinder.

51-3. Steps in using the turning rolls to form a wired edge.

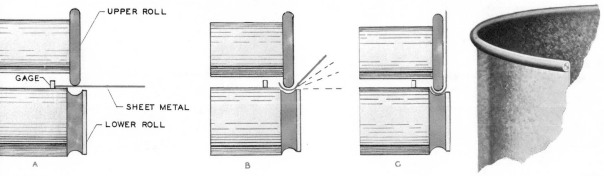

SINGLE BEAD   OGEE BEAD

TRIPLE BEAD

51-6. Types of beads made in a beading machine.

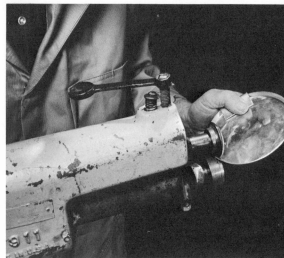

51-9. Combination beading and crimping rolls.

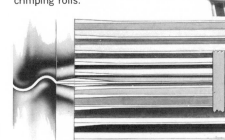

51-7. A section of crimped pipe.

51-8. Crimping.

51-10. Rolls for burring an edge.

51-11. Starting the burring operation. Note the hand guard as described in the text.

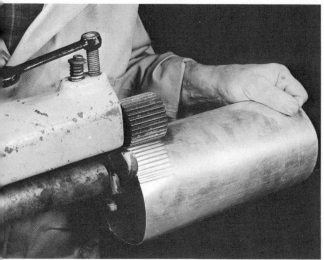

The three types of beads commonly used are (1) the single bead, (2) the ogee bead, and (3) the triple bead. Fig. 51-6.

1. Place the proper beading rolls on the machine and set the gage to locate the position of the bead.

2. Lower the upper roll by turning the crank screw until a slight impression is made in the metal.

3. Turn the crank handle and pass the metal through. Continue tightening the upper rolls a little at a time until the bead is completely formed.

Crimping

Crimping is used to corrugate and reduce the size of one end of a pipe, so it will fit into another pipe of the same dimension. Fig. 51-7.

To crimp, proceed as follows:

1. Place the crimping rolls on on the rotary machine. Adjust the gage to the desired length of the crimp.

2. Slip the metal between the rolls with the edge held tightly against the gage.

3. Lower the upper roll with a moderate amount of pressure and turn the crank handle to form an impression. Fig. 51-8.

4. Continue lowering the rolls to deepen the crimp. Fig. 51-9 shows a combination crimping and beading machine.

Forming a Flange or Burr

Burring rolls, Fig. 51-10, can be used to turn a flange on a cylinder and to turn a burr on the bottom of an article in making a double seam to attach a cylinder. NOTE: Turning a burr on a round bottom is an operation that re-

51-12. Completing the burring operation.

quires a great deal of practice to achieve skill. The procedure is as follows:

1. Insert burring rolls on the rotary machine. Set the gage for the required width of the burr. NOTE: For a ¼″ burr set the gage to slightly less than ¼″, and the same for other sizes.

2. Place the disc between the rolls. To protect the hand, bend a small rectangle of sheet metal into a U shape and place this between the thumb and forefinger.

3. Holding the disc against the gage, lower the upper roll until a slight pressure is applied to the metal. Fig. 51-11.

4. Make one revolution, scoring the edge slightly.

5. Tighten the crank screw. Make a number of revolutions, raising the disc slightly after each revolution, until the burr is turned to the proper angle. This operation is shown in Fig. 51-12.

Slitting and Trimming

Operations such as slitting and trimming can be performed on a combination machine. Fig. 51-13 shows a trimming operation and Fig. 51-14 examples of trimming and slitting.

51-13. Trimming on a hand operated, deep-throated combination machine.

51-14. Examples of trimmed and slit metal.

197

52 ▷ Fastening Sheet Metal

52-1. (A)   Rivet set.

Sheet metal parts may be fastened together by riveting, by using sheet metal screws, and by soldering. The soldering method will be described in Unit 53.

Riveting Tools and Rivets

A rivet set, Fig. 52-1 (A), has two different purposes, pressing the metal around the rivet and forming a round head, commonly known as heading the rivet. Rivet sets are made in sizes to match the rivets. Select the correct rivet set by number or by trying the rivet shank in the hole.

One end of a rivet set has a deep hole and a shallow, cup-shaped hole. The cup-shaped hole forms the head on the rivet while the deep hole binds the sheets of metal and rivet snugly together. Another type of rivet set is shown in Fig. 52-1 (B). Here both ends are used.

• The **riveting hammer,** Fig. 52-2, has a slightly convex face with the corners beveled to prevent them from digging into the metal. The peen end is double-tapered and slightly rounded for spreading the rivet. Riveting hammers range in size (weight) from 4 oz. to 30 oz.

• A **solid punch,** Fig. 52-3, is used to punch holes in sheet metal for soft tinner's rivets. Solid punches have solid or flat cutting ends. They punch holes from 3/32″ to 3/8″ in diameter. They are numbered from 6 to 10, or some companies letter their punches

from B to I. Each numbered punch fits a certain size rivet.

The hand lever punch is used when numerous small holes are to be punched. Fig. 52-4.

Rivets

Sheet metal or tinner's rivets are used to join sheet metal. They are made of soft iron coated with tin to prevent corrosion. Sheet metal rivets are also made with a black iron oxide and zinc coating. If made of copper, they are called copper tinner's rivets.

The size of tinner's rivets is determined by the weight per thou-

52-1. (B)   A hand forming rivet set.

52-2.   Riveting hammer.

52-3.   Solid punch.

52-4.   Hand lever. Note the different sized punches.

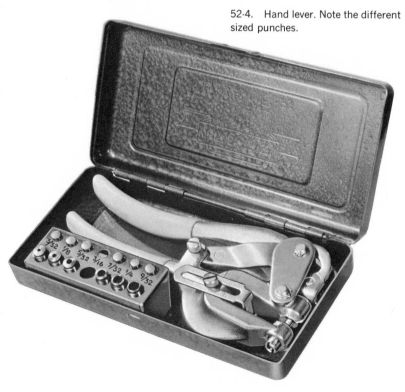

sand. For example, 1 lb. rivets weigh 1 lb. per thousand, 2 lb. rivets, 2 lbs. per thousand, etc. Tinner's rivets are made in only a flat-head style. Table 52-A shows their size range.

The rivet selected for the job must be long enough so that the proper head shape may be obtained. A rivet that is too short makes it very difficult to shape the head properly. On the other hand, if the rivet is too long it has a tendency to bend when headed. To assure the proper length rivet, add the total thickness of the metal sheets plus 1½ times the diameter of the rivet. Fig. 52-5.

EXAMPLE:

Total thickness of two 27-gage metal
sheets $= 2 \times .0164 = .0328$
Rivet diameter $= 3 \times$ total thickness
$\qquad = .0984$
$\qquad = 10$ oz. tinner's rivets
Rivet length $= 1½ \times$ diameter of rivet
plus thickness of metal.
Thickness of two 27-
gage metal sheets
$\qquad = .0328''$
$1½ \times (.0984) + .0328$
$\qquad = 0.1804$
$\qquad = 11/64''$.

Riveting Procedure

1. Space the rivet holes according to requirements of the job. The space from the edge of the metal to the center of the rivet line should be twice the diameter of the rivet, Fig. 52-6, to prevent it from tearing out. The minimum distance between rivets should be about three times the rivet diameter to allow the rivets to be driven without interference. The maximum distance should never exceed 24 times the thickness of the metal sheets.

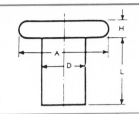

Size numbers refer to the approximate weight of 1,000 rivets.

Diameter of Body D			Diameter of Head A		Height of Head H		Length L		
Size	Max.	Min.	Max.	Min.	Max.	Min.	Nom.	Max.	Min.
6 oz	0.081	0.075	0.213	0.193	0.028	0.016	⅛	0.135	0.115
8 oz	0.091	0.085	0.225	0.205	0.036	0.024	⁵/₃₂	0.166	0.146
10 oz	0.097	0.091	0.250	0.230	0.037	0.025	¹¹/₆₄	0.182	0.162
12 oz	0.107	0.101	0.265	0.245	0.037	0.025	³/₁₆	0.198	0.178
14 oz	0.111	0.105	0.275	0.255	0.038	0.026	³/₁₆	0.198	0.178
1 lb	0.113	0.107	0.285	0.265	0.040	0.028	¹³/₆₄	0.213	0.193
1¼ lb	0.122	0.116	0.295	0.275	0.04:	0.033	⁷/₃₂	0.229	0.209
1½ lb	0.132	0.126	0.316	0.294	0.046	0.034	¹⁵/₆₄	0.244	0.224
1¾ lb	0.136	0.130	0.331	0.309	0.049	0.035	¼	0.260	0.240
2 lb	0.146	0.140	0.341	0.319	0.050	0.036	¹⁷/₆₄	0.276	0.256
2½ lb	0.150	0.144	0.311	0.289	0.069	0.055	⁹/₃₂	0.291	0.271
3 lb	0.163	0.154	0.329	0.303	0.073	0.059	⁵/₁₆	0.323	0.303
3½ lb	0.168	0.159	0.348	0.322	0.074	0.060	²¹/₆₄	0.338	0.318
4 lb	0.179	0.170	0.368	0.342	0.076	0.062	¹¹/₃₂	0.354	0.334
5 lb	0.190	0.181	0.388	0.362	0.084	0.070	⅜	0.385	0.365
6 lb	0.206	0.197	0.419	0.393	0.090	0.076	²⁵/₆₄	0.401	0.381
7 lb	0.223	0.214	0.431	0.405	0.094	0.080	¹³/₃₂	0.416	0.396
8 lb	0.227	0.218	0.475	0.445	0.101	0.085	⁷/₁₆	0.448	0.428
9 lb	0.241	0.232	0.490	0.460	0.103	0.087	²⁹/₆₄	0.463	0.443
10 lb	0.241	0.232	0.505	0.475	0.104	0.088	¹⁵/₃₂	0.479	0.459
12 lb	0.263	0.251	0.532	0.498	0.108	0.090	½	0.510	0.490
14 lb	0.288	0.276	0.577	0.543	0.113	0.095	³³/₆₄	0.525	0.505
16 lb	0.304	0.292	0.597	0.563	0.128	0.110	¹⁷/₃₂	0.541	0.521
18 lb	0.347	0.335	0.706	0.668	0.156	0.136	¹⁹/₃₂	0.603	0.583

Table 52-A.

52-5. (A) Determining rivet length, (B) determining rivet diameter.

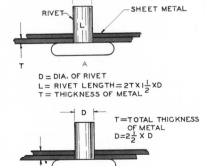

D = DIA. OF RIVET
L = RIVET LENGTH = 2 T X 1½ X D
T = THICKNESS OF METAL

T = TOTAL THICKNESS OF METAL
D = 2½ X D

52-6. (A) Lap required for riveting, (B) the correct method of spacing rivets.

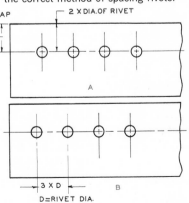

D = RIVET DIA.

2. Drill or punch the holes by placing the sheet metal on a lead cake or the end grain of a block of wood. Fig. 52-7.

3. Select the correct rivets.

4. Rest the head of the rivet on a stake or metal bar and slip the metal sheets over the rivet so that the shank comes through the matching holes.

5. Draw the metal sheets and the rivet head together by using the rivet set and striking with a hammer. Fig. 52-8 (A).

6. Remove the rivet set and upset the rivet with a ball-peen or riveting hammer. Hit the rivet shank squarely. Fig. 52-8 (B).

7. Using the cup-shaped depression strike the rivet set one or two sharp blows to head up the rivet. Fig. 52-8 (C). Be sure to hold the rivet set at a right angle to avoid denting the metal.

If it becomes necessary to remove a rivet the following procedure may be used. Fig. 52-9.

1. Place the rivet on a solid stake with the formed head upward.

2. Center punch the center of the formed head.

3. Place the head of the rivet over a hole drilled in a solid block of steel or over a nut with a hole slightly larger than the head of the rivet.

4. Drive out the rivet with a solid punch of the correct size.

Fastening with Tapping Screws

The tapping screw is designed especially for joining metal sheets. Also some types can be used to fasten sheet metal to heavier material. The threads extend over the entire length of the screw, making it possible to join metal that is held tightly against the underside of the head. These screws are used in the sheet metal trade to install ducts for air-conditioning, heating, and other work.

Tapping screws fall into two general classifications: Thread-cutting and thread-forming. Thread-cutting screws remove metal during the forming of mating threads in drilled or punched holes. Thread-forming screws displace metal when driven, instead of removing it, thus forming a chip-free mating thread.

Illustrated in Fig. 52-10 (see following page) are the common types of tapping screws, both thread-cutting and thread-forming. Each is designed to perform a special function or to meet a particular requirement. A description follows:

Type A—Thread-Forming

Sharp gimlet point for use in light gage sheet metal for pierced or punched holes, when exposed point is acceptable.

Type B—Thread-Forming

Blunt point for use on light and heavy sheet metal and non-ferrous castings. The slight taper makes driving easier.

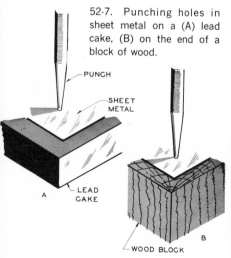

52-7. Punching holes in sheet metal on a (A) lead cake, (B) on the end of a block of wood.

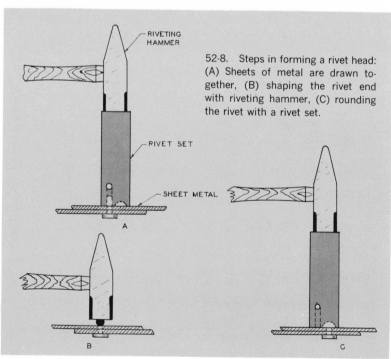

52-8. Steps in forming a rivet head: (A) Sheets of metal are drawn together, (B) shaping the rivet end with riveting hammer, (C) rounding the rivet with a rivet set.

Type AB—Thread-Forming

Similar to type B except that that this screw has a sharp gimlet starting point.

Type TEKStm—Self-Drilling

Also cuts or forms its own mating threads. Eliminates hole preparation and tapping operations.

Type C—Thread-Forming

Blunt point with machine screw threads for use in soft metals from .030″ to .100″ in thickness.

Type F—Thread-Cutting

Blunt point with cutting grooves and chip cavities.

Type 1—Thread-Cutting

Off-center slot, blunt point, provides true cutting action.

To use sheet metal screws, the following procedure is recommended:

1. Lay out the required holes and prick punch the centers.

2. Choose the correct size drill as shown in Tables 52-B and 52-C.

3. Line up the hole and start the screw. Hold the two pieces together and drive the screw into place with a screwdriver.

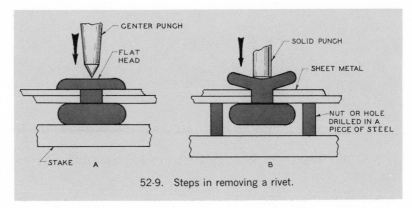

52-9. Steps in removing a rivet.

RECOMMENDED DRILL SIZES FOR SELF-TAPPING, SHARP-POINTED SHEET METAL SCREWS

Screw Size	Thickness of Metal	Drill Size
No. 4	.018	44
	.024	43
	.030	42
	.036	42
No. 6	.018	37
	.024	36
	.030	36
	.036	35
No. 8	.024	32
	.030	31
	.036	31
No. 10	.024	27
	.030	27
	.036	26

Table 52-B

RECOMMENDED DRILL SIZES FOR SELF-TAPPING, BLUNT-END SHEET METAL SCREWS

Screw Size	Thickness of Metal	Drill Size
No. 4	.018	44
	.024	42
	.030	42
	.036	40
No. 6	.018	39
	.024	39
	.030	38
	.036	36
No. 8	.018	33
	.024	33
	.030	32
	.036	31
No. 10	.018	30
	.024	30
	.030	30
	.036	29

Table 52-C

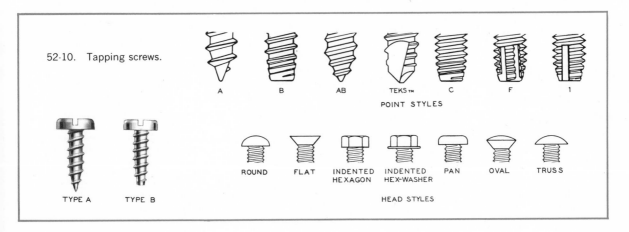

52-10. Tapping screws.

POINT STYLES
A   B   AB   TEKStm   C   F   1

TYPE A   TYPE B

HEAD STYLES
ROUND   FLAT   INDENTED HEXAGON   INDENTED HEX-WASHER   PAN   OVAL   TRUSS

53 ▷ Soft Soldering Sheet Metal

Soldering, as you know, consists of joining two or more metal surfaces by means of another metal which is applied in a molten condition.

The metal which forms the joint is an alloy called solder. In order to do a good job of soldering, you must know the following:
• The kind or kinds of material to be soldered.
• The kind of solder and flux to use.
• The proper soldering device for each job.
• How to clean.
• How to hold in juncture while soldering.

Soft Solders

Since soft soldering is generally used in sheet metalwork, this unit will deal primarily with this type.

Most soft solders are composed of a mixture of tin and lead. The melting point is largely determined by the proportions of these two elements. Solder consisting of half tin and half lead, called "half-and-half" or "50-50," melts at about 415°F.

If the proportion of lead and tin is changed to 60% tin and 40% lead, the melting point is about 370°F.

Pure tin melts at 450°F. but, surprisingly enough, if another metal, lead, which liquefies at 620°F., is mixed with the tin—for example, in the proportion of 63 parts of tin by weight to 37 parts of lead by weight—a fusible alloy results which melts at an even lower temperature, 361°F. This is the lowest melting point of tin-lead mixtures.

Tin mixes with lead in all proportions. The most common compositions are 40/60, 50/50, and 60/40. Tin, contrary to popular belief, is an expensive metal. It is imported from countries in Asia, Africa, and South America. Lead, on the other hand, is less expensive, so the more tin in the solder the more expensive it is.

A good solder is 40/60. It gives all-around service well suited for non-professional use. The first number is always tin. As noted, this type of solder starts to soften at 361°F. It then goes through a mushy or plastic stage and becomes completely liquid at 460°F. Solders in the form of wire are of this type. Wire solders come plain or with acid or rosin core centers. In addition, soft solders are available in bar, cake, ribbon, powder, pig, and slab.

Fluxes

To secure good adherence, you know that the surface of the metal and solder must be free of oxide, rust, or dirt.

Practically all clean metals, when exposed to the atmosphere, acquire a film of oxide or tarnish. The thickness of this film tends to increase as time goes on, especially with unalloyed iron and steel. Moisture and heat help speed it up. It is difficult or impossible to get metal to adhere unless clean because the solder must penetrate the metal to be effective.

To prepare for the "wetting" or alloying of metal with molten solder, a chemical material is used—a soldering flux. This does three things: (1) Removes tarnish or metallic oxide, (2) prevents further oxide from forming while the metal is being heated to soldering temperature, (3) lowers the surface tension of the molten solder enabling it to spread about the area and penetrate.

Fluxes are classified as corrosive or non-corrosive. Fluxes that are ordinarily used for soft soldering are pastes or solutions containing zinc chloride. Zinc chloride fluxes have a corrosive action. The common fault of most corrosive fluxes is that, after the soldering operation, the flux residues will attract moisture unless they are removed. This moisture causes the metals nearby to rot or corrode.

Rosin flux must be used in soldering the wiring on all types of electronic equipment: radio, television, meters, telephones, and computers or electronic instruments. The residue of rosin flux is inert, non-corrosive, and electrically non-conductive. It does not attract dust and will not harm delicate wiring.

As a flux, rosin works best only on clean tin plate, solder-coated surfaces, and clean copper.

There are many types of commercial fluxes available. Among these are paste, liquid, powder, and cake. Use as convenient.

A *corrosive* flux penetrates best. It cannot be used on electrical

53-1. Pointed copper and a bottom copper.

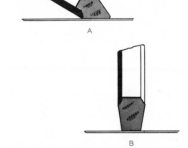

53-2. (A) Pre-heating work with a pointed copper, (B) with a bottom copper.

work. It is prepared by adding small pieces of zinc to muratic acid (hydrochloric acid). The acid dissolves the zinc, forming zinc chloride. Mix half and half with water.

(Always pour the acid into the water.)

Preparation of the zinc chloride should always be done out of doors or near an open window.

Acid-core (corrosive) solder is an all-purpose choice wherever a chemically active flux is desired for a strong joint, and electrical work is not involved.

It can be purchased in wire form.

Soldering Devices

There are many heating devices that can be used in soldering. The most common are: electric soldering copper and soldering furnace, blowtorch, electric soldering iron, soldering gun, Bunsen burner, or bottled-gas soldering torch.

Successful soldering requires heat—enough to raise the temperature of the metals to be joined to a melting point in the area concerned. The most popular and preferred method of transferring heat is by means of the soldering copper or iron.

Soldering irons are available in many weights or sizes. Forge-heated soldering irons or coppers, are sold singly or by the pair.

NOTE: Sometimes it is desirable to have one of these irons heating-up while the other one is in use, to avoid interruption of the work.

A copper weighing ½ lb. is suitable for light work; use a 1 lb. iron for medium weight soldering and a 1½ lb. iron for heavier soldering. Coppers may be purchased that weigh 4 to 5 lbs. to the pair, for even heavier work.

The pointed copper and the bottom copper, Fig. 53-1, are the types used most commonly in the school. The pointed copper has a pyramid-shaped point, while the bottom copper has a broad, wedge-shaped tip. It is used in an upright position to utilize the broad tip best. Fig. 53-2. Soldering irons can be forged to any desired shape.

The usual method of heating a soldering copper is in a gas furnace of the type shown in Fig. 53-3 (A), which is a combination

53-3. (A) Combination soldering and melting furnace.

53-3. (B) A typical school soldering section.

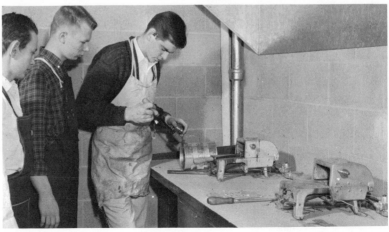

203

soldering and melting furnace. It will quickly produce a heat of 1,800° F. and comes equipped with either a single or double burner, each controlled by a separate valve. The furnace is also equipped with a pilot light. Fig. 53-3 (B) shows a typical school soldering section. (See page 203.)

A blowtorch can be used to heat a soldering iron or for direct soldering with heat. The one shown in Fig. 53-4 is fueled with gasoline mixed with air, making a gas which produces a hot flame. Air pressure is provided in the tank by means of a hand pump. When the valve is opened the gas mixture is made.

53-4. A gasoline blowtorch can be used to heat a soldering copper.

53-5. Small soldering iron.

53-6. Electric soldering pencil.

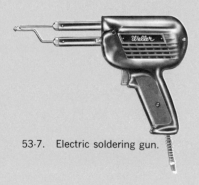

53-7. Electric soldering gun.

Electric Soldering Irons

Electric soldering irons are convenient for many types of soldering operations. They are made in sizes from 25 to 550 watts. Fig. 53-5.

A 100 watt iron is recommended for electrical work and practically all home soldering.

A 200 watt iron is recommended for heavier soldering, and for rugged work a 350 watt iron should be used.

It is not enough to have a high temperature capable of melting solder, but there also must be a great enough volume of heat transmitted by the iron to the work, to quickly raise the temperature of the metals to be joined to solder-melting temperature.

It is this step in soldering that amateurs often fail to grasp. Too light a soldering iron will often cause trouble.

Not only must a soldering iron be hot and heavy enough, but its faces must be smooth and well tinned.

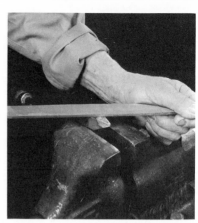

53-8. Filing a soldering copper to remove corrosion and secure a clean, well-shaped point.

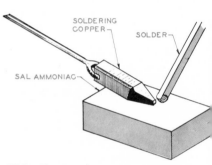

53-9. Tinning a copper on a cake of sal-ammoniac.

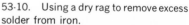

53-10. Using a dry rag to remove excess solder from iron.

53-11. Material used in cleaning sheet metal before soldering: Cleaning fluid (dangerous fumes—use only with proper ventilation); wire brush; file; abrasive cloth; steel wool.

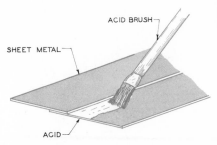

53-12. Applying soldering flux to a seam.

Soldering pencils, Fig. 53-6, being convenient, are used a great deal in electric and electronic work. Soldering guns, Fig. 53-7, have advantages because they provide instant heat and are equipped with a prefocused spotlight which illuminates the work and eliminates shadows. Two trigger positions permit instant switching to high 140 watt or low 100 watt heat as the job requires.

Tinning a Soldering Copper

Tinning provides for the quick transfer of heat into the metal to be joined and also enables the iron to glide along smoothly.

If the faces of the soldering copper tips are oxidized or pitted so as to prevent the rapid flow of heat, they must be filed flat or smooth, down to the bare, bright copper. Overheating will cause the point to be coated with oxide. The process of tinning a copper is as follows:

1. Heat copper in a gas furnace. Remove and clamp in vise.

2. File each side of the point with a mill file to remove oxide and pits. Fig. 53-8.

3. Replace the copper in the furnace and reheat to a degree that will just melt solder.

4. Remove from furnace and rub each side on a block of sal-ammoniac. Apply a little solder as you rub. Fig. 53-9.

CAUTION: *Don't shake the iron in the air if you have too much solder on the tip. Use a dry rag to push off any excess molten solder. Fig. 53-10. The soldering iron should now be tinned and ready for use.*

When rosin is used as a flux on tin plate, rub the copper back and forth in powdered rosin and add a small amount of solder.

Another method is to dip the point in paste or liquid flux and apply solder.

Soldering a Seam or Joint

The parts to be soldered must be held firmly while the soldering operation is going on.

Avoid using a metal-top bench or vise if there is any danger of robbing the job of the heat that is applied.

In soldering parts of unequal size, favor the thicker or heavier part because it does require more heat and molten solder runs toward the hottest part, which is most likely to be the smallest or lightest.

Keep the work *level;* otherwise you will discover that molten solder, like water, flows away.

1. Select the proper soldering copper for the job to be done.

2. Clean the area of the metal to be soldered. Fig. 53-11 shows various cleaning materials.

3. Place the parts to be soldered on a table that has a nonconductor top.

4. Apply flux to the seam as in Fig. 53-12 with a brush or swab. NOTE: A raw-acid flux should be used on galvanized iron.

5. Heat the soldering iron to the correct temperature. This temperature can be determined by touching the solder to the point, as in Fig. 53-13. If the solder melts quickly the iron is ready

205

53-13. Testing a soldering copper for the proper temperature.

53-16. Hold the copper until the solder begins to flow into the seam.

53-14. Hold the copper at one end of the seam until the heat penetrates the metal.

53-17. Hold the copper on the seam and draw it towards you.

53-18. Tin the joint area in preparation for marking a sweat-soldered joint.

53-15. Tack the seam in several places.

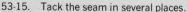

for use. Never overheat the copper or its surface will be ruined. If this occurs the copper will have to be filed and tinned again.

6. Pick up the solder with the soldering copper and hold the copper at one end of the seam until the heat penetrates through the metal. Fig. 53-14.

7. Tack the seam in several places, Fig. 53-15, to hold the parts in the proper position.

8. Starting at one end of the seam and with the tapered side of the head flat along the seam, hold the copper in this position until the solder starts to flow into the seam. Fig. 53-16.

9. Hold the copper against the seam and draw it slowly towards you. More solder can be added in front of the point if it is needed. Be sure parts are held together until the solder turns a dull color. For simple work use the tang of a file, as in Fig. 53-17.

Once the iron has been removed, the work should be allowed to cool undisturbed until the solder solidifies. Jarring the parts during this cooling or pasty stage can result in a weak joint. Tiny fractures sometimes set themselves up inside the joint and weaken it. Don't apply any water to speed up the chilling of a soldered joint. Clean the seam with hot water. Baking soda can be added to the water to counteract excess acid.

Sweat Soldering

When two parts need to be soldered together so that no solder can be seen it is called sweat soldering. Success in sweat soldering depends upon a constant supply of even heat. To sweat solder a joint the procedure is as follows:

1. Tin one side of each part to be joined. Fig. 53-18.

2. Place the tinned surfaces together.

3. Heat the seam with a hot soldering copper by placing the flat surface of the copper on one end of the seam. Hold the parts together while soldering.

4. When the solder between the two pieces begins to melt and flow out from under the edges, press steadily down on the metal with a file tang and draw the copper slowly along the seam. Keep a constant pressure on the seam so that a good contact is obtained.

Torch Soldering

Some soldering jobs are difficult to accomplish with a soldering copper. Projects such as parts of bowls and lamps are good examples. Copper plumbing pipes are also soldered by using a torch.

A gas-air or bottled-gas soldering torch, Fig. 53-19, will do a good job of joining the above kinds of projects. With a torch, the correct size flame can be obtained and directed to an exact spot.

The parts are heated first to the proper temperature and the solder applied.

Soldering Aluminum

The soldering operations for soldering aluminum are the same as for other metals. However, a suitable solder has to be used consisting of an alloy of zinc with one or more parts of aluminum, tin, lead, or copper. The oxide has to be first removed with abrasive cloth or steel wool. Some commercial aluminum solders have the necessary flux in with the solder.

Resistance Soldering

Resistance soldering does what all other soldering systems do. It furnishes heat to activate flux and melt solder on the metal parts to be joined .

But resistance soldering is unique in this respect: The electrodes actually conduct low-voltage, high-amperage current. This current is conducted through the workpiece, confining the heat to a specific area between the electrodes.

Three pieces of equipment are necessary for the basic system: (1) A step-down transformer, called the power unit, Fig. 53-20; (2) tool, called the handpiece, to hold the electrodes and place them in contact with the work being soldered, Fig. 53-20, (3) the electrodes, Fig. 53-20.

Power Units

Resistance-soldering power units are commonly divided into four classes, based on their output in watts.

Miniature power unit—up to 100 watts.

Medium power unit—between 100 and 250 watts.

Standard power unit—between 250 and 500 watts.

Heavy-duty power unit—over 500 watts.

Handpieces

Handpieces are of two main types for resistance soldering: (1) Single-electrode, (2) Dual-electrode.

When either handpiece is used, ground is made by means of an additional clamp attached to the work itself.

53-19. Propane bottled-gas torch.

53-20. Step-controlled electric pencil-type soldering unit.

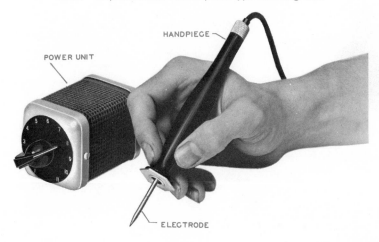

HANDPIECE

POWER UNIT

ELECTRODE

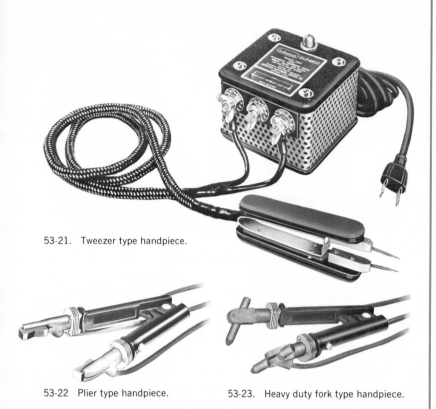

53-21.　Tweezer type handpiece.

53-22　Plier type handpiece.

53-23.　Heavy duty fork type handpiece.

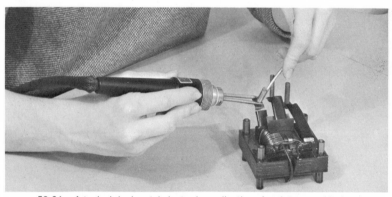

53-24.　A typical dual-metal-electrode application of resistance soldering.

53-25.　Electrode placed in contact with the work while solder is fed to the joint.

The most common types of handpieces are: (1) pencil, Fig. 53-20, (2) tweezer, Fig. 53-21, and (3) plier, Figs. 53-22 and 53-23.

Electrodes

Resistance-soldering electrodes are of two types: (1) carbon, (2) metal alloy.

Carbon electrodes are usually used in single-electrode handpieces while metal alloy electrodes are used in dual-electrode handpieces.

Electrodes vary in size from metal alloy of .078″ diameter for miniature work to large carbon blocks used with plier-type handpieces, Fig. 53-23.

The Soldering Operation

In resistance soldering the electrode is always held in contact with the work, which differs from welding operations where an arc has to be formed. There is no arcing because of the contact and the low voltages used.

Generally, a small diameter, flux core solder is used.

There are five basic steps in the resistance-soldering operation.

1. Adjust the power unit for the job. NOTE: Experimentation with similar set-ups is the best way to ascertain the exact output for a job.

2. Place electrodes in contact with the work.

3. Press switch to complete the circuit.

4. Feed solder to the joint.

5. Release the switch when the solder begins to flow and remove the tool.

Resistance soldering is used in industrial applications, Figs. 53-24 and 53-25, because it provides instant heat, without warm-up periods before or between jobs as is required with a regular soldering copper. A No. 20 gage wire joint normally requires 1.1 seconds soldering time. Parts to be soldered are heated thoroughly, providing complete "wetting" for uniform connections. In electronic work where a fast heat factor is important, resistance soldering makes it possible to get the connection made before any appreciable amount of heat has been conducted away from the joint being soldered.

NOTE: No pre-heating of soldering iron tips is necessary in resistance soldering.

There is less expense in replacing resistance-soldering electrodes than maintaining and replacing conduction soldering iron tips. This is an important item in industrial applications.

No heating elements are contained in handpieces, which are extremely light. The handpiece does not get uncomfortably warm, which is a considerable factor in the comfort of operators on high-production soldering jobs.

Check Your Knowledge

1. What is the basic operation in most sheet metalwork?

2. Name some of the most widely used metals in sheet metalwork.

3. Describe how a zinc coating is applied to galvanized iron.

4. What is tin plate? What is the difference between "coke tin plate" and "charcoal tin plate"?

5. What is a stretchout?

6. What are seams and hems?

7. How are raw edges and overlapping seams eliminated?

8. Name three types of notches.

9. How are the sizes of seams and hems determined?

10. What is a wired edge?

11. Name typical projects with a wired edge.

12. What is a sheet metal pattern?

13. What are the four types of pattern development?

14. How do you figure the amount of metal required for a wired edge?

15. What tools are used for cutting sheet metal by hand?

16. Straight lines and outside curves are cut with what tools? Inside curves?

17. What type of machine will cut large sheets?

18. What part of the snips should be used in cutting notches?

19. What tool is used to punch holes in sheet metal?

20. Name main types of sheet metal stakes. Describe their uses.

21. What is a hand seamer?

22. Explain three methods of making an angular bend by hand.

23. What degrees of bend can be made on a bar folder?

24. What type of hem will greatly strengthen an edge?

25. What bends can be made on a box and pan brake?

26. How many rolls does a roll-forming machine have?

27. Which one does the forming?

28. Describe the steps in forming a cylinder.

29. How are cone-shaped pieces formed on a roll forming machine?

30. After a cylinder is formed, how is it removed from the machine?

31. Name some of the common types of seams.

32. How do grooved and folded seams differ?

33. When is a double seam needed?

34. What tool is used to lock the grooved seam?

35. Is it necessary to use solder or rivets on a double seam? Explain.

36. Draw a diagram of a double seam.

37. What type of hammer is needed in closing a double seam?

38. How is the disc size determined for the bottom of a round container?

39. What is the function of a setting-down machine?

40. A Pittsburgh lock seam is often used for what type of work?

41. For what is a cap-strip seam used?

42. Is it possible to do wiring, beading, and crimping on the same machine? Which machine?

43. Why is beading done?

44. What is meant by turning a burr?

45. Name three methods of fastening sheet metal.

44. What is a rivet set? Explain how used.

47. What is the use of a solid punch.

48. What are tinner's rivets?

49. What determines the size of tinner's rivets?

50. Does riveting make a permanent joint? Explain.

51. What tool is used to punch holes for tinner's rivets?

52. How is the rivet set?

53. Name two types of sheet metal screws.

54. Define soldering.

55. What is the composition of most soft solders?

56. Why must solders melt at a lower temperature than the metal being joined.

57. What is flux and why is it needed?

58. Name the most important soldering devices.

59. What must be done when the soldering copper becomes coated with oxide?

60. Describe metal cleaning methods in readiness for soldering?

61. What is a soldering pencil? How used?

62. Describe the process of tinning a soldering copper.

63. Describe the process of sweat soldering.

64. How does resistance soldering differ from the conventional methods? Tell its advantages.

Terms to Know and Spell

flanging	cornice	soldering
galvanized	burr	rosin flux
corrosion	cylindrical	acid-core flux
annealed	frustum	sweat soldering
galvannealed	triangulation	grooved
notching	transition	offset
development	truncated	nonferrous
stretchout	disc	resistance soldering
radial	crank screw	furnace

Section 6, Project 1
PLANTER

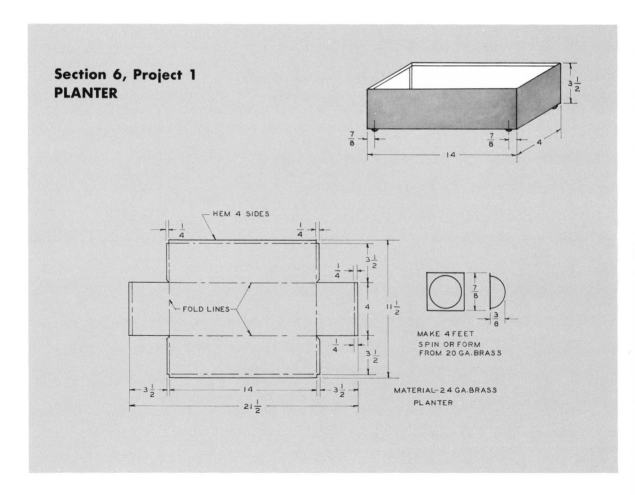

Section 6, Project 2
NAIL TRAY

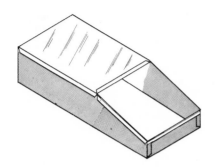

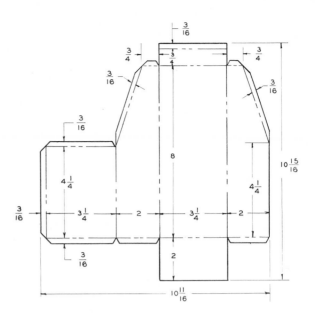

Section 6, Project 3
DUST PAN

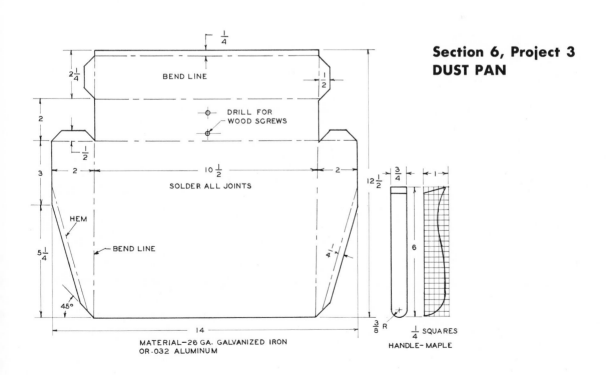

BEND LINE

DRILL FOR
WOOD SCREWS

SOLDER ALL JOINTS

HEM

BEND LINE

45°

MATERIAL—26 GA. GALVANIZED IRON
OR .032 ALUMINUM

$\frac{1}{4}$ SQUARES
HANDLE—MAPLE

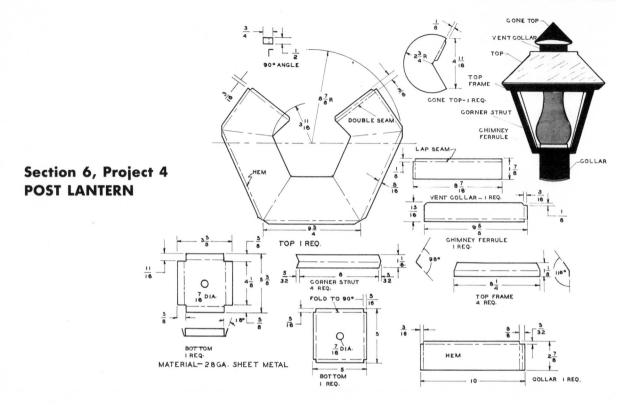

Section 6, Project 4
POST LANTERN

MATERIAL—28 GA. SHEET METAL

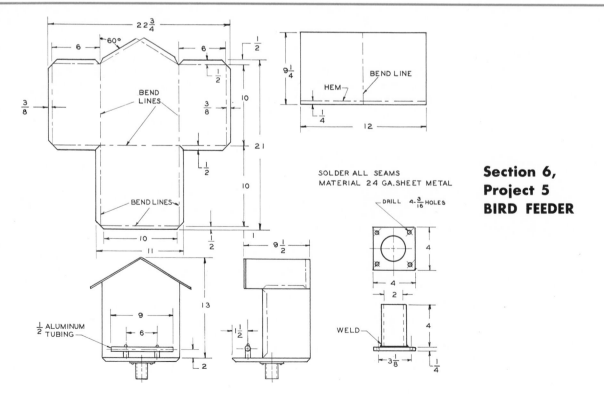

SOLDER ALL SEAMS
MATERIAL 24 GA. SHEET METAL

Section 6,
Project 5
BIRD FEEDER

Section 6, Project 6—BIRD FEEDER

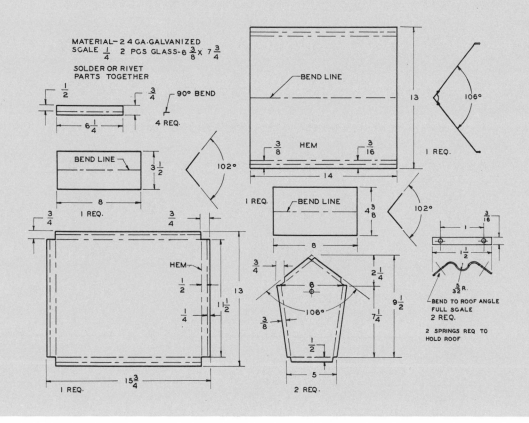

MATERIAL— 2 4 GA.·GALVANIZED
SCALE $\frac{1}{4}$ 2 PCS GLASS— 6$\frac{3}{8}$ X 7$\frac{3}{4}$

SOLDER OR RIVET
PARTS TOGETHER

90° BEND
4 REQ.

BEND LINE

BEND LINE   HEM

BEND TO ROOF ANGLE
FULL SCALE
2 REQ.

2 SPRINGS REQ TO
HOLD ROOF

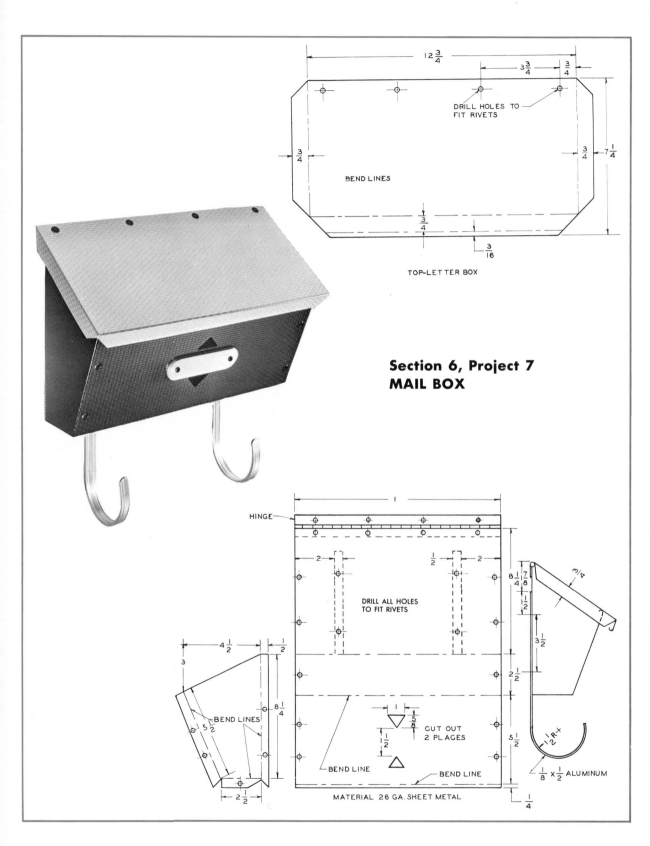

TOP-LETTER BOX

Section 6, Project 7
MAIL BOX

DRILL HOLES TO FIT RIVETS

BEND LINES

HINGE

DRILL ALL HOLES TO FIT RIVETS

BEND LINES

CUT OUT 2 PLACES

BEND LINE

BEND LINE

$\frac{1}{8} \times \frac{1}{2}$ ALUMINUM

MATERIAL 2 6 GA. SHEET METAL

Forging

F ORGING is the process of shaping metal to a desired form by means of pressing or hammering. Most of the work today requires hot forging. Some softer metals can be forged without heating, which is known as cold forging.

Mechanical forging press, used in making automotive, aircraft, and agricultural machine parts.

Forging dates from the early dawn of civilization and is one of the oldest metalworking processes. Man discovered he could form metal to various shapes by hammering it and almost every community had a blacksmith whose work grew in importance as civilization progressed.

Most forging today is done in industrial plants by specialists. This type of forging will be explained in Unit 55.

54 ▷ Hand Forging

54-2. Gas forge unit.

Although hand forging does not play the important part in our everyday living that it once did, it still has a great deal of value in the teaching of hand skills in our schools. You develop an understanding of the properties of metals and learn to shape and fabricate small parts such as cold chisels and center punches. You also can learn to make repairs at home or on the farm.

Equipment Used in Hand Forging

Although the coal forge has been largely replaced by gas or oil-burning forges, it is still in some use today. Fig. 54-1 illustrates a gas type furnace used in schools. It is made ready instantly by turning on the blower and lighting the gas. Another type of furnace for schools is shown in Fig. 54-2. A gas furnace eliminates the building of fires, disposal of ashes, fuel storage, and tending the forge when not in use. The work is always visible to the operator, thus helping to prevent the burning and wasting of valuable materials.

Fig. 54-3 shows a type of gas furnace used in industrial forging.

ANVILS

Anvils are made of cast steel, cast iron, or have a cast iron base with a welded steel face. The steel faced anvil is the best type. For heavy forging operations, an anvil weighing 100 lbs. is preferred. Fig. 54-4.

HAMMERS

Fig. 54-5 shows some of the hammers used in forging. Set hammers are used for work such as grooving, fluting, and squaring. Hammers of 1½ to 2 lbs. are used for light work and those of 3 to 3½ lbs. for heavy work.

ANVIL TOOLS

Anvil tools come equipped with a square shank to fit into the "hardy" hole of the anvil. The bottom *fuller*, bottom *swage*, and hot and cold hardies are useful

54-1. Modern type of forge set-up for school learning.

54-3. Industrial type gas furnace. The weight on the chain serves as a counterbalance.

CROSS PEEN HAMMER

SLEDGE

SET HAMMER

FLATTER

54-5. Types of hammers used in forging.

BOTTOM SWAGE

HOT HARDY

COLD HARDY

BOTTOM FULLER

54-6. Anvil tools.

tools for the shaping and stretching of metal. Fig. 54-6.

Tongs

Tongs are used for holding hot metal while it is being forged. They are made in several sizes and shapes. Some of the most common are illustrated in Fig. 54-7. Straight lip tongs are used to hold flat, round, and square shapes. They have a V-notch in each jaw. Gad tongs are designed for general forging purposes. Curved lip tongs have fluted jaws to assure a firm hold on bolts and irregular shapes. Single pick-up tongs can be used for picking up either round or flat stock. In order

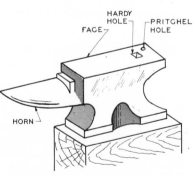

54-4. Anvil. Details are explained in the procedures.

54-7. Tongs: (A) Straight lip with V-notch, (B) gad tongs, (C) curved lip with fluted jaws, (D) single pick-up.

for the work to be held securely, the jaws of the tongs must close evenly on the work throughout their length. Fig. 54-8. The jaws can be heated and bent to fit the stock.

Hand Forging Operations

Keep the workpiece heated to the proper temperature during the forging process. It may be necessary to reheat several times before the forging is completed. *Mild steel* should be heated to a bright red heat. It is not necessary to heat *tool steel* to as high a temperature. If using a gas or oil furnace, adjust the flame so that it burns with a blue neutral flame to avoid the formation of a heavy scale. If a coal forge is used, avoid thrusting the metal in from the top with one end at the bottom of the fire. Place the workpiece in a horizontal position. Fig. 54-9.

Tapering

Tapering refers to stretching and lengthening the metal by hammering. The tapered end of a cold chisel is a good example.

1. Heat one end of the piece to be tapered.

2. Hold the other end firmly in the tongs with the heated section on the face of the anvil. Fig. 54-10.

CAUTION: *Wear protective clothing and safety glasses when working around hot metal.*

3. Hold the metal at an angle to the face of the anvil equal to about one-half the amount of the required taper. Strike the heated portion with the flat of the hammer, turning the metal to keep the taper even. Flatten the sides of the taper after every few blows

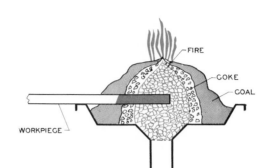

54-8. The proper method of gripping flat metal with tongs.

54-9. The correct method of heating a workpiece in a coal forge. Hold in the forge horizontally.

so that the proper shape will be obtained. In shaping round stock, turn the workpiece slightly after each blow of the hammer.

4. Reheat the metal to a dull red, keeping it at forging temperature. Use light hammer blows to smooth out the tapered portion to the desired shape.

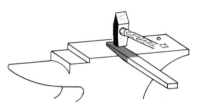

54-10. Tapering.

Drawing Out

Drawing out consists of forging

54-11. Drawing out a piece on the anvil, using a fuller and a bottom fuller.

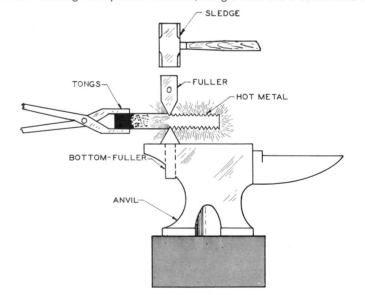

to make a piece longer and thinner. Flat pieces are drawn out more easily by first notching them with fullers, Fig. 54-11, and then removing the notches by reheating the metal and hammering the workpiece on the face of the anvil. To draw a round piece to shape, the following steps should be followed:

1. Heat the workpiece to a high red.

2. Hammer out the section to a square shape.

3. Place in the furnace and reheat the metal. Form it into an octagon.

4. Round off the workpiece as the metal is rotated on the anvil face. Fig. 54-12.

A punch may be drawn to shape as shown in Fig. 54-13.

Bending

Sharp, square bends may be formed in the following manner.

1. Place the heated metal on the anvil face with the portion to be bent over the rounded corner of the anvil face.

2. Strike the extended part of the stock glancing blows to bend the stock down to the desired angle.

3. Square off the bend over the square edge of the anvil by alternately striking the vertical and horizontal faces of the stock. Fig. 54-14.

4. The workpiece can also be bent by placing it in the hardy hole and pulling toward you. If the end of the bar is hot, use tongs. Fig. 54-15.

5. Square the metal off by hammering as in Fig. 54-14.

6. A curved shaped can be formed by hammering over the horn of the anvil. Fig. 54-16. Heat

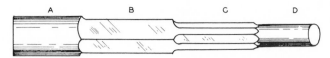

54-12. Steps in drawing out a round to a smaller diameter: (A) Round, (B) square, (C) octagon, (D) round.

ROUND TO SQUARE   SQUARE TO OCTAGON   OCTAGON TO CONE

54-13. Steps in drawing a round piece of stock to a point, to make a punch.

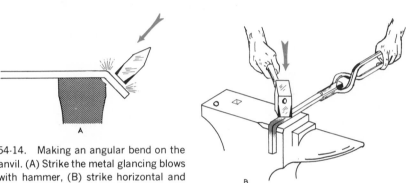

54-14. Making an angular bend on the anvil. (A) Strike the metal glancing blows with hammer, (B) strike horizontal and vertical faces alternately to square off bend.

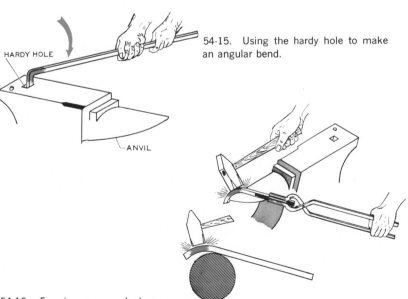

54-15. Using the hardy hole to make an angular bend.

54-16. Forming a curved shape over the horn of the anvil.

the area of the metal to be bent and strike the workpiece with overlapping blows as you form the desired curve.

BENDING AN EYE

1. Measure the length of material needed to make the eye and mark with a prick punch. Heat and bend this section over the edge of the anvil. Fig. 54-17 (A).

2. Reheat and start bending the end to form the eye. Fig. 54-17 (B).

3. Continue heating, if necessary, and forming the eye over the anvil horn. Fig. 54-17 (C).

4. Close the eye by holding over the edge of the anvil, striking it firmly with a hammer. Fig. 54-17 (D).

Upsetting

Upsetting may be described as the process of broadening the end of the workpiece while shortening its length.

1. Heat the section to be upset to the proper forging temperature.

2. If the workpiece is long it may be held in a vise. Fig. 54-18 (A). Strike the end of the heated portion with a hammer to increase the breadth.

3. If the piece is short and both ends are to be upset, hold the workpiece with a pair of tongs on the face of the anvil and strike one end to obtain the desired result. Fig. 54-18 (B). If the metal bends, lay it flat on the anvil and hammer it back to shape.

4. If only one end is to be upset, heat one end, hold the heated end with tongs on the face of the anvil, and upset. Fig. 54-18 (C).

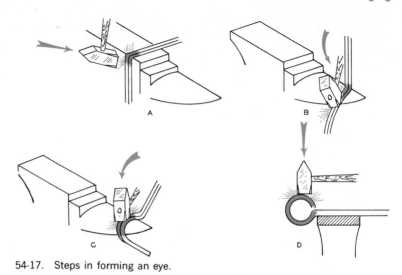

54-17. Steps in forming an eye.

54-18. (A) Holding the workpiece in a vise for upsetting operation, (B) upsetting both ends of the workpiece, (C) upsetting one end of the workpiece on the anvil.

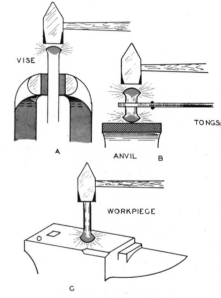

Twisting

1. Heat the area of the metal to be twisted.

2. Clamp securely in a vise, with the starting point of the twist even with the top edge of the vise jaws.

3. Place an adjustable wrench on the other end and rotate it the number of turns required to obtain the desired twist.

55 ▷ Machine Forging

Forging improves metals in all directions. It concentrates grain structure and fiber formation at points of greatest shock and stress to obtain the utmost strength and toughness a specific metal affords.

The resulting uniformity renders the metal remarkably free of concealed, internal defects. Here is "predictable resistance" to "calculated stresses," as well as ample reserve strength and toughness.

Forgings often permit reduction of dead weight in parts because their higher strength-to-weight ratio allows the use of lighter sectional thickness at no sacrifice in strength. Often improvements in product design are the result. Forging to uniform shapes and close dimensional tolerances eliminates machining operations and results in a reduction in the amount of machine time required for necessary finishing. Fig. 55-1 illustrates the typical grain characteristics of a casting, of a workpiece machined from a solid, and of a forging. Draft or taper must be provided in all forgings. Although the draft angles are not usually shown in drawings of sand castings, they are always

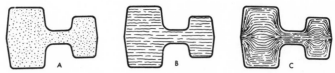

55-1. Typical grain characteristics of (left to right): (A) casting, machined from (B) solid, and a (C) forging. The forging is much stronger at points of stress because of the grain contour or flow.

shown on forging drawings. Fig. 55-2 is typical of this. It is necessary where strength must be calculated.

Types of Forging

Metal can be forged by impact or pressure. When forged by impact in hammers, the part can be formed by dies. These are either flat, slightly shaped (smith forged), or have a closed impression. Fig.

55-3 (drop forging). Presses can also be used for flat-die forging. The largest work is done on hydraulic presses.

SMITH FORGING

Smith forgings are commonly produced with steam hammers, which imitate the blacksmith. Small forgings are generally made on motor driven pneumatic or helve hammers. A smith forging,

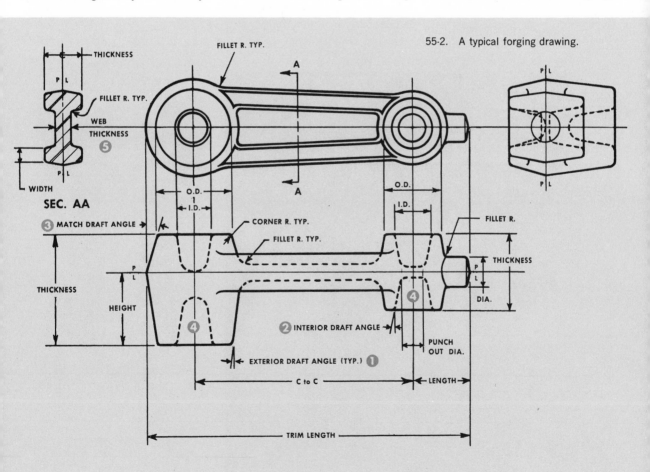

55-2. A typical forging drawing.

221

55-3.   A forging die.

55-5.   Industrial type gas forge furnace.

55-4.   Smith forging. Drawing out a tapered wedge.

55-6.   Drop hammer.

55-7. Straight side mechanical press used for trimming, forging, blanking, piercing, drawing, and forming.

55-8. Basic unit for forging operations.

55-9. Forging hammer operated by one man.

Fig. 55-4, is principally used where quantity is too low to justify dies or a "pilot" product is needed too quickly to permit the making of dies. For large production, dies may be made later, after the forging has been tested.

Drop Forging

The simplest drop-forging process employs a basic producing unit—a heating furnace, Fig. 55-5, a drop hammer, Fig. 55-6, and a trimming press, Fig. 55-7. In some heavy forging operations, as many as three men are needed to complete the cycle. Fig. 55-8. In other forging operations, one man can handle everything. Fig. 55-9. A normal cycle is as follows: The operator, gripping the bar, manipulates the hot end through die impressions, trims the forging, cuts the flash (spread) from the end of the bar, and returns the shortened bar to the furnace. Tongs are used only for the last operation. Fig. 55-10, page 224.

A few of the thousands of drop forgings produced in such basic units include surgical instruments, hammers, pliers, wrenches, cutlery, and a host of machinery parts. Figs. 55-11 (A) and (B) show some of the parts produced. See following pages.

Machine Forging

Machine forgings or upset forgings are produced on horizontal,

double-acting forging machines or upsetters. The heated bar stock is placed between a pair of gripper dies which close on the work before the header slide pushes a punch against the soft, heated metal to force it into the die impression.

PRESS FORGING

Press forgings are formed in mechanical or hydraulic presses. The action is similar to that of the regular forging machine except that the ram movement is vertical.

The dies used in press forging are similar to those used in drop forging, but there are variations in design and the construction is more flexible. Individual die sections can be mounted in a bolster plate and die inserts can be used.

Each method of forging can be used independently or combined with other methods.

Smith forging is frequently a preliminary to drop or press forging.

Types of Hammers

STEAM FORGING HAMMERS

The steam forging hammer, Fig. 55-12, is used for preliminary forging operations and for small-quantity productions. The hammers are made in single and double-frame styles and, though called steam hammers, can operate on either steam or compressed air.

Single-frame forging hammers, Fig. 55-12, are built in two types—self-contained and standard. The self-contained, in sizes from 50 lbs. to 300 lbs., includes the anvil as an integral part of the frame. The standard type, in sizes from 250 lbs. to 6,000 lbs., has a separately mounted anvil.

55-11. (A) Examples of the numerous types of forgings that are produced by machine or upset forging.

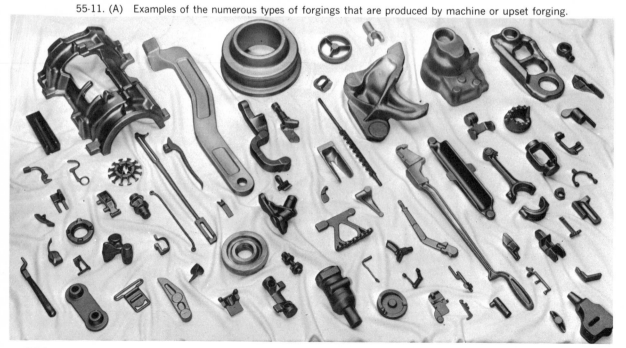

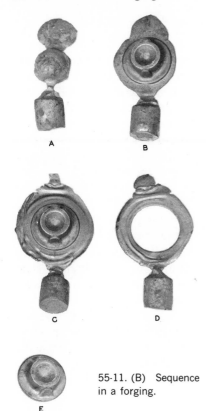

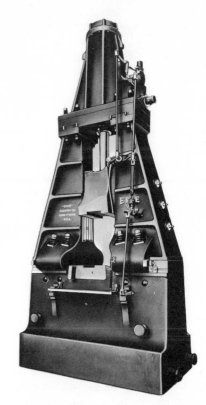

55-11. (B) Sequence in a forging.

Forging hammers are rated by the "nominal scale weight of the reciprocating parts," including the ram, top die, piston rod, and piston.

Double-frame hammers are generally made in larger sizes, suited to heavier work. The dies are not as accessible as they are in the single-frame hammer. Sizes of double-frame hammers range from 1,000 to 25,000 lbs. Fig. 55-13.

The ram is raised and lowered by pressure of steam or compressed air in the cylinder above it. The piston is double-acting, so steam can be used to raise the ram and also augment or retard the force of gravity in lowering the ram. The force can be controlled from a light tap to a giant maximum force.

BOARD DROP HAMMERS

The force of gravity is employed in the board drop hammer. The ram is raised to striking position by means of boards, the lower ends of which are wedged into the ram. Fig. 55-14. The upper ends of the boards pass between one or two pairs of rolls. With the two rolls in a pair rotating in opposite directions, the boards and ram are raised when the rolls move together. When the ram reaches the top of the stroke the rolls separate and the boards are released.

The board drop hammer will automatically deliver blows at a uniform rate when the treadle is depressed and held down.

STEAM DROP HAMMERS

The steam drop hammer, Fig.

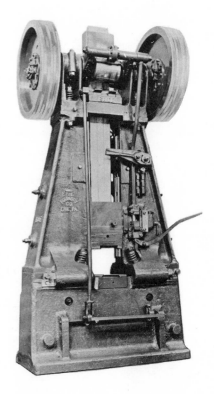

55-13. Double-acting steam or air powered drop hammer.

55-12. Single-frame forging hammer upsetting a single square steel bar.

55-14. Board lift gravity drop hammer.

55-15. Steam or air drop hammers.

55-15, is similar in operation to the steam forging hammer except that the frame is mounted on the anvil so that the top and bottom dies can be held in alignment.

Steam drop hammers are made in sizes from 400 lbs. to 50,000 lbs. although no hammer larger than 35,000 lbs. is used in the United States.

Pneumatic Hammers

See Fig. 55-16. These are used for both job and production work. The machine delivers a sharp, lively blow like that of a steam hammer. The ram pulls away quickly so that the operator can turn or move the work. Both the lightest taps and full blows are delivered at a constant speed. This machine has a built-in compression chamber, engineered to deliver the exact amount of air required to lift the upper die and ram.

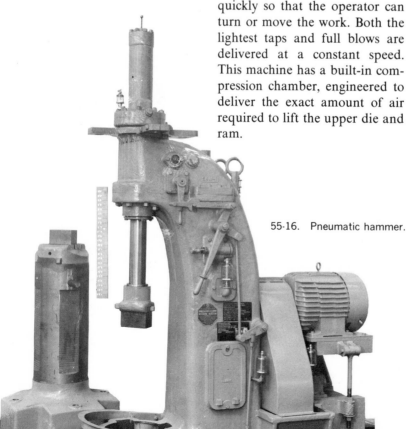

55-16. Pneumatic hammer.

Cold Forging Machines

See Fig. 55-17. Known as "cold headers," these are built for working cold stock. Cold headers are automatic, with stock fed from a reel. The machine can forge products such as cap screws or bolts, and can upset the heads and trim the bar, roll the threads, and chamfer the ends.

Forging Presses

Forging presses, Fig. 55-18, are designed for high volume forging of a variety of parts, such as connecting rods, gear blanks, stem pinions, ring gears, track links, and hub caps.

These presses are of massive, rigid construction with steel frames and heavy crankshafts. The heated metal is placed between the two dies which are then closed by a steady application of hydraulic pressure.

Check Your Knowledge

1. What is forging?

2. What is the fundamental difference between the work of the blacksmith and of the modern industrial forge?

3. What can you learn that is of practical value from hand forging?

4. What type of furnace is most commonly used for heating metal for forging operations?

5. What type of material makes the best anvil?

6. Name some types of hammers most commonly used in hand forging.

7. What is a set hammer? Explain its uses.

8. Name four different anvil tools in common use.

9. Name four types of tongs.

10. Why is it important that the

226

metal be heated to the proper temperature for forging?

11. What does the term "tapering" refer to?

12. Explain the process of tapering a piece of stock.

13. What is meant by drawing out metal? How is it done?

14. How are sharp bends made?

15. Describe the process of bending an eye.

16. Define upsetting. How is it done?

17. Describe the process of twisting.

18. What is cold forging?

19. Explain how forging uses the grain of metal for added strength.

20. List some of the advantages of forging over machining processes.

21. What is drop forging?

22. Give the normal cycle in a forging operation.

23. Name several products that are produced in industry by forging.

24. What types of dies are commonly used in drop forging?

25. Explain the difference between press forging and drop forging.

55-18. Forging press.

55-17. Horizontal cold forming press.

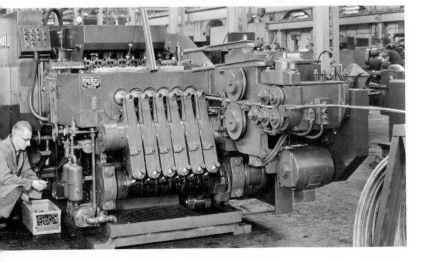

Terms to Know and Spell

pneumatic
anvil
tongs
hardy
upsetting
drop forging
machine forging
dimensional tolerances
flat-die forging
helve hammer
smith forging
die impressions
press forging

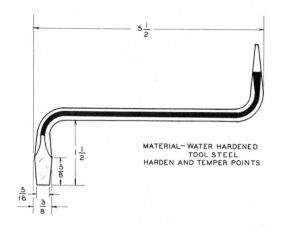

MATERIAL— WATER HARDENED
TOOL STEEL
HARDEN AND TEMPER POINTS

Section 7, Project 1
OFFSET SCREWDRIVER

Section 7, Project 2
CENTER PUNCH

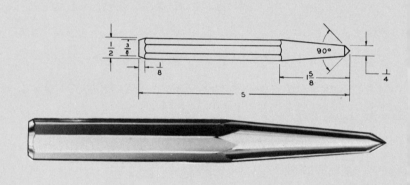

Section 7, Project 3
COLD CHISEL

MATERIAL—TOOL STEEL

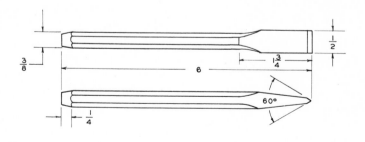

**Section 7, Project 4
WRECKING BAR**

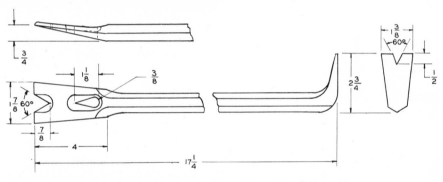

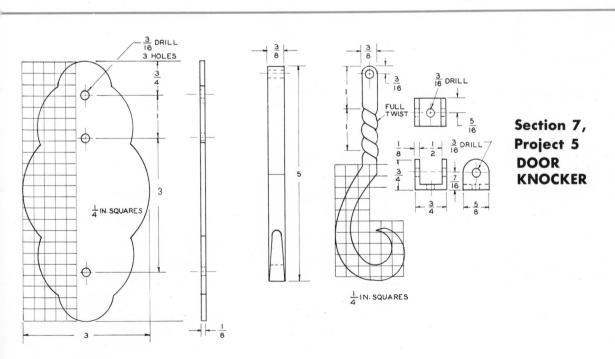

**Section 7,
Project 5
DOOR
KNOCKER**

229

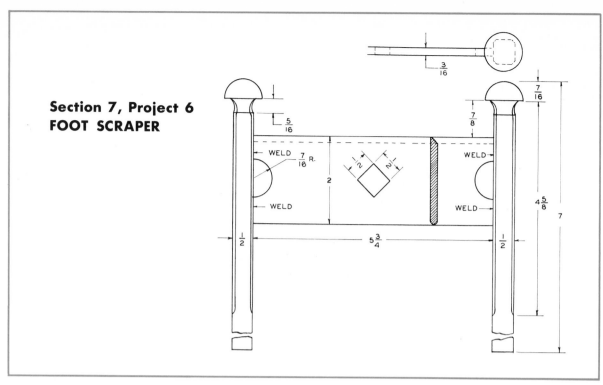

Section 7, Project 6
FOOT SCRAPER

WELD $\frac{7}{16}$ R.

WELD

$\frac{5}{16}$

$\frac{7}{16}$

$\frac{7}{8}$

WELD

WELD

$\frac{1}{2}$

2

$\frac{1}{2}$

$\frac{1}{2}$

$5\frac{3}{4}$

$4\frac{5}{8}$

7

$\frac{3}{16}$

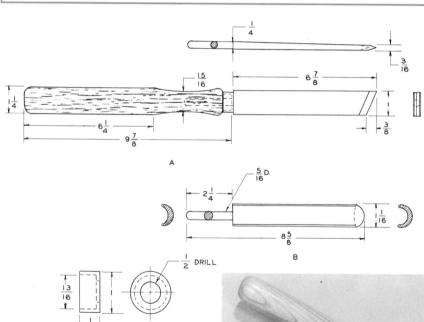

$\frac{1}{4}$

$\frac{3}{16}$

$\frac{15}{16}$

$6\frac{7}{8}$

$1\frac{1}{4}$

$6\frac{1}{4}$

$9\frac{7}{8}$

$\frac{3}{8}$

A

$\frac{5}{16}$ D.

$2\frac{1}{4}$

$\frac{1}{16}$

$8\frac{5}{8}$

B

$\frac{1}{2}$ DRILL

$\frac{13}{16}$

$\frac{1}{2}$

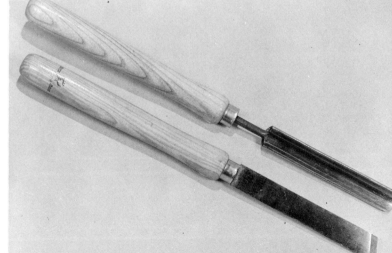

Section 7, Project 7
WOODTURNING CHISELS
(A) Skew chisel
(B) Gouge

Foundry

ONE of the oldest industries in the world is the casting of metals. Metal castings were made by the Egyptians about the year 4,000 B.C. The columns that supported King Solomon's Temple were made of bronze 27' high and 5'9" in diameter, the thickness of the metal being about 4". The Greeks and the Romans cast metal bells and ornaments for temples of worship.

Production molding.

The first use of foundry work was for ornamental purposes. Then as man became more skillful, he developed weapons.

The art of founding progressed slowly until cast iron was developed. In the year 1642 the first Colonial American iron casting was made by the Saugus Iron Works. It was an iron cooking pot. From this single foundry engaged in the manufacture of cooking utensils has developed one of the largest industries in the United States.

Today foundry work is a basic industry, dealing with the melting of metals and the pouring of molten metal into molds from which castings are obtained.

There are an estimated 386,000 workers employed in our nation's more than 5,000 foundries.

Most foundries specialize in casting a particular metal, since somewhat different methods and equipment are needed for others. However, there are foundries that do cast several types of metals.

Some foundries use very little mechanized equipment. These are usually small, and ordinarily use the sand molding method to produce assorted orders of different kinds of castings.

Other types of foundries are highly mechanized and have typically large shops that produce great quantities of identical castings. For example, such a foundry may produce thousands of identical automotive parts. Materials and castings in these plants are moved with mechanized conveyers and cranes.

The conveniences of the modern home depend to a large extent on foundry products, such as bathtubs, sinks, wash basins, soil pipe, furnaces, cooking utensils, and parts for washers and dryers, which are made from gray iron castings.

56 ▷ Foundry Materials and Equipment

A great deal of special equipment is used in industrial foundries because molding operations are performed by machines.

Much of the equipment used in the school in hand molding can be made. The molding benches, molding tools, and even the crucible furnace can be produced in the shop. Described in this unit are some of the basic items needed for hand molding.

• A **flask** is a boxlike container in which the sand mold is made, either of wood with metal fittings, or entirely of metal. The flask is made in two parts, the upper section being called the **cope**, and the bottom section the **drag**.

• A **snap flask**, Fig. 56-1, has a hinge on one corner so that the flask may be removed from the mold before the metal is poured. Then the mold is enclosed with a wood or metal frame called a jacket.

• The **sponge bulb** or **water brush** is used to moisten the sand around the pattern. This prevents the sand edges from crumbling when the pattern is removed from the mold. Fig. 56-2 (A).

• A **strike-off bar** is a metal bar used to remove the surplus sand from the mold after the ramming has been completed. Fig. 56-2 (B).

• **Draw screws**, Fig. 56-2 (C), and **draw pins**, Fig. 56-6 (C), are drawing devices used to lift the pattern from the sand after it has been rammed. The draw screw is screwed into a draw plate fastened to the pattern.

• The **draw pin** is a pointed steel rod which is stabbed into the wooden pattern to lift the pattern from the mold.

• A **gate cutter**, Fig. 56-2 (D), is a metal device used to cut an opening between the sprue and mold cavity.

• A **bellows**, Fig. 56-2 (E), blows loose sand from the mold. It is often more satisfactory to use the bellows or the air hose to blow out loose sand than to try to remove these particles with lifters or a brush.

• **Riddles**, Fig. 56-2 (F), are used by the molder to sift sand over the pattern in order to insure a smooth casting. Riddles are usually round in shape. Sizes are de-

56-1. Snap flask.

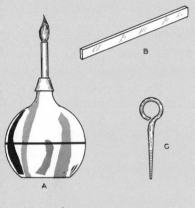

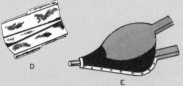

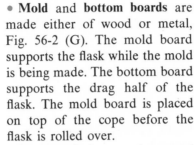

56-2. (A) Bulb sponge, (B) strike-off bar, (C) draw screw, (D) gate cutter, (E) molder's bellows, (F) riddle, (G) molding board, (H) sprue-and-riser pin.

noted by the diameter of the frame and the coarseness of the wire screen. The size of the screen is determined by the number of meshes per inch it contains. A No. 10 mesh has ten openings per lineal inch. For the majority of bench molding operations, No. 4 to No. 12 meshes are common. For general-purpose molding, a riddle with No. 12 or No. 14 mesh is recommended.

● **Mold** and **bottom boards** are made either of wood or metal, Fig. 56-2 (G). The mold board supports the flask while the mold is being made. The bottom board supports the drag half of the flask. The mold board is placed on top of the cope before the flask is rolled over.

● A **sprue pin** is a wood or metal pin placed in the cope of the mold to make an opening through which the metal is poured. Fig. 56-2 (H).

● **Steel flasks**, Figs. 56-3 and 56-4, are used in industrial foundries because of their durability.

For some complicated molding operations, a three-part flask is often used. It is made up of a third section called a **cheek**, in addition to the cope and drag.

For industry, a motor driven riddle, Fig. 56-5, is commonly used.

● **Sprue cutters** are used instead of the sprue pin in production molding because they save time in ramming the mold. A sprue cutter is a tapered hollow tube which is pushed through the cope to the joint of the mold. When withdrawn from the sand the tube removes it, leaving an opening for the metal to be poured.

● A **riser pin** is similar to a sprue pin except that it is somewhat

56-3 and 4. Steel flasks.

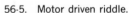

56-5. Motor driven riddle.

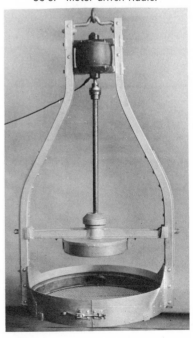

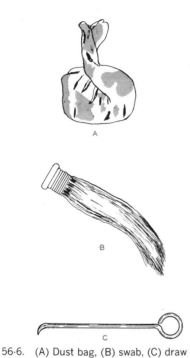

56-6. (A) Dust bag, (B) swab, (C) draw spike. (See reference to C on page 232.)

larger in diameter. It forms an opening to supply the mold with additional metal to compensate for metal shrinkage.
• A **shake bag**, Fig. 56-6 (A), is used to dust *parting compound* on the mold and pattern, for ease in removal.

• A **swab**, Fig. 56-6 (B), is made of camel's hair or flax. It is used to moisten the sand around the pattern, in place of a bulb sponge.
• **Rammers** are often used in pairs for packing sand in the mold around the pattern. Fig. 56-7. Molder's bench rammers are turned from choice hard maple, smoothly sanded, and dipped in heavy paraffin oil. They are made in standard sizes, with either square or round shoulders in 3″, 3½″, 4″, and 4½″ by 14″ sizes.

The job molder uses one in each hand to ram up the mold.

Pneumatic rammers are used in industrial foundries to speed up the work. Fig. 56-8.

Slicks, Spoons, Lifters, and Trowels

• **Slicks** are small tools used for repairing and finishing molds. There are many types, as shown in Fig. 56-9. The oval spoon is most commonly used.
• **Lifters** are for patching deep sections of a mold and removing loose sand from the pockets of the mold.
• **Trowels** are for making joints

and finishing flat surfaces of a mold. Although the round-end finishing trowel is probably the most commonly used, there are other trowels such as the square-end, heart, and spear.
• A **vent wire** is a wire rod for making openings or vents in the mold. These allow gas and steam to escape during the pouring operation.

Molding Bench

In the school foundry, bench molding is commonly practiced because machine methods are not economical. The molding is done on a bench or shelf about 30″ high. The bench should have a sand bin to help prevent tracking sand to other parts of the shop and for convenience. A rack should be built above the bench so that the molding tools will be accessible for use.

Melting Furnace

• **Crucible furnaces** melt *non-ferrous* metals such as aluminum, brass, bronze, tin, lead, and zinc.

The most common method of melting nonferrous metals in

56-7. Rammers.

56-8. Pneumatic sand rammer being used to pack sand into a foundry mold.

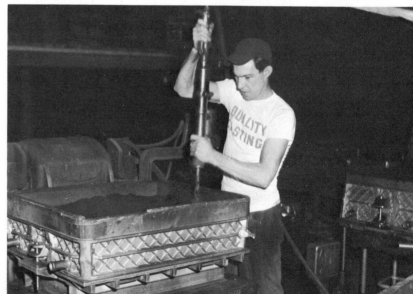

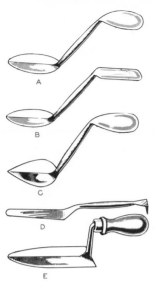

56-9. Tools used to shape and smooth the surfaces of the mold: (A) Slick-and-oval spoon, (B) slick-and-square spoon, (C) heart-and-oval spoon, (D) bench lifter (bent), (E) No. 2 finishing trowel.

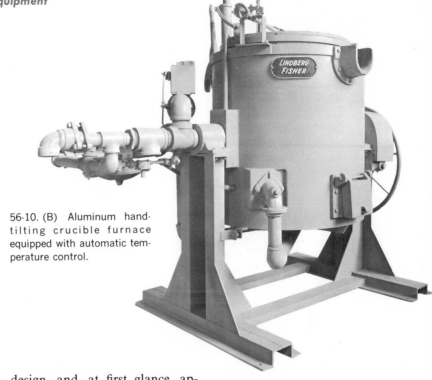

56-10. (B) Aluminum hand-tilting crucible furnace equipped with automatic temperature control.

the school is by using a gas-fired furnace. Fig. 56-10 (A). In this furnace, the burning gas does not come in direct contact with the metal charge. The metal is placed in a crucible where it is melted. A blast of burning gas and air is blown around the crucible until the charge is melted. Fig. 56-10 (B) shows a hand-tilting crucible furnace for larger production.

While the furnace is simple in

56-10. (A) Gas-fired melting furnace, showing crucibles and crucible shank.

design, and, at first glance, apparently easy to build and operate, it is a piece of equipment in which dimensional relations are important if the melting process is to be carried out so as to obtain both economy of operation and good metallurgical quality. The inside diameter of the lining should be enough larger than the bilge of the crucible to provide proper combustion space for efficient melting and allow room for application of the tongs. The lining should be free from holes or projections which will divert the flame from its normal course and result in uneven heating. Unless the flame has an unrestricted path around the crucible, incomplete combustion may occur with the result that hydrogen can be absorbed by the charge. This can cause porous, weak castings.
• In general, *ferrous* metals are melted in a **cupola furnace**, Fig. 56-11. This is a vertical steel

56-11. An industrial complex of cupola furnaces.

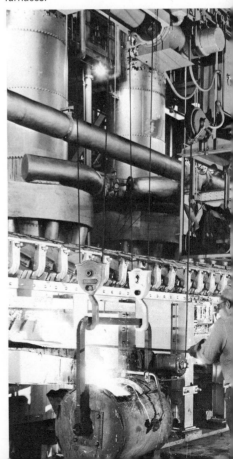

235

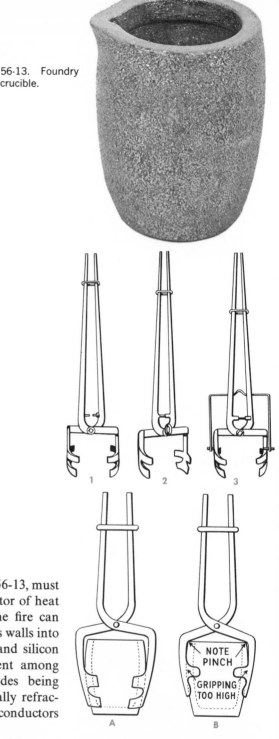

56-13. Foundry crucible.

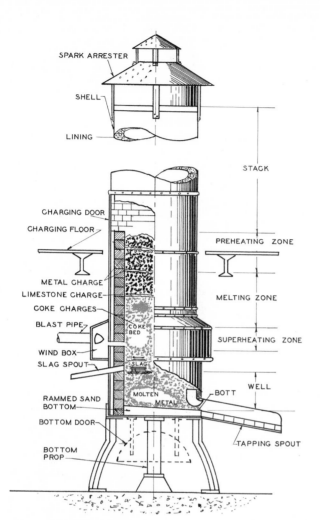

56-12. Cross-section of cupola furnace, for melting ferrous metals.

56-14. (1) Hand lift tongs, (2) with eye bolt for mechanical hoist, (3) with side trunnions and bail for lifting. Above: Tongs that fit will increase crucible life and correct fit of tongs shown at (A). A crucible may be cracked by tongs pinching across the top, as at (B).

structure lined with refractory material. The cupola furnace is fired with coke to produce the high temperature required for melting iron. The furnace is charged with alternate layers of coke, metal, and flux. The molten metal collects at the bottom and flows out through a hole and down the tapping spout into a receiving ladle. Fig. 56-12.

Crucibles

Besides not being subject to melting itself and being chemically inert to molten metals, a foundry crucible, Fig. 56-13, must also be a good conductor of heat so that the heat of the fire can flow rapidly through its walls into the charge. Graphite and silicon carbide are pre-eminent among materials which, besides being thermally and chemically refractory, are also good conductors of heat.

The particles of graphite and silicon carbide are bonded with either clay or carbon.

● **Clay-bonded** graphite crucibles, taken from warm, dry storage, may immediately be put into

56-15. Molten metal in crucible being poured from carrying shank.

56-16. Ladle.

56-18. Standard crane ladle, with riveted construction.

Hardware

● **Tongs and shanks.** The hardware or equipment used to *carry* the crucible to where it is to be poured consists of the tongs, Fig. 56-14. Tong jaws should be shaped so as to cradle the crucible just below the bilge and should not rest or pinch the rim of the crucible. Fig. 56-14 (A). NOTE: Sometimes the crucible is poured from the carrying shanks, but in most cases, after being taken from the furnace with tongs, it is transferred to shanks. The latter is a rigid hoop with steel rods which extend from opposite ends of the hoop and serve as carrying handles. Fig. 56-15.

service. On the first heat, the temperature should be brought up slowly with a low gas flame and with reduced air supply. Larger sizes will naturally require a little slower rate of initial heating.

● **Carbon-bonded** silicon carbide crucibles may be brought up to melting temperature as rapidly as possible.

56-19. Trolley ladle, with detachable bail.

● A **ladle**, Fig. 56-16, is constructed from steel, with a lining such as fire clay. Molten metal is transferred from the furnace to the ladle and then poured into molds.

Of course, the hand type is most commonly used in schools. In mechanized foundries, ladles are transported on roller conveyers, Fig. 56-17, for pouring the molds. Fig. 56-18 illustrates a standard-pour crane ladle and Fig. 56-19 a trolley ladle.

56-17. Pouring molds on a roller conveyor with ladle handlers and trolley ladles.

57 ▷ Patterns

A pattern is a form used to make a cavity of the desired size and shape in a mold from which a casting can be obtained. A pattern may be made from wood, metal, plaster, plastic, or any other material that will retain its shape during the molding process. Metal patterns are used when production runs are high, due to the fact that a metal pattern has a much longer life than a wood pattern. However, a wood pattern is made first—as the master pattern—and the permanent metal pattern cast from it.

In general, metals expand when heated and contract when cooled. It is therefore necessary to provide *shrinkage* allowance in constructing the pattern. Different metals, when being cast, have different shrinkages. This shrinkage allowance is readily calculated by the patternmaker, so he constructs the pattern oversize to allow for it.

The patternmaker also has to make allowances for *machining* the finished casting. This allowance is controlled by the degree of finish required, the type of metal used, and the shape, and size of the casting.

All vertical surfaces of patterns must be provided with *draft* to facilitate their being drawn from the mold. The verticals are slightly tapered to permit releasing the pattern without injury to the mold. Fig. 57-1.

Types of Patterns

The most common types of patterns are: flat-back, solid, split, cored, and match-plate patterns.
- **Flat-back patterns**, Fig. 57-2, have a large flat surface on the cope side, making possible a straight line parting on the joint between the cope and drag of the mold.

- **Solid** or **single-piece patterns**, Fig. 57-3, consist of a single unit made of wood. This is the most economical pattern when only a few castings are required.
- **Split patterns**, Fig. 57-4, are made in two parts, split at a flat parting line to facilitate molding. A split pattern is molded with the upper half in the cope and the lower half in the drag. The cope and drag portions are fitted together accurately with wood or metal pins.
- **Cored patterns**, Fig. 57-5. Many castings require holes, recesses, or indentations of various sizes and shapes. Some patterns are made with parts added to the surface, called core prints. These form a seat in the mold to support and locate the core.
- A **core print** is an added projection on a pattern which forms a seat in the mold, in which the core rests during the pouring operation. Fig. 57-5.
- **Match-plate patterns**, Fig. 57-6, are used on molding machines for quantity production of castings. Either a single pattern or a num-

57-2.   Flat-back pattern.

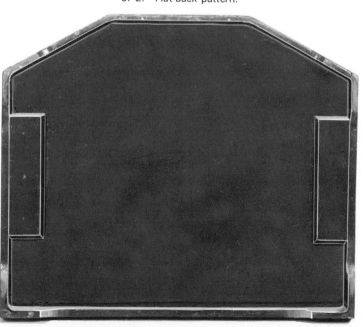

57-1.   Taper is put on the sides of a pattern so that it can easily be withdrawn from the sand.

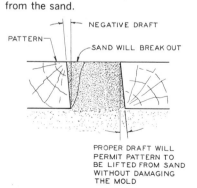

NEGATIVE DRAFT

PATTERN

SAND WILL BREAK OUT

PROPER DRAFT WILL PERMIT PATTERN TO BE LIFTED FROM SAND WITHOUT DAMAGING THE MOLD

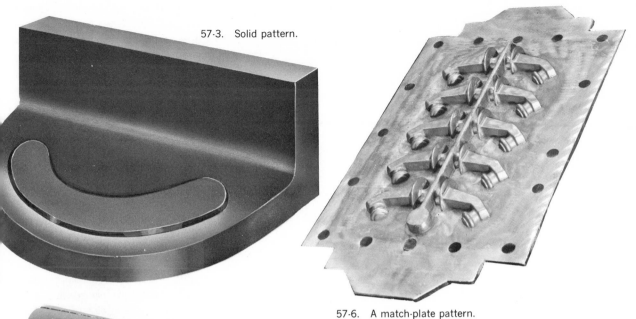

57-3. Solid pattern.

57-6. A match-plate pattern.

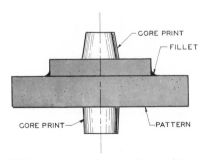

57-4. Split pattern.

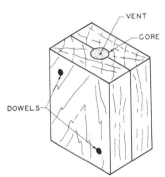

57-7. Sand is rammed into a two-part core box to form a core.

CORE PRINT

FILLET

CORE PRINT

PATTERN

57-5. Core prints on a one-piece pattern.

ber of patterns may be mounted on a match plate. Part of the pattern can be located on the cope and the remainder on the drag side.

Patterns for gates and runners are fastened on the match plate, thereby eliminating the necessity of cutting flow channels by hand.

Cores

• A **core** is a body of specially prepared sand used to form the desired opening in the casting. The core prevents the molten metal from flowing into cavities of the casting that are to remain open.

Cores are made by ramming sand into core boxes, Figs. 57-7 and 57-8, formed to produce the required shape. After ramming, the mold is removed from the core box and baked in an oven until it hardens. Fig. 57-9 shows how various types of cores are used in the mold. See page 240.

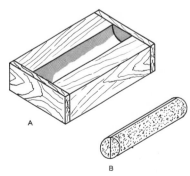

57-8. Half-core box and a sand core.

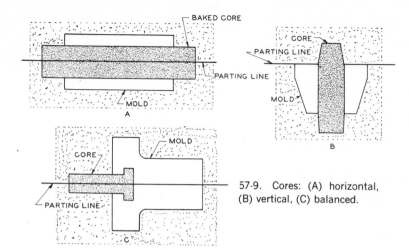

57-9. Cores: (A) horizontal, (B) vertical, (C) balanced.

• **Chaplets**, Fig. 57-10, are small metal parts used to support a core prior to and during the pouring operation.

Molding Sand

The greatest percentage of casting is done with "green" or moist sand. This is a mixture of silica, clay, and water. It should possess three different qualities: (1) The required chemical composition to resist fusion from the high tem-

RADIATOR CHAPLET PLAIN STEM WITH SHOULDER

NICKED STEM WITH SHOULDER

ANGLE STEM

57-10. Some types of chaplets used in foundry work.

TWISTED STEM

peratures of molten metal, (2) enough bond (clay) to hold the shape of the mold during the process of pouring, (3) possess the proper porosity to enable the free escape of gases which have a tendency to form when molten metal comes in contact with moisture.

Dry sand cannot be used for molding. The sand must be dampened for proper working consistency. Metals which have high melting points must be poured into molds containing sands of greater refractoriness. Clay gives the sand a bond, but care should be taken that the sand does not contain too much clay, as it may make the mold too tight and not permit gases to escape. NOTE: Too little bond can cause the mold to fall apart when it becomes partially dried.

Water tempered sand has to be used, and properly cared for, each day if good castings are to be obtained. Difficulties are often encountered if the sand becomes dry because it is not used for several days at a time.

A type of *waterless* sand that is near-ideal for use in schools is a sand-oil-binder combination.

With this type of sand, water tempering is not used, as even a ¼ of 1 percent moisture is detrimental to the mixture. The grade and type of sand is very instrumental in controlling the surface finish of the casting. A wash silica sand with a fineness number of 100 to 180 is satisfactory. Use a sand with a low clay content, as clay has a tendency to absorb moisture during the molding operation and release it during the pouring of the metal.

The binders for waterless sand can be purchased from foundry supply houses.

The oil used in oil-bonded sand has a viscosity index of less than 50 or 55 and an aromatic content of 10-20 percent. This type of oil can be obtained from a local oil station.

A small quantity of methyl alcohol should be mixed with the sand as a catalyst.

Below is given the proper amounts of materials to prepare a waterless sand.
• 100 lbs. of sand.
• 5 lbs. of "Neo-Bond" or "Petro-Bond" binder.
• 3 lbs. oil.
• 4 oz. methyl alcohol.
   1. Mix the sand and binder *dry* for at least two minutes.
   2. Add 3 lbs. of oil to the sand binder mixture and mull for 5 minutes.
   3. Add the methyl alcohol and mull for 15 minutes.

The sand may be stored until ready for use. Any type of flask may be used with oil-bonded sands but a steel flask will give the best results.

The molder will get better results if a dry parting agent is used and the parting agent spread evenly over the pattern.

CAUTION: *Do not open oil-bonded molds too quickly as there is always the possibility of fire if they are shaken out while hot.*

● **Facing Sand.** To give the casting a smoother surface, materials in the form of graphite or sea coal are added to the sand. The addition of foundry flour or cereal to facing sand adds body. The finer texture of facing sand will produce a smoother surface on

the casting. In the school, riddled sand from the molding bin is satisfactory for facing purposes if shaken through a No. 16 riddle.

● **Core Sand.** Core sand has a very low clay content and the grain size is somewhat larger than regular molding sand. A binder has to be added because of this low clay content.

Core sand must resist fusion to the casting in order to procure a smooth surface and prevent sandy inclusions in the castings.

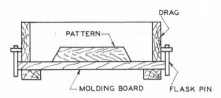
58-1. Testing the temper of molding sand.

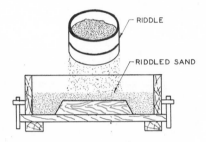
58-2. Pattern placed on a molding board with the parting surface face downward.

58 ▷ Making a Mold with a One-piece Pattern

To make a green sand mold, the sand must be properly "tempered." To temper, wet the outside of the pile and, by cutting the sand over from one pile to another, distribute the moisture evenly. To check the sand for proper temper, a handful is grasped in the fist. The pressure is released and the sand broken into two sections as shown in Fig. 58-1. If the edges do not crumble but remain sharp and firm, the sand is in proper condition to use.

1. Place the pattern with the parting surface face downward on the molding board. Check the pattern to see if the draft is pointing upward, so that when the flask is turned the pattern may be removed without breaking out the mold. Fig. 58-2.

2. Place the drag half of the flask on the molding board with

the pins pointing downward. Fig. 58-2.

3. Dust parting compound over the pattern and bottom board.

4. Riddle fine facing sand to a depth of about 1″ over the pattern. Fig. 58-3.

5. Fill the flask level full with unriddled, tempered sand from the bin or floor. Peen ram around the outer edge of the pattern and inside edge of the flask. Fig. 58-4.

6. After the peen ramming is completed, fill the flask heaping full with sand. Fig. 58-5. NOTE: Correct ramming is important as a sand packed too hard will have insufficient openings to permit gases and steam to escape.

7. Strike off surplus sand, level with the top of the flask, using a strike-off bar. Fig. 58-6.

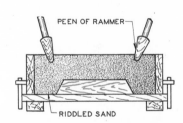
58-3. Fine facing sand being riddled over the pattern.

58-4. Peen ramming around the edge of the pattern.

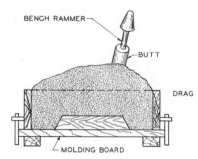
58-5. Fill flask heaping full and butt ram to pack the sand.

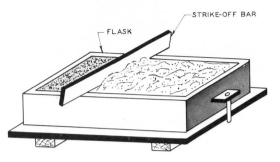

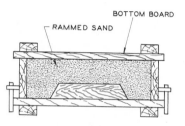

58-7. Place the bottom board on the sand and rub firm to bed.

8. Place ¼″ loose sand on top of the flask to form a bed for the bottom board. Place the bottom board on the sand and rub it firm to the bed. Fig. 58-7. Grip the bottom board and molding board and lift all, including the drag, off the bench as a unit and roll over. Fig. 58-8.

9. Remove the mold board and smooth the surface of the mold with a trowel. Place the cope part of the flask in position.

58-8. Student hand molding, showing rollover of the mold.

58-6. After the sand is packed, it is leveled with the strike-off bar.

Be sure the guide pins fit properly and slide easily.

10. Push the sprue pins into the drag, Fig. 58-9, about 1″ from the pattern. Near the heaviest section, insert a riser pin in the drag about the same distance from the pattern.

11. Sift parting compound over the pattern and the parting surface of the mold. The compound will prevent the tempered sand from sticking to the pattern when the cope is rammed and will also enable the cope to be lifted from the drag without sticking.

12. Riddle sand over the pattern. Then fill the cope with sand, and ram. Fig. 58-10 (A). Strike off with the strike-off bar.

13. Vent the cope with a vent wire to permit gases to escape. NOTE: Do not strike the pattern with the wire.

14. Remove the sprue and

riser pins from the cope. Form a funnel-shaped pouring basin over the sprue with the fingers, being careful that no sand falls into the sprue hole. Fig. 58-10 (B).

15. Carefully lift the cope from the drag and set it on its side.

16. Dampen the sand around the edge of the pattern with a swab or molder's bulb. This will prevent the sand from breaking away when the pattern is withdrawn. Fig. 58-11.

17. Insert a draw spike into the pattern and tap gently to loosen the pattern. Fig. 58-12. Draw the pattern straight upward to avoid breaking the sand.

18. Repair any damage to the mold with a slick or lifter. Remove the sharp edges on the bottom of the sprue and riser holes to avoid any sand entering the

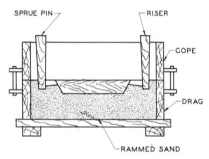

58-9. The cope part of the flask in position, with sprue and riser pins in place.

58-10. (A) Completed mold with sprue and riser in place. (B) Sprue and riser pins removed from the cope.

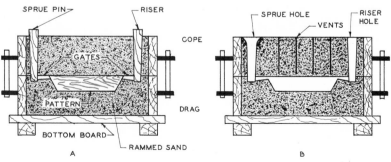

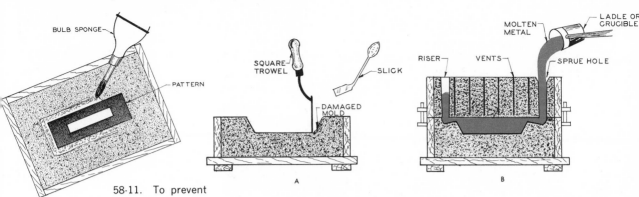

58-11. To prevent sand from breaking up when the pattern is removed from the mold, dampen around the pattern.

58-13. (A) Repairs being made on a damaged mold. (B) Pouring the molten metal into the cavity left by removal of the pattern.

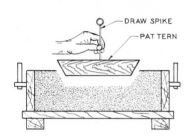

58-12. Pattern being drawn from the mold with a draw spike.

cavity when the molten metal is poured. Fig. 58-13 (A).

19. Cut a gate with a gate cutter, from the mold cavity to the sprue hole. Do the same for the riser. NOTE: The cross-section area of the gate should be less than that of the sprue in order to flow clean metal to the mold. Smooth the gates with the fingers or a slick.

20. Blow out all loose sand from the sprue and mold, using bellows or air hose.

21. Carefully replace the cope on the drag, being sure they line up properly. The mold is then ready to be poured. Fig. 58-13 (B).

In pouring heavy metal it may be necessary to place a weight on the mold or clamp the cope and drag together to prevent the cope from floating.

58-14. Lance pyrometer.

Melting and Pouring Metal

Most castings made in school are nonferrous. Scrap aluminum can be secured from local junk yards or auto shops. Aluminum automobile engine heads, when melted and cast to shape, make good castings as this metal is alloyed and machines much better than pure aluminum.

1. Select a crucible that will hold the amount of metal needed to pour the mold.

2. Pre-heat the crucible, if necessary. The heat will evaporate any moisture that may have been absorbed.

3. Cut the metal to sizes that will fit into the crucible and light the furnace. For aluminum the melting temperature should be from 1,252° - 1,400° F. The temperature can be tested with a lance pyrometer. Fig. 58-14.

The melting temperature and shrinkages of common metals are shown in Table 58-A.

Metals	Melting Temperatures in Degrees F.	Shrinkages in Fractions of an Inch Per Foot
Aluminum	1252	3/16
Babbitt	462	1/8
Brass	1616-1949	3/16
Bronze	1800	3/16
Cast iron	1990-2260	1/8
Copper	1870	5/32
Garalloy	800	3/16
Lead	630	5/16
Magnesium	1200	3/16
Tin	455	1/2
Zinc	787	5/16

Table 58-A.

243

58-15. Protective clothing and safety goggles must be worn during the pouring operation.

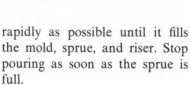

58-16. Removing the sprues, gates, and risers on a metal-cutting band saw.

4. To obtain the best results in a casting, the metal should be heated and poured at a predetermined temperature. Test the metal frequently with the lance pyrometer.

CAUTION: *Overheating the metal can produce a defective casting.*

5. When the metal has reached the proper pouring temperature, shut off the furnace. Add flux to the molten metal, which will bring the impurities to the surface so that slag can be skimmed off.

6. Place the mold on the floor. It is now ready to pour.

CAUTION: *Never pour the mold on a wooden floor.*

7. Remove the crucible from the furnace with tongs. Transfer to a ladle or pouring shank.

CAUTION: *Stand to one side of the mold when pouring.*

8. Begin pouring the metal as rapidly as possible until it fills the mold, sprue, and riser. Stop pouring as soon as the sprue is full.

When the metal has solidified, shake out the mold and remove the casting with tongs.

SAFETY PRECAUTION. *Do not add wet metal to the pot or crucible. Wet metal can create an explosion. Proper clothing and goggles must be worn. Fig. 58-15.*

Finishing the Casting

1. After the casting has cooled enough to be held in the bare hands, remove the sprues, gates, and risers, using a hand hacksaw or on a metal-cutting band saw, as shown in Fig. 58-16. Any projection left on the casting can be removed with a file or on the grinder. Fig. 58-17.

2. Small cast projects can be finished by brushing with a wire brush, abrasive cloth, or steel wool. Other castings may call for machining operations.

58-17. Removing projections on castings by grinding.

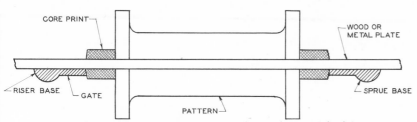

59-1. Showing how a pattern is mounted to make a match plate.

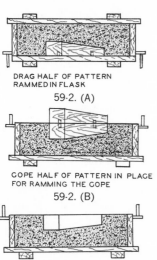

DRAG HALF OF PATTERN RAMMED IN FLASK

59-2. (A)

COPE HALF OF PATTERN IN PLACE FOR RAMMING THE COPE

59-2. (B)

PATTERN DRAWN FROM DRAG

59-2. (C)

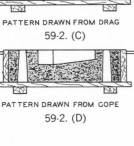

PATTERN DRAWN FROM COPE

59-2. (D)

59-2. (E)

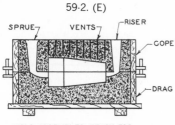

MOLD ASSEMBLED READY FOR POURING

The chief purpose of a two-piece split pattern is to make the molding easier. Split patterns are sometimes fastened to a match plate for production molding. Fig. 59-1.

A split pattern is molded with the lower half in the drag and the upper half in the cope.

1. Place the drag half of the pattern on the molding board with the flat side down.

2. Ram up the drag, using the same method as for a one-piece pattern. Fig. 59-2 (A).

3. Remove the molding board and then dust parting compound on the surface of the mold. Put the cope half of the pattern in place. Fig. 59-2 (B). Be sure the cope half of the pattern withdraws easily, Fig. 59 (C). If not, sand the pins slightly. Fig. 59-2 (D) shows the pattern drawn from the cope.

4. Shake parting compound over the pattern.

5. Place the cope half of the flask on the drag and the riser and sprue in place as described in Unit 58.

6. Ram the mold, as previously described for a flat-back pattern.

7. Vent the mold and remove sprue and riser pins. Remove the cope and set on edge.

8. With a bulb swab moisten the edges of the mold around the pattern.

9. Draw each half of the pattern with a draw spike.

10. Cut the gates with a gate cutter and place the cope in position. The molten metal is then ready to be poured into the mold. Fig. 59-2 (E).

60 ▷ **Machine Molding**

In modern foundries, speed in production of castings is highly important. A molding machine with efficient pattern and flask equipment can produce castings that will meet the high production demands of industry.

There are many types of molding machines used in our foundries, each one of which is adaptable to a special type of mold. The sizes of these machines range from one capable of ramming a mold 12″ x 14″ to a machine that will ram, rollover, and draw a pattern up to 12′ in length.

60-1. Jolt rollover machine. The man on the right is ramming the drag. On the left, the drag is being rolled over.

60-2. Portable jolt-squeeze molding machine.

The jolt rollover, Fig. 60-1, and the jolt-squeeze molding machines, Fig. 60-2, are commonly used for many molding operations.

Modern Molding Machine Operations

1. The drag and match-plate pattern are assembled on the molding machine table. After the drag is filled with molding sand, a valve is pressed by the operator, causing the machine to jolt-ram the drag.

2. The bottom board is bedded and clamped to the drag and rolled over, using the trunnion on the flask.

3. The cope is then lowered on the flask and filled by hand or from an overhead sand hopper. Fig. 60-3.

4. The squeeze board is then set in place, and the sand squeezed by operating a hand valve, which actuates the squeeze piston. Fig. 60-4.

5. The squeeze board is removed and the sprue is cut in the cope. The cope is lifted from the drag on the return stroke of the piston.

6. The cope is then swung to one side and the pattern is vibrated, which gives a clean, accurate lift to the pattern. Fig. 60-5.

7. If core holes are required, they are set in the mold. Loose sand is blown from the mold.

8. The next operation swings the cope back to a closing position. The drag is raised until the mold is closed. Finally, the clamps on the cope are released and the table lowered. The mold is then completed and another mold is ready to be made. Fig. 60-6.

60-3. Molder fills cope with sand from overhead hopper.

246

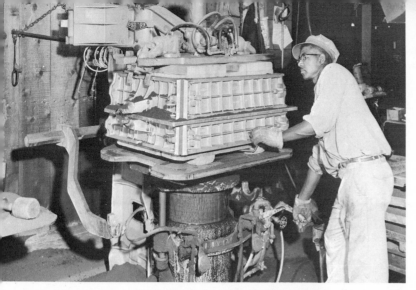

60-4. After the cope is filled with sand and rammed, the machine squeezes cope and drag. The flask being run here is 24" x 33" with 8" cope over 6" drag.

60-5. With the cope clamped, drawn, and swung out of way at the left, the heavy pattern plate is easily drawn by the operator.

60-7. Blast cleaning small castings.

Mechanical Cleaning of Castings

Industry uses many types of mechanical devices for cleaning castings. One such device is called a *tumbling barrel*, which is a cylindrical drum mounted in a horizontal position, rotated at a slow speed. Pieces of wood and small cast metal stars are placed in the tumbler with the castings. As the tumbler rotates, the castings rub against each other and the points of the metal stars. The wood pieces absorb the shock and prevent the breakage of the castings.

Another device for cleaning small castings is the *blasting barrel*. The castings are cleaned by a blast of sand. Fig. 60-7.

60-6. Completion of a mold on the portable jolt-squeeze molding machine.

247

Castings are also cleaned on *sand blast tables.* The tables rotate slowly under a series of sand blast nozzles. After one revolution, the castings are turned over and the underside cleaned as shown in Fig. 60-8.

Large castings such as cylinder blocks, Fig. 60-9, are cleaned in *shot-blast cabinets.* The cylinder blocks are hung on a conveyer. Different cleaning operations can be applied to each block by using separate shot-blast cleaning systems.

When the castings have been cleaned, the rough spots are removed by an emery wheel. Airless blast cleaning is done in a special tumbler.

60-8. Cleaning castings with rotary blast equipment.

60-9. Blast cleaning of engine block castings.

61 ▷ Special Casting Processes

Castings are made by other methods than sand molding. Such processes include permanent mold, shell molding, and precision investment. Descriptions of these special processes are given.

Permanent Mold

When a large quantity of small aluminum or zinc castings is to be made, a permanent mold is preferred.

This is made of two pieces of metal, iron or steel, which can be clamped together to form the cavity desired. Fig. 61-1. Because of the mold, castings have extremely close grain characteristics and are usually free from the more common surface defects of sand castings. They insure better machining qualities and allow closer tolerances.

Pistons for motorcycles, automobile, marine, and diesel engines account for a large percentage of the aluminum castings produced with permanent molds. Cooking utensils, bodies for housings, motor housings, and nozzles for vacuum cleaners are also produced by this method.

This process differs from die casting in that the metal is fed into the mold by gravity rather than by pressure. Fig. 61-2.

61-1. Showing the two parts of a permanent molding machine. The top half has been lifted away.

61-3. Simple permanent mold for a screwdriver handle, which can be cast in the school.

DRILL 4 HOLES FOR $\frac{1}{4}$" DOWEL PINS

WHEN POURING MOLTEN METAL, CLAMP TWO SECTIONS TOGETHER WITH C-CLAMPS

DRILL HOLE FOR DRILL-ROD BLADE

61-4. A brightly polished metal master pattern used in dip molding.

61-2. Permanent mold as it is positioned for the pouring operation.

Industrial permanent molds are made from special alloy cast iron. For school use, molds made from cold-rolled steel will prove very satisfactory. These molds may consist of two or more pieces. Two-piece molds are held together by metal dowels or a hinge.

Sprues and gates are cut along the parting line of the mold, with part of the gate in each mold half. The molds are designed to promote progressive freezing of coats. Permanent metal cores are used in this type of molding.

Fig. 61-3 shows a permanent mold for a screwdriver handle. The mold can easily be constructed in the school from cold-rolled steel. The screwdriver shown in the project section is made by this process.

Dip Molding

Dip molding—otherwise known as the slush casting process of making molds for electronic components with epoxy resins—is quite simple. A brightly polished master pattern, Fig. 61-4, is dipped into a vessel of molten metal, Fig. 61-5, and immediately removed. A discarded cook pot, Fig. 61-5, can be used for melting, but for a long period of time it is recommended that a thermostatically controlled heating pot be used. During the brief period of immersion, a shell of metal freezes to the pattern. This shell is easily removed, Fig. 61-6, and forms a perfect mold for the casting resin.

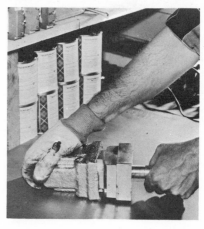

61-5. Melting pot used in dip molding.

61-6. Removing shell from the master pattern.

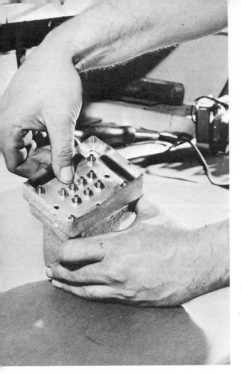

61-7. Components being positioned inside the molds.

61-8. After the components are positioned, the resin is poured in.

(The highly polished metal of the master die imparts a smooth finish to the inside of the mold shell and allows it to be withdrawn easily from the master. This shell forms the resin mold.)

Removal of the shell mold from the master pattern is a simple process. The operator grasps the die handle, Fig. 61-6, with one hand and pulls the shell away from the mold with the other. As soon as molds are taken from the master die they are ready for use. Components are positioned inside of molds, and resin poured in. Figs. 61-7 and 61-8. Units are baked and, after curing, components are extracted from molds by peeling or sawing. Fig. 61-9.

Shapes which do not have projections or re-entrant angles can be made single, one-piece fashion. Two-piece molds can be made by forming the master dies on exactly opposite sides of a match plate.

Die-Castings

Die-castings are produced by forcing hot metal under pressure into water-cooled dies which are held in a machine. Fig. 61-10.

Die-casting is the fastest method of casting metal because all operations are automatic. Fig. 61-11 illustrates the process. In

61-9. Cast units are trimmed for flash and the pouring face is finished to the proper dimension on a belt sander.

Fig. 61-11 (A), the two-piece die is closed. The metal is poured into the "cold chamber" through a port or pouring slot from a ladle which holds enough metal for one filling. The plunger advances, seals the port, and forces the metal into the die.

As the molten metal does not remain long in the cold chamber, higher melting point metals can be cast in this type machine. A slug is left at the end of the cylinder and is either sheared off or ejected from the casting.

61-10. Die-casting machine.

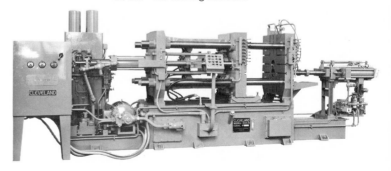

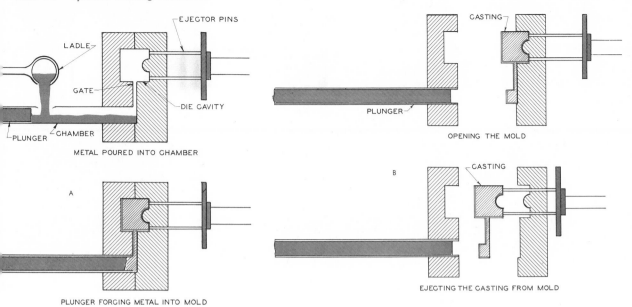

EJECTOR PINS

LADLE

GATE

DIE CAVITY

PLUNGER CHAMBER

METAL POURED INTO CHAMBER

CASTING

PLUNGER

OPENING THE MOLD

A

B

CASTING

EJECTING THE CASTING FROM MOLD

PLUNGER FORCING METAL INTO MOLD

61-11.   Cold chamber die casting.

Fig. 61-12 shows a product that has been die-cast.

Shell Molding

Shell molding is a foundry process that involves the making of thin molds from a mixture of phenolic resin binder and fine sand. This gives a finer finish and dimensional accuracy than green sand molds. Shell molding process permits production of castings with thin sections and intricate designs because they contain little moisture to chill the metal.

To produce a casting by this process, a metal pattern such as shown in Fig. 61-13 is inserted in the molding machine, Fig. 61-14. A mixture consisting of thermosetting resin and sand is deposited on the cope and drag halves of the metal pattern plate that has been heated to 400° to 600° F.

61-12.   Sample of workpieces made in a die-casting machine.

61-13.   Metal pattern for shell molding process.

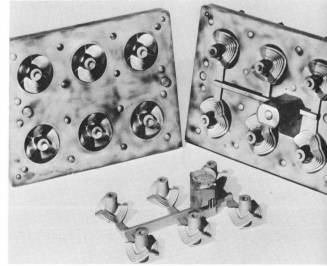

61-14.   Metal pattern inserted in the shell molding machine.

61-16.   Example of finished shell mo[...]

After the pattern has been heated, a release agent is sprayed over the surface to prevent the shell from sticking to the pattern. The resin melts and coats the grains of sand, causing them to adhere and form the shell. Excess sand is removed by a rollover operation. From ¼″ to ½″ of the mix sticks to the hot pattern. The pattern is then rolled back and moved to an oven to allow the resin to harden. The finished mold, Fig. 61-15, is ejected from the machine in a hardened condition. Fig. 61-16.

At the closing machine, Fig. 61-17, the cope is placed on the drag and cores set in place with adhesive applied to the two mold halves, bonding them together. The molten metal is then poured and, after the mold has solidified, it is broken free from around the casting.

Precision Investment Casting

The investment process is used when high precision must be maintained or for products that are too difficult to machine.

Almost any shape of casting can be made from an investment mold. Draft does not have to be taken into consideration, as the pattern is not drawn as in sand molding.

In investment casting, sometimes known as the "lost wax" process, a pattern molded from wax the shape of the part to be cast is made. Fig. 61-18 (A). A die is then made from two or more matching steel blocks, with the cavity in the blocks cut to the shape of the pattern to be cast. Melted wax is poured into the cavity and, after the wax has hardened, the pattern is removed.

The pattern is then placed in a steel flask, Fig. 61-18 (B) and a slurry made up of silica and a hardener is poured around the wax pattern. The flask is vibrated on a vibrating table to pack the slurry around the pattern and remove any air bubbles which may have formed.

61-15.   One type of shell mold being lifted from the pattern.

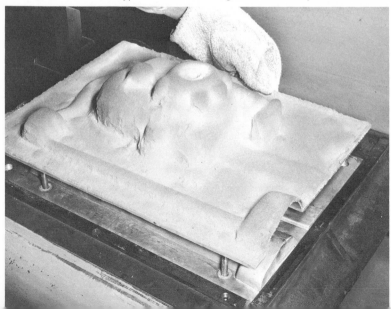

61-17. Bonding press.

After this mixture has hardened, the flask is placed in a furnace and heated to 1,500° F. The heat causes the wax to melt and run out of the mold, leaving the shape of the pattern in the investing slurry. Fig. 61-18 (C).

While the mold is still hot, the molten metal is poured into the cavity, where it hardens. Fig. 61-18 (D). Due to the fact that the mold is still hot, the metal does not cool or chill quickly, allowing it to flow into very thin, delicate cavities of the mold before it solidifies. When the metal has cooled, the investment material is broken away and the finished casting removed.

A high degree of accuracy is obtained in this type of casting because the investing slurry provides a smooth surface.

Many useful products are produced, such as surgical instruments, jewelry, blades for gas turbines (which are difficult to cast by other methods), movie machine projector parts, and business machine parts.

Plaster Mold Casting

This is a foundry process for casting metal in molds made of a combination of plaster and sand. Intricate designs can be molded.

The mold is made by mixing plaster of paris with water. The wet plaster is poured over a pattern and allowed to harden. The pattern can then be removed and the mold fired in a low temperature oven to remove all traces of moisture. Some castings are so complex that it becomes necessary to make them in sections. These sections are then assembled with plastic-resin cement and fired to set the cement. After the casting is poured the mold is broken up to remove the casting. Figs. 61-19 to 61-23 illustrate the plaster cast process for making a tire mold tread ring.

Smooth surface finishes can be obtained with this method of casting, readily adapted to production techniques. Turbines in the automatic transmission of an automobile can successfully be produced by this process. Thinner sections can be cast by plaster mold casting than by the sand or permanent mold method.

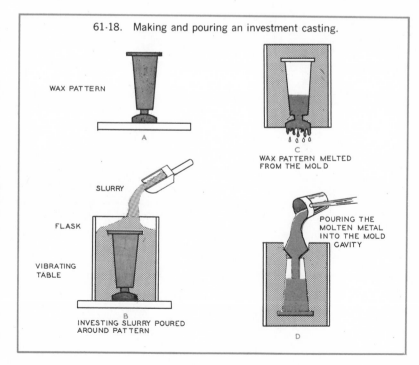

61-18. Making and pouring an investment casting.

WAX PATTERN

A

SLURRY

FLASK

VIBRATING TABLE

B
INVESTING SLURRY POURED AROUND PATTERN

C
WAX PATTERN MELTED FROM THE MOLD

POURING THE MOLTEN METAL INTO THE MOLD CAVITY

D

61-21. Assembling plaster cores into the mold for a tire mold tread ring.

61-19. Pouring plaster into the core box to make a core for aluminum tire mold tread ring.

61-20. Aluminum tire mold ring made by the plaster cast process.

61-22. Vapor blasting an aluminum tire mold tread ring made by the plaster cast process.

61-23. (A) Checking dimensional accuracy of aluminum tire mold tread ring made by the plaster cast process.

Sand Testing Equipment

Controlling sand mixtures in modern foundry operations is an important part of the casting industry. At one time the molder was responsible for testing the quality of the sand he was to use. His experience had to guide him as to the quality of the molding sand. Today, high production quotas and competitive costs have made it necessary to use more selective and scientific methods. Modern mechanized foundries have installed sand-testing laboratories.

Testing for Sand Strength

The Universal sand strength machine, Fig. 61-24, is used to test the hardness and strength of sand, governed by the correct amount of bonding material in the sand. This particular machine can be used for testing green core sand and for measuring the dry compression strength of molding sand. A sand specimen is prepared in a rammer and transferred to the strength machine where tensile, shear, and compression tests can be made.

Testing for Moisture Content

Fig. 61-25 shows a machine that tests the moisture content of molding sand. In its operation a fan drives air down past large capacity heating elements. The heated air is dispersed through the sand sample and out through the 500 mesh bottom of the drying pan. The high velocity of the air dries the 50 gram sample of molding sand in 3 or 4 minutes. A precision balance registers the loss of weight after the moisture is removed. See page 256 for Fig. 61-25.

61-23. (B) Worker gages an aluminum tire mold produced at Cleveland (Ohio) Works of Aluminum Company of America. This premium engineered casting is used to cure tires for trucks and similar vehicles.

61-24. Universal sand strength machine.

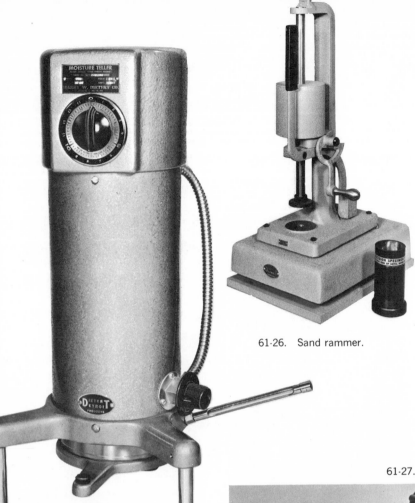

61-25.   Moisture teller.

ness. The sand is then placed in a tube in an electric permmeter. Fig. 61-27. A simple lever arrangement is used to expand a ring to form an airtight seal within the specimen tube. The required pressure (10 cm of water) is maintained by a high speed fan with a rheostat-controlled universal motor. An air floating release mechanism keeps the air pressure constant. The time required for the air to pass through the specimen is then read directly on the dial. The value must conform to permeability standards.

The reason for this test is to measure that physical property which permits gas to pass through the molded mass of sand.

Check Your Knowledge

1. What are some of the common products made in the industrial foundry today?

61-26.   Sand rammer.

61-27.   Electric permmeter.

Testing for Permeability

Sand is given a permeability test to determine its porosity. A sand specimen is prepared in a machine known as a sand rammer. Fig. 61-26. A pre-determined weight is placed in a steel specimen tube. The tube is placed in the rammer and a 14 pound weight is dropped on the sand three times. This operation compacts the sand to a standard hard-

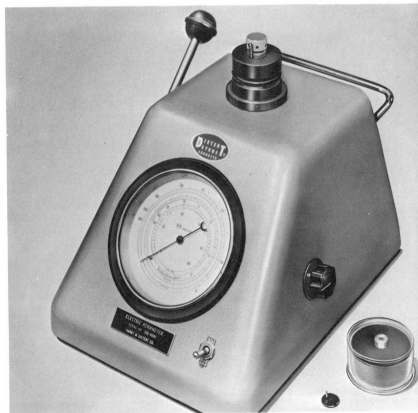

2. What are the two main sections of a flask?

3. What is a riddle used for?

4. What are draw screws used for?

5. What is a swab? Explain its uses.

6. Explain the function of a sprue and riser.

7. How are rammers used?

8. Why is it necessary to place draft on a pattern?

9. Explain the differences between a solid and a split pattern.

10. Why is it necessary to vent a mold?

11. What is a match-plate pattern?

12. Explain the difference between a cupola and a crucible melting furnace.

13. What is a crucible?

14. How are ladles transported in a mechanized foundry?

15. What is a core box?

16. Explain the function of a core print.

17. What is a core? From what is it made?

18. Under what circumstances would a core be used in a molding operation?

19. What are chaplets? Explain how they are used.

20. What is meant by green sand and dry sand?

21. Why is a waterless sand the best type of sand for use in the school?

22. What is facing sand used for?

23. Is it necessary to use a different type of sand in making cores than the sand used in molding operations? Explain.

24. Explain the process of making a mold with a one-piece pattern.

25. Why is parting compound dusted over the pattern?

26. Why is sand riddled over the pattern before the flask is filled with backing sand?

27. Explain a simple method of testing the sand for moisture content.

28. What tool is used to ram the mold?

29. Why should a mold be vented?

30. What safety precautions should be taken while pouring the mold?

31. How is the mold tested for the correct pouring temperature?

32. Does the shrinkage of the metal have any importance in the construction of the master pattern? Why?

33. What is the shrinkage per foot of the following metals: cast iron, aluminum, brass, and bronze?

34. Why is a split pattern used in some molding operations?

35. Explain the important differences between hand molding and machine molding.

36. How are castings cleaned?

37. How does permanent-mold casting differ from sand casting?

38. What is precision-investment casting? Under what circumstances would it be used?

39. What is die-casting? Is it in common use?

40. Explain the technique used in this type of casting. What are its advantages?

41. What is shell-molding?

42. What industry uses plaster-mold casting to a large extent?

43. What are some of the different types of equipment used in testing sand?

44. What tests are made on sand? Why are such tests necessary?

Terms to Know and Spell

flask	graphite
draft	mechanized
riddle	cavity
bellows	chaplet
rammer	methyl
pneumatic	catalyst
crucible	pyrometer
combustion	pattern
cupola	shrinkage
refractory	solidified
investment	resin
precision	slurry
electronic	silica
re-entrant	rheostat
thermosetting	permeability

See next seven pages for sample projects.

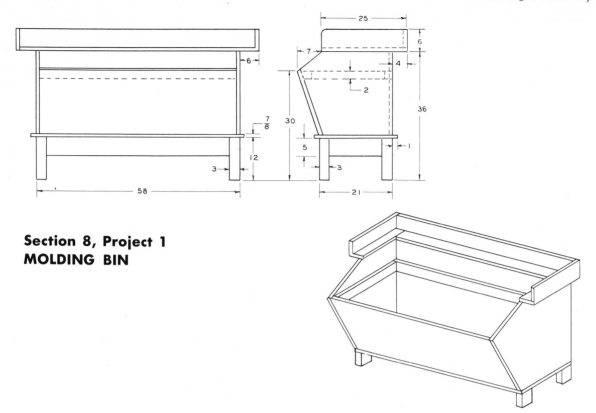

Section 8, Project 1
MOLDING BIN

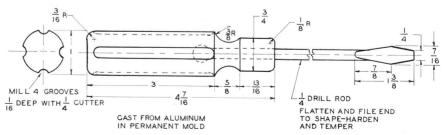

Section 8, Project 2
SCREWDRIVER

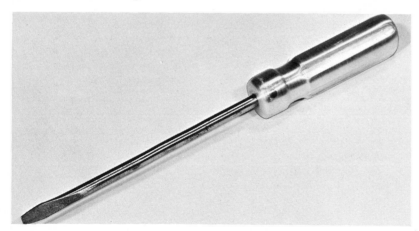

MILL 4 GROOVES
$\frac{1}{16}$ DEEP WITH $\frac{1}{4}$ CUTTER

CAST FROM ALUMINUM
IN PERMANENT MOLD

$\frac{1}{4}$ DRILL ROD
FLATTEN AND FILE END
TO SHAPE-HARDEN
AND TEMPER

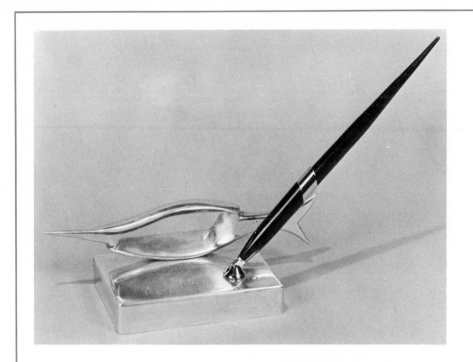

Section 8, Project 3
PEN STAND

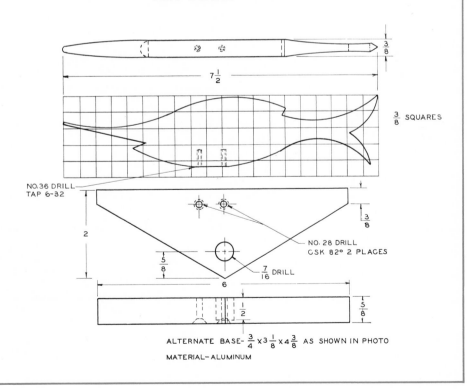

$7\frac{1}{2}$

$\frac{3}{8}$

$\frac{3}{8}$ SQUARES

NO. 36 DRILL
TAP 6-32

2

NO. 28 DRILL
CSK 82° 2 PLACES

$\frac{3}{8}$

$\frac{5}{8}$

$\frac{7}{16}$ DRILL

6

$\frac{1}{2}$

$\frac{5}{8}$

ALTERNATE BASE— $\frac{3}{4}$ x $3\frac{1}{8}$ x $4\frac{3}{8}$ AS SHOWN IN PHOTO

MATERIAL—ALUMINUM

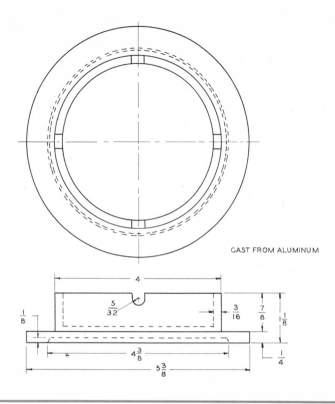

CAST FROM ALUMINUM

Section 8, Project 4
ASH TRAY

Section 8, Project 5
DISC SANDER

*Drawings for the Disc Sander
will be found on the
next four pages.*

Disc Sander Drawings

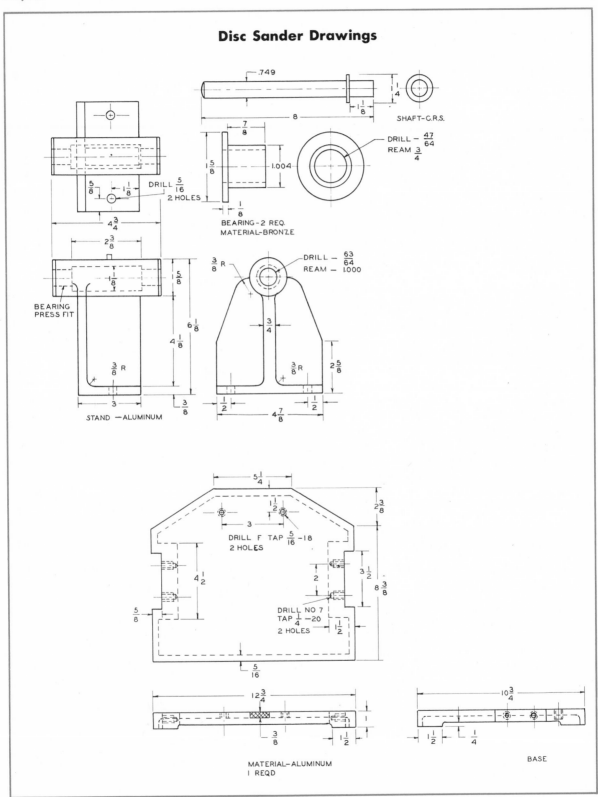

.749

8

$1\frac{1}{8}$

4

SHAFT–C.R.S.

$\frac{5}{8}$ $1\frac{1}{8}$

DRILL $\frac{5}{16}$
2 HOLES

$4\frac{3}{4}$

$\frac{7}{8}$

$1\frac{5}{8}$ 1.004

$\frac{1}{8}$

DRILL – $\frac{47}{64}$
REAM $\frac{3}{4}$

BEARING–2 REQ.
MATERIAL–BRONZE

$2\frac{3}{8}$

$1\frac{1}{8}$ $\frac{5}{8}$

BEARING
PRESS FIT

$6\frac{1}{8}$

$4\frac{1}{8}$

$\frac{3}{8}$ R

3

$\frac{3}{8}$

STAND –ALUMINUM

$\frac{3}{8}$ R

DRILL – $\frac{63}{64}$
REAM – 1.000

$\frac{3}{4}$

$\frac{3}{8}$ R

$2\frac{5}{8}$

$\frac{1}{2}$ $\frac{1}{2}$

$4\frac{7}{8}$

$5\frac{1}{4}$

$2\frac{3}{8}$

$1\frac{1}{2}$

3

DRILL F TAP $\frac{5}{16}$ –18
2 HOLES

$4\frac{1}{2}$

2

$3\frac{1}{2}$

$8\frac{3}{8}$

$\frac{5}{8}$

DRILL NO 7
TAP $\frac{1}{4}$ –20
2 HOLES

$1\frac{1}{2}$

$\frac{5}{16}$

$12\frac{3}{4}$

$\frac{3}{8}$

$1\frac{1}{2}$

MATERIAL–ALUMINUM
I REQD

$10\frac{3}{4}$

$1\frac{1}{2}$ $\frac{1}{4}$

BASE

261

Disc Sander Drawings (continued)

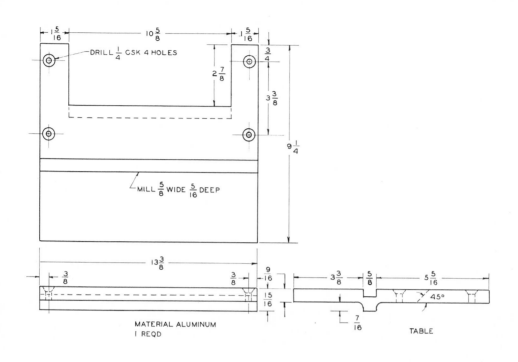

MATERIAL ALUMINUM
I REQD

TABLE

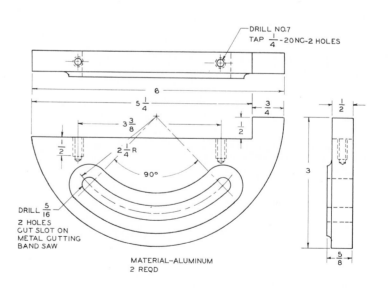

DRILL NO.7
TAP $\frac{1}{4}$-20NC-2 HOLES

DRILL $\frac{5}{16}$
2 HOLES
CUT SLOT ON
METAL CUTTING
BAND SAW

MATERIAL—ALUMINUM
2 REQD

TRUNNION

Disc Sander Drawings (continued)

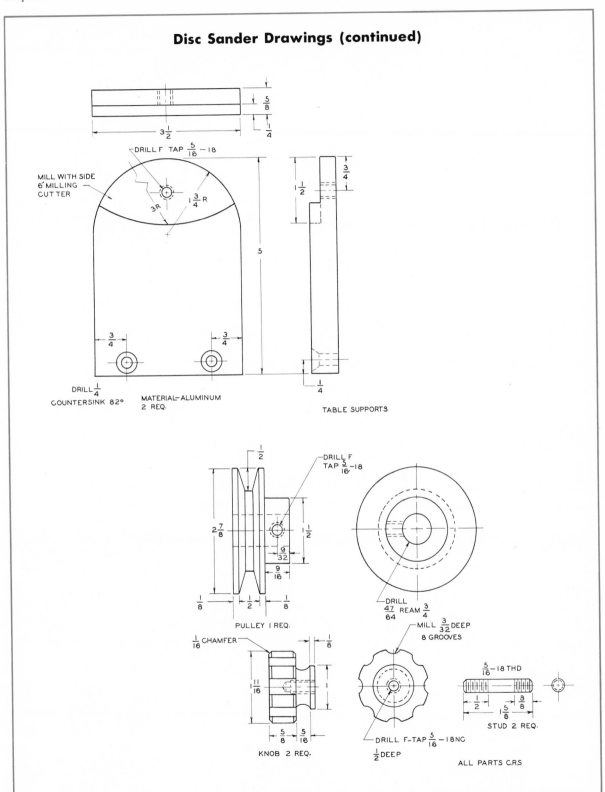

DRILL F TAP $\frac{5}{16}$ – 18

MILL WITH SIDE 6" MILLING CUTTER

3R $1\frac{3}{4}$ R

$3\frac{1}{2}$

$\frac{5}{8}$ $\frac{1}{4}$

5

$\frac{3}{4}$ $\frac{3}{4}$

DRILL $\frac{1}{4}$
COUNTERSINK 82°

MATERIAL—ALUMINUM
2 REQ.

$\frac{3}{4}$ $1\frac{1}{2}$ $\frac{1}{4}$

TABLE SUPPORTS

$\frac{1}{2}$

DRILL F
TAP $\frac{5}{16}$ – 18

$2\frac{7}{8}$ $1\frac{1}{2}$

$\frac{9}{32}$

$\frac{9}{16}$

$\frac{1}{8}$ $\frac{1}{2}$ $\frac{1}{8}$

PULLEY 1 REQ.

DRILL $\frac{47}{64}$ REAM $\frac{3}{4}$

MILL $\frac{3}{32}$ DEEP
8 GROOVES

$\frac{1}{16}$ CHAMFER $\frac{1}{8}$

$\frac{11}{16}$

$\frac{5}{8}$ $\frac{5}{16}$

KNOB 2 REQ.

DRILL F-TAP $\frac{5}{16}$ –18NC
$\frac{1}{2}$ DEEP

$\frac{5}{16}$ –18 THD

$\frac{1}{2}$ $\frac{3}{8}$

$1\frac{5}{8}$

STUD 2 REQ.

ALL PARTS C.R.S

Disc Sander Drawings (continued)

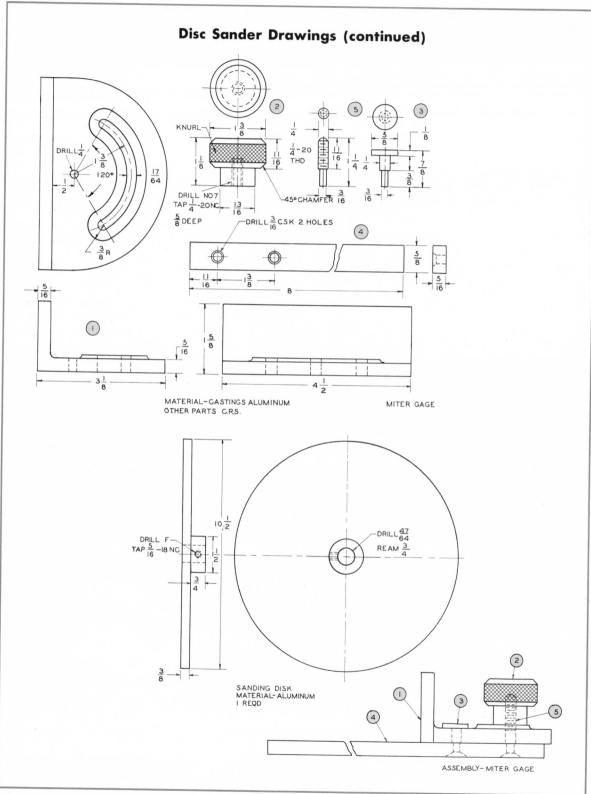

KNURL

DRILL NO 7
TAP ¼-20NC
⅝ DEEP

DRILL ¼
⅛
1⅜
120°
½
17/64
⅜ R

¼-20 THD

45° CHAMFER

DRILL 3/16 CSK 2 HOLES

MATERIAL–CASTINGS ALUMINUM
OTHER PARTS C.R.S.

MITER GAGE

DRILL F
TAP 5/16 –18 NC

DRILL 47/64
REAM ¾

SANDING DISK
MATERIAL– ALUMINUM
1 REQD

ASSEMBLY– MITER GAGE

Welding

WELDING is the process of joining metal by melting and fusion. Of the more than 35 different ways of welding metals, most fall under three categories: arc, gas, and resistance. Arc welders perform their work either by hand or with

machine methods. Gas welders do on-the-job work, which means hand operations, although industry uses automatic and semi-automatic gas-welding equipment.

Resistance welding is mainly a machine process performed by semi-skilled resistance-welding operators. They work with machines that are designed for this type of welding.

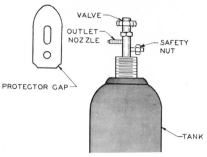

62-2. Oxygen cylinder showing safety device.

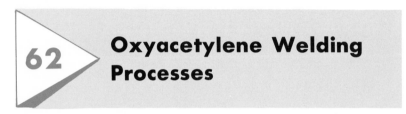

62 ▷ Oxyacetylene Welding Processes

Oxyacetylene welding utilizes a mixture of acetylene and oxygen in the correct proportions to produce a flame hot enough to melt specific types of metals—steel, iron, cast iron, copper, brass, aluminum, and alloys.

Welding Equipment

The basic oxyacetylene equipment, Fig. 62-1, consists of an oxygen cylinder, an acetylene cylinder, two regulators, two lengths of hose, a welding torch with an assortment of welding tips, and hose fittings. The cylinders are mounted on a two-wheel truck to permit the moving of the equipment. Cylinders should always be secured to a cart or some fixed object to prevent them from tipping over.

Oxygen Cylinders

Oxygen cylinders are charged with oxygen at a pressure of 2,200 lbs. per sq. in. at 70° F. The pressure in a cylinder will increase and decrease as the temperature changes, since the volume remains constant. To provide against dangerously excessive pressures, such as could occur if the cylinder were exposed to fire, every valve has a safety device to release the oxygen before there is any danger of rupturing the cylinder. Fig. 62-2.

62-1. Standard hand welding outfit.

General Safety Precautions

1. Keep cylinders chained to a cart or a fixed object in an upright position.

2. Keep oxygen cylinder fittings away from oil or grease, which may ignite violently in the presence of oxygen under pressure.

3. Never use oxygen from a cylinder except through an oxygen regulator.

4. Do not store cylinders where there is excessive heat.

5. Avoid rough handling of cylinders.

6. Never use a cylinder that is leaking acetylene.

7. Always turn off torch when you have completed a weld.

8. Always wear goggles when welding.

9. Use a spark lighter to light the torch. Never use matches.

10. Do not let others watch you weld unless they wear suitable goggles.

11. Never light the torch with both valves open.

12. For added protection, wear welder's gloves, leather apron, and sleeves when welding.

13. Never attempt to blow dirt off your clothing with gas pressure. The clothing can become saturated with oxygen or acetylene and will burst into flame if a spark comes in contact with it.

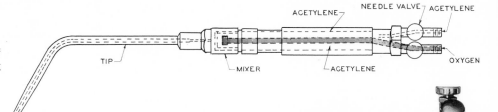

62-3. Basic elements of an oxyacetylene welding torch.

There are three sizes of cylinders used for welding and cutting. The small size contains about 80 cu. ft. of oxygen, the medium 122 cu. ft., and the large size 244 cu. ft.

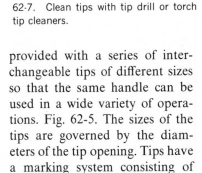

62-4. Welding torch.

ACETYLENE CYLINDERS

Acetylene cylinders are strong steel containers filled with a porous substance which is saturated with acetone. This absorbs large quantities of acetylene. Acetylene is an explosive gas that becomes very unstable beyond a pressure of 15 lbs. per sq. in. As a safeguard, the cylinder is equipped with a fusible plug that releases in case it is subjected to undue heat. Dissolved acetylene is sold in cylinders having rated capacities of 60, 100, or 300 cu. ft.

Acetylene is drawn off through a valve located in the top of the cylinder. The valve is operated by means of a key handle which is left in place during the use of the cylinder.

WELDING TORCH

Welding torches have a handle with two inlet sections at one end. Each inlet has a valve that controls the volume of oxygen or acetylene passing through. The two gases are fed independently to a mixing chamber and then flow out through the tip. Figs. 62-3 and 62-4.

• *Welding Tips*

The typical welding torch is

62-5. Welding tips.

62-6. Standard tip cleaners.

62-7. Clean tips with tip drill or torch tip cleaners.

provided with a series of interchangeable tips of different sizes so that the same handle can be used in a wide variety of operations. Fig. 62-5. The sizes of the tips are governed by the diameters of the tip opening. Tips have a marking system consisting of numbers varying from 0, the smallest, to 15, the largest.

Welding tips are designed to produce correct flames and proper capacity for heat output. These characteristics depend upon polished internal surfaces, so tip bores must be properly cleaned and maintained. Use standard tip cleaners. Fig. 62-6. Cleaning tips with sharp or rough wires will result in ragged and distorted flames. Bumping the tip on rough, hard surfaces will distort the tip end. Fig. 62-7.

62-8.   Regulator and gages for an oxygen tank.

62-9.   Regulator and gages for an acetylene tank.

62-10.   Acetylene welding goggles.

REGULATORS

Oxygen and acetylene regulators, Figs. 62-8 and 62-9, are used to reduce cylinder pressure to the required working rate, and also to produce a steady flow of gas under varying pressures. However, the regulator must be more than a simple reducing valve, for the cylinder pressure does not remain constant while the torch is in operation.

Let us assume that welding requires a 10 lb. oxygen pressure at the torch, while the oxygen in the cylinder is compressed to a pressure of 2,200 pounds per sq. in. It is then necessary to have a regulator that can be adjusted to 10 lb. pressure at the outlet side of the regulator, while the oxygen enters the regulator at 2,200 pounds per sq. in.

Regulators are equipped with two gages, one indicating the pressure in the cylinder and the other the working pressure at the torch.

HOSE

Two lengths of hose, one for oxygen and one for acetylene, are required to connect the regulators and the torch. Green is the standard color for oxygen hose and red for acetylene, the same as the colors of the respective regulators.

For connecting the hose to torches and regulators, only standard connectors of the correct size should be used. NOTE: To prevent interchange of hoses, the standardized *oxygen* thread is right-hand and the *acetylene* thread is left-hand.

Examine the hose frequently for leaks and worn places. The hose can be immersed in water under normal working pressure to detect the location of leaks.

SAFETY GOGGLES

Safety goggles, Fig. 62-10, should be worn at all times while welding or cutting, or observing such work. Goggles will protect the eyes from flying sparks and bits of spattered metal. They also protect the eyes from reflected heat and the intensity of the flame.

Goggle lenses are made of a special, shatter-resistant, colored optical glass that cuts the glare and at the same time permits the operator to view the work clearly.

GLOVES

It is advisable to have some protection for the hands, using leather, asbestos, or other fire-resistance material.

CAUTION: *Gloves must be kept free of oil or grease.*

WELDING BENCH

A gas welding bench ideal for schools is shown in Fig. 62-11. This type has two work stations equipped with regulators, shelf for holding cleaning brush, welding tips, lighter, and flux. Rod tubes keep rods sorted and ready at bench level.

62-11.   Two-station gas welding bench.

RECOMMENDED ROD SIZES FOR OXYACETYLENE WELDING

Thickness of Metal	Diameter of Rod in Inches
18 gage	1/16
16 gage	1/16 to 3/32
10 gage	1/32 to 1/8
3/16 in.	1/8 to 5/32
1/4 and heavier	3/16 to 1/4

Table 62-A.

FRICTION LIGHTERS

Friction lighters, Fig. 62-12, should be used for lighting torches.

CAUTION: *Matches should not be used. Using a match to light the torch brings the hand too close to the flame. It may be burned when the gases ignite. Friction lighters are safe.*

WELDING ROD AND FLUXES

A mild-steel welding rod is best for beginners. It has a copper coating which prevents rusting of the rod. See Table 62-A.

Brazing rod, or bronze rod, is used for bronze welding or brazing. A commercial flux, that makes a weld run together easily and prevents oxide from forming, is used.

Setup and Operation of Equipment

ATTACHING THE REGULATOR AND CONNECTING THE TORCH

1. Open the oxygen cylinder valve slightly to blow out any foreign matter. Close the valve and wipe with a clean rag. Repeat on acetylene valve.

2. Attach oxygen and acetylene regulators, being sure that inlets are clean. Never tighten the regulators by pulling on the gages.

3. Attach hoses to regulator outlets and tighten connections securely. Release the tension on the regulator adjusting screws. Open the oxygen cylinder valve a little and, when full pressure is shown on the gage, open fully. Blow any powder from hose by tightening the regulator adjusting screw. Cut off the flow of oxygen valve slowly (about 2½ turns). Repeat for the acetylene hose.

4. Connect hoses to the torch and tighten the hose nuts securely. Select the proper tip size for the thickness of metal to be welded.

5. Connect the tip and mixer to the torch, tighten securely, position and tighten the tip.

6. Consult tip chart for the size of tip to be used. Table 62-B. Open the acetylene needle valve on the torch one turn. Adjust acetylene regulator to the recommended pressure. Close acetylene needle valve and open oxygen valve on torch one turn. Adjust oxygen regulator to the recommended pressure. Permit oxygen to flow momentarily to purge air from hose. Close oxygen needle valve.

RECOMMENDED TIP SIZES FOR OXYACETYLENE WELDING

Tip Number	Thickness of Metal (inches)	Oxygen Pressure (pounds)	Acetylene Pressure (pounds)
00	1/64	1	1
0	1/32	1	1
1	1/16	1	1
2	3/32	2	2
3	1/8	3	3
4	3/16	4	4
5	1/4	5	5
6	5/16	5	5
7	3/8	7	7
8	1/2	7	7
9	5/8	7½	7½
10	3/4 and up	9	9

Table 62-B.

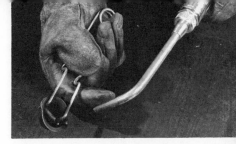

62-12. Position for lighting the torch.

LIGHTING THE TORCH AND ADJUSTING THE FLAME

Open the acetylene needle valve ½ turn. Hold the tip away from you and ignite the torch with a spark lighter. Fig. 62-12. Adjust the needle valve until the flame starts breaking or jumping away from the tip end. Open the oxygen needle valve slowly and as oxygen is mixed with the burning acetylene, the flame will change to a blue color. Continue opening the oxygen valve until a well-defined, blue-white cone forms at the tip. This is known as a neutral flame. Fig. 62-13.

A *neutral flame* is produced by burning the *correct mixture* of oxygen and acetylene. Welds made with it should be thoroughly fused and free from burned metal or hard spots.

An *oxidizing flame,* Fig. 62-13,

62-13. Types of oxyacetylene welding flames.

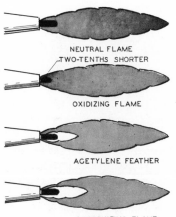

INNER CONE

NEUTRAL FLAME
TWO-TENTHS SHORTER

OXIDIZING FLAME

ACETYLENE FEATHER

CARBONIZING FLAME

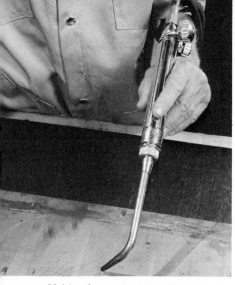

62-14. One method of holding the torch.

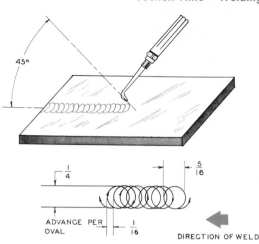

62-16. Proper angle of the torch. Rotate while moving the puddle forward.

ADVANCE PER OVAL

DIRECTION OF WELD

is produced when a mixture has an *excess amount* of oxygen. This type of flame resembles the neutral flame but has a shorter cone with purple coloring.

• *Controlling the Flame*

1. If there is too much acetylene the flame has an intermediate cone between the envelope and inner cone. The correct adjustment of acetylene pressure is denoted by the flame just jumping away from the tip. NOTE: The acetylene should be lighted and adjusted before the oxygen needle valve is opened.

62-15. Another method of holding the torch.

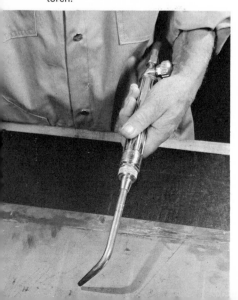

2. If the flame starts "popping," open both the oxygen and acetylene needle valves on the torch slightly to permit a better flow of gases.

3. In shutting off the torch, *always close the acetylene needle valve first* and then close the oxygen needle valve. Release the regulator pressure adjusting screws.

If the apparatus is not to be used for some time, open the acetylene valve. Remove the pressure on the working gages by opening the needle valves to drain the hoses. Close the needle valves. Release the adjusting screws on the pressure regulators.

Torch Welding Procedures

TYPES OF OXYACETYLENE WELDED JOINTS

Before a joint can be welded the proper preparation must be made. The thickness, the type of material to be welded, and the type of joint are important. Rust and scale have to be cleaned from the base metal to secure a satisfactory joint.

In oxyacetylene welding, the torch may be held much the same

as a pencil. Fig. 62-14. The tip should be positioned so that the flame points in the direction you are going to weld and at an angle of about 45° with the seam. Fig. 62-15 shows another method of holding the torch.

Before any welding is done on a project some practice welds should be made to become familiar with the operation of the equipment. The following procedure should be followed:

• *Running a Bead Without a Rod*

The speed at which welding can progress is determined by the rate at which the desired amount of base metal can be melted into the welding puddle. A puddle that has been moved at the proper rate will show an even ripple effect of uniform width.

1. Place a sheet of hot rolled steel on the welding table so that one edge faces you.

2. Light the torch with the friction lighter and adjust to a neutral flame. Fig. 62-13. Hold the torch so that the flame points in the direction you are going to weld and at a 45° angle with the completed part of the weld.

270

62-17. Position of rod on a repair job.

3. With the inner cone of the flame held about ⅛″ away from the metal, hold the torch still until a pool of molten metal about ³⁄₁₆″ to ¼″ in diameter is formed.

4. Move the puddle across the sheet in the desired direction, making a series of overlapping ovals. Fig. 62-16. NOTE: If the puddle is moved too slowly, the flame will burn a hole through the metal. If the flame is moved too rapidly, the heat will not penetrate enough to melt the metal properly.

● *Running a Bead with Welding Rod*

The position of the metal sheet

62-18. Starting, movement of torch, and position of rod and torch.

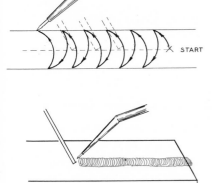

and of the torch should be the same as in the previous exercise. The welding rod (filler rod) is held in the left hand, Fig. 62-17, at a 45° angle with the line of weld.

1. Start just inside the edge of the sheet. Hold the torch still until the pool begins to form; then place the end of the rod in the puddle and start the weld across the sheet. NOTE: The diameter of the rod used should be equal to the thickness of the base plate to be welded. On plate ¼″ or more, a rod ⅛″ to ³⁄₁₆″ diameter is used.

2. While the torch is being moved continuously, the end of the rod should be raised and lowered into the puddle as necessary to build up the weld to the desired height. Fig. 62-18. When the rod is not in the puddle, the tip is held in the outer envelope of the flame. If the rod sticks to the metal, move the flame so that it will play directly upon the tip, freeing it.

● *Butt Joint*

1. Place two ¹⁄₁₆″ or ⅛″ steel sheets on the welding table, spaced ¹⁄₁₆″ apart.

2. Hold the flame still so that it will play upon the two corners at the starting end of the seam. Just as two small spots of molten metal begin to form, add molten metal from the mild steel welding rod so that it will bridge the gap between the puddles.

3. Tack the other end in the same manner.

4. Remelt a small puddle on the first tacked end. Add metal and build it up above the surface of the base metal.

5. Weave the torch back and forth, making the puddle move along the seam to produce the

desired weld. The bead is formed as shown in Fig. 62-19 (A).

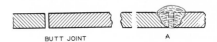

Fig. 62-19. (A)

● *Tee Joint*

Tack together two metal sheets, with one on edge. Fig. 62-19 (B). Hold the tip of the torch at a 45° angle to the flat plate and the rod 15° to 20° to the horizontal plate. Complete the weld.

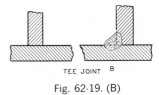

Fig. 62-19. (B)

● *Corner Welds*

1. Mount the two steel sheets on the welding table to form an open corner.

2. Tack the pieces together in much the same way as for a flange joint, and weld. NOTE: It may be found necessary to add filler rod. Fig. 62-19 (C).

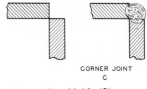

Fig. 62-19. (C)

● *Lap Joint*

A lap joint, Fig. 62-19 (D), is one piece of metal welded flat over another. Direct more heat on the lower surface, since less heat is required to melt the edge of the upper piece than the flat surface of the flat plate. Use a filler rod.

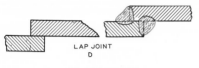

LAP JOINT
D

Fig. 62-19. (D)

● *Edge Joint*

In welding an edge joint, Fig. 62-19 (E), filler rod is not necessary, as the surfaces are flat and the base metal can serve as filler material.

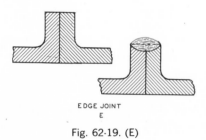

EDGE JOINT
E

Fig. 62-19. (E)

● *Flange Weld*

In making a flange weld, no welding rod need be used, as the flanges melt down to fill in the joint. Fig. 62-19 (F).

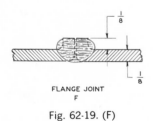

FLANGE JOINT
F

Fig. 62-19. (F)

1. Bend a flange on each sheet equal to its thickness.

2. Place the two sheets on the welding table with the flanges up and edges just touching. Position the torch as described in previous operations.

3. Hold the torch flame until a puddle of the right size is obtained. Move the puddle along the seam.

Brazing

Two things distinguish brazing from welding and soldering: (1) The temperature at which it is done and (2) the principle of the joint.

Soldering uses low temperatures, below 800° F. Soldered joints are not very strong. They rely largely on the "gripping action" or adhesion of the molten solder in the surface irregularities of the metals.

Welding, on the other hand, produces joints as strong as the metals themselves.

Brazing starts at a temperature of about 800° F. Its upper range is indefinite, but always below the melting point of the base metal. Brazing, like soldering, never melts the base metal. Yet it does not tend to warp or burn the metal, since the application of heat is general. Fig. 62-20. Brazed joints, despite common misconceptions, can be as strong as welds.

1. Clean the base metal thoroughly of all rust, scale, oil, grease, or other foreign substances.

2. Heat the metal with a torch until it just begins to glow.

3. Heat the bronze rod slightly and dip in powdered flux which will adhere to the surface of the rod and can be transferred to the weld. The flux will remove any oxide present.

4. Hold the end of the rod just ahead of the torch and apply heat until the flux and rod start to flow. NOTE: The rod should

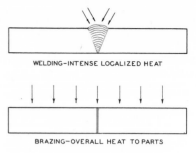

WELDING-INTENSE LOCALIZED HEAT

BRAZING-OVERALL HEAT TO PARTS

62-20. Brazed joints.

never be melted directly with the torch. If you start to apply the rod before the base metal is hot enough, the molten bronze will not flow over the base metal surface but will form into drops.

Welding Aluminum

The welding of aluminum presents certain considerations of design and technique which are considerably different in some aspects from steel.

Preparation for Welding

After the edges to be welded have been prepared in accordance with the joint design selected, the following steps must be performed before welding starts.

1. Clean grease, oil, or dirt from surfaces to be welded. Remove oxide from metal to insure a good weld.

2. Preheat the material to a temperature not to exceed 700° F. with city gas, kerosene torch, or a second oxyacetylene torch. Proper heating can be checked with carpenter's blue chalk. The chalk will turn white at the proper temperature for welding.

Welding Sheet Aluminum

1. Mix the flux with water so as to form a thin paste. With the flux mixture, paint both sides of the sheet and along the edges to be welded.

2. Clamp the sheet in a jig.

3. Hold the blowpipe at an angle of about 30° with the weld and with the tip of the inner cone, about ⅛″ away from the metal.

4. Using the forehand technique, melt a small puddle of metal and carry the puddle along the flanged edges in the same manner as steel.

5. As soon as the weld has cooled, remove the sheets from the jig and scrub off all extra flux with hot water and a stiff brush.

Welding Stainless Steel

There are so many different types of alloy steels that it would not be practical to describe all the welding processes in a book of this type. However, a description of the most common method of welding stainless steel is given.

In welding stainless steel a tip that is one or two sizes smaller than one used for welding steel is used. This reduces the possibility of destroying the properties of the metal, which might occur if a larger flame were employed. *Special stainless steel filler rod and flux are needed.* To perform the welding operation proceed as follows:

1. Flux the surfaces of the rod and metal to be welded.

2. The tip of the inner cone of the flame should be kept about ¹⁄₁₆″ from the pool of molten metal. This assists in preventing oxidation. The angle at which the flame is held should be steeper than that used for carbon steel; an angle of about 80° is recommended.

3. The welding rod, when not being fed into the puddle, should be *withdrawn completely* from the

welding flame. When it is held in the flame it should be held close to the inner cone. The heat used in welding stainless steel should be the minimum amount that will give the results desired.

4. The choice between forehand and backhand welding partially depends upon the operator.

Forehand welding is preferable on light gauge metal, while backhand is used for heavier materials.

5. Should both ends of the weld terminate at the edges, begin the weld an inch or two from one edge, weld out to the edge, and then return to the starting point to complete.

63 ▷ Flame Cutting

Metal cutting can be done with an oxyacetylene flame. Industry uses the flame cutting process to a great extent.

Flame cutting consists of heating metal and then directing a stream of oxygen on the spot, which causes a rapid oxidation that reduces the metal to iron oxide.

Since the cutting action is dependent upon the chemical reaction between the metal and the oxygen, any dirt or scale along the cutting line should be scraped or otherwise removed.

The Cutting Torch

Oxyacetylene cutting torches, Fig. 63-1, are designed to provide both a stream of pure oxygen that does the actual cutting and small acetylene flames that are used both to accomplish the original heating of the material and supply additional heat so that the

cutting will be a continuous operation.

The cutting tip has an orifice in the center surrounded by several smaller holes. These are for preheating the metal. Table 63-A.

TIP SIZES AND CUTTING PRESSURE

Tip No.	Thickness of Metal (inches)	Acetylene Pressure (pounds)	Oxygen Pressure (pounds)
0	¼	3	30
1	⅜	3	30
1	½	3	40
2	¾	3	40
2	1	3	50
3	1½	3	45
4	2	3	50
5	3	4	45
5	4	4	60

Table 63-A.

Procedure for Cutting Steel

1. Start with a clean plate of mild steel ½″ thick and 12″ square.

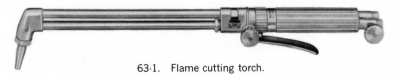

63-1. Flame cutting torch.

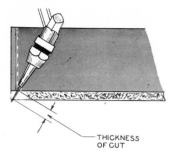

63-2. When a bevel cut is made, it frequently is necessary to preheat a slightly longer time than for a square cut. A straight edge against which to rest the blowpipe assists in keeping the bevel cut straight.

2. With chalk rule a line about 1″ from one edge of the plate. Let the plate overhang the far side of the welding table about 1″.

3. Insert the proper size cutting tip in the cutting torch and adjust the oxygen and acetylene pressures for ½″ steel in accordance with Table 63-A. *Put on goggles, gloves, and other suitable clothing.*

4. Light the torch, and adjust the preheating flames to neutral, with the cutting-oxygen valve open. Then close the valve.

5. Hold the torch in the right hand (or left hand if left-handed) so that you can control the oxygen lever. The other hand should be used to steady the torch. A clean straight cut depends upon your steadiness.

6. Hold the torch with the nozzle perpendicular to the metal's surface and with the inner cones of the heating flames about ¹⁄₁₆″ above the end of the chalk line at the edge of the plate.

7. Hold the torch until this spot turns a bright red, then slowly press down the cutting-oxygen valve lever.

63-3. Cutting a round opening with a torch.

8. There will be a shower of sparks from the lower side as the cutting starts. The cutting-oxygen lever should be pressed down all the way.

9. As soon as the cut has been made through the plate, move the torch slowly along the chalk line.

BEVELING

In beveling it will be necessary to hold the torch as shown in Fig.

63-2. Torch control during beveling is more difficult than when making a straight cut. The speed at which the torch is moved and the steadiness of the movement are of great importance in obtaining a smooth cut.

CUTTING HOLES

1. Place the steel on two fire bricks on top of welding table.

2. Hold the torch nozzle over the plate until the pre-heating flames have produced a round, red-hot spot.

3. Open the cutting valve slowly and at the same time raise the nozzle away from the plate slightly so that slag formed will not blow back into the torch nozzle.

4. To cut a small circle, locate the circle so that the cut can be started at the edge of the plate. Start the cut in the scrap material and then move into the line of cut. The torch should rest lightly upon the left hand and be moved forward and backward. Fig. 63-3.

64 ▷ Arc Welding

The process of joining metal by means of heat created by an electric arc is known as arc welding. Additional metal melted in with the base metal fills the bond.

Welding Equipment

Welding machines in common use are of two basic types: D.C. welders, Fig. 64-1, using direct current, and A.C. welders, using

alternating current. Fig. 64-2. Some welding machines provide both D.C. and A.C. welding current. Fig. 64-3.

The D.C. welder has a generator to produce the required current in much the same manner as an automobile generator, and can be driven by an electric motor or a gasoline engine. This type of machine can use a wider variety

64-1. A compact D.C. arc welder.

64-2. Fully equipped A.C. arc welder.

64-3. A.C.-D.C. arc welder.

of electrodes and can do certain types of jobs that A.C. welders cannot do. Output can be controlled to better advantage because the polarity in the circuit can be changed, which permits the use of a wider selection of electrodes.

The A.C. or alternating current welder uses a built-in transformer to furnish the current. The polarity in this machine is constantly reversing itself, minimizing its importance.

The amount of current output is regulated on both types of machines by controls of various types to suit the size and type of electrodes, for the specific job to be done.

Safe Practices in Arc Welding

In arc welding it is essential that the eyes be protected from the glare and heat of the arc, and also particles of hot metal which can fly up from the work.

In addition to the eyes, it is also imperative that the skin be protected from the intensity of the ultraviolet and infrared rays.

Instantaneous flashes, if repeated, will result in eye burn which is very painful. A 2% solution of butyn sulphate offers excellent relief for eye burns, but avoid all such possibilities!

Two types of face shields are available. The hood type, Fig. 64-4, is worn like a helmet, leaving both hands free. The hand type is held before the face with one hand while you weld with the other.

To protect the operator from flying globules of molten metal, *gauntlet gloves* and *aprons* of chrome leather or spark-resisting duck should be worn during welding operations.

Proper ventilation is necessary during welding. Smoke and heat can be removed by exhaust equipment.

ELECTRODE HOLDER

The electrode holder, Fig. 64-5, used to hold the electrode while welding, is attached to the cable.

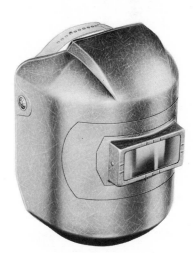

64-4. Hood type face shield.

64-5. Electrode holder.

CAUTION: *Make certain that electrode holders are in good condition and insulated to protect the operator. Never lay the holder on the metal bench top while the welder is running.*

64-6. Ground clamp.

64-7. Two-station arc welding bench.

64-8. Wire brush used to clean the bead.

64-9. Chipping hammers.

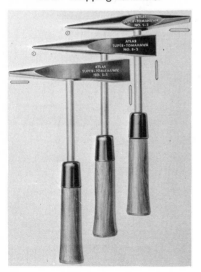

SPECIAL
MANUFACTURER'S
CHARACTERISTIC

ELECTRIC
WELDING

TENSILE
STRENGTH

WELDING POSITION

64-10. Symbols used to designate the specifications of electrodes.

GROUND CLAMP AND CABLES

In arc welding, two cables are used to carry the current through a complete circuit. One is attached to the electrode holder and the second is fastened to the ground clamp. Fig. 64-6. Of course, a good ground is necessary in all heavy electrical work. The clamp is attached to the workpiece or to a table of the type shown in Fig. 64-7. The cable can also be bolted, tack welded, or fastened with a C-clamp to the table.

CLEANING TOOLS

A wire brush, Fig. 64-8, and a chipping hammer, Fig. 64-9, are necessary tools for cleaning the weld. The chipping hammer is used to remove the slag from the

bead and should then be brushed with the wire brush.

Selection of Electrodes

Electrodes are made both for A.C. and D.C. machines, to weld specific metals. The American Welding Society has established classifications for identifying and standardizing electrodes. There is also a uniform color code for electrodes. Symbols are used to designate the specifications of electrodes such as E-6011, E-6012, etc. Fig. 64-10.

Electrodes are metal rods covered with a hard-baked chemical coating. The size of the electrode is determined by the diameter of the core rod or wire, in fractions of an inch. The purpose of the chemical-flux coating is as follows: (1) As part of the coating burns, it forms a blanket of gas that acts as a shield around the arc. (2) Part of the flux melts and mixes with the weld metal and floats impurities to the surface which forms a slag. (3) It shields

64-11. (A) Light-coated electrode, (B) heavy-coated electrode.

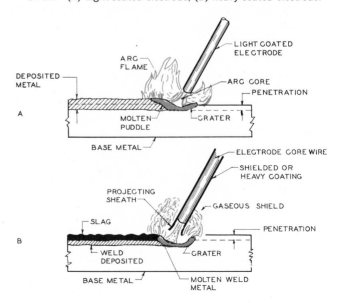

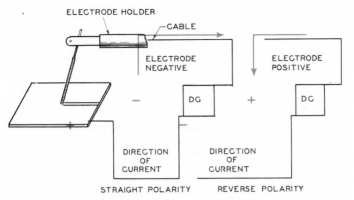

64-12. D.C. arc welding circuits.

the molten metal from the air to prevent nitrogen and oxygen from forming impurities in the weld. (4) It slows the hardening rate of the metal.

The coatings on light-coated electrodes serve not only as a fluxing agent to aid the flow of molten metal or in cleaning the surface of the base metal when welding, but also they increase the arc stability. Fig. 64-11 (A) shows the action in an arc ob-tained with a light-coated electrode.

Shielded-arc or. heavy-coated electrodes, are made in two forms, with cellulose and mineral coatings. Cellulose-coated elec-trodes depend upon a gaseous shielding for protection around the arc stream as well as a slag covering over the weld deposit. The mineral type depends entirely upon the slag as a shield. The general type of shielded-arc,

heavy-coated electrode is illus-trated in Fig. 64-11 (B).

When a D.C. welder is used it is important that the electrode cable is attached to the correct output pole. By connecting the cable to the negative terminal, straight (negative) polarity is obtained. If the electrode cable is connected to the positive terminal of the D.C. welder it has reverse (positive) polarity. Fig. 64-12. It would be very difficult to get a satisfactory weld if an electrode was being used on straight polarity but was intended for reverse polarity. The same would be true if an electrode intended for horizontal welding was being used in flat position welding. Table 64-A lists the most commonly used mild steel elec-trodes.

Welding Procedure

HOW TO STRIKE AN ARC

1. Check the machine and adjust to the right amperage. This is determined by the size of rod to be used. Generally, *the larger the electrode the higher the amperage.*

2. Select a piece of steel, mak-ing sure that it is clean. Place it upon the welding table and turn on the welder.

3. Put on welding gloves and helmet.

There are two methods of strik-ing an arc, (1) the scratch method, Fig. 64-13 (A), and (2) the down-up or tapping method. Fig. 64-13 (B). In using the tapping method lower the electrode and touch the steel plate lightly. Then raise the electrode quickly away from the metal and lower it again until the proper arc length is obtained. See illustration, next page.

COMMON MILD STEEL ELECTRODES

AWS No.	Welding Current	Welding Position	Primary (P) Secondary (S) color marking	Penetration & Characteristics
E6010	D.C. reverse polarity	All	None	Deep penetra-tion; thin slag, easy to remove: forceful arc.
E6011	A.C. or D.C. reverse polarity	All	Blue (S)	Deep penetra-tion; thin slag, easy to remove; forceful arc.
E6012	D.C. straight polarity or A.C.	All	White (S)	Medium pene-tration; heavy slag; soft arc.
E6013	A.C. or D.C. straight polarity	All	Brown (S)	Medium to shallow pene-tration; light slag, easy to re-move; soft arc.

Courtesy American Welding Society

Table 64-A.

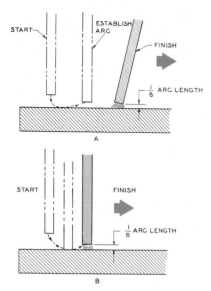

64-13. (A) The scratch method for starting a weld, (B) tapping or down-up method for starting a weld.

The scratch method is easier for beginners to learn. This resembles the action of striking a match. Raise the electrode as in the tapping method, to prevent it from sticking to the metal. If the electrode sticks, break it loose by twisting or bending the holder. Try to maintain the correct arc length. A wide spattered bead is obtained if the arc is too long. If the arc is too short the electrode is likely to stick frequently because insufficient heat is built up to melt the base metal.

WELDING A CORRECT BEAD

A bead weld is that type of weld made by one passage of the electrode without weaving or oscillating.

1. After the fundamentals of

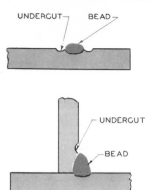

64-15. Undercutting.

obtaining the correct arc are learned, attention should be centered on the welding current. Fig. 64-14 shows examples of properly and improperly formed beads and the effects that various currents can produce. Too high a current will cause the electrode to melt too fast and create a pool that is too large and irregular. Undercutting, Fig. 64-15, is also a result of too high a current. Too low a current results in overlapping. Fig. 64-14 (A). No fusion with the base metal is obtained if this occurs.

2. After the arc is started, try to hold it from $1/16''$ to $1/8''$ in length to obtain the best results. Move the arc at a steady, uniform rate and, as the electrode shortens in length, feed it down to maintain the same arc length. Too slow movement of the electrode will build up the metal excessively and create a rough and uneven weld.

3. The correct welding speed is important. By watching the puddle of molten metal directly behind the arc and the ridge where the metal has solidified, the correct speed can be determined. This is acquired only through practice.

64-14. Characteristics of beads under various conditions: (A) Welding current too low; excessive piling up of metal. (B) Welding current too high, causing excessive splatter. (C) Voltage too high; bead irregular with poor penetration. (D) Welding speed too fast and bead too small. (E) Welding speed too slow, causing excessive piling up of weld metal. (F) Proper current and timing create a smooth, regular, well-formed bead.

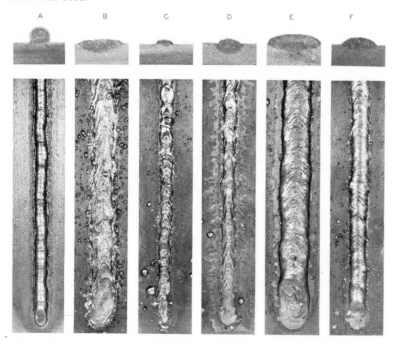

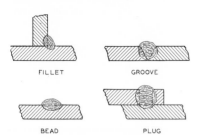

64-16. Typical beads.

Various types of bead welds are shown in Fig. 64-16.

4. Clean the slag from the weld with a chipping hammer so that if additional layers of weld metal are to be laid a strong joint will be obtained. Fig. 64-17.

5. For deep grooves or fillet welds where several passes must be made, a weaving motion of the electrode is used. Fig. 64-18.

RUNNING BEAD WELDS— FLAT POSITION

To weld beads in the flat position, a short arc is essential where strength, ductility, and appearance are required. Table 64-B shows the approximate arc lengths for metallic electrodes of the most commonly used diameters.

APPROXIMATE ARC LENGTHS	
For ¹⁄₁₆″ dia.	¼″ arc length
For ⅛″ and ⁵⁄₃₂″ dia.	⅛″ arc length
For ³⁄₁₆″ and ¼″ dia.	³⁄₁₆″ arc length

Table 64-B.

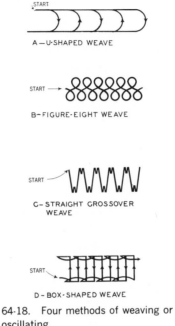

A—U-SHAPED WEAVE

B—FIGURE-EIGHT WEAVE

C—STRAIGHT CROSSOVER WEAVE

D—BOX-SHAPED WEAVE

64-18. Four methods of weaving or oscillating.

A short arc with the proper electrode, current, and polarity will give out a sharp, crackling sound. Examination of the deposited bead shows deep penetration within the crater. There is very little overlap along the sides of the bead weld, deposited as shown in Figs. 64-19 (A), (B), and (C), and there is very little spatter.

A long arc will never give off a sharp, crackling sound but will be distinguished by a steady hiss. Penetration in the crater will be poor and overlap will be noticeable along the sides of the bead weld. Figs. 64-19 (E) and (F). Spatters are in the form of large globules of molten metal from an uncontrolled arc deposit. Fig. 64-19 (D).

64-19. Depositing bead welds in a flat position.

64-17. Cleaning slag from weld.

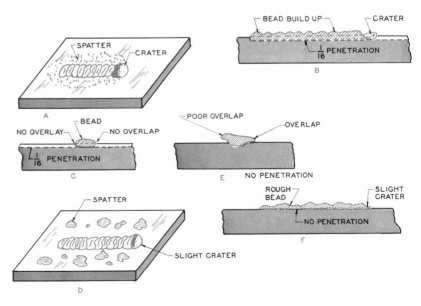

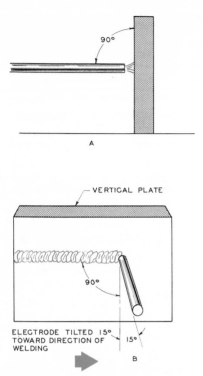

64-20. Horizontal bead weld on a vertical plate.

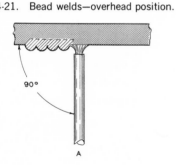

64-21. Bead welds—overhead position.

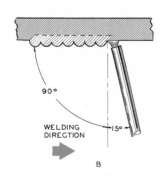

64-22. Five basic welding joints: (A) Corner, (B) edge, (C) butt, (D) lap, (E) tee.

RUNNING A HORIZONTAL BEAD ON A VERTICAL PLATE

1. When depositing a bead weld in the horizontal plane on a vertical plate, the electrode is held at right angles to the vertical. Fig. 64-20 (A).

2. Tilt the electrode about 15° towards the direction of welding, Fig. 64-20 (B). The current should be slightly less than when welding in a flat position.

BEAD WELDS— OVERHEAD POSITION

1. Place a practice plate in an overhead jig, being sure the metal surfaces are clean.

2. Practice striking an arc and depositing short bead welds.

3. Hold the electrode as in Fig. 64-21 (A). For viewing, the electrode may be held at a 15°

angle into the crater. Fig. 64-21 (B).

4. Deposit bead welds from left to right and right to left, away from and towards you. Hold a short arc and acquire the technique of metal transfer, by quickly shortening and pulling out slightly at frequent intervals.

Basic Joints in Arc Welding

There are five basic joints in arc welding: the corner weld, edge weld, butt weld, fillet or lap weld, and the tee-joint. Fig. 64-22.

BUTT WELD

A butt weld is used to fuse two plates, having surfaces approximately in the same plane with each other. Fig. 64-23.

1. Prepare two ¼″ plates with square edges, space them from ³/₃₂″ to ⅛″ apart, and tack weld.

2. With a ⁵⁄₃₂″ electrode, deposit a single pass, Fig. 64-24. A miniature crescent weave should be used, with a slight hesitation on the edges, to insure good fusion and penetration.

3. Clean the first layer of weld and apply a second pass, weaving the electrode from side to side. The width of the second should be about ¼″. Steel plates over ⅜″ thick are beveled on both sides. Fig. 64-25 illustrates various types of butt joints.

FILLET WELDS

1. Set the polarity switch on the welding machine to straight polarity—electrode negative (−). For fillet welds in a tee-joint, use two plates.

2. Place one flat plate on the welding table and the other at a right angle and in the middle of the flat plate; then tack each end.

3. First, practice making a ¼″ *single-pass* fillet weld of the tee-joint in the flat position, using a ⁵⁄₃₂″ electrode with a slight weaving motion. Use a short arc to obtain fusion into the corner of the weld.

4. Hold the electrode at a 45° angle, bisecting the right angle made by the surfaces of the two plates. The electrode should be tilted about 15° in the direction of travel, with the arc pointed into the crater.

5. In making a *multiple-pass* fillet weld in a tee-joint, apply the first pass as a bead with no weaving. Apply the second pass with a weave, using a semi-circular crescent with a slight hesitation at the end of each crossover motion to insure good fusion.

For fillet welds in a lap joint, overlap the two edges, Fig. 64-26,

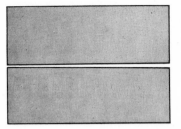

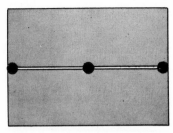

64-23. Butt weld.

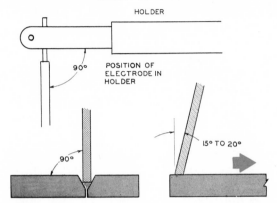

64-24. Position of electrode when running a butt weld.

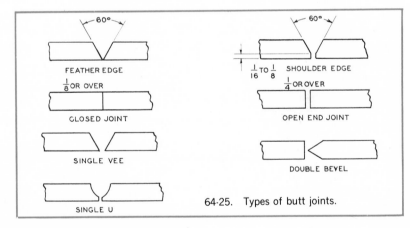

64-25. Types of butt joints.

about two inches, tack weld, and proceed as in a tee-weld.

Arc Welding Alloy Steels

In welding alloy steels, such as stainless, the diameter of the electrode or filler rod should be approximately equal to, or slightly less than, the thickness of the metal to be welded. Electrodes larger than ³⁄₁₆″ are seldom used.

64-26. Fillet weld on a lap joint.

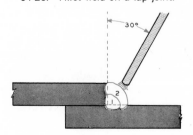

Short electrodes are preferred, since electrical resistance of stainless steels is much greater than that of carbon steel.

In metal-arc welding, coated electrodes are used in order to deposit a solid, nonporous weld metal. Electrode coatings are made of materials that will steady the arc, protect the stream of molten metal from the atmosphere, and at the same time form a fusible slag that will cover and protect the molten metal against oxidation. This slag should be easily removable.

Electrode coatings must be free from undesirable elements that might combine with the deposited weld metal and alter its composition.

In setting up for welding, light material (.050″ and under) should be clamped firmly to prevent buckling, and edges should be butted tightly together. It is advisable to tack weld at short intervals in addition to using clamping devices.

Heavier gage sheets (.0625″ to about .1875″) are set up for welding with an opening equal to about one-half the gage thickness. The heavy gages should be beveled with a 30° angle on each edge so that when placed together the beveled edges form a 60° V.

The electrode should always point into the weld and the "figure eight" or excessive side weaving motion, such as used in welding carbon steel, should be avoided. A slight weaving motion and steady forward travel with the electrode sloped back about 60° will give best results.

The arc should always be as short as possible. Correct voltage is indicated if a slight withdrawal

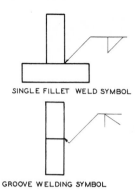

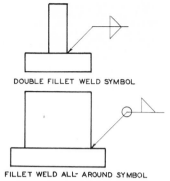

64-27. Welding symbols.

of the electrode breaks the arc. The following table will serve as a guide when commencing operations. Some experimentation and adjustment will usually determine proper welding conditions.

Too large an electrode creates a pool of molten metal which is likely to show shrinkage cracks on cooling.

Excessive arc length tends to produce surface pin holes. Sputtering of the arc may be caused by excessive moisture in the coat-

ing. Store rods in a warm, dry location.

For vertical or overhead welding, use small size electrodes—not exceeding ⅛″ diameter—and the current ratings in Table 64-C.

Welding Symbols

A series of symbols has been developed by the American Welding Society for the purpose of giving the welder specific instructions. These are shown in Fig. 64-27.

Metal Thickness	Electrode Dia.	Amperage	Voltage Open Circuit
.050″ and lighter	⁵⁄₆₄″	25-50	30-25
.050″ to .0625″	³⁄₃₂″	30-90	35-40
.0625″ to .140625″	³⁄₃₂″-⅛″	50-100	40-45
.250″ and heavier	⅛″-⁵⁄₃₂″	80-125	45-50
	³⁄₁₆″	100-175	55-60

Table 64-C.

65 ▷ Industrial Welding Processes

The efficient joining of metals has been responsible for many of our recent technological advances. High-strength, lightweight missile cases and fuel tanks employed in

our space programs involve high-precision welding processes.

Although the average school does not have available machines for the special welding processes

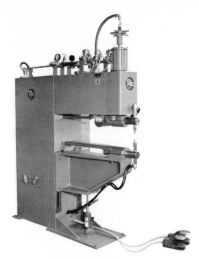

65-1. Spot welder.

described in this unit, it is important that you have a basic understanding of some of the production arc-welding processes used in industry today.

Spot Welding

This form of resistance welding is done on a machine called a spot welder. Fig. 65-1. Spot welding is used mostly in sheet-metal fabrication. It consists of applying pressure to two or more sheets by means of conducting electrodes, and then passing a high current at low voltage through the sheets from one electrode to the other. The electrical resistance of the materials causes the metal to become heated at the juncture of the two parts and take on a plastic state. This action, combined with correct amount of pressure, causes fusion. Fig. 65-2.

The welding time is controlled by a timer built into the machine. It controls the squeeze, weld, hold, and off periods. Calculations of the exact time of each stage for different types and thicknesses of metals can be obtained from tables which are furnished with the machine.

Seam Welding

Seam or line welding is an adaption of spot welding, employing continuously rotating rollers for electrodes. Fig. 65-3 shows the type of machine used for this method and Fig. 65-4 illustrates the welding operation.

Successive impulses of electrical current produce, in effect, a series of overlapping spots. The current is automatically turned on and off as the electrode revolves, corresponding to the speed at which the work is set to move.

This type of welding is used to make airtight seams on fuel tanks, water heaters, and similar products. Instead of intermittent spots as in spot welding, it makes a continuous weld.

Butt or Flash Welding

In butt or flash welding, a low voltage, heavy-current transform-

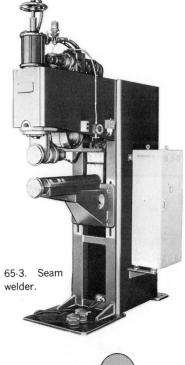

65-3. Seam welder.

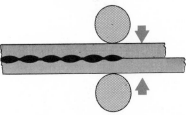

65-4. In seam welding, the spots overlap each other.

er is connected to the two pieces to be welded. An intense arc forms as the parts are moved together endwise at a relatively slow speed. When this occurs long enough for the ends of the pieces to become molten, the current is turned off, the pieces are punched together, and held in position under pressure. Fig. 65-5.

65-5. Flash and butt welder.

65-2. Periods of spot welding.

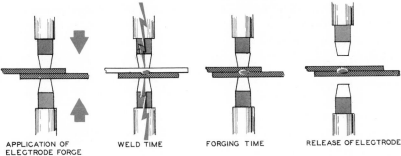

APPLICATION OF ELECTRODE FORCE   WELD TIME   FORGING TIME   RELEASE OF ELECTRODE

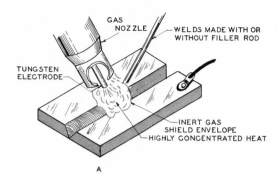

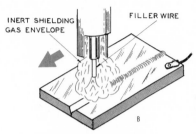

MIG ARC INERT GAS SHIELDED
METAL ARC

65-6. (A) Gas tungsten-arc welding (TIG), (B) gas metal arc-welding—inert shielding (MIG).

65-9. Submerged arc welder.

65-7. Gas tungsten-arc welding machine.

65-8. Gas metal-welding gun.

Gas Tungsten-Arc Welding (TIG)

This is a gas shielded arc welding process which uses the intense heat of an electric arc between a non-consumable tungsten electrode and the work to be welded. Shielding is obtained from a single inert gas, such as CO_2, or from a mixture of inert gases. Filler metal may or may not be used; it is usually fed manually into the weld pool. Fig. 65-6 (A).

TIG welding (1) produces the highest quality welds in *nonferrous* metals, (2) requires practically no post (or after) welding. (3) The arc and pools are clearly visible. (4) The metal does not transfer through the arc, and (5) welding is possible in all portions. TIG welding is used primarily for welding aluminum, magnesium, silver, copper, stainless steels, nickel, cast iron, and mild steel. Fig. 65-7.

Gas Metal-Arc Welding— Inert Shielding (MIG)

MIG arc welding is a gas shielded metal-arc welding which

also uses the intense heat of an electric arc between a continuously fed, consumable electrode wire and the workpiece. Shielding is obtained with a single inert gas or with an inert gas mixture. Fig. 65-6 (B) shows the electrode wire and the inert shielding gas being directed into the arc area. The process may either be semi-automatic or automatic, with the semi-automatic method being most widely used.

The special wire feeder and the constant voltage welding machine constitute the heart of the MIG welding process. There is a fixed relationship between the rate of wire burn-off and the welding current.

Since the MIG process can be either semi-automatic or automatic, a manually controlled welding gun or a fixtured welding torch is used, depending upon the method of process. The welding gun can be either air or water cooled. Fig. 65-8.

Submerged Arc Welding

Submerged welding speeds

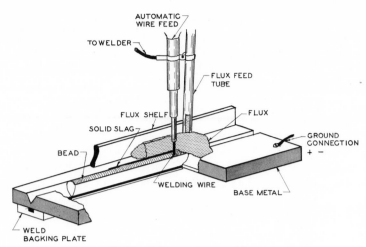

65-10.   Submerged arc welding.

65-11.   The sections to be welded are clamped tightly, one in a stationary chuck, the other in a rotating chuck.

65-12.   Abutting ends brought together to consummate a weld.

deep penetration and gives smooth weld on a wide range of materials. This process uses the intense heat of an electric arc between a continuously fed consumable electrode wire and the workpiece. Fig. 65-9. Metal is transferred through the arc to the workpieces. Shielding is obtained from a blanket of granular, fusible material directly upon the work. Fig. 65-10. This process produces no arc rays, smoke, spatter, or radiant heat.

Electron-beam Welding

Electron-beam welding, a process normally performed in a vacuum, is accomplished by an electro bombardment of a workpiece seam. The "tool" used is essentially a stream of pure energy focused on a very small area of the seam. Upon contact with the adjoining surfaces of the workpieces, the beam energy is converted to heat. This action causes the seam to melt and become mutually soluble. Upon solidification, the fusion zone becomes a weld seam.

The electron beam is capable of melting any known material. This makes it possible to join high melting temperature metals like tungsten (4760°) and molybdenum (6170°) needed for work in space equipment.

Inertia Welding

Inertia welding, a relatively simple process, produces a superior weld. Stored kinetic energy generates all the heating and most of the forging necessary to create a full, sound interface weld. In the process, one of the members to be welded (bar, plate, casting, tube, formed piece) is placed in a secondary chuck, or fixture. The other member—which must have a reasonably cylindrical surface for welding—is securely clamped in a rotating spindle. Fig. 65-11. Attached to this spindle is a flywheel of a specified amount of inertia.

The clamped part, spindle, and flywheel are rotated by an external energy source. Members to be welded are not yet in contact. When a predetermined rpm has

been reached, the drive source is disconnected. The freely rotating mass contains a specific amount of kinetic energy.

Now the members are brought into contact, Fig. 65-12, under a precomputed thrust load. The kinetic energy in the rotating mass converts to frictional heat. The heating rate for a particular application is always the most favorable since inertia can be controlled to supply whatever energy is needed.

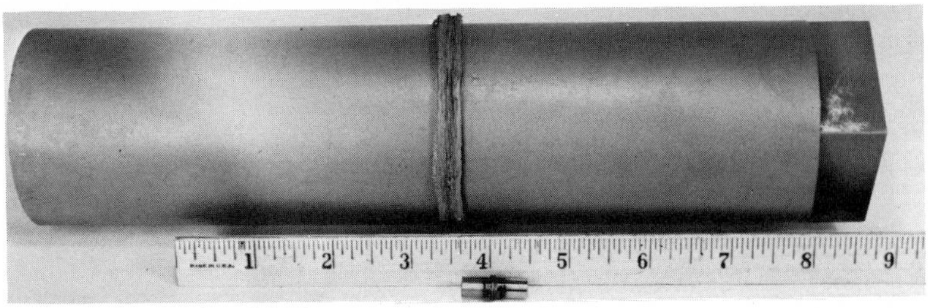
1
2
3
4
5
6
7
8
9

65-13. Parts that have been welded together by inertia welding—low carbon steel ¼″ dia. and 2½″ dia.

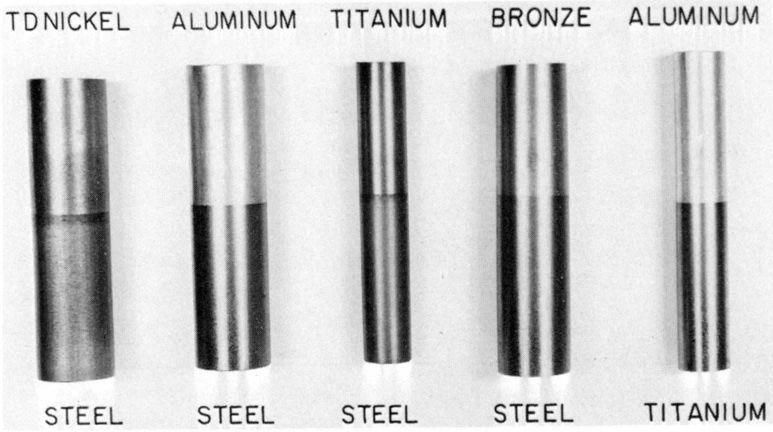
TD NICKEL
ALUMINUM
TITANIUM
BRONZE
ALUMINUM
STEEL
STEEL
STEEL
STEEL
TITANIUM

65-14. Various types of metals can be welded together.

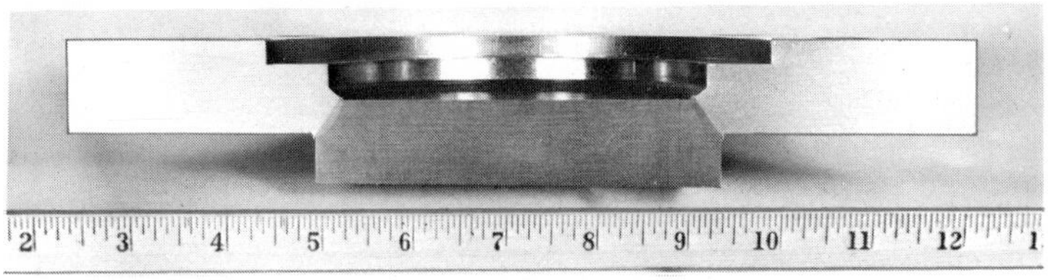
2
3
4
5
6
7
8
9
10
11
12
1

65-15. Carbon steel shaft welded to stainless steel flange.

65-16. Steel welded to steel. A complete interface weld.

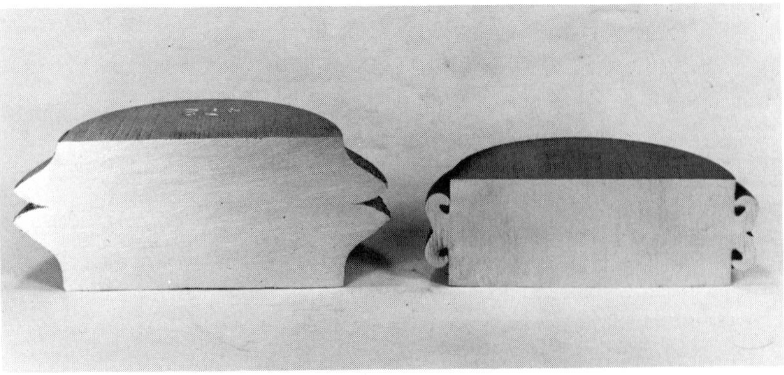

Welding occurs as friction ceases. The process produces plastic deformation in the weld zone, resulting in grain refinement, favorable flow line orientation, and flash expulsion. The heat-affected zone is narrow. Fig. 65-13 shows two parts that have been welded by this process.

A wide variety of metals which are normally difficult to join together can be effectively welded in seconds. Fig. 65-14. A carbon steel shaft that has been welded to a stainless steel flange is shown in Fig. 65-15.

Fig. 65-16 is an example of two pieces of steel of the same type welded together. A complete interface weld has been obtained rather than a perimeter weld, as with a submerged arc or stick electrode welding.

Check Your Knowledge

1. *Define welding.*
2. *What safety devices are used to prevent cylinders from exploding when subjected to intense pressure?*
3. *Describe the safety precautions that should be taken in handling cylinders.*
4. *What danger is involved when grease and oil come in contact with the oxygen cylinder valve?*
5. *Why are torches supplied with interchangeable tips?*
6. *How are sizes of tips indicated?*
7. *What is the function of a regulator on a cylinder?*
8. *How is an oxygen hose distinguished from an acetylene hose?*
9. *Why should the adjusting screw on a regulator be released before opening a cylinder valve?*
10. *Why should a friction lighter, instead of a match, be used to light a torch?*

11. How is a neutral flame produced?

12. What determines the correct tip size?

13. What is a carbonizing flame?

14. What causes "popping" of the flame?

15. Why should the acetylene valve be closed first?

16. Name two methods of holding the acetylene torch.

17. Name some types of oxyacetylene welded joints.

18. What is brazing?

19. Compare the strength of welded joints with brazed joints.

20. What is flame cutting?

21. How does the tip of a cutting torch differ from a welding tip?

22. What procedure is used for cutting holes?

23. How does arc welding differ from acetylene welding?

24. Describe the difference between a D.C. welder and an A.C. welder.

25. Why is it dangerous to watch a welding arc without proper eye protection?

26. What is an electrode holder?

27. What tools are used to clean the weld?

28. What is an electrode?

29. How do you determine the correct size of electrodes suitable for a specific job?

30. Why are electrodes coated?

31. What is polarity?

32. Explain two methods of striking an arc.

33. What is undercutting?

34. Why is the correct welding speed important in obtaining a good weld?

35. Why is it necessary to clean the slag from a weld? What tools are used?

36. Why is a weaving motion used in welding?

37. What is "overlap"?

38. What is spot welding?

39. How does seam welding differ from spot welding?

40. What is submerged arc welding?

41. What is CO_2 welding?

42. What are some of the advantages of this type of welding?

43. Describe two other production welding processes.

Terms to Know and Spell

fusion	electrode	infrared
homogeneous	transformer	ultraviolet
acetylene	flux	porosity
regulator	shielded	plastic
spatter	polarity	voltage
oxyacetylene	slag	shielded
oxidizing	fillet	inert
puddle	direct current	tungsten
oxygen	alternating current	granular
generator	globules	

On the following pages are projects requiring the use of welding.

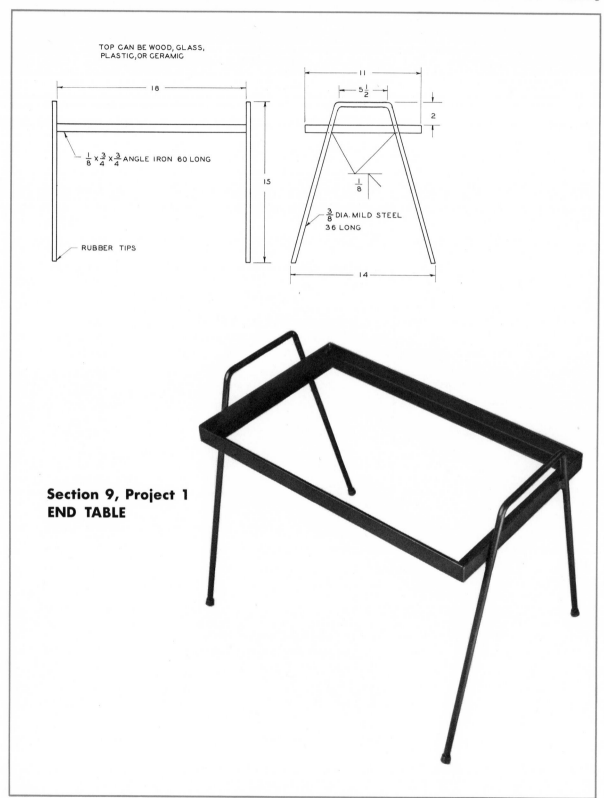

TOP CAN BE WOOD, GLASS, PLASTIC, OR CERAMIC

18

$\frac{1}{8} \times \frac{3}{4} \times \frac{3}{4}$ ANGLE IRON 60 LONG

RUBBER TIPS

15

11

$5\frac{1}{2}$

2

$\frac{1}{8}$

$\frac{3}{8}$ DIA. MILD STEEL 36 LONG

14

**Section 9, Project 1
END TABLE**

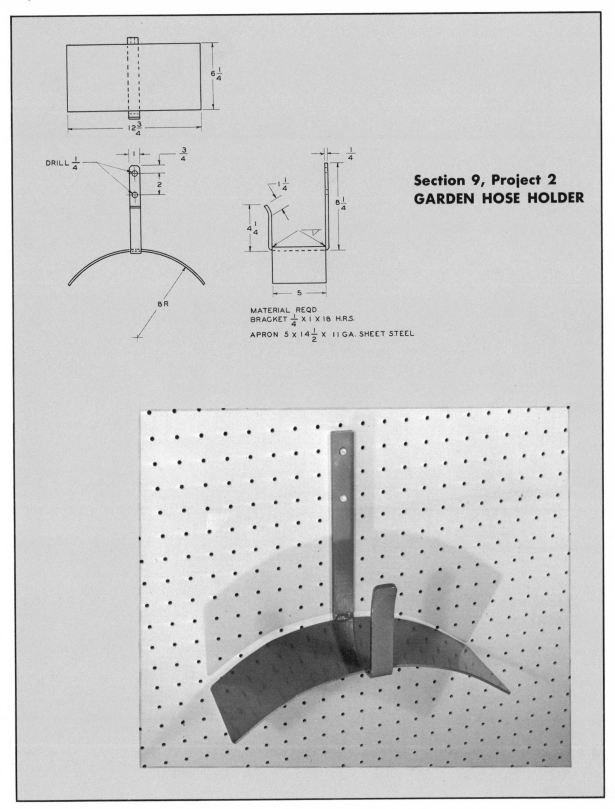

6 $\frac{1}{4}$

12 $\frac{3}{4}$

DRILL $\frac{1}{4}$

1

$\frac{3}{4}$

2

8 R

$\frac{1}{4}$

1 $\frac{1}{4}$

8 $\frac{1}{4}$

4 $\frac{1}{4}$

5

**Section 9, Project 2
GARDEN HOSE HOLDER**

MATERIAL REQD
BRACKET $\frac{1}{4}$ X 1 X 18 H.R.S.

APRON 5 X 14 $\frac{1}{2}$ X 11 GA. SHEET STEEL

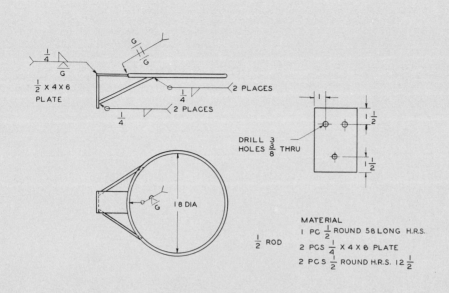

$\frac{1}{4}$

$\frac{1}{2}$ X 4 X 6 PLATE

G
G
G

2 PLACES

$\frac{1}{4}$ 2 PLACES

$\frac{1}{4}$

DRILL $\frac{3}{8}$ HOLES THRU

1

$1\frac{1}{2}$

$1\frac{1}{2}$

18 DIA

G

$\frac{1}{2}$ ROD

MATERIAL
1 PC $\frac{1}{2}$ ROUND 58 LONG H.R.S.
2 PCS $\frac{1}{4}$ X 4 X 6 PLATE
2 PCS $\frac{1}{2}$ ROUND H.R.S. 12 $\frac{1}{2}$

Section 9, Project 3
BASKETBALL GOAL

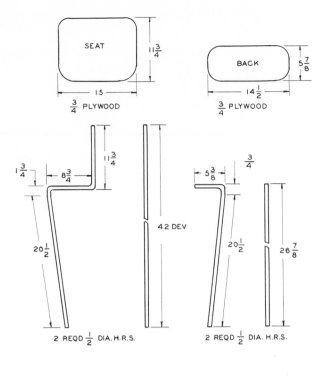

SEAT

$11\frac{3}{4}$

15

$\frac{3}{4}$ PLYWOOD

BACK

$5\frac{7}{8}$

$14\frac{1}{2}$

$\frac{3}{4}$ PLYWOOD

$11\frac{3}{4}$

$1\frac{3}{4}$

$8\frac{3}{4}$

$\frac{3}{4}$

$5\frac{3}{8}$

42 DEV

$20\frac{1}{2}$

$20\frac{1}{2}$

$26\frac{7}{8}$

2 REQD $\frac{1}{2}$ DIA. H.R.S.

2 REQD $\frac{1}{2}$ DIA. H.R.S.

Section 9, Project 4
CHAIR

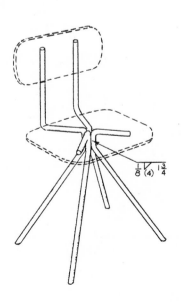

$\frac{1}{8}$ (4) $1\frac{3}{4}$

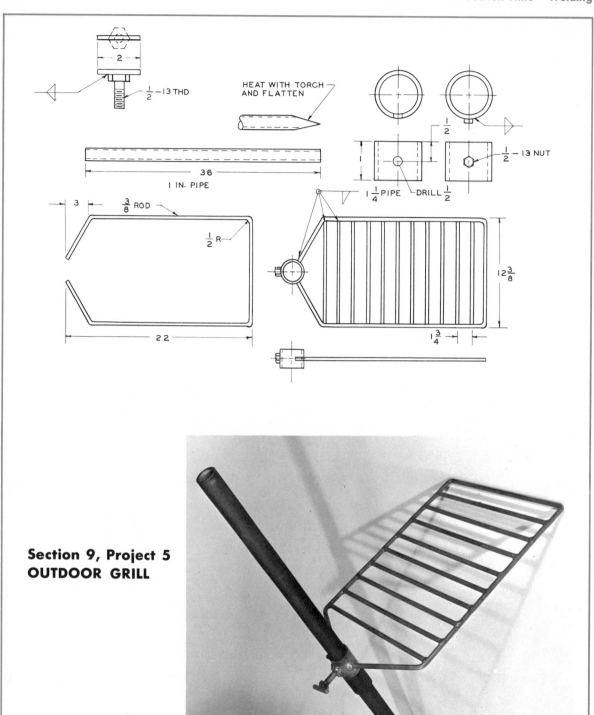

$\frac{1}{2}$ –13 THD

HEAT WITH TORCH
AND FLATTEN

36
1 IN. PIPE

$\frac{1}{2}$
1$\frac{1}{4}$ PIPE   DRILL $\frac{1}{2}$
$\frac{1}{2}$ –13 NUT

3
$\frac{3}{8}$ ROD
$\frac{1}{2}$ R

22

12$\frac{3}{8}$
1$\frac{3}{4}$

**Section 9, Project 5
OUTDOOR GRILL**

Metal Finishing

M OST metals have a natural color and texture that can be beautified by polishing and buffing. Smooth surfaces can be obtained by hand polishing with abrasive cloth. However, more commercial-like quality calls for machine methods.

Final inspection. This requires highly skilled inspectors who can detect even the most minute scratch or discoloration. Such pieces are marked and returned for correcting and refinishing.

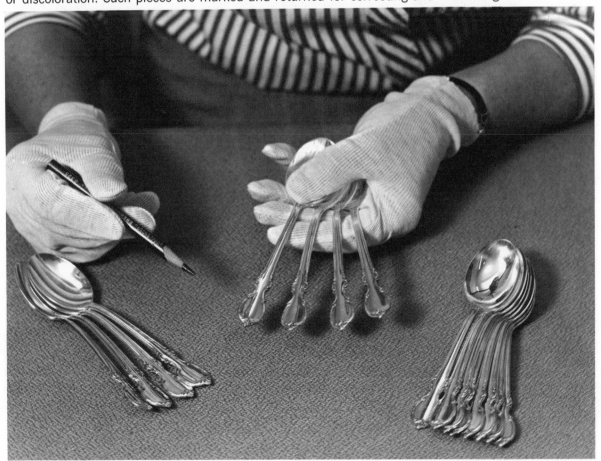

Abrasives for Polishing

An abrasive is any hard, sharp material that wears away another material when one, the other, or both move in pressure contact. Thus, stones tumbled together will polish each other. Abrasive stones were used by early man to sharpen tools and spears. Bonded abrasives were used by the Chinese in the 13th century when crushed seashells were bound to parchment with natural gums. Abrasives today are used in making abrasive papers, cloths, liquids, powders, grinding wheels, and compounds of various types.

66-2. Polishing a curved surface by hand.

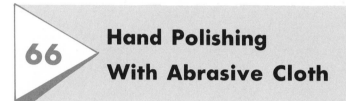

66 ▷ Hand Polishing With Abrasive Cloth

In schools where a polishing lathe is not available the work can be done by hand with abrasive cloth and steel wool. Naturally, a higher polish can be obtained on a polishing lathe, but interesting contrasts are possible in art metal work for the hand craftsman.

See the section on Abrasives in selecting abrasive cloths. To review, emery is a natural composite of corundum and iron oxide. Emery cloth is used in maintenance work for polishing metals but has largely been replaced by *synthetic aluminum oxide* and *silicon carbide* whereever appreciable removal of metal is required. Aluminum oxide abrasives are produced in electric furnaces by purifying bauxite to a crystalline form and adding various amounts of titania to impart extra toughness. It is made in much finer grades than that of emery cloth. The different grades of fineness are designated by numbers. The grades of emery cloth run from 4/0 to No. 3, while aluminum oxide runs from 4½, or 12 mesh to 600 mesh.

In hand polishing with abrasive cloth, the first abrasive used should be a coarse grit to remove excess metal quickly. NOTE: A proper selection of grit should be used to avoid deep scratches that are hard to remove with a finer grade.

A few drops of oil when polishing with finer grits will produce better results.

The following grits can be used satisfactorily:

Coarse: 60 to 80
Medium coarse: 100 to 120
Medium fine: 150 to 180
Fine: 220 to 240
Very fine: 280 and up
High polish: crocus cloth

1. To polish a flat surface, wrap the abrasive cloth on a flat wooden block and stroke the abrasive cloth back and forth. Fig. 66-1. As polishing progresses use a finer grade of cloth to obtain the desired polish.

2. Irregular and curved surfaces can be polished by holding the abrasive cloth as shown in Fig. 66-2.

Steel Wool

Steel wool can also be used in hand polishing and cleaning metal. Fig. 66-3. It is made in seven grades—from 0000, which is the finest, to No. 3, the coarsest. NOTE: Deep scratches cannot be removed with steel wool.

It is commonly used with liquid or powdered abrasives.

66-1. Polishing a flat surface by hand.

66-3. Polishing with steel wool.

Machine Polishing and Buffing

FINISHING CHARACTERISTICS—
POLISHING

A metal form may have been produced by machining, heat-treating, forging, casting, forming, or grinding. These give different surfaces.

Polishing is usually undertaken to make metal smoother or to produce a more uniform surface. The amount and degree of polishing is determined solely by the characteristics of the metal surface. The rougher the metal to start with, and the finer the finish specified, the greater amount of work is required. It is also determined by the hardness of the metal itself; for instance, stainless steel is harder to finish than brass.

Another feature which has to be observed in the finishing of metals is whether the surface has hard and soft crystals. Care must be taken not to use methods which gouge out the soft crystals, leaving the hard areas high, thus producing a mottled effect.

As the polishing progresses, the original roughness is eliminated, so the roughness of polishing materials must be decreased. Finer materials must be used.

Economical finishing requires a thorough understanding of polishing, buffing, and burring, using the proper materials so the desired surface can be produced with a minimum of work and waste.

Such operations are influenced greatly by (1) the metal itself, (2) the method and amount of forming, (3) the condition of the surface prior to finishing, and (4) the character of the surface finish desired.

Table 66-A shows the distinguishing appearance of selected metal finishes.

Polishing refers to the process of the rapid cutting away of the surface of the metal to remove blemishes that a buffing wheel is unable to tone out. The operation *follows grinding* and *precedes buffing*. Sometimes in place of rigid, felt-covered abrasive-coated wheels, flexible wheels are used. Fig. 66-4.

Buffing

The function of the buffing operation is to produce a smooth, uniform surface with a high, bright luster. To do this it is obvious that the abrading action must be reduced to a minimum. Therefore, a lubricant is usually blended with abrasive particles.

Buffing can be divided into two operations—(1) cutting down and (2) coloring. The first operation smooths the surface more than polishing. The second operation—coloring—produces a high finish or luster. As with polishing operations, many variations are obtainable, depending upon the grade of compound and type of buff.

Polishing and buffing wheels are mounted on polishing lathes of the type illustrated in Fig. 66-5, which is a bench polishing

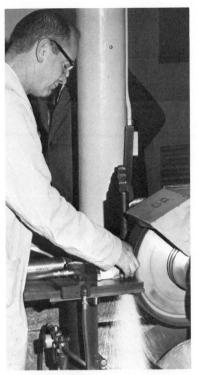

66-4. Polishing on a polishing wheel. Note the use of a simple jig and air-powered feed stroke which controls the extent of the grinding cut.

66-5. Bench polishing lathe suitable for schools.

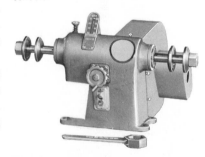

Table 66-A.

FINISH APPEARANCE FROM BRIGHT TO DULL

Mirror	No surface defects visible.
Buffed bright	No surface defects visible but less brilliant.
Bright satin	No surface defects visible but fine finishing lines show.
Regular satin	No surface defects visible—heavier finishing lines.
Satin	Some slight defects, heavy lines.
Dull satin	Very heavy lines.
Bright matte	Etched or frosted finish with some luster, but no lines visible.
Dull matte	Dead etched or frosted finish with no luster and no lines visible.

66-6. Large polishing lathe used in industrial applications.

66-7. Production finishing. A bright surface is given the handles of flatware with a fine abrasive on a high-speed revolving belt.

66-8. Tapered spindle.

66-9. Tapered arbor with buffing wheel. Can be used on a lathe.

lathe. Fig. 66-6 shows a large polishing and buffing lathe of the type used in industry. A great deal of polishing today is done on abrasive belt polishing machines of the type illustrated in Fig. 66-7.

Schools that are not equipped with polishing lathes can use wheels mounted on any lathe, grinder, or drill press. Polishing and buffing spindles of the types shown in Figs. 66-8 and 66-9 can be used to adapt motors, grinders, and other machines for polishing and buffing.

Polishing and Buffing Wheels

POLISHING WHEELS

Commonly used polishing wheels are constructed of muslin, canvas, felt, and leather, which, by changes in construction, offer varying flexibility to suit the particular article to be finished and its surface condition.

In general, the more rigid polishing wheels are indicated where there is either a need for rapid metal removal or where there are

66-10. Felt polishing wheel.

66-11. Loose buffing wheel.

66-12. Greaseless polishing and buffing compound is clearly labeled.

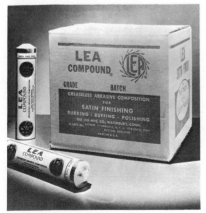

no contours and a flat surface is to be maintained. Fig. 66-10. Conversely, softer types of polishing wheels are used where there are irregularities in the surface and the fast removal of metal is not a prime requisite.

Felt polishing wheels are coated with hot hide glue and, when almost dry, rotated, scraped smooth, and the wheel shaped with a file that has been ground to the proper shape. When the wheel is dry it is recoated with hot glue or waterglass and, while it is wet, rolled in aluminum oxide grain. NOTE: Silicon carbide may be preferred because of its faster cutting properties but it does not bond well to the conventional wheel.

For the polishing operation, generally a felt wheel, charged with No. 100 to 220 grit, is used. Buffing tallow, oil, or beeswax serves as a lubricant.

BUFFING WHEELS

Buffs are flexible wheels made of cloth, paper, or sheepskin discs. Those made of high-count cotton cloth are generally used. Canton flannel or wool cloth buffs are used for high coloring on the

noble metals (gold, silver, and platinum). In addition loose buffs made of sheepskin are used for final coloring of the precious metals.

The material most widely used for buffs is muslin, bleached and unbleached, with thread counts up to 86 x 93. Fig. 66-11. Higher count sheeting is of course more expensive, but the greatly increased wearing quality makes buffs of this material more economical.

The high thread count buffs are used for heavy, hard service on large brass, copper, or nickel-silver surfaces, as well as on heavy nickel stock.

Polishing and Buffing Compounds

Polishing and buffing compounds, like wheels, are usually divided into two broad categories, (1) cutting down—removing scratches and grain lines from previous operations—and (2) coloring, which gives the product the final bright, deep luster. Buffing compounds can either be greaseless, Fig. 66-12, or have a grease base. Fig. 66-13. (Compounds that *combine* cut and color

66-13. Grease-type buffing compounds.

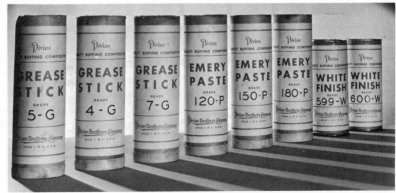

are usually medium to dry as far as greasiness is concerned.)

A mixture of glue base, a softening agent, and a mineral makes up a greaseless compound. This generates a satin finish and is also used in cutting down prior to coloring. Sometimes a greaseless compound is followed by a cutting compound and then a coloring mixture. Many different abrasive elements are used for the coloring compound, such as emery, tripoli, crocus, chrome rouge, jeweler's rouge, and white coloring compounds.

Grease type buffing compounds use oil, tallow, and other bonds. The bonding material not only serves as a lubricant but causes the abrasive to adhere to the wheel. The selection depends upon the type of work to be done, the type of equipment available, and the finish required. For cutting operations, emery abrasives and tripoli will do a good job. Generally limes and rouge can be used for coloring.

66-14.   The method of holding the work-piece on the wheel.

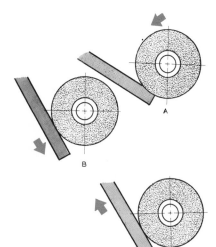

66-15.   Polishing a thin, flat piece held on a block of wood.

66-16.   Gloves protect the hands and prevent finger marks on the polished surface.

66-17.   Applying buffing compound to a wheel.

66-18.   Hold the workpiece with con-siderable pressure.

Polishing Procedures

1. Place a felt polishing wheel that has been properly prepared on the spindle of the polishing lathe. This is used to remove deep scratches that cannot be buffed out.

2. The correct positioning of the workpiece is important in this operation. Hold below the centerline of the wheel. Fig. 66-14 (A).

3. **Caution:** *Pull the workpiece up against the rotation of the wheel, Fig. 66-14 (C), as this prevents the hands from being pulled down in. Avoid placing either the top or bottom edge in the workpiece against the wheel. It can catch on the wheel and be pulled from the operator's hands.*

Flat pieces can be polished by holding the workpiece on a block, as in Fig. 66-15.

4. **Caution:** *It is a good idea to wear cotton gloves as the metal becomes heated during the polishing operation and can burn the hands. Fig. 66-16. Never hold the workpiece with a cloth when polishing or buffing.*

Buffing Procedures

1. Select the wheel and compound.

2. Press the bar or stick of compound lightly against the rotating wheel until the entire edge is coated. Fig. 66-17.

3. Hold the workpiece against the wheel with considerable pressure, so that black streaks and other deposits of compound will not be left on. Fig. 66-18. Rotate the workpiece so that the surface will be polished in several directions.

66-19. Manually operated abrasive-belt polishing machine.

66-20. Operator loads plates onto the belt polishing machine. Parts are previously stamped, milled, and hardened. Four different aluminum oxide belts are used for achieving the desired finish.

66-21. Automatic abrasive-belt polishing machine.

66-22. Backstand idler kit which can be assembled in the school.

66-23. The assembled backstand idler polishing kit in use.

66-24. Edge polishing. Fine abrasive belts are used to polish edge surfaces of flatware.

4. Wash the metal with soap and hot water after buffing. Dry with a clean, soft cloth, being careful not to touch the surface with the fingers to avoid grease marks. To prevent oxidation of the surface, spray with a clear metal lacquer. Spraying does a better job than trying to apply the lacquer with a brush.

Polishing Metals with Abrasive Belts

Coated abrasives have become a major production cutting tool accepted by the modern metal industry for polishing metals.

Coated abrasive machines are of various types: manually operated, Fig. 66-19, semi-automatic, Fig. 66-20, and fully automatic, Fig. 66-21. Coated abrasive machines are also classified as drum, disc, sheet, and roll.

Coated abrasive belts and brushes are the most versatile for metal polishing. One very important benefit provided by abrasive belts is the quick change that is possible from a used belt to a new one, or from one grade to another.

The belts used for polishing are coated with resins and hide glues. The belts are then coated with either emery, flint, crocus, garnet, aluminum oxide, or silicon carbide.

Belts can be made in any desired length. Their widths range from ⅛″ to 86″.

For schools, a backstand idler kit, shown in Figures 66-22 and 66-23, can be assembled in a short time.

Fine abrasive belts are used by the silverware industry to polish edges of flatware to a smooth finish. Fig. 66-24.

66-25. Silverware that has been polished and buffed with production methods.

The combination of various polishing methods produces a product that is beautiful as well as useful. Fig. 66-25 illustrates silverware that has been polished and buffed by a combination of the methods described in this unit.

Power Brush Finishing

Power brushing methods are finding considerable extension of uses as production tools for metal finishing operations.

One of the major advantages of the power brush is that it can be used in manually, in semi-automatic, or integrated methods.

Polishing, as a part of the finishing process, has a double meaning. One meaning is broad, "preparation of any surface for further treatment." The other meaning is narrower and deals with "the final preparation of the surface."

Two basic factors generally control the finish of any product.

• *The material being finished.* It is generally known that hard material such as steel will take a higher luster than soft material such as aluminum. Treatments that affect the hardness of metal—such as drawing, rolling, and heat-treating—have a bearing on the luster. Brushes are selected accordingly.

• *The selection of a proper power brush.* The correct brush with the proper buffing compound is important for a good finish.

Many types of brushes are used for polishing metals. These include wire, cord, and tampico fiber brushes.

All common metals can be brushed but proper brush selection depends upon hardness and electrolytic corrosion characteristics. Only **fiber brushes** are used for relatively soft metal such as zinc. For stainless steel, aluminum, and magnesium, fiber brushes can be used alone or after previous wire brushing.

Wire wheel brushes are best for general purpose jobs, and such metals as steel, stainless steel, nickel alloys, brass, bronze, and copper.

Cord brushes are used with abrasive compounds for polishing, finishing, and burring metal parts.

Treated **tampico fiber brushes**

66-27. Power brushing has removed tiny burrs and polished an electric shaver head.

used with abrasive compounds are outstanding for removing burrs and tool marks, and for blending surface junctures. In the latter stages of the polishing procedure, these brushes are used more like a buffing wheel, in that the compound is applied loosely rather than as a fixed abrasive.

Fig. 66-26 illustrates a casing ring before power brushing and after the ring has been brushed. Fig. 66-27 shows that power brushing can remove minute burrs and also produce a high finish on delicate electric shaver heads.

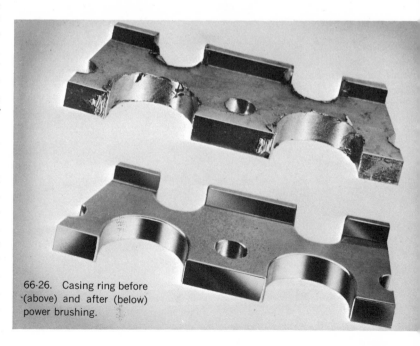

66-26. Casing ring before (above) and after (below) power brushing.

Decorative and Protective Metal Finishes

Electroplating

Electroplating consists of covering by electro-deposit a surface or object (usually metallic) with a thin adherent coating of the same *or other* metal. The form and details of the original surface are retained.

Equipment

1. Wooden rinse tanks were formerly used exclusively in the plating industry and are still in common use. They are lined with asphalt, sheet lead, or rubber. Steel tanks are now used for cleaners and for alkaline plating solutions; wood, steel, or concrete tanks lined with lead are used for solutions containing sulphuric or chromic acid. Rubber linings are usually applied to steel tanks in the form of hard or soft rubber sheets cemented to the steel, or rubber is sprayed on to produce seamless coatings. Containers made of earthenware can also be used in plating operations.

2. There are many types of electrolyte plating solutions. A different one is necessary for each kind of metal plating. The electrolyte must contain a chemical compound of the metal, to be deposited on the surface.

3. All electroplating is done with the use of direct current electricity at low voltages. For much plating a 6 volt line is sufficient. NOTE: It is necessary to either generate direct current or to convert alternating current to direct current by the use of a rectifier.

Proper current density, expressed in amperes per square foot, is important in obtaining smooth, dense deposits; thus, in addition to a rheostat for each tank, it is desirable also to have an ammeter and a voltmeter in the line.

Preparation for Plating

Electro-deposited metal will adhere firmly only to a clean surface. Also, the deposited metal is a thin film that reproduces an almost precise image of the surface on which it is deposited, making thorough cleaning even more necessary. All surface irregularities will be carried through to the finished product. Operations of cleaning and polishing may involve any, or all of the following steps:

1. Removal of oil, grease, or any organic material.

2. Removal of surface irregularities, scale, and oxides by solution of pickling acids, or by use of a file, abrasive wheel, wire brush, or polisher.

3. Since the compounds used in polishing are greasy in character, polishing must be followed by a soap or alkali wash and a rinse in cold water.

Plating—General

Fig. 67-1 illustrates an electroplating set-up.

1. The plating solution (electrolyte) is placed in the tank. The electrolyte contains some salt of the metal to be plated and usually other salts, acids, or alkalies, to improve the action of the electrolyte.

2. The positive electrodes (anodes of pure metal are suspended in the bath from suspension bars connected to the negative terminal.

67-1. Electroplating set-up.

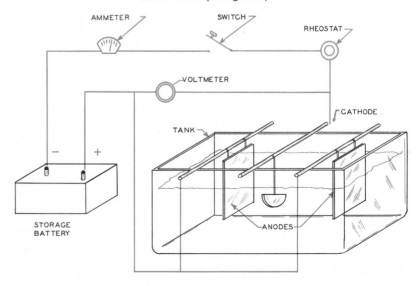

67-2. Silverplating. Forks rotate in plating tank containing cyanide solution and bars of pure silver. The amount of electric current and length of time the pieces remain in the tank determine the amount of silver on each piece.

3. The object (cathode) to be plated is connected to the negative terminal and suspended in the plating bath.

4. As the current is passed through this circuit the metal from the electrolyte is deposited upon the workpiece.

● *Copper Plating*

The greater portion of copper plating is done in one or both of two types of baths—the copper cyanide or alkaline solution.

In depositing copper on an iron base, the plating solution would contain copper sulphate. Upon the addition of water, positive copper ions and negative sulphate ions are formed. When direct current is passed through this bath, the copper ions will be attracted to the negative electrode—the workpiece—and the sulphate ions will be attracted to the positive electrode of pure copper. The positive copper ions obtain electrons from the workpiece and neutral copper atoms are formed which adhere to the surface of the iron, forming a copper coat. NOTE: The negative sulphate ions are transferred to the positive anode and unite with the copper to form a fresh supply of copper sulphate. The copper sulphate is renewed in this manner and the process continues with other metal pieces until the copper anode has been used up.

● *Silver Plating*

Silver is seldom plated directly on steel, but is added to a cheaper deposit of copper, nickel, or tin. This is commonly followed by a "strike" solution, which is a preliminary plating solution low in metal ions, used where difficulty is experienced because of deposition by immersion, if the article is to go directly into the regular plating solution.

If silver is to be plated directly on steel it is usually given a first strike in a solution containing less than 2 grams of silver per liter (0.2 ounce per gallon), followed by a second strike. NOTE: This is the first and only strike for plating on brass, copper, nickel, and britannia metal.

Fig. 67-2 shows the method of silver plating a quantity of forks. Where points of wear occur on such articles as forks and spoons they are spot plated. Fig. 67-3.

● *Gold Plating*

Gold plating is used for decorative purposes and for resistance to corrosion. Jewelry, musical instruments, pen points, and some table service ware may be gold plated.

Gold can satisfactorily be deposited on copper, brass, nickel, and silver. Steel, like silver, is usually given an undercoat of these metals for gold plating.

Anodes of high-purity rolled gold—with insoluble anodes of *platinum, stainless steel, nichrome, or carbon*—are used. If gold alone is used, the gold content of the

67-3. Spot plating. The back of forks are placed on these racks so the most used sections to be overlaid with pure silver are in a silver cyanide solution. This gives the wear points overlaid reinforcement.

solution tends to increase. In order to maintain a fairly uniform gold concentration in the bath, both gold and insoluble anodes therefore are necessary.

Cyanide baths are used for practically all gold plating.

● *Chromium Plating*

Chromium plating is used as a bright decorative finish on metal articles. When iron or steel is chromium plated, undercoats of copper and then nickel are deposited on the metal.

In industrial chromium plating, where wear resistance and corrosion resistance are required, hard chromium deposits are plated directly on the steel.

The plating tanks are of lead-lined steel and plating is done at elevated temperatures.

Chromium metal is seldom used in anodes; insoluble lead anodes are used, antimonial lead being preferable to pure lead.

Color Anodizing Aluminum

This gives intense chemical dye-coloring to aluminum. The procedures that follow can successfully be used in the school for color-anodizing aluminum.

1. The article to be anodized should be cleaned with an aluminum degreasing agent or a hot household detergent solution. Rinse in cold running water.

2. Prepare a caustic solution by dissolving 2½ ounces of sodium hydroxide (NaOH) in 1 quart of cool water. Use an oven-glass or enameled container. *This solution should be used hot.*

3. Immerse the aluminum article in this solution for about 15 to 60 seconds to etch the metal slightly. Rinse in cool running water. *Do not etch the article for too long a time.*

4. Make an anodizing solution of 60 cc. of concentrated sulphuric acid and 475 cc. of distilled water. Place the solution in an oven-glass or stoneware jar.

CAUTION: *Always add the acid to the water.*

5. Connect the article to the positive terminal of a 12-volt D.C. power source, using aluminum clips.

6. Connect the negative terminal of the power source to an electrode of sheet lead. NOTE: The surface area of the lead sheet must be greater than the article to be anodized.

7. Oxygen is deposited during the anodizing operation. It combines with the aluminum to form aluminum oxide.

8. Place the article in the tank and adjust the power source to 15 volts. Leave the article in the solution for about 20 minutes while anodizing takes place. NOTE: The color of the dye to be used will have some influence on the anodizing time.

9. The solution must be kept at room temperature of 70° to 75° F. During the anodizing process the temperature of the solution will rise, but care must be taken to keep it within the above limits.

10. Rinse the article in cold running water after anodizing has taken place. Be sure all acid has been removed.

11. Commercial dyes can be obtained. Mix in the proportion of 2 grams of dye per 1 liter of water. Heat the dye solution to 150° F. and immerse the article for 10 minutes in the solution.

NOTE: By varying the immersion time, lighter or darker shades can be obtained.

12. After removing the article from the dye solution rinse in cold, running water for about 1 minute.

13. Apply a coat of clear metal lacquer with a spray gun or use a chemical sealing process. Chemical sealing is more durable. The solution may be made by mixing 5 grams of nickel acetate and 5 grams of boric acid per liter of water. This must be kept heated to 180° to 200° F. The article must remain in this bath from 5 to 10 minutes.

14. Rinse the article in hot running water, dry, and buff lightly on a clean buffing wheel, *using no compound.*

Protective Metal Finishes

Most metals will tarnish or oxidize when exposed to moisture and air. Silver, copper, and aluminum are no exceptions. It is therefore necessary to apply some protective coating to preserve the surface and finish.

Among the many protective coatings are primers, metal fillers, enamels, and lacquers.

PRIMERS

In order to secure the proper cohesion of most paints and enamels to metal surfaces, a primer has to be applied first. There are many types. Some are made especially for application to steel, such as automobile bodies. This is lead primer. Zinc and lead chromate primers can be used on steel, zinc, and aluminum for satisfactory results—for instance, on aluminum siding before enamel is baked on.

METAL FILLERS

Blemishes such as pits, dents, and tool marks may be filled with a metal filler after primer has been applied. The fills can then be sanded smooth by hand or with a power sander, using Nos. 280 or 320 abrasive paper or cloth. This type of work is done in repairing automobile bodies.

METAL ENAMELS

Enamels are used for decorating and protecting metal surfaces. They are highly durable and resistant to moisture. Enamels may be flat, semi-gloss, or gloss, depending upon the type of product and the finish desired. Today they are made from synthetic resins, mixed with agents to facilitate the drying process. "Porcelain" enamels are baked on.

A better job can be secured by spraying than by brush application. Curing can be done in a kiln or oven.

LACQUERS

Lacquers provide a durable finish, but a considerable amount of skill is required in their application. Due to fast-drying qualities they are best applied by spraying. Applying lacquer by brushing techniques is very difficult. The fast-drying qualities cause the brush to drag, almost preventing an even application.

Lacquers provide a harder finish than enamels and are more mar and abrasion resistant. They resist fading, wear, and most mild chemicals.

Either colored or clear lacquers may be applied.

In order to preserve the finish and prevent the oxidation on copper and brass art metal projects, a clear metal lacquer is used.

Small hand sprays do an excellent job. In spraying, the lacquer should be thinned with a metal lacquer thinner or, if using *instrument lacquer,* a 50-50 solution of lacquer and amyl acetate is required.

1. The project to be sprayed should be thoroughly cleaned and degreased. All buffing compound should be removed and the project handled with cotton gloves to prevent grease marks from the fingers.

2. Hold the spray gun at the proper distance from the project, being careful that the coating is not so heavy that it will run. If this occurs, the lacquer will have to be removed with a thinner and the project repolished and buffed.

Check Your Knowledge

1. What is the advantage of machine polishing over the hand method?

2. What is an abrasive?

3. Why should abrasive cloth be wrapped around a wood block when polishing a flat surface?

4. Define the term polishing.

5. What is buffing?

6. What types of machines are used in polishing and buffing?

7. What types of wheels are used in polishing and buffing operations?

8. Explain how a polishing wheel is prepared for use.

9. How does a polishing wheel differ from one used in buffing?

10. Buffing compounds are placed in what two categories?

11. Name typical buffing compounds.

12. Why should the article be held below the center of the buffing wheel?

13. Explain the difference between coated abrasive machines and conventional polishing machines.

14. What is power brushing?

15. What is electroplating? Explain the process.

16. Describe tanks used in this process.

17. What is a plating solution?

18. What type of current is used in the electroplating process?

19. Describe the method of preparing the article for plating.

20. Explain the copper plating process.

21. Why is steel given a deposit of copper, nickel, or tin before silver plating?

22. What types of articles are gold plated?

23. What types of articles are chromium plated?

24. What is color anodizing? Why is it used?

25. What is a protective metal finish?

26. What is the best method of applying lacquer?

Terms to Know and Spell

polishing	*lubricant*	*rectifier*
buffing	*concentric*	*electrolyte*
adhesive	*garnet*	*anode*
oxide	*crocus*	*cathode*
bauxite	*silicon*	*electron*
spindle	*electroplating*	*anodizing*

Heat-Treating and Testing Metals

THE effect of heat treatment on metal is very great indeed. The metal may become harder than it was before, or softer, tougher, and stronger. It all depends upon how the treatment is carried out and on the nature of the metal that is being treated.

A piece of steel may be so hard that it can be used as a cutting tool or it may be treated so that it can be machined. Industrial heat-treating is for the most part intended either to harden the steel or make it tough and soft.

Success in heat-treatment depends largely upon understanding the process involved and the use of proper equipment.

Only the basic processes are described in this section.

68 ▷ Heat-Treating

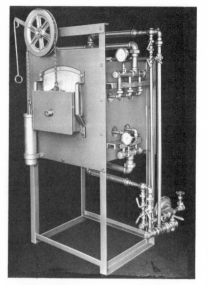

68-1. High-speed oven furnace.

Heat-treatment of metals involves a combination of heating and cooling operations timed and applied to a solid metal or alloy in a way that will produce the desired properties. NOTE: Heating for the sole purpose of hot working is excluded from the meaning of this definition.[1]

The desired properties may be hardness, improvement of the grain structure, and resistance to shock. Metals may also be treated to soften (anneal), making them easier to machine or form.

Heat-treatment can be applied to both ferrous and nonferrous metals. Because each area is so broad this unit will be confined to the basic heat-treating operations such as hardening, tempering, annealing, normalizing, and casehardening.

Furnaces

The source of heat may be oil, gas, or electricity, all of which can be controlled automatically. The choice of fuel depends upon the availability, economic consid-

erations, and the location of equipment.

CAUTION: *Both oil and gas must have provisions for exhausting waste fumes.*

There are a great many designs and shapes of furnaces but in general they may be classified as the tool-room oven furnace, Fig. 68-1, and the pot-type furnace, Fig. 68-2.

The tool-room oven furnace is designed for use in the tool department where occasional tools and parts must be heat-treated. This type of furnace is popular in schools. Fig. 68-3. It employs a standard combustion system with burners mounted in the side wall of the heating chamber to achieve positive control of the furnace atmosphere. The casing is fabricated of welded steel plate and angles. The lining is molded and pre-burned, and has lightweight insulating refractory.

The pot-type hardening furnace is designed for heat-treating parts, with lead, cyanide, neutral salt,

68-2. Pot-type hardening furnace.

68-3. A simpler, smaller tool-room oven furnace can be used in the schools.

[1]ASM Metals Handbook.

68-4. Industrial pot-type hardening furnace using a salt bath in the heating medium.

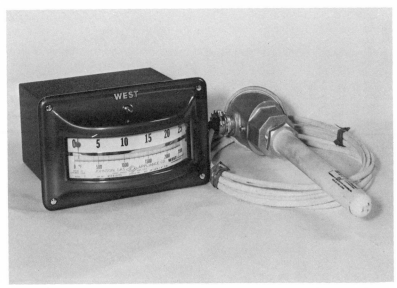

68-5. Indicating pyrometer with lead wire and thermocouple.

or carburizing salt as a heating vehicle. This type of furnace is shown above. Fig. 68-4.

Modern furnaces contain devices to regulate the heating or cooling. A pyrometer, Fig. 68-5, gives accurate control of temperatures. It consists of a thermocouple, which projects into the furnace, Fig. 68-6, connected by lead wires to an instrument that indicates the temperature. A thermocouple consists of two wires which are welded together at the hot end and electrically insulated from each other throughout the rest of their length. When the welded points are heated they generate a small amount of voltage, which activates the instrument.

Quenching Tanks

In the heat-treatment of steel it is necessary that quenching tanks or baths be located close to the furnace to prevent too much air cooling of the metal before it

reaches the quenching medium. In industrial heat-treating practice, the tanks are equipped with circulating pumps and coolers to provide a constant temperature to the quench.

The quenching bath may consist of a variety of liquids depending upon the heat-treatment method used. Oil, brine, and water are the most commonly used. The oil baths consist of fish oil, paraffin oil, machine oil, or cottonseed oil. The type of steel governs the type of bath to be used.

Hardening

Tools are hardened to develop their strength and wear resistance. The operation consists in heating

the steel to some temperature above the critical point and then cooling rapidly enough to cause molecular tension. The degree of hardness that can be obtained depends upon the amount of carbon in the steel.

Some types of steels with a low carbon content (.10 to .30 percent) cannot be hardened by regular heat-treating methods. These types of steels have to be casehardened or cold-worked.

The critical temperature is the temperature above which a steel must be heated in order that it will harden when quenched. Steels have temperatures at which some definite change takes place in their physical properties.

68-6. A pyrometer indicates the temperature inside the furnace.

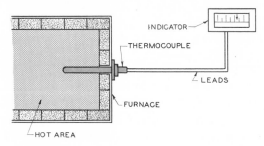

INDICATOR

THERMOCOUPLE

LEADS

FURNACE

HOT AREA

68-7. Workpiece being held by tongs and placed in the furnace for heating.

These temperatures vary, depending upon the type of steel. The more carbon the steel contains, the lower its critical temperature and the less it should be heated for hardening.

Changes in grain structures of steel take place during the heat-treating process; these changes govern the quality of hardness. The temperature at which steel will harden is called the critical temperature and may range from 1,400° to 2,400° F., depending upon the carbon and alloy content. Temperatures at which the steel should be heated to bring about the changes in grain structure are indicated by the manufacturer. Heating steel to the recommended temperature is very important. If the metal is overheated, it has a tendency to warp and become distorted.

Following is a quick review of the basic principles that must be followed in hardening steel:

1. The steel must be heated to the required temperature. This temperature is called the critical point. It is at this point that the steel has the best characteristics.

2. The more carbon the steel contains, the lower will be its critical temperature and the less heat will be needed for hardening.

3. The steel must be cooled by quenching in order to make changes permanent. The cooling has to be rapid enough so that the desired changes will hold.

4. In order to relieve the hardening strain and increase toughness, it is necessary to reheat the metal mildly and "let down" the hardness by tempering and drawing.

Hardening Carbon Tool Steels

1. Bring the furnace heat up to the correct temperature.

2. Place the workpiece in the furnace with tongs, and heat to the critical temperature. For high carbon steels, allow about 20 to 30 minutes per inch of thickness for coming up to heat. Fig. 68-7.

3. When the hardening temperature has been reached, allow 10 to 15 minutes per inch for "soaking" at this temperature.

4. Remove the workpiece from the furnace with tongs and plunge into the quench. Fig. 68-8. Move the workpiece in a figure eight style so the metal will cool evenly.

5. Remove metal from quenching solution.

6. Test for hardness with a file.

Quenching

Quenching refers to the rapid cooling of metal—usually by immersion in a liquid. Its major application is to steel, which is the only widely used metal hardened by a quench alone.

As said, the most widely used liquid quenching materials are water and oil. Carbon steels, in general, require a fast rate of cooling. They are classified as water-hardening steels. Oil quenching of plain carbon steels is sometimes used in the stress relieving heat-treatment of cold-worked parts, such as cold-headed bolts. Some steels of the low alloy type require a slower rate of cooling and are often quenched in various types of oils. Steels that have a slow rate of transformation, such as used in blanking dies, must be hardened with a still milder quench such as air or gas.

The use of salt brine in quenching water-hardening steels is better than fresh water, as the action of the salt inhibits the water from dissolving into atmospheric gas. Mineral oils are used for steels requiring an oil quench.

Tempering

The high tension produced by quenching is practically always relieved to some extent by a tempering or drawing operation conducted as soon as possible after quenching. Extreme hardness of carbon steels leaves the steel much too brittle without tempering.

Tempering is accomplished by heating the steel below the low critical temperature point. The reheating relieves the strains and serves to break down any austenite—produced by the quench—to martensite. The tempering range can be from 400° to 1,250° F.

The tempering operation can be carried out with many quenches, depending upon the temperatures involved. Salt baths, oil, and molten lead are used. Air circulated by fans in special furnaces is most important for close control of final hardness.

Hardening and Tempering Small Tools

1. Heat the tool to the critical temperature.

2. Remove from the furnace with tongs and plunge the point in the quenching bath. Move the tool around in the bath for uniform cooling.

3. Remove the tool from the bath and polish the point with abrasive cloth.

4. Watch the temper colors (see Table 68-A) move toward the point and, when the correct color reaches the point, quench only the point of the tool.

68-9.   Continuous annealing line.

TEMPERING COLORS

Deg. F.	Color	Tool
375	Yellow	Center punches, lathe centers, scrapers.
425	Light straw	Tool bits, hammers.
465	Dark straw	Drills, taps, reamers, and dies.
490	Yellowish brown	Drill drifts, wood chisels.
525	Purple	Cold chisels, wood carving tools.
590	Pale blue	Screwdrivers, springs.

Table 68-A.

Annealing

Annealing softens steel so that it can be machined easily or fabricated by cold working. Annealing removes internal strains produced by previous forging, working, or heating operations. Fig. 68-9.

The annealing process is accomplished by heating the metal part to a point above the critical range, which realigns the previous grain structure.

The "soaking time" depends upon the particular type of steel involved and the size of the furnace charge. One small piece does not require the time of a large batch, even though the steel is of the same type. When the heating is completed the metal is allowed to cool slowly. Two methods of cooling are: (1) furnace cooling and (2) packing. If the piece is to be cooled in the furnace, the heat is turned off and the part is left to cool in the oven. NOTE: If packing is used, the steel parts are placed in a pot or box. The parts are then covered with ashes, mica, spent carburizing compound, lime, or any insulating material. The parts are then allowed to remain until they have cooled.

Normalizing

Normalizing is a process closely related to annealing. It removes any previous undesirable or non-uniform structure or stresses produced by forging, casting, welding, or machining. Normalizing is accomplished by heating the material to about 100° F. above the upper critical temperature and cooling in air.

68-8.   Removing heated workpiece from the furnace preparatory to quenching.

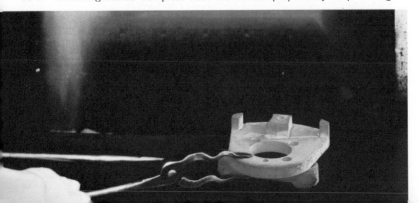

Case-Hardening

Steel with a low carbon content cannot be hardened to any great degree by conventional heat-treatment. However, a hard, wear-resistant surface (case) can be put on the surface of the metal by heating the piece to red hot and introducing small quantities of carbon or nitrogen to its surface.

The three principal processes used in case-hardening are: (1) carburizing, (2) cyaniding, and (3) the nitriding or gas method.

Carburizing

Low carbon steel is tough but does not harden, whereas high carbon steel develops high hardness when quenched but is brittle. By increasing the carbon content on the surface layers of low carbon steel, the advantages of both low and high carbon metal are obtained.

Carburizing materials may be solid, liquid, or gaseous in form.

The amount of carbon that is absorbed and the penetration depth are dependent upon the time and temperature used in the process.

Pack Method

1. Pack the parts in a steel container with a carbonaceous material, such as bone charcoal, wood charcoal, or charred leather.

2. Seal the container, place in the furnace, and bring the heat up to carburizing temperature.

3. Hold this temperature to the required time specified by the manufacturer for the particular type of steel being carburized.

4. Remove from furnace and cool by quenching in oil or water or let cool in air. NOTE: Air cooling reduces warpage.

Cyaniding

The cyanide method is used when only a shallow surface hardness is required. The work is placed in a bath of molten sodium cyanide or potassium cyanide and heated to 1,550° F. for 15 minutes. Then it is removed and quenched in water or brine.

CAUTION: *This method is dangerous and should not be used in the schools.*

Nitriding or Gas Method

In nitriding, the parts are placed in a special, air-tight, muffle-type furnace, where ammonia gas is introduced at a high temperature and produces nitrogen and hydrogen. The nitrogen passes into the steel to form nitrides; this imparts a high wear resistance and gives an extreme hardness to the surface. NOTE: This method is not suitable for low-carbon steels but is used for hardening special steel alloys.

Simple Case-Hardening

Workpieces can be case-hardened under average school conditions using two methods:

METHOD A

1. Place the workpiece in a covered metal box. Surround with a commercial case-hardening compound such as "Kasenite."

2. Place the box in the furnace and heat to the required time as specified by the manufacturer of the compound. Leave in the furnace for from 15 minutes to one hour, depending upon the depth of the case desired.

3. Remove the box from the furnace and allow to cool slowly.

4. After the workpiece is sufficiently cool, remove from the compound and reheat to the critical temperature.

5. Quench in cold water.

When a deeper case is desired the following method can be used.

METHOD B

1. Place the workpiece in the furnace and heat to a bright red —about 1,650-1,700° F. Check the temperature with a pyrometer.

2. Remove the workpiece with tongs and roll or dip in the compound. The powder will melt and adhere to the work, forming a shell around it.

3. Reheat the piece to a bright red and hold the work at this temperature for 10 to 15 minutes.

4. Remove from the furnace and quench in *clean, cold* water.

69 ▷ Testing and Inspecting Metals

It is important that the physical characteristics of metals be known so that they may be utilized to the greatest advantage. The effect of various methods of fabrication, heat-treating, and melting upon these characteristics may be measured by testing.

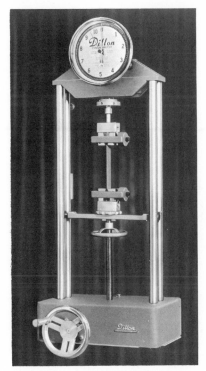

69-1. Tensile testing machine.

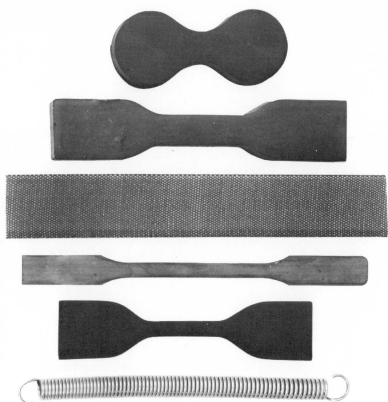

69-2. Special specimens prepared for testing.

There are many types of tests, the main ones being chemical, physical, and metallurgical. Chemical tests are used to determine the chemical identity or composition. Physical tests are conducted on special machines, mechanically. Metallurgical tests depend upon the skill and judgment of individuals conducting the tests. Many other tests use a combination of these methods.

Tensile and Compression Tests

TENSILE TESTS

The tensile test mechanically determines certain characteristics of the material when it is subjected to a slowly applied force tending to pull it apart. A machine employed for this purpose is shown in Fig. 69-1. Special specimens are prepared, as in Fig. 69-2, for conducting the tests.

The machine shown in Fig. 69-1 will test materials such as rubber, plastics, or soft annealed brass. The specimen to be tested is loaded in the machine and tension applied until it is pulled apart.

Tensile strength, elastic limit, and yield point are expressed in unit terms—pounds per square inch.

The stretch occurring over the actual length of the test piece during extension is measured by instruments called *extensometers.* From the measurement of strain or elongation which occurs as the load is applied, a stress-strain diagram is made. Fig. 69-3. NOTE: If the load is removed at any point below the elastic limit, the

69-3. Stress-strain diagram of wrought iron.

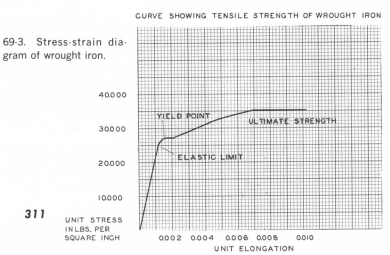

CURVE SHOWING TENSILE STRENGTH OF WROUGHT IRON

YIELD POINT

ULTIMATE STRENGTH

ELASTIC LIMIT

40.000

30.000

20.000

10.000

UNIT STRESS IN LBS. PER SQUARE INCH

0.002 0.004 0.006 0.008 0.010

UNIT ELONGATION

311

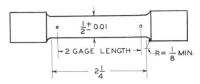

69-4. Tension test specimen dimensions for general testing of metals.

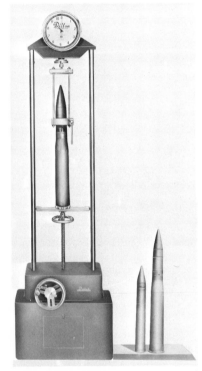

69-5. Testing machine used for determining the effectiveness of the crimp of a projectile. The projectile is pulled from its case to determine the strength of crimp.

material returns to its original length. Beyond the elastic limit, the material does not return to its original length.

Increasing the load too much will cause rupture of the piece. The highest load recorded before the piece breaks is called the ultimate strength. When the two broken pieces of a test bar are placed together, the distance between the two punch marks is

remeasured. Fig. 69-4. Comparing this distance with the original acting length gives the ultimate elongation expressed in percentage of the original length.

Fig. 69-5 shows the application of a tester as a projectile is pulled from the case, to determine the effectiveness of the crimp.

TORSION TESTS

Shafts that must withstand twisting in service are given torsion tests. Fixtures grip the metal and the material is slowly twisted until failure occurs. The stress load is then plotted—or laid out—against the angle of deflection, and stress-strain curves are developed on a chart.

COMPRESSION TESTS

The compression test closely resembles the tensile test excepting that there is a squeeze employed instead of a pull. The test is used for determining general compression properties such as elasticity or "give" of bearing metals.

Bend and Transverse Tests

The cold bend properties of metals can be determined by bending the piece around a mandrel or bar, having a defined radius, until a rupture in the metal

occurs. The transverse test is valuable in testing a welded joint.

Impact Tests

The purpose of these tests is to note the behavior of steels under impact loads. The test is performed by a machine which subjects the specimen to a single blow and measures the energy in foot-pounds required to break it. The specimen is usually notched to concentrate the stresses at the base of the notch. There are two common impact tests, (1) the Izod test, where the specimen is gripped by one end and the blow struck 22 millimeters above the notch, and (2) the Charpy test, where the specimen is supported at the ends and the blow is made just behind the notch at the middle of the span. A freely swinging pendulum is used to apply the blow.

Testing for Hardness

Hardness is the resistance of metal to penetration, an index of wear resistance and strength. The harder the metal, the greater the strength.

In the school where no hardness testing machine is available, a file can be used. This is only an approximate method but can give some indication as to machinability. Table 69-A compares

HARDNESS COMPARISONS	
Brinell Hardness No.	**Action of File**
152	Easily filed—metal rubs off.
200	More pressure required to remove metal.
300	Resistance to file felt.
400	Filing becomes more difficult.
500	File barely removes metal.
750	No metal can be removed by file. Wear is on file.

Table 69-A.

hardness ratios of the Brinell testing machine with the action of a machinist's file.

There are several testing machines used to determine the hardness of metal. The Brinell, the Rockwell, and the Shore scleroscope are the most common.

BRINELL HARDNESS TESTER

The Brinell hardness tester, Fig. 69-6, measures the resistance the material offers to the penetration of a steel ball under constant pressure (about 3,000 kilograms, 3¼ tons) for a definite time (about 30 seconds minimum). The diameter of the impression is measured microscopically; then the Brinell number is checked on a standard chart. The wider the impression, the softer the metal and the lower the number. Brinell numbers range from 152—for annealed high-carbon steel—to 750, for hardened high-carbon steel.

ROCKWELL HARDNESS TESTER

The Rockwell hardness tester, Fig. 69-7, uses a 120° diamond cone for hard metals and a 1/16" steel ball for softer metals. The method is based upon resistance-to-penetration measurement. The hardness is read directly from a dial on the tester, and the depth of the impression is measured instead of the diameter. It has two scales for reading hardness, called the "B" and "C" scales. The "C" scale is used for harder materials and the "B" scale for softer metals.

In conducting hardness tests, it is essential that all of the test specimens be properly prepared. Remove all burrs. Scale and deep marks must be removed from the surface under test. Care must be taken so that work-hardening is

69-6. Brinell hardness tester. The hardness of the metal is based on the size of the impression made by the steel ball.

not introduced during the preparation of the specimen. The specimen must be homogeneous, unless the test is being conducted to determine decarburization, segregations, or inclusions. The grain size of the test specimen must also bear proper relationship to the size of the indentation.

Accuracy of testing is dependent on many factors that can affect indentation hardness of metallic materials under test conditions. For example, one point of hardness on the Rockwell scale represents a penetration of only 0.00008 inch, so extreme care must

69-7. Rockwell hardness tester.

be exercised in performing the test.

Fig. 69-8 illustrates the operation of the Rockwell hardness test. The test specimen is placed on

69-8. The principle of the Rockwell hardness test.

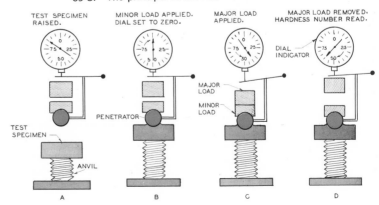

the anvil as in A and then elevated until it touches the penetrator. A minor load of 10 kg is applied to indent the test piece and to insure a well-defined point from which to start measuring the penetration of the test load. The dial indicator is then set to zero, or to the set point, as in B. A major load of 60, 100, or 150 kg, depending upon the expected hardness of the material, is then applied, as at C, and removed, leaving a minor load still applied (D). The hardness number, read from the dial indicator, is a relative hardness value which is proportional to the change in indentation of the penetrator as the major load is applied and removed.

THE SHORE SCLEROSCOPE

The Shore scleroscope is a portable instrument, especially useful in hardness testing of fixed parts or tools. The device, Fig. 69-9, has a diamond-tipped hammer which is dropped through a guiding glass tube by gravity, from a fixed height, upon the specimen being tested. The resulting rebound is registered on a graduated scale. The accuracy of the reading depends upon the operator's technique.

Magnaflux Testing

Magnaflux testing is used to detect surface cracks and defects in thousandths of an inch below the surface, such as forging laps, quenching cracks, surface seams, or fatigue cracks.

This type of testing is carried out by magnetizing in a special apparatus. The part is then dusted with a very fine iron-oxide powder or immersed in a suspension of the powder in fine oil. Any defect

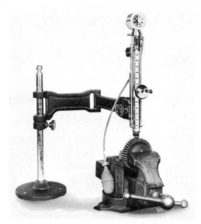

69-9. The Shore scleroscope with swing arm and post. A portable instrument for hardness testing of fixed parts. The hammer is lifted to a predetermined height and dropped on material to test hardness.

or crack acts as a tiny magnet, the opposite sides having a different polarity. The powder accumulates locally around the crack or defect. This is a nondestructive test used a great deal in the aircraft industry.

Check Your Knowledge

1. What is the purpose of the heat-treatment of ferrous metals?

2. Name two types of furnaces used in the heat-treatment of steel.

3. How does the tool-room oven furnace differ from the pot type?

4. What is the function of the pyrometer?

5. Why is a quenching tank used in the heat-treatment of steel?

6. Why should the quenching tank be located close to the furnace?

7. What types of liquids are used in the quenching bath?

8. Why are tools hardened?

9. Describe the hardening process.

10. What is meant by "cold-working" steel?

11. What is meant by critical temperature?

12. What is meant by drawing?

13. Why is salt brine better than fresh water in quenching water-hardening steels?

14. What is meant by the term tempering?

15. Describe this process.

16. Why is tempering necessary?

17. What is the difference between annealing and normalizing?

18. Describe the case-hardening process.

19. What are the three principal case-hardening processes?

20. What is carburizing?

21. Why shouldn't the cyanide method be used in the school?

22. Name three main methods of testing metals.

23. How is tensile strength of a material determined?

24. What is the function of a torsion test?

25. How does the Brinell hardness test differ from the Rockwell test?

26. Describe the function of the Shore scleroscope.

Terms to Know and Spell

tempering	*thermocouple*	*austenite*
annealing	*voltage*	*martensite*
normalizing	*quenching*	*cyaniding*
combustion	*molecular*	*nitriding*
refractory	*critical*	*carbonaceous*
carburizing	*magnaflux*	*molten*
pyrometer	*brittle*	*cold-working*

Section Twelve

Precision Measurement

TODAY, accuracy of measurement is of first importance as economical production of automobiles, planes, ships, and all machinery would be impossible without it.

Through the years, limits of measurements have been reduced so that while 8ths, 16ths, 32nds, and 64ths of an inch were the limits in the past, hundredths, thousandths, and ten-thousandths are now in common use.

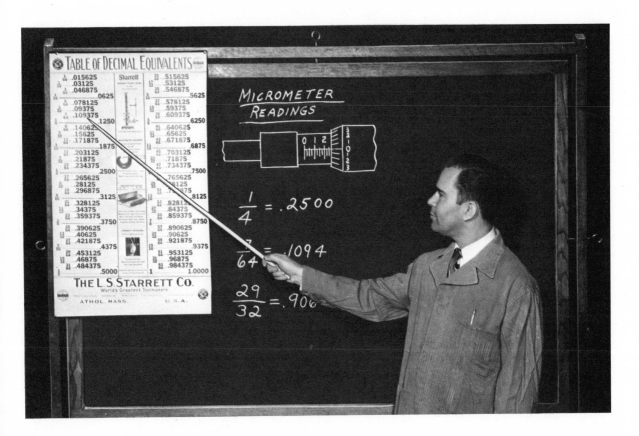

Science has made great strides toward establishing absolute laboratory standards which will permit working to close tolerances with greater ease and accuracy. In industry, it will lead to the development of better, more accurate inspection of measuring tools themselves. This is in line with the current trend toward greater economy and efficiency through better standards of dimensional control in production and inspection.

Unit 7 of this text described the use of some of the more simple measuring tools. This section will deal with the type of tools needed for precision measurement necessary in machining of metal. See Section Thirteen.

EXAMPLE 1.

What is the reading if the edge of the thimble is between the .125″ and the .50″ lines, Fig. 70-2 (A), and the line on the thimble is the coinciding line?

SOLUTION:

$$\text{Micrometer reading}$$
$$= \text{sleeve} + \text{thimble}$$
$$= .125 + .015 = .140$$

EXAMPLE 2.

Find the reading if the thimble is between .450 and .475 and the line .015 coincides. Fig. 70-2 (B).

SOLUTION:

$$\text{Micrometer reading}$$
$$= \text{sleeve} + \text{thimble}$$
$$= .450 + .015 = .465$$

In effect, a micrometer caliper combines the double contact of a slide caliper with a precision screw adjustment which may be read with great accuracy.

Dirt between the anvil and spindle will cause a micrometer to read incorrectly. The test is to clean and bring the anvil and spindle together carefully. If the zero line on the thimble and the axial line on the sleeve fail to coincide, wear has taken place either in the screw or contact surfaces.

70 ▷ Calipers and Gages

The smallest measurement that can be made with the caliper and steel rule is, in common fractions, 64ths of an inch. To measure in thousandths and ten-thousandths, a micrometer caliper is necessary.

Fig. 70-1 shows a one-inch micrometer and names the principal parts.

The device operates on the principle that a screw accurately made with 40 threads to the inch will advance 1/40″ or .025″ with each complete turn. On a micrometer caliper of one inch capacity, the sleeve is marked longitudinally with 40 lines to the inch corresponding with the number of threads on the spindle. Every fourth line is made longer and is numbered 1, 2, 3, 4, etc., to indicate 1/10″, 2/10″ etc.

The beveled edge of the thimble is marked into 25 divisions around a circumference and numbered from 0 to 25. When the caliper is closed, only the 0 line on the sleeve can be seen next to

the beveled edge of the thimble, and the 0 line on the thimble is aligned with the horizontal or axial line on the sleeve. Every complete revolution of the thimble from 0 to 0 advances or retracts the spindle 1/40″ or .025″. Rotation of the thimble from 0 on the beveled edge to the first graduation will retract the spindle 1/25 of 1/40—or 1/25 of .025—which is .001.

70-1.   A one-inch micrometer caliper.

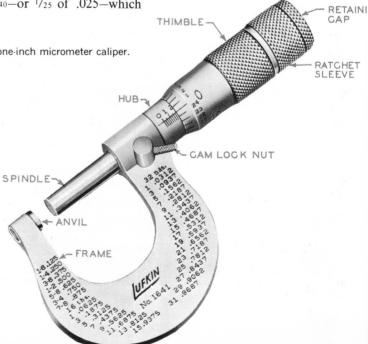

THIMBLE

RETAINING CAP

RATCHET SLEEVE

HUB

CAM LOCK NUT

SPINDLE

ANVIL

FRAME

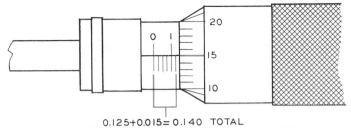

0.125+0.015= 0.140 TOTAL

70-2. (A) Reading the micrometer. The reading is 0.140.

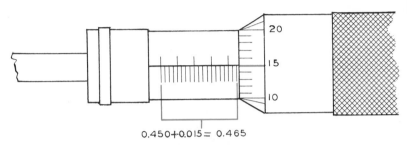

0.450+0.015= 0.465

70-2. (B) Another reading of the micrometer. Note that eighteen full divisions on the sleeve scale are visible. Since each represents 0.025 inch, this reading equals 0.450. The spindle has also advanced an additional 0.015, making the reading a total of 0.450 + 0.015, or 0.465.

Micrometer calipers are made in a wide range of sizes and in matched sets.

Those shown in Fig. 70-3 come equipped with a ratchet stop and lock nut. The ratchet stop is used to rotate the spindle in taking a measurement and insures a consistent, accurate gaging by limiting the spindle pressure on the workpiece to a definite amount. The lock nut makes it possible to lock the micrometer spindle at any desired setting. A slight turn of the knurled lock nut ring contracts a split bushing around the spindle and makes the micrometer a solid gage.

Fig. 70-4 shows the correct method of holding an outside mi-

70-3. Outside micrometer calipers equipped with ratchet stop and lock nut.

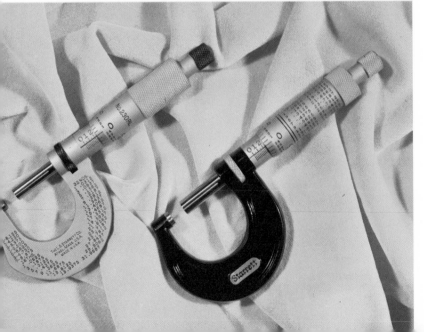

70-4. Correct method of holding a micrometer.

crometer caliper when checking the diameter of stock held between centers on the lathe.

The Vernier Micrometer

When very accurate measurements are required, employ a micrometer which has an extra scale added to the sleeve, enabling you to read ten-thousandths of an inch. This scale consists of a series of lines on the sleeve parallel to its axis.

On the vernier micrometer, Fig. 70-5, ten divisions on the sleeve mark the same spaces as nine divisions on the beveled edge of the thimble. Therefore the difference between the width of one of the ten spaces on the sleeve and one of the nine spaces on the thimble is one tenth of a division on the thimble. Since the thimble is graduated to read in thousandths, $\frac{1}{10}$ of a division would be .0001 or one ten-thousandth.

To make the reading, first read as with a regular micrometer; then see which of the horizontal lines on the sleeve coincides with a line on the thimble. Add to the previous reading the number of ten-thousandths indicated by a line on the sleeve which exactly coincides with a line on the spindle.

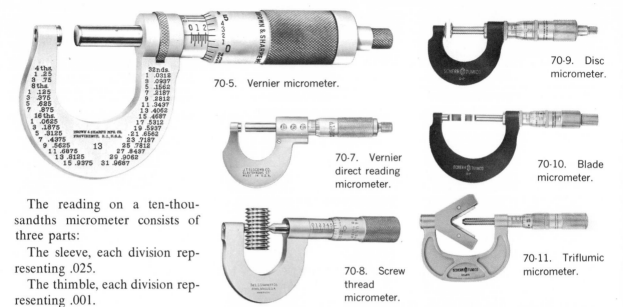

70-5. Vernier micrometer.

70-7. Vernier direct reading micrometer.

70-8. Screw thread micrometer.

70-9. Disc micrometer.

70-10. Blade micrometer.

70-11. Triflumic micrometer.

The reading on a ten-thousandths micrometer consists of three parts:

The sleeve, each division representing .025.

The thimble, each division representing .001.

The vernier, each division representing .0001.

EXAMPLE:

In Fig. 70-6 find the line on the thimble that matches the numbered straight line on the vernier. The number on that line is a ten-thousandths (.0001) reading.

SOLUTION:

Hub reading	= .150
Thimble reading	= .004
Vernier reading	= .0006
Total	= .1546

70-6. Reading the vernier scale.

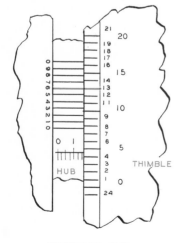

READING TO 1.546

DECIMAL EQUIVALENTS OF COMMON FRACTIONS

		1/64	0.015625				33/64	0.515625
	1/32		0.03125		17/32			0.53125
		3/64	0.046875				35/64	0.546875
	1/16		0.0625		9/16			0.5625
		5/64	0.078125				37/64	0.578125
	3/32		0.09375		19/32			0.59375
		7/64	0.109375				39/64	0.609375
1/8			0.125	5/8				0.625
		9/64	0.140625				41/64	0.640625
	5/32		0.15625		21/32			0.65625
		11/64	0.171875				43/64	0.671875
	3/16		0.1875		11/16			0.6875
		13/64	0.203125				45/64	0.703125
	7/32		0.21875		23/32			0.71875
		15/64	0.234375				47/64	0.734375
1/4			0.25	3/4				0.75
		17/64	0.265625				49/64	0.765625
	9/32		0.28125		25/32			0.78125
		19/64	0.296875				51/64	0.796875
	5/16		0.3125		13/16			0.8125
		21/64	0.328125				53/64	0.828125
	20/32		0.34375		27/32			0.84375
		23/64	0.359375				55/64	0.859375
3/8			0.375	7/8				0.875
		25/64	0.390625				57/64	0.890625
	13/32		0.40625		29/32			0.90625
		27/64	0.421875				59/64	0.921875
	7/16		0.4375		15/16			0.9375
		29/64	0.453125				61/64	0.953125
	15/32		0.46875		31/32			0.96875
		31/64	0.484375				63/64	0.984375
1/2			0.5	1				1.

Table 70-A.

Direct Reading Micrometers

The direct reading micrometer is read directly from the numbers appearing in three round windows on the frame. This micrometer offers constant reading, eliminating .025 errors, cuts waste, and can be used by semi-skilled operators. Numbers are expressed in thousandths of an inch (.000), but graduations on the thimble provide for simple interpolation to read ten-thousandths (.0000) of an inch. Fig. 70-7.

Screw Thread Micrometers

The screw thread micrometer, Fig. 70-8, is used for checking pitch diameters of screw threads. The spindle and anvil ends conform to the standard shapes of threads for which they are selected. At a direct reading, the micrometer gives the pitch diameter, which equals the basic outside diameter of one thread. The 1″ micrometer is made to check threads within four ranges—that is, 8 to 13 threads per inch, 14 to 20, 22 to 30, and 32 to 40 threads per inch.

Disc or Flange Micrometer

This caliper has ½″ diameter discs which are ground to a shallow angle, permitting them to enter a ¹/₃₂″ slot. Fig. 70-9.

Precision measuring of extruded metal sections, forming tools, lands, cutting edges, and difficult-to-gage sections, is made possible by this disc design.

The spindle and one disc are integral, while the second disc replaces the conventional micrometer anvil.

Blade Micrometer

This caliper is used for measuring narrow grooves, keyways, splines, recesses, and similar hard-to-measure indentations. Fig. 70-10.

Having a blade thickness of .030″, this tool accurately gages depths to ¼″. The spindle does not rotate in the conventional manner but travels straight in and out on a splined key in order to maintain perfect alignment.

Triflumic Micrometer

This is used for measuring the diameter of three-fluted cutting tools, such as end mills, taps, and reamers. It reads directly in .001-inch and can be used while the cutting tool is set up in the machine; true roundness of cylindrical work can also be determined. Fig. 70-11.

Inside Micrometer

The inside micrometer caliper, Fig. 70-12, is an application of the micrometer screw principle to adjustable end-measuring gages. The distance between the ends or contacts is changed by rotating the sleeve on the micrometer head up to the extent of the screw length, usually ½″ or 1″. The thimble is graduated to read in thousandths of an inch. In the smaller sets, measuring rods enable a maximum measurement of up to 8″. In the larger sets, measurements can be taken to 32″. This tool is used for checking internal and lineal measurements and for setting calipers.

Micrometer Depth Gage

A micrometer depth gage, as the name implies, was designed to measure depths such as in holes, slots, recesses, and keyways.

The tool consists of a hardened, ground and lapped base combined with a micrometer head. Fig. 70-13. Measuring rods with individual length adjustment are inserted through a hole in the micrometer screw and brought to a positive seat by a knurled nut. The screw is precision ground and has a 1″ movement. The rods are furnished to measure in increments of 1″. Each rod protrudes through the base and moves as the thimble is rotated.

The reading is taken exactly the same as with an outside micrometer except that the sleeve graduations run in the opposite direction. In obtaining a reading using a rod other than the 0-1″, it is necessary to consider the additional rod length. For example, if the 1-2″ rod is being used, one inch must be added to the reading on the sleeve and thimble.

70-12. Inside micrometer caliper with extension to measure up to 4″.

70-13. Micrometer depth gage.

70-14. Measuring the depth of a recess with a micrometer depth gage.

70-17. The reading is 1.436″.

EXAMPLE:

In Fig. 70-17 the vernier has been moved to the right 1.000″ plus .400″ plus .025, which equals 1.425″ as shown on the beam, and the eleventh line on the vernier coincides with a line on the beam as indicated by the stars. Therefore .011″ is to be added to the reading on the beam and the total reading is 1.436″.

Fig. 70-14 shows how the gage is used. Fig. 70-15 shows a direct reading depth gage.

Vernier Caliper

A vernier sliding caliper consists basically of a main scale with a sliding jaw. On the main scale, each unit is divided into 40 parts, so that each part is 1/40 or .025″. For convenience in reading, every fourth division is numbered 1, 2, 3, 4, etc. Fig. 70-16.

The zero of the sliding scale is the gage line; its location—in reference to the main scale—determines part of the reading. The remainder of the reading is determined by the vernier scale, which is constructed as follows:

A length equal to 24 main scale divisions or .600″ is divided into 25 equal parts on the vernier scale, every fifth division being numbered. Each space on the vernier is therefore equal to 1/25 of .600″ or .024. The difference between the scale division and a vernier division is .025-.024″ or .001″. If the tool is set so that the 0 line on the vernier scale coincides with the 0 line on the beam, the line to the right of the 0 on the vernier will differ from the line to the right of the 0 on the bar by .001″, the second line by .002″, and so on. The difference will continue to increase .001″ for each division until the 25 on the vernier coincides with line 24 on the beam.

To read the tool, note how many inches, tenths (or .001″) and fortieths (or .025″) the 0 mark on the vernier is from the 0 mark on the beam; then add the number of thousandths indicated by the line on the vernier which exactly coincides with a line on the beam.

The Vernier Height Gage

The vernier height gage, Fig. 70-18, is a precision instrument that marks off vertical distances from a plane.

The gage consists of a steel bar

70-18. Vernier height gage.

70-15. Direct-reading micrometer depth gage.

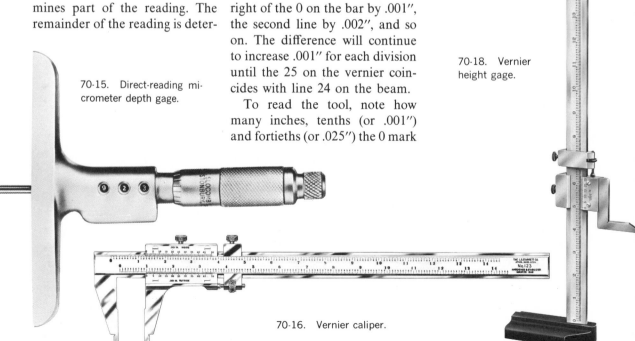

70-16. Vernier caliper.

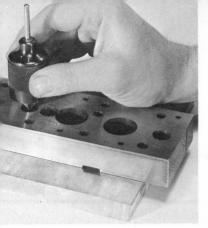

70-19. Transfer punch.

70-21. The reading is 50° 20′.

mounted on a heavy base. The bar varies in length from 10″ to 36″. The gage reads to thousandths by means of a vernier sliding jaw. It is designed for use in tool rooms and in inspection departments on layout, jig, and fixture work.

Transfer Punch

This tool is used in layout work to accurately transfer holes of any diameter from 3/16″ to 1 3/16″. NOTE: There is no need for a collection of expensive transfer punches in increments of 1/64″ graduations.

The punch is accurate to .002″. It precisely centers any shape hole —round, rectangular, square, even

70-20. Universal bevel protractor.

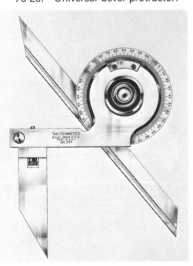

elongated or tear-shaped—in material up to 2″ thick. Layout time is cut by 90%. Fig. 70-19 shows the operation of the tool.

Universal Bevel Protractor

This type of protractor can be accurately read to five minutes or 1/12°. The dial of the protractor is graduated both to the right and left of zero up to 90°. The vernier scale is also graduated to the right and left of zero up to 60 minutes, each of the 12 vernier graduations representing 5 minutes. Any size angle can be measured, and it should be remembered that the vernier reading must be read in the same direction from zero as the protractor, either right or left. Fig. 70-20.

Since 12 graduations on the vernier scale occupy the same space as 23 graduations or 23° on the protractor dial, each vernier graduation is 1/12° or 5 minutes shorter than 2 graduations on the protractor dial. Therefore, if the zero graduation on the vernier scale coincides with a graduation on the protractor dial, the reading is in exact degrees, but if some other graduation on the vernier scale coincides with a protractor graduation, the number of vernier graduations multiplied by 5 minutes must be added to the number of degrees read between

the zeros on the protractor dial and the vernier scale.

Gear Tooth Vernier Caliper

The gear tooth vernier caliper, Fig. 70-22, measures chordal thickness at the pitch line of a gear tooth to one-thousandth of an inch. Chordal tooth thickness is the thickness of the tooth as measured on the chord of an arc on the pitch circle.

70-22. Vernier gear tooth caliper.

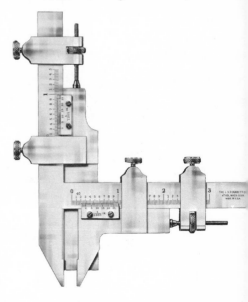

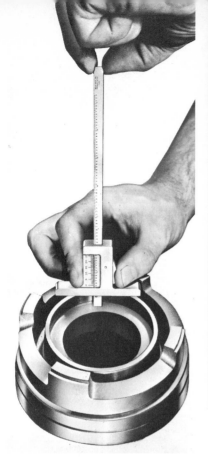

70-23. Vernier depth gage.

70-24. (B) Electronic dial indicator designed to replace mechanical indicators. Remote readings can be taken.

70-24. (A) Dial indicator.

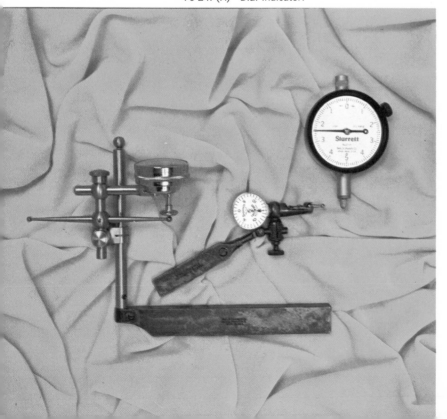

The vertical slide is set to a depth by means of its vernier plate fine-adjusting nut so that when it rests on top of the gear tooth, the caliper jaws will be correctly positioned to measure across the pitch line. The horizontal slide is then used to obtain the chordal thickness of the gear tooth.

The procedure for reading these gages is exactly the same as for vernier calipers and height and depth gages.

Vernier Depth Gage

The vernier depth gage, Fig. 70-23, differs slightly from the vernier caliper in that the vernier slide remains fixed while the graduated slide is moved to obtain desired measurement in thousandths of an inch. The vernier slide also forms the base which is held on work by one hand while the blade is operated with the other.

Obtaining a measurement is accomplished the same as with a vernier caliper. After the blade is brought into contact with the bottom of the slot or recess, the clamp screw adjacent to the fine adjusting nut is locked. The nut is turned to obtain exact measurement, then locked into position by clamp screw beside the vernier plate.

The Dial Indicator

The dial indicator, Fig. 70-24, is used for testing the alignment of machine parts on either exterior or interior surfaces of workpieces and for inspection purposes. Fig. 70-25.

In appearance the indicator resembles a watch and is made to the same fine standards. Indicators not only have carefully finished gears, pinions, and other working parts, but the best contain jeweled movements. The dials are calibrated in different ways: either from direct or continuous reading, as from 0-10-10, to 50, etc., or for balanced plus

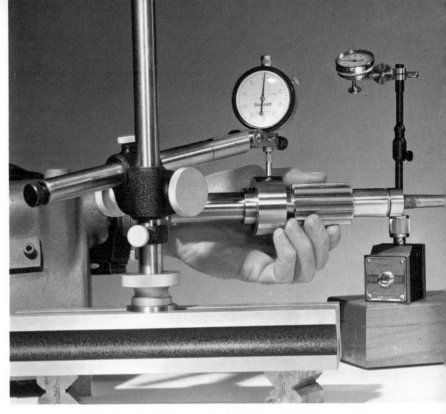

70-25.   Dial indicator used for inspection purposes.

or minus readings, as 0-50-0, 0-25-0, etc. Dial indicators are widely used in the machine tool industry as a part of machine tools, jigs, fixtures, and on production machines. To use the indicator, bring the workpiece so that the needle on the indicator registers at "0." As the workpiece is moved under the indicator, Fig. 70-26, or the indicator moved along inside the bored hole, Fig. 70-27, any variation will show on the dial. (As the workpiece is turned slowly by hand, the indicator shows in thousandths the difference between the high and low points or its total run-out.)

70-26.   Any variation in the diameter of the workpiece will show on the dial indicator.

70-27.   Checking the inside of a bored hole with a dial indicator.

323

Telescoping Gages

Telescoping gages may be preferred to ordinary calipers for the precision measuring of internal diameters, because the head of the telescoping gage expands across the inside of the hole and may be locked and measured with a micrometer caliper. Fig. 70-28. The ends of the telescoping heads are ground with a special radius, equal to the radius of the smallest hole in which it can be used. Table of sizes is above.

TELESCOPING GAGES

No.	Gage Closed	Gage Open
A	½″	¾″
B	¾″	1¼″
C	1¼″	2⅛″
D	2⅛″	3½″
E	3½″	6″

Table 70-B.

70-28.   Telescoping gage.

70-29.   Planer gage being used to set a cutting tool to proper height.

Planer or Shaper Gage

A planer gage has many applications. Some are: setting the cutting tool on a shaper or planer, Fig. 70-29; using with gage blocks in building up work on a surface plate, Fig. 70-30; using with a sine bar in grinding angles, Fig. 70-31; using with an indicator for transferring measurements; and using as an adjustable parallel.

The planer gage can be used on its base or end, also flat on either side, as both nut and slide are within the outside width of the base and both sides are ground square with the working edges.

Protractor

The protractor, Fig. 70-32, is used for setting bevels, transferring angles, and many other classes of work.

The head is semi-circular and its back is flat. It is graduated at the edge from 0° to 180° and has two rows of figures reading in opposite directions. The indicating arm of the blade has a line graduation for accurately setting and reading the protractor.

Thickness Gages

Thickness gages, Fig. 70-33, also called feeler gages, are extensively used not only in the manufacturing and servicing of automobiles, but by toolmakers, machinists, and others in jig and fixture work; in the making of gages, in experimental work, etc. Thickness gages are usually arranged in leaf form and the thickness of each leaf is indicated.

70-30.   A shaper gage being used with gage blocks.

70-31.   A shaper gage being used with a sine bar.

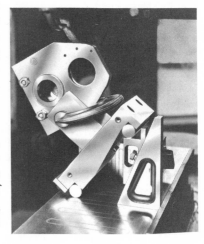

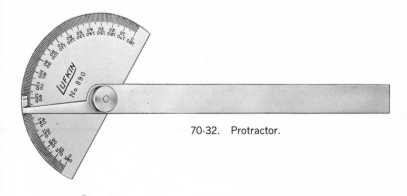

70-32.   Protractor.

70-33.   Thickness gage.

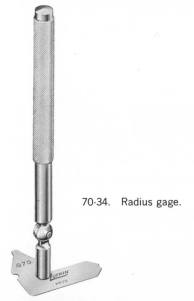

70-34.   Radius gage.

70-35.   Some uses of the radius gage.

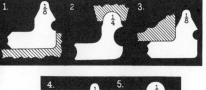

Fillet and Radius Gages

The fillet and radius gages shown in Fig. 70-34 are used to check concave and convex radii on corners or against shoulders. Radii or fillets from $\frac{1}{64}''$ to $\frac{1}{2}''$ can be checked or laid out easier, faster, and more accurately in any machining, layout, inspection, or patternmaking job. Fig. 70-35 shows some of the uses of the radius gage.

71 ▷ Inspection Gages

While you may not have the opportunity to use some of the gages described in this unit, it will be worthwhile to become acquainted with them.

Many measuring tools are used by machinists and inspectors to judge a semi-finished or finished part. A great many specialized gages are not to be found in the average machinist's tool box. These instruments are usually the property of the concern that employs the machinist, because they are too costly for him to own.

Inspection gaging operations consist of comparing dimensions of a part with the required dimensions given on the drawing or blueprint. There is always a certain amount of interchangeability required, and therefore it is essential that some reference to the standard inch be available. Gage blocks can be used as such a reference.

The use of gage blocks in industry today is a necessity.

Gage Blocks

Gage blocks are made of hardened alloy steel, ground and lapped so that the surfaces are flat and accurate to within millionths of an inch of the specified size. These gages when "wrung" together will hold as if magnetized. Fig. 71-1. They have been known to hold as much as 200 pounds on a direct pull. The blocks are sold under various trade names, as Johansson blocks, "Jo" blocks, Hoke blocks, or merely gage blocks. Fig. 71-2.

With special accessories, the blocks can be used as inside or outside calipers, trammels, and height gages. Figs. 71-2 and 71-3. See next pages for illustrations.

They may be obtained in sets ranging from a few blocks to complete sets of 83. The full set makes it possible to obtain over 200,000 different combinations of sizes.

Classification of Gages

Inspection equipment can be

71-1. Hoke precision gage blocks.

broadly divided into two classifications: (1) fixed gages or adjustable limit gages, (2) indicating types of measuring instruments and comparators.

FIXED GAGES

- *Plug Gages*

The commonest type of gage used for inspection purposes is the plug gage, which consists of a cylindrical plug of hardened steel, accurately ground to a specific size. Fig. 71-4. Many plug gages are made double-ended with a GO on one end and a NOT GO on the other. Due to the fact that the GO end must fit into the hole, it is always made to the low limit of the dimension. The NOT GO end is always made to the high limit of the dimension and must not fit into the hole. The hole is undersize when the GO end will not fit.

71-2. Sets of gage blocks and some uses as measuring tools.

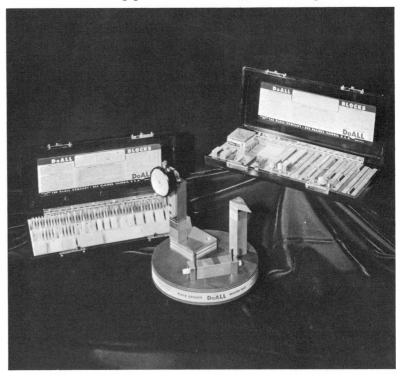

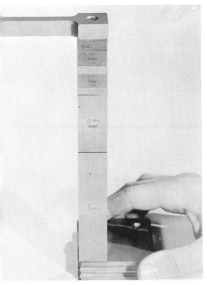

71-3. Gage blocks used as a height gage.

71-4. GO and NOT GO plug gage.

71-5. (A) Indicating snap gage.

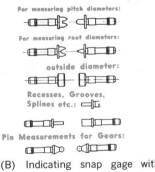

INTERCHANGEABLE ANVILS

For measuring pitch diameters:

For measuring Root diameters:

outside diameter:

Recesses, Grooves, Splines etc.:

Pin Measurements for Gears:

71-5. (B) Indicating snap gage with interchangeable anvils.

71-6. Ring gages.

71-7. Ring thread gage.

71-8. Thread plug gages.

● *Snap Gages*

Snap gages are used for gaging diameters, lengths, and thicknesses of parts. Fig. 71-5 (A). The gages can be fixed, adjustable, or of the indicating type. Fig. 71-5 (B). Adjustable snap gages have a C frame, very similar to a micrometer, with gaging pins in both the upper and lower arms. Such gages are usually set to gage blocks or other "masters."

● *Ring Gages*

Ring gages are used for the purpose of gaging outside diameters of cylindrical parts. Fig. 71-6. They are hardened steel rings that have been bored, ground, and lapped to the desired dimensions. The gages are used in pairs, one a GO and the other a NOT GO.

● *Thread Gages*

These resemble plain plug and ring gages except that they are threaded. Thread ring gages are provided with an adjusting and locking screw. They are usually of the split variety. Fig. 71-7. The locking screw permits fine adjustment by the manufacturer of the gage. An inspection thread plug gage is shown in Fig. 71-8.

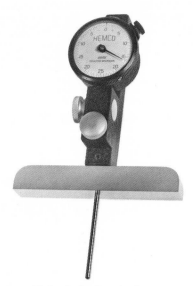

71-9.   Indicating depth gage.

71-10.   Indicating adjustable depth gage.

DIAL SNAP GAGES
0″ to 4″ BY .0001″
WIDE FLAT ANVILS
POSITIVE PARALLEL LOCKING
UNIFORM MEASUREMENTS
CARBIDE MEASURING FACES

71-11.   Dial snap and bore gages.

DIAL BORE GAGES
⅛″ to 13″ BY .0001″
FEWER EXTENSIONS
POSITIVE CENTRALIZING
THERMAL INSULATION
ACCURACY WITH GAGE TIPPED

INDICATING GAGES

An indicating gage is one that exhibits visually the variations in the uniformity of dimensions. The amount of variation above or below the required dimension is indicated by a lever on a graduated scale dial, flush pin, or plunger. The dial is set to zero and the workpiece is set under the contact point. Any variation is shown on the indicating hand. The dial depth gage, Figs. 71-9 and 71-10, is a good example of an indicating gage. This is used where extreme accuracy in measuring the depths of holes or slots is required. Extra rods to measure from 2″ to 6″ can be secured with the gage.

● *Dial Snap and Bore Gages*

These gages provide a quick method of checking inside and outside dimensions accurately. They are set easily to the desired dimensions with gage blocks, plugs, or masters and indicate exactly how much the workpiece is undersize or oversize, eliminating trial and error methods. Fig. 71-11.

For fast and accurate inspection of bores on a production basis, dial bore gages greatly simplify the operation. They determine quickly whether the bore diameters are within tolerances and disclose conditions such as bellmouth, out-of-roundness, or barrel shape. Their use eliminates the sense-of-feel method. A slight rocking motion of the gage gives true bore measurement. No special skill is required in its use. These gages are extremely sensitive and give exact duplication.

COMPARATORS

For inspection purposes, the simple comparator is widely used, Fig. 71-12. The comparator is made up of a finished bed plate upon which is located a vertical column. An adjustable bracket, bearing a dial indicator, slides upon the column. The dial is adjusted to a suitable master; then the part being inspected is rolled or slid under the dial.

• *Air Gages*

The air gage is a form of comparison device designed to measure the inside characteristics of holes. It indicates the amount of air escaping between the sides of the hole and a standard gaging spindle, which has been inserted in the hole.

A metal plug, which is slightly smaller than the minimum diameter of the workpiece, carries two or more accurately calibrated jets through which air is blown at carefully controlled pressure. Fig. 71-13.

Both the velocity and the pressure of the air at a given instant depend upon the clearance between the gaging spindle and the hole. The greater the clearance, the higher will be the velocity and the lower the back pressure. The smaller the clearance, the less velocity and the greater the back pressure. Therefore a comparison may be made by measuring either the air velocity or the air pressure. Two types of air gages are based on this principle.

71-12. Comparator.

71-13. Air gage, which permits measuring jobs more accurately than by other gaging methods.

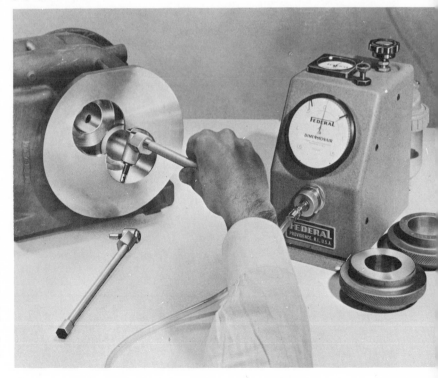

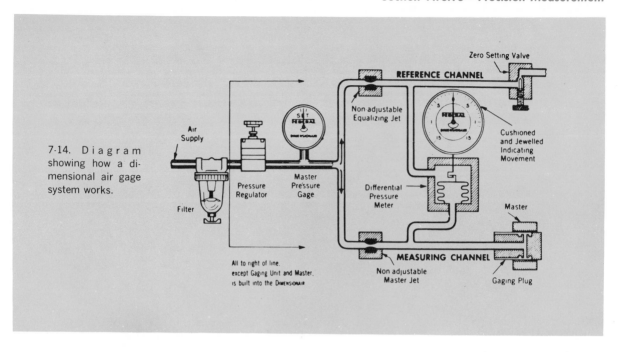

7-14. D i a g r a m showing how a dimensional air gage system works.

71-15. Transistorized electronic comparator.

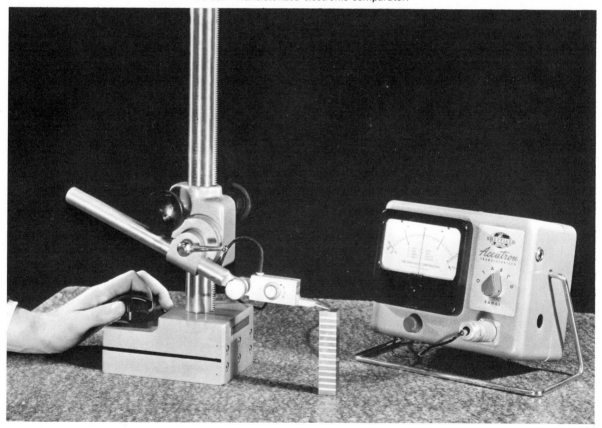

71-16.   Optical flats.

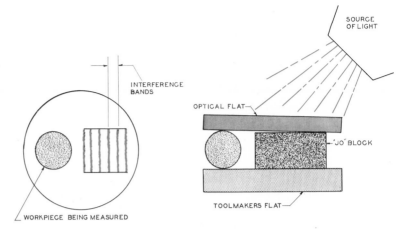

71-17.   Interference bands indicate differences in size between the workpiece and gage block.

The gaging spindle does not contact the surface being measured. The escaping air creates a cushion between the surface and the spindle so that soft, even surfaces are not marred or scratched in the measuring operation. Fig. 71-14.

• *Electronic Comparator*

The electronic comparator, Fig. 71-15, is used to make extremely close measurements. It is a comparison type gage and must be set by means of master gage blocks.

• *Optical Flats*

Optical flats make use of light waves as a measuring standard. Fig. 71-16. These flats are of quartz with one face ground and polished to optical flatness. The ground face is placed upon a machined surface and a special light passed through the flat. Bands are set up by the light on the machined surface, producing a shape which indicates to the inspector the accuracy of the measurement

from millionths to hundred millionths of an inch. Fig. 71-17.

• *Optical Comparator*

The optical comparator, Fig. 71-18, is used in production inspection. An enlarged image of the workpiece is projected on a screen where it is superimposed upon a drawing that is the correct size and shape. A visual comparison is then made. A skilled operator can note variations as small as .0005 of an inch.

71-18.   Optical comparator.

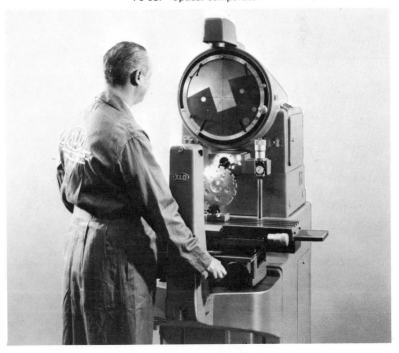

71-19. Horizontal measuring machine.

Horizontal Measuring Machine

The horizontal measuring machine, Fig. 71-19, is used for checking gages and allied parts. The measuring heads consist of a micrometer on one of the columns and a .00002 micro-indicator that has a pressure measuring control mounted on the other column. Gage blocks are used to make accurate measurements of the parts being checked. The work table raises and lowers for positioning.

Check Your Knowledge

1. Why is accuracy in measurement so important?

2. Why are precision measurements expressed in decimals rather than in fractional values?

3. Why does the spindle of a micrometer caliper contain 40 threads to the inch?

4. What is the purpose of the ratchet stop on a micrometer caliper?

5. Explain the vernier principle.

6. What is the advantage of a direct reading micrometer?

7. What is a blade micrometer used for?

8. What is the difference between a vernier caliper and a height gage?

9. Name some uses of the vernier height gage.

10. How accurate is a universal bevel protractor?

11. What does the gear tooth caliper measure?

12. Name some of the uses of a dial indicator.

13. How is the dial indicator calibrated?

14. Name some of the applications of a planer gage?

15. What is another name for a thickness gage?

16. What is meant by inspection gaging operations?

17. Name some of the uses of gage blocks.

18. Name the two general classifications of gages.

19. Explain the difference between an adjustable type snap gage and an indicating type.

20. Why is fast and accurate inspection of parts necessary?

21. Describe a comparator and explain its uses.

22. Explain the working principle of an air gage.

23. What is an optical flat?

24. What is meant by the term "optical flatness"?

Terms to Know and Spell

vernier	*telescoping*	*calibrated*
lineal	*three-fluted*	*thimble*
increments	*indicator*	*interpolation*
micrometer	*sine bar*	*integral*
protractor	*trammel*	*splines*
chordal	*comparator*	*bored hole*
alignment	*optical flatness*	*interchangeability*
inspection gaging	*dial indicator*	*indicating gage*
snap gage	*planer gage*	*transistorized*
fillet	*tolerance*	

Machining Metal

Broadly speaking, the purpose of all machine tools is to produce metal parts by changing the shape, size, and finish of metal pieces.

To accomplish its function of changing the dimensions and shape of a workpiece by cutting a quantity of the metal away,

the machine tool must first move either the tool or the workpiece by either a rotating or a straight line motion, to accomplish a single cut. A series of cuts is then produced by reciprocating either the tool or the workpiece. The speed and movement of both must be accurately controlled. The direction of movement—forward or backward, left or right in a horizontal plane—must also be precisely controlled as well as the up and down or vertical movement. The movement of the tool must be coordinated with the movement of the workpiece.

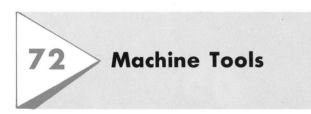

72 ▷ Machine Tools

Machine tool motion control and application may be identified by the type of motion produced in either the cutting tool and the material, or both, and the direction in which that motion is applied as in Fig. 72-1. The necessity for controlling the two basic forms of motion—reciprocating and rotating—in different directions, in either the vertical or · horizontal plane, is the fundamental reason for variations in machine tool construction.

● In a **lathe,** the workpiece is rotated and the tool is reciprocated to complete a given sequence of cuts as in Fig. 72-1 (A).

● In a **planer,** both the workpiece and the tool are reciprocated to complete a given sequence of cuts. Fig. 72-1 (B).

● In a **milling machine,** the workpiece is reciprocated as in Fig. 72-1 (C) and the cutter is rotated.

● In **drilling** operations the workpiece is stationary and the tool rotated and advanced to the workpiece, Fig. 72-1 (D).

In a **shaper,** Fig. 72-1 (E), both the workpiece and the tool are reciprocated to complete a given sequence of cuts.

In **grinding,** the workpiece is rotated or reciprocated and the wheel is rotated to complete a given sequence of cuts. Fig. 72-1 (F).

Machinability of Metals

Cutting metal requires pressure and motion of the tool applied to the material being cut. The value of the tool's cutting action depends upon: (1) the velocity of motion, (2) keenness of the tool edge, and (3) degree of pressure involved.

A cutting edge may be used to cut an object in one of three different ways: (1) by a slicing action, (2) by a wedging action, (3) by a scraping action.

The first type of cutting motion can be compared to slicing bread.

The second cutting motion is a "wedging action" compared to the action of a cold chisel on a workpiece.

The "scraping" action as used in lathe operation has the pressure applied to the cutting edge, and the speed of the cutting motion is rather high.

Formation of Chips

Three types of chips are formed when metal is machined:

● A discontinuous chip is formed when metal separates into small chips. Fig. 72-2 (A).

● A continuous chip, Fig. 72-2 (B), is formed by the metal ahead of the tool being removed with-

72-1. Machine tool motion control and application may be identified by the type of motion produced either in the cutting tool, the material, or both.

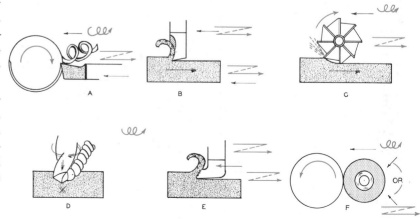

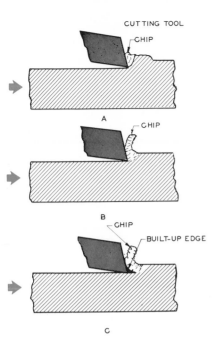

72-2. (A) Discontinuous chip formed when machining brittle metals. (B) Continuous chip formed when machining ductile metals. (C) Continuous chip with built-up edge formed when machining wear-resistant metals.

out fracture. Ductile metals such as copper and aluminum form a continuous chip.

• A continuous chip with built-up edge also forms on metals that are ductile. The metal in front of the tool becomes compressed and adheres to the face of the cutting edge of the tool. Fig. 72-2 (C). The chip is then formed and begins to flow away. Small particles of metal from the workpiece adhere to the point of the cutting tool. Part of the built-up edge breaks off and is carried away with the chip. Other portions of the built-up edge cling to the workpiece, causing a rough surface. Soft or mild steel usually forms a continuous chip with a built-up edge when machined with high-speed tools.

73 ▷ The Engine Lathe

The engine lathe, Fig. 73-1, is used to shape metal by revolving the workpiece against the cutting edge of the tool.

Lathe Parts and Classification

The operating principles of each part should be carefully studied before operating the lathe. Oftentimes this prevents damage to valuable equipment and avoids a waste of materials. The parts of a lathe can be readily memorized if you divide them into two main classifications. Fig. 73-2, page 336.

1. The lathe parts that hold the workpiece and control its motion.

2. The parts that hold the cutting tool and control its movement.

LATHE SIZE AND CAPACITY

The size of a screw cutting lathe is designated by the swing and the length of the bed. Fig. 73-3. A 13″x5′ lathe is one having a swing over the bed, A, sufficient to take a workpiece up to 13″ in diameter and having a bed length, C, of 5′. The maximum distance between centers, B, determines the length of a workpiece that can be turned between centers.

THE LATHE BED

The lathe bed, a casting of rigid construction, is the foundation on which the lathe is built. It usually has four prismatic V ways, which have been found to be the most accurate and serviceable. The two outer ways guide the lathe carriage, while the inner ways and the flat way align the heatstock and tailstock. All modern lathes have a combination of flat ways and V ways.

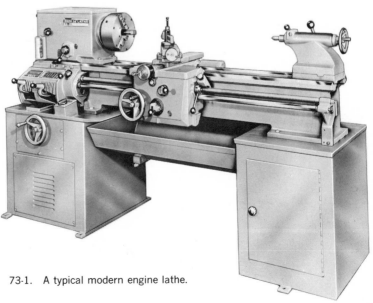

73-1. A typical modern engine lathe.

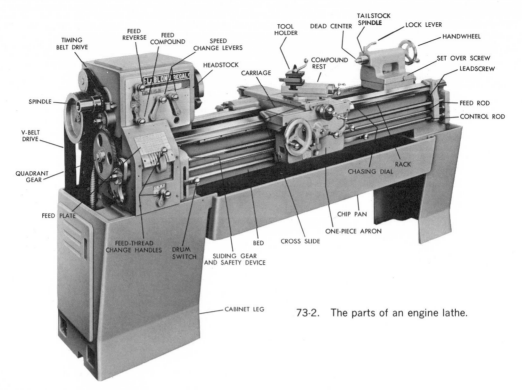

73-2.   The parts of an engine lathe.

THE HEADSTOCK

The headstock is fastened to the inner ways on the left end of the bed.

The spindle that rotates the workpiece revolves in bearings that are built into the headstock. The spindle is rotated by gears or a combination of gears and pulleys. The spindle holds attachments, which, in turn, hold and turn the workpiece. A hole extends through the spindle. The front end is tapered for holding centers and other tools having a tapered shank. A taper sleeve fits into the taper spindle hole. The live center fits into the sleeve and turns with the workpiece.

Some types of lathes come equipped with a common screw nose, Fig. 73-4, and other types have a standard key-drive taper nose, Fig. 73-5.

The headstock unit also contains the back gears. Slower

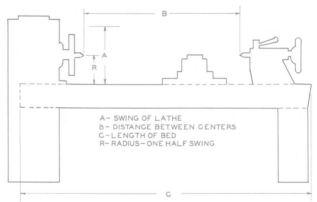

73-3.   The size of a lathe is designated by the swing and length of bed.

A— SWING OF LATHE
B— DISTANCE BETWEEN CENTERS
C— LENGTH OF BED
R— RADIUS— ONE HALF SWING

speeds on belt driven lathes can be obtained by engaging the back gears. The large gear (bull gear) is keyed to the spindle and is locked to the cone pulley with a bull gear lock pin. The back gears can be disengaged by disconnecting the bull gear lock pin. *The back gears should never be engaged while the spindle is rotating.*

On some types of lathes the

73-4.   Threaded type spindle nose.

73-5.   Long taper key spindle nose.

73-6.   The gear train and drive mechanism with variable speed drive.

spindle speed can be changed by shifting the driving belt to a pulley of smaller or larger diameter. Other types of lathes come equipped with a variable speed drive, Fig. 73-6, with infinite choice of speeds from 40 to 1,600 rpm.

THE TAILSTOCK

The tailstock supports an adjustable spindle, which moves in and out of the upper casting when the tailstock handwheel is turned. This spindle has a tapered hole which holds the tapered dead center (called "dead center" because it does not revolve). Taper shank drills, reamers, and similar tools can be mounted in the tailstock center. The tailstock shown in Fig. 73-7 has a quick-acting cam lock that clamps the tailstock to the bed. Also note the easy accessibility of the ram clamp lever. A large micrometer collar with .001″ decimal graduations is provided in addition to the $\frac{1}{16}$″ graduations on the ram. The tailstock has an offset feature for taper turning, an ejection feature for centers, and wipers for both V ways and flat ways.

THE CARRIAGE

The lathe carriage, Fig. 73-8, which is attached to the lathe

73-7.   The tailstock.

bed, is made up of the saddle, apron, cross slide, compound rest, and the tool post.

The saddle is an H-shaped casting that fits over the bed and slides along the ways.

The apron is fastened to the saddle and is mounted over the front of the bed. It contains the levers, clutches, and gears that control the movement of the carriage either by hand or power feeds. The handwheel is attached to a pinion gear that meshes with a rack under the front of the bed. The apron also contains friction clutches for the automatic operation of the carriage. A split nut is also contained in this unit that can be closed over the lead screw threads and is used for thread cutting.

The saddle contains the cross slide; it can be moved in and out perpendicular to the center of the lathe, with the cross feed lever.

The compound rest, mounted on top of the cross slide, can be swiveled in a full circle and locked in any position. Both the

73-8.   The lathe carriage.

cross slide and the compound rest screws are equipped with micrometer collars divided into thousandths of an inch. These are used when turning workpieces to close measurements, and when cutting screw threads.

Most modern lathes have a separate rod that is used for all power feeding. The lead screw is used for thread cutting only.

FEED AND THREAD CUTTING MECHANISMS

Modern lathes come equipped with feeding and threading mechanisms that consist of a quick-change gear box, lead screw, feed rod, and the gears and clutches in the apron. The quick-change gear box is directly below the headstock assembly. This gear box, Fig. 73-9, contains a number of different size gears which provides a means of changing the rate of feed and the rotation between the revolutions of the headstock spindle and the movement of the carriage for thread cutting.

Most gear boxes contain two levers to obtain the correct feed or number of threads. Faster or slower tool movements, in relation to the rotating speed of the spindle, are accomplished by moving the control levers which engage the proper gear trains. This makes it possible to change the longitudinal movement of the carriage.

An index plate or chart is attached to the gear box for use in selecting the proper feed or threads per inch.

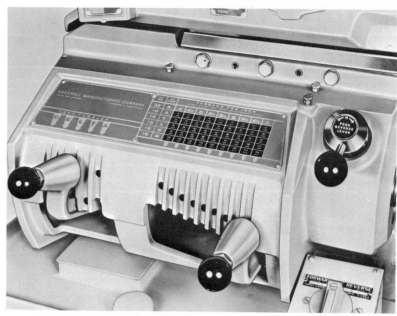

73-9.   The quick-change gear box with feed reverse lever.

74 ▷ Lathe Cutting Tools

Tools used for cutting on the lathe are generally made of high speed steel—an alloy of iron, carbon, tungsten, and vanadium.

Lathe tools are also made of "stellite," a combination of cobalt, chromium, and tungsten. Stellite will stand higher speeds and feeds than will high-speed-steel cutter bits.

Tungsten-carbide tipped tools are used for manufacturing operations requiring maximum cutting speeds and feeds.

Cutter bits are usually purchased unground and can be purchased by the pound. The bits are then ground to the desired shape for cutting operations. Cutter bits may also be purchased ground to shape, Fig. 74-1. These bits are more expensive.

74-1.   Typical lathe cutter bits ground to shape.

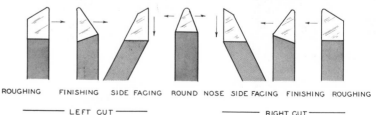

ROUGHING   FINISHING   SIDE FACING   ROUND NOSE   SIDE FACING   FINISHING   ROUGHING

———— LEFT CUT ————   ———— RIGHT CUT ————

Cutting Tool Shapes

The parts of a cutter bit are shown in Fig. 74-2, with their angles. The cutting efficiency of any lathe tool depends upon the proper design and location of the cutting edges.

Left- and Right-Cut Roughing Tools

The left-cut roughing tool, Fig. 74-3, cuts from left to right. The right-cut roughing tool operates just the opposite. The shape of the tool permits deep cuts at heavier feeds. This tool will cut freely but does not produce a very smooth finish.

Finishing Tools

The right- and left-cut finishing tool, Fig. 74-3, has a rounded nose which produces a smooth finish. This tool is used in making a light finish cut. After grinding, the cutting edge should be honed with a fine oilstone which will improve the final cut.

Boring and Inside Threading Tools

The boring tool, Fig. 74-3, is ground the same as a left-cut turning tool, except that the front clearance must be ground at a slightly greater angle so that the heel of the tool will not rub in the hole of the workpiece.

The inside threading tool is ground the same as the screw thread cutting tool, except that the front clearance must be increased for the same reason as for the boring tool.

Facing Tools

The right-cut side facing tool, Fig. 74-4, is used for facing the ends of shafts and for machining

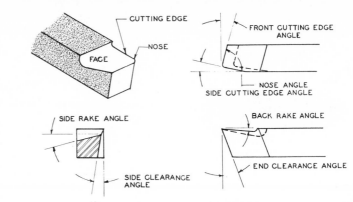

74-2. Angles at which a lathe cutter bit is ground.

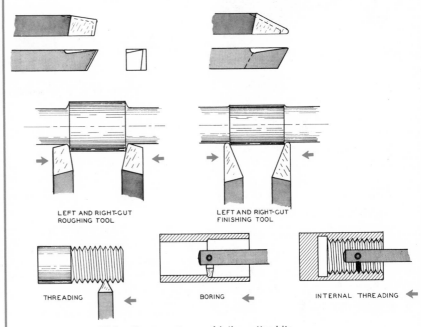

74-3. Common types of lathe cutter bits.

74-4. Other lathe cutter bits.

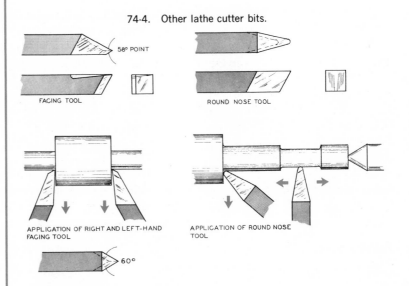

74-5. Formed threading tool.

74-6. Cut-off tool holder and tool.

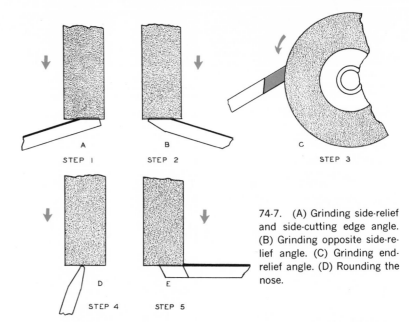

74-7. (A) Grinding side-relief and side-cutting edge angle. (B) Grinding opposite side-relief angle. (C) Grinding end-relief angle. (D) Rounding the nose.

the right side of a shoulder. This tool is fed outward from the center. The point of the tool is sharp and is ground to an angle of 58° to prevent interference with the tailstock center.

The left-cut side facing tool is just the reverse, it is used for facing the left side of the workpiece.

Round Nose Turning Tools

This tool is ground flat on top so that the tool may be fed in either direction as indicated by the arrows in Fig. 74-4. This is a very convenient tool for reducing the diameter of a shaft in the center.

Threading Tool

The screw thread cutting tool is usually ground flat on top and the point must be ground to an included angle of 60° as shown in Fig. 74-4. Careful grinding and setting of this cutter bit will result in perfectly formed screw threads. Always keep the workpiece flooded with lard oil to obtain a smooth thread when cutting threads. Fig. 74-5 shows a formed threading tool.

Parting Tool

The parting tool, Fig. 74-6,

should always be set exactly on center. It may be sharpened by grinding the end of the cutter blade to an angle of 5°. The sides of the blade have sufficient taper to provide side clearance, so do not need to be ground. NOTE: Flood the workpiece with oil when cutting steel.

Grinding Lathe Cutter Bits

Learning to grind lathe cutter bits is as important as learning how to operate the lathe itself. To grind a cutter bit for straight turning, five angles are involved: (1) the angle of keenness, (2) end relief angle, (3) side relief angle, (4) back rake, and (5) side rake. Fig. 74-7 shows the steps in grinding a *round nose* turning tool.

The procedure is as follows:

1. Dress the grinding wheel to eliminate all grooves and uneven surfaces. Use a coarse-grit wheel for roughing the tool bit to shape and a fine-grit wheel for finishing.

2. Grind the left side of the cutter bit, holding the bit at the correct angle against the wheel to form the side cutting edge angle. Fig. 74-7 (A). This angle should be about 6° for cutting mild steel. Move the cutter bit back and forth across the wheel to prevent grooving. Dip tool in water frequently to prevent overheating. A *tool bit grinding gage* can be used to check the angles.

3. Grind the right side or side-relief angle as shown in Fig. 74-7 (B).

4. To grind the end-relief angle, hold the tool with the end up, Fig. 74-7 (C). Swing the tool bit in a semicircle. Do not round off the nose too much. Fig. 74-7 (D).

5. Grind the side and back rake angles. Table 74-A gives the correct angle. When grinding the back rake angle, remember the tool is held in the toolholder at an angle.

6. Hone the cutting edge with a medium fine oilstone.

Lathe Toolholders

There are three common types

RAKE ANGLES FOR COMMON METALS

Material	Back Rake Deg.	Side Rake Deg.
Aluminum and alloys	8	18
Cast iron:		
Soft	5	5
Medium	4	4
Hard	3	3
Steel:		
Low-carbon	8	14
Medium-carbon	10	12
High-carbon	5	10
Tool and die	8	12
Alloy	8	12
Copper	16¼	20
Brass and bronze	2	2
Malleable iron	4	5

Table 74-A.

of lathe toolholders: (1) straight, Fig. 74-8 (A), (2) right-hand off-set, Fig. 74-8 (B), left-hand offset, Fig. 74-8 (C). If the shank is set to the right, it is a right-hand off-set holder. If the shank is offset to the left, it is a left-hand. NOTE: The straight toolholder is used for most types of work.

74-8. (A)   Straight toolholder.

74-8. (B)   Right-hand offset.

74-8. (C)   Left-hand offset toolholder.

Speeds, Feeds, Depth of Cut

One sign of a lathe expert is the ability to balance the speed, feed, and depth of cut.

Cutting speed, measured in surface feet per minute (sfm), refers to the distance the workpiece moves past the cutter in one minute as measured on the circumference. It is the total length of the chip taken off by the tool bit in one minute. The cutting speed depends upon the rpm of the spindle and the diameter of the workpiece. For instance, if the speed of the spindle remained constant but the diameter of the workpiece were changed from ¾″ to 1½″, the cutting speed would be doubled. Therefore any increase in the diameter of the workpiece would necessarily mean that the spindle speed must be slowed.

Cutting speed is influenced by:

1. Type of cutter bit.
2. Type of material.
3. Condition of the lathe.
4. Amount of feed.
5. Depth of cut.
6. Whether doing roughing or finishing cuts.

The spindle speed can be calculated by the following:

$$rpm = \frac{12 \times sfm}{3.1416 \times d} \quad \text{or} \quad \frac{3.82 \times sfm}{d}$$

sfm = surface feet per minute
d = diameter

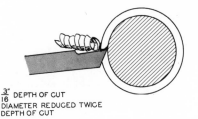

3/16″ DEPTH OF CUT
DIAMETER REDUCED TWICE DEPTH OF CUT

74-9. The diameter of the workpiece being turned is reduced twice the depth of the cut.

Feed and *depth* of cut are always considered together. Feed is the distance the tool moves longitudinally along the workpiece with each revolution of the spindle. Feed varies with (1) depth of cut, (2) kind of material, (3) condition of the lathe. Depth of cut is the distance from the bottom of the cut to the uncut surface of the workpiece measured at right angles to the machined surface. To reduce the diameter of the workpiece by ⅜″ the depth of cut would have to be ³⁄₁₆″, Fig. 74-9.

The depth of cut may vary from as little as a thousandth of an inch to as much as ¾″. It determines the thickness of the chip removed. On some jobs, the depth of cut is subject to more variations than speed or feed.

A heavy cut should be taken at the start to bring the workpiece down to dimensions, and a lighter cut be taken to bring the work to exact dimensions and finish.

TABLE FOR CHOOSING CORRECT RPM

Material	sfm	½″	1″	1½″	2″
Low carbon steel	100	800	400	266	200
Tool steel	50	400	200	133	100
Cast iron	75	600	300	200	150
Brass	200	1,600	800	533	400
Aluminum	300	2.400	1,200	800	600

Table 74-B.

75 ▷ Mounting Workpieces on an Engine Lathe

The manner in which a workpiece should be mounted on a lathe for the most efficient production results is determined by the following factors: (1) the size and shape of the workpiece, (2) nature of operation to be performed, (3) the area and location of the workpiece surface to be machined.

There are four methods of transmitting the turning power of the spindle to the workpiece: (1) with the face plate, (2) with the lathe dog, (3) with the lathe chuck, and (4) with the collet chuck.

Face Plate and Lathe Dog

The function of the lathe dog is to transmit the rotating motion of the driving plate to the workpiece. It must grip the workpiece firmly enough to withstand the pressure of the tool. For round workpieces, dogs with tear-shaped openings are generally used. Three types of dogs can be used on the lathe, Fig. 75-1. Select a dog with an opening just slightly

75-2. Face plates.

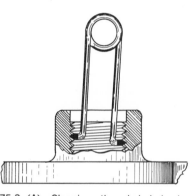

75-3. (A) Cleaning threaded hole in face plate.

75-3. (B) Workpiece can be bolted on the face plate.

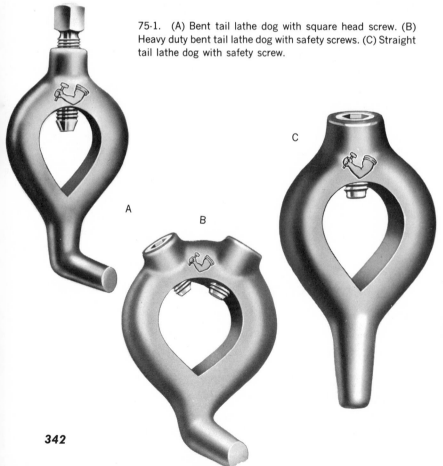

75-1. (A) Bent tail lathe dog with square head screw. (B) Heavy duty bent tail lathe dog with safety screws. (C) Straight tail lathe dog with safety screw.

A

B

C

75-4. Draw-in chuck with collet.

larger than the diameter of the workpiece.

The driving or face plate, Fig. 75-2, is screwed to the spindle of the headstock. The threads should be free of dirt and chips before mounting the face plate on the spindle nose. The threads can be cleaned with a tool as shown in Fig. 75-3 (A). The slots in the plate are used to receive the tail of the dog for driving the work between centers.

Workpieces can also be bolted to the face plate. Fig. 75-3 (B).

The Collet Chuck

Stock of small diameter, whether round, hexagonal, or octagonal, can be held in a draw-in collet chuck, Fig. 75-4. This chuck is made with extreme accuracy which makes it possible to chuck the workpiece accurately without adjustment. Collets for this type of chuck are interchangeable, to fit different shapes and dimensions of stock.

Workpieces are commonly turned between centers. There are many advantages if the size and the nature of the operation will permit.

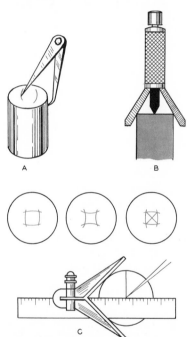

76-1. (A) Locating the center with a hermaphrodite caliper. (B) Using a bell center punch to locate center. (C) Using the center head of a combination square to locate center.

Locating and Drilling Center Holes

Before the workpiece can be mounted, the centers of both ends have to be countersunk with a 60° combination countersink drill. This operation provides bearing holes for the lathe centers.

1. Remove the burrs from each end of the workpiece.

2. Locate the center of the workpiece by one of the following methods:

- Use a hermaphrodite caliper as shown in Fig. 76-1 (A).
- Locate the center with a bell center punch as shown in Fig. 76-1 (B). This method is limited by the size of the stock.
- Hold a center head of a combination square on the end of the workpiece and scribe two lines that cross. Fig. 76-1 (C).

3. Prick-punch the center and then center punch.

4. Select the proper size combination countersink center drill. Table 76-A. Figs. 76-2 (A) and (B) show a combination center drill and countersink. See the next page.

SIZE OF CENTER HOLE FOR $^3/_{16}$'' TO 4'' DIA. WORKPIECES			
Dia. of workpiece D	Large dia. of countersunk hole C	Dia. of drill P	Dia. of body F
$^3/_{16}$'' to $^5/_{16}$''	$^1/_8$''	$^5/_{64}$''	$^3/_{16}$''
$^3/_8$'' to 1''	$^3/_{16}$''	$^7/_{64}$''	$^1/_4$''
1$^1/_4$'' to 2''	$^1/_4$''	$^1/_8$''	$^5/_{16}$''
2$^1/_4$'' to 4''	$^5/_{16}$''	$^3/_{16}$''	$^7/_{16}$''

Table 76-A.

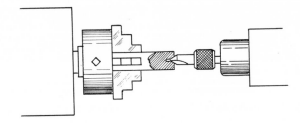

76-3. One method of drilling a center hole in the end of the workpiece.

76-2. (A) Combination center drill and countersink.

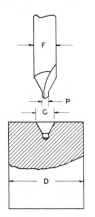

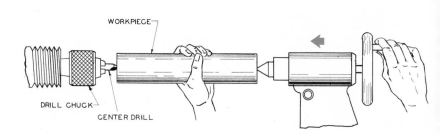

WORKPIECE

DRILL CHUCK
CENTER DRILL

76-2. (B) Size of countersink drill.

76-4. Center drill mounted in the headstock in a drill chuck to countersink hole.

5. Drill the center holes on the lathe as shown in either Figs. 76-3 or 76-4, or on the drill press, Fig. 76-5. Fig. 76-6 shows correctly and incorrectly drilled center holes.

Facing the Workpiece

1. Place the tailstock centers in alignment with each other. Fig. 76-7.

2. Fasten the lathe dog on one end of the workpiece.

3. Insert the tail of the dog in the opening in the face plate. Apply lubricant to the workpiece dead center hole. Tighten the tailstock spindle until the workpiece is held in place. *Do not* tighten the tailstock spindle too tightly as it will cause the dead center to burn. *Readjust* after a few cuts because the workpiece has a tendency to expand when heated.

4. Insert a right-cut side-facing tool in the toolholder.

5. Adjust the toolholder so that the cutting edge of the tool

is at an approximate right angle to the center line.

6. Square up the end by moving the carriage to the left, so as to contact the workpiece and move the cross-feed towards you. The *first cut* will be a roughing cut from the outside towards the center. For the *finish cut,* feed the cross-feed from the center to the outside of the workpiece. NOTE: Facing the ends between centers is greatly facilitated by using a half center in the tailstock. Fig. 76-8.

7. Reverse the workpiece and face the other end. NOTE: Short pieces of stock can be held in a chuck and faced.

Rough Turning

1. Select a right-cut roughing tool for this operation.

2. Mount the toolholder in the tool post. NOTE: Beginners have an inclination to set the **toolholder out too far. Too much** overhang causes the tool to spring.

3. Set the tool on center and

turned slightly *away from* the headstock. Any toolholder slippage will cause the tool to gouge into the workpiece if it is mounted toward the headstock. Fig. 76-9.

4. Set the lathe for the correct

76-5. Drilling a center hole on the drill press.

speed and feed. Move the carriage towards the headstock to see if it can travel the required distance without the lathe dog striking the compound rest.

5. Determine the depth of the roughing cut and adjust an outside caliper to $\frac{1}{32}''$ of the finish size. The depth of the roughing cut depends upon the size and condition of the lathe and the type of tool being used.

6. Adjust the micrometer collar on the cross-feed to zero and lock in position. Back the tool off and move the carriage to clear the end of the workpiece at the right. Turn the cross-feed in for the desired depth of cut.

7. Turn the power on and engage the carriage clutch. Make a trial cut and check the diameter with an outside micrometer caliper.

8. After the cutting has reached the halfway point, back off the tool, stop the feed, and return the carriage to the starting point. Reverse the workpiece and return the cross-feed to the starting point. Rough-turn the second half to size. NOTE: Some operators do not back off the tool but turn off the power and remove the workpiece. They then return the carriage to the starting position and machine the second half without changing the setting. You may like this method. Try both.

Finish Turning

1. For the finish turning operation check the diameter with a micrometer caliper to determine the amount of stock to finish-turn to the required dimensions.

2. Insert a right-cut finishing

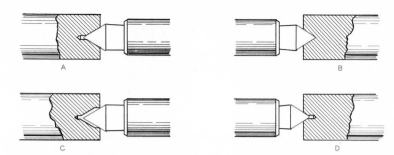

76-6. Correct and incorrectly drilled center holes. (A) Properly drilled. (B) No pilot. (C) Countersunk too deep. Center rides on lip of hole. (D) Hole not deep enough. Small bearing surface.

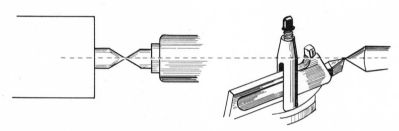

76-7. When a live and dead center are in alignment with each other, then center lines must meet and form a straight line.

tool in the toolholder. The tool must have a keen cutting edge.

3. Turn the power on, move the tool so that it just touches the workpiece, and move the carriage to the right until it clears the end of the stock.

4. Turn the power off and adjust the cross-feed collar to zero. Turn the feed in for the desired depth of cut. Start the lathe and take a trial cut about $\frac{1}{2}''$ long. Turn off the power and check the diameter with an outside micrometer. If the diameter is 0.010 oversize, turn the cross-feed in 0.005 and take a cut. Check the diameter again to see if the correct diameter has been obtained. Turn the second half to size.

76-9. The angle of tool setting in relation to the center line of the workpiece determines whether or not the turned surface will become damaged if the tool swivels.

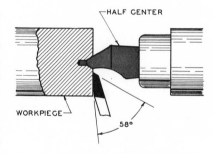

76-8. Application of half center.

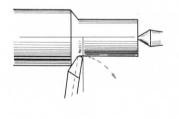

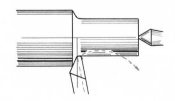

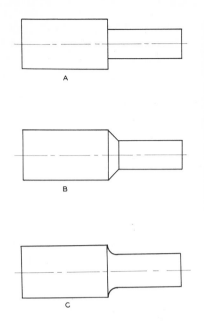

76-10. Four different types of shoulders: (A) Square, (B) angular, (C) filleted, (D) undercut.

Turning to a Shoulder

Workpieces that are turned to more than one outside diameter are said to be "turned to a shoulder." The four general types of shoulders are: (1) square shoulder, (2) angular shoulder, (3) filleted shoulder, (4) undercut. Fig. 76-10.

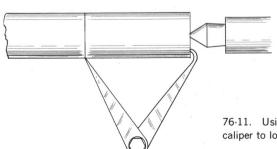

76-11. Using a hermaphrodite caliper to locate reference points.

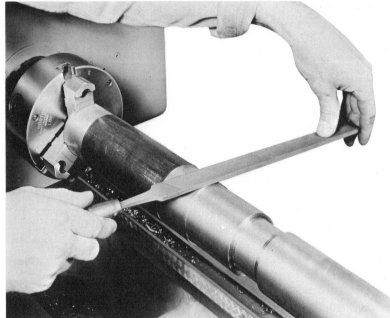

76-12. Right hand method of filing. The left arm is held high to avoid the chuck.

1. Face the right end of the workpiece, as all measuring will be done from this end.

2. Lay off a specified distance with a hermaphrodite caliper. Fig. 76-11.

3. Place a right-cut roughing tool in a toolholder.

4. "Neck" (recess) the workpiece at the place marked, and rough-turn the first diameter to 1/32" oversize.

5. Insert the properly ground finishing tool and turn the type of shoulder desired.

Filing and Polishing

A file and fine abrasive cloth can be used to obtain a smooth finish on the workpiece. Use a long angle lathe file or mill file for this operation.

1. Remove the tool post and use a high spindle speed.

2. If using the right-hand method of filing, be careful to keep your arm away from the revolving lathe dog. Fig. 76-12. NOTE: The left hand is more awkward but much safer.

Turning Tapers

A workpiece may be tapered by any of three different methods: (1) by setting the tailstock over the amount required, (2) by using the taper attachment, (3) by setting the compound rest at the proper angle for short tapers.

Most taper turning in the schools is done by offsetting the tailstock. The tailstock is made in

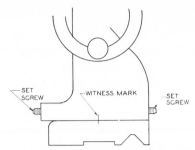

76-13. Witness marks on the tailstock are used to measure the amount of set-over. Note adjusting screws on each side of base for moving the upper part of the tailstock.

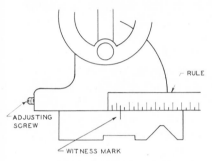

76-14. Measuring setover on the tail-stock with a rule.

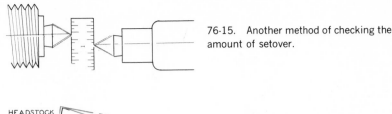

76-15. Another method of checking the amount of setover.

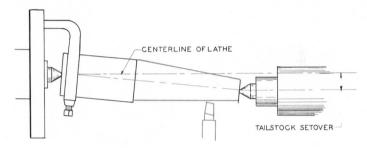

76-16. The length of the workpiece varies the taper even though the tailstock offset remains the same.

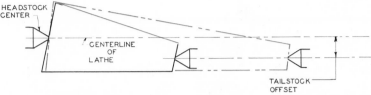

76-17. Showing a portion of the workpiece being tapered.

two sections, which permits the upper half to be moved toward or away from the operator to obtain the desired amount of setover.

TAILSTOCK SETOVER METHOD OF TURNING A TAPER

Condition 1: When the full length of the workpiece and the diameters of both ends are known. First calculate the amount of setover by using the following formula:

$$\frac{\text{large diameter} - \text{small diameter}}{2} = \text{setover}$$

1. Loosen the anchor bolt that locks the tailstock to the ways. Move the upper part toward you to the required setover by the adjusting screws on each side of the base. Fig. 76-13. The small end of the taper will then be at the tailstock end.

2. There are two witness or index lines on the end of tailstock. Measure the distance between these two lines with a rule or set a pair of dividers to the correct length; then measure, Fig. 76-14. A rule can also be used for measuring the distance between the live and dead centers. Fig. 76-15.

Condition 2: When a portion of the workpiece length is to be tapered and the diameter of both ends of the taper is known. The offset must be calculated for each job, as the length of the workpiece is important in figuring the setover. Fig. 76-16.

Calculate the amount of setover by using the following formula:

$$\frac{\text{length of workpiece}}{\text{length of taper}} \times \frac{\text{large dia.} - \text{small dia.}}{2}$$
$$= \text{setover}$$

Condition 3: When the full length of the workpiece is to be tapered and the taper per foot is known.

$$\frac{\text{Taper per foot} \times \text{length of taper in inches}}{24}$$
$$= \text{setover}$$

3. To turn taper, place workpiece between centers. Fig. 76-17.

4. Select the tool of suitable shape and set its point even with the centerline of the workpiece.

5. Start the lathe and take a moderately heavy cut.

6. When the working length of the taper is cut, measure the actual length and the large and small diameter.

7. Make adjustment of tailstock if the taper is not correct.

8. Take a light finishing cut for reducing the workpiece to the exact dimensions.

76-20. A pair of standard face knurls, diamond pattern fine (33 pitch).

76-21. Knurling tool.

76-22. Three-jaw universal chuck.

76-23. Four-jaw independent chuck.

76-18. Turning a taper with the taper attachment.

76-19. Knurling on the lathe.

Taper Turning with the Taper Attachment

The taper attachment consists of a swivel bar mounted on the back of the bed. The cross-feed screw is removed and the cross-feed is attached to the swivel bar, Fig. 76-18. The bar is set to the taper required either in taper per foot or in degrees. One end of the bar is marked for taper per foot and the other end in degrees. The cross-feed will move in or out as the carriage is moved longitudinally.

Knurling

Knurling is the process of embossing the surface of a workpiece with a knurling tool. Fig. 76-19. Knurling is used to provide a better grip as well as for decorative purposes.

Fig. 76-20 shows a set of standard knurls. They are held in a special holder, Fig. 76-21, in the tool post of the lathe. To knurl a workpiece, proceed as follows:

1. Select the knurling tool with the degree of coarseness wanted.

2. Mount the knurling tool in the tool post and adjust so that the line of thrust will pass through the center of the work and between the two knurls when forced

76-24. The different methods for gripping a workpiece in a chuck: (A) Outside grip with jaws reversed, (B) inside grip, (C) outside grip.

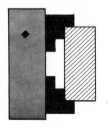

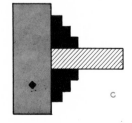

into the workpiece. Turn the tool very slightly toward the head-stock.

3. Place the lathe in back gear and adjust the longitudinal feed for a slow travel.

4. Check to see if the right pattern is being obtained. If the right pattern is not obtained, release the cross-feed pressure, move the tool a little to the left, and start over again.

5. When the correct pattern is obtained, start the lathe, turn the cross-feed, and apply a gener-ous amount of cutting fluid. NOTE: Clean the knurls frequently with a wire brush.

6. As the tool reaches the end of the part to be knurled, release the feed. If the knurl is not deep enough, reverse the direction of the feed and engage the power feed. Apply more pressure to the cross-feed and run the tool back.

Using Chucks

Workpieces that cannot be readily mounted between centers on a lathe can be held in a chuck and machined.

TYPES OF CHUCKS

There are two types of chucks in common use: the three-jaw universal chuck, Fig. 76-22, and the four-jaw independent chuck. Fig. 76-23.

The three-jaw universal chuck grips the workpiece from three sides and all the jaws are actuated by a single scroll mechanism. This type of chuck comes equipped with two sets of jaws, as the jaws are not reversible. The jaws are moved in and out by a single screw. Fig. 76-24.

The four-jaw independent chuck is equipped with four jaws

that are reversible; they are op-erated independently of each other. This type of chuck is more difficult to adjust.

Centering Work in an Independent Chuck

The following method can be used to center the workpiece in a four-jaw independent chuck:

1. Check to see that the threads on the lathe spindle are clean. Free the threads on the chuck from chips. Fig. 76-25.

2. Mount the chuck on the spindle and line up the jaws with the concentric circles on the face of the chuck so the opening fits the workpiece. Clamp the work-piece by tightening each jaw a little at a time.

3. Mount a toolholder as shown in Fig. 76-26 (A), and move it close to the workpiece. Rotate the chuck by hand and check the distance between the toolholder and the workpiece. Keep adjusting the jaws until the stock is centered.

Another method is shown in Fig. 76-26 (B). Hold a piece of chalk lightly against the work-piece. The length of line drawn on the workpiece that is out of true indicates the extent and the direction of adjustment to be made.

A *dial indicator* makes possible maximum accuracy in checking the on-center position of the workpiece. Any variation from center is visibly recorded.

Facing

1. In facing operations the cut can be made in either direc-tion. For large diameter stock it is usually made from the center to the outside. Fig. 76-27, page 350.

76-25.   Cleaning the threads in a chuck.

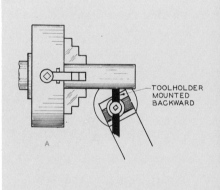

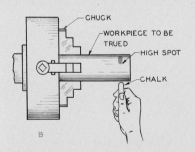

76-26.   (A) The alignment can be checked by the method shown in this illustration. (B) Aligning the workpiece in a four-jaw chuck by using a piece of chalk.

349

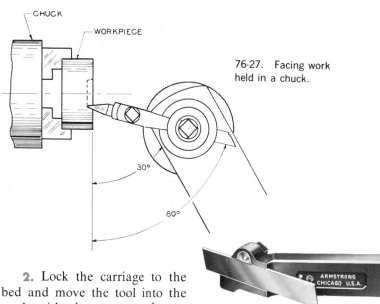

CHUCK

WORKPIECE

30°

80°

76-27. Facing work held in a chuck.

76-29. Drilling a workpiece on the lathe.

76-28. Parting tool and holder.

2. Lock the carriage to the bed and move the tool into the work with the compound rest. For work over 1½″ in diameter, use the power cross-feed.

Parting Operations

Parting refers to cutting off stock after it has been machined.

The parting tool, Fig. 76-28, must be ground with the correct clearance on the front, sides, and end. The blade is set at 90° to the workpiece. The cutting edge of the blade should be set on center when cutting stock 1″ or less in diameter, and ¹⁄₁₆″ above center for each additional inch in diameter. Use an ample supply of cutting fluid and set the spindle speed at about one third the speed used in turning. *No attempt* should be made to cut off work held between centers with this tool.

Drilling on the Lathe

Most drilling operations on the lathe are done with the workpiece mounted in a chuck. If the twist drill has a tapered shank, it can be mounted in the tailstock spindle. If a straight shank

76-30. Reaming on the lathe.

76-31. Boring operation being performed on the lathe.

drill is used, the drill can be held in a chuck mounted in the tailstock.

1. Center-drill the workpiece.

2. Replace the center drill with a twist drill of the required size.

3. Advance the drill slowly into the revolving workpiece by turning the handwheel of the tailstock spindle. Apply cutting fluid. Back the drill frequently to free from chips. Fig. 76-29.

Reaming

Reaming on the lathe can be done with either a hand or a machine reamer. A taper shank reamer can be inserted in the tailstock spindle and the workpiece reamed in this manner. Fig. 76-30. Adjust the lathe for a very slow speed. Advance the tailstock spindle in a slow, steady manner. Withdraw the reamer before stopping the lathe and *do not* turn the reamer backwards.

Boring

It is often necessary to enlarge or true a drilled or cored hole. Boring is also done to cut nonstandard holes—holes too large to be drilled and holes that must be very accurate in size. A boring bar with a tool ground like a left-cut turning tool is used for this operation. In stock where there is no existing hole, one is drilled large enough to admit the boring bar. The hole can then be bored to the required size. Fig. 76-31 shows a boring bar set-up.

How To Cut Sharp V Threads on the Lathe

The following procedure can be used to cut sharp V threads on the lathe:

1. Sharpen the tool to the proper angle for cutting this type of thread. Use a center gage for checking the angle. Fig. 76-32 (A).

2. Set the work up in much the same manner as for straight turning.

3. Make the proper gear and apron adjustments and pivot the compound rest 29° to the right.

4. Set the tool at a 90° angle to the centerline of the workpiece. Fig. 76-32 (B).

5. Fasten a thread cutting stop to the saddle dovetail. After the point of the tool is set so that it just touches the workpiece, the stop is locked to the saddle dovetail, with the adjusting screw just bearing on the stop.

6. After a cut has been made, move the tool back from the workpiece with the cross-slide screw.

7. Move the carriage back to the starting point for another cut and feed the tool into the workpiece with the cross-slide until the adjusting screw again bears on the stop.

8. Advance the compound rest about 0.002″ so the next cut can be taken.

9. Repeat this process with subsequent cuts of about 0.005″ until the last two passes are to be made. The final cuts should be about 0.002″ deep. Check the depth of the threads with a pitch gage. Fig. 76-33. Internal threading set-up is shown in Fig. 76-34.

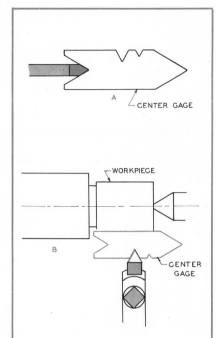

76-32. (A) Cutting tool ground and checked with a center gage for sharp V threads. (B) Using the center gage to position the threading tool.

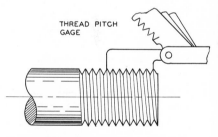

76-33. Checking the number of threads per inch with a screw-pitch gage.

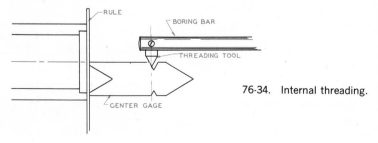

76-34. Internal threading.

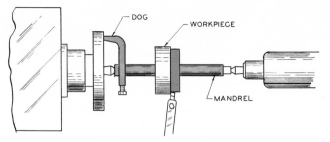

76-37. Turning a workpiece mounted on a tapered mandrel.

76-38. Large lathe with tracer control.

76-35. Cutting internal threads on the lathe with a tap.

76-39. Heavy duty type engine lathe for large turning operations.

Cutting Threads with Taps and Dies on the Lathe

External and internal threads can be cut on the lathe with a tap and die. Fig. 76-35 shows threading with a tap. The tailstock center aligns the tap with the drilled hole. It is threaded into the hole by hand.

An external thread can be obtained on the workpiece with a die and diestock. A drill pad is placed in the tailstock to hold the diestock flat until the thread is started. The pad is then removed and replaced with a dead center to support the center-drilled end of the stock. The compound rest is used to support the tap wrench and the diestock handles.

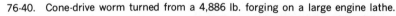

76-40. Cone-drive worm turned from a 4,886 lb. forging on a large engine lathe.

76-36. Solid mandrel.

Turning Work on a Mandrel

Sometimes it is necessary to machine the outside diameter of a workpiece that has a hole in its center, such as a bearing, pulley, or wheel. A mandrel—which is an accurately ground and centered shaft with a slight taper—is pressed into the hole with an arbor press. Fig. 76-36. It can then be set up between centers and turned. Fig. 76-37.

Industrial Lathes

There are many basic variations of the engine lathe used in industrial applications when the product requires several turning, facing, drilling, reaming, and threading operations.

● **Tracer lathes,** Fig. 76-38, are basically engine lathes modified with duplicating equipment to produce predetermined contours by following a template. Either flat or round templates can be used to guide the cutting tool, which is mounted on a slide, feeding at 45 or 90 degrees to the axis of workpiece rotation. Tracer lathes are intended for repetitive production.

● **Heavy duty** type engine lathes, such as the one shown in Fig. 76-39, are used to turn large products. Fig. 76-40. **Turret lathes,** Fig. 76-41, were developed for production work and designed for multiple tooling. They are distinguished by a turret of hexagonal shape mounted on a vertical axis in place of the tailstock of a standard engine lathe. Six types of tools can be mounted on the turret.

Multiple tooling is accomplished by mounting tools on both the front and rear of the carriage cross-slide.

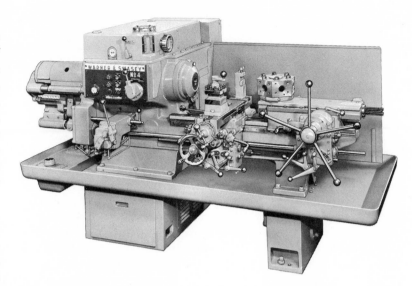

76-41. Turret lathe, horizontal type, for bar stock and chuck work. A six-position toolholder replaces the tailstock.

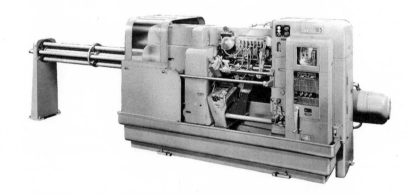

76-42. Five-spindle automatic bar machine for high production use.

● **Automatic screw machines,** either single or multiple-spindle, are fully automatic high production machines.

Multiple-spindle bar-feed machines represent an extremely fast method of producing parts from bar stock, actually machining 4, 5, 6, or more bars simultaneously. Fig. 76-42.

Check Your Knowledge

1. What is a discontinuous chip?

2. How is the size of a lathe designated?

3. What is the function of the quick-change gear box?

4. Give the reasons for grinding a lathe cutter bit to a certain form.

5. Describe the procedure for grinding a lathe cutting tool.

6. What is meant by the feed on a lathe?

7. Name standard methods of locating the center of a round piece of stock.

353

8. Describe three methods of drilling center holes.

9. Why should the workpiece be faced before it is finish-turned?

10. Describe three methods of checking the alignment of centers.

11. What is rough turning?

12. Name three types of chucks.

13. What is the difference between drilling and boring?

14. What precaution should be observed in reaming?

15. What is knurling?

16. In starting a knurl, what precautions should be observed?

17. What is a taper?

18. Explain the procedure for cutting a taper on the lathe.

19. Name three methods of cutting a taper.

20. How are short tapers turned?

21. Explain the difference between a right- and left-hand thread.

22. Why is the compound rest set at 29° for most thread cutting operations?

23. Describe how to cut internal threads.

24. How is a center gage used in thread cutting?

25. What are the advantages in using a thread stop?

Terms to Know and Spell

reciprocating	taper
rake	prismatic
longitudinal	fillet
adhere	tailstock
roughing	saddle
spindle	clutch
collet	mechanism
knurling	"stellite"
headstock	tungsten
compound	overhang
carriage	

77 ▷ The Shaper

The shaper is used less than in the past but still has its place. Many shops continue to do much work with it.

The shaper is used primarily for the production of flat surfaces which may be in a horizontal, vertical, or an angular plane. However, a skilled operator can manipulate a shaper to cut curved and irregular shapes, grooves, slots, and keyways. The cutting tool travels back and forth over the workpiece, Fig. 77-1, which is held stationary. The length of the cutting stroke can be 7" on small shapers to a maximum length of 36" on heavy duty machines. The main parts are shown in Fig. 77-2.

Shaper Work—Mounting Workpieces

The workpiece must be held securely and solidly while being machined. Grinding tools properly and setting them correctly mean nothing if the workpiece is not correctly supported and secured.

Fig. 77-3 shows a vise with the base graduated in degrees. The top of the vise can be rotated so that the jaws can be set at various angles. Fig. 77-4 shows a workpiece mounted in a vise with two parallels beneath the workpiece to raise it above the top of the vise jaws and provide a solid seat.

Hold-downs are used to grip the workpiece firmly against the parallels while it is being ma-

chined. They are either wedge-shaped or round. Fig. 77-4. The hold-down should always be placed between the movable jaw and the workpiece.

Work may also be clamped directly to the table as shown in Fig. 77-5, or fastened to an angle plate and bolted to the table. Fig. 77-6.

Shaper Toolholders

Most machining done on the shaper requires a toolholder. Several types are in common use: (1) regular lathe toolholder, Fig. 77-7, (2) swivel head, Fig. 77-8, and (3) the extension type, Fig. 77-9.

The lathe toolholder and tool make a satisfactory shaper combination, provided the tool bit is not given too much clearance. The swivel head (universal) toolholder permits the tool to be held securely in any one of five positions, Fig. 77-8. See page 356.

The extension toolholder is used for cutting internal shapes, Fig. 77-9. There are many different types of tool bits that can be

77-1. Tool is reciprocated and table moves horizontally.

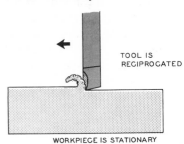

TOOL IS RECIPROCATED

WORKPIECE IS STATIONARY

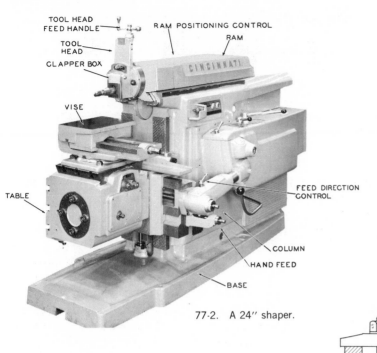

77-2. A 24" shaper.

77-5. The workpiece clamped directly to the table.

77-3. Shaper vise with swivel base.

77-6. Two methods of mounting work on the shaper for machining.

77-4. Hold-downs are used to hold work in the vise.

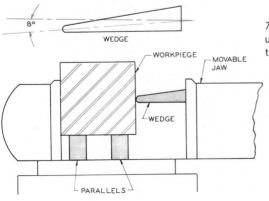

77-7. Straight shaper toolholder.

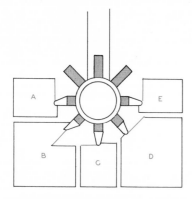

77-8. The tool can be held in different positions in the swivel head: (A) For vertical cuts, (B) for angular cuts, (C) for horizontal cuts, (D) for angular cuts, (E) for vertical cuts.

used to machine metal on a shaper. The shaper tool's rake, cutting angle, and clearances are governed by the material being cut, Fig. 77-10. The shape of the cut, the material being machined, and the degree of finish desired have a bearing on how the tool is to be ground. Fig. 77-11 shows some types of tools commonly used in shaper work.

Machining a Horizontal Surface

Since most shaper work consists of machining a flat surface, a single point tool is used. A good finish depends upon the following factors: (1) shape of the tool, (2) speed, (3) rate of feed, (4) depth

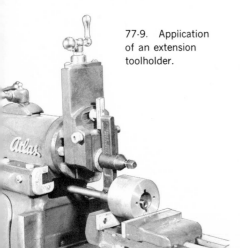

77-9. Application of an extension toolholder.

77-10. Various shaper tool angles.

of cut, (5) type of material being machined, and (6) condition of the machine. The following procedure should be followed:

1. Place thin strips of paper under each corner of the workpiece on the parallels. Clamp the workpiece with the long side parallel to the jaws. Fig. 77-12. Tighten the vise and tap the work lightly with a lead hammer to seat the workpiece on the parallels. Test the work, to see if it is seated properly, by pulling on the paper strips.

2. Set the tool head at right angles to the machine table. (Vertically.)

3. Run the tool slide up on the head so that it will not extend below the swivel block.

4. Mount the toolholder with a properly ground tool placed vertically in the tool post. If the cut is to be heavy, clamp the tool slightly away from the workpiece so that if the toolholder moves it will not dig into the work. Fig. 77-13.

5. Adjust the cross-rail on the column so that the surface to be machined is about 2″ below the ram. Do not attempt to raise or lower the cross-rail until its bolts have been loosened. Move the table up or down as required. Tighten all bolts.

6. Measure the length of the surface to be machined. Allow ¼″ clearance at the end of the stroke

and ½″ at the start of stroke, to permit the clapper box to drop back for the start of the next stroke. Fig. 77-14.

7. Adjust the length of stroke by placing the crank on the square end of the stroke adjusting shaft. Turn the crank until the required length is obtained.

8. Adjust the position of the stroke by moving the ram to the extreme forward position.

9. Loosen the clamping block on top of the ram until the cutting tool extends about ¼″ beyond the front edge of the surface to be machined. Turn the binding lever and lock the ram in position.

10. Move the ram to the extreme end of its return stroke, which should be about ½″ from the end of the work.

11. Adjust the speed by whatever means is employed on the shaper you are using. The speed needed is determined by the type of material being machined.

12. Adjust for the correct feed. A heavy feed is used for a roughing cut and a finer feed for a finishing cut.

13. Move the workpiece and table by means of the cross-feed screw to bring it into position with the cutting tool.

14. Move the ram so that the tool is over the workpiece. Lower the tool until it touches the work and adjust the micrometer collar at the zero graduation.

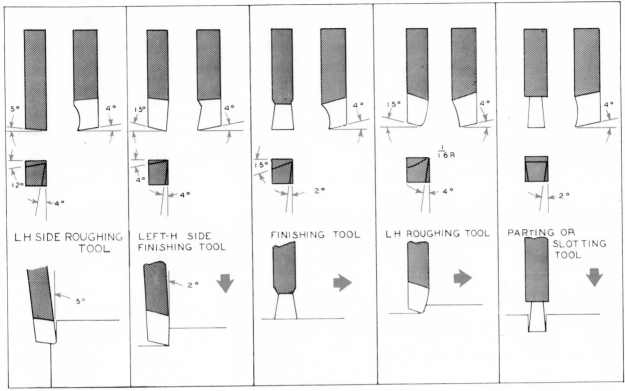

5°   4°   12°   4°   4°

15°   4°   15°   4°   4°

4°   2°

15°   4° $\frac{1}{16}$R   4°

4°   2°

5°   2°

L H SIDE ROUGHING TOOL

LEFT-H SIDE FINISHING TOOL

FINISHING TOOL

L H ROUGHING TOOL

PARTING OR SLOTTING TOOL

77-11.   Tool shapes for machining mild steel.

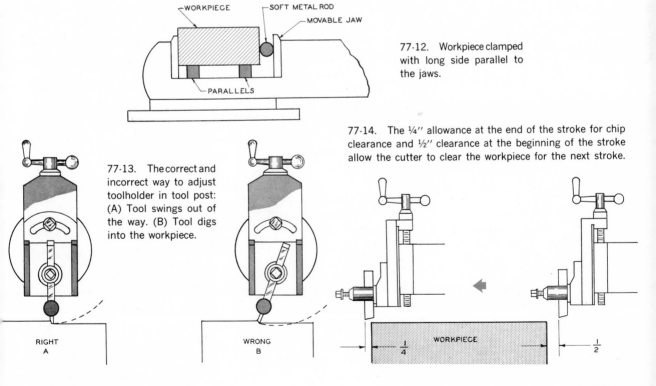

WORKPIECE — SOFT METAL ROD — MOVABLE JAW

PARALLELS

77-12.   Workpiece clamped with long side parallel to the jaws.

77-14.   The ¼″ allowance at the end of the stroke for chip clearance and ½″ clearance at the beginning of the stroke allow the cutter to clear the workpiece for the next stroke.

77-13.   The correct and incorrect way to adjust toolholder in tool post: (A) Tool swings out of the way. (B) Tool digs into the workpiece.

RIGHT
A

WRONG
B

WORKPIECE

$\frac{1}{4}$ $\frac{1}{2}$

77-15. Vertical surface has been machined. Note the clapper box has been turned away from the direction in which cut was made.

15. Lift the tool and move the work to the left of the tool. Set the tool to remove the required amount of metal.

16. Turn the shaper on and feed the tool by hand until the cut is just started and its depth can be determined.

17. Stop the shaper and check the cut.

18. Start the shaper, engage the automatic feed, and complete the cut.

19. Disengage the feed and bring the table back to the starting point. Allow between 0.010″ to 0.015″ for the finishing cut.

77-16. The toolholder is swiveled to take an angular cut.

20. Increase the speed if machining steel; use a fairly fine feed per stroke.

21. Engage the automatic feed and take the finishing cut.

Machining a Vertical Surface

1. Swivel the vise so that the jaws are at right angles to the stroke.

2. Lay out the workpiece and place it in the vise so that the end which is to be squared extends about ½″ beyond the right side of the vise. Tap the work with a lead hammer to seat it in the vise.

3. Turn the clapper box away from the direction in which the cut is to be made. Fig. 77-15. This makes it possible for the tool to clear the end of the work and prevents it from digging in on the return stroke.

4. Mount the cutting tool in the toolholder and fasten securely in the tool post.

5. Run the tool slide up far enough at the start of the cut so that when it is completed the slide will extend only slightly below the swivel block.

6. Move the table to the left until there is clearance between the tool and the workpiece.

7. Adjust the shaper for the proper speed and feed.

8. Turn on the shaper. Feed the tool down by hand until the cut is started. Stop the machine and measure the workpiece to make certain that the proper cut is being made.

9. Start the shaper again and feed the tool down 0.010″ at the end of each return stroke.

10. File burrs from the work. Check with a square to see if the end has been machined true.

77-17. Head revolved through the number of degrees necessary to produce the required angle.

77-18. Layout of contour.

77-19. Shaping the contour.

77-20. Machining a slot.

11. If a finish cut is to be taken, replace the cutter with a finish tool.

Making Angular Cuts

Angular cuts may be made either by (1) setting the cutting edge of the tool at an angle corresponding to the angle to be produced on the workpiece, (2) by setting the workpiece at an angle, and (3) by swiveling the toolhead to guide the tool in an angular direction. The third method is described below. Fig. 77-16.

1. Carefully lay out the cut to be made.

2. Clamp the workpiece in vise so that the layout line is visible above the jaws.

3. Revolve the head through the number of degrees necessary to produce the required angle. Fig. 77-17.

4. Offset the clapper box away from the surface to be cut.

5. Insert a properly ground tool for the job to be done.

6. Adjust the stroke for correct length and clearance.

7. Check the tool slide to make certain that the tool can be moved the full length of the cut.

8. Lower the tool slide until the point is about 0.002″ below the surface of the workpiece and move the work table until the

starting point is aligned with the cutting tool.

9. Adjust the shaper for correct cutting speed.

10. Feed the tool down just a few thousandths at a time for each cut.

11. Check the angular surface with a protractor.

How To Do Contour or Form Cutting

1. Lay out the contour or form. Fig. 77-18.

2. Set up the machine as in cutting a conventional horizontal surface.

3. A left-hand cutting tool is used to remove metal from the right side and a right-hand cutting tool to remove metal from the left side.

4. After the workpiece has been roughed to approximate shape, insert a round nose cutting tool in the toolholder.

5. Engage the automatic feed and machine to the contour line, Fig. 77-19, by feeding the tool up or down as it progresses across the workpiece.

Slots which may vary in shape, width, and depth can be cut in a shaper. Fig. 77-20.

Squaring a Piece of Stock

A definite sequence of operations must be followed to square a piece of stock.

1. Secure the workpiece in the vise and machine the face surface. Fig. 77-21, Step 1.

2. Place the workpiece in the vise with the face surfaces against the solid jaw and place a rod between the workpiece and adjustable jaw. Machine this surface. Fig. 77-21, Step 2.

3. Lay out the correct width. Place the face surface against the solid jaw, with the first edge down. Fig. 77-21, Step 3.

4. Place the workpiece with the face on two parallels or on the first surface and machine to correct thickness. Fig. 77-21, Step 4.

5. Machine the ends as explained under Machining a Vertical Surface.

Check Your Knowledge

1. What is the primary function of a shaper?

2. What types of cuts can be taken on the shaper?

3. Why is the shaper called a reciprocating tool?

4. What purpose do paper

77-21. The proper steps in squaring the workpiece on a shaper.

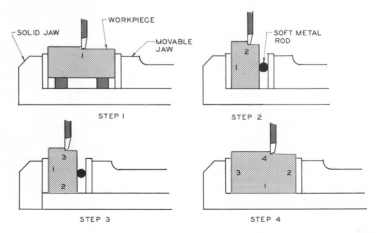

strips placed under the workpiece serve?

5. What are the two adjustments that can be made to the ram stroke?

6. Why must excessive overhang be avoided?

7. What purpose does a holddown serve when mounting the workpiece in the vise?

8. Explain how an angular surface is machined on a piece of stock.

9. Name standard methods of holding the workpiece for machining on the shaper.

10. A good finish depends upon what factors?

11. Why is a soft metal rod often placed between the work and the vise jaw?

12. Why is the toolholder clamped slightly away from the workpiece when taking a heavy cut?

78 ▷ The Milling Machine

In this unit only the basic uses of the milling machine will be discussed.

Milling machines are used in one form or another in nearly every metalworking operation from the toolroom to the high-speed production line. Whereas other machines are refinements of primitive processes using single point tools, milling machines use complex, multiple-tooth rotary cutters. Lathes, shapers, and drilling machines are designed for simple cutting motions. Milling machines make use of compound cutting motions.

Types of Milling Machines

Milling machines have been developed along several lines. As a result there are four major groups of standard machines and many special-purpose machines using the milling principle.

The four standard types consist of: (1) the knee-and-column machine, Fig. 78-1, (2) the vertical milling machine, Fig. 78-2, (3) fixed bed, Fig. 78-3, and (4) the planer type milling machine, Fig. 78-4.

The horizontal milling machine —either plain or universal—and the vertical machine (both being

---

Terms to Know and Spell

manipulate
keyway
grooves
graduated
rake
machined
parallel
tighten
swivel
clapper
adjusting
automatic
saddle
sequence
wedge
angular
protractor
contour

78-1. Horizontal milling machine.

78-2. Vertical milling machine.

78-4. Aluminum plate gets a smooth surface in a milling machine. The surface cutter already has finished the right side of the plate with a characteristic milling pattern. The left side is unmilled. Capable of handling plate up to 10 feet wide and 40 feet long, the mill shapes, routs, contours and surfaces metal. It produces aircraft plate, milled shapes, etc.

78-3. Fixed-bed type milling machine.

the knee-and-column type) are the two most commonly found in schools.

The spindle is fixed in the column, horizontally on the plain machine and vertically on the vertical machine. The table can be adjusted longitudinally, transversely, and vertically. The head on the vertical machines can be swiveled 180° in a horizontal plane and, on many machines, adjusted in a vertical plane to any angle. The vertical milling machine can do a wide variety of end or face milling operations, die-sinking, template milling, and boring.

Milling Cutters

Milling cutters usually take their names from the type of operation being performed. They may be listed in several general classifications. However, there are also different kinds of cutters designed for specific jobs. The seven general types are:

- Plain milling cutters
- Side milling cutters
- Angular milling cutters
- End mills
- Formed cutters
- Face milling cutters
- Special cutters

The cutters are made in many sizes and shapes. They are usually made of high speed steel or have carbide tips. See these tooth forms, Fig. 78-5. The nomenclature shown can also be applied to high-speed steel cutters.

78-5. Nomenclature of carbide-tipped, staggered-tooth side-milling cutter.

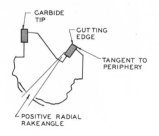

CARBIDE TIP
CUTTING EDGE
TANGENT TO PERIPHERY
POSITIVE RADIAL RAKE ANGLE

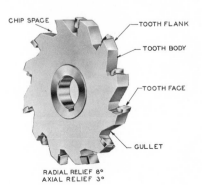

CHIP SPACE
TOOTH FLANK
TOOTH BODY
TOOTH FACE
GULLET
RADIAL RELIEF 8°
AXIAL RELIEF 3°

78-6. Plain milling cutter.

78-9. Metal slitting saw.

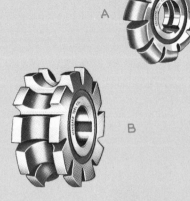

A

B

78-7. Side milling cutter.

78-10. Carbide-tipped angular cutters.

C

78-13. Formed cutters: (A) Convex, (B) concave, (C) corner-rounding.

78-11. Double-end, helical-flute end mill.

78-12. Shell mill.

78-8. Staggered-tooth milling cutter.

78-14. Carbide-tipped face milling cutter.

78-15. Carbide-tipped woodruff key-seat cutter.

PLAIN MILLING CUTTERS

Plain milling cutters are of plain cylindrical form with teeth only on the periphery or outer edge. They are used to produce a flat surface parallel to the axis of rotation, Fig. 78-6.

• **Side milling cutters** have teeth around the periphery and protruding at one or both sides, Fig. 78-7.

• The **staggered-tooth side milling cutter** is designed for heavy cutting and deep slotting, Fig. 78-8. Side milling cutters are also made with interlocking teeth so that two cutters may be placed side by side to mill slots of standard widths.

• Essentially, **slitting saws** are thin plain milling cutters. Fig. 78-9. They are made thinner at the center than at the outer edge for clearance purposes. They are used for sawing and cutting narrow grooves.

• **Angular milling cutters** are made as single or double-angle cutters, used to machine angles other than 90°, Fig. 78-10.

• **End mills** have cutting teeth on the ends as well as at the periphery. They may be solid, Fig. 78-11, and have straight or taper shanks. Some types have helical flutes. *Shell* end mills are made with a separate cutter and shank, Fig. 78-12.

• **Formed cutters** are made in various shapes to mill irregular surfaces, Fig. 78-13.

• **Face milling cutters**, a solid type, may have inserted teeth, Fig. 78-14. The teeth are cut on the face and periphery.

• **Key-seat cutters**, of course, are used for milling key seats, Fig. 78-15.

There are many types of special cutters made for specific jobs. These cutters are made up to meet the various manufacturers' specifications.

Workpiece Holding Devices

There are various methods of holding workpieces while doing milling operations. The work must be well supported so it will not shift.

• The **plain flanged vise**, Fig. 78-16, is made with flanges for clamping to the table. The **adjustable swivel vise** is fitted into a base which is graduated in degrees on the full circle. This permits the jaws to be set at any angle. Fig. 78-17.

• The **cam-lock vise**, Fig. 78-18, is built to hold pieces for machining duplicate parts for production work. The jaws can be quickly opened and closed.

78-16.   Plain flanged vise.

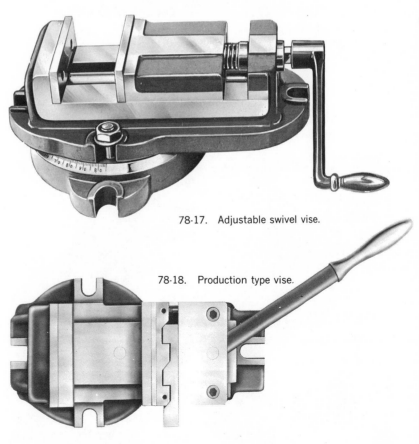

78-17.   Adjustable swivel vise.

78-18.   Production type vise.

78-19. Vertical mill with dividing head mounted on table. Spindle of head in vertical position.

78-20. Dividing head used to cut a spur gear.

● The **dividing head**, Fig. 78-19, or **indexing head**, is used to hold the workpiece and divide work into equally spaced sections such as teeth on reamers and gears of various types. Fig. 78-20.

The **rotary attachment** is used for circular milling of recesses, T-slots, and semi-circular pockets. It is generally fitted with an indexing unit. Fig. 78-21.

● A **universal chuck** is generally fitted to the dividing head spindle for holding round workpieces as shown in Fig. 78-22.

Cutting Speeds and Feeds

● The best cutting speed for a workpiece depends upon a number of factors. These are:
● Material used in the cutting tool.
● Kind of metal to be milled.
● The feed.
● Depth of cut.
● Condition of machine.

Table 78-A lists the speeds in surface feet per minute for various materials.

SPEEDS
SURFACE FEET PER MINUTE*

Material	H.S.S. Cutter S.F.M. Range	Carbide Cutter S.F.M. Range
Aluminum	1,000-550	4,000-2,700
Brass and bronze	650-250	2,600- 100
Low carbon steel	325-100	1,300- 400
Free cutting steel	250-150	1,000- 600
Alloy steel	175-70	700- 280
Cast iron	100-60	400- 240

*Based on recommendations of the Brown & Sharpe Mfg. Co.

Table 78-A.

The usual procedure is to start at the middle of the range listed and increase or reduce speeds to get proper character of cut and chip. Reduce speeds for hard

78-21. Precision rotary table with indexing plate.

Table 78-B. **FEEDS***

Type of Cut	Trial Feed per Tooth-Inches	
Face milling	.008	*For end mills smaller
Straddle milling	.008	than ½″ dia., feeds per
Slot milling	.008	tooth must be much lower
Slab milling	.007	than figure given.
End milling	*.004	
Sawing	.003	

Based on recommendations of Brown & Sharpe Mfg. Co.

materials, abrasive materials, deep cuts, and high alloy content.

Increase speeds for soft materials, better finishes, light cuts, frail workpieces and setups, and fine pitch thread milling.

Cutting speed is expressed in terms of surface feet per minute (sfm), using a point on the circumference of the milling cutter. The speed at which the point on the circumference is traveling is directly dependent, of course, upon the rpm of the cutter. The cutting speed is found by multiplying rpm × 3.1416 × D and then dividing by 12.

$$CS \text{ or } SFM = \frac{rpm \times 3.1416 \times D}{12}$$

The following formula can be used to determine the rpm of cutter when the cutting speed is known.

$$RPM = \frac{CS \times 4}{\text{Dia. of cutter in inches}}$$

Feeds

The feed on a milling machine is the rate that the workpiece advances with each succeeding tooth of the cutter. It is really the most important single factor in determining how fast metal can be machined from the workpiece. Table 78-B gives the approximate feeds for different types of milling.

Plain or Slab Milling

One of the simplest operations that is performed on the milling machine is plain or slab milling. It consists of milling a broad surface by means of a plain or helical cutter, Fig. 78-23, whose length is greater than its diameter. The following procedure can be used:

1. Clean the surface of the table and mount the vise.

2. Check the solid jaw of the vise. Fig. 78-24. The vise jaws should be either at right angle to the face of the column or exactly

78-23. Slab milling cutter.

78-24. Two methods for squaring a milling machine vise: (A) Squaring solid vise jaw with column by using a solid square, (B) arbor being used to square vise.

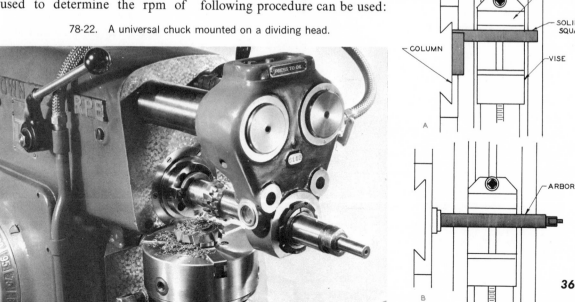

78-22. A universal chuck mounted on a dividing head.

365

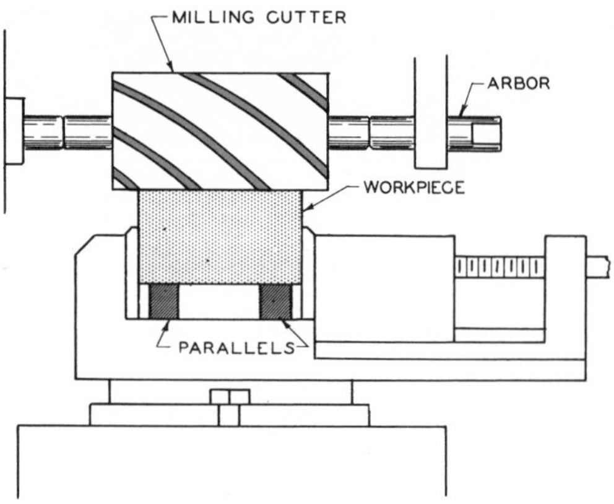

78-25. Vise set at right angles to column.

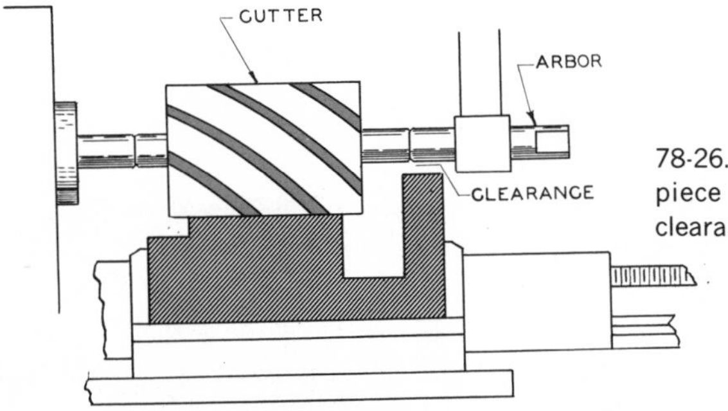

78-26. Set up the workpiece so that adequate clearance is provided.

CONVENTIONAL MILLING   CLIMB MILLING

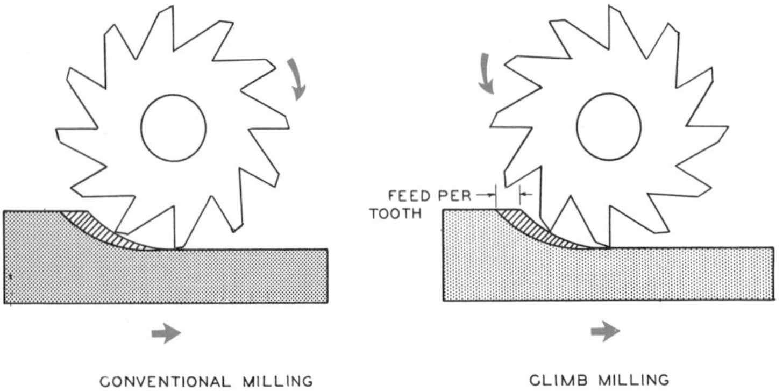

78-27. Two methods of milling.

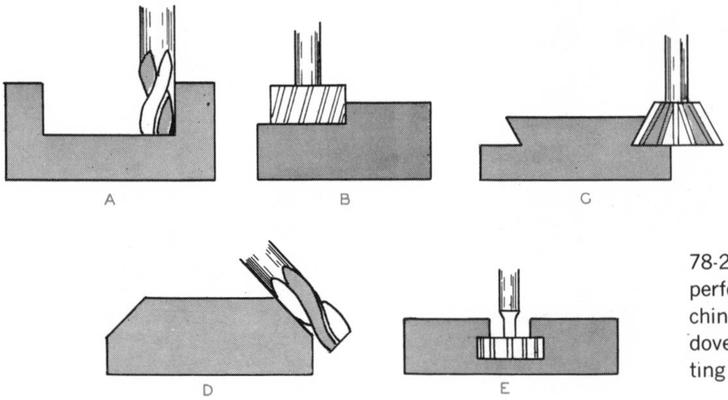

78-28. Typical operations that can be performed on the vertical milling machine: (A) Shaping, (B) surfacing, (C) dovetailing, (D) angular milling, (E) cutting T slots.

parallel to it. Fig. 78-25. Bolt the vise to the table.

3. Place parallels in the vise with paper strips on them.

Mount the workpiece on the parallels and tighten the jaws. Tap the workpiece with a lead hammer to seat it. Pull on the paper strips to check further.

4. Mount the arbor in the spindle and draw it in tightly with the draw-in bar.

5. Select the proper size cutter, using the smallest diameter possible but large enough to provide adequate clearance. Fig. 78-26.

6. Place the cutter on the arbor and key it to the arbor.

7. Swing the overarm in place and lock it. Tighten the arbor nut.

8. Adjust the correct speed and feed. The feed should be opposite to the direction of cutter rotation which is known as conventional milling. Fig. 78-27. NOTE: Climb milling should not be attempted by beginners.

9. Position the workpiece under the rotating cutter until it just touches the surface. Set the micrometer collar to 0. Back the workpiece away from the cutter and raise the table for the depth of cut desired for roughing out.

10. Tighten all locks and turn on the coolant and power feeds. *Do not* stop the feed during the machining operation. A slight depression will be made in the work surface if the feed is stopped.

11. After the first cut is complete, stop the machine. If a second cut is necessary, move the

78-29. One of the many operations that can be performed on the vertical mill.

workpiece to the starting position and raise the table for the next cut. *Never* feed the workpiece back under the rotating cutter.

12. Repeat the above operations until the required dimensions are obtained.

The Vertical Milling Machine

The vertical milling machine is a useful piece of equipment in the school. A great variety of operations can be performed. Fig. 78-28.

MACHINING A FLAT SURFACE ON A VERTICAL MILL

1. Select an end mill of the proper size.

2. Mount the milling cutter in the spindle and check to see that the spindle is at right angles to the table.

78-30. Machining an angle.

3. Set the workpiece in the vise and lock in place.

4. Adjust the machine for the correct speed and feed.

5. Check the length of cut to be taken; adjust the trip dogs.

6. Move the workpiece under the cutter; start the machine.

7. Raise the knee until the cutter touches the workpiece.

8. Set the micrometer dial to 0 on the index line.

9. Move the table so that the workpiece clears the cutter; raise the knee to the required height.

10. Move the table by hand until the cut is started; then turn on the power feed.

11. After the cut has been taken, measure the workpiece.

12. Take a second cut if necessary.

BORING

Boring operations on the vertical mill require a special chuck that permits the tool to be moved eccentrically (off center) for making the correct size hole. The toolholder is arranged so that the tool may be moved while held in the sliding jaw with a set screw.

The workpiece should be supported on parallels to avoid boring into the table. Workpieces are prepared for boring by: (1) laying out the location of the holes and test boring or (2) by using toolmaker's buttons. Fig. 78-29 shows one of the many operations that can be performed on the vertical milling machine.

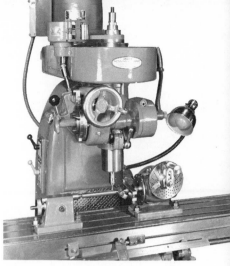

78-31. A slot being cut on a vertical mill.

Machining an Angle on a Surface with an End Mill

1. Place layout lines on the workpiece to locate a taper, chamfer, or bevel.

2. Mount the workpiece in the vise and check the angle with a protractor or surface gage.

3. Insert the proper cutter in the spindle. Some work will require head to be tilted.

4. Proceed as in machining a flat surface. Fig. 78-30.

A slot or keyway can be milled on the vertical milling machine, Fig. 78-31. A two-flute end mill, Fig. 78-32, is used when a blind keyway must be cut; otherwise, a four-flute end mill is used. Fig. 78-33.

78-32. Two-flute end mill.

78-33. Four-flute end mill.

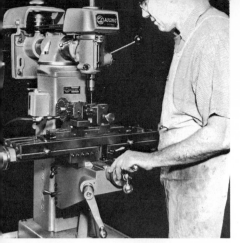

78-34. Drilling can be done on the vertical mill.

Drilling, Fig. 78-34, is often done on the vertical mill. After the first hole has been located by using a "wiggler," Fig. 78-35, and drilled, it is possible to locate the remaining holes by using the micrometer feed dials on the table movement screws.

Check Your Knowledge

1. What are the two basic types of milling machines?

2. Name four standard variations of milling machines.

3. Explain the difference between a plain milling cutter and a side milling cutter.

4. What are the advantages of a carbide-tipped cutter over a high-speed steel cutter?

5. Name some of the operations that can be performed with an end mill.

6. What is the difference between a plain flanged vise and a swivel base vise?

7. Explain some of the uses of a rotary attachment.

8. What factors must be considered when determining the best cutting speed on a milling machine?

9. How does the condition of the machine affect the cutting speed?

10. Define feed in milling.

11. What is the effect of cutting speeds that are too high?

12. Name some of the operations that can be performed on the vertical milling machine.

13. Explain the difference between climb milling and conventional milling.

14. Why is a vertical mill more versatile than a horizontal milling machine?

15. How is boring done on the vertical mill?

Terms to Know and Spell

universal	*periphery*	*dividing*
column	*axial*	*helical*
horizontally	*carbide*	*vertical*
longitudinally	*staggered*	*adapter*
radial	*interlocking*	*angular*
tangent	*specifications*	*overarm*

78-35. Mill wiggler.

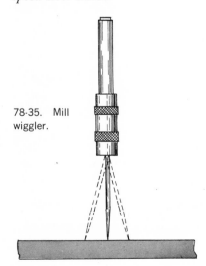

79 ▷ Drilling Machines and Drills

Drilling machines are used mainly for the purpose of removing metal by drilling holes. Many operations can be performed, such as reaming, countersinking, boring, spotfacing, honing, tapping, and lapping.

Drilling machines are made in many types and sizes. The bench drill press, Fig. 79-1, and the floor type, Fig. 79-2 are the most common for schools. The size of a drill press is determined by the largest diameter of a circular piece that can be drilled *on center.*

Fig. 79-3. Because the floor type drill press does not require a bench, it can be placed at convenient locations.

The radial drilling machine, Fig. 79-4, has the capability of handling large workpieces. The head is mounted on a radial arm that may be swung about a column or raised and lowered. The length of which varies from 3′ to 12′ or more.

Standard gang drilling machines are composed of two or more standard columns, heads,

79-1. Bench type drilling machine.

79-2. Floor model drilling machine.

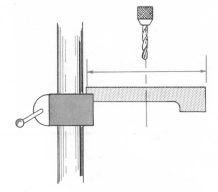

79-3. The size of a drilling machine can be determined by the largest diameter workpiece that can be drilled on center.

and spindles, mounted on a common base. Fig. 79-5. The most common application of this type of machine is to eliminate the changing of tools for different operations. NOTE: Turret drilling machines are rapidly replacing gang drillers.

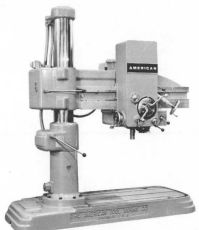

79-4. Radial drilling machine.

79-5. Gang drilling machine.

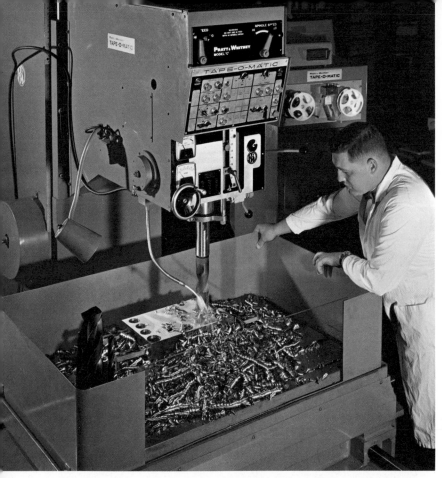

79-6. Numerically controlled drilling machine.

Fig. 79-6 is an example of a numerically controlled drilling machine. This machine has a 5 hp motor with a 45″ x 29″ table, 20″ x 15″ table travel, and a #4 Morse spindle. Milling and boring operations can also be performed. The machine is equipped with six-position depth control and manual data input.

Twist Drills

The tool most commonly used in a drilling machine is the twist drill. Twist drills come with shanks either straight, Fig. 79-7, or tapered, Fig. 79-8. *Straight* shank drills are held in a chuck. The *taper* shank drill fits a tapered hole in the spindle, with the tang of the drill engaging a slot. A *drill drift,* Fig. 79-9, is used to remove the drill from the spindle.

DRILL PARTS

A twist drill is divided into three principal parts: (1) the point, (2) the body, and (3) the shank. These have several features. Fig. 79-10 (A and B).

79-7. Straight shank drill.

79-8. Taper shank drill.

79-9. Automatic drill drift.

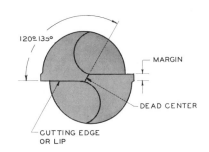

79-10. (A) Parts of a twist drill.

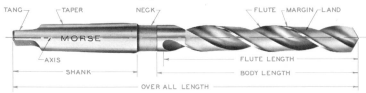

79-10. (B) Section of a drill cut from near the point.

WEB IS THICKER TOWARDS SHANK

79-11. Drill gage for numbered drills, 1 to 60.

DRILL SIZES

80	0.0135	49*	0.073	20	0.161	I	0.272
79	0.0145	48	0.076	19	0.166	J	0.277
1/64	0.0156	5/64	0.0781	18	0.1695	9/32	0.2813
78	0.016	47	0.0785	11/64	0.1719	K	0.281
77	0.018	46	0.081	17	0.173	L	0.290
76	0.02	45	0.082	16	0.177	M	0.295
75	0.021	44	0.086	15	0.18	19/64	0.2969
74	0.0225	43	0.089	14	0.182	N	0.302
73	0.024	42	0.0935	13	0.185	5/16	0.3125
72	0.025	3/32	0.0938	3/16	0.1875	O	0.316
71	0.026	41	0.096	12	0.189	P	0.323
70	0.028	40	0.098	11	0.191	21/64	0.328
69	0.0292	39	0.0995	10	0.1935	Q	0.332
68	0.031	38	0.1015	9	0.196	R	0.339
1/32	0.0313	37	0.104	8	0.199	11/32	0.34375
67	0.032	36	0.1065	7	0.201	S	0.348
66	0.033	7/64	0.1094	13/64	0.203	T	0.358
65	0.035	35	0.11	6	0.204	23/64	0.359
64	0.036	34	0.111	5	0.2055	U	0.368
63	0.037	33	0.113	4	0.209	3/8	0.375
62	0.038	32	0.116	3	0.213	V	0.377
61	0.039	31	0.12	7/32	0.21875	W	0.386
60	0.04	1/8	0.125	2	0.221	25/64	0.3906
59	0.041	30	0.1285	1	0.228	X	0.397
58	0.042	29	0.136	A	0.234	Y	0.404
57	0.043	9/64	0.1406	15/64	0.2344	13/32	0.4063
56	0.0465	28	0.1405	B	0.238	Z	0.413
3/64	0.0469	27	0.144	C	0.242		
55	0.052	26	0.147	D	0.246		
54	0.055	25	0.1495	1/4	0.250		
53	0.0595	24	0.152	E	0.250		
1/16	0.0625	23	0.154	F	0.257		
52	0.0635	5/32	0.15625	G	0.261		
51	0.067	22	0.157	7/64	0.2656		
50	0.07	21	0.159	H	0.266		

Table 79-A.

The general-purpose drill is made with two spiral grooves. Other types have three or four grooves or flutes running around the body to permit the chips to escape from the hole and to permit the lubricant to flow down to the cutting edge.

Drills are made of either carbon or high speed steel (HSS). The high speed steel drills have a longer life and, of course, can be operated at a higher speed.

DRILL SIZES

Twist drills are made in many different sizes, designated under four types as follows:

• Wire-gage sizes: (number drills) #80 the smallest, to #1, the largest (0.0135 to 0.228). Table 79-A.

• Alphabetical: letter A to letter Z (0.234 to 0.413).

• Fractional: 1/64″ to 4″ and over, by 64ths.

• Millimeter: from .5 to 10.0 mm. by 1 mm., and larger than 10.0 by .5 mm.

The drill size is usually stamped on the shank. All number, letter, and some fractional drills up to ½″ in diameter are made with straight shanks. Drill gages as shown in Fig. 79-11 can be used to check the drill size. There is a drill gage for each size classification. Table 79-A shows drill sizes.

79-12. Three-flute drill.

79-13. Drill chuck.

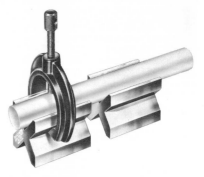

79-18. Round work can be held in V blocks for drilling.

79-16. This drill press vise can be tilted from 0° to 90°.

79-14. (A) Drill sleeve.

79-14. (B) Drill socket.

79-17. Wedge vise for production work.

Three- and four-flute drills enlarge or rough-ream holes which have been previously drilled, punched, or cored. Fig. 79-12. *Oil hole* drills are used on turret lathes and similar equipment.

DRILL HOLDING DEVICES

Straight shank drills must be held in a drill chuck, Fig. 79-13. The chuck has three jaws that are tightened against the drill with a chuck key. Drill chucks can be fitted with a taper shank or directly on the end of the drill press spindle.

DRILL SOCKETS AND SLEEVES

A drill with a taper shank smaller than the spindle taper may be fitted with a sleeve. Fig. 79-14 (A). A drill socket is used for drills with shanks larger than the opening in the spindle. The taper opening in the socket is larger than the taper on the socket shank. Fig. 79-14 (B).

WORKPIECE HOLDING DEVICES

In drilling any material on a drilling machine, the workpiece has to be properly secured. Several types of holding devices may be used: (1) drilling machine vises, (2) V blocks, (3) step blocks, (4) clamps, (5) angle plates, (6) jack screws, and jigs and fixtures. Figs. 79-15, 79-16 and 79-17 show typical drill press vises. V blocks are used to hold round work-

79-15. Drill press vise.

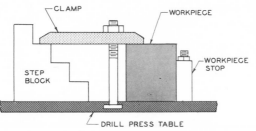

79-19. Workpiece being held by clamp strap and step block.

79-24. Holding the workpiece in two toolmaker's vises while drilling.

79-20. One type of clamp used to hold work on the table.

pieces. A U-shaped clamp helps hold the work in place. Fig. 79-18. The workpiece can be placed upon the table and supported against a stop at one end and a step block at the other. Fig. 79-19. Clamps, straps, and bolts are sometimes used to hold work directly on the table. It is important that the bolts should be as close to the work as possible. Figs. 79-20, 79-21 and 79-22 show an assortment of various clamps. Drill jigs are used in mass production work. Figs. 79-23 (A) and 79-23 (B). They can be designed so that several holes of different sizes are drilled rapidly in the same jig.

The size and shape of the workpiece govern to a large extent the method of clamping the work. It is necessary to support the work so that it will not bend when pressure is applied when drilling. Be sure and protect the table from being drilled. Figs. 79-24, 79-25 and 79-26 illustrate some of the methods of holding the work while being drilled.

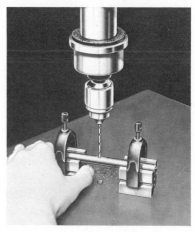

79-25. Holding the workpiece in a V block while drilling.

79-26. Straight shank drill held in a drill chuck. The rotary device is clamped to the table.

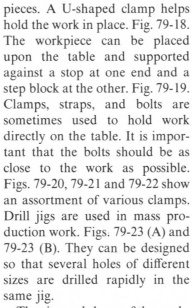

79-21. C-clamp.

79-22. Drill press clamp. It can be fastened to the drill press column to hold work to the table.

79-23. (A) Drill jig to hold parts while being drilled. (B) Drill jig or fixture. Used to hold work while drilling.

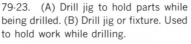

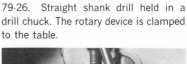

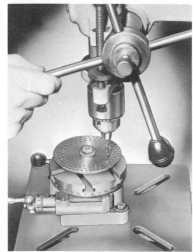

SPEEDS FOR HIGH SPEED DRILLS*

(Both rpm and sfm should be reduced 50 percent for carbon steel drills)

Drill dia.	Aluminum, brass, bronze 300 ft. per min.	Cast iron, hard steel 70 ft. per min.	Mild steel 100 ft. per min.	Mal. iron 90 ft. per min.	Tool steel 50 ft. per min.	Feed per rev. (general)
⅛	9170 rpm	2139 rpm	3057 rpm	2745 rpm	1528 rpm	.002
¼	4585	1070	1528	1375	764	.004
⅜	3056	713	1019	915	510	.006
½	2287	535	764	688	382	.007
1	1143	267	382	349	191	.012

Based upon recommendations of the Cleveland Twist Drill Co.

Table 79-B.

FEEDS FOR DIFFERENT SIZE DRILLS

Dia. of drill in inches	Feed in inches per revolution
under ⅛″	.001-.002
⅛″ to ¼″	.002-.004
¼″ to ½″	.004-.007
½″ to 1″	.007-.015
1″ and over	.015-.025

Table 79-C.

Table 79-C can be used in general practice.

SPEEDS AND FEEDS

The speed of a drill is usually measured in terms of the rate at which the outside or periphery of the drill moves in relation to the workpiece being drilled. This is expressed as surface feet per minute (sfm).

Because so many variables affect the results, no hard and fast rule for determining the exact cutting speed can be given. Several factors affect the choice of the best cutting speed: (1) kind of drill being used, (2) composition and hardness of material, (3) amount of feed, (4) condition of the machine, and (5) use of coolant.

Table 79-B shows the suggested drilling speeds for different materials.

To find the rpm at which to run the drilling machine for a given cutting speed, find the circumference of the drill in inches (circumference = dia. × 3.1416). Then the cutting speed in feet per minute must be changed into inches per minute by multiplying by 12. The rpm would then be the cutting speed in inches per minute divided by the circumference of the drill in inches.

The formula would be:

$$rpm = \frac{cutting\ speed \times 12}{dia. \times 3.1416}$$

FEED

Drilling feed is the distance that the drill advances into the workpiece for each revolution. The distance varies with each size drill, the material being drilled, and the rpm. The feeds shown in

79-27. Drill grinder.

Sharpening a Twist Drill

Many difficulties encountered in drilling arise from improper grinding of either the point or lip clearance.

Drills can be sharpened either by hand on an off-hand grinder, or on a drill grinder. Fig. 79-27.

Three separate, distinct steps are followed in reconditioning a drill: (1) removal of worn section, (2) web thinning, and (3) regrinding the point.

GRINDING A DRILL BY HAND

1. Dress and true up the grinding wheel.

2. Check the drill to see if it is dull or the margins located near the point are worn. If the drill is in this condition, it will be necessary to grind off the entire point and regrind a new one.

3. Grasp the drill near the point, in your right hand, with the left hand holding the shank. Fig. 79-28.

4. Hold the lip of the drill at an angle of 59° to the grinding wheel.

5. Move the hand, holding the shank downward. Do not twist the drill. As your hand goes down it will follow a natural arc. This motion will grind the correct curve on the surface back of the cutting

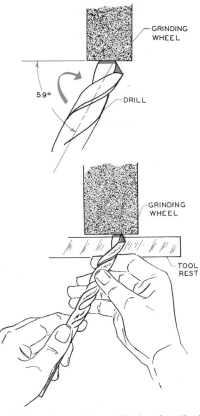

79-28. Sharpening a drill—hand method.

79-29. Checking the angle of the drill point with a drill grinding gage.

edge. Keep the end of the shank below the level of the cutting lip. Avoid grinding a negative angle, as the drill will not cut but will rub back of the cutting edge. The clearance behind the cutting edge should be about 12°.

6. Grind the other lip in the same manner.

7. Check the drill point with a drill-grinding gage to make sure that the cutting edges are the same length and at the same angle with the axis—59°. Fig. 79-29.

In Fig. 79-30 is shown a drill with the point having lips of equal length, but which make unequal angles with the axis of the drill. It will cause an oversize hole.

79-30. INCORRECT point. Lips equal length but have unequal angles.

79-31. INCORRECT. Angles are not equal and lengths are different, making the hole larger than the drill.

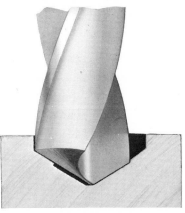

Much the same result is obtained if the angles are equal but the lips are of unequal length. A combination of both unequal lengths and angles is shown in Fig. 79-31.

Fig. 79-32 shows the results of giving a drill too much lip clearance. The edges of the cutting lips have broken down because of insufficient support.

Fig. 79-33 illustrates insufficient lip clearance. As a result there ceased to be any cutting edges whatsoever, and, as the feed-pressure was applied, the drill could not enter the workpiece. As a result the drill will split up the center.

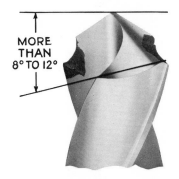

79-32. INCORRECT. Too much lip clearance. Edges have broken down due to insufficient support.

79-33. Drill with insufficient lip clearance. The drill has split up the center. As feed pressure was applied, the drill could not enter the workpiece.

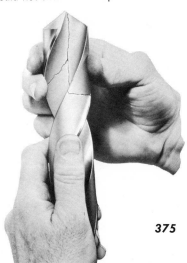

375

79-34. INCORRECT. Lips of unequal length and unequal angles.

Be sure that the lips are ground with equal angles and equal lengths or a hole will be obtained as shown in Fig. 79-34.

Layout for Drilling

The first operation in drilling is laying out the workpiece. This requires three major steps: (1) blueprint interpretation, (2) preparation of the workpiece, and (3) knowledge and use of proper layout and measuring tools.

1. Coat workpiece with layout dye.

2. Draw two lines at right angles in the proper location.

3. Use prick and center punch to make indentation at the intersection of two lines. Fig. 79-35 (A).

4. With a divider, scribe a circle the same size as the hole to be drilled. Fig. 79-35 (B). Scribe a smaller circle inside the first one. This is called the "proof" circle. This circle helps to center the drill exactly as it begins the cut.

Operations on the Drilling Machine

DRILLING

1. Select the proper drill.

2. If a straight shank drill is used, mount the drill in a drill chuck. If a taper shank drill is used, insert it directly in the spindle, or in a drill sleeve and then in the spindle.

3. Turn on the power to see if the drill is running straight.

4. Adjust the machine for the correct speed.

5. Mount the workpiece in a vise, or clamp to the table.

6. Move the point of the drill with the hand-feed lever and line it up with the punch mark on the workpiece. Check to see that the depth of cut will be correct.

7. Turn on the power and feed the drill into the workpiece to enlarge the punch mark. Apply cutting fluid and begin drilling.

8. Check to see if the circle cut by the drill is true with the proof circle. If not, cut a groove in the side toward which the drill should be moved. Fig. 79-36. Use a round nose chisel. The groove should be cut directly opposite the point where the drill touches the layout circle and should extend to the circle in depth.

9. Apply even pressure. Too much pressure will cause the smaller size drill to break.

10. Raise the drill occasionally to clear the hole of chips. Apply plenty of cutting fluid. As the drill begins to break through the lower side of the workpiece, release the pressure slightly to prevent the drill from catching.

11. Raise the drill from the work and turn off the power.

12. In drilling large holes a pilot or lead hole should be

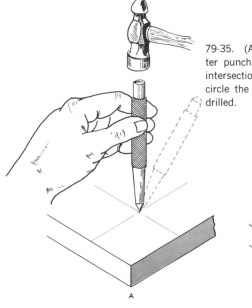

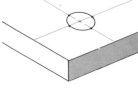

79-35. (A) Using a prick punch and center punch to make indentation at the intersection of two lines. (B) Scribe the circle the same size as the hole to be drilled.

A

B

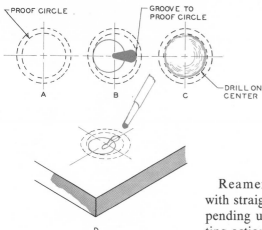

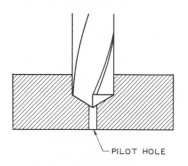

79-36. Chipping a groove to draw the drill back when it has started inaccurately.

drilled equal to or slightly larger than the web of the drill. Fig. 79-37.

Round workpieces can be clamped for drilling in V blocks.

REAMING

Reaming is the process of sizing an existing hole to a given diameter. Correct reaming assures the machinist of a straighter, smoother, and more accurate hole.

79-37. The pilot or lead hole is drilled first for large holes.

79-38. Jobbers' reamer with taper shank.

79-39. Taper reamer with taper shank.

Reamers are manufactured with straight or taper shanks, depending upon their size and cutting action.

● *Jobbers' reamers,* Fig. 79-38, have a tapered shank and are designed for machine reaming.

● *Taper reamers* are used for reaming tapered holes for taper pins, etc. Fig. 79-39.

● The *chucking reamer,* Figs. 79-40 (A) and 79-40 (B) is made with straight and tapered shanks. It is similar to a jobbers' reamer, except that the flutes are shorter and deeper.

● The *rose chucking reamer* is designed to cut on its end. The flutes provide chip clearance and are ground to serve as guides. Fig. 79-40 (C).

● *Expansion chucking reamers,* Fig. 79-40 (D), are made with either a straight or taper shank. Note the slots in the body which permit the reamer to expand when the adjusting screw on the end is tightened.

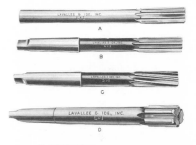

79-40. (A) Straight shank chucking reamer. (B) Tapered shank chucking reamer. (C) Rose chucking reamer. (D) Expansion chucking reamer.

Using a Machine Reamer

1. Mount the reamer in the drilling machine.

2. Drill the hole so that the reamer will cut instead of burnishing.

For a 1¼" reamed hole, allow 0.010". ¼" to ½" diameter allow 0.015". ½" to 1" diameter allow 0.020". 1" to 1½" allow 0.025".

3. Turn on the power. NOTE: Run the drilling machine at a reduced speed.

4. Feed slowly into the hole, applying cutting oil generously.

5. Remove the reamer from the hole before shutting off the power.

Countersinking

Countersinking is the machining of metal at the end of a hole to a cone shape for the seating of a flathead screw.

377

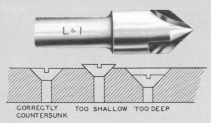

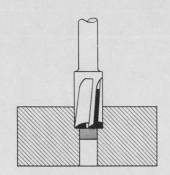

79-41. Countersink tool and correctly and incorrectly countersunk holes.

79-42. Counterboring.

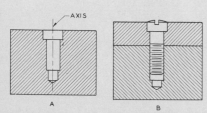

79-43. (A) Counterbored hole. (B) Fillister head cap screw set flush with hole.

79-44. Spotfacing.

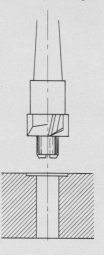

The tool used for this operation is a countersink tool, Fig. 79-41, and is available with cutting edges of 60°, 82°, 90°, 100°, 110°, and 120° included angles. Fig. 79-41 shows correctly and incorrectly countersunk holes.

Counterboring

The counterbore tool, Fig. 79-42, is used to enlarge a hole to a given depth, as for fillister head machine screws. Figs. 79-43 (A) and 79-43 (B). The tool has a guide, called a pilot, which positions the counterbore in the hole.

Spotfacing

Spotfacing is the process of smoothing off and squaring the surface of the workpiece around a hole to seat a washer, Fig. 79-44, or to seat a nut or a bolt.

Spot Finish

The spot finish, sometimes called an engine finish, is an operation that can easily be done on the drill press. A rod of hard rubber or a hardwood dowel is used. Fig. 79-45.

1. Mix abrasive grains of emery, aluminum oxide, or silicon carbide, of about 150 grit, with oil.

2. Spread evenly over the surface of the metal.

3. Turn on the power—about 1,200 rpm—and bring the rod in contact with the work. The rod tip grinds abrasive grains into the work, producing a circular spot. Repeat the operation overlapping the rings a trifle, until the whole surface is covered.

Check Your Knowledge

1. How is the size of a drill press determined?

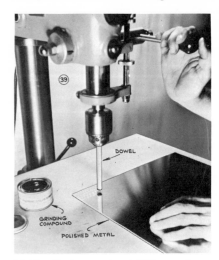

79-45. Spot or engine finishing on the drill press.

2. What is a gang drilling machine?

3. What are the three principal parts of a twist drill?

4. What advantages do high-speed drills have over carbon steel drills?

5. How are the sizes of drills designated?

6. Why is it important to hold the work securely while drilling?

7. Explain the difference between a drill socket and a drill sleeve.

8. Name several types of holding devices used on the drill press.

9. What factors govern the method of clamping the work?

10. Why are speed and feed important factors in drilling?

11. What determines the speed at which a drill should run?

12. What causes a large percentage of difficulties encountered in drilling?

13. What three main steps should be followed in reconditioning a drill?

14. Why must a drill have proper lip clearance?

15. What is the result if the

angles of a drill are equal but the lips are of unequal length?

16. *What is the result of insufficient lip clearance?*

17. *Describe the process of laying out a hole for drilling.*

18. *What is the function of a reamer?*

19. *What is the difference between countersinking, counterboring, and spotfacing?*

20. *What is spot finishing?*

Terms to Know and Spell

radial	*socket*	*clearance*
shank	*composition*	*reamer*
spiral	*margin*	*countersink*
flutes	*axis*	*counterbore*
fractional		

---

80 ▷ Machine Grinding

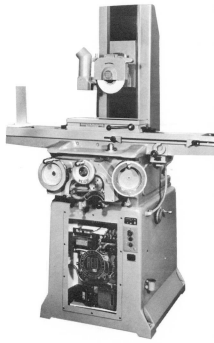

80-1. Toolroom power-feed surface grinder.

80-2. Massive face grinding machine in operation.

A grinder is a machine employing an abrasive wheel for removing excess stock and at the same time producing a finish.

At one time the grinder was used only in the toolroom for the purpose of grinding cutting tools and producing fine finishes. The grinder is now also a production machine.

The grinder cuts with a grinding action removing chips. It is readily applied to most metal surfaces. It is not only used to finish pieces that have been formed on the shaper, milling machine, etc., but high powered surface grinders are taking over stock removal operations not too long ago reserved for cutter type machine tools. The reasons: (1) The cost of wheels can be lower than the cost of cutting tools, (2) no sharpening costs, (3) fixture costs are small, (4) part handling and loading of magnetic chucks are fast and easy, and (5) heavy stock removal and final finish can often be accomplished in one setup.

The Surface Grinder

Surface grinding produces and finishes flat surfaces. The term "surface grinding" has gained general acceptance as meaning grinding of plane surfaces only.

Types of Machines

Surface grinders vary in size from small toolroom machines using 7½″ wheels, Fig. 80-1, to massive face grinding machines mounting 48″ to even 60″ segmental chucks. Fig. 80-2. There are two types with respect to the movement of the work table:

• **Planer type**—the work table reciprocates.

• **Rotary type**—the work table revolves.

80-3.   Hand-fed surface grinder.

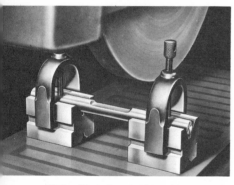

80-4.   Workpiece held in a V block while being ground on a surface grinder.

80-5.   Workpiece held on a magnetic chuck while being ground.

The *planer* type of surface grinder has three classes: (1) Using the periphery or O.D. of the grinding wheel, mounted on a horizontal spindle; (2) using a cup, cylinder, or segmental type wheel mounted on a horizontal spindle; and (3) using a cup, cylinder, or segmental type wheel mounted on a vertical spindle at right angles to the work.

The *rotary* type surface grinder has two classes: (1) Using the periphery of the grinding wheel mounted on a horizontal spindle, and (2) using a cup, cylinder, or segmental wheel mounted on a vertical spindle.

In planer type surface grinding, the reciprocating table movement can be controlled manually or by means of a mechanical or hydraulic drive. A manually operated machine is shown in Fig. 80-3. This is generally used in schools.

Several methods are employed to hold the workpiece while surface grinding. It may be bolted directly to the table, held in a vise, or held in V blocks. Fig. 80-4. However, much of the work done on the surface grinder is held in position by a permanent magnetic chuck, of the type shown in Fig. 80-5. The electromagnetic chuck, Fig. 80-6, makes use of electric current to create a magnetic field.

CYLINDRICAL GRINDING

Fig. 80-7 shows a cylindrical grinder reducing the outside diameter of a revolving cylindrical workpiece. The work is mounted between centers, and rotates while in contact with the grinding wheel, Fig. 80-8.

It does two kinds of jobs, traverse and plunge grinding.

80-6.   Electromagnetic chuck.

TRAVERSE GRINDING

In traverse grinding, the work table on which the headstock and tailstock centers are located reciprocates past the grinding wheel. The work passes the wheel which removes a fixed amount of metal (the infeed) from the diameter. At the end of the pass, the wheel is advanced another increment of distance to remove the same amount of stock on the succeeding pass. Fig. 80-7.

Traverse grinding is favored where the workpiece is longer than the maximum width of the wheel that can be mounted on the machine.

PLUNGE GRINDING

Plunge grinding is accomplished by using a wheel that is at least as wide as the area to be ground. The wheel is fed into the work, which is mounted between

80-7.   Plain hydraulic cylindrical grinding machine traverse grinding a workpiece.

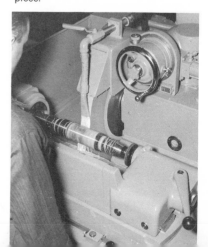

centers and does not reciprocate past the wheel. Fig. 80-9. In this type of grinding the infeed rate is continuous rather than intermittent.

FORM GRINDING

In form grinding, the wheel is shaped to produce the required design on the workpiece. Thread grinding is an example of form grinding. The shape desired is cut into the face of the grinding wheel either by diamond truing or crush truing.

CENTERLESS GRINDING

Centerless grinding is the method of grinding cylindrical surfaces without rotating the work between fixed centers. This is accomplished by supporting the work between three fundamental machine components—the grinding wheel, the regulating or feed wheel, and the work blade. The relationship to each other is shown in Fig. 80-10.

The grinding wheel at the left does the actual grinding, while the work support blade positions the workpiece for grinding. The regulating wheel has a three-fold job to do: (1) Govern the speed of work rotation, (2) govern sizing of the work, and (3) govern the rate of work travel through the machine in through-feed grinding.

THROUGH-FEED GRINDING

In this type of grinding only cylindrical shapes can be produced.

The work is fed by hand, or from a feed hopper, into the gap between the grinding wheel and the regulating wheel.

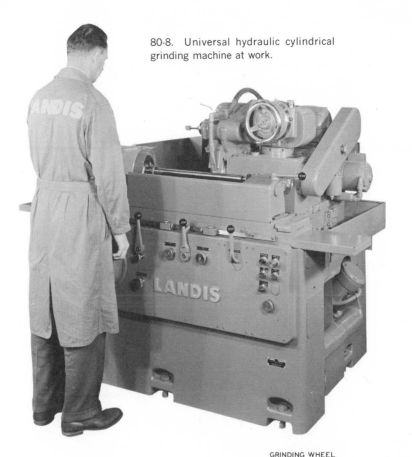

80-8. Universal hydraulic cylindrical grinding machine at work.

80-9. Plunge grinding.

80-10. The relationship of the various units in centerless grinding.

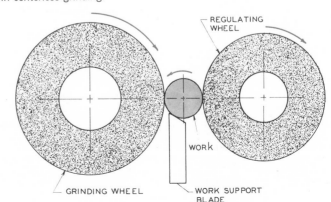

80-11. (A) Through-feed grinding on a centerless grinder, (B) infeed grinding, (C) end-feed grinding done to produce a tapered surface.

When the grinding operation is completed, the workpiece drops off the work support blade. Fig. 80-11 (A). Infeed grinding is similar to plunge or form grinding. It is used when the workpiece has a head or shoulder, and for simultaneous grinding of several diameters of a workpiece. Fig. 80-11 (B).

The end-feed method is used only on taper work. The grinding wheel, regulating wheel, and blade are set in a fixed relation to each other; the work is fed in from the front, manually or mechanically. Either the grinding wheel, regulating wheel, or both are dressed to the proper taper. Fig. 80-11 (C).

Internal Grinding

Internal grinding machines are used for the finishing of holes to accurate diameters, as for bushings, gears, bearing races, cutters, and gages. Fig. 80-12.

The modern internal grinding machine has reduced the necessity of lapping, except as a finishing operation where extreme accuracy or a high finish beyond the usual limits of commercial work is required.

80-12. Universal grinding machine equipped with internal grinding fixture. Face grinding is being done.

80-13. Grinding a tapered workpiece with table swiveled. Note the internal grinding spindle on this Universal grinder.

Types of Machines

Internal grinding may be done on universal grinding machines or on machines designed especially for that purpose. Fig. 80-13.

There are three types of internal grinding machines:

• The work is rotated and held in a chuck.
• The work can be revolved or held by the outside diameter between rolls.
• The work is stationary.

Toolroom internal grinding is

generally done dry, but common practice on production work is to grind soft steel and hardened steel work wet; bronze, brass, and cast iron dry.

The wheel on the grinder is mounted on a slender spindle and runs at a very high speed in order that a necessary peripheral speed of 4,000 to 6,000 surface fpm may be obtained.

TOOL AND CUTTER GRINDING

Tool and cutter grinding is done on a machine as shown in Fig. 80-14. Cutter grinding may be divided into two general classifications, depending upon the design of the milling cutter teeth and the method used to sharpen.

1. Cutters having teeth which must be sharpened on either the periphery or sides, such as slab milling cutters, side mills, face mills, and machine reamers. Figs. 80-15 and 80-16.

2. Formed cutters such as gear cutters, convex and concave cutters, etc. Fig. 80-17.

There are two methods of grinding tools and cutters based upon the rotation of the grinding wheel in relation to the cutting edges of the tool or the teeth.

1. The grinding wheel rotates from the body of the cutter tooth off the cutting edge.

2. The grinding wheel rotates from the cutting edge toward the body of the tooth.

FLEXIBLE SHAFT HAND GRINDERS

Flexible shaft hand grinders, Fig. 80-18, perform many grinding jobs from light de-burring and polishing to light milling operations. They are used a great deal in finishing dies.

80-14. Tool and cutter grinder.

80-17. A formed cutter being sharpened on a precision tool and cutter grinder.

80-18. Flexible shaft hand grinding unit.

80-15. Grinding an angular milling cutter. Note the position of the tooth rest.

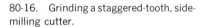

80-16. Grinding a staggered-tooth, side-milling cutter.

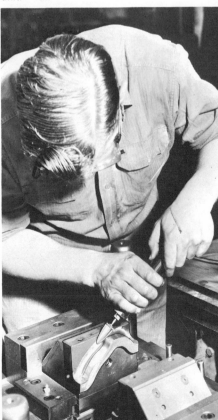

383

80-19.   Deep hole internal grinding in a lathe with a tool post grinder.

Many schools are not equipped with grinding machines. However, a tool post grinder, Fig. 80-19, can be used on the lathe to do cylindrical, external, and internal grinding operations.

Grinding Wheels

Grinding wheels are made of small, sharply crushed abrasives held together by strong, porous bonds. Each grain cuts a very small chip from the workpiece, leaving a smooth, accurate finish that varies with the size of the granules. As the abrasive particles are used, they tend to fracture away from the bond to expose new, sharp cutting edges. Fig. 80-20.

Composition of Grinding Wheels

Grinding wheels have five distinguishing characteristics: (1) type of abrasive, (2) grain, (3) grade, (4) structure, and (5) bond.

To aid in duplicating grinding performance, a standard system of marking grinding wheels has been adopted by the abrasive industry:

• Manufactured abrasives fall in two main groups. Letter symbols are used to identify them: *A.* Aluminum oxide. *C.* Silicon carbide.

A prefix *number* is also used to designate a particular type of these two materials, as *32A* or *37C.*

• Grain size—indicated by number from 10 (coarse) to 600 (fine).

• Grade—the strength of the bond holding the wheel together ranges from A (soft) to Z (hard).

• Structure—the grain spacing. It is numbered from 1 to 12. The higher the number the more "open" the structure.

• Bond—the material that holds the grains together. There are five types: (V) vitrified, (B) resinoid—synthetic resins, (R) rubber, (E) shellac, and (S) silicate.

The standard system for marking grinding wheels is shown in Fig. 80-21.

Grinding wheels are made in nine standard shapes with twelve basic face shapes. *Some* of these are shown in Fig. 80-22.

How To Mount the Grinding Wheel

Wheels can break if not correctly mounted. Fig. 80-23.

80-20.   Proper distribution of abrasive grains.

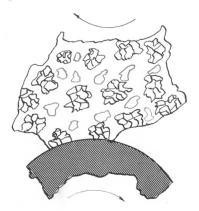

80-21.   Standard system for marking grinding wheels.

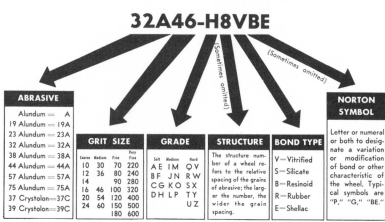

32A46-H8VBE

(Sometimes omitted)   (Sometimes omitted)

ABRASIVE				
Alundum = A				
19 Alundum = 19A				
23 Alundum = 23A				
32 Alundum = 32A				
38 Alundum = 38A				
44 Alundum = 44A				
57 Alundum = 57A				
75 Alundum = 75A				
37 Crystolon = 37C				
39 Crystolon = 39C				

GRIT SIZE			
Coarse	Medium	Fine	Very Fine
10	30	70	220
12	36	80	240
14		90	280
16	46	100	320
20	54	120	400
24	60	150	500
		180	600

GRADE		
Soft	Medium	Hard
A E	I M	Q V
B F	J N	R W
C G	K O	S X
D H	L P	T Y
		U Z

STRUCTURE
The structure number of a wheel refers to the relative spacing of the grains of abrasive; the larger the number, the wider the grain spacing.

BOND TYPE
V—Vitrified
S—Silicate
B—Resinoid
R—Rubber
E—Shellac

NORTON SYMBOL
Letter or numeral or both to designate a variation or modification of bond or other characteristic of the wheel. Typical symbols are "P," "G," "BE."

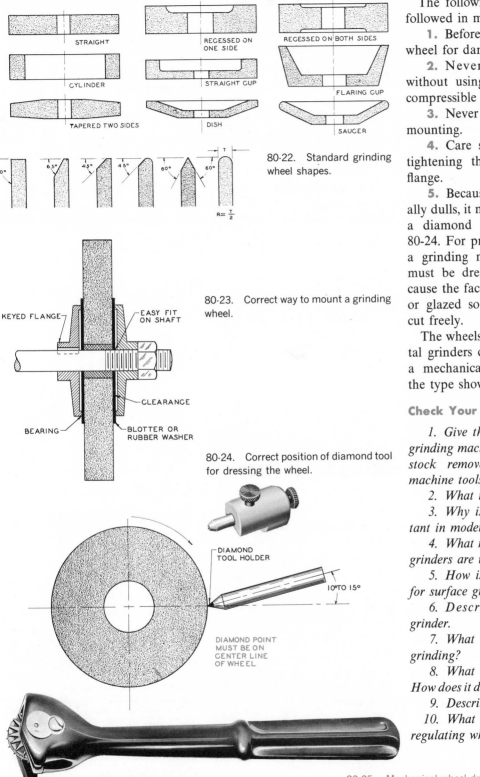

STRAIGHT

RECESSED ON ONE SIDE

RECESSED ON BOTH SIDES

CYLINDER

STRAIGHT CUP

FLARING CUP

TAPERED TWO SIDES

DISH

SAUCER

$R = \frac{T}{2}$

80-22.   Standard grinding wheel shapes.

KEYED FLANGE

EASY FIT ON SHAFT

CLEARANCE

BEARING

BLOTTER OR RUBBER WASHER

80-23.   Correct way to mount a grinding wheel.

80-24.   Correct position of diamond tool for dressing the wheel.

DIAMOND TOOL HOLDER

10° TO 15°

DIAMOND POINT MUST BE ON CENTER LINE OF WHEEL

80-25.   Mechanical wheel dresser.

The following rules should be followed in mounting wheels:

1. Before mounting, test the wheel for damage.

2. Never mount a wheel without using washers or some compressible material.

3. Never force wheels on the mounting.

4. Care should be taken in tightening the nut against the flange.

5. Because the wheel eventually dulls, it must be dressed with a diamond dressing tool. Fig. 80-24. For precision grinding on a grinding machine, the wheel must be dressed frequently because the faces become "loaded" or glazed so that they will not cut freely.

The wheels on bench or pedestal grinders can be dressed with a mechanical wheel dresser of the type shown in Fig. 80-25.

Check Your Knowledge

1. Give the main reasons why grinding machines are taking over stock removal from cutter-type machine tools.

2. What is surface grinding?

3. Why is grinding so important in modern production?

4. What main types of surface grinders are used in industry?

5. How is the workpiece held for surface grinding?

6. Describe a cylindrical grinder.

7. What is meant by traverse grinding?

8. What is plunge grinding? How does it differ from other types?

9. Describe centerless grinding.

10. What is the function of the regulating wheel?

385

11. Explain the difference between through-feed, infeed, infeed rate, and end-feed grinding.

12. What types of products are finished on an internal grinder?

13. What type of machine is used for sharpening milling cutters?

14. What is a formed cutter?

15. Explain the two methods of grinding tools and cutters based upon the rotation of the grinding wheel in relation to the cutting edges of the cutter teeth.

16. Name five distinguishing characteristics of grinding wheels.

17. What is meant by the term bond as applied to grinding wheels?

18. List the standard grinding wheel shapes.

19. Explain the method of mounting a grinding wheel.

Terms to Know and Spell

abrasive	plunge	concave
plane	regulating	structure
magnetic	cylindrical	porous
electromagnetic	internal	resinoid
traverse	universal	vitrified
reciprocate	convex	synthetic resins
increment		

PROJECTS—SECTION 13

Machine Shop Project Suggestions

Some of the projects shown in the following pages have handles that are built up of plastic. "Plexiglas" or "Lucite" is recommended.

One of the easiest methods of constructing a handle is to cut the plastic in squares about ⅛" to 3/16" larger than the finished diameter handles. A hole is then drilled through the plastic of the proper diameter to fit the handle. A nice effect can be obtained by combining different colors that go together.

After the handle has been assembled, the hold nut must be screwed up tightly. Otherwise, the plastic section will revolve when the turning tool contacts it. The nut is countersunk on one end so that the handle can be turned between centers. Take a light cut and use a fine feed until the plastic has been turned to a round shape.

The handle may then be chucked and the countersunk center removed.

CAUTION: *Protect the plastic with soft metal while holding the handle in the chuck for finishing the end.*

Note on the Soldering Iron

In constructing the electric soldering iron, a 100 watt heating element can be purchased from a manufacturer of soldering irons and inserted in the iron. The copper tip is drilled as shown in the drawing to fit the heating element. The element has two leads which can be connected to the cord.

TO OBTAIN CASTINGS

The castings for the **block plane** and **paper punch** can be purchased from the Gemaco Genevro Machine Co., Box 295, Garden Grove, California.

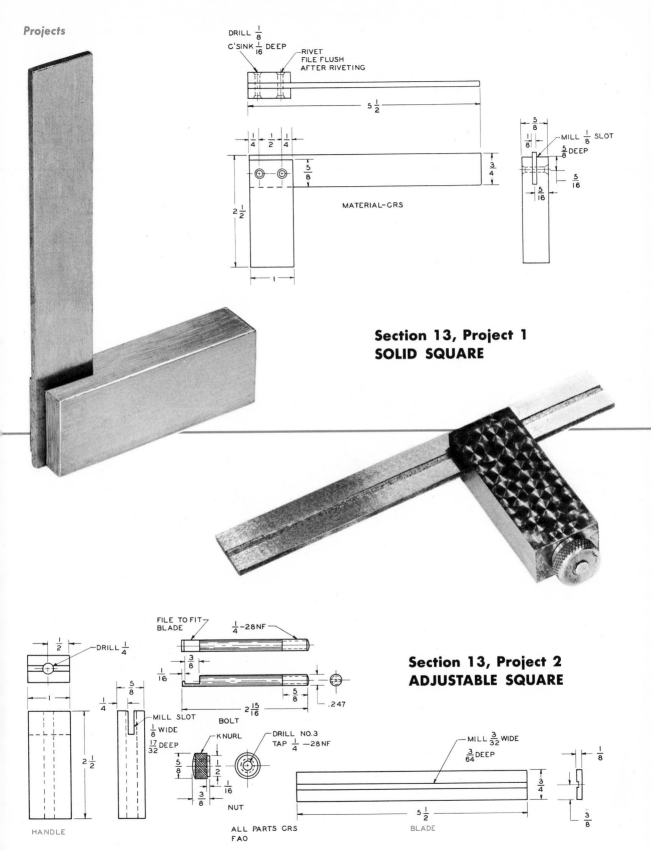

DRILL $\frac{1}{8}$
C'SINK $\frac{1}{16}$ DEEP
RIVET
FILE FLUSH
AFTER RIVETING

$5\frac{1}{2}$

$\frac{1}{4}$ $\frac{1}{2}$ $\frac{1}{4}$

$\frac{5}{8}$

$\frac{3}{4}$

$2\frac{1}{2}$

MATERIAL-CRS

1

$\frac{5}{8}$

$\frac{1}{8}$

MILL $\frac{1}{8}$ SLOT

$\frac{5}{8}$ DEEP

$\frac{5}{16}$

$\frac{5}{16}$

Section 13, Project 1
SOLID SQUARE

Section 13, Project 2
ADJUSTABLE SQUARE

FILE TO FIT
BLADE

$\frac{1}{4}$ –28NF

$\frac{1}{2}$

DRILL $\frac{1}{4}$

$\frac{3}{8}$

$\frac{1}{16}$

$\frac{5}{8}$

.247

$2\frac{15}{16}$

BOLT

1

$\frac{1}{4}$

$\frac{5}{8}$

MILL SLOT
$\frac{1}{8}$ WIDE
$\frac{17}{32}$ DEEP

$2\frac{1}{2}$

KNURL

DRILL NO.3
TAP $\frac{1}{4}$ –28NF

$\frac{5}{8}$

$\frac{1}{2}$

$\frac{1}{16}$

$\frac{3}{8}$

NUT

MILL $\frac{3}{32}$ WIDE
$\frac{3}{64}$ DEEP

$\frac{1}{8}$

$\frac{3}{4}$

$5\frac{1}{2}$

$\frac{3}{8}$

HANDLE

ALL PARTS CRS
FAO

BLADE

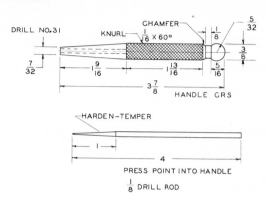

Section 13, Project 3
SCRIBER #1

DRILL NO. 31

KNURL

CHAMFER
$\frac{1}{16}$ X 60°

$\frac{5}{32}$

$\frac{1}{8}$

$\frac{3}{8}$

$\frac{7}{32}$

$\frac{9}{16}$

$\frac{13}{16}$

$\frac{5}{16}$

$3\frac{7}{8}$

HANDLE CRS

HARDEN—TEMPER

1

4

PRESS POINT INTO HANDLE

$\frac{1}{8}$ DRILL ROD

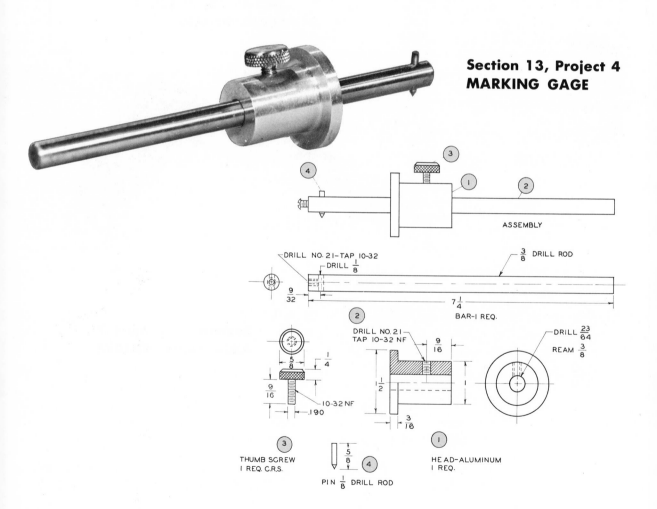

Section 13, Project 4
MARKING GAGE

4

3

1

2

ASSEMBLY

DRILL NO. 21—TAP 10-32

DRILL $\frac{1}{8}$

$\frac{3}{8}$ DRILL ROD

$\frac{9}{32}$

$7\frac{1}{4}$

BAR—1 REQ.

2

DRILL NO. 21
TAP 10-32 NF

$\frac{9}{16}$

DRILL $\frac{23}{64}$

REAM $\frac{3}{8}$

$\frac{5}{8}$

$\frac{1}{4}$

$1\frac{1}{2}$

$\frac{9}{16}$

10-32 NF

.190

$\frac{3}{16}$

3

THUMB SCREW
I REQ. C.R.S.

$\frac{5}{8}$

4

PIN $\frac{1}{8}$ DRILL ROD

1

HEAD—ALUMINUM
I REQ.

388

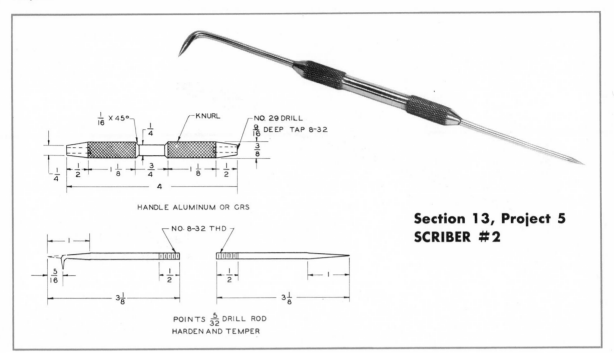

$\frac{1}{16}$ X 45°

KNURL

NO. 29 DRILL
$\frac{9}{16}$ DEEP TAP 8-32

$\frac{1}{4}$

$\frac{3}{8}$

$\frac{1}{4}$ $\frac{1}{2}$ $1\frac{1}{8}$ $\frac{3}{4}$ $1\frac{1}{8}$ $\frac{1}{2}$

4

HANDLE ALUMINUM OR CRS

Section 13, Project 5
SCRIBER #2

NO. 8-32 THD

1

$\frac{5}{16}$ $\frac{1}{2}$ $\frac{1}{2}$ 1

$3\frac{1}{8}$ $3\frac{1}{8}$

POINTS $\frac{5}{32}$ DRILL ROD
HARDEN AND TEMPER

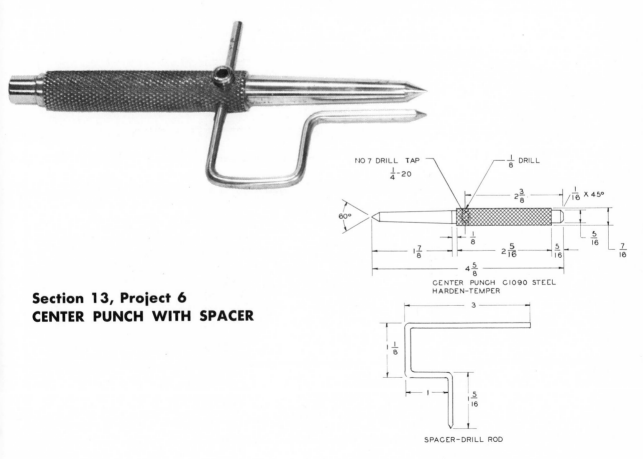

Section 13, Project 6
CENTER PUNCH WITH SPACER

NO 7 DRILL TAP
$\frac{1}{4}$-20

$\frac{1}{8}$ DRILL

$2\frac{3}{8}$

$\frac{1}{16}$ X 45°

60°

$\frac{1}{8}$

$\frac{5}{16}$

$\frac{7}{16}$

$1\frac{7}{8}$ $2\frac{5}{16}$ $\frac{5}{16}$

$4\frac{5}{8}$

CENTER PUNCH C1090 STEEL
HARDEN-TEMPER

3

$1\frac{1}{8}$

1

$\frac{5}{16}$

SPACER-DRILL ROD

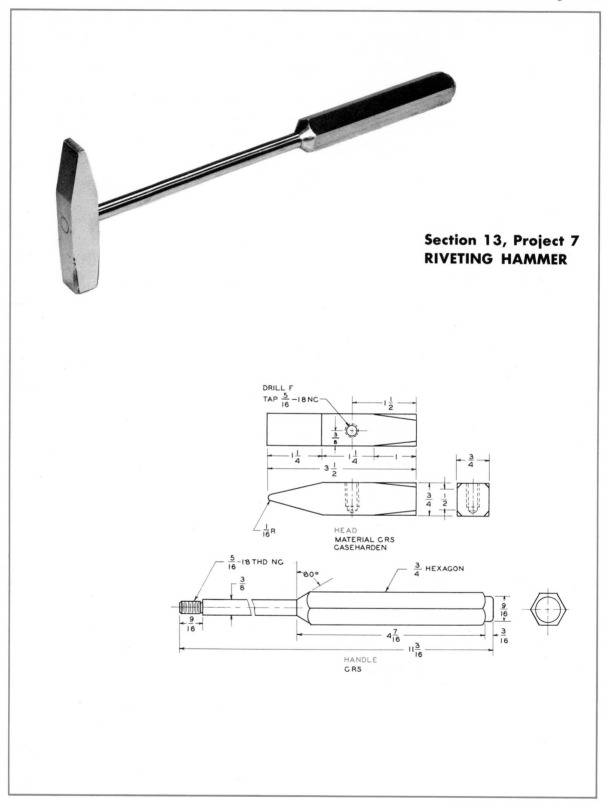

Section 13, Project 7
RIVETING HAMMER

DRILL F
TAP $\frac{5}{16}$ —18 NC

$1\frac{1}{2}$

$\frac{3}{8}$

$1\frac{1}{4}$ $1\frac{1}{4}$ 1

$3\frac{1}{2}$

$\frac{3}{4}$

$\frac{3}{4}$ $1\frac{1}{2}$

$\frac{1}{16}$ R

HEAD
MATERIAL CRS
CASEHARDEN

$\frac{5}{16}$ —18 THD NC

$\frac{3}{8}$

80°

$\frac{3}{4}$ HEXAGON

$\frac{9}{16}$

$\frac{9}{16}$

$\frac{3}{16}$

$4\frac{7}{16}$

$11\frac{3}{16}$

HANDLE
CRS

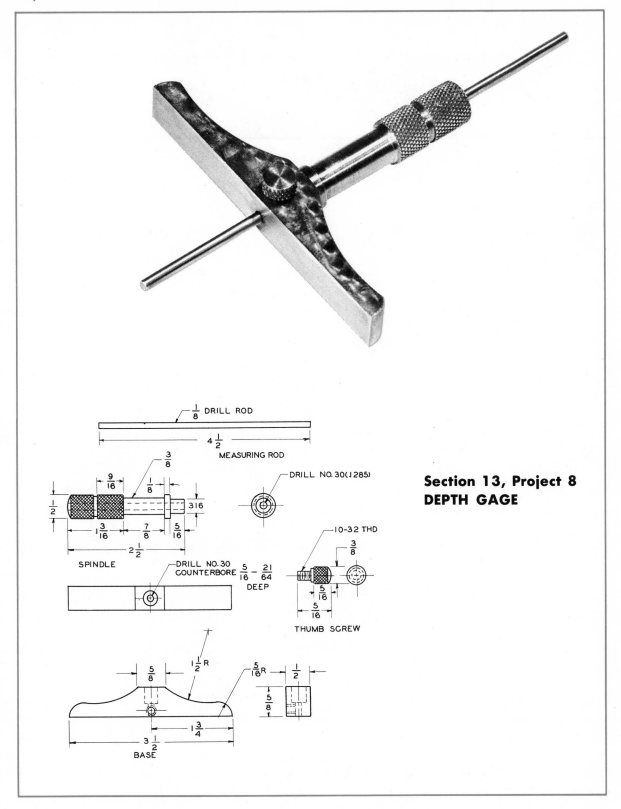

$\frac{1}{8}$ DRILL ROD

4 $\frac{1}{2}$

MEASURING ROD

$\frac{9}{16}$

$\frac{3}{8}$

$\frac{1}{8}$

$\frac{1}{2}$

3 16

$1\frac{3}{16}$

$\frac{7}{8}$

$\frac{5}{16}$

2 $\frac{1}{2}$

SPINDLE

DRILL NO. 30 (.1285)

DRILL NO. 30
COUNTERBORE $\frac{5}{16} - \frac{21}{64}$
DEEP

10-32 THD

$\frac{3}{8}$

$\frac{5}{16}$

$\frac{5}{16}$

THUMB SCREW

Section 13, Project 8
DEPTH GAGE

$1\frac{1}{2}$ R

$\frac{5}{8}$

$\frac{5}{16}$ R

$\frac{1}{2}$

$\frac{5}{8}$

$1\frac{3}{4}$

$3\frac{1}{2}$

BASE

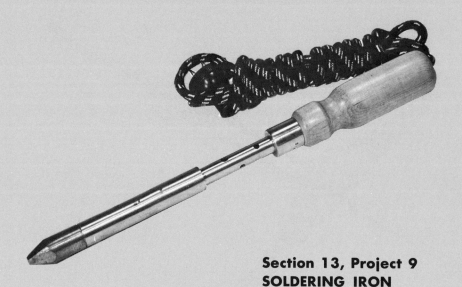

Section 13, Project 9
SOLDERING IRON

A jig can be made for drilling
the holes in the barrel.

A 100-watt heating element must be purchased for this project.
A suitable one is available from Wall Mfg. Co., Kinston, N. C.

Section 13, Project 10
TAP WRENCH

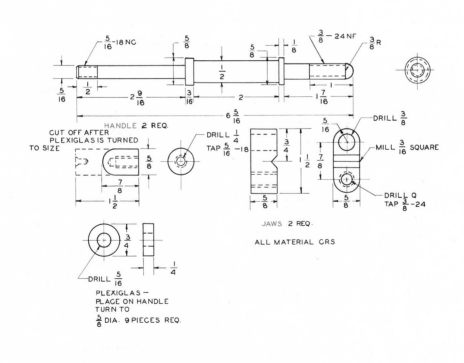

$\frac{5}{16}$–18 NC

$\frac{5}{8}$

$\frac{5}{8}$

$\frac{1}{8}$

$\frac{3}{8}$–24 NF

$\frac{3}{8}$R

$\frac{1}{2}$

$\frac{5}{16}$

$\frac{1}{2}$

$2\frac{9}{16}$

$\frac{3}{16}$

2

$1\frac{7}{16}$

1

$6\frac{5}{16}$

HANDLE 2 REQ.

CUT OFF AFTER
PLEXIGLAS IS TURNED
TO SIZE

DRILL $\frac{1}{4}$
TAP $\frac{5}{16}$–18

$\frac{5}{8}$

$\frac{7}{8}$

$1\frac{1}{2}$

$\frac{3}{4}$

$1\frac{1}{2}$

$\frac{5}{8}$

$\frac{5}{16}$

DRILL $\frac{3}{8}$

MILL $\frac{3}{16}$ SQUARE

$\frac{7}{8}$

$\frac{5}{8}$

DRILL Q
TAP $\frac{3}{8}$–24

JAWS 2 REQ.

ALL MATERIAL CRS

$\frac{3}{4}$

$\frac{1}{4}$

DRILL $\frac{5}{16}$

PLEXIGLAS —
PLACE ON HANDLE
TURN TO
$\frac{5}{8}$ DIA. 9 PIECES REQ.

Section 13, Project 11
MEAT TENDERIZER

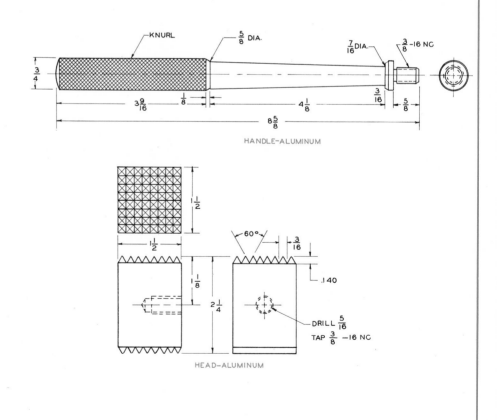

KNURL

$\frac{5}{8}$ DIA.

$\frac{7}{16}$ DIA.

$\frac{3}{8}$ -16 NC

$\frac{3}{4}$

$3\frac{9}{16}$

$\frac{1}{8}$

$4\frac{1}{8}$

$\frac{3}{16}$

$\frac{5}{8}$

$8\frac{5}{8}$

HANDLE—ALUMINUM

$1\frac{1}{2}$

$1\frac{1}{2}$

60°

$\frac{3}{16}$

$1\frac{1}{8}$

$2\frac{1}{4}$

.140

DRILL $\frac{5}{16}$

TAP $\frac{3}{8}$ -16 NC

HEAD—ALUMINUM

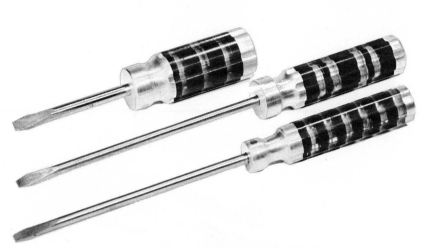

Section 13, Project 12
SCREWDRIVERS

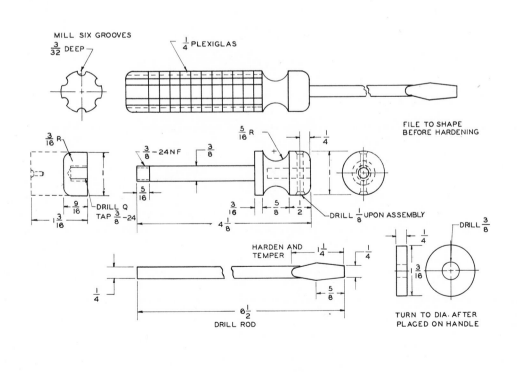

MILL SIX GROOVES
$\frac{3}{32}$ DEEP

$\frac{1}{4}$ PLEXIGLAS

FILE TO SHAPE
BEFORE HARDENING

$\frac{3}{16}$ R

$\frac{9}{16}$

$1\frac{3}{16}$

DRILL Q
TAP $\frac{3}{8}$-24

$\frac{3}{8}$ -24 NF

$\frac{5}{16}$

$\frac{3}{8}$

$\frac{5}{16}$ R

$\frac{1}{4}$

$\frac{3}{16}$ $\frac{5}{8}$ $\frac{1}{2}$

$4\frac{1}{8}$

DRILL $\frac{1}{8}$ UPON ASSEMBLY

HARDEN AND
TEMPER

$1\frac{1}{4}$ $\frac{1}{4}$

$\frac{1}{4}$

$\frac{5}{8}$

$6\frac{1}{2}$

DRILL ROD

DRILL $\frac{3}{8}$

$\frac{1}{4}$

$\frac{3}{16}$

TURN TO DIA. AFTER
PLACED ON HANDLE

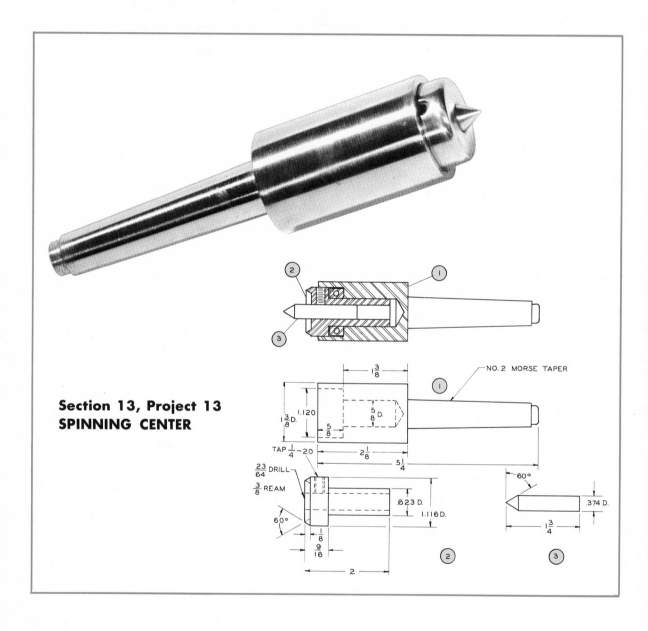

Section 13, Project 13
SPINNING CENTER

NO. 2 MORSE TAPER

TAP $\frac{1}{4}$-20

$1\frac{3}{8}$

$1\frac{3}{8}$ D. 1.120

$\frac{5}{8}$ D.

$\frac{5}{8}$

$2\frac{1}{8}$

$5\frac{1}{4}$

$\frac{23}{64}$ DRILL

$\frac{3}{8}$ REAM

60°

$\frac{1}{8}$

$\frac{9}{16}$

2

.623 D.

1.116 D.

60°

.374 D.

$1\frac{3}{4}$

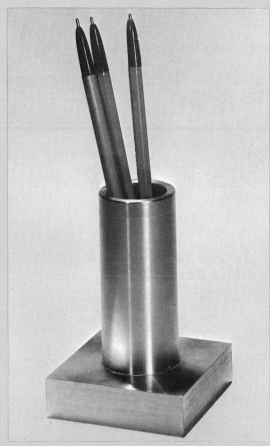

Section 13, Project 14
PEN AND PENCIL HOLDER

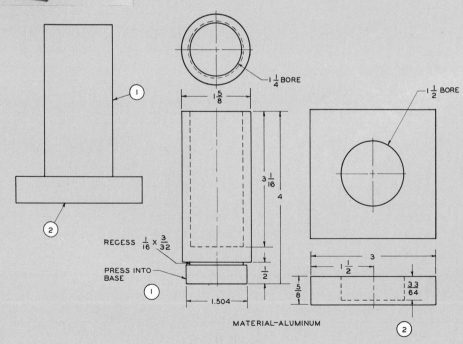

$1\frac{1}{4}$ BORE

$1\frac{5}{8}$

$1\frac{1}{2}$ BORE

$3\frac{1}{16}$

4

REGESS $\frac{1}{16} \times \frac{3}{32}$

PRESS INTO BASE

$\frac{1}{2}$

1.504

MATERIAL–ALUMINUM

3

$1\frac{1}{2}$

$\frac{5}{8}$

$1\frac{33}{64}$

397

Section 13, Project 15
DRILL PRESS VISE

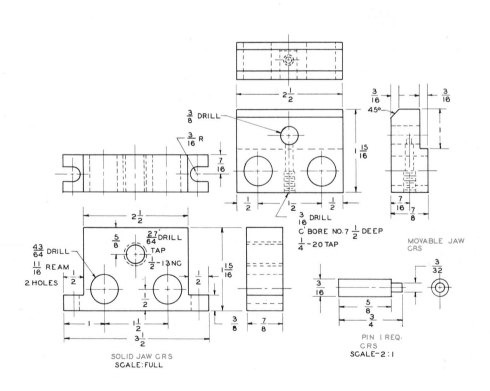

DRILL PRESS VISE (continued)

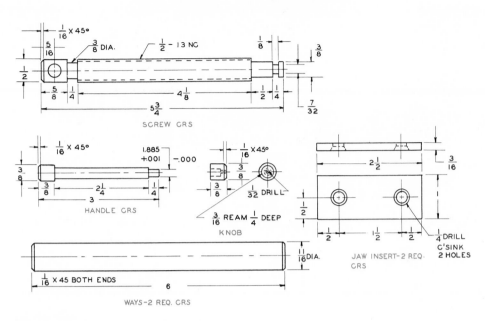

$\frac{1}{16}$ X 45°

$\frac{5}{16}$

$\frac{3}{8}$ DIA.

$\frac{1}{2}$ - 13 NC

$\frac{1}{8}$

$\frac{3}{8}$

$\frac{1}{2}$

$\frac{5}{8}$ $\frac{1}{4}$

$4\frac{1}{8}$

$\frac{1}{2}$ $\frac{1}{4}$

$\frac{7}{32}$

$5\frac{3}{4}$

SCREW CRS

$\frac{1}{16}$ X 45°

$\frac{3}{8}$

$\frac{3}{8}$

$2\frac{1}{4}$

$\frac{1}{4}$

3

HANDLE CRS

1.885 +001 -.000

$\frac{1}{16}$ X 45°

$\frac{3}{8}$

$\frac{3}{8}$

$\frac{1}{32}$ DRILL

$\frac{3}{16}$ REAM $\frac{1}{4}$ DEEP

KNOB

$2\frac{1}{2}$

$\frac{3}{16}$

$\frac{1}{2}$

$\frac{1}{2}$ $1\frac{1}{2}$ $\frac{1}{2}$

$\frac{1}{4}$ DRILL C'SINK 2 HOLES

JAW INSERT-2 REQ. CRS

$\frac{11}{16}$ DIA.

$\frac{1}{16}$ X 45 BOTH ENDS

6

WAYS-2 REQ. CRS

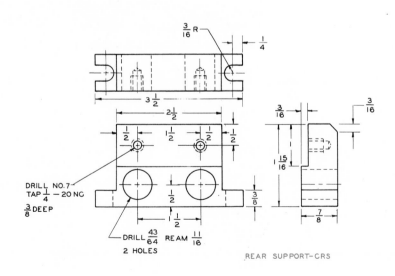

$\frac{3}{16}$ R

$\frac{1}{4}$

$3\frac{1}{2}$

$\frac{3}{16}$

$\frac{3}{16}$

$2\frac{1}{2}$

$\frac{1}{2}$ $\frac{1}{2}$ $\frac{1}{2}$ $\frac{1}{2}$

$1\frac{15}{16}$

DRILL NO.7 TAP $\frac{1}{4}$ - 20 NC $\frac{3}{8}$ DEEP

$\frac{1}{2}$

$\frac{3}{8}$

$1\frac{1}{2}$

DRILL $\frac{43}{64}$ REAM $\frac{11}{16}$ 2 HOLES

$\frac{7}{8}$

REAR SUPPORT-CRS

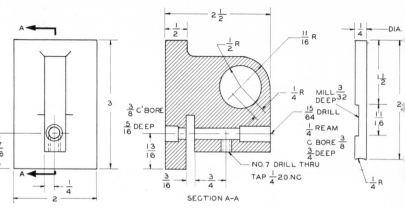

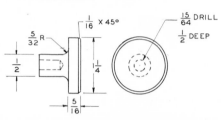

SECTION A-A

Section 13, Project 15
PAPER PUNCH

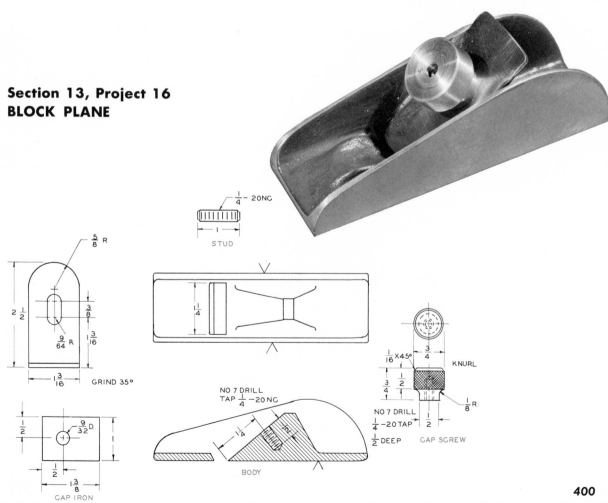

Section 13, Project 16
BLOCK PLANE

Mathematics and Science
in Metalworking

METALWORK calls for an understanding of mathematics and science. You must learn to take accurate measurements and lay out the work properly to avoid waste. Industry places the same requirements upon the worker because their specifications in making products are even more stringent.

The mathematics you will study in this section will simply identify the kinds of problems you will face. If you are particularly weak in mathematics, you would do well to take as much math as possible in high school or in the technical center where you study.

It would be well also to take a course in physics and other special courses having to do with metalworking and the structure of metals.

When you are machining, grinding, or performing other metalworking operations, heat and stress cause changes that you must understand to do a good job. Also you must know the nature of the metal you are working with so that you can do soldering or welding and so that the product will perform the service required of it.

Scientific features covered in this section will not fill in a weak background knowledge of physics. But the formulas and other information cover the points that you should know in handling metals as taken up in this book.

81 ▷ **Mathematics**

Having a good knowledge of mathematics is essential to the worker in metalworking industries. Whether you work in sheet metal, machining, patternmaking, or other trades, it is necessary to use mathematics in the laying out or production of the product.

Only a few examples of the type of problems you will have to solve are given in this unit.

Fractions

An understanding of what a fraction is may be obtained by the examination of an inch measurement as found on an ordinary 12 inch rule. You may wish to review this, even though you have previous knowledge.

In Fig. 81-1, it will be seen that each inch is divided into 16 equal parts, or divisions. Each one of these divisions equals $\frac{1}{16}$ (a fraction) of the whole unit, the inch.

Five $\frac{1}{16}$'s would accordingly be expressed in fractional form as $\frac{5}{16}''$.

It will be noted that each fraction is made up of two parts. The number above the line is the numerator (number of parts) and the figure below the line is the denominator.

81-1. Showing part of an ordinary 12″ rule.

ADDITION OF FRACTIONS

Adding fractions has a wide application in practical shop problems. You must often figure material or a job with pieces having fractional measurements added together.

RULE FOR ADDITION OF FRACTIONS. Reduce the fractions to equivalent fractions having the least common denominator, add their numerators, and write their sum over the common denominator.

When fractions, mixed numbers, and whole numbers occur in addition, add the whole numbers and fractional parts separately and unite their sums. If the fractional part of the result is an improper fraction, it should be changed to a mixed number, the whole number of which should be added to the rest of the whole numbers.

In the problem below it may be seen that 16 is the least common denominator of the fractions.

Decimal Fractions

Decimal fractions are used to a great extent in the metalworking trades.

A decimal fraction is a fraction whose denominator is 10 or some multiple of 10. The denominator of a simple decimal fraction is always omitted but is expressed by a dot called a decimal point.

ADDITION OF DECIMALS

Since it is necessary to have a common denominator when adding or subtracting common fractions, and since decimal fractions are only a modified form of common fractions, it becomes evident that to add decimals the decimal points must be placed in a column directly under each other. The same method is used as in adding whole numbers.

EXAMPLE:
What is the total length of the pin shown in Fig. 81-2?

SOLUTION: $\frac{5}{16}$
$\frac{3}{16}$
$1\frac{7}{16}$
$\frac{13}{16}$
Sum $=1\frac{28}{16}$ or $2\frac{3}{4}$

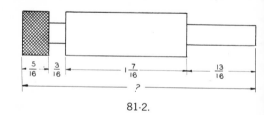

81-2.

EXAMPLE:
Determine the length of the part shown in Fig. 81-3.

SOLUTION: $\frac{1}{4} = \frac{4}{16}$
$\frac{7}{8} = \frac{14}{16}$
$1\frac{9}{16} = 1\frac{9}{16}$
Sum $= 1\frac{27}{16}$ or $2\frac{11}{16}$

81-3.

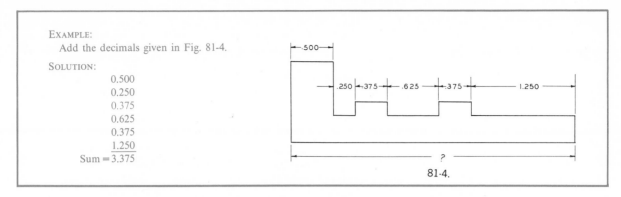

EXAMPLE:
Add the decimals given in Fig. 81-4.

SOLUTION:

$$
\begin{array}{r}
0.500 \\
0.250 \\
0.375 \\
0.625 \\
0.375 \\
\underline{1.250} \\
\text{Sum} = 3.375
\end{array}
$$

81-4.

SUBTRACTION OF DECIMALS

Subtracting decimals is the same as in subtracting whole numbers.

EXAMPLE:
Subtract 3.4750 from 5.6237.

SOLUTION:
As shown below, the decimal points lie in the same vertical line.

$$
\begin{array}{r}
5.6237 \\
\underline{3.4750} \\
\text{Ans.} = 2.1487
\end{array}
$$

MULTIPLICATION OF DECIMALS

Multiplication is actually the process of adding a number as many times as there are units in the quantity by which it is multiplied. The *multiplicand* is the number which is to be multiplied. The *multiplier* is the number by which the multiplicand is to be multiplied. The *product* is the result.

Proceed as in the multiplication of whole numbers. Since the product of two common fractions whose denominators are 10 will produce a fraction whose denominator is 100, the product of two decimal fractions stated in tenths will produce a decimal fraction stated in hundredths. From this it is evident that the number of decimal places in the product is equal to the sum of the decimal places in the multiplicand and the multiplier.

EXAMPLE:
Multiply 2.5 by .7854.

SOLUTION:

$$
\begin{array}{ll}
.7854 & \text{4 decimal places} \\
\underline{2.5} & \text{1 decimal place} \\
39270 & \\
\underline{15708} & \\
1.96350 & \text{5 decimal places. Therefore}
\end{array}
$$
place the decimal point 5 decimal places from right to left in the product.

DIVISION OF DECIMALS

Division of decimals is a special application of long division. When a decimal is divided by another decimal, it is important that the decimal point in the quotient is placed in the proper location. For each place that it is moved to the right, the value of the decimal is multiplied by 10; for each place it is moved to the left, the value is divided by 10.

In dividing decimals the divisor may be reduced to a whole number. In order to do this, move the decimal point to the right as many places as there are figures to the right of the decimal point. Next, move the decimal point in the dividend the same number of places to the right, counting from the original position.

The decimal quantity is always read from left to right, annexing the name corresponding to the last decimal figure. For example: the figure 25.5637 is read twenty-five and five-thousand six-hundred thirty-seven ten-thousandths.

EXAMPLE:
Divide 124.625 by 48. Carry out to four decimal places.

SOLUTION:

$$
\begin{array}{r}
2.5963 \\
48 \overline{)\ 124.6250} \\
\underline{96} \\
286 \\
\underline{240} \\
462 \\
\underline{432} \\
305 \\
\underline{288} \\
170 \\
\underline{144} \\
26
\end{array}
$$

TO CONVERT A DECIMAL FRACTION TO A COMMON FRACTION

EXAMPLE:
Convert 0.250 to a common fraction.

SOLUTION:
The number after the decimal point is the numerator of the fraction, while the denominator is a 1 with ciphers, due to the fact that there are three figures to the right of the decimal point. Reduce to the lowest terms. This can be done by dividing both the numerator and denominator by 125.

$$
\frac{250}{1000} = \frac{250}{1000} \div \frac{125}{125} = \frac{2}{8} = \frac{1}{4}
$$

To Convert a Common Fraction to a Decimal

EXAMPLE:

Convert ¾ to a decimal fraction. Since a fraction is an indicated division, divide 3 by 4. Since 4 does not go into 3, place a decimal point after the 3, annex ciphers, and carry out the division as shown.

SOLUTION:

$$\begin{array}{r} .75 \\ 4\,)\overline{3.00} \\ \underline{28} \\ 20 \\ \underline{20} \end{array}$$

Figure the decimal point in the quotient as many places as the number of decimal places in the dividend exceed those in the divisor.

Many different types of formulas are used in metalworking trades. A shop formula is a mathematical statement of a rule in which letters, symbols, or figures are used separately or in a combination with each other. Such formulas aid in the solution of problems by substituting for these symbols their equivalent numerical values.

There are a great variety of these formulas but it is not within the scope of this text to cover them all. Only the most elementary ones as applied to metalworking will be considered.

Formulas

FINDING THE CIRCUMFERENCE AND DIAMETER OF A CIRCLE

There are many occasions when the metalworker has to find the circumference of a circle. The formula for finding the circumference of a circle is given below.

$c = 3.1416 \times d$

Circumference $= c$

Diameter $= d$

Sometimes the decimal is expressed by the symbol π, called pi (3.1416 +).

EXAMPLE:

If the diameter of a piece of pipe is 5″, what is the circumference?

SOLUTION:

$c = 3.1416 \times 5''$
$c = 3.1416 \times 5 = 15.7080''$

The circumference would be approximately 15⁴⁵⁄₆₄″.

The diameter of a circle can also be found by dividing the circumference by 3.1416, as:

$$d = c \div 3.1416 = \frac{c}{3.1416}$$

EXAMPLE:

Find the diameter of a circle whose circumference is 42.5″.

SOLUTION:

$$d = \frac{c}{3.1416} = \frac{42.5}{3.1416} = 13.54''$$

The machinist should know how to run his machines at various speeds and feeds, depending upon, (1) the nature of the metal being worked, (2) nature of the cut (roughing or finishing), (3) the feed and depth of cut, (4) the material and shape of cutting tool and, (5) the strength and condition of the machine.

Finding Cutting Speed on the Lathe

The cutting speed is the rate at which a tool passes over a piece of work. In the case of the lathe, cutting speed may be defined as the number of linear feet on the surface of the work that passes the point of the tool in one minute. Therefore the cutting speed in feet per minute is found by multiplying the circumference of the workpiece expressed in fpm by the number of rpm.

EXAMPLE:

Find the cutting speed of a piece of steel ⅞″ in diameter turned in a lathe at 180 rpm.

SOLUTION:

cs = 3.1416 × d in feet × rpm.
$$= \frac{3.1416 \times \frac{7}{8} \times 180}{12} = 41\frac{1}{4} \text{ fpm.}$$

Finding Surface or Rim Speed

By surface or rim speed is meant the number of feet that a point on the rim or circumference of a wheel travels in one minute.

EXAMPLE:

Find the surface speed of an emery wheel 8″ in diameter running at a rate of 240 rpm.

SOLUTION:

$$s = \frac{8 \times 3.1416}{12} \times 240$$
$$= \frac{25.1328}{12} \times 240 = 503 \text{ fpm.}$$

Finding Cutting Speed of Shapers

The method of finding the cutting speed of a crank shaper is illustrated in the following example:

EXAMPLE:

Find the cutting speed of a shaper making 30 rpm with a reverse of 2:1 with a stroke length of 14 inches.

SOLUTION:

Length of stroke = 1⅙′.
Total length of metal cut in one minute = 30 × 1⅙ = 35′.
cs = 35 × ½ = 52.5′ per minute.

Finding Cutting Feed of a Lathe

The cutting feed of a lathe is the distance the tool travels horizontally along a workpiece while the workpiece makes one revolution. For example, if the tool moves ¹⁄₃₂″ while the piece turns around once, the feed is ¹⁄₃₂″.

Screw Thread Formulas

One of the common jobs in a machine shop is that of cutting screw threads on the lathe. The threads have definite proportions which may be calculated by simple formulas.

Screw threads are referred to by the number of threads per inch, such as 16 threads per inch. Of course, this means that for each inch there are 16 threads.

The length of the bolt or screw is the length of the shank measured from the underside of the head. Fig. 81-5.

The distance from the top of one thread to the top of the next thread is called the pitch. The *pitch* is found by dividing 1″ by the number of threads per inch.

EXAMPLE:

$$p = \frac{1}{n}$$

p = pitch. n = no. of threads per inch.
What is the pitch of a thread on a bolt having 8 threads per inch?

SOLUTION:

$$p = \frac{1}{8} \text{ or } 1 \div 8 = 0.125 \text{ or } \tfrac{1}{8}''.$$

EXAMPLE #2:

How many threads per inch on a screw having a pitch of .0625 inch?

SOLUTION:

$$\text{No. of thds. per inch} = \frac{1}{p} = \frac{1}{.0625} = 16$$

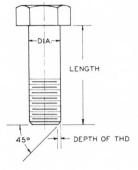

81-5. Parts of a bolt that are dimensioned.

EXAMPLE:

A piece of work revolves 90 times while the tool travels ¾″. Find the feed.

SOLUTION:

Feed = $90 \div \frac{3}{4} = 90 \times \frac{4}{3} = 120$

Finding Drill Press Feed

Feed on the drill press is the distance the drill penetrates the workpiece in one revolution. If the drill revolves 150 times while it penetrates 1″ into the metal, the feed is $\frac{1}{150}''$ per revolution.

EXAMPLE:

Find the time required to drill through a piece of stock 2″ thick with a drill making 280 rpm, if the feed per revolution is 0.006″.

SOLUTION:

Penetration in one minute
  = 280 × 0.006
  = 1.680

Time to drill through 2″
  = 2 ÷ 1.680
  = 1.181 minutes.

Finding Milling Machine Feed

Feed on the milling machine is the distance traveled by the table while the cutter makes one revolution. If the cutter revolves 60 times while the table moves 1″, the feed is $\frac{1}{60}''$.

EXAMPLE:

Find the feed per minute of a milling cutter if the feed is 0.03″ per revolution and the cutter makes 180 rpm.

SOLUTION:

Feed per min. = 180 × 0.03 = 5.4″.

Computing Tapers

A tapered workpiece gradually decreases in diameter so that it assumes a conical shape. It is common practice to refer to this as "taper per inch" or "taper per foot." For example, a taper of ¾″ in the length of 6″ would be expressed as ⅛″ taper per inch. The taper per foot would be 12 × ⅛″, or 1½″.

Formulas for calculating such tapers are given below:

$$\text{Taper per inch} = \frac{\text{large dia.} - \text{small dia.}}{\text{length in inches}}$$

$$\text{Taper per foot} = \frac{\text{large dia.} - \text{small dia.} \times 12}{\text{length in inches}}$$

These terms may be abbreviated as below:

$$\text{tpi} = \frac{D - d}{L} \qquad \text{tpf} = \frac{D - d \times 12}{L}$$

EXAMPLE:

A workpiece being turned in the lathe has the following dimensions. What is its taper? D = 4, d = 2, L = 16.

$$\begin{aligned} \text{tpi} &= \frac{D - d}{L} \\ &= \frac{4 - 2}{16} = \frac{2}{16} = \tfrac{1}{8} \text{ tpi} \end{aligned}$$

EXAMPLE:

If the taper per foot were desired, the following formula would be used.

$$\begin{aligned} \text{tpf} &= \frac{(D \div d)}{L} \times 12 \\ &= \frac{4 - 2}{16} \times 12 = 1\tfrac{1}{2} \text{ tpf} \end{aligned}$$

Tapers are turned by "setting over" the tailstock a definite amount. The method of determining this offset can be found in the unit on taper turning.

Finding the Depth of an American National Thread

The depth of this thread is equal to the pitch multiplied by 0.866.

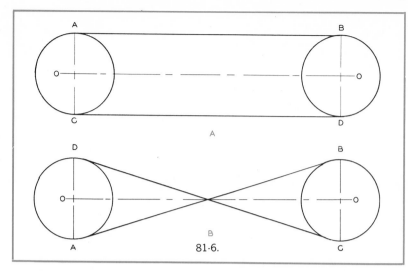

EXAMPLE:

Find the depth of an American National thread of $1/12$ pitch.

SOLUTION:

$$\text{Depth} = p \times 0.866$$
$$= 1/12 \times 0.866 = 0.0722''.$$

Belting

In calculating the length of an open belt connecting two equal pulleys as in Fig. 81-6, we have the simple rule:

Length = 2 × center distance + circumference of pulley.

EXAMPLE:

Find the length of an open belt connecting two 18″ pulleys 6′-6″ center-to-center.

SOLUTION:

$6'-6'' = 78''$

length of straight pieces
$$= 2 \times 78'' = 156''$$

circumference of 18″ pulleys
$$= 3.1416 \times 18'' = 56.54''$$
$$= 156'' + 56.54'' = 212.54''$$

total length of belt $= 17'-8''$

While there are several formulas for the length of crossed belts, the following is among the simplest and most accurate for ordinary purposes:

$$\text{Length} = \frac{3.25}{2}(D+d) + 2L$$

which in turn reduces to
$$= 1.625(D+d) + 2L$$

EXAMPLE:

Determine the length of a crossed belt needed in connecting two pulleys that measure 12″ and 14″ in diameter and whose centers lie 18′ apart.

SOLUTION:

$$L = 1.625(14'' + 12'') + 2(18' \times 12'')$$
$$= 1.625(26'') + 2(216'')$$
$$= 42.25'' + 432''$$
$$= 474.25'' \text{ or } 39.5208 \text{ ft.}$$

Finding Tap Drill Size for American National Threads

In practice, the amount of material left for tapping, after the hole has been drilled with a tap drill, equals approximately three-fourths the double depth of the thread. This produces an internal thread approximately 75 percent of full depth.

If d denotes the diameter of the tap and n the number of threads per inch, the tap-drill size may be found by the formula:

$$\text{Tap-drill size} = d - \frac{1}{n}$$

EXAMPLE:

What is the commercial tap-drill size to produce approximately 75 percent full thread for a $5/16$-18 NC thread?

SOLUTION:

$$\text{Tap-drill size} = d - \frac{1}{n}$$
$$= d - \frac{1}{18}$$
$$= .312 - .055,$$
$$= .257 \text{ or an F drill.}$$

82 ▷ Science

Science has a close relationship with metalworking. Tools and machines employ principles of science. Information that you acquire in your science classes can be applied in metalworking to good advantage. Some applications will be covered in this unit.

Machines

From the very earliest times man has used machines to help him in his work.

Machines transform energy.

For instance, a steam turbine transforms heat energy into mechanical energy and a generator transforms mechanical energy into electrical energy. Machines transform energy from one place to another. For instance, drive shafts, crankshafts, and rear axles transfer energy from the combustion in the cylinders of an automobile to the tires on the rear wheels.

Machines can be used to multiply force—to speed and change

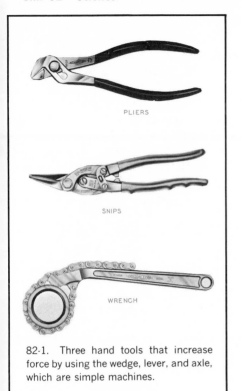

PLIERS

SNIPS

WRENCH

82-1. Three hand tools that increase force by using the wedge, lever, and axle, which are simple machines.

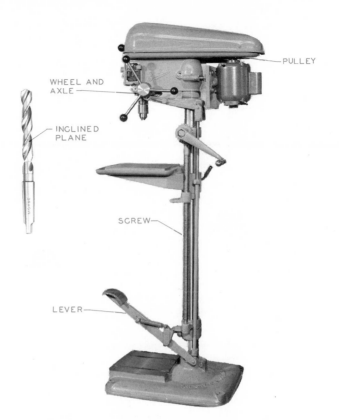

PULLEY

WHEEL AND AXLE

INCLINED PLANE

SCREW

LEVER

82-2. The drill press is a complex machine made up of a number of simple machines.

the direction of a force. Hand tools are an example. Some are cleverly designed. Fig. 82-1.

Large power machines are made of holding devices, electric controls, and simple machines. These are the lever, the pulley, the wheel and axle, the inclined plane, the screw, and the wedge. Fig. 82-2.

Following is a review of simple machines, worth your study even if you have previous knowledge:

THE LEVER

A lever is a rigid bar which is free to turn about a fixed point called a fulcrum. When we row a boat we are using the oars as levers. The fulcrum is the pivot point. The *effort* force is exerted upon one lever arm and tends to rotate the lever in one direction. The *resistance* force is exerted

upon the other lever arm and tends to rotate the lever in the opposite direction.

There are three kinds of levers: (1) first class, (2) second class, and (3) third class. Fig. 82-3. Examples of first class levers are pliers, tin-snips, and pry bars. The wheelbarrow and nutcracker are examples of second class levers. A shovel is an example of a third class lever. Most tools in the metal shop use first class levers.

Levers make it possible to exert a great deal of force for lifting weights, cutting, and as an *aid* in holding objects tightly. Learning to recognize the principles of the lever can make working with metal more efficient.

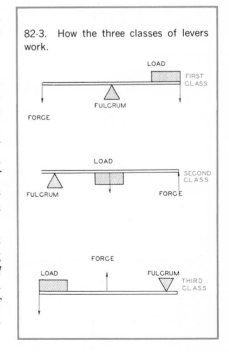

82-3. How the three classes of levers work.

LOAD

FIRST CLASS

FULCRUM

FORCE

LOAD

SECOND CLASS

FULCRUM

FORCE

FORCE

LOAD

FULCRUM

THIRD CLASS

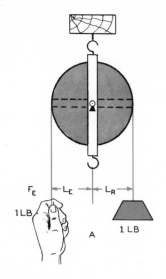

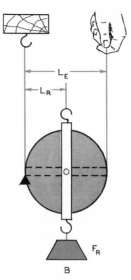

82-4. (A) The mechanical advantage of a single fixed pulley is one. (B) The mechanical advantage of a single movable pulley is two.

THE PULLEY

A pulley is a wheel that turns readily on an axle, which in turn is mounted on a frame. One or more pulleys enclosed in a frame is usually called a block. A series of pulleys with attached rope, or chain is known as the familiar block and tackle.

Fig. 82-4 (A) shows a single fixed pulley. This acts like a lever in which L_e equals L_r, and the ideal mechanical advantage is 1. If we neglect friction, an effort force of 1 lb., pulling downward

through a distance of 1 ft. raises a resistance force of 1 lb. through a distance of 1 ft. A single pulley gains neither force nor speed. It merely changes the direction in which the force is applied.

A single movable pulley is shown in Fig. 82-4 (B). The force F_e acts upon arm L_e, which is the diameter of the pulley. F_r acts upon the arm L_r, which is the radius of the pulley. Since the diameter is twice the radius, the ideal mechanical advantage of a single movable pulley is two. When the effort force moves 2′, the resistance force is lifted 1′.

Many different combinations of fixed and movable pulleys are possible.

THE WHEEL-AND-AXLE

A wheel-and-axle is a wheel or crank rigidly attached to an axle. Both the wheel and axle have the same angular velocity.

In Fig. 82-5 we have two wheels of unequal diameters, fastened together so that they turn on the same axis. In one revolution, F_e moves a distance equal to the outer circumference (C) of the wheel. During this time, F_r will also travel a distance equal to the inner circumference (c). The ideal mechanical advantage $= \frac{C}{c}$. The control and adjustment devices on drill presses, lathes, milling machines, and hand drills are examples of the wheel-and-axle.

THE INCLINED PLANE

When we wish to elevate an object without lifting it vertically, we may use an inclined plane.

When an inclined plane is used, less effort force is required because we can move the object

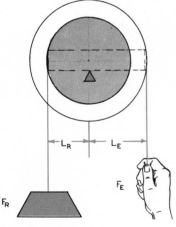

82-5. The wheel-and-axle is similar to a lever with unequal arms.

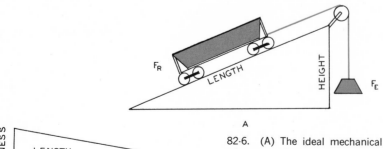

82-6. (A) The ideal mechanical advantage of an inclined plane is the length of the plane divided by its height. (B) The wedge is a double inclined plane.

up a long slanted surface more easily than trying to lift it a short distance vertically. The force needed is reduced in proportion to the distance. The effort force must be applied over the entire length of the plane to raise the load through the height. Fig. 82-6 (A).

$$IMA = \frac{length}{height}$$

IMA means mechanical advantage.

THE WEDGE

The wedge is really a double inclined plane. Fig. 82-6 (B). There is so much friction in using a wedge that an ideal or perfect machine advantage is never reached. However, the force is multiplied greatly as the wedge moves at a slant into the object, rather than "crushing" its way in. The cold chisel, axe, and knife are wedges.

THE SCREW

A screw is an inclined plane wound about a cylinder. Fig. 82-7. Bolts, nuts, and screws of all types utilize this type of simple machine. The screw multiplies force like the wedge. In one turn a bolt will move only a short distance into a nut, at a slant. The force that pulls the bolt through the nut is much greater than the effort required to turn it. A machinist's vise is an example of effort force applied to the handle attached to the screw. While the force makes a complete turn or circle, the head and axis of the screw also make one complete turn, and the resistance force moves a distance equal to the pitch of the screw, which is the distance from the top of one screw thread to the top of the next thread.

82-7. The screw is a spiraling inclined plane.

Compound Machines

Many machines are combinations of simple machines. A food chopper is a good example. The crank works on the principle of the wheel-and-axle. The crank has a screw which, when turned, forces the food along to a plate that has small holes located in its face. The pressure of the screw forces the food through these holes and the food is reduced to strands by the action of the cutting disc and force applied gradually by the screw and the crank.

The Transmission of Mechanical Power

On most machines used in schools, power is transmitted by means of a belt and pulleys. The manner in which belts are usually connected is shown in Fig. 82-8 (A). The drive wheel and the driven wheel rotate in the same direction. The pulleys can be made to turn in opposite directions by twisting the belt as in Fig. 82-8 (B). The ratio of the angular velocities of the pulleys is inversely proportional to the ratio of their radii, diameters, or circumferences.

Extracting Metals by Electrolysis

Although many metals are extracted by heating the ores in the presence of carbon or coke, this method cannot be used for the extraction of aluminum. Aluminum is obtained by electrolysis.

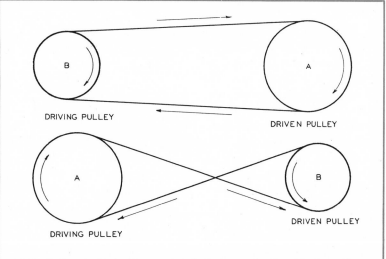

82-8. Pulleys in the top figure rotate in the same direction. The lower figure shows crossed belt pulleys which rotate in opposite directions.

The ore is cleaned and then dissolved in fused cryolite and sodium aluminum fluoride. Finally it is decomposed by electrolysis.

Metals such as copper are also refined by electrolysis. Copper ore is treated by using a bar of impure copper as an anode of an electrolytic cell, and a thin sheet of pure copper as the cathode. Cupric sulphate in a solution of sulphuric acid is used as the electrolyte. A small difference of potential is maintained across the cell. During the electrolysis, copper and other metals are oxidized from the anode and enter the solution in ionized form.

Oxyacetylene Welding

In oxyacetylene welding of metals, oxygen and acetylene gases are combined to produce a hot flame of approximately 6,000° F. The proportion needed for complete combustion is about 2½ parts of oxygen to 1 part of acetylene. However, 1½ parts of the necessary oxygen is supplied by the air surrounding the flame, so that only one part of oxygen need be supplied to the torch. Acetylene is made up of 2 parts of carbon and 2 parts of hydrogen. In the combustion of acetylene and oxygen in the neutral flame, carbon unites with oxygen to form carbon monoxide. Carbon monoxide is unstable and will unite with oxygen from the air to form carbon dioxide, so becomes harmless. The layer of carbon monoxide tends to keep the molten puddle from oxidizing.

The flame produced by the welding torch enables the operator to melt and control the fusion of metals of almost all kinds.

Check Your Knowledge

1. Why is it necessary for a metalworker to have a knowledge of mathematics?

2. A boy attending the stockroom of a machine shop fills out an order for a lathe job requiring one piece of round stock 10¹⁄₁₆″ long; one piece 4⅞″ long; and one piece 9¼″ long. What would be the total length of the material given out on this particular job?

3. Subtract ¹³⁄₄₀ from ²⁹⁄₄₀.

4. After clipping ⁷⁄₃₂″ from a piece of aluminum ²⁹⁄₃₂″ wide, what is the width of the piece remaining?

5. Define a decimal fraction.

6. What is the fractional equivalent of .625?

7. Find the sum of each of the following:
   (a) $7.2 + 0.076 + 1.09 + 3 = ?$
   (b) $6 + 3 + 5.0002 + 11.8 + 0.4 = ?$

8. Subtract 0.7754 from 5.

9. What is the weight of a bar of 1″ square iron that measures 6¾′ long when the stock weighs 3.33 lbs. per foot?

10. Divide 3.14 by 5.024.

11. What is the cross-section area of a shaft which measures 2.625 in diameter?

12. Find the circumference of a 16″ circle.

13. A countershaft pulley 10″ in diameter runs at 320 rpm. What is the surface speed of this pulley?

14. What is meant by cutting speed?

15. What is surface or rim speed?

16. Define taper.

17. What is the taper per foot of a piece 4″ long measuring .330″ diameter on the small end and .580″ diameter on the large end?

18. How is the length of a bolt measured?

19. Name six simple machines.

20. Name three kinds of levers.

21. Examine the kitchen in your home and identify all the devices which are applications of one or more of the machines studied in this unit.

22. Examine the various devices in your metal shop used for exerting large forces with little expenditure of effort.

23. An emery wheel having an allowable surface speed of 4500 feet per minute makes 15 r.p.m. What is its diameter?

24. A 1¾ in. hole is drilled with a drill running at 80 r.p.m. Find the cutting speed.

25. A crank shaper with a 2 to 1 return makes 28 strokes of one foot length in a minute. Find the cutting speed.

Terms to Know and Spell

mathematics	quotient	lever
fraction	symbols	fulcrum
division	circumference	resistance
numerator	linear	mechanical
denominator	science	pulley
decimal	energy	wedge
equivalent	transfer	force
multiplication	inclined	compound
multiplicand	axle	

Chipless Machining and Controls

"CHIPLESS MACHINING" describes other methods, besides using cutting tools. Actually, in some ways, these methods are related to forming, raising, etching, and use of heat, which are done by hand. The difference is that the results are somewhat like machining metal.

All the following types of chipless machining are covered here:

Metal can be formed on the lathe by pressure, which gives us *power spinning.* Metal can also be built up by *flame spraying* —another industrial method. By using *electrical discharge,* metal can be eroded and thus quickly machined industrially.

Cold-heading, another form of pressure shaping, is done without cutting or without heating the metal. *Explosive forming* is a method of changing the shape of metal by carefully controlled use of explosives. *Chemical milling* employs etchants, 86 to 90 parts caustic and 4 to 10 parts wetting sequestering agents and special chemicals that attack alloy elements, for modern production work.

No course in metalworking techniques would be complete without presenting the principles of *automation* and numerical controls, as here done. All methods can be accelerated and precision controlled by use of these principles.

You should give special attention to the unit on *quality controls,* or inspection and testing, which is the key to achieving the best possible results with your projects. Industry could not rely on its products without this very important factor—each item must be carefully inspected and tested, especially when used as a machine part or when it must stand up against destructive forces.

83-1. Conventional spinning.

tained consistently and the parts are not always uniform.

In power spinning, the diameter of the blank to be spun is exactly that of the finished part, plus trim, and a very large reduction in material thicknesses can be accomplished.

Power spinning and conventional spinning are often combined in production of certain parts. One example is the Explorer spacecraft nose cone.

Metal thickness can be reduced 75 percent or more in one pass, to a minimum included angle of 30°, depending upon the type of metal being spun. (Table 83-A.)

Each manufacturer has a different name for the power spinning operation. For one, Floturning,

83 ▷ Power Spinning

Power spinning is the cold rolling process of plastically deforming metal to the shape of a rotating mandrel, using a power-fed roll or rolls.

This process is known by a variety of processes such as spin-forging, Floturning, Hydrospinning, shear spinning and power roll forming.

Hollow parts with a circular cross-section and straight sides, such as cones and cylinders, can be produced quickly and accurately by these methods.

Power spinning is much different from the conventional method of metal spinning. As shown in Fig. 83-1, the diameter of the conventional blank must be considerably larger than that of the finished part, and hand tools must be skillfully used to shape the metal over the chuck or mandrel under pressure. By this method close tolerances cannot be main-

CAPACITY—THICKNESS RANGE

Metal	Dia. up to 36″	37″-48″	49″-72″	73″-144″
Aluminum	2½″	2″	1½″	1″
Copper base alloy	⅞″	⅝″	½″	⅜″
Steel— low alloy	1″	⅞″	¾″	⅝″
Stainless steel	¾″	½″	⅜″	¼″
Steels— ultra	⅞″	¾″	⅝″	½″

Table 83-A.

83-2. Floturn machine for power spinning.

TOLERANCES

Diameters	Commercial	Space, missile, aircraft
Up to 12″	± 1/64″	.008″
13″ to 36″	± 1/32″	.015″
37″ to 54″	± 1/16″	.020″
55″ to 96″	± 1/8″	.030″
97″ to 144″	± 1/4″	.040″

Table 83-B.

the machine shown in Fig. 83-2, has been developed.

In the middle and late forties, Floturning was used to produce the round TV picture tube and now turns out such utensils as mixing bowls, pails, cocktail shakers, and other products of stainless steel. Fig. 83-3. Floturning is an easy way to overcome common problems in spin-turning stainless. It produces a more precise tolerance and better finish than drawing.

Floturning is accomplished by squeezing or "flowing" thick metal over a revolving mandrel with high-pressure rollers which are tracer-controlled to follow the required contour. Much industry depends on this process.

Close tolerances and unusual shapes, inconceivable before, are now found in standard specifications. Some missile skin thicknesses, for example, are held at 0.100″±0.003 in diameters up to 30″ or 40″. (Table 83-B.)

As said above, Floturning is not a process limited to the science-fiction industries or glamour metals. Typical products which can benefit from power spinning techniques are down-to-earth items like fire extinguishers, stainless tanks for soft drink containers, cylindrical air filters, and many other items.[1]

Many products used in hospitals and laboratories are power spun, such as the automatic speed-filter, double-tank unit used for pressure filtration. Fig. 83-4.

[1] Source, Machine Tool Blue Book.

83-4. Automatic speed-filter, double-tank filtration unit.

83-3. Display of typical small parts made by power spinning—difficult forms at production rates at close tolerances, from an exceptional range of metals.

83-5. Rotating display light used primarily by jewelers and display houses.

A rotating display light is another example of power spinning. Fig. 83-5. Die casting ladles are another item made by the power spinning method. These ladles are produced in 23 sizes for the aluminum and zinc die casting industry. Fig. 83-6.

The Hydrospin, Fig. 83-7, has a hydraulically operated tailstock, with positive advance and retraction. Also the tailstock can be offset .3″ for venturi-type work to eliminate the need for offset mandrels.

Fig. 83-8 shows the tracer control for automatic tracing on a wide range of simple or complex contoured parts.

Why Power Spinning Has Advantages

Cold-working during power spinning refines and elongates the grain structure in the direction of flow, resulting in increases in the tensile strength and fatigue resistance of the metal. Spinning removes no metal from the workpiece. It merely pushes the metal

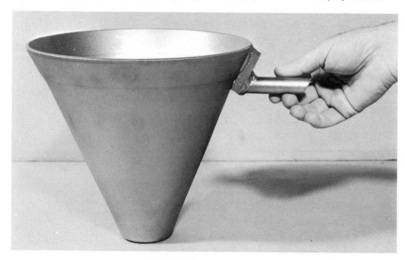

83-6. Die casting ladle produced for aluminum and die casting industry, made in stainless and mild steel. Note the thickness of the metal.

83-7. Power spinning lathe being used to spin a bowl out of 3/16″ thick aluminum. Operator is using hand guided tracer movements against a template.

83-8. Power spinning lathe features hydraulic "muscle" (4000 lbs. force from main slide and cross slide) to power spin a variety of medium sized parts—ceiling diffuser cones, lamp bases, collars, strainers, bowls, light reflectors, etc.

from one area to another—"flowing" it into the desired shape and thickness. The thickness will vary according to the shape, size, and kind of metal from which the part is spun. For this reason, parts requiring maximum *uniformity* of wall thickness are produced by a controlled series of processing. This makes possible the maintenance of a specified thickness limit either by spinning, by supplementary methods. Fig. 83-9.

For many years the only metals which were spun were copper, brass, aluminum, and soft steel. Now any metal that can be wrought-formed can be spun, such as:

    copper alloys
    magnesium
    steels—high strength
    steels—super strength
    nickel base stainless
    stainless alloy
    titanium alloy
    refractory metals

The Future of Power Spinning

There is no doubt that bigger, more powerful machines will be built for power spinning. Missile airframes are a natural for this process. One manufacturer has proposed a machine that will spin parts up to 120″ in diameter by 120″ long. Cylindrical shapes as small as 3″ in diameter can be formed on this same machine.

Power spinning will undoubtedly become automated. The combining of power spinning with other operations in automated machines is a possibility.

Check Your Knowledge

1. What is power spinning?

2. How does it differ from the conventional spinning process?

83-9. 70″ dia. hemispheres power spun from ⅜″ thick carbon steel plate.

3. What are some of the trade names given to power spinning?

4. List some of the products that are made by the power spinning process.

5. Give some of the advantages of power spinning over all other methods.

6. What types of metals can be spun? What are the size limits?

Terms to Know and Spell

spinning	*maximum*	*venturi*
blank	*cylindrical*	*stainless*
reduction	*tolerance*	*refractory*
flowing		

---

84 ▷ Flame Spraying

Flame spraying has evolved in industry to a distinct, widely recognized process. It can be defined as the process of melting materials in a heating zone and propelling them in a molten, or heat-softened condition onto a target to form a coating.

There are three types of flame spraying processes:
- Metallizing
- ThermoSpray
- Plasma Flame

Metallizing

Metallizing is the process of:

84-1. Three metallizing machines used to deposit 5,000 lbs. of 3/16" gage bronze metallizing wire over prepared surfaces of cast iron machine rolls.

Sprayed metal is used for building up worn parts and salvaging mis-machined parts. It is also used to apply corrosion-resistant material to iron or steel. Aluminum and zinc are used for this purpose on structural steel elements such as bridges, lock gates, ships, and other marine structures.

There are many other uses, such as electrical shielding, making electrical conductive elements for radiant heaters, and soldering connections for carbon resistors and brushes.

In the metallizing process the metal to be sprayed is fed into a gun by an automatic feed mechanism and through the gun into a gas-oxygen flame. Compressed air restricts the flame and causes it in turn to blast the molten tip of the wire, producing a fine metal spray which interlocks or meshes to produce a coating. Fig. 84-2.

The structure of sprayed metal is quite different from that found in rolled, drawn, or cast form. As the small molten particles are sprayed from the gun, they strike the surface, flatten out, and cool almost instantly. Wear resistance usually exceeds that of the same metal in wrought or cast form.

84-2. Lathe mounted wire metallizing gun spraying a shaft.

spraying a molten metal onto a surface to form a coating. Fig. 84-1. Pure or alloyed metal is melted in a flame and atomized by a blast of compressed air into a fine spray. This spray builds up on a surface that has been prepared in advance and forms a solid metal coating. The object being sprayed does not heat very much due to the fact that the molten metal is cooled by a strong blast of air.

The metallizing process should not be used where the sprayed metal will be subjected to sharp impact, edge strain, or continued pounding at one point. For use on crankshaft bearings, Fig. 84-3, where there is considerable vibration and where there is full bearing surface, it is entirely satisfactory.

ThermoSpray

The ThermoSpray processes employ a technique which permits the application of metals,

84-3. Metallizing process as used on crankshaft bearings.

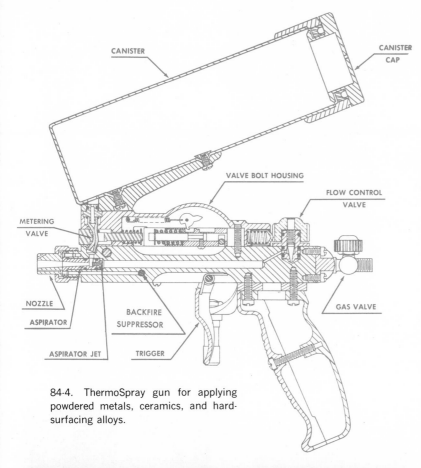

CANISTER

CANISTER CAP

VALVE BOLT HOUSING

FLOW CONTROL VALVE

METERING VALVE

NOZZLE

ASPIRATOR

ASPIRATOR JET

BACKFIRE SUPPRESSOR

TRIGGER

GAS VALVE

84-4. ThermoSpray gun for applying powdered metals, ceramics, and hard-surfacing alloys.

84-5. ThermoSpray gun spraying alumina onto a pump part for protection against corrosion and abrasion.

ceramics, alloys, and cermets—available in powder form.

The type of equipment used makes it possible to flame-spray materials that cannot be drawn into wire. Special alloys are used for hard-facing critical areas of parts that must operate under severe conditions.

The powder is applied with a gun, Fig. 84-4. Ordinarily the gun requires no air, and only two lightweight hoses are used to supply oxygen and fuel gas. The powder is fed from a canister attached directly to the gun, Fig. 84-5, eliminating separate hoppers and hoses.

An air cooler may be attached, to reduce overheating on small workpieces or thin sections. A trigger-actuated vibrator is used with ceramic powders.

Many special-purpose refractory and cermet (titanium carbide) coatings may be sprayed, but alumina and zerconia are the materials most widely favored. Zerconia is used principally as a thermal barrier for high temperature service. Alumina is used as a heat barrier and for wear resistance.

Plasma Flame Process

"Plasma" is the name used to describe vapors of materials which are raised to a higher energy level than the ordinary gaseous state. Ordinary gases consist of separate molecules, while "plasma" consists of these same gases which have been broken up and disassociated so that some of the electrically charged particles have been separated.

The plasma flame spray process is accomplished through the use of a spray gun which utilizes an electric arc that is contained within a water-cooled jacket. Fig. 84-6 shows a cross-section of this gun. The plasma flame permits the selection of an inert or chemically inactive gas for the flame medium so that oxidation can be controlled during the heating and application of the spray material. Passing the gas through the electric arc makes it possible to obtain temperatures to 30,000° F.

The powder used is fed into the plasma flame through the side of the nozzle. The high velocity of the flame propels the powder toward the surface to be coated. While doing so, the ions and electrons are recombining into atoms, releasing energy as heat which is absorbed by the powder until the particles reach a molten state. Fig. 84-7.

The flame spraying technique is used for spraying missile nose cones and rocket nozzles with high melting point materials.

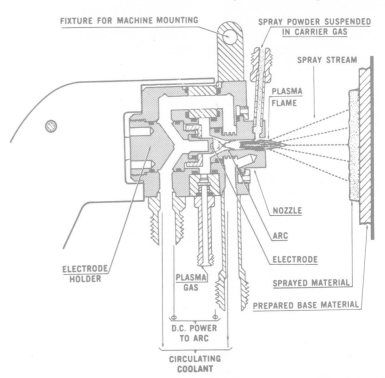

FIXTURE FOR MACHINE MOUNTING

SPRAY POWDER SUSPENDED IN CARRIER GAS

SPRAY STREAM

PLASMA FLAME

NOZZLE

ARC

ELECTRODE

SPRAYED MATERIAL

PREPARED BASE MATERIAL

ELECTRODE HOLDER

PLASMA GAS

D.C. POWER TO ARC

CIRCULATING COOLANT

84-6.   Cross-section of plasma flame spray gun.

Check Your Knowledge

1. What is flame spraying?

2. Name three flame spraying processes.

3. What is metallizing?

4. Explain this process.

5. What are some of its disadvantages?

6. Explain the ThermoSpray process. How does it differ from metallizing?

7. What type of spraying material is used in the ThermoSpray technique?

8. Give an explanation of the "plasma" flame process.

9. What are some of the advantages of this technique?

84-7.   Plasma flame gun applying a self-bonding undercoat.

Terms to Know and Spell

metallizing	resistors	oxidation
atomized	critical	electrodes
shielding	plasma	cermet

Electrical Discharge Machining

In electrical discharge machining (spark-arc disintegration), pulsating discharges of electrical energy pass from a shaped electrode and through a dielectric fluid to the workpiece, the surface of which is progressively eroded.

This process is suitable for forming irregular-shaped cavities in very hard materials that could not previously be machined. They are worked to tolerances as small as 0.0005″ with very fine surface finishes.

Electrical discharge machining works on the principle that when an electrical switch is turned on and off, sparking and arcing takes place. "Pulling" or "burning" from the arc removes a small amount of metal.

Figs. 85-1 and 85-2 illustrate electrical discharge units. They are composed of a power supply to provide direct current and a method of controlling voltage and frequency, and an electrode of brass, tungsten, or other materials listed later in this unit. The electrode can be compared with the cutting tool in conventional machining. Fig. 85-3.

In machining it is necessary to know the depth of cut and speed at which materials can be removed. Rate in electrical discharge machining is dependent upon the amount of electric current used. As the amperes are increased, metal removal rates increase. These rates have been calculated by using a graphite electrode on a steel workpiece.

85-2. Power supply unit for electrical discharge machining.

To illustrate the way in which current regulates metal removal rate, consider three similar machining conditions as in Fig. 85-4. In each case, there is only one spark. Electrode and workpiece materials remain the same.

85-1. Electrical discharge units.

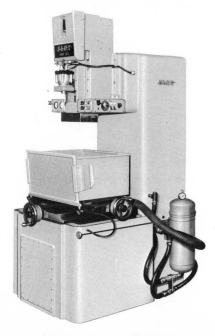

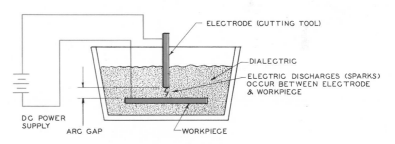

85-3. Basic electrical machining circuit.

85-4. Metal removal, one discharge.

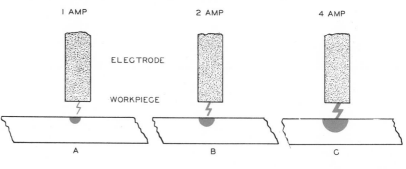

The only factor that changes is the current (amperes). A spark of one ampere, Fig. 85-4 (A), contains a certain amount of energy; consequently, it will remove a certain amount of material from the workpiece. When the current is doubled, as in Fig. 85-4 (B), twice the volume of material is removed, etc.

One other condition has changed with the increasing amperes. That is surface finish. As the amperes are increased, the spark cavity size in the workpiece also increases, which roughens the surface finish more.

As with any machining operation, surface finish of the machine area is a prime consideration. Rough cutting of any kind is normally accompanied by a rough surface finish. Finish machining calls for a fine surface finish. Electrical discharge machining is no different, and so a "surface finish selector" is built into each power supply. The frequency is controlled by the number of sparks per second between the electrode and workpiece, with frequencies ranging from 2,000 to 1,000,000 sparks per second.

Electric discharge machining requires that the user visualize the way in which clearance between the electrode and workpiece is obtained and how it is controlled. An electronic envelope or cloud (thin gas) surrounds the electrode. The size of this envelope or cloud is controlled by a servomechanism and is determined by the amount of machining amperes, spark frequency, and condenser value manufactured. Fig. 85-5.

The *dielectric* is more commonly called a coolant since this is one of the functions it serves. However, there are really three functions: The coolant (1) forms a dielectric barrier between the electrode and the workpiece at the arc gap; (2) "cools" the eroded particles of the workpiece; (3) flushes the eroded workpiece particles out of the arc gap.

Several types of coolants can be used: oil, distilled water, or certain compressed gases.

Electrode Materials

Ideal electrode material has to have the following characteristics:
- A high melting point.
- Be a good conductor of heat and electricity.

Some electrode materials have good wear rates but are difficult to fabricate and may be quite expensive. Other materials have poorer wear rates but may be cast from existing cavities using inexpensive materials. A list of known acceptable electrode materials is given below:

tungsten carbide	brass
tungsten	copper
silver tungsten	graphite
copper tungsten	copper
graphite	zinc alloys

New electrode materials are constantly being developed. However, most of these are refinements.

Workpiece Materials

The material being machined is the factor over which there is the least control. The material simply must be a conductor of electricity. Unlike regular machining, the hardness of the workpiece does not determine whether or not it can or cannot be machined. For instance, a brass electrode may be used to machine soft steel, hardened steel, or even carbide. This is one of the greatest advantages of electrical discharge machining. If you try to cut or shape materials in their hardened state it is possible to have breakage and distortion that could destroy the part. Use of even such hard materials as tungsten carbide is practical with electrode machining.

A list of recommended materials would include:

aluminum	molybdenum
beryllium	stainless steel
brass	steel
carbide	tungsten
magnesium	titanium

This list is by no means complete. Many "exotic" materials are being machined by this method, though considered unmachinable by conventional methods.

85-5. Round, square, and irregular shapes show that the envelope follows the shape of the electrode. Electrodes may be any shape.

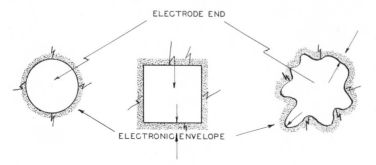

ELECTRODE END

ELECTRONIC ENVELOPE

Check Your Knowledge

1. Define electrical machining.

2. Describe the process of electrical discharge machining.

3. What effect does the increase in amperage have on the spark cavity size?

4. What is an electronic envelope?

5. What is meant by dielectric?

6. Name some of the characteristics of electrode material.

7. Name main types of electrode materials.

8. Why does the material being machined have to be a conductor of electricity? Explain why hardness is not a problem.

Terms to Know and Spell

dielectric	graphite	eroded
voltage	electronic	tungsten
electrode	servomechanism	titanium
frequency		

---

86 ▷ Cold-Heading

Cold-heading is a process whereby unheated metal is deformed beyond its elastic limit to take a permanent set to the particular shape desired. It is also referred to as cold upsetting, cold forming, and cold forging. It is widely used in making nails, rivets, bolts, screw blanks, and many other parts. Fig. 86-1. It is a high speed process of the shaping of metal between dies without preheating.

Most cold-headed parts are made of wire. The wire is supported on a reel in front of the machine as shown in Fig. 86-2 and passes through straighteners and feed rolls, coming to rest against a stop. The wire is then sheared to size and formed.

There are two basic cold-heading machines, the solid die and open die types.

The solid die machine, Fig. 86-3, uses a cylindrical block with an axial hole through its center. A knockout pin extends partially into the hole from the rear. A wire "blank" is automatically cut and pushed into the open end of the hole until it is halted by the knockout pin. A portion of the blank which extends beyond the die is hit by a heading punch. In a single-blow machine this completes the forming operation. The knockout pin then advances, ejecting the part. Fig. 86-4. When larger heads and collars are formed they may be struck by two or more punches before being completed. Fig. 86-5 illustrates the die-box area of the seven-station, six-die cold former shown in Fig. 86-7.

The open die-header uses a pair of identical blocks with mating grooves which form an axial hole when the two blocks are placed together. Wire is fed into the parted dies. The wire is halted with a portion extending beyond the forward ends of the dies. The dies now come together.

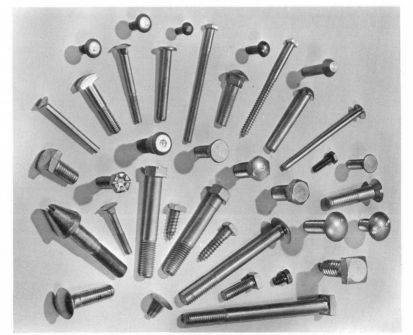

86-1. Various fasteners headed by the cold-heading process.

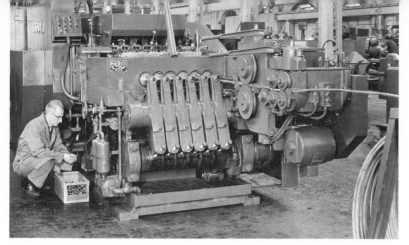

86-2. A seven-station, six-die cold former, latest in cold-heading type machinery.

The dies clamp on the wire, which is then sheared by a lateral movement of the dies. The head or collar is then cold-headed in the same manner. The dies then open and the formed piece drops out.

Cold-heading was first used for making nails. The procedure varies slightly from the above, as the head is formed prior to shearing. After that, the dies open, permitting the wire to travel forward and then be cut to the proper length. The points are formed in the cut-off process.

There are several methods of forming the head. See Fig. 86-6.

The cold-heading process takes place at a speed that can turn out 400 parts per minute on such machines as shown in Fig. 86-7.

When cold-heading does not involve parts over 1″ in diameter, it is the preferred process for much work.

86-3. This cold header is a two-die, three-punch, solid-die machine engineered to utilize an advanced impact extrusion die design in combination with the conventional two-blow heading sequence.

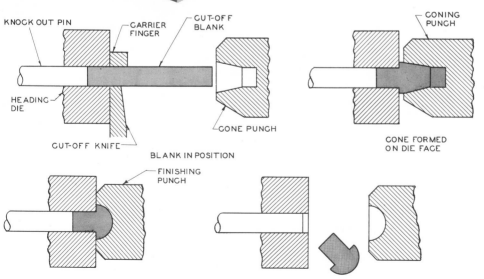

86-4. The operations performed in a cold-heading sequence.

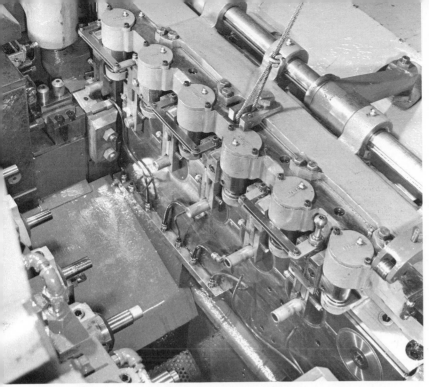

86-5. Die-box area. Blanks are automatically transferred from die to die between blows. Different operations are performed simultaneously at the various stations. Completed part is ejected from the final die with each stroke.

Hot-heading is used for heading bar stock 1″ or more in diameter and where large heads are required. In hot-heading, of course, the stock has to be heated to a high temperature.

There are certain *shapes* which are best made by cold-heading. Parts having non-symmetrical offsets cannot be machined but do lend themselves to the cold-heading process. Cold-heading, in comparison to machining, produces no waste while a machining part produces a considerable amount of waste material in the form of chips, as shown in the comparison of the two methods, Fig. 86-8. The flow lines as shown in the same figure indicate that they follow the contour of the upset and produce a much stronger part than machining, which cuts across these lines.

86-6. Four methods of forming the head or collar.

BODY DIE

PUNCH

KNOCKOUT PIN

SHAPED BY PUNCH

SHAPED BY DIE

SHAPED BY BOTH

SHAPED BETWEEN PUNCH AND DIE

86-7. A cold-header.

86-8. Savings can be obtained in raw material by cold working. Better quality and greater strength are also obtained.

MACHINED

COLD-HEADED

SCRAP

SCRAP

ROD DIAMETER

WIRE DIAMETER NO SCRAP

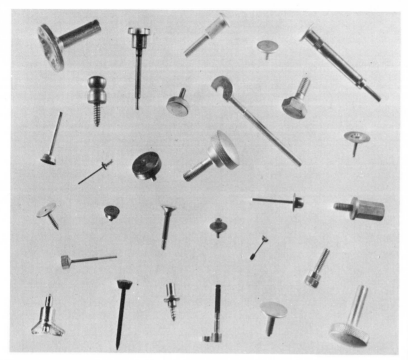

86-9. A great variety of parts such as shown in this illustration can be produced with cold-headers.

86-10. A universal cold-header. This machine is actually four headers in one. Designed as a four-blow machine with two solid dies, it converts to two-blow heading plus extruding and trimming tubular rivets.

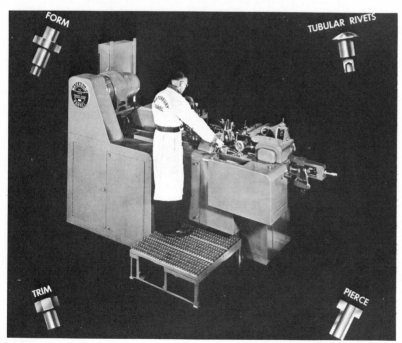

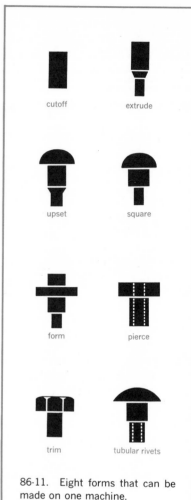

cutoff

extrude

upset

square

form

pierce

trim

tubular rivets

86-11. Eight forms that can be made on one machine.

Cold-heading machines can produce parts at a much faster rate than automatic screw machines. Fig. 86-9 is an illustration of parts that were formerly made by slower and more costly machining operations. These parts can now be made by the extrusion principle coupled with cold forming on the same machine. This process makes it possible to produce 50 to 150 parts per minute.

Fig. 86-10 shows a universal header that can do all the eight operations shown in Fig. 86-11, using either ferrous or non-ferrous wire. This machine is designed as a two-die, four-blow header, but quickly converts to two-blow heading plus extruding, trimming, and tubular rivet heading. Many secondary operations on other machines, such as drilling, trimming, and shaving, are eliminated.

The industrial fastener industry today is made up of some 400 companies producing about 400,000 different types and sizes of fasteners.

Check Your Knowledge

1. *What is meant by the term cold-heading?*

2. *What type of products can be made by this process?*

3. *Explain the cold-heading process on a solid die machine.*

4. *What is an open-die header and how does it differ from a solid-die type?*

5. *Name the main methods of forming a head on a part.*

6. *Give some of the advantages of cold-heading over the machining process.*

7. *What is "hot-heading"?*

8. *Why are certain shapes best made by cold-heading? Give examples.*

9. *What are flow lines?*

Terms to Know and Spell

deformed
elastic
axial
ejecting
shearing
offset
extrusion
header

---

87 ▷ Explosive Forming

Explosive forming is a high-energy-rate method of forming metal by the sudden high-velocity release of the powerful energy of explosives. The rapidly applied shock waves and gas pressures caused by the explosive charges are great enough to shape the metal upon which they act. This process is being used in the aircraft and missile industry to shape the high-strength materials that are being used in these industries today. It is especially useful for shaping materials that are difficult to form by conventional methods or parts that are too large to be formed in existing presses. A great deal of welding is also eliminated.

Explosive forming may be done by gas pressure, shock wave, or a combination of the two. The method used is largely controlled by the shape of the cavity in the die in which the explosive charge is fired. There are two distinct methods of explosive forming:

- Pressure forming with a propellant type explosive.

- Shock forming with detonating explosives.

In **pressure forming** a closed system is necessary. The propellant must be confined in order to burn and control the pressure generated.

Open and semi-open systems are generally used with the **shock forming** method in forming large parts. Fig. 87-1. Pressure can be applied directly. The media through which the energy of the explosion is transmitted include air, oil, water, plastics, and talc.

87-1.   Forward head closure for Polaris missile. 1. Sized in an open die. 2. Die with workpiece lowered into a tank of water, which was the transfer medium for the shock wave from the explosive.

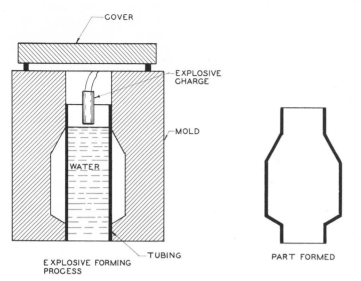

87-2. How a piece of tubing is explosively formed with water as a medium.

87-3. Explosively assembled tubing and coupling.

87-4. (A) Explosively assembled tubing and coupling. (B) Mechanically joined.

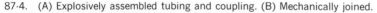
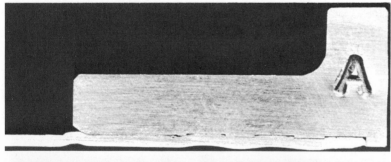
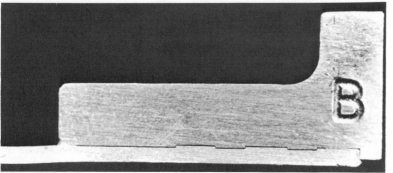

These pressure-transfer media also serve as a shock and noise dampener. In using this technique the bottom of the die is vented to remove the air between the workpiece and the die to prevent surface damage to the work. Sometimes a vacuum pump is employed to remove the air.

The type of explosive mixture and container size controls the gas pressure and deformation rate, which is critical in this type of forming.

One of the most common methods used in the aircraft industry in forming cones, cylinders, tanks, etc., is shown in Fig. 87-2. In this explosive process, water was used as the intermediate medium.

In this technique, explosive forming utilizes the pressure wave generated by the explosion in the water to force the material being formed against the walls of the die. The explosive is placed in the center at approximately water level, and a cover placed on top of the die. The air is pumped from between the die and the workpiece and the explosive is detonated. The cylindrical part is forced against the walls of the die.

Under water it is possible to duplicate such operations as stretching, shrinking, bending, and shearing, that were formerly done with presses, drop hammers, brakes, and similar less efficient equipment.

There are two basic types of explosives: (1) low-energy, (2) high-energy. Low-energy explosives are materials which *burn* rapidly rather than explode. This produces a gas which expands, causing a pressure. Powders such

426

as smokeless, black, and ball are used in shotgun shells, blank cartridges, and similar containers.

High-energy or detonating explosives are set off by the shock of a primary explosive. They expand more rapidly and create a great deal of shock per unit of weight. Some types of high-energy explosives are based on nitroglycerin or TNT.

A great deal of progress is now being made in the assembly of parts by the explosive method. Figs. 87-3 and 87-4.

Check Your Knowledge

1. What is explosive forming?

2. What industries, especially, are using this method of forming metal?

3. What are some of the advantages of forming metal by this process?

4. Name two distinct methods of explosive forming.

5. When are open and semi-open systems used?

6. How is the pressure applied in this method of forming?

7. What machine operations can be duplicated by this method?

8. Explain the important difference between low-energy and high-energy explosives.

Terms to Know and Spell

explosive
propellant
detonating
deformation
medium
shock
low-energy
high-energy

---

88 ▷ Chemical Milling

Chemical milling is the process used to shape metals to an exacting tolerance by the chemical removal of material, or deep etching, rather than by conventional mechanical milling or machining operations. This permits the fabrication of lightweight, high strength parts which heretofore were either too expensive or practically impossible to manufacture.

Chemical milling and machine milling have one thing in common: both are basic production methods of removing metal. However, the two techniques are so different that neither one entirely replaces the other.

But mechanical methods of removing metal are limited to the removal of metal from simple planes. In the chemical method, metal can be removed from all surfaces of an entire part at one time and also from the most complex surfaces. Fig. 88-1.

88-1. A typical deep-draw part that has been chemically milled. Compare with the heavier, formed part below.

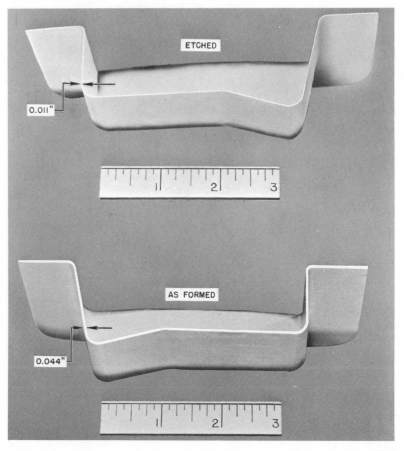

ETCHED

0.011"

AS FORMED

0.044"

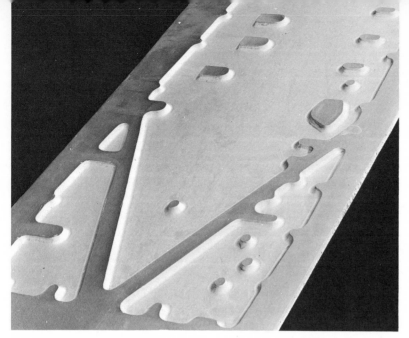

88-2. "Sandwich" panel with integrally milled inserts.

88-3. Steps in chemical milling an aircraft heat exchanger.

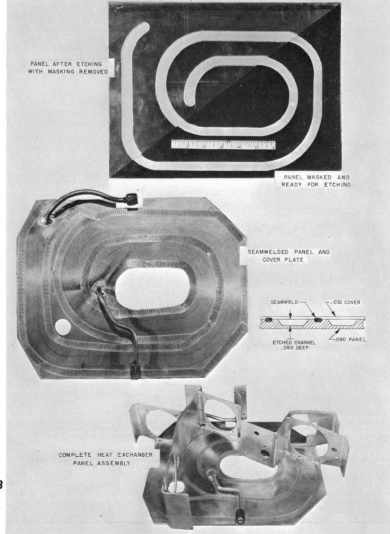

PANEL AFTER ETCHING
WITH MASKING REMOVED

PANEL MASKED AND
READY FOR ETCHING

SEAMWELDED PANEL AND
COVER PLATE

SEAMWELD   .032 COVER

ETCHED CHANNEL   .090 PANEL
.060 DEEP

COMPLETE HEAT EXCHANGER
PANEL ASSEMBLY

As said, the greatest advantage of chemical milling is that it is possible to perform operations that cannot be done successfully with conventional machine tools. Fig. 88-2.

Chemical milling is being used extensively in the fabrication of Apollo and Saturn hardware in our space program. The Apollo Command Module, which will make the journey to the moon and back, will be a structure that will meet all the requirements for lightweight strength through chemical milling processes.

The basic chemical milling applications have three uses: (1) weight removal, (2) cutting, and (3) tapering. The most important of the three is weight reduction.

Tapering by the chemical milling process is being done on 55' long aluminum wing stringers for the Boeing Airplane Co., on their 727 jet aircraft. These stringers are placed in a tank 60' deep and 8' in diameter. This tapers the basic shapes, which include tie, zees, channels, and box sections, in quantities from 4 to 24 at a time.

Where chemical milling was previously limited to shallow cuts on thin sheets, work is now being done on "gore segments" of 33' diameter fuel-and-oxidizer-tank bulkheads, where the depths of cut by etching exceed ½". Stainless steel parts are chemically milled to tolerances of plus or minus .001 on a production basis.

Procedure Used in Chemical Milling

The entire part is cleaned to remove all dirt and grease that will affect the etching process. It is generally degreased with

428

trichlorethylene and then alkaline cleaned for 15 min. in aviation cleaner.

Part is rinsed for 5 min., at 110° to 120° F.

It is then deoxidized for 10 min. in chromic deoxidant, rinsed, and dried.

A key step in professional chemical milling is proper masking. Fig. 88-3. Technicians apply a rubber coating material to the part. Maskant is applied by "flow coating" to attain a uniform film of controlled thickness. Large parts are masked by using electrospraying, which produces a smooth, uniform coating. Maskants are also applied by airless spraying or flow coating. Cure part for 1 hour at 210° F.

A template is placed over the part, and areas to be exposed to the etch are scribed by trained workers using scribing tools to remove cured rubber coating only in areas to be milled.

The part is then lowered into the caustic etchant at 195° F. long enough to dissolve the indicated metal. Temperature control is maintained thermostatically. Fig. 88-4 shows the part being lowered into an etchant tank.

Due to the fact that the etchant removes metal at an equal rate in all directions, the maskant must extend onto the etch area for a distance equal to the total depth of the etched portion. This allowance is the "eat back." Fig. 88-5.

After rinsing in cold water, the part is lowered into a solvent tank which releases the maskant bond. The maskant is stripped off.

The part is then brightened by dipping in chromic deoxidant 3 to 5 min. and rinsed.

88-4. Chemcial milling etchant tank. These great tanks are constructed in underground excavations covered by a heavy concrete craneway structure for supporting handling equipment and etching baskets. This tank has a 12,000 gal. capacity. In it were milled the long skins of the B-70 bomber.

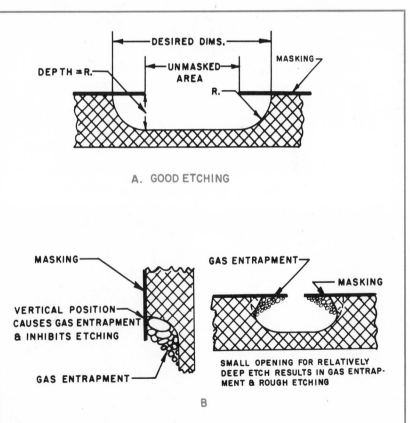

88-5. (A) Shows how chemical milling eats back under the masking just as far as it etches down into the metal. Allowances must be made in the template to allow for eat-back. (B) Undesirable etching conditions.

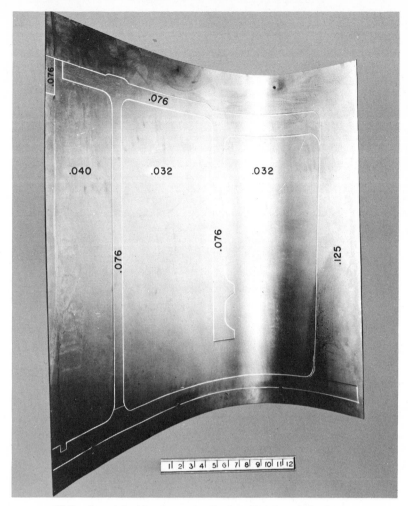

88-6. A part that has been chemically milled to various depths.

88-7. Checking a chemically milled part with an etching-depth-limit monitor.

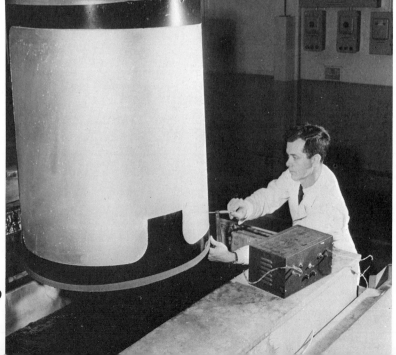

88-8. Senior Research Engineer Clayton Shepherd compares test specimens etched by means of the Chem-Mill process.

Next, the part is dried in an oven.

NOTE: If the part is to be etched at several depths, the maskant is removed from the deepest part first and other areas are then unmasked at the time intervals proportionate to the differences in depth. Fig. 88-6 shows a part that has different etched depth areas.

After the part has been etched, it is given a final inspection using a Vidigage to check thickness. Fig. 88-7. Parts are also checked for surface flaws—blemishes and scratches—by the use of fluorescent dye and ultraviolet light.

Constant efforts are being made to develop new and improved etching solutions, Fig. 88-8.

As this process is further developed it will continue to replace machining operations that cannot be performed best by conventional methods. Fig. 88-9 shows comparative chemically milled and machine-milled surfaces.

Chemical milling has been a valuable aid in helping aircraft designers in achieving finer details for some aircraft parts. Figs. 88-10 and 88-11.

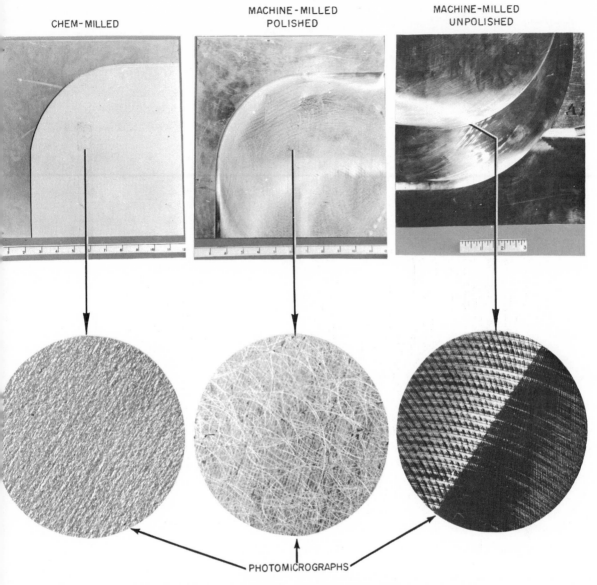

CHEM-MILLED

MACHINE-MILLED
POLISHED

MACHINE-MILLED
UNPOLISHED

PHOTOMICROGRAPHS

88-9.   Comparative machine milled and chemically-milled surfaces.

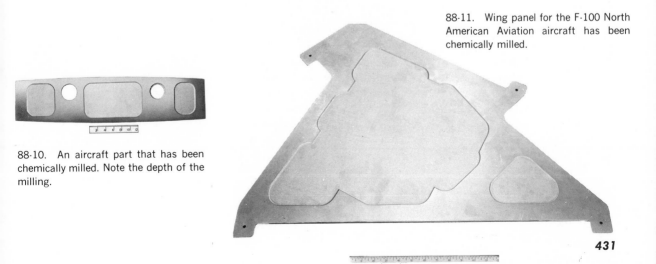

88-11.   Wing panel for the F-100 North American Aviation aircraft has been chemically milled.

88-10.   An aircraft part that has been chemically milled. Note the depth of the milling.

1. What is chemical milling?

2. Why is this process of removing metal used?

3. What are some of its advantages?

4. Chemical milling applications have three basic uses. What are they?

5. Explain the procedure of this process.

Terms to Know and Spell

chemical	*alkaline*	*solvent*
milling	*deoxidized*	*caustic*
etching	*maskant*	*thermostatically*
contoured	*template*	

89 ▷ Automation

The lathe, shaper, drill press, milling machine, and grinder are still the basic machine tools of industry and will be found in manufacturing plants.

Yet radical changes are being made in machine tools and the various processes of machining. New products are being developed that require the services of highly skilled technicians, engineers, and electronics experts. This has been necessary because the machining industry is a highly competitive one and production and costs have to be taken into serious consideration.

Due to the fact that numerically controlled machines are so expensive, it is rather doubtful that this type of equipment will find its way soon into the typical school metalworking center. However, the author feels it is important that the metalworking student should have at least some knowledge of the fundamentals.

Automation has become an important part of metal processing. Most plants today have some type of automatic equipment at work. Common examples are cutting-type machine tools with automatic loading and unloading devices. Other types of automation found are transfer lines between cutting-type machine tools and between presses; automatic plating, heat treating, and welding lines. We have had automation for a great many years turning out products on automatic screw machines controlled by a series of cams on a revolving drum.

Many improvements have been made on modern machine tools. A machine of the type shown in Fig. 89-1 is used for operations such as boring, milling, drilling, and tapping. All types of jigs, fixtures, and product parts can be machined without special operator skill which is normally required for this type of work.

Reliance on the "human element" to produce close tolerance work is largely eliminated by automatic machine functions.

Numerical control is the most significant breakthrough in manufacturing technology since the invention of production line techniques to mass-produce identical, interchangeable parts. The primary machine functions have not changed, but in the past, if the operator wished to make certain movements, he turned cranks and read scales to be sure the machine did the specified work. Numerical control tells the machine to move to a specific point to perform some operation. The machine automatically measures, knows when it reaches the specified point, and relates back to control, through the "closed loop" system, that it has completed the instructions fed in through the tape.

Types of Numerically Controlled Machines

There are many types of machine tools that can be adapted to numerical control methods of machining. In 1964-65 there were about 3,600 N/C machine tools built and delivered, compared to about 7,000 in operation. Estimates are that by the late 1970's 30 to 40% of all machine tools built will be numerically controlled.

Drills, milling machines, jig borers, turret lathes, and many other machines are produced to operate on the N/C system.

The turret lathe shown in Fig. 89-2 can be set up in a very short time with simple standard tooling and visual readout.

This machine has a presetting selector system, Fig. 89-3, and

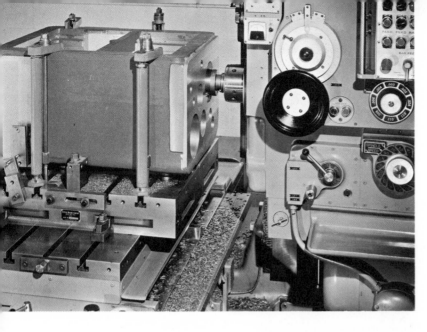

89-1.   A DeVlieg Jigmil.

transistorized memory control of all the machine functions and operation sequences. Except for loading and unloading, all operations are completely automatic. The back of the machine console is shown in Fig. 89-4. Fig. 89-5 shows parts that have been produced on this machine.

Jig boring requires extreme machining accuracy. The machine shown in Fig. 89-6 is an N/C jig borer with positioning accuracy to ± millionths of an inch, with repeatability the same. It is also equipped with fully transistorized, or "logic," circuitry.

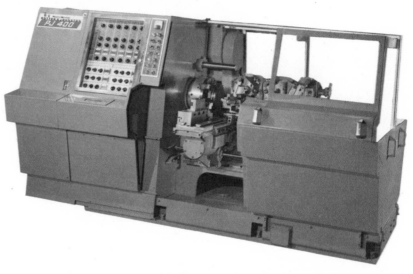

89-2.   Numerically controlled automatic turret lathe. Sets up with standard tooling and visual readout. Operations are completely automatic.

89-3.   Control panel on a numerically controlled turret lathe.

433

89-4. Back of the console of the automatic N/C turret lathe.

Understanding Numerical Control

Numerical control is the control by numbers. This takes a giant step beyond conventional automatic control, because it minimizes jigs, fixtures, and set-up. The short-cut handling of tooling and set-up gives a practical answer for production when it is needed, whether it involves 10 pieces or 10,000 pieces. It cuts down large inventories and production costs, because the "stored" knowledge can be used for any run, short or long, almost instantly.

The idea of numerical control is to use simple basic machine tools in which one, two, or more multiple motions are easily coordinated, sequenced, or otherwise manipulated from the nec-

89-6. Numerically controlled jig borer.

89-5. Parts that can be made on an N/C turret lathe.

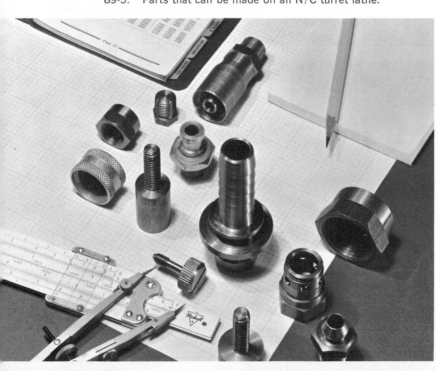

essary data prepared in advance. In the broad sense N/C requires only the counting and measuring functions of numbers. It directly converts *symbolic* numerical values into *physical* values—such as quantities or dimensions. (When a machinist operates a machine in the conventional manner, he is putting in a physical value, not a numerical value.) Once set up, machines controlled by tape do not need skilled operators.

Programming

Point-to-point is the simplest form of numerical control. Programming can be accomplished by anyone having a basic knowledge of conventional machining practices along with the ability to read a working drawing. Point-to-point programming does not require the use of a computer.

A numerical control system follows the instructions that are programmed on the tape. It is important to prepare the tape program carefully, as the system is unable to think for itself and cannot overcome errors made in the tape program.

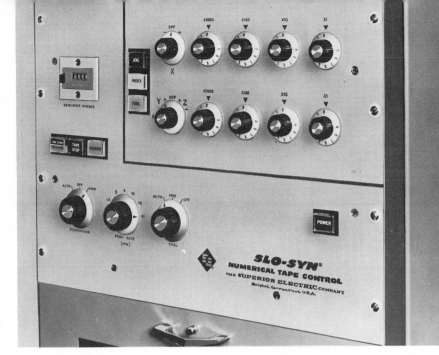

89-8. Example of a numerical tape control unit.

Cartesian, or rectangular, coordinates are used for programming. The X and Y axes represent horizontal table movements while the Z axis represents a vertical motion of the spindle or tool, whether it is a drilling machine or a vertical milling machine. Fig. 89-7. With two-axis numerical control, Z-axis motion is generally controlled by a mechanical or hydraulic actuator energized by commands from a controller, which is shown in Fig. 89-8.

Numerical controls may use either incremental or absolute positioning. With incremental positioning, each movement is programmed from the last position. When programming for absolute positioning, each machining location is given in relation to the zero point of origin.

Numerical control systems also differ in the way information is presented on the tape for entry into the controller. Although the

use of eight-channel tape, Fig. 89-9, and binary decimal coding is almost standard, the tape format may be fixed sequential, tab sequential, word address, or variable block, depending upon the control system used. All can be

89-7. Three dimensional coordinates. X and Y axes are horizontal table motions; Z axis is a vertical tool motion.

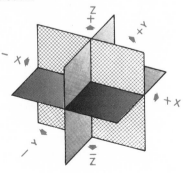

89-9. Eight channel tape with binary code value of holes. All holes punched in channel #1 = 1, #2 = 2, #3 = 4, #4 = 8, and #6 = 0.

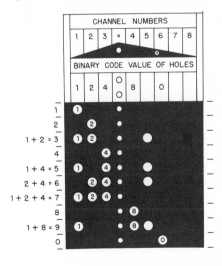

prepared on a special typewriter or a standard tape-punching unit. Fig. 89-10 shows a chart of type codes for a typical controller which uses the tab sequential format.

Preparing The Program

Before preparing a tape program, the programmer must know whether the program is for an incremental or an absolute positioning system. He should also be familiar with the required tape format and codes.

A rough sketch of the part should be made, redimensioning as required for purposes of programming and showing tool changes and the order in which machining operations will take place. Fig. 89-11. As you can see, the part shown requires six holes. The sketch shows the dimensions, point-to-point increments for programming, and the setup point. The holes are numbered to indicate drilling order.

The following procedures should be used by the programmer:

1. Plan the method of locating and holding the workpiece on the machine table. This might require making a special fixture to hold the part.

2. Select a setup point. This point can be located at a corner of the part, at the reference point on the fixture, or at some other reference point.

3. Select the first tool change point where the finished part will be removed and a new workpiece inserted at the completion of the tape program. The setup point can be selected for this location if desired. Sometimes it is neces-

EIA STANDARD RS-244 KEYBOARD SYMBOLS	ALTERNATE KEYBOARD SYMBOLS	CODE ON TAPE									SYSTEM FUNCTION
		1	2	3	•	4	5	6	7	8	
TAPE FEED	SPACE, BUZZ, FEED										LEADER
	RWST, %, $										RWS (REWIND STOP)
TAB											TAB
+											+ (OPTIONAL)
−											−
1											1
2											2
3											3
4											4
5											5
6											6
7											7
8											8
9											9
0											0
CAR. RET. OR EOB											EOB (END OF BLOCK)
DELETE	TAPE FEED										DELETE

89-10. Typical tape codes for a numerical controller employing the tab-sequential format.

sary to select a second point so that sufficient clearance is provided when loading or unloading workpieces.

4. The sequence of operations is determined next and additional tool change points should

be selected as required. Make sure that the tool will not hit the fixture or workpiece during any positioning motion.

5. Record the sequence of operations, together with any operations, on a program sheet. Fig.

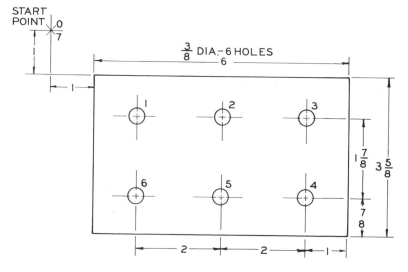

89-11. Programmer's sketch of drilling operation.

89-12. Filling out the tape preparation sheet from the part print.

89-12. The program sheet must be compatible with the tape format used.

6. When the program is complete, a copy of it is given to a typist who makes the tape on a tape-punching machine with a keyboard similar to that of a typewriter, Fig. 89-13, or on a machine like the one shown in Fig. 89-14.

To see the steps a programmer must follow in a sample point-to-point drilling program

89-13. Information typed on a special typewriter with tape attachments, the result being completely coded and punched tape.

using the tab-sequential format and codes, refer back to Fig. 89-10.

Fig. 89-15 shows a completed program for the drilling job. Since the holes are center-drilled, a tool change will be needed. Each horizontal line of information, together with any miscellaneous functions such as tool changes, makes up one positioning movement. The drilling operations will be performed by the controller after positioning has been completed. The controller automatically actuates the tool after positioning unless inhibited in the tape program.

Starting from zero (start point), each line has a sequence number, labeled "Seq. No.," placed in the first column. The sequence number marked zero contains no positioning information. The Rewind Stop (RWS) instructions to the tape reader and the End of Block (EOB) code are entered here.

With the tab-sequential format, X-axis positioning commands follow the second command. A tab should be entered in the second column and the direction (+ or −) and magnitude (distance) entered in the third and fourth columns. A Tab is entered in the fifth column to indicate that the X command is complete and the Y command is to follow. The Y-axis commands are entered in the sixth and seventh columns and a Tab code is entered in column eight. Rewind, Tool Change and any other micellaneous function codes are entered in column nine and an EOB code is placed in column ten, conveying to the control unit that the block of information is complete.

Drilling Operation

The tape has been completed and the job is ready to be run.

89-14. Converting machine operations to N/C tape.

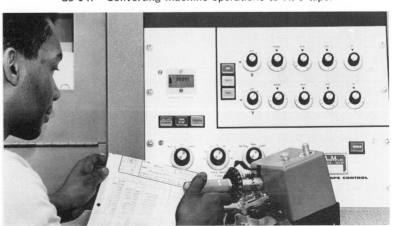

SLO-SYN™ NUMERICAL TAPE CONTROL PROGRAM

COMPANY NAME _____ ADDRESS _____

PREPARED BY DATE	PART NAME	PART NO.	OPER. NO.
CK'D BY DATE	Plate	Sample Drilling Program No. 3	
SHEET OF	REMARKS:		
DEPT	Tool Switch—Auto	Tools: Center-Drill	
	Feed Rate—Hi	3/8″ Drill	
TAPE NO.	Backlash—No. 2 or No. 3	Run Program For Each Tool	

SEQ. NO.	TAB OR EOB	+ OR −	"x" INCREMENT	TAB OR EOB	+ OR −	"y" INCREMENT	TAB OR EOB	"m" FUNCT.	EOB	INSTRUCTIONS
									EOB	
0	RWS								EOB	Change Tool, Load, Start
1	TAB		2000	TAB	−	1875			EOB	
2	TAB		2000						EOB	
3	TAB		2000						EOB	
4	TAB			TAB	−	1875			EOB	
5	TAB	−	2000						EOB	
6	TAB	−	2000						EOB	
7	TAB	−	2000	TAB		3750	TAB	02	EOB	

89-15. Completed program for drilling job.

89-16. Inserting tape in the tape reader.

The tape is placed in the control unit, Fig. 89-16, and is ready to be fed through the tape reader. In operation, the tape passes under a series of wire "fingers" and the circuit is operated by compressed air or a photoelectric cell. Each time a hole in the tape appears, a wire finger drops through a hole and actuates a key. An electrical pulse is transmitted by the pressure of the key to a sensing device on the controls which transmits a signal to the machine table, telling it when, in what direction, and how far to move. The basic drilling procedure is as follows:

1. Center-drill each hole with a ½″ drill before automatic drilling.

2. Console presets tool switch, feed rate-Hi, and backlash #2 or #3. Fig. 89-17.

3. Operator starts program with a center drill mounted in a toolholder.

4. Sequence #1 through #6 statements move the tool to the first hole and to each of the remaining holes. The holes are center-drilled automatically.

5. Sequence #7 statement returns the tool from the last hole to the starting point and signals the reader to rewind the tape.

6. The operator changes to a ⅜″ drill and reruns the program to accomplish final drilling.

7. At the end of this cycle, the operator changes back to a

89-17. Manual programming of the basic sequence.

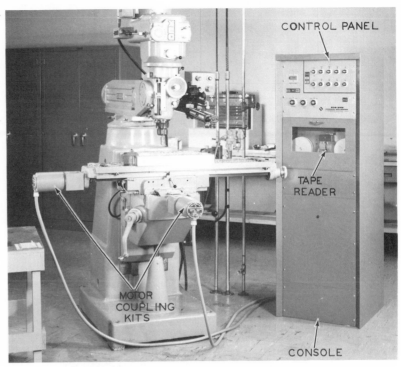

89-18. This job is complete. Tape is being removed and will be filed.

89-19. Vertical Milling machine equipped with numerical controls for straight line milling.

center drill and places a new workpiece in the holding fixture, ready for the next run.

When the order is filled, the tape is removed from the tape reader and stored until the part is to be run again. Fig. 89-18.

Straight line milling programs can also be easily programmed with the point-to-point system. For milling, the tool must be raised or lowered. When this tool movement occurs, an appropriate "M" function code can be inserted in the program. In preparing a program for milling a slot or similar configuration, compensation must be made for the diameter of the milling cutter. Fig. 89-19 shows a vertical milling machine set up for a numerically controlled milling operation.

Check Your Knowledge

1. What is automation?

2. What main significance has numerical control in manufacturing technology?

3. What are the greatest advantages of numerical control?

4. Can production be increased by this method of machine control? How?

5. Are jigs and fixtures necessary for this type of machine operation? Why or why not?

6. What is the difference between incremental and absolute positioning?

7. Briefly describe the procedure followed by programmers.

8. What happens as the finished tape feeds through the tape reader?

Terms to Know and Spell

automation	*programming*	*magnitude*
numerical	*tape*	*specific*
symbolic	*coded*	*setup point*
sequence	*point-to-point*	*computer*
incremental	*coordinate*	*axis*
absolute	*controller*	*positioning*

90 ▷ Inspection

The inspection and testing of parts has become very important in industry. Equipment loads and operating speeds are being stepped up, so it is imperative that fatigue cracks and other flaws in parts be detected before they can result in equipment failure, resultant expense, delay, and possible injury to operating personnel. This testing of parts and materials is commonly known as quality control.

The testing and inspection of parts can be done by: (1) destructive testing and (2) non-destructive testing.

In destructive testing the part is destroyed during the testing process and cannot be used again. Non-destructive testing does not damage the part being tested yet it will furnish information about performance capability.

The three most commonly used tests and the ones that will be described in this unit are: (1) magnetic particle testing [Magnaflux], (2) penetrant testing, and (3) ultrasonic testing.

Magnetic Particle Testing

This magnetic test method uses finely divided ferromagnetic particles to produce indications of defects, only on magnetic material. Fig. 90-1.

A magnetic field is induced in a part by passing an electric current through or around it. The magnetic field is always at right angles to the direction of current flow. It registers an abrupt change in the resistance in the path of the magnetic field, such as would be caused by a crack lying at an angle to the direction of the magnetic field with the magnetic poles

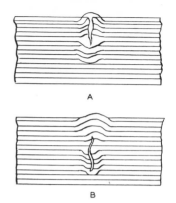

90-2. (A) Magnetic flux distribution at a surface defect. (B) Magnetic flux distribution at a sub-surface defect.

at the crack. Finely divided ferromagnetic particles applied to the area of leakage field will be attracted and outline the crack. Fig. 90-2.

There are many special magnetizing techniques used on such things as gears, welds, etc.

Penetrant Testing

The use of aluminum, magnesium, stainless steel, and other nonmagnetic materials grew rapidly during the late 1930's and at the beginning of World War II. This growth created an urgent need for a sensitive, reliable, fast and inexpensive means of finding surface flaws and other defects in nonferrous materials. The most popular methods at the time were radiography, etching, anodizing, oil and whiting, brittle lacquer, and simple visual inspection. However, none of these could do what penetrants could—locate minute surface cracks and porosity under all circumstances.

Types of Dye Penetrant

There are two types of penetrants now in use—the color-contrast and the fluorescent versions.

90-1. Testing large turbine blades on a Magnaflux machine.

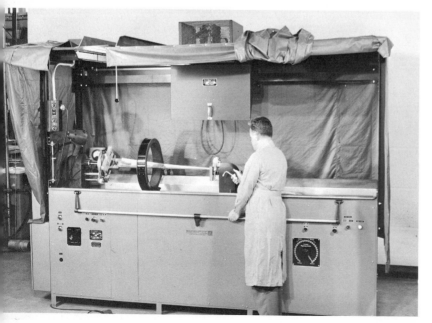

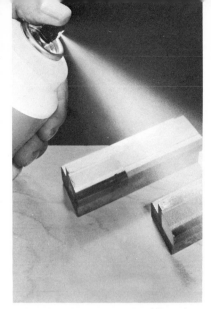

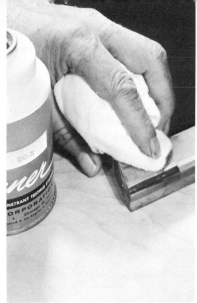

90-3. Spray-on penetrant. Allow short penetration time. (Pre-clean part with spray cleaner if necessary.)

90-4. Use cleaner to remove penetrant from surface.

90-5. Shake can and apply a thin film of developer. Allow a short developing time.

Color-contrast penetrants incorporate a colored dye sufficiently intense to show under ordinary white light.

Fluorescent penetrants contain a more effective fluorescent dye that shows under black "light."

Most penetrants have an oil base. For surfaces on which oil may be considered a serious contaminant, water based penetrants are available. The procedure for using a penetrant follows:

• **Pre-cleaning:** The test surface must be clean and dry. Suspected flaws must be free of water, oil, or other contaminants. Solvents are often used. Sometimes the part is sand or grit blasted to remove scale, paint, and other foreign substances.

• **Application and penetration:** The test surface must be covered with a film of penetrant by dipping, bathing, spraying, or brushing. Sufficient time must be allowed for the penetrant to enter any flaws. Fig. 90-3.

• **Cleaning and drying:** The test surface must be wiped, washed, or rinsed free of excess penetrant. Drying with cloths or hot air follows. Fig. 90-4.

• **Developing:** A developing powder applied to the test surface acts like a blotter to speed the penetrant's tendency to exude from any flaws on the test surface. Fig. 90-5.

• **Inspection:** Depending upon the type of penetrant, visual inspection is made under ordinary white light, or under "black" light if a fluorescent penetrant is used.

In basic theory fluorescent penetrant inspection is very simple indeed. It is the most widely used to find pores, cracks, and cracklike defects. Fig. 90-6.

The test's effectiveness is based upon an infallible natural phenomenon—capillary action. This is the same force that draws water and sap to the top of the tallest trees.

While the fluorescent penetrant solution is applied to a part surface by dipping, spraying, or brushing, it does not "seep" into any defects that may be present.

It is literally pulled into them by capillary action. Surface penetrant drains away, leaving the penetrant in the defects. The surface is rinsed clean with water and, before or after drying, a wet or dry developer is applied. This acts like a blotter, and draws the penetrant back to the surface. Fig. 90-7. See page 442.

90-6. Inspection under black light. Cracks will show as glowing lines; porosity as spots.

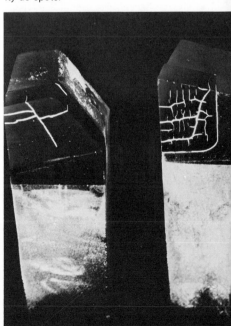

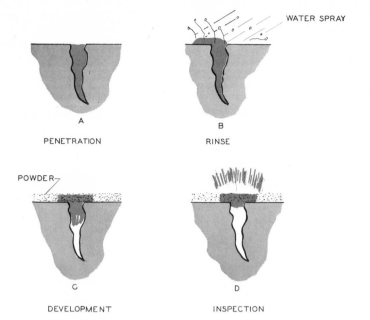

A
PENETRATION

B
RINSE

WATER SPRAY

POWDER

C
DEVELOPMENT

D
INSPECTION

90-7. (A) Fluorescent penetrant on the surface is drawn down into the crack by strong capillary forces. (B) Water spray removes the penetrant from the outer surface, but not from cracks and pores. (C) Developer acts like a blotter, to draw the penetrant out of the crack and hold it on the surface. (D) Black light causes the penetrant to glow in the hole.

sprayed on the part and a developer makes the flaw visible. Fig. 90-9.

Ultrasonic Testing

The third and newest method is ultrasonic testing. This technique utilizes a high frequency sound beam to detect cracks and flaws in a part. The depth of the flaw is shown by a gage on a trace screen. Fig. 90-10.

Chrysler's Indianapolis foundry uses a portable ultrasonic measuring device supplied by Magnaflux Corp. to measure wall thickness of rough castings for engine blocks. Formerly this was measured only by destructive testing.

The instrument works according to resonant frequencies, which are proportional to thickness.

90-8. When part is inspected under black light, all defects glow with fluorescent brilliance.

When inspected under black light, Fig. 90-8, every defect glows with fluorescent brilliance. This glowing line or spot marks each defect.

The detection of *leaks* represents a major use of penetrants. Leak detection applications range from the closed systems of nuclear power generators to the miniature semiconductor devices used in modern electronic circuits.

"SPOTCHECK"
(Trademark: Magnaflux Corp.)

Spotcheck is a penetrant which is sprayed on a part for inspection purposes to detect any flaws. This penetrant does not need a black light to bring out the flaws. A cleaner is applied to loosen grease and dirt. The penetrant is then

90-9. "Spotcheck" penetrant being sprayed on a suspended area of casting to find any possible cracks, before failure on the job itself.

Sound energy is sent from a contacting transducer through a couplant (such as oil, glycerin, or soap film). When the constantly varying frequency of the wave meets the resonant frequency of the workpiece, the thickness of the workpiece is read out on the calibrated dial of the test instrument.

X-ray Testing

Welds have been inspected by x-ray or gamma ray devices for many years.

However, x-ray testing has its disadvantages. Costs can run as high as $4.00 per foot of weld inspected, and the area must be cleared of all personnel because of radiation hazards. This can mean production delays and excessive production costs.

Ultrasonic testing of welds is rapidly taking the place of x-ray testing.

Check Your Knowledge

1. What is meant by the term "quality control?"

2. How can the testing and inspection of parts be accomplished?

3. Name one of the disadvantages of destructive testing.

4. Name three of the most important and most commonly used methods of testing materials.

5. Explain each method.

6. What is a penetrant? How is it used?

7. What is ultrasonic testing?

8. What are some of the disadvantages of x-ray testing?

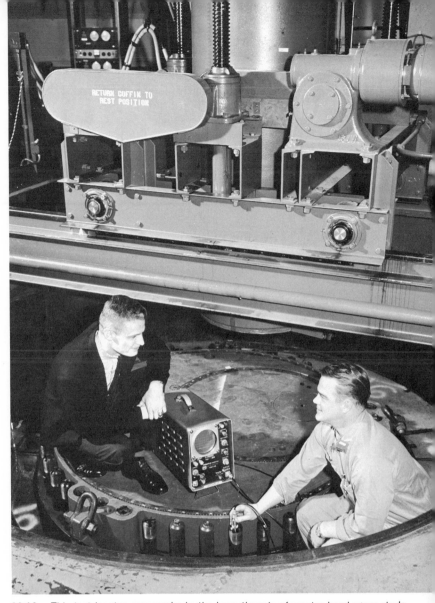

90-10. This test locates any cracks in the base threads of reactor head-cover studs.

Terms to Know and Spell

destructive	*radiography*	*ultrasonic*
magnetic	*anodizing*	*transducer*
particle	*fluorescent*	*resonant*
ferromagnetic	*developer*	*calibrated*
penetrant	*capillary*	

The Metric System

MANY TIMES during the last two centuries, the Congress of the United States considered the merits of adopting the metric system as America's primary language of measurement. Each time action was postponed, often because the metric system was not then in use by our major trading partners abroad. Now, with every other major nation converted to metric or committed to conversion, this obstacle has been removed.

No other system of measurement that has been actually used can match the inherent simplicity of International Metric. It was originally designed to fill all the needs of scientists and engineers, although the average individual need only know and use a few simple parts of it.

It is a foregone conclusion that eventually the United States will join the rest of the world in the use of the metric system as the common language of measurement.

It is with this thought in mind that a section on the metric system has been added to this text, so that students may obtain some knowledge and understanding of the metric system as it relates to industry as well as everyday living.

A scale showing metric measurements.

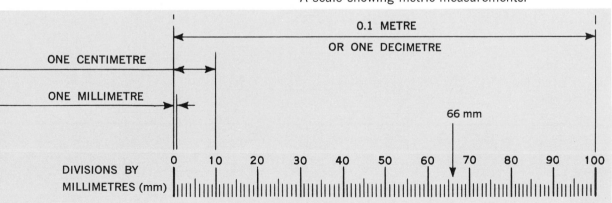

91 ▷ The Basics of the Metric System

COMPARING THE MOST COMMON MEASURING UNITS

Approximate conversions from customary to metric and vice versa

	WHEN YOU KNOW	YOU CAN FIND	IF YOU MULTIPLY BY
LENGTH	inches	millimetres	25
	feet	centimetres	30
	yards	metres	0.9
	miles	kilometres	1.6
	millimetres	inches	0.04
	centimetres	inches	0.4
	metres	yards	1.1
	kilometres	miles	0.6
AREA	square inches	square centimetres	6.5
	square feet	square metres	0.09
	square yards	square metres	0.8
	square miles	square kilometres	2.6
	acres	square hectometres	0.4
	square centimetres	square inches	0.16
	square metres	square yards	1.2
	square kilometres	square miles	0.4
	square hectometres	acres	2.5
MASS	ounces	grams	2.8
	pounds	kilograms	0.45
	short tons	megagrams	0.9
	grams	ounces	0.035
	kilograms	pounds	2.2
	megagrams	short tons	1.1
LIQUID VOLUME	ounces	milliliters	3.0
	pints	liters	0.47
	quarts	liters	0.95
	gallons	liters	3.8
	milliliters	ounces	0.034
	liters	pints	2.1
	liters	quarts	1.06
	liters	gallons	0.26
TEMPERATURE	degrees Fahrenheit	degrees Celsius	5/9 (after subtracting 32)
	degrees Celsius	degrees Fahrenheit	9/5 (then add 32)

Table 91-A

There are only six basic units in the International Metric system: (1) length—metre, (2) mass—kilogram, (3) time—second, (4) electric current—ampere, (5) temperature—kelvin (which in common use is translated into the degree Celsius, formerly called Centigrade) (6) luminous intensity—candela. All other units are derived from these six units.

Metric is based on the decimal system. Multiples and submultiples of any given unit are always related by powers of 10. As an example, there are 10 millimetres in one centimetre; 100 centimetres in one metre; 1,000 metres in one kilometre. This greatly simplifies converting larger to smaller measurements. In order to calculate the number of metres in 3.794 kilometres, multiply by 1,000 (move the decimal point three places to the right), making the answer 3,794. For comparison, in order to find the inches in 3.794 miles, it is necessary to multiply first by 5,280 and then by 12. See Table 91-A.

Moreover, multiples and submultiples of all of the International Metric units follow a consistent naming scheme, which consists of attaching a prefix to the unit, whatever it may be. Micro is the prefix for one millionth: one metre equals one million micrometres, and one gram equals one million micrograms. For the meaning of other prefixes, see Table 91-B.

Metric calculations are so much easier, in fact, that one authority is convinced the aerospace industry alone would save about $65 million a year in en-

**NAMES AND SYMBOLS FOR
METRIC PREFIXES**

PREFIX		MEANS
Tera	(10^{12})	One trillion times
giga	(10^9)	One billion times
mega	(10^6)	One million times
kilo	(10^3)	One thousand times
hecto	(10^2)	One hundred times
deca	(10)	Ten times
deci	(10^-)	One tenth of
centi	(10^{-2})	One hundredth of
milli	(10^{-3})	One thousandth of
micro	(10^{-6})	One millionth of
nano	(10^{-9})	One billionth of
pico	(10^{-12})	One trillionth of

Table 91-B

gineers' time by converting entirely to metric.

Many manufacturing concerns are now in the process of changing drawings to show decimal equivalents in place of fractions. Some are also converting decimal dimensions to millimetres, showing both the inch dimensions as well as metric. This system is known as "dual dimensioning."

Use Of Dual Dimensioning*

Most industries using dual dimensioning on their drawings show metric sizes above the dimension line and inch dimensions below. The unit of measure on all metric drawings is the millimetre (mm).

EXAMPLE: $\dfrac{72 \pm 0.1 \text{ mm}}{2.835'' \pm .004''}$

Some plants also use a slash (/) to separate the inch dimension from the metric.

EXAMPLE:
$72 \pm 0.1 / 2.835'' \pm .004''$

The metric equivalent should be shown first. The decimal sign (dot) for metric values is the

*Beloit Tool Corporation, U.S.A. Goes Metric, Swani Publishing Company, Roscoe, Illinois, 1970.

same as now used for the inch decimal dimension.

In the metric system, a decimal point is never used with a whole number. A zero, which is placed to the left of the decimal point, is used for metric dimensions of less than one millimetre. For example: point 3 millimetre should be written 0.3 mm instead of just .3 mm. A comma is never used to show thousands; use a space instead.

EXAMPLE: 1,500 pieces should be written 1 500 pieces; 8,000 rpm should be written 8 000 rpm.

In the inch system, nonsignificant zeros are usually added to the right of the decimal point so as to have the same number of digits in both the dimension and the tolerance.

EXAMPLE: $2.8055'' \pm .0050$

In the metric system, nonsignicant zeros are not added to the right of the decimal point. This means the dimension and the tolerance may or may not have the same number of digits after the decimal point (except for limit dimensions).

EXAMPLE: 72.25 ± 0.127

However, when showing limit dimensions in metric, and either the maximum or minimum dimension has digits after the decimal point, the other value should have zeros added for uniformity.

EXAMPLE: $\dfrac{18}{18.35}$ should be written $\dfrac{18.00}{18.35}$

When showing unequal or bilateral tolerance, both the plus

and minus figures should have the same number of decimal places, adding zeros where necessary.

EXAMPLE: $18 \dfrac{+ 0.15}{- 0.1}$ should be written $18 \dfrac{+ 0.15}{- 0.10}$

This symbol—Ø—designates a diametral value and should be shown on drawings either before or after the diametral dimension.

EXAMPLE: $\varnothing \dfrac{25.4}{1.00}$ or $\dfrac{25.4}{1.00} \varnothing$

As an example, let's take a milling cutter, Fig. 91-1, with the size 4″ O.D. × ½″ wide × 1½″ hole. Converted to our decimal system, it becomes 4.000″ × .500″ × 1.500″. Converted to millimetres, it becomes 101.6 mm × 12.7 mm × 38.1 mm. A dual dimensioned drawing will show this milling cutter as follows:

$$\dfrac{101.6 \times 12.7 \times 38.1}{4.000'' \times .500'' \times 1.500''} \varnothing$$

Fig. 91-2 (Page 448) shows a dual dimensioned drawing. All drawings should illustrate how to identify the inch and millimetre dimensions, by a note adjacent to, or within, the title block. Fig. 91-3(A) shows a drawing using the customary method of dimensioning a drawing using whole num-

91-1.   Milling cutter.

bers and fractions. Fig. 91-3(B) is the same drawing; however, on this drawing the numbers have been converted to their metric equivalents.

As people become more familiar with the metric designations, the inch reference will be dropped completely and only the metric dimension used.

Let's take a standard ¼-20 UNC tap, Fig. 91-4, as an example. Converted to decimal, it becomes .250″-20 UNC (.0500″ pitch). Converted to metric, it is 6.350 mm-1.270 mm. A dual dimensioned drawing would show this tap as follows:

$$\frac{6.35\text{-}1.27}{.250\text{-}20 \text{ UNC}}$$

The ISO (International Standards Organization) has developed very workable standards in most areas; however, for fasteners and screw threads, the ISO proposed standard is incomplete and produces assemblies unsatisfactory to American industry.

The dual-designation code developed in this country will help engineers determine and designate the best screw thread assembly. Most imported thread tools and fasteners do not provide accepted assemblies and often do not fit in present toolholders. In order to minimize the impact of metrification on industry, many tool companies are at present making American metric taps, drills, gages, end mills, and milling cutters for use in present machine tools.

Metric Precision Measuring Instruments

Many different types of precision measuring instruments are manufactured today. Manufacturers in America, who produce goods for overseas use, have indicated the need for metric precision instruments to eliminate costly manufacturing errors caused through confusion or conversion of product specifications and tolerances. Many of the precision measuring instruments used

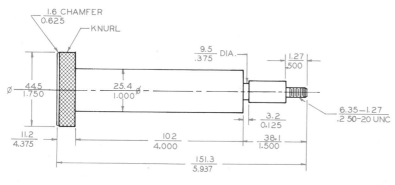

91-2. Typical dual dimensioned drawing.

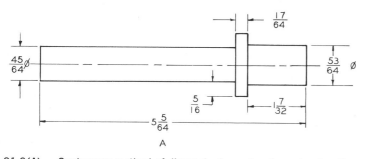

A

91-3(A). Customary method of dimensioning a drawing using fractions.

91-3(B). The same drawing shown in 91-3(A), using the metric system of dimensioning.

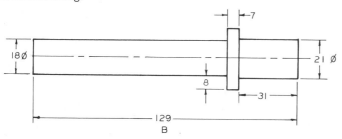

B

91-4. A 1/4-20 tap.

448

in this country today are manufactured by European countries and distributed by American tool suppliers.

Most of these instruments are of the dual dimensioned type to aid workers as the changeover to the metric system becomes a reality in the United States.

Fig. 91-5 shows a tempered steel rule. This rule is double sided—a 15.2 cm scale on one side and a 6″ scale with ⅟₁₆″ and ⅛″ graduations on the other.

A dual dimensioned micrometer known as an "Anglometric" micrometer is shown in Fig. 91-6. This precision instrument is uniquely designed to provide capabilities of two micrometers in one. Metric readings of 0.01 mm are in red and inch readings to .0004″ are in black, eliminating the chance for confusion. These micrometers are available in three sizes: (1) 0-1″/0-25 mm; (2) 1-2″/25-50 mm; and (3) 2-3″ /50-75 mm. Fig. 91-7 (A & B) shows how these micrometers are read (Fig. 91-7B shown on page 450).

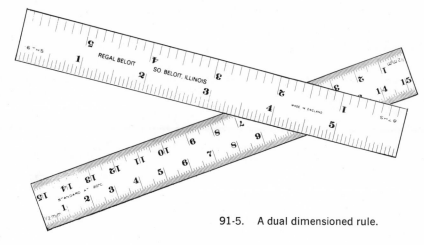

91-5.   A dual dimensioned rule.

91-6.   A dual dimensioned micrometer.

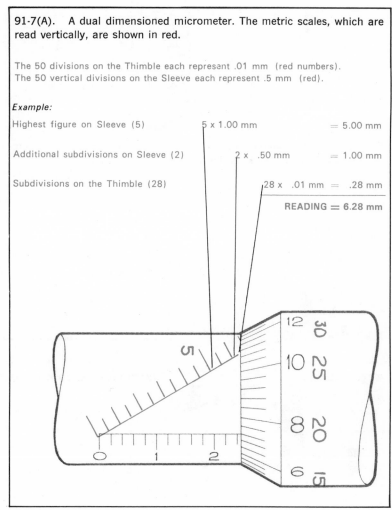

91-7(A).   A dual dimensioned micrometer. The metric scales, which are read vertically, are shown in red.

The 50 divisions on the Thimble each represent .01 mm (red numbers).
The 50 vertical divisions on the Sleeve each represent .5 mm (red).

Example:

Highest figure on Sleeve (5)	5 x 1.00 mm	= 5.00 mm
Additional subdivisions on Sleeve (2)	2 x .50 mm	= 1.00 mm
Subdivisions on the Thimble (28)	.28 x .01 mm =	.28 mm

READING = **6.28 mm**

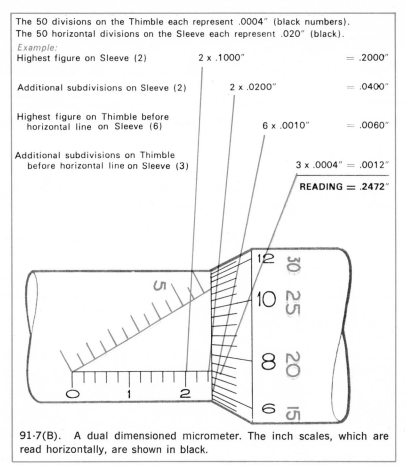

The 50 divisions on the Thimble each represent .0004″ (black numbers).
The 50 horizontal divisions on the Sleeve each represent .020″ (black).

Example:

Highest figure on Sleeve (2)	2 x .1000″	= .2000″
Additional subdivisions on Sleeve (2)	2 x .0200″	= .0400″
Highest figure on Thimble before horizontal line on Sleeve (6)	6 x .0010″	= .0060″
Additional subdivisions on Thimble before horizontal line on Sleeve (3)	3 x .0004″ = .0012″	
	READING = .2472″	

91-7(B).   A dual dimensioned micrometer. The inch scales, which are read horizontally, are shown in black.

Vernier calipers, Fig. 91-8, metric dial calipers, dual dimensioned vernier height gages, gage blocks, and dial indicators are also among the metric measuring instruments now available in this country.

Conversion tables, such as 91-C, 91-D, and 91-E, will probably have to be used by most Americans during the changeover until we all become accustomed to the metric system.

"The U.S.A. must and will convert much more rapidly than generally anticipated, and . . . . most problems will be a result of failure to understand this new simple effective method of measurement. Although Congress approved the metric system over 100 years ago, we have failed to follow through and metrification will be more difficult as each day passes."*

K. Y. Taylor, President, Beloit Tool Corporation, South Beloit Illinois.

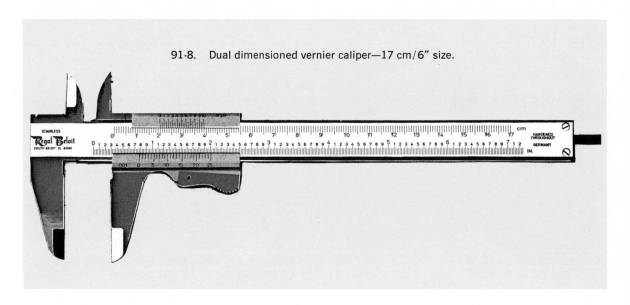

91-8.   Dual dimensioned vernier caliper—17 cm/6″ size.

METRIC EQUIVALENTS

Inches	mm	Inches	mm	Inches	mm
0.001	0.03	7/32	5.6	2½	63.5
0.002	0.05	¼	6.4	3	76.2
0.005	0.13	9/32	7.1	4	102
0.01	0.3	5/16	8.0	4¼	108
1/64	0.4	0.315	8.0	5	127
1/32	0.8	11/32	8.7	5½	140
3/64	1.2	3/8	9.5	6	152
1/16	1.6	0.394	10.0	7	179
5/64	2.0	½	12.7	8	203
3/32	2.4	¾	19.1	9	229
0.1	2.5	1	25.4	10	254
7/64	2.8	1¼	31.8	11	280
1/8	3.2	1½	38.1	12	305
9/64	3.6	2	50.8	14	356
5/32	4.0	2.165	56.0	16	406
3/16	4.8	2¼	57.2	18	457

Table 91-C

or become obsolete, according to Catepillar's engineering department.

All machine tools can be placed in one of two categories: (1) those in which the measurement system of the machine determines the finished dimensions of the workpiece or (2) those in which the finished dimensions of the workpiece are determined by separate gaging equipment (the dials or scales of the machines are used only for making adjustments).

The first type includes tool room jig borers, jig mills, other precision horizontal bar machines, and most tape-controlled machines. If the measuring system of such a machine is in the inch system, the dimensional input to it must be in inches. For a number of years engineering drawings of metric piece parts will carry a chart of inch equivalents of the metric dimensions. This will permit toolmaking and N/C tape preparation on existing machines and will permit con-

Industrial Conversion To The Metric System*

The Caterpillar Tractor Company began converting to the metric system in the early 1950's when the company began selling sizable quantities of their products overseas. The parts books and service information prepared for dealers and customers have listed equivalent metric measurements for inches, feet, gallons, quarts, and other units.

This company is using a "soft" conversion. This means the physical size of the products will change little, if at all. No changes will be made from the use of U.S. engineering standards for thread sizes, sheet and plate thicknesses, bar diameters, etc. These standards will all remain the same.

New tooling and gages purchased for manufacturing new parts will have metric calibration. Inch-calibrated machine tools used on current designs will not be replaced until they wear out

Victor Schellschmidt, Supervising Engineer of Planning in Manufacturing, Catepillar Tractor Co., Peoria, Illinois.

DECIMAL EQUIVALENTS OF MILLIMETRES

mm	Inches	mm	Inches	mm	Inches	mm	Inches	mm	Inches
.01	.00039	.41	.01614	.81	.03189	21	.82677	61	2.40157
.02	.00079	.42	.01654	.82	.03228	22	.86614	62	2.44094
.03	.00118	.43	.01693	.83	.03268	23	.90551	63	2.48031
.04	.00157	.44	.01732	.84	.03307	24	.94488	64	2.51968
.05	.00197	.45	.01772	.85	.03346	25	.98425	65	2.55905
.06	.00236	.46	.01811	.86	.03386	26	1.02362	66	2.59842
.07	.00276	.47	.01850	.87	.03425	27	1.06299	67	2.63779
.08	.00315	.48	.01890	.88	.03465	28	1.10236	68	2.67716
.09	.00354	.49	.01929	.89	.03504	29	1.14173	69	2.71653
.10	.00394	.50	.01969	.90	.03543	30	1.18110	70	2.75590
.11	.00433	.51	.02008	.91	.03583	31	1.22047	71	2.79527
.12	.00472	.52	.02047	.92	.03622	32	1.25984	72	2.83464
.13	.00512	.53	.02087	.93	.03661	33	1.29921	73	2.87401
.14	.00551	.54	.02126	.94	.03701	34	1.33858	74	2.91338
.15	.00591	.55	.02165	.95	.03740	35	1.37795	75	2.95275
.16	.00630	.56	.02205	.96	.03780	36	1.41732	76	2.99212
.17	.00669	.57	.02244	.97	.03819	37	1.45669	77	3.03149
.18	.00709	.58	.02283	.98	.03858	38	1.49606	78	3.07086
.19	.00748	.59	.02323	.99	.03898	39	1.53543	79	3.11023
.20	.00787	.60	.02362	1.00	.03937	40	1.57480	80	3.14960
.21	.00827	.61	.02402	1	.03937	41	1.61417	81	3.18897
.22	.00866	.62	.02441	2	.07874	42	1.65354	82	3.22834
.23	.00906	.63	.02480	3	.11811	43	1.69291	83	3.26771
.24	.00945	.64	.02520	4	.15748	44	1.73228	84	3.30708
.25	.00984	.65	.02559	5	.19685	45	1.77165	85	3.34645
.26	.01024	.66	.02598	6	.23622	46	1.81102	86	3.38582
.27	.01063	.67	.02638	7	.27559	47	1.85039	87	3.42519
.28	.01102	.68	.02677	8	.31496	48	1.88976	88	3.46456
.29	.01142	.69	.02717	9	.35433	49	1.92913	89	3.50393
.30	.01181	.70	.02756	10	.39370	50	1.96850	90	3.54330
.31	.01220	.71	.02795	11	.43307	51	2.00787	91	3.58267
.32	.01260	.72	.02835	12	.47244	52	2.04724	92	3.62204
.33	.01299	.73	.02874	13	.51181	53	2.08661	93	3.66141
.34	.01339	.74	02913	14	.55118	54	2.12598	94	3.70078
.35	.01378	.75	.02953	15	.59055	55	2.16535	95	3.74015
.36	.01417	.76	.02992	16	.62992	56	2.20472	96	3.77952
.37	.01457	.77	.03032	17	.66929	57	2.24409	97	3.81889
.38	.01496	.78	.03071	18	.70866	58	2.28346	98	3.85826
.39	.01535	.79	.03110	19	.74803	59	2.32283	99	3.89763
.40	.01575	.80	.03150	20	.78740	60	2.36220	100	3.93700

L. S. Starrett Company

Table 91-D

tinued use of such machines used for production work.

Using Conversion Scales

The majority of production machines are of the second type. For these, setups are made with the aid of tool-setting gages, sample parts, tracer templates, or N/C tapes. A trial cut is taken, the piece part is measured with a separate gage or micrometer, and the amount of the required adjustment is determined. If a piece part is metric, the gage used will be metric. However, if a machine has inch calibration, the operator must convert the adjustment value into decimal inches. This does not involve converting piece part dimensions, but only the small adjustment values. Normally, this will be a few hundredths of a millimetre to be converted into thousandths of an inch. This conversion can be instantly done with the aid of a simple conversion scale like the one shown in Fig. 91-9.

This scale may be used to make quick—but not highly accurate—conversions from metric to inches. Numbers across the top are metric units; those across the bottom are inch units. Following is a list of conversions you can make with just these two scales.

- Centimetres to inches.
- Millimetres to tenths of an inch.
- Tenths of a millimetre to hundredths of an inch.
- Hundredths of a millimetre to thousandths of an inch.
- Thousandths of a millimetre to ten-thousandths of an inch.

This conversion list must be followed when using this scale.

Most conversions involve three steps:

- Step 1. Find the number you are converting and note its relationship to the other scale. It will usually fall between two numbers on the other scale, so write down the lower of those two numbers. This will be referred to as the *rough conversion.*
- Step 2. Consult the conversion list and express the rough conversion accordingly. (Remember that for metric numbers smaller than one, a zero is placed to the left of the decimal point.)
- Step 3. Refine by adding the desired number of decimal places to the rough conversion.

For example, suppose you want to convert 9 hundredths of a millimetre to some measurement in inches. Proceed as follows:

- Step 1. Note that 9 on the metric scale falls between 3 and 4 on the inch scale. Write down 3 (because it is lower).
- Step 2. The conversion list shows that hundredths of a millimetre convert to thousandths of

an inch, so express the rough conversion accordingly—0.003.

- Step 3. Refine to 0.0035, because 9 on the metric scale falls roughly halfway between 3 and 4 on the inch scale.

The above procedure assumes that you are trying to achieve the greatest accuracy possible within the limitations of this method. Sometimes you may want to simplify. For instance, 13 millimetres might be simply converted to half an inch, since the 13 on the metric scale corresponds so closely with the 5 on the inch scale.

Conversions to inch units smaller than 1 might seem confusing at first, but they follow the rules given previously. For example, to convert 2 millimetres, first write down 0, because it is the digit lower than 1. Express it in tenths—.0—as the list shows. Then refine to about 0.075.

Examples given thus far have dealt with converting metric to inch units. The process works equally well in reverse. Thus 4 inches can be converted to about 10.2 centimetres by following the steps given earlier.

Figures larger than those shown on the scales can be converted by the use of simple ratios. Thus 18 millimetres would convert to about 0.7″. This is determined by simply doubling the conversion of 9 millimetres.

METRIC UNITS

91-9. Conversion scale for machine adjustments.

Table 91-E

THE METRIC SYSTEM

WEIGHTS

Metric Denominations and Values			Equivalents in Denominations in use.			
Names		No. Grams	Quantity of water at maximum density		Avoirdupois Weight	
Millier or tonneau	=	1,000,000	=	1 cubic metre	=	2204.6 pounds
Quintal	=	100,000	=	1 hectoliter	=	220.46 pounds
Myriagram	=	10,000	=	10 liters	=	22.046 pounds
Kilogram or kilo	=	1,000	=	1 liter	=	2.2046 pounds
Hectogram	=	100	=	1 deciliter	=	3.5274 ounces
Dekagram	=	10	=	10 c. centimetres	=	0.3527 ounce
Gram	=	1	=	1 c. centimetre	=	15.432 grains
Decigram	=	.1	=	.1 c. centimetre	=	1.5432 grains
Centigram	=	.01	=	10 c. millimetres	=	0.1543 grain
Milligram	=	.001	=	1 c. millimetre	=	0.0154 grain

MEASURES OF LENGTH

Metric Denominations and Values				Equivalents of Denominations in use	
Myriametre	=	10,000 metres	=	6.2137 miles	
Kilometre	=	1,000 metres	=	0.62137 mile, or 3,280 feet 10 inches	
Hectometre	=	100 metres	=	328 feet and 1 inch	
Dekametre	=	10 metres	=	393.7 inches	
Metre	=	1 metre	=	39.37 inches	
Decimetre	=	.1 metre	=	3.937 inches	
Centimetre	=	0.1 metre	=	0.3937 inch	
Millimetre	=	.001 metre	=	0.0394 inch	

MEASURES OF SURFACE

Metric Denominations and Values				Equivalents in Denominations in use	
Hectare	=	10,000 square metres	=	2.471 acres	
Are	=	100 square metres	=	119.6 square yards	
Centare	=	1 square metre	=	1550 square inches	

MEASURES OF CAPACITY

Metric Denominations and Values					Equivalents of Denominations in use			
Names		No. Liters		Cubic Measure	Dry Measure		Wine Measure	
Kiloliter	=	1,000	=	1 cubic metre	=	1.308 cubic yards	=	264.17 gallons
Hectoliter	=	100	=	.1 cubic metre	=	2 bush. 3.35 pecks	=	26.417 gallons
Decaliter	=	10	=	10 c. decimetres	=	9.08 quarts	=	2.6417 gallons
Liter	=	1	=	1 c. decimetre	=	0.908 quart	=	1.0567 quarts
Deciliter	=	.1	=	.1 c. decimetre	=	6.1022 cubic inches	=	0.845 gill
Centiliter	=	.01	=	10 c. centimetres	=	0.6102 cubic inch	=	0.338 fluid oz.
Milliliter	=	.001	=	1 c. centimetre	=	0.061 cubic inch	=	0.27 fluid oz.

Stanley Tools, Division of Stanley Works

Table 91-E cont'd.

UNITED STATES AND METRIC CONSTANTS

LONG MEASURE

Millimetres	×	.03937	=	Inches
Millimetres	÷	25.4	=	inches
Centimetres	×	.3937	=	inches
Centimetres	÷	2.54	=	inches
Metres	=	39.37	=	Inches (Act of Congress)
Metres	×	3.281	=	feet
Metres	×	1.094	=	yards
Kilometres	×	.621	=	miles
Kilometres	÷	3280.7	=	feet
Kilometres	÷	1.6093	=	miles

SQUARE MEASURE

Square millimetres	×	.0015	=	square inches
Square millimetres	÷	645.1	=	square inches
Square centimetres	×	.155	=	square inches
Square centimetres	÷	6.451	=	square inches
Square metres	×	10.764	=	square feet
Square kilometres	×	247.1	=	acres
Hectares	×	2.471	=	acres

CUBIC MEASURE

Cubic centimetres	÷	16.383	=	cubic inches
Cubic centimetres	÷	3.69	=	fluid drachms (U.S.P.)
Cubic centimetres	÷	29.57	=	fluid ounce (U.S.P.)
Cubic metres	×	35.315	=	cubic feet
Cubic metres	×	1.308	=	cubic yards
Cubic metres	×	264.2	=	gallons (231 cubic inches)

LIQUID MEASURE

Liters	×	61.022	=	cubic inches (Act of Congress)
Liters	×	33.84	=	fluid ounces (U.S. Phar.)
Liters	×	.2642	=	gallons (231 cubic inches)
Liters	÷	3.78	=	gallons (231 cubic inches)
Liters	÷	28.316	=	cubic feet
Hectoliters	×	3.531	=	cubic feet
Hectoliters	×	2.84	=	bushels (2150.42 cubic inches)
Hectoliters	×	.131	=	cubic yards
Hectoliters	÷	26.42	=	gallons (231 cubic inches)

WEIGHTS

Grams	×	15.432	=	grains (Act of Congress)
Grams	×	981.	=	dynes
Grams (water)	÷	29.57	=	fluid ounces
Grams	÷	28.35	=	ounces avoirdupois
Grams per cubic centimetre	÷	27.7	=	pounds per cubic inch
Joule	×	.7373	=	foot pounds
Kilograms	×	2.2046	=	pounds
Kilograms	×	35.3	=	ounces avoirdupois
Kilograms	÷	1102.3	=	tons (2,000 pounds)
Kilograms	× per square centimetre	14.223	=	pounds per square inch

Stanley Tools, Division of Stanley Works

Check Your Knowledge

1. What advantages does the metric system of measurement have over the customary system?
2. Name the six basic units in the International Metric System.
3. Upon what system is metric based?
4. What is meant by dual dimensioning?

Problems

1. There are 4,000 liters in 4 cubic metres (m^3). How many are there in one kilogram?

2. Determine the following decimal equivalents, putting your answers on separate paper:

1 mm =   m
1 cm =   m
1 m =   km

1 ml =   l
1 cl =   l

1 mg =   g
1 g =   kg
1 kg =   g

3. A contractor removed the following amounts of gravel per hour: 225 cubic metres, 215 cubic metres, 213 cubic metres, 197 cubic metres, 240 cubic metres. What was the hourly removal of gravel?

4. Determine the following, putting your answers on separate paper:

0.001 metre =   mm
0.021 metre =   mm
0.321 metre =   mm
1   cm =   mm
1   cm =   m
12   cm =   m
0.9 metre =   cm

METALWORKING TABLES

BASIC THREAD DIMENSIONS AND TAP DRILL SIZES

AMERICAN NATIONAL FINE THREADS

Formerly A. S. M. E. Special for Sizes 0-12; S. A. E. Standard for Sizes ¼ in. and larger

Size of Thread and Threads per Inch	Major Diameter D Inches	Pitch Diameter E Inches	Minor Diameter Internal Threads Kn Inches	Commercial Tap Drill to Produce Approx. 75% Full Thread	Decimal Equivalent of Tap Drill Inches	Size of Thread and Threads per Inch	Major Diameter D Inches	Pitch Diameter E Inches	Minor Diameter Internal Threads Kn Inches	Commercial Tap Drill to Produce Approx. 75% Full Thread	Decimal Equivalent of Tap Drill Inches
0 x80	.0600	.0519	.0465	³/₆₄	.0469	³/₈ x24	.3750	.3479	.3299	Q	.3320
1 x72	.0730	.0640	.0580	¹/₁₆	.0625	⁷/₁₆ x20	.4375	.4050	.3834	²⁵/₆₄	.3906
2 x64	.0860	.0759	.0691	No. 49	.0730	½ x20	.5000	.4675	.4459	²⁹/₆₄	.4531
3 x56	.0990	.0874	.0797	No. 44	.0860	⁹/₁₆ x18	.5625	.5264	.5024	³³/₆₄	.5156
4 x48	.1120	.0985	.0894	No. 42	.0935	⁵/₈ x18	.6250	.5889	.5649	³⁷/₆₄	.5781
5 x44	.1250	.1102	.1004	No. 36	.1065	³/₄ x16	.7500	.7094	.6823	¹¹/₁₆	.6875
6 x40	.1380	.1218	.1109	No. 32	.1160	⁷/₈ x14	.8750	.8286	.7977	¹³/₁₆	.8125
8 x36	.1640	.1460	.1339	No. 29	.1360	1 x12	1.0000	.9459	.9098	⁵⁹/₆₄	.9219
10 x32	.1900	.1697	.1562	No. 20	.1610	1⅛ x12	1.1250	1.0709	1.0348	1³/₆₄	1.0469
12 x28	.2160	.1928	.1773	No. 14	.1820	1¼ x12	1.2500	1.1959	1.1598	1¹¹/₆₄	1.1719
¼ x28	.2500	.2268	.2113	⁷/₃₂	.2188	1⅜ x12	1.3750	1.3209	1.2848	1¹⁹/₆₄	1.2969
⁵/₁₆ x24	.3125	.2854	.2674	I	.2720	1½ x12	1.5000	1.4459	1.4098	1²⁷/₆₄	1.4219

Courtesy of The Cleveland Twist Drill Co.

Length of effective thread
Imperfect thread
Engagement

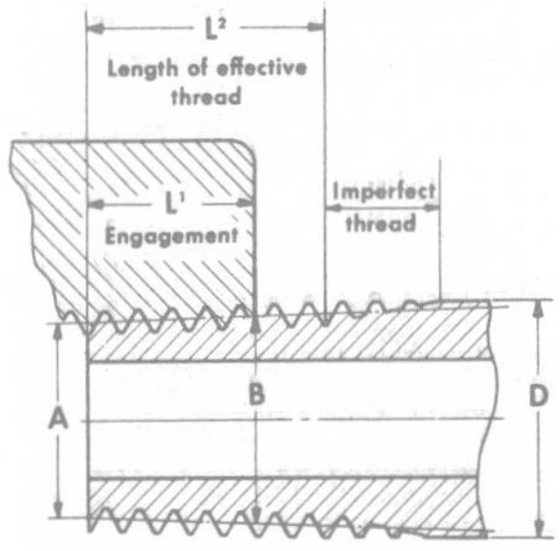

Taper ¾ inch per foot on diameter

AMERICAN NATIONAL PIPE THREADS

A = Pitch Diameter of thread at end of pipe

B = Pitch Diameter of thread at gauging notch

D = Outside Diameter of pipe

L¹ = Normal Engagement by hand between external and internal thread.

Nominal Size Inches	No. of Threads per Inch	Pitch Diameter A Inches	Pitch Diameter B Inches	Length L2 Inches	Length L1 Inches	Pipe O.D. D Inches	Depth of Thread Inches	Tap Drills for Pipe Threads Minor Diameter Small End of Pipe	Tap Drills for Pipe Threads Size Drill
⅛	27	.36351	.37476	.2639	.180	.405	.02963	.3339	R
¼	18	.47739	.48989	.4018	.200	.540	.04444	.4329	⁷/₁₆
⅜	18	.61201	.62701	.4078	.240	.675	.04444	.5676	³⁷/₆₄
½	14	.75843	.77843	.5337	.320	.840	.05714	.7013	²³/₃₂
¾	14	.96768	.98887	.5457	.339	1.050	.05714	.9105	⁵⁹/₆₄
1	11½	1.21363	1.23863	.6828	.400	1.315	.06957	1.1441	1⁵/₃₂
1¼	11½	1.55713	1.58338	.7068	.420	1.660	.06957	1.4876	1½
1½	11½	1.79609	1.82234	.7235	.420	1.900	.06957	1.7265	1⁴⁷/₆₄
2	11½	2.26902	2.29627	.7565	.436	2.375	.06957	2.1995	2⁷/₃₂
2½	8	2.71953	2.76216	1.1375	.682	2.875	.10000	2.6195	2⅝
3	8	3.34062	3.38850	1.2000	.766	3.500	.10000	3.2406	3¼
3½	8	3.83750	3.88881	1.2500	.821	4.000	.10000	3.7375	3¾
4	8	4.33438	4.38712	1.3000	.844	4.500	.10000	4.2344	4¼

Courtesy Cleveland Twist Drill Co.

AMERICAN NATIONAL COARSE SCREW THREADS

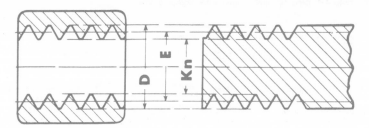

D = Major Dia.
E = Pitch Dia.
Kn = Minor Dia.

Size of Thread and Threads per Inch	Major Diameter D Inches	Pitch Diameter E Inches	Minor Diameter Internal Threads Kn Inches	Commercial Tap Drill to Produce Approx. 75% Full Thread	Decimal Equivalent of Tap Drill Inches	Size of Thread and Threads per Inch	Major Diameter D Inches	Pitch Diameter E Inches	Minor Diameter Internal Threads Kn Inches	Commercial Tap Drill to Produce Approx. 75% Full Thread	Decimal Equivalent of Tap Drill Inches
1 x64	.0730	.0629	.0561	No. 53	.0595	$1\frac{1}{8}$x 7	1.1250	1.0322	.9704	$\frac{63}{64}$	.9844
2 x56	.0860	.0744	.0667	No. 50	.0700	$1\frac{1}{4}$x 7	1.2500	1.1572	1.0954	$1\frac{7}{64}$	1.1094
3 x48	.0990	.0855	.0764	No. 47	.0785	$1\frac{3}{8}$x 6	1.3750	1.2667	1.1946	$1\frac{7}{32}$	1.2188
4 x40	.1120	.0958	.0849	No. 43	.0890	$1\frac{1}{2}$x 6	1.5000	1.3917	1.3196	$1\frac{11}{32}$	1.3438
5 x40	.1250	.1088	.0979	No. 38	.1015	$1\frac{3}{4}$x 5	1.7500	1.6201	1.5335	$1\frac{9}{16}$	1.5625
6 x32	.1380	.1177	.1042	No. 36	.1065	2 x $4\frac{1}{2}$	2.0000	1.8557	1.7594	$1\frac{25}{32}$	1.7812
8 x32	.1640	.1437	.1302	No. 29	.1360	$2\frac{1}{4}$x $4\frac{1}{2}$	2.2500	2.1057	2.0094	$2\frac{1}{32}$	2.0312
10 x24	.1900	.1629	.1449	No. 25	.1495	$2\frac{1}{2}$x 4	2.5000	2.3376	2.2294	$2\frac{1}{4}$	2.2500
12 x24	.2160	.1889	.1709	No. 16	.1770	$2\frac{3}{4}$x 4	2.7500	2.5876	2.4794	$2\frac{1}{2}$	2.5000
$\frac{1}{4}$x20	.2500	.2175	.1959	No. 7	.2010	3 x 4	3.0000	2.8376	2.7294	$2\frac{3}{4}$	2.7500
$\frac{5}{16}$x18	.3125	.2764	.2524	F	.2570	$3\frac{1}{4}$x 4	3.2500	3.0876	2.9794	3	3.0000
$\frac{3}{8}$x16	.3750	.3344	.3073	$\frac{5}{16}$	.3125	$3\frac{1}{2}$x 4	3.5000	3.3376	3.2294	$3\frac{1}{4}$	3.2500
$\frac{7}{16}$x14	.4375	.3911	.3602	U	.3680	$3\frac{3}{4}$x 4	3.7500	3.5876	3.4794	$3\frac{1}{2}$	3.5000
$\frac{1}{2}$x12	.5000	.4459	.4098	$\frac{27}{64}$	.4219	4 x 4	4.0000	3.8376	3.7294	$3\frac{3}{4}$	3.7500
$\frac{1}{2}$x13	.5000	.4500	.4167	$\frac{27}{64}$	.4219						
$\frac{9}{16}$x12	.5625	.5084	.4723	$\frac{31}{64}$	.4844						
$\frac{5}{8}$x11	.6250	.5660	.5266	$\frac{17}{32}$	.5312						
$\frac{3}{4}$x10	.7500	.6850	.6417	$\frac{21}{32}$	.6562						
$\frac{7}{8}$x 9	.8750	.8028	.7547	$\frac{49}{64}$	.7656						
1 x 8	1.0000	.9188	.8647	$\frac{7}{8}$	.8750						

Courtesy Cleveland Twist Drill Co.

Lubricants for Cutting Tools

Material	Turning	Chucking	Drilling Milling	Reaming	Tapping
Tool Steel	Dry or Oil	Oil or Soda Water	Oil	Lard Oil	Oil
Soft Steel	Dry or Soda Water	Soda Water	Oil or Soda Water	Lard Oil	Oil
Wrought Iron	Dry or Soda Water	Soda Water	Oil or Soda Water	Lard Oil	Oil
Cast Iron	Dry	Dry	Dry	Dry	Oil
Brass	Dry	Dry	Dry	Dry	Oil
Copper	Dry	Oil	Oil	*Mixture	Oil
Babbitt	Dry	Dry	Dry	Dry	Oil
Glass				Turpentine or Kerosene	

*Mixture is ⅓ Crude Petroleum, ⅔ Lard Oil. When two lubricants are mentioned the first is preferable.

Courtesy The L. S. Starrett Company

AMERICAN STANDARD TAPER DIMENSIONS

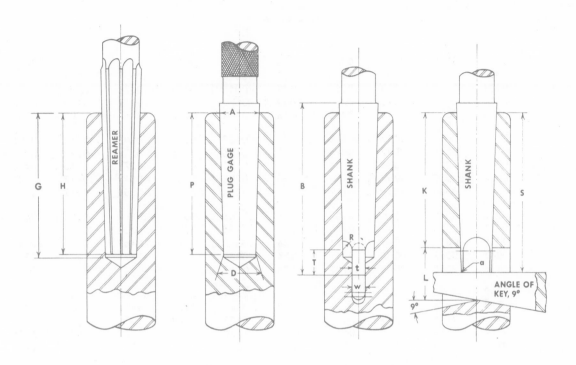

Detail Dimensions*

American Standard Taper Number	Diam. of Plug at Small End	Diam. at End of Socket	SHANK		Depth of Drilled Hole	Depth of Reamed Hole	Standard Plug Depth	TANG				TANG SLOT		End of Socket to Tang Slot	Taper per Inch	Taper per Foot	American Standard Taper Number
			Whole Length	Depth				Thickness	Length	Radius	Radius	Width	Length				
	D	A	B.	S	G	H	P	t	T	R	a	W	L	K			
†0	.25200	.35610	$2\frac{11}{32}$	$2\frac{7}{32}$	$2\frac{1}{16}$	$2\frac{1}{32}$	2	$\frac{5}{32}$	$\frac{1}{4}$	$\frac{5}{32}$	$\frac{3}{64}$	$\frac{11}{64}$	$\frac{9}{16}$	$1\frac{15}{16}$	.052050	.62460	†0
1	.36900	.47500	$2\frac{9}{16}$	$2\frac{7}{16}$	$2\frac{3}{16}$	$2\frac{5}{32}$	$2\frac{1}{8}$	$\frac{13}{64}$	$\frac{3}{8}$	$\frac{3}{16}$	$\frac{3}{64}$	$\frac{7}{32}$	$\frac{3}{4}$	$2\frac{1}{16}$	.049882	.59858	1
2	.57223	.70000	$3\frac{1}{8}$	$2\frac{15}{16}$	$2\frac{21}{32}$	$2\frac{39}{64}$	$2\frac{9}{16}$	$\frac{1}{4}$	$\frac{7}{16}$	$\frac{1}{4}$	$\frac{1}{16}$	$\frac{17}{64}$	$\frac{7}{8}$	$2\frac{1}{2}$	.049951	.59941	2
3	.77800	.93800	$3\frac{7}{8}$	$3\frac{11}{16}$	$3\frac{5}{16}$	$3\frac{1}{4}$	$3\frac{3}{16}$	$\frac{5}{16}$	$\frac{9}{16}$	$\frac{9}{32}$	$\frac{5}{64}$	$\frac{21}{64}$	$1\frac{3}{16}$	$3\frac{1}{16}$	.050196	.60235	3
4	1.02000	1.23100	$4\frac{7}{8}$	$4\frac{5}{8}$	$4\frac{3}{16}$	$4\frac{1}{8}$	$4\frac{1}{16}$	$\frac{15}{32}$	$\frac{5}{8}$	$\frac{5}{16}$	$\frac{3}{32}$	$\frac{31}{64}$	$1\frac{1}{4}$	$3\frac{7}{8}$	.051938	.62326	4
$4\frac{1}{2}$	1.26600	1.50000	$5\frac{3}{8}$	$5\frac{1}{8}$	$4\frac{5}{8}$	$4\frac{9}{16}$	$4\frac{1}{2}$	$\frac{9}{16}$	$\frac{11}{16}$	$\frac{3}{8}$	$\frac{1}{8}$	$\frac{37}{64}$	$1\frac{3}{8}$	$4\frac{5}{16}$	.052000	.62400	$4\frac{1}{2}$
5	1.47500	1.74800	$6\frac{1}{8}$	$5\frac{7}{8}$	$5\frac{5}{16}$	$5\frac{1}{4}$	$5\frac{3}{16}$	$\frac{5}{8}$	$\frac{3}{4}$	$\frac{3}{8}$	$\frac{1}{8}$	$\frac{21}{32}$	$1\frac{1}{2}$	$4\frac{15}{16}$	.052626	.63151	5
6	2.11600	2.49400	$8\frac{9}{16}$	$8\frac{1}{4}$	$7\frac{13}{32}$	$7\frac{21}{64}$	$7\frac{1}{4}$	$\frac{3}{4}$	$1\frac{1}{8}$	$\frac{1}{2}$	$\frac{5}{32}$	$\frac{25}{32}$	$1\frac{3}{4}$	7	.052138	.62565	6
7	2.75000	3.27000	$11\frac{5}{8}$	$11\frac{1}{4}$	$10\frac{5}{32}$	$10\frac{5}{64}$	10	$1\frac{1}{8}$	$1\frac{3}{8}$	$\frac{3}{4}$	$\frac{3}{16}$	$1\frac{5}{32}$	$2\frac{5}{8}$	$9\frac{1}{2}$	.052000	.62400	7

*Table agrees with American Standards for Taper Shanks except for angle and undercut of tang.
†Size 0 taper shank not listed in American Standards.

Courtesy Cleveland Twist Drill Co.

TAPERS

Tapers from ¹⁄₁₆ to 1¼ Inch per Foot—Amount of Taper for Lengths Up to 24 Inches

Length Tapered, Inches	TAPER PER FOOT									
	¹⁄₁₆	³⁄₃₂	⅛	¼	⅜	½	⅝	¾	1	1¼
¹⁄₃₂	.0002	.0002	.0003	.0007	.0010	.0013	.0016	.0020	.0026	.0033
¹⁄₁₆	.0003	.0005	.0007	.0013	.0020	.0026	.0033	.0039	.0052	.0065
⅛	.0007	.0010	.0013	.0026	.0039	.0052	.0065	.0078	.0104	.0130
³⁄₁₆	.0010	.0015	.0020	.0039	.0059	.0078	.0098	.0117	.0156	.0195
¼	.0013	.0020	.0026	.0052	.0078	.0104	.0130	.0156	.0208	.0260
⁵⁄₁₆	.0016	.0024	.0033	.0065	.0098	.0130	.0163	.0195	.0260	.0326
⅜	.0020	.0029	.0039	.0078	.0117	.0156	.0195	.0234	.0312	.0391
⁷⁄₁₆	.0023	.0034	.0046	.0091	.0137	.0182	.0228	.0273	.0365	.0456
½	.0026	.0039	.0052	.0104	.0156	.0208	.0260	.0312	.0417	.0521
⁹⁄₁₆	.0029	.0044	.0059	.0117	.0176	.0234	.0293	.0352	.0469	.0586
⅝	.0033	.0049	.0065	.0130	.0195	.0260	.0326	.0391	.0521	.0651
¹¹⁄₁₆	.0036	.0054	.0072	.0143	.0215	.0286	.0358	.0430	.0573	.0716
¾	.0039	.0059	.0078	.0156	.0234	.0312	.0391	.0469	.0625	.0781
¹³⁄₁₆	.0042	.0063	.0085	.0169	.0254	.0339	.0423	.0508	.0677	.0846
⅞	.0046	.0068	.0091	.0182	.0273	.0365	.0456	.0547	.0729	.0911
¹⁵⁄₁₆	.0049	.0073	.0098	.0195	.0293	.0391	.0488	.0586	.0781	.0977
1	.0052	.0078	.0104	.0208	.0312	.0417	.0521	.0625	.0833	.1042
2	.0104	.0156	.0208	.0417	.0625	.0833	.1042	.125	.1667	.2083
3	.0156	.0234	.0312	.0625	.0937	.1250	.1562	.1875	.250	.3125
4	.0208	.0312	.0417	.0833	.125	.1667	.2083	.250	.3333	.4167
5	.0260	.0391	.0521	.1042	.1562	.2083	.2604	.3125	.4167	.5208
6	.0312	.0469	.0625	.125	.1875	.250	.3125	.375	.500	.625
7	.0365	.0547	.0729	.1458	.2187	.2917	.3646	.4375	.5833	.7292
8	.0417	.0625	.0833	.1667	.250	.3333	.4167	.500	.6667	.8333
9	.0469	.0703	.0937	.1875	.2812	.375	.4687	.5625	.750	.9375
10	.0521	.0781	.1042	.2083	.3125	.4167	.5208	.625	.8333	1.0417
11	.0573	.0859	.1146	.2292	.3437	.4583	.5729	.6875	.9167	1.1458
12	.0625	.0937	.125	.250	.375	.500	.625	.750	1.000	1.250
13	.0677	.1016	.1354	.2708	.4062	.5417	.6771	.8125	1.0833	1.3542
14	.0729	.1094	.1458	.2917	.4375	.5833	.7292	.875	1.1667	1.4583
15	.0781	.1172	.1562	.3125	.4687	.625	.7812	.9375	1.250	1.5625
16	.0833	.125	.1667	.3333	.500	.6667	.8333	1.000	1.3333	1.6667
17	.0885	.1328	.1771	.3542	.5312	.7083	.8854	1.0625	1.4167	1.7708
18	.0937	.1406	.1875	.3750	.5625	.750	.9375	1.125	1.500	1.875
19	.0990	.1484	.1979	.3958	.5037	.7917	.9806	1.1875	1.5833	1.9792
20	.1042	.1562	.2083	.4167	.625	.8333	1.0417	1.250	1.6667	2.0833
21	.1094	.1641	.2187	.4375	.6562	.875	1.0937	1.3125	1.750	2.1875
22	.1146	.1719	.2292	.4583	.6875	.9167	1.1458	1.375	1.8333	2.2917
23	.1198	.1797	.2396	.4792	.7187	.9583	1.1970	1.4375	1.9167	2.3058
24	.125	.1875	.250	.500	.750	1.000	1.250	1.500	2.000	2.500

Courtesy of Lufkin

TAPERS PER FOOT AND CORRESPONDING ANGLES

Taper per Foot	INCLUDED ANGLE			ANGLE WITH CENTER LINE			Taper per Foot	INCLUDED ANGLE			ANGLE WITH CENTER LINE			Taper per Foot	INCLUDED ANGLE			ANGLE WITH CENTER LINE		
	Deg.	Min.	Sec	Deg.	Min.	Sec.		Deg.	Min.	Sec.	Deg.	Min.	Sec.		Deg.	Min.	Sec.	Deg.	Min.	Sec.
1/64	0	4	28	0	2	14	31/32	4	37	20	2	18	40	3 3/4	17	45	40	8	52	50
1/32	0	8	58	0	4	29	1	4	46	18	2	23	9	3 7/8	18	20	34	9	10	17
1/16	0	17	54	0	8	57	1 1/16	5	4	12	2	32	6	4	18	55	28	9	27	44
3/32	0	26	52	0	13	26	1 1/8	5	21	44	2	40	52	4 1/8	19	30	18	9	45	9
1/8	0	35	48	0	17	54	1 3/16	5	39	54	2	49	57	4 1/4	20	5	2	10	2	31
5/32	0	44	44	0	22	22	1 1/4	5	57	48	2	58	54	4 3/8	20	39	44	10	19	52
3/16	0	53	44	0	26	52	1 5/16	6	15	38	3	7	49	4 1/2	21	14	2	10	37	1
7/32	1	2	34	0	31	17	1 3/8	6	33	26	3	16	43	4 5/8	21	48	54	10	54	27
1/4	1	11	36	0	35	48	1 7/16	6	51	20	3	25	40	4 3/4	22	23	22	11	11	41
9/32	1	20	30	0	40	15	1 1/2	7	9	10	3	34	35	4 7/8	22	57	48	11	28	54
5/16	1	29	30	0	44	45	1 9/16	7	26	58	3	43	29	5	23	32	12	11	46	6
11/32	1	38	22	0	49	11	1 5/8	7	44	48	3	52	24	5 1/8	24	6	28	12	3	14
3/8	1	47	24	0	53	42	1 11/16	8	2	38	4	1	19	5 1/4	24	40	42	12	20	21
13/32	1	56	24	0	58	12	1 3/4	8	20	26	4	10	13	5 3/8	25	14	48	12	37	24
7/16	2	5	18	1	2	39	1 13/16	8	38	16	4	19	8	5 1/2	25	48	48	12	54	24
15/32	2	14	16	1	7	8	1 7/8	8	56	2	4	28	1	5 5/8	26	22	52	13	11	24
1/2	2	23	10	1	11	35	1 15/16	9	13	50	4	36	55	5 3/4	26	56	46	13	28	23
17/32	2	32	4	1	16	2	2	9	31	36	4	45	48	5 7/8	27	30	34	13	45	17
9/16	2	41	4	1	20	32	2 1/8	10	7	10	5	3	35	6	28	4	2	14	2	1
19/32	2	50	2	1	25	1	2 1/4	10	42	42	5	21	21	6 1/8	28	37	58	14	18	59
5/8	2	59	2	1	29	31	2 3/8	11	18	10	5	39	5	6 1/4	29	11	34	14	35	47
21/32	3	7	56	1	33	58	2 1/2	11	53	36	5	56	48	6 3/8	29	45	18	14	52	39
11/16	3	16	54	1	38	27	2 5/8	12	29	2	6	14	31	6 1/2	30	18	26	15	9	13
23/32	3	25	50	1	42	55	2 3/4	13	4	24	6	32	12	6 5/8	30	51	48	15	25	54
3/4	3	34	44	1	47	22	2 7/8	13	39	42	6	49	51	6 3/4	31	25	2	15	42	31
25/32	3	43	44	1	51	52	3	14	15	0	7	7	30	6 7/8	31	58	10	15	59	5
13/16	3	52	38	1	56	19	3 1/8	14	50	14	7	25	7	7	32	31	12	16	15	36
27/32	4	1	36	2	0	48	3 1/4	15	25	24	7	42	42	7 1/8	33	4	8	16	32	4
7/8	4	10	32	2	5	16	3 3/8	16	0	34	8	0	17	7 1/4	33	36	40	16	48	20
29/32	4	19	34	2	9	47	3 1/2	16	35	40	8	17	50	7 3/8	34	9	50	17	4	55
15/16	4	28	24	2	14	12	3 5/8	17	10	40	8	35	20							

Courtesy of Lufkin

SPEEDS IN SURFACE FEET PER MINUTE FOR CARBIDE TWIST DRILLS

Material	Speed	Material	Speed
Aluminum	150-500	Copper	200-300
Brass	150-300		
Bronze	150-300	Nonferrous alloys	150-200
Cast Iron (soft)—Size 1/8" to 7/16"	90-165	Plastic (phenolic, etc.)	100
Cast Iron (soft)—Size 9/16" to 1"	90-125	Plastic (Glass-bonded)	50
Cast Iron (soft)—Size 1" or larger	125	Rubber	200-300
Cast Iron (chilled)	30	Wood	200

Courtesy Cleveland Twist Drill Co.

Material Cutting Chart—Hand Hacksaw Blades

Material	Type	Teeth per Inch
Aluminum	Solids	14
Angles	Heavy	18
Angles	Light	24
Babbitt		14
Brass	Solids up to 1″	18
Brass Pipe		24
Brass Tubing		24
Bronze	Solids up to 1″	18
BX Cable	Heavy	24
BX Cable	Light	32
Cast Iron	Up to 1″	18
Channel	Heavy	18
Channel	Light	24
Cable	Heavy	18
Copper	Solids up to 1″	14
Drill Rod	Over ¼″	18
Drill Rod	No. 30 to ¼″	24
Drill Rod	No. 30 and smaller	32
General Purpose Cutting		18
Iron Pipe		24
Metal Conduit		24
Sheet Metal	Over 18 gage	24
Sheet Metal	Under 18 gage	32
Steels	¼″ to 1″	18
Steels	¼″ and under	24
Tubing	Over 18 gage	24
Tubing	Under 18 gage	32

Material Cutting Chart—Power Hacksaw Blades

Material	Teeth per Inch	Strokes per Minute	Feed Pressure
Aluminum Alloy	4-6	150	Light
Aluminum, Pure	4-6	150	Light
Brass Castings, Soft	6-10	150	Light
Brass Castings, Hard	6-10	135	Light
Bronze Castings	6-10	135	Medium
Cast Iron	6-10	135	Medium
Copper, Drawn	6-10	135	Medium
*Carbon Tool Steel	6-10	90	Medium
*Cold Rolled Steel	4-6	135	Heavy
*Drill Rod	10	90	Medium
*High Speed Steel	6-10	90	Medium
*Machinery Steel	4-6	135	Heavy
Manganese Bronze	6-10	90	Light
*Malleable Iron	6-10	90	Medium
*Nickel Silver	6-10	60	Heavy
*Nickel Steel	6-10	90	Heavy
Pipe, Iron	10-14	135	Medium
Slate	6-10	90	Medium
*Structural Steel	6-10	135	Medium
Tubing, Brass	14	135	Light
*Tubing, Steel	14	135	Light

*Use cutting compounds or coolant.

High Temperatures Judged by Color, and Colors for Tempering

Degrees Centigrade	Degrees Fahrenheit	High Temperatures Judged by Color	Degrees Centigrade	Degrees Fahrenheit	Colors for Tempering
400	752	Red heat, visible in the dark	221.1	430	Very pale yellow
474	885	Red heat, visible in twilight	226.7	440	Light yellow
525	975	Red heat, visible in daylight	232.2	450	Pale straw-yellow
581	1077	Red heat, visible in sunlight	237.8	460	Straw-yellow
700	1292	Dark red	243.3	470	Deep straw-yellow
800	1472	Dull cherry-red	248.9	480	Dark yellow
900	1652	Cherry-red	254.4	490	Yellow-brown
1000	1832	Bright cherry-red	260.0	500	Brown-yellow
1100	2012	Orange-red	265.6	510	Spotted red-brown
1200	2192	Orange-yellow	271.1	520	Brown-purple
1300	2372	Yellow-white	276.7	530	Light purple
1400	2552	White welding heat	282.2	540	Full purple
1500	2732	Brilliant white	287.8	550	Dark purple
1600	2912	Dazzling white (bluish-white)	293.3	560	Full blue
			298.9	570	Dark blue

WIRE GAGE STANDARDS

Wire Gage No.	Decimal Parts of an Inch						
	American or B&S Gage	Birmingham or Stubs Wire Gage	Washburn Moen Steel Wire Gage	A.S.&W. Music Wire Gage	British Imp. Wire Gage	U. S. Std. Revised	U. S. Std. for Plate Gage
0000000	—	—	.4900	—	.500	—	—
000000	.580049	—	.4615	.004	.464	—	.46875
00000	.516549	.500	.4305	.005	.432	—	.4375
0000	.460	.454	.3938	.006	.400	—	.40625
000	.40964	.425	.3625	.007	.372	—	.375
00	.3648	.380	.3310	.008	.348	—	.34375
0	.3249	.340	.3065	.009	.324	—	.3125
1	.2893	.300	.2830	.010	.300	—	.28125
2	.25763	.284	.2625	.011	.276	—	.265625
3	.22942	.259	.2437	.012	.252	.2391	.250
4	.20431	.238	.2253	.013	.232	.2242	.234375
5	.18194	.220	.2070	.014	.212	.2092	.21875
6	.16202	.203	.1920	.016	.192	.1943	.203125
7	.1443	.180	.1770	.018	.176	.1793	.1875
8	.1285	.165	.1620	.020	.160	.1644	.171875
9	.11443	.148	.1483	.022	.144	.1495	.15625
10	.1019	.134	.1350	.024	.128	.1345	.140625
11	.090742	.120	.1205	.026	.116	.1196	.125
12	.080808	.109	.1055	.029	.104	.1046	.109375
13	.0720	.095	.0915	.031	.092	.0897	.09375
14	.0641	.083	.0800	.033	.080	.0747	.078125
15	.0571	.072	.0720	.035	.072	.0673	.0703125
16	.0508	.065	.0625	.037	.064	.0598	.0625
17	.0453	.058	.0540	.039	.056	.0538	.05625
18	.0403	.049	.0475	.041	.048	.0478	.050
19	.0359	.042	.0410	.043	.040	.0418	.04375
20	.0320	.035	.0348	.045	.036	.0359	.0375
21	.0285	.032	.0317	.047	.032	.0329	.034375
22	.0253	.028	.0286	.049	.028	.0299	.03125
23	.0226	.025	.0258	.051	.024	.0269	.028125
24	.0201	.022	.0230	.055	.022	.0239	.025
25	.0179	.020	.0204	.059	.020	.0209	.021875
26	.0159	.018	.0181	.063	.018	.0179	.01875
27	.0142	.016	.0173	.067	.0164	.0164	.017875
28	.0126	.014	.0162	.071	.0148	.0149	.015625
29	.0113	.013	.0150	.075	.0136	.0135	.0140625
30	.0100	.012	.0140	.080	.0124	.0120	.0125
31	.0089	.010	.0132	.085	.0116	.0105	.0109375
32	.0080	.009	.0128	.090	.0108	.0097	.01015625
33	.0071	.008	.0118	.095	.0100	.0090	.009375
34	.0063	.007	.0104	.100	.0092	.0082	.00859375
35	.0056	.005	.0095	.106	.0084	.0075	.0078125

DOUBLE DEPTH OF THREAD

Threads Per In. N	V Threads DD	Am. Nat. Form DD U. S. Std.	Whitworth Stand. DD	Threads Per In. N	V Threads DD	Am. Nat. Form DD U. S. Std.	Whitworth Standard DD
2	.86650	.64950	.64000	28	.06185	.04639	.04571
2¼	.77022	.57733	.56888	30	.05773	.04330	.04266
2⅜	.72960	.54694	.53894	32	.05412	.04059	.04000
2½	.69320	.51960	.51200	34	.05097	.03820	.03764
2⅝	.66015	.49485	.48761	36	.04811	.03608	.03555
2¾	.63019	.47236	.46545	38	.04560	.03418	.03368
2⅞	.60278	.45182	.44521	40	.04330	.03247	.03200
3	.57733	.43300	.42666	42	.04126	.03093	.03047
3¼	.53323	.39966	.39384	44	.03036	.02952	.03136
3½	.49485	.37114	.36571	46	.03767	.02823	.02782
4	.43300	.32475	.32000	48	.03608	.02706	.02666
4½	.38488	.28869	.28444	50	.03464	.02598	.02560
5	.34660	.25980	.25600	52	.03332	.02498	.02461
5½	.31490	.23618	.23272	54	.03209	.02405	.02370
6	.28866	.21650	.21333	56	.03093	.02319	.02285
7	.24742	.18557	18285	58	.02987	.02239	.02206
8	.21650	.16237	.16000	60	.02887	.02165	.02133
9	.19244	.14433	.14222	62	.02795	.02095	.02064
10	.17320	.12990	.12800	64	.02706	.02029	.02000
11	.15745	.11809	.11636	66	.02625	.01968	.01939
11½	.15069	.11295	.11121	68	.02548	.01910	.01882
12	.14433	.10825	.10666	70	.02475	.01855	.01728
13	.13323	.09992	.09846	72	.02407	.01804	.01782
14	.12357	.09278	.09142	74	.02341	.01752	.01729
15	.11555	.08660	.08533	76	.02280	.01714	.01673
16	.10825	.08118	.08000	78	.02221	.01665	.01641
18	.09622	.07216	.07111	80	.02166	.01623	.01600
20	.08660	.06495	.06400	82	.02113	.01584	.01560
22	.07872	.05904	.05818	84	.02063	.01546	.01523
24	.07216	05412	.05333	86	.02015	.01510	.01476
26	.06661	.04996	.04923	88	.01957	.01476	.01454
27	.06418	.04811	.04740	90	.01925	.01443	.01422

$$DD = \frac{1.733}{N} \text{ For V Thread}$$

$$DD = \frac{1.299}{N} \text{ For American Nat. Form, U. S. Std.}$$

$$DD = \frac{1.28}{N} \text{ For Whitworth Standard}$$

DECIMAL EQUIVALENTS OF NUMBER SIZE DRILLS

No.	Size of Drill in Inches	No.	Size of Drill in Inches	No.	Size of Drill in Inches	No.	Size of Drill in Inches
1	.2280	21	.1590	41	.0960	61	.0390
2	.2210	22	.1570	42	.0935	62	.0380
3	.2130	23	.1540	43	.0890	63	.0370
4	.2090	24	.1520	44	.0860	64	.0360
5	.2055	25	.1495	45	.0820	65	.0350
6	.2040	26	.1470	46	.0810	66	.0330
7	.2010	27	.1440	47	.0785	67	.0320
8	.1990	28	.1405	48	.0760	68	.0310
9	.1960	29	.1360	49	.0730	69	.0292
10	.1935	30	.1285	50	.0700	70	.0280
11	.1910	31	.1200	51	.0670	71	.0260
12	.1890	32	.1160	52	.0635	72	.0250
13	.1850	33	.1130	53	.0595	73	.0240
14	.1820	34	.1110	54	.0550	74	.0225
15	.1800	35	.1100	55	.0520	75	.0210
16	.1770	36	.1065	56	.0465	76	.0200
17	.1730	37	.1040	57	.0430	77	.0180
18	.1695	38	.1015	58	.0420	78	.0160
19	.1660	39	.0995	59	.0410	79	.0145
20	.1610	40	.0980	60	.0400	80	.0135

Courtesy The L. S. Starrett Co.

DECIMAL EQUIVALENTS OF LETTER SIZE DRILLS

Letter	Size of Drill in Inches	Letter	Size of Drill in Inches
A	.234	N	.302
B	.238	O	.316
C	.242	P	.323
D	.246	Q	.332
E	.250	R	.339
F	.257	S	.348
G	.261	T	.358
H	.266	U	.368
I	.272	V	.377
J	.277	W	.386
K	.281	X	.397
L	.290	Y	.404
M	.295	Z	.413

Courtesy The L. S. Starrett Company

FEEDS FOR MILLING CUTTERS

The following table of suggested feeds should prove of value in setting up initial jobs.

TYPE OF CUT	STARTING FEED PER TOOTH, INCHES
Face milling	.008
Straddle milling	.008
Channel or slot milling	.008
Slab milling	.007
End milling or profiling	*.004
Sawing	.003
Thread milling	.002

*For end mills smaller than ½ inch diameter, feeds per tooth must be much lower than the figure given.

Courtesy Brown & Sharpe

TABLE OF DECIMAL EQUIVALENTS OF SCREW GAGE

FOR MACHINE AND WOOD SCREWS

The difference between consecutive sizes is .01316″
for American Screw Co. Standard;
.013″ for A.S.M.E. Standard

No. of Screw Gage	Size of Number in Decimals		No. of Screw Gage	Size of Number in Decimals		No. of Screw Gage	Size of Number in Decimals
	American Screw Co. Standard	A.S.M.E. Basic and Maximum Outside Diameter		American Screw Co. Standard	A.S.M.E. Basic and Maximum Outside Diameter		American Screw Co. Standard
000	.03152		16	.26840	.268	34	.50528
00	.04468		17	.28156		35	.51844
0	.05784	.060	18	.29472	.294	36	.53160
1	.07100	.073	19	.30788		37	.54476
2	.08416	.086	20	.32104	.320	38	.55792
3	.09732	.099	21	.33420		39	.57108
4	.11048	.112	22	.34736	.346	40	.58424
5	.12364	.125	23	.36052		41	.59740
6	.13680	.138	24	.37368	.372	42	.61066
7	.14996	.151	25	.38684		43	.62372
8	.16312	.164	26	.40000	.398	44	.63688
9	.17628	.177	27	.41316		45	.65004
10	.18944	.190	28	.42632	.424	46	.66320
11	.20260		29	.43948		47	.67636
12	.21576	.216	30	.45264	.450	48	.68952
13	.22892		31	.46580		49	.70268
14	.24208	.242	32	.47896		50	.71584
15	.25524		33	.49212			

HARDNESS CONVERSION TABLES

BRINELL 10 MM Std. Ball 3000 KGM load		ROCKWELL		Approx. Tensile Strength	BRINELL 10 MM Std. Ball 3000 KGM load		ROCKWELL		Approx. Tensile Strength
			Diamond Brale					Diamond Brale	
Dia. of Ball Impression in MM	Hardness Number	1/16 Ball 100 KGM B Scale	150 KGM C Scale	Equiv. 1000 lb. Sq. In.	Dia. of Ball Impression in MM	Hardness Number	1/16 Ball 100 KGM B Scale	150 KGM C Scale	Equiv. 1000 lb. Sq. In.
			58	315	4.30	197	93	(13)	95
			56	295	4.35	192	92	(12)	93
			54	278	4.40	187	91	(10)	90
2.75	495		52	262	4.45	183	90	(9)	89
2.80	477		50	247	4.50	179	89	(8)	87
2.85	461		49	237	4.55	174	88	(6)	85
2.90	444		47	226	4.60	170	87	(5)	83
2.95	429		46	217	4.65	167	86	(4)	81
3.00	415		45	210	4.70	163	85	(3)	79
3.05	401		43	202	4.75	159	84	(2)	78
3.10	388		42	195	4.80	156	83	(1)	76
3.15	375		40	188	4.85	153	82		75
3.20	363		39	182	4.90	149	81		73
3.25	352	(110)	38	176	4.95	146	80		72
3.30	341	(109)	37	170	5.00	143	79		71
3.35	331	(109)	36	166	5.05	140	78		69
3.40	321	(108)	34	160	5.10	137	76		67
3.45	311	(108)	33	155	5.15	134	75		66
3.50	302	(107)	32	150	5.20	131	74		65
3.55	293	(106)	31	145	5.25	128	73		64
3.60	285	(106)	30	141	5.30	126	72		63
3.65	277	(105)	29	137	5.35	124	71		62
3.70	269	(104)	28	133	5.40	121	70		60
3.75	262	(103)	27	129	5.45	118	69		59
3.80	255	(102)	25	126	5.50	116	68		58
3.85	248	(101)	24	122	5.55	114	67		57
3.90	241	100	23	118	5.60	111	66		56
3.95	235	99	22	115	5.65	109	64		55
4.00	229	98	21	111	5.70	107	63		54
4.05	223	97	(19)	108	5.75	105	62		53
4.10	217	96	(18)	105	5.80	103	61		52
4.15	212	96	(16)	102	5.85	101	59		51
4.20	207	95	(15)	100	5.90	99	58		50
4.25	201	94	(14)	98	5.95	97	57		49

These tables are established for homogeneous steels.
Bold face figures are derived from A.S.T.M. Spec. E 48-47.
Figures in parentheses are beyond normal range and offered for comparison only.

Decimal Equivalents of 8ths, 16ths, 32nds, 64ths

8ths	32nds	64ths	64ths
1/8 = .125	1/32 = .03125	1/64 = .015625	33/64 = .515625
1/4 = .250	3/32 = .09375	3/64 = .046875	35/64 = .546875
3/8 = .375	5/32 = .15625	5/64 = .078125	37/64 = .578125
1/2 = .500	7/32 = .21875	7/64 = .109375	39/64 = .609375
5/8 = .625	9/32 = .28125	9/64 = .140625	41/64 = .640625
3/4 = .750	11/32 = .34375	11/64 = .171875	43/64 = .671875
7/8 = .875	13/32 = .40625	13/64 = .203125	45/64 = .703125
16ths	15/32 = .46875	15/64 = .234375	47/64 = .734375
1/16 = .0625	17/32 = .53125	17/64 = .265625	49/64 = .765625
3/16 = .1875	19/32 = .59375	19/64 = .296875	51/64 = .796875
5/16 = .3125	21/32 = .65625	21/64 = .328125	53/64 = .828125
7/16 = .4375	23/32 = .71875	23/64 = .359375	55/64 = .859375
9/16 = .5625	25/32 = .78125	25/64 = .390625	57/64 = .890625
11/16 = .6875	27/32 = .84375	27/64 = .421875	59/64 = .921875
13/16 = .8125	29/32 = .90625	29/64 = .453125	61/64 = .953125
15/16 = .9375	31/32 = .96875	31/64 = .484375	63/64 = .984375

Courtesy The L. S. Starrett Co.

SUGGESTED CUTTING SPEEDS FOR DRILLS

A feed per revolution of .004 to .007 for drills ¼ inch and smaller, and from .007 to .015 for larger drills is about all that should be required.

This feed is based on a peripheral speed of a drill equal to:

30 feet per minute for steel; 35 feet per minute for iron; 60 feet per minute for brass.

It may also be found advisable to vary the speed somewhat as the material to be drilled is more or less refractory.

We believe that these speeds should not be exceeded under ordinary circumstances.

Drill Diam., Inches	FEET PER MINUTE										
	15	20	25	30	35	40	45	50	60	70	80
	REVOLUTIONS PER MINUTE										
¹/₁₆	917.	1223.	1528.	1834.	2140.	2445.	2751.	3057.	3668.	4280.	4891.
⅛	459.	611.	764.	917.	1070.	1222.	1375.	1528.	1834.	2139.	2445.
³/₁₆	306.	408.	509.	611.	713.	815.	917.	1019.	1222.	1426.	1630.
¼	229.	306.	382.	458.	535.	611.	688.	764.	917.	1070.	1222.
⁵/₁₆	183.	245.	306.	367.	428.	489.	550.	611.	733.	856.	978.
⅜	153.	204.	255.	306.	357.	408.	458.	509.	611.	713.	815.
⁷/₁₆	131.	175.	218.	262.	306.	349.	393.	437.	524.	611.	699.
½	115.	153.	191.	229.	268.	306.	344.	382.	459.	535.	611.
⅝	91.8	123.	153.	184.	214.	245.	276.	306.	367.	428.	489.
¾	76.3	102.	127.	153.	178.	203.	229.	254.	306.	357.	408.
⅞	65.5	87.3	109.	131.	153.	175.	196.	219.	262.	306.	349.
1	57.3	76.4	95.5	115.	134.	153.	172.	191.	229.	267.	306.
1⅛	51.0	68.0	85.0	102.	119.	136.	153.	170.	204.	238.	272.
1¼	45.8	61.2	76.3	91.8	107.	123.	137.	153.	183.	214.	245.
1⅜	41.7	55.6	69.5	83.3	97.2	111.	125.	139.	167.	195.	222.
1½	38.2	50.8	63.7	76.3	80.2	102.	115.	127.	153.	178.	204.
1⅝	35.0	47.0	58.8	70.5	82.2	93.9	106.	117.	141.	165.	188.
1¾	32.7	43.6	54.5	65.6	76.4	87.3	98.2	100.	131.	153.	175.
1⅞	30.6	40.7	50.9	61.1	71.3	81.5	91.9	102.	122.	143.	163.
2	28.7	38.2	47.8	57.3	66.9	76.4	86.0	95.5	115.	134.	153.
2¼	25.4	34.0	42.4	51.0	59.4	68.0	76.2	85.0	102.	119.	136.
2½	22.9	30.6	38.2	45.8	53.5	61.2	68.8	76.3	91.7	107.	122.
2¾	20.8	27.8	34.7	41.7	48.6	55.6	62.5	69.5	83.4	97.2	111.
3	19.1	25.5	31.8	38.2	44.6	51.0	57.3	63.7	76.4	89.1	102.

Courtesy The L. S. Starrett Company

Decimal Equivalents of 7ths, 14ths, and 28ths

7th	14th	28th	Decimal	7th	14th	28th	Decimal
		1	.035714			15	.535714
	1		.071429	4			.571429
		3	.107143			17	.607143
1			.142857		9		.642867
		5	.178571			19	.678571
	3		.214286	5			.714286
		7	.25			21	.75
2			.285714		11		.785714
		9	.321429			23	.821429
	5		.357143	6			.857143
		11	.392857			25	.892857
3			.428571		13		.928571
		13	.464286			27	.964286
	7		.5				

Decimal Equivalents of 6ths, 12ths, and 24ths

6th	12th	24th	Decimal	6th	12th	24th	Decimal
		1	.041667	3			.5
	1		.083333			13	.541666
		3	.125		7		.583333
1			.166666			15	.625
		5	.208333	4			.666666
	3		.25			17	.708333
		7	.291666		9		.75
2			.333333			19	.791666
		9	.375				
				5			.833333
	5		.416666			21	.875
	11		.458333		11		.916666
						23	.958333

Courtesy The L. S. Starrett Company

SPEEDS AND FEEDS FOR MILLING CUTTERS
(Basic Recommendations for Milling Cutter Footage)

This table contains basic recommendations for milling cutter surface feet per minute for various common materials within Brinell hardness range. The range of surface feet per minute is in relation to the Brinell range of the material.

Cutter type, holding device, condition of equipment, horsepower and finish requirements will have considerable effect on the use of these recommendations.

These figures do not take into consideration feed or horsepower, as each type of milling operation would cause variation to these recommendations.

		SPEEDS		
Material	Brn. Range	H.S.S. Cutter S.F.M. Range	Cast Alloy Cutter S.F.M. Range	Carbide Cutter S.F.M. Range
Aluminum	100-150	1000-550	2000-1100	4000-2000
Brass	100-175	650-250	1300-500	2600-1000
Low carbon steel	100-200	325-100	650-200	1300-400
Free cutting steel	150-200	250-150	500-300	1000-600
Alloy steel	150-250	175-70	350-140	700-280
Alloy steel	250-350	70-40	140-80	280-160
Cast iron	125-175	100-60	200-120	400-240
Cast iron	175-200	60-45	120-90	240-180
Cast iron	200-225	45-40	90-80	180-160
Cast iron	225-250	40-35	80-70	160-140

Courtesy Brown & Sharpe

GUIDE TO THE USE OF CARBIDE END MILLS

SPEEDS AND FEEDS

The proper feed and speed together with a good vibration free set-up are essential for economical usage of carbide end mills. The end mills should be gripped as short as possible to increase rigidity.

Below is listed a table of feeds and speeds which may serve as a starting point. The final consideration of feed and speed depend upon the finish desired, depth of cut, width of cut, and condition of the machine.

Material	Speed in Surface Feet Per Minute	Feed in Inches Per Minute			
		Cutter Diameter To $3/16$	Cutter Diameter $1/4 — 1/2$	Cutter Diameter $9/16 — 1$	Cutter Diameter $1\frac{1}{8} — 2$
Cast Iron	90-200	1-5	2-15	4-15	4-30
Malleable Iron	90-200	1-5	2-15	4-15	4-30
Brass	100-300	1-6	3-20	4-20	4-30
Bronze	100-300	1-6	3-20	4-20	4-30
Aluminum (and Alloys)	200-1000	2-12	4-25	4-60	4-60
Zinc	200-1000	2-12	4-25	4-60	4-60
Copper	100-300	1-6	3-20	4-20	4-30
Rubber	100-500	2-12	4-25	4-40	4-60
Fibre	200-500	2-12	4-25	4-40	4-60
Plastics	200-1000	2-15	5-40	6-60	6-60
Stainless Steel	75-200	$5/8$-4	2-10		
Carbon Steels	150-250	$5/8$-4	2-10	3-12	3-12
Free Cutting Steels	150-300	$5/8$-4	3-15	4-15	4-15

Courtesy Cleveland Twist Drill Co.

MATERIALS USED IN METALWORKING

BAR MATERIALS	CHARACTERISTICS
High carbon and tool steel	AISI C1095 or tool steel
Flats Sizes: 1/8″ x 1/2″, 1/8″ x 3/4″, 1/4″ x 3/4″, 1/4″ x 1″	Same
Squares Sizes: 3/8″ to 3/4″	Same
Rounds Sizes: 1/4″ to 1″	Same
Octagons Sizes: 1/4″ to 3/4″	Same
Drill rods Sizes: 1/8″ to 1″	Polished round; smooth finish
Mild steel and non-ferrous	
Band iron—cold-rolled Sizes: 1/8″ x 1/2″, 1/8″ x 5/8″, 1/8″ x 3/4″, 1/8″ x 1″	AISI C1018 rolled mild steel with oxide coating
Squares—cold-rolled, hot-rolled, and aluminum	AISI C1018 or SAE 1020
Rounds—cold-rolled, hot-rolled, and aluminum Sizes: 1/4″ to 1 1/2″	AISI C1018 or SAE 1020
Hexagons—cold-rolled Sizes: 3/8″ to 3/4″	SAE 1020
Flats—cold-rolled Sizes: 1 1/8″ x 1 1/4″, 1/2″ x 2″, 3/8″ x 2″	AISI C1018 or SAE 1020
Angles Sizes: 1/2″ x 1/2″, 3/4″ x 3/4″	AISI C1015 hot-rolled or aluminum

(Continued on next page)

MATERIALS USED IN METALWORKING

(Continued from previous page)

FASTENERS

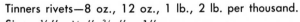

Machine screws—steel, aluminum & brass.
Sizes: 6-32, 8-32, 10-32, 10-24
Lengths: ½'', ¾'', 1'', 1½''

Tinners rivets—8 oz., 12 oz., 1 lb., 2 lb. per thousand.
Sizes: ⅛'' x ¹/₁₆'', ³/₁₆'' x 1''

Rivets—Aluminum, brass, copper, and soft iron.
Sizes: ⅛'' x ½'', ⅛'' x 1'', ³/₁₆'' x 1''

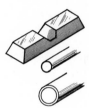

Foundry metal—Aluminum or brass.

Miscellaneous items
Wire—USS gage Nos. 10, 12, 14, 18 black soft annealed wire
Tubing—Flexible copper for art metal projects, ⅛'', ³/₁₆'', ¼'', ⁵/₁₆''
Pipe—⅛''—black iron and brass for lamps.

SHEET MATERIALS

MATERIAL	COMMON SIZES	CHARACTERISTICS
Galvanized steel (iron)	USS gage Nos. 28 to 30	Mild steel with zinc coating
Tin plate	USS gage No. 30 or 28 also IC or IX	Mild steel with tin coating
Black annealed sheet (iron)	USS gage 26 to 18	Hot-rolled or cold-rolled mild steel with oxide coating
Copper (soft)	B&S gage 16 to 24	Pure metal
Brass (soft)	B&S gage 18 to 20	Pure metal
Aluminum (1100s or 3003s)	B&S gage 18 to 24	Commercially pure metal

THREAD CONSTANTS CHART

FOR VARIOUS THREAD PERCENTAGES

FORMULA FOR OBTAINING TAP DRILL SIZES
(Select nearest commercial stock drill)

$$\text{Outside Diam. of Thread} - \frac{.3300mm \times \text{Amount of percentage of full thread}}{mm \text{ Pitch}} = \text{Drilled Hole Size}$$

PERCENTAGE OF FULL THREAD FOR OTHER DRILL SIZES

$$\frac{mm}{\text{Pitch}} \times \frac{\text{Outside Diam. of thread} - \text{Drill Diam.}}{.3300} = \text{Percentage of Full Thread}$$

Figures in table show amount to subtract from O. D. of screw to obtain specific percentage of thread.

EXAMPLE: To find the hole size for obtaining 75% of thread in a 6.5mm – 1.25mm tapped hole, follow first column to 1.25 threads, then across to 75% of thread. This figure (1.2177) when subtracted from the 6.5000 diameter is 5.2823, which is the required diameter of hole.

mm Pitch	Double Depth	50% Thread	55% Thread	60% Thread	65% Thread	70% Thread	75% Thread	80% Thread	85% Thread
4.00	5.1963	2.5982	2.8580	3.1178	3.3776	3.6374	3.8972	4.1570	4.4169
3.50	4.5466	2.2733	2.5006	2.7280	2.9553	3.1826	3.4100	3.6373	3.8646
3.00	3.8969	1.9485	2.1433	2.3381	2.5330	2.7278	2.9227	3.1175	3.3124
2.50	3.2476	1.6238	1.7862	1.9486	2.1109	2.2733	2.4357	2.5981	2.7605
2.00	2.5979	1.2990	1.4288	1.5587	1.6886	1.8185	1.9484	2.0783	2.2082
1.75	2.2733	1.1367	1.2503	1.3640	1.4776	1.5913	1.7050	1.8186	1.9323
1.50	1.9487	.9744	1.0718	1.1692	1.2667	1.3641	1.4615	1.5590	1.6564
1.25	1.6236	.8118	.8930	.9742	1.0553	1.1365	1.2177	1.2989	1.3801
1.00	1.2990	.6495	.7145	.7794	.8444	.9093	.9743	1.0392	1.1042
.90	1.1687	.5844	.6428	.7012	.7597	.8181	.8765	.9350	.9934
.80	1.0394	.5197	.5717	.6236	.6756	.7276	.7796	.8315	.8835
.75	.9743	.4871	.5359	.5846	.6333	.6820	.7307	.7794	.8282
.70	.9093	.4547	.5001	.5456	.5910	.6365	.6820	.7274	.7729
.60	.7793	.3897	.4286	.4676	.5065	.5455	.5845	.6234	.6624
.50	.6421	.3211	.3532	.3853	.4174	.4495	.4816	.5137	.5458
.45	.5847	.2924	.3216	.3508	.3801	.4093	.4385	.4678	.4970
.40	.5197	.2599	.2858	.3118	.3378	.3638	.3898	.4158	.4417
.35	.4547	.2274	.2501	.2728	.2956	.3183	.3410	.3638	.3865
.30	.3896	.1948	.2143	.2338	.2532	.2727	.2922	.3117	.3312
.25	.3246	.1663	.1785	.1948	.2110	.2272	.2434	.2597	.2759

Courtesy Beloit Tool Corp.

BIBLIOGRAPHY

METALWORKING TEXTS

Bench Work, Delmar Publishers, Inc., Albany, New York.

Drill Press Work, Delmar Publishers, Inc., Albany, New York.

Heat Treatment of Metals, Delmar Publishers, Inc., Albany, New York.

How to Run a Lathe, South Bend Lathe Co., Inc., South Bend, Ind.

How to Run a Shaper, South Bend Lathe Co., Inc., South Bend, Ind.

How to Run a Drill Press, South Bend Lathe Co., Inc., South Bend, Ind.

Lathe Work, Delmar Publishers, Inc., Albany, New York.

Lectures in Grinding, Norton Company, Worcester, Mass.

Numerical Control, American Machinist, McGraw-Hill Publishing Co., Inc., New York.

Flame Spray Handbook, Vols. I, II, and III, Metco Inc. Westbury, Long Island, New York.

Milling Machine Work, Delmar Publishers, Inc., Albany, New York.

Modern Steels and Their Production, Bethlehem Steel Co., Bethlehem, Pa.

Machine and Tool Blue Book, Hitchcock Publishing Co., Wheaton, Ill.

Procedure Handbook of Arc Welding Design and Practice, The Lincoln Electric Co., Cleveland, Ohio.

Hobart Welding School, *Welding Processes,* Troy, Ohio.

Coated Abrasives, Modern Tool of Industry, McGraw-Hill Book Company, New York.

A. D. Althouse and C. H. Turnquist: *Modern Welding Practice,* Goodheart Willcox Co., Inc., Homewood, Ill.

T. Gardner Boyd: *Metalworking,* Goodheart-Willcox Co., Inc., Homewood, Ill.

Leroy F. Bruce: *Sheet Metal Shop Practice,* American Technical Society, Chicago, Ill.

Henry Burghardt: *Machine Tool Operations,* Parts I and II, McGraw-Hill Book Co., New York.

John L. Feirer: *General Metals,* McGraw-Hill Book Co., New York.

John L. Feirer and John R. Lindbeck: *I. A., Metalwork,* Chas. A. Bennett Co., Inc., Peoria, Ill.

John L. Feirer and Earl E. Tatro: *Machine Tool Metalworking,* McGraw-Hill Book Co., New York.

Roland R. Frazer and Earl L. Bedell: *General Metal,* Prentice-Hall, Inc., Englewood Cliffs, N.J.

J. W. Giachino and Neil L. Schoenhals: *General Metals for Technology,* The Bruce Publishing Co., Milwaukee, Wis.

Everett R. Glazner: *Basic Metalwork,* The Steck Co., Austin, Texas.

Douglas B. Hobbs: *Aluminum,* Bruce Publishing Co., Milwaukee, Wis.

Harold V. Johnson: *Metal Spinning Techniques and Projects,* Bruce Publishing Co., Milwaukee, Wis.

Harold V. Johnson: *General Industrial Machine Shop,* Chas. A. Bennett Co., Inc., Peoria, Ill.

Emil F. Kronquist: *Art Metalwork,* McGraw-Hill Book Co., New York.

Rupert Le Grand, Editor: *The American Machinist Handbook,* McGraw-Hill Book Co., New York.

Oswald A. Ludwig: *Metalworking Technology and Practice,* McKnight and McKnight Publishing Co., Bloomington, Ill.

Harvey D. Miner and John G. Miller: *Exploring Patternmaking and Foundry,* D. Van Nostrand Co., Inc., Princeton, N.J.

Eric Oberg and F. D. Jones: *Machinery's Handbook,* The Industrial Press, New York, N.Y.

Harold W. Porter, Charles H. Lawshe, Orville D. Lascoe: *Machine Shop, Operations and Setups,* American Technical Society, Chicago, Ill.

S. E. Rusinoff: *Automation in Practice,* American Technical Society, Chicago, Ill.

J. T. Sherman: *Machine Shop Work,* American Technical Society, Chicago, Ill.

Robert E. Smith: *Forging and Welding,* McKnight and McKnight Publishing Co., Bloomington, Ill.

Emanuele Stieri: *Fundamentals of Machine Shop Practice,* Prentice-Hall, Inc., Englewood Cliffs, N.J.

Tustison, Kranzusch, Blide: *Metalwork Essentials,* Bruce Publishing Co., Milwaukee, Wis.

Chas. W. Wick: *Chipless Machining,* The Industrial Press, 93 Worth Street, New York.

METALWORKING PROJECT BOOKS

Wm. J. Becker: *Metalworking Made Easy,* Bruce Publishing Co., Milwaukee, Wis.

J. W. Bollinger: *Fun with Metalwork,* Bruce Publishing Co., Milwaukee, Wis.

Chris Harold Groneman: *Bent Tubular Furniture,* Bruce Publishing Co., Milwaukee, Wis.

Algot E. Anderson: *56 Problems in Elementary Sheet Metal Work,* McKnight and McKnight Publishing Co., Bloomington, Ill.

Harold V. Johnson: *Metal Spinning Techniques and Projects,* Bruce Publishing Co., Milwaukee, Wis.

Roy E. Knight: *Machine Shop Projects,* McKnight and McKnight Publishing Co., Bloomington, Ill.

E. B. Mattson, *Creating with Aluminum,* Bruce Publishing Co., Milwaukee, Wis.

E. B. Mattson: *Creative Metalworking,* Bruce Publishing Co., Milwaukee, Wis.

M. J. Ruley: *Practical Metal Projects,* McKnight and McKnight, Bloomington, Ill.

Dezso Sekely: *Contemporary Industrial Arts Projects,* McKnight and McKnight, Bloomington, Ill.

Donald G. Lux and Edward R. Towers: *Contemporary Metal Home Furnishings,* McKnight and McKnight Publishing Co., Bloomington, Ill.

INDEX

TABLES AND CHARTS

PROJECT SUGGESTIONS